The Call of Classical Literature in the Romantic Age

Edited and with an Introduction by
K. P. Van Anglen and James Engell

EDINBURGH
University Press

Edinburgh University Press is one of the leading university presses in the UK. We publish academic books and journals in our selected subject areas across the humanities and social sciences, combining cutting-edge scholarship with high editorial and production values to produce academic works of lasting importance. For more information visit our website: edinburghuniversitypress.com

© editorial matter and organisation K. P. Van Anglen and James Engell, 2017
© the chapters their several authors, 2017

Edinburgh University Press Ltd
The Tun—Holyrood Road, 12(2f) Jackson's Entry, Edinburgh EH8 8PJ

Typeset in 11/13 Adobe Sabon by
IDSUK (DataConnection) Ltd

A CIP record for this book is available from the British Library

ISBN 978 1 4744 2964 1 (hardback)
ISBN 978 1 4744 2966 5 (webready PDF)
ISBN 978 1 4744 2967 2 (epub)

The right of K. P. Van Anglen and James Engell to be identified as the editors of this work has been asserted in accordance with the Copyright, Designs and Patents Act 1988, and the Copyright and Related Rights Regulations 2003 (SI No. 2498).

Contents

Acknowledgments — v

Introduction: The Call of Classical Literature in
the Romantic Age — 1
K. P. Van Anglen and James Engell

Part I: Classical Practice, Romantic Concerns, and Genre

1. William Gilpin: A Classical Eye for the Picturesque — 35
   Margaret Doody

2. Phillis Wheatley and the Political Work of Ekphrasis — 53
   Mary Louise Kete

3. "Past ruin'd Ilion": The Classical Ideal and the Romantic
   Voice in Landor's Poetry — 80
   Steven Stryer

4. "Larger the shadows": Longfellow's Translation of
   Virgil's *Eclogue 1* — 103
   Christoph Irmscher

5. Changes of Address: Epic Invocation in Anglophone
   Romanticism — 126
   Herbert F. Tucker

Part II: Wider Romantic Engagements with the Classical World

6. Thoreau's Epic Ambitions: "A Walk To Wachusett" and
   the Persistence of the Classics in an Age of Science — 153
   K. P. Van Anglen

7. Pilgrimage and Epiphany: The Psychological and Political
   Dynamics of Margaret Fuller's Mythmaking — 193
   Jeffrey Steele

8. Remaking the Republic of Letters: James McCune Smith
   and the Classical Tradition   220
   John Stauffer

9. "In the face of the fire": Melville's Prometheus,
   Classical and Romantic Contexts   241
   John P. McWilliams

10. Coleridge's Rome   267
    Jonathan Sachs

11. The Classics and American Political Rhetoric in a
    Democratic and Romantic Age   289
    Carl J. Richard

12. Gibbon, Virgil, and the Victorians: Appropriating the
    Matter of Rome and Renovating the Epic Career   313
    Edward Adams

Coda

13. The Other Classic: Hebrew Shapes British and American
    Literature and Culture   341
    James Engell

Contributor List   404
Index   409

Acknowledgments

The editors would like to thank the staff of Edinburgh University Press for their unfailing professionalism, learning, courtesy, and skill—qualities they displayed at each stage of the publication process. We owe a special debt to our two editors, Michelle Houston and Adela Rauchova, who answered every question and found a way through—or around—every difficulty. We extend our gratitude as well to Saskia van der Lingen and Camilla Rockwood. The essays collected here were revised and improved for having been made subject to evaluation by the readers appointed by the Press. We thank them for their time, care, and helpful knowledge. In reading the draft manuscript of this collection, they provided important suggestions for improvement.

The Robinson and Rollins Funds of the Department of English at Harvard University helped to support the editorial and publication expenses of this volume. The editors are also grateful for publication support provided by the Anne and Jim Rothenberg Fund of Harvard. James Engell thanks his teachers, colleagues, and former students in the Classics, especially Glen Bowersock, Wendell Clausen, and Richard Thomas, also Leah Whittington and Victoria Moul, as well as the following individuals, who assisted with "The Other Classic": Charles Berlin, Eric Nelson, and Shaye Cohen. Kevin Van Anglen thanks Richard Thomas, Jan Ziolkowski, Richard Hunter, Maurice Lee, Wai Chee Dimock, and Laura Dassow Walls for their advice, and notes his general debt to Robert Fitzgerald and Seamus Heaney. Finally, we thank Amelie Prusik and Sol Kim-Bentley for their assistance in preparing the manuscript of this book.

In Chapter 11, "The Classics and American Political Rhetoric in a Democratic and Romantic Age" by Carl J. Richard, some material is, by kind permission of Harvard University Press, excerpted and reproduced from *The Golden Age of the Classics in America: Greece, Rome, and the Antebellum United States* by Carl J. Richard, Cambridge, MA: Harvard University Press, copyright © 2009 by the President and Fellows of Harvard College.

Introduction: The Call of Classical Literature in the Romantic Age

K. P. Van Anglen and James Engell

This book reveals the pervasive extent to which, on both sides of the Atlantic, classical texts deeply inform and shape the cultural period we now call Romanticism, a term and period label established only many decades after the end of the era that it describes. Throughout the later eighteenth and earlier nineteenth centuries, the presence of classical texts, genres, values, and attitudes flows strongly through a wide range of authors working in many modes: poetry, history, essays, politics, aesthetics, and life-writing. The classics remain vibrant and appealing as a ready resource. The classics establish a pervasive, essential presence in the literary and cultural fabric of the Romantic period. Far from being inimical to romantic attitudes, classical inheritances often enrich those attitudes. Moreover, the study of Hebrew—designated and studied as a classical language—significantly changes poetry and literary criticism, as well as inflecting political discourse and cultural debate.

Classical strains found in major British poets—especially in Wordsworth, Coleridge, Shelley, Keats, and Byron—have long been recognized and studied. Scholars such as David Fairer, Stephen Gill, Bruce Graver, Nicholas Halmi, James Mays, Jacob Risinger, and others have illuminated the extent to which these poets loved and variously incorporated classical texts and ideas in their own verse, criticism, and letters. The present volume moves beyond and supplements these studies to demonstrate how thoroughly an entire literate culture, one that we now call romantic, exhibited close knowledge of the classics and turned to classical literature habitually as a resource for poetry, the revitalization of genres, historical understanding, biographical presentation, critical principles, and political reform.

Romanticism and classicism, the romantic and the classic, are so habitually paired, primarily by placing them in contrast or opposition, that it has become hard to imagine how thoroughly classical literature permeated and informed what we now call the Romantic Age. In that era, very few writers in Great Britain or America refer to themselves or their contemporaries as *romantics*, and virtually none of them use the term *Romanticism* for what William Hazlitt calls "the spirit of the age." If they seem to quarrel with the classical inheritance that many of them knew so well, their fight is more with the narrowed transmission of that inheritance found in strictures of high neoclassic literary theory that had dominated criticism and practice since the later seventeenth century than it is with classical literature itself. Such theory demanded strict adherence to conventions and genres whose existence it could proclaim as immutable and "natural." While romantic writers regarded what they were doing as new, this attitude in no way prompted them to abjure valuable lessons of expression, judgment, and genre flowing from the classical authors they loved. This volume disturbs categories that have become too settled.

In recent national conventions of ASECS, BARS, and NASSR, despite hundreds of panels on various subjects and more than one thousand papers, virtually no panels and very few papers engage the presence of the classical world in either eighteenth-century or romantic literature. There are exceptions, of course, especially in the community of romantic scholars who love and venerate the classics and who may attend more specialized gatherings. Yet, these individuals are now (and increasingly) outnumbered in a proportion that undercuts the presence and influence of classical texts in romantic literature itself. One might then conclude, why study or call attention to the presence of the classics in the Romantic era? Who will care? The counter to this is simply that such classical presence is, in fact, pervasive and vital. Romanticism cannot be properly known or understood for what it is without examining, appreciating, and even theorizing its classical presence, which is an essential, abiding aspect of Romanticism. To do otherwise passes over the deep force exerted by the classics in literature, culture, and personal life.

This volume presents the Romantic emulation and incorporation of classical texts as part of a broader, Janus-faced response to significant forces of change, among them democracy, egalitarianism, individualism, and abolition. Rather than placing these forces in opposition to the values of antiquity, authors whom we now call romantic regard ancient Greek, Roman, and Hebrew culture—Hebrew is consistently regarded as a *classical* language and exerts large influence on both sides the Atlantic—as enabling adaptation to a new cultural milieu without abandoning an allegiance to themes and forms of the past.

This is why writers we now regard as romantic so often turn for guidance in genre, style, shaping of literary career—and even in life—to classical writers. They are radical traditionalists responding to great shifts in their own times. Their Janus-faced stance pervades patterns of quotation, allusion, imitation, and emulation found in the texts they produce under classical influence. Their careers reflect the continuing impact of concepts such as the Virgilian *cursus honorum*. The classics empower these writers to address politics, morality, spirituality, history, aesthetics—even constitution-making, for the ancients had been there before them and had left a record of excursions into these matters from which the romantic writers learn, whether they are novelists or historians, poets or essayists. It might be observed that the presence of the classics is more prevalent in the literature of the romantic era than it has been at any time since. This impact fell on both sides of the Atlantic.

One could produce a series of volumes on the call of the classic, separate ones on translation, politics, allusion, critical theory, and life-writing, to name a few areas where the classical presence looms in Romantic writing. The present volume offers the variety of that presence and therefore strives to represent, in so far as a single volume can, the reach and diversity inherent in the call of the classic. Through a series of individual studies treating a wide range of writers on both sides of the Atlantic, this volume reconstructs complex relationships that bind the ancient classics to what we now call the Romantic Age. It is not intended as a comprehensive history of the classics and their reception during the late eighteenth and early nineteenth centuries.[1] Instead, these thirteen previously unpublished essays focus on specific instances of that reception, as well as on the application of the classics to produce a new literature that we have come to call Romantic.

Each essay describes why and how the texts, thought, and history of classical antiquity became a presence in the life and writings of one or more modern authors; how this presence complicates and redefines the terms and assumptions by which we understand the relationship between classic and romantic; and how the presence of the classics enabled romantic poets and historians to address their own situations while retaining a formative connection to the cultural past. That situation included not only literary concerns but also wider issues of politics, history, and the conduct of life. In other words, use of the classics was not here confined to experiments in genre, imitation, translation, allusion, or the shape of a literary career. Historical perspectives, political and social convictions, judgment of aesthetic forms generally, and the expression of personal values all came into play. Such use encompassed multiple aspects of experience transmitted by the written word. This, after all, is why the classics had been regarded as holding perennial value: as a guide to literary form and expression, yes, but, just as importantly, as a rich record touching almost every aspect of human thought, feeling, and conduct. The presence of the classical in whatever form it takes (e.g., quotation, translation, use of a rhetorical device, source of a critical or generic model, or exemplar of certain values) enables romantic authors to develop a revolutionary traditionalism and apply it to the writing they produced about and for their own age. Many of them believed the classics eminently helpful in meeting the challenges of modernity—challenges they faced as writers but also as human beings, individual, social, and mortal.

To speak of classical reception as revolutionary as well as traditional may strike some readers as counterintuitive. Using terms like *the classical* or *the classics* implies, after all, a concern at some level with ranking works, languages, or authors hierarchically. Etymologically, the literary term *classic* is related to classism and class struggle. It arose by analogy to the supposed division of the early Romans "into five classes by their sixth king, Servius Tullius": a superior text being described, like "a citizen of the highest grade[,] . . . as *classicus* '[above] grade,'" i.e., of the first or highest rank.[2] In particular, a "classic" was superior to other texts because it expressed the greater moral authority and influence (*auctoritas*) of its author, who was accorded a higher degree of *dignitas* or prestige than his contemporaries.[3] Moreover, such a work was often considered a "classic" because it implicitly or explicitly affirmed a political and social hierarchy. T. S. Eliot made this point in his 1944 address to the Virgil Society, entitled "What is a Classic?" Sir Frank Kermode expanded Eliot's theme in 1975 when he suggested that "the notion of a literary classic requires for its very existence one form or another of imperialism." For both critics, furthermore, Virgil, the defender alike of Roman *imperium* and the Augustan regime—though, we might add, not without hinting at his own reservations and even sadness—was "the foundational type of such a classic."[4]

The existence of texts, languages, or linguistic forms that a culture regards as "classical" affirms the connection between the classics and hierarchy in another way. It tends to make knowing those texts or acquiring those languages or linguistic forms a prerequisite for membership in a dominant class. In England, for instance, from the Middle Ages to the eighteenth century, access to the Latin and (later also) Greek languages, and so to direct knowledge of classical authors and texts, was traditionally restricted to those groomed for admission to the male political, ecclesiastical, social, and cultural elite by the grammar and public schools, and by the ancient universities. Whether in the Church, as a fellow at Oxford or Cambridge, or in a parliamentary debate, one's membership in the establishment—especially what Coleridge would later call "the clerisy," the intellectually engaged portion of the dominant class—depended to some degree on one's knowledge of Latin and Greek and the corpus of texts in those languages. Further, this use of the classics to reinforce a social and political hierarchy, as well as a certain degree of intellectual conformity, tended to produce texts that reflected dominant class values and interests. Yet, writers could and did turn to the classics to see examples of republicanism, resistance to tyranny, and even rebellion against unjust gods.

We have tended for a long time to associate Romanticism with the revolutionary and to oppose it to classicism, often seen as traditional and conservative. We need, though, to reckon with the term *Romanticism* in a more nuanced way. As a label or "-ism," the writers in the era to which we now affix that name would barely recognize our use of it. Their views of what that word meant were widely divergent and not infrequently negative. Their usage of it was comparatively rare. They could speak of "the romantic" or use *romantic* as an adjective in various ways, often meaning something exotic, wild, or filled with extraordinary emotion, but as the designation of a period or movement it was foreign to them. Many British and American writers openly revolted against certain eighteenth-century, *neoclassical* structures and rules, against the blind use of classical mythology and pastoral conventions, and especially against narrow critical practices that codified the writing of the ancients in order to show the supposed superiority of their inheritors in systematic theory. (*Neoclassical* itself was a term introduced only in the late nineteenth century.) In this manner Blake rejected the criticism of Sir Joshua Reynolds, though Blake seems to have overlooked the significant shift in Reynolds' criticism from the earlier to the later *Discourses*. Byron, however, continued to defend the three dramatic unities, a triad not found in Aristotle (only the unity of action is).

Thus, one point often overlooked is that what we now call Romanticism or the Romantic period is largely a literary-historical term and formation established only in the later nineteenth century and refined in the twentieth. Authors who fall within what we now accept as this literary-historical period were far more informed by, and engaged with, classical literature than many latter-day critics and students realize. Through a variety of genres that convey literary connection, cultural resonance, and biographical import, this formative engagement took place on both sides of the Atlantic. Many of these writers did not regard themselves self-consciously as belonging to a "Romantic" period, least of all to a style or orientation that disavowed the classics.

Writers we now call romantic rarely dismissed the achievements of eighteenth-century English verse. Pope, Thomson, Gray, Cowper, Crabbe, and others remained popular and admired well into the nineteenth century. At times invoking romances and the romantic (earlier authors such as Pope, Collins, Hurd, and the Wartons had done so, too), writers in English from the 1790s through the 1830s nevertheless did not regard themselves as forming a unified cultural movement called "Romanticism." To repeat, *Romanticism* and *romantic poets* became standard terms for literary and cultural history only in the later nineteenth century. Before that, most discussion, at least in Great Britain, analyzed literary expression of the era with categories such as the "Lake school." Writing in 1864 and looking back on the poetry of the earlier part of the century, one British commentator, reprinted in Boston, stated, "There used to be three schools of poetry,—the Byronic school, heroic and passionate; the Lake school, long identified with Coleridge's 'Ode to an Ass;' and the Cockney school, artificial and far removed from nature."[5] Certain writers, such as Byron, enjoyed their own "circles" or "schools." This followed ways of categorizing styles and affinities taken from the criticism of painters and visual artists in the Renaissance. As David Perkins notes, "In England between 1798 and 1824, the term *romantic* did not designate a contemporary literary movement or period. The adjective was widely current and meant wonderful, exotic, like a medieval romance."[6] This is how Coleridge uses the adjective—though very sparingly—in *Biographia Literaria* (1817). The word cannot be found in Wordsworth's Preface to *Lyrical Ballads* (1800 or 1802). In the poems of that collection the word appears only once ("visions of romantic joy") in verses about a rustic shelter for animals and the poet, "on the Island at Grasmere," an "Out-house" built by "the poor / Vitruvius of our village." Even there, a classical reference. Shelley does not employ *romantic* or *Romanticism* in his *Defence of Poetry* (composed 1821). Nor had Peacock done so in *The Four Ages of Poetry* (1820), which prompted Shelley's response. In America, the Transcendentalists had to outgrow the didacticism of their Boston Unitarian predecessors, who treated the romantics not as one group, but as two: one that was powerful but conventionally moral (like Wordsworth and Sir Walter Scott) and another (e.g., Byron), which used its power to transgress the limits of the moral order, and so possessed a demonic attraction.[7] If the romantics became—as Emery Neff once suggested—the classics of the modern world, it was to a significant degree because many of them knew the classics of the ancient world and loved them deeply enough to apply them in new contexts—even in America, as Walt Whitman demonstrated by his renovation of the pastoral elegy in "When Lilacs Last in the Dooryard Bloom'd" to honor the assassinated Abraham Lincoln.

Moreover, from the later nineteenth until the earlier twentieth century, in literary studies as well as in music and the visual arts, Romanticism was often widely received as designating almost the entire nineteenth century. As late as 1930, for example, one of the most influential and widely used literary anthologies and textbooks of pre-World War II America, *Poetry of the Victorian Period*, compiled by George B. Woods, stated at the outset that, "Down to the [18]90's Victorian poetry is in the main, though with significant new shadings, a continuation of the romantic tradition founded in the first third of the century."[8] T. E. Hulme in "Romanticism and Classicism" (1914, published posthumously in 1924) set classicism against the whole nineteenth century, as Irving Babbitt did, too. For Hulme and especially T. S. Eliot, classicism was an ally of modernism in siding against practices that predominated throughout the entire romantic nineteenth century. Hulme began his essay, "I want to maintain that after a hundred years of romanticism, we are in for a classical revival."[9]

Our present academic periodization, especially in English-speaking literary studies, thus restricts Romanticism in a strong way and departs from the terms that the practitioners and creators of what we now generally accept as romantic literature had themselves employed to describe their own activities. Our current use of Romanticism is doubly retroactive, first adopted around 1880 and then later further refined in academic study by dividing the nineteenth century into "romantic" and "Victorian" or "Romanticism" and "the Nineteenth Century." All this has tended to set the romantic in direct opposition to the classical and to reduce the degree to which we think of the presence of the classics in the earlier nineteenth century. Studies in the latter part of the twentieth century, among them W. J. Bate's *From Classic to Romantic* (1946), M. H. Abrams' *The Mirror and the Lamp* (1953), and James Engell's *The Creative Imagination: From Enlightenment to Romanticism* (1981), tended by their titles, if not always by their content, to draw a line between literature anchored to the classics and literature that was not. However, to take just one example, the criticism of Coleridge cleaves to some broadly classical principles while at the same time introducing new ones as well. It is neither mirror nor lamp but more akin to a crystal chandelier. Kathleen Wheeler has argued convincingly that the classic and romantic are not so much oppositions as they are differing emphases that often co-exist even while stressing different qualities.[10]

Divisions in college and graduate courses, as well as the categories followed by many academic journals and presses, have helped to cement a sharp distinction between the classics and romantic studies. The presence of "the long eighteenth century" as an expanded period has not significantly reinserted the classics into study of its later decades (and often not into its earlier ones either). A general decline in the knowledge of the classical languages by those pursuing modern English studies has exacerbated the false sense that romantic writers rejected classical literature. In many doctoral programs today not even rudimentary knowledge of Latin or Greek is expected.

While most romantic writers had ceased to produce imitations of classical works in the way practiced through the first half of the eighteenth century, they nevertheless cared about and often venerated classical literature. Their use of the classics was less direct imitation than it was a broad, imaginative application of classical literature and classical principles. This is what Edward Gibbon praised in Burke, the "sense and spirit of the Classics," and what Burke hoped his son Richard might follow when reading the Greek tragedians.[11] The Stoicism and absence of Christian orthodoxy in classical writers appealed to many in the Romantic Age, at least at certain stages of their careers. To put it in simplest terms, many romantic writers knew and loved the classics. The classics permeated the literary culture of the era we have come to call Romanticism.

The poets we call the romantics were almost all well educated in the classics, in the original languages, no matter what their social background. For instance, even though John Keats (1795–1821) came from humble origins, and even though he went to Enfield School, not among the more elite or classically oriented institutions, while there he translated much—perhaps the entirety—of the *Aeneid*. He absorbed the venerable Virgilian *cursus honorum* that provided a model of the poet's career still as relevant to him as it had been to Spenser and Milton. Little wonder, then, that the "melodious plot / Of beechen green" in "Ode to a Nightingale" likely owes something to Virgil's first Eclogue; or that Keats's early *Sleep and Poetry*, as well as his later *Hyperion* and *Fall of Hyperion*, reveal the pressure that the teleology of Virgil's career model continued to exert on later poets as they emulated him, moving from pastoral to georgic to epic.[12] For, "within this pattern, which distinguishes Virgil from his contemporaries and makes of him a paradigm for his successors, the *Eclogues*, the *Georgics*, and the *Aeneid* become part of one text, which we might call 'the Book of Virgil.'" Indeed, by Keats's time "'the poetic career'" of Virgil had become synonymous with the ambition and subjects of any great poet; and so, Virgil could serve the romantics as precedent for their own attempts at greatness, whatever their subject matter or political position.[13] These poems also reflect Keats's imaginative engagement with classical mythology and, building on that, his commitment to emulate—rather than imitate—his classical predecessors by engaging in mythmaking of his own.[14]

Very early in his poetic career, Wordsworth translated from Virgil's *Georgics* lines that would inform his verse for decades. Next to Milton, Dryden, and Tennyson, Wordsworth became one of the greatest—and greatest, in part, because understated—of English poets suffused with a Virgilian spirit and, at times, with the English equivalent of Virgil's style. Wordsworth translated several books of the *Aeneid*, too. His treatment of the story of Laodamia entailed much reading in ancient texts, including Pliny's *Historia Naturalis*. When Coleridge was at Christ's Hospital School, his older "patron and protector," as he later called him, Thomas Middleton, discovered him reading Virgil, an author thought too difficult for boys in the lower school. The encounter led to Coleridge's elevation and successful early education. Without this, it is doubtful if he would have succeeded and gone to university. Coleridge never forgot the classics, either in literature or philosophy, especially Plato and Plotinus, but also Pythagoras and many others as well. As with Hazlitt, Coleridge's literary criticism may be called romantic, yet it reflects multiple tenets of a broadly classical (rather than neoclassical) outlook. Byron in his letters and journals so often quotes Horace and other Latin authors that it is impossible to imagine him without that ballast and resource. His favorite play, from the time he attended Harrow, where he studied the Greek tragedians in the original, was the *Prometheus* of Aeschylus, a revolutionary figure prompting some of his best poetry, just as it did with Shelley and Goethe. A strong stoic impulse rooted in its ancient expression informs the lives and work of Wordsworth, Southey, Byron—and Coleridge, too, if we consider his intellectual engagement rather than his own temperament and behavior. Such a catalogue could go on, through Macaulay's *Lays of Ancient Rome* (1842), in which the author never employs the word *romantic* or *Romanticism*, and barely invokes the terms *classic* or *classical* either. It is possible for Macaulay to envision a world, and to assume a learned world, that pays attention to the classic and romantic without the necessity of oppositional distinctions. (Macaulay's essay on Warren Hastings paints the youthful and "romantic" plans and aspiration of Hastings in a manner far from disapproving.) The *Lays* enjoyed great popularity through the early twentieth century.

Major figures of the American Renaissance, as well as other important writers such as Longfellow, were conversant with classical literature and loved it. The essays in this volume reveal many fruitful connections. Thoreau, the most devoted of the Transcendentalists to the literature and thought of antiquity, began his career translating two plays of Aeschylus, as well as selections from Pindar and the *Anacreontea*, for publication. His Journal, commonplace books, unpublished nature writings, and literary works are later filled with allusions to and quotations from a wide range of classical texts. Jones Very explored the nature of epic and of tragedy in his critical essays; Margaret Fuller adapted and in many ways went beyond the boundaries of classical mythology in order to come to terms with her experience of being a woman in the nineteenth century; and Ralph Waldo Emerson was especially interested in the philosophers of ancient Greece—above all, Plato and Plotinus. Outside Transcendentalist circles, the old ambition to write a foundational epic motivated post-revolutionary Americans to create numerous imitations of Homer and Virgil, with titles like *The Conquest of Canaan*, *The Columbiad*, and *The Fredoniad*. Other poets, including Longfellow and Whitman, explored strands of the epic genre that had emerged since the Renaissance, from the religious or biblical epic of Milton, to the bardic or primitive epic of "Ossian," to the psycho-autobiographical epics of Wordsworth. Likewise, the shift from heroic verse to novelistic prose as the medium in which writers chose to treat the fundamental concerns and destiny of a culture found Americans such as James Fenimore Cooper and Herman Melville more than simply willing to follow the lead of British predecessors such as Sir Walter Scott. Throughout all these works, classical presences of various sorts provoked American writers to respond centrally, both in literary and broadly cultural contexts.

Margaret A. Doody's essay in this volume, "William Gilpin: A Classical Eye for the Picturesque," provides a good example of how the classical presence in an eighteenth-century text reveals Gilpin's ideological loyalties through the simple act of quoting classical poetry. Doody examines a series of books by Gilpin (1724–1804) on "the Picturesque," each centering on a different region of Britain and based on the Anglican clergyman's own travels. In these works, Gilpin taught several generations of aspiring tourists how to see. He also taught his readers three other things. First, writing in an age of accelerating intellectual and political change, he defends the classical tradition as capable of comprehending new genres, experiences, and subjects. This is meant to reassure his readers about the ability of traditional learning and its institutional guardians to respond to innovation. Throughout, Gilpin quotes Horace and other classical writers to lend authority to his descriptions of the landscape, themselves examples of at least two relatively novel prose forms: the nature essay and travel literature, as well as to the recent rise of tourism. The literary canon thus expands to bless and include the new; it does not crumble before the challenges presented by social change and a rising allegiance to individual experience.

Second, Gilpin's classical quotations invest his experiences as a tourist and his descriptions of landscapes with the force of a philosophical revelation into the nature and power of the Picturesque: namely, the way it lends the evocative and revelatory force of elemental time and mortality to a specific ruined or crumbling wall, or a particular dead branch. Death is always near at hand to sweep away the past, and the reverse of timelessness is part of the timeless appeal of the Picturesque. So, by celebrating the triumph of the transitory, the varied, the mutable and mortal, the form also celebrates the survival of the transcendent and unchangeable and immortal, albeit via a back door.

Third, and perhaps more obviously, the survival of the old order in literary and philosophical terms is reinforced by the way that Gilpin uses the classics to give contemporary Protestant English readers permission to enjoy the Gothic remains of monasteries and churches. Gilpin loved English ecclesiastical foundations, particularly abbeys, but only in their ruined state. Like a good eighteenth-century Protestant, he repeatedly decries monasteries for having fostered ignorance, idleness, and begging. But in their present collapsed, abandoned condition in England, they are admirable. Indeed, he regarded their desolation as an extra, since it afforded the visitor an experience lacking in Catholic Europe, where the abbeys lacked the fragmented, decorative, and picturesque effect of the English foundations.

The classical quotations interspersed throughout Gilpin's guidebooks therefore exhibit the author as culturally "safe" from an eighteenth-century English establishmentarian point of view, signaling that his aesthetic has not wandered far from the truly central Greco-Roman aesthetic any more than his faith has become tainted with sympathy for mediaeval Catholicism. Here, in the language of Horace and Virgil, we find verbal analogues for the strong columns, round domes, proportions, and assertive civilized power from which the Gothic was a wondrous but freakish departure. Moreover, the fact that the abbeys are in ruins proves that classicism, like Protestantism, has won, and that the Gothic and the Catholic are forever—however elegantly—dying. Quotation thus not only gives Gilpin's novel genre, travel writing or the tourist guide, something of the authority of the poetry of his classical predecessors, it reassures his readers that he owes allegiance alike to literary tradition, to philosophical moderation, and to Protestant England and a Whig view of its history.

Yet, even by the middle of the eighteenth century, it was clear that the attempt to use "formal education" to maintain "knowledge of the classics" as "a 'preserve,' with strong class and gender associations," was starting to fail. Due to the value of familiarity with ancient texts as a sign of social respectability, market pressures increased to create "more than one route . . . to knowledge of" the classics. The publishing industry, for example, undermined the long association of Latin and Greek with "British aristocratic culture" by making the main classical authors available in English for the rising middle classes. Publishers printed textbooks that did the same. "Publishing in the classics" during the age of Dryden and Pope and beyond thus marked "an opening out, or extension of access, beyond that élite—a process of removing barriers (specifically, of linguistic and cultural barriers related to gender and class) which also points towards the construction of a new national literary identity" for Britain,[15] an identity that, as with Gilpin, could be expanded to comprehend and control new types of literature and experience.

As English writers imaginatively drew on the classics that they knew well, so did their American contemporaries. For example, in "The Classics and American Political Rhetoric in a Democratic and Romantic Age," historian Carl J. Richard demonstrates that the difference in class structure between the two countries does not seem to have affected the popularity of the classics. While the extension by about 1830 of the suffrage to most white males resulted in a more democratic style of politics in America, paradoxically, it was accompanied by a simultaneous expansion of interest in antiquity. Despite calls that the nation's colleges reform their course offerings and become more practical and egalitarian, emphasizing modern foreign languages and the natural sciences, the classical curriculum held sway at American institutions of higher education till after the Civil War; the same was true in the secondary schools of the period.[16] Far from being discarded as a holdover from the culturally aristocratic colonial past, classical texts retained their prestige and (as in England) either in translation or in the original became familiar to the middle classes. American courtrooms, legislatures, newspapers, and private letters continued to bristle with classical allusions, even as the early republic quickly evolved into a mass democracy. Classically trained, most American politicians had to learn to live a kind of double rhetorical life, attempting to assure common voters of their ability to empathize with their concerns, while simultaneously demonstrating their learning, wisdom, and virtue to constituents of all classes through their knowledge of the classics. Typically, this political conundrum drove members of the educated elite—schooled in a Ciceronian style of rhetoric long associated with aristocracy—to choose the ancient, "democratic" Athenian republic and its parallels with the new United States as their subject matter, even as they eschewed the Attic style for Ciceronianism. In like manner, the choice of intellectual and oratorical borrowings from the thought and rhetoric of antiquity by both sides in the debate over slavery stemmed from the non-literary concerns of politicians caught between the opposing forces of cultural prestige and leveling, democratic politics.

Moreover, as Richard also shows, the antebellum standing of the classics was such that African Americans in particular were attracted to the study of Latin and Greek; for in a culture that—north or south—daily proclaimed their inferiority if not subhuman or nonhuman status, fluency in the ancient languages suggested that African Americans were not only the equal of whites in terms of their intellectual capability, they had already in many individual cases mastered one of the iconic fields within Western high culture. African Americans, where they were given the chance, therefore tended to flock to schools featuring a classical curriculum. Their reception of classical texts bespeaks the way in which a would-be emergent class might try to gain access to a previously forbidden, dominant-class body of knowledge.

For example, Mary Louise Kete's essay, "Phillis Wheatley and the Political Work of Ekphrasis," reveals that this strategy was central to Wheatley's self-presentation as America's first published, black, enslaved—and female—poet. Kete begins by asserting that her subject enacts one of the less obvious aspects of the poetics of ekphrasis: the political. For whether we think of ekphrasis broadly as a mode defined by the rhetorical re-depiction and commentary on one work of art by another, or more narrowly as a genre of poetry about visual images, it is generally imagined to be, most simply, art about art. This inherently critical or theoretical dimension makes it a useful mode for artists who want to reflect on the nature and function of images as depictions of reality (to "picture theory" as W. J. T. Mitchell puts it).[17] Ekphrasis, in this sense, is a mode of poetics that poses questions and answers about representational art. However, late eighteenth- and early nineteenth-century Americans, including Wheatley, exposed its political dimension, for they were asking the same questions before and after the American Revolution in the political realm as they asked poetically: who or what can be represented, by whom, in what circumstances, in what manner, and to what end?

In the poem, "To Maecenas," that she herself insisted be added at the start of her collection, *Poems on Various Subjects* (1773), Wheatley uses ekphrasis to transform and re-direct the force of the poem's Horatian model radically. Allying it to her effort to discover what the broader relationship is between the self, as subject, and the world, as object, the ekphrastic mode is key to Wheatley's pursuit of what John Shields has elsewhere described as her "theoretics of the imagination," for through it she renders her theory of the conditions and consequences of successful verbal images.[18] As such, ekphrasis also helps Wheatley articulate the parameters of her own poetic project, free from the contingencies of race, gender, and her enslaved status. Her response to the powerful, verbal images of other poets and the aesthetic argument Wheatley makes—one predominantly concerned with poetic ethos and affect—thus simultaneously advance and shield a revolutionary political argument: the necessity of freedom as a precondition for great literature.

Likewise, Wheatley in the same poem proclaims her rejection of earlier forms of patronage, whether local or transatlantic, resting her future career on an American belief in autonomy and self-reliance instead. If her verse has the look and feel of eighteenth-century neoclassical imitations, its themes and personal investment reflect attitudes often associated with romantic tendencies toward liberation and self-reliance. The first and most important expression of her genius is to correct a misrepresentation about the identity of the authorizing agent of *Poems on Various Subjects*. "To Maecenas" suggests that her historical masters and patrons mistake both themselves and her by depicting her as being in need of them to speak out, or to speak for her. Whether because of her age, gender, or race—and despite the impulses of their politics, religion, and affection—Wheatley's patrons cannot seem to imagine her as other than an owned self. But Wheatley can; and this ability to imagine her self in a radically new way stems, as she depicts it in "To Maecenas," from her active and voluntary engagement with the powerful verbal images made by famous poets of the classical era.[19] Although written a good thirty years before John Keats would depict the revolutionary, personal consequences of "First Looking into Chapman's Homer," Wheatley's poem, like Keats's, posits a claim to poetic authority inspired by her engagement with that authority as an achieved reality in the classical poets she cites. The poetry of Homer, Virgil, Horace, and especially (the former African slave) Terence depicted in Wheatley's "To Maecenas" results in the recognition—if not the immediate declaration—of the speaker's self as an autonomous subject rather than an object, and as a person rather than a thing. Wheatley implies that she is free to create her own character, as a poet and as a woman and as a person of color, and need not wait for her learning or her character to be recognized by her white masters and English patrons, no matter how benevolent their intentions. In this, she is typical of the revolutionary generation in America.

John Stauffer presents the first full treatment of James McCune Smith's classicism. McCune Smith, a leading abolitionist and the foremost black intellectual before W. E. B. Du Bois, was in love with the classics and believed that studying the literature, history, and languages of Greece and Rome was especially relevant in antebellum America. For Greece and Rome had established republics, but ones fatally flawed by slavery. They thus illuminated the predicament in the United States, a slave republic that explicitly saw itself as a successor to these classical societies. The histories of Greece and Rome represented cautionary tales for Americans. In particular, they served as warnings of what would happen if slavery persisted. For McCune Smith, the writings of the ancients emphasized the urgency to abolish slavery in America and to establish a "pure Republic" in which all people would enjoy the right of citizenship. For such a transformation to occur, however, he believed that Americans first needed to create a new "republic of letters," one inspired by the classical tradition, one that would provide them with a new social vision and encourage the creation of a virtuous and uncorrupted republic. Through his essays, McCune Smith led the way in the effort to create this new "republic of letters," a domain including, for instance, the antebellum novelist, historian, and abolitionist William Wells Brown, whose *Clotel, or, The President's Daughter* (1853) seems indebted to McCune Smith. Keeping, as Wheatley did, the example of Terence firmly in mind, McCune Smith was as much a classicist as an abolitionist, and he was an abolitionist in part because he was a classicist.

In England as in America, the tendency among writers generally categorized as "romantic" is, in fact, to combine what are commonly described as both "classical" and "romantic" elements. For example, as Steven Stryer shows in his essay "'Past ruin'd Ilion': The Classical Ideal and the Romantic Voice in Landor's Poetry," even more than the other romantics, Walter Savage Landor (1775–1864) has been praised by critics and fellow poets ranging from Ezra Pound to Robert Pinsky for his classicism. By labeling Landor in this way, critics seek to capture two aspects of Landor's work. The first is the objective fact of his immersion in the classical world—something revealed by his composition of a large body of poetry in Latin as well as by the sheer number of his explicit invocations of Greek and Latin writers, myths, names, settings, and historical events within his English poems. The second aspect is the widely shared sense that his lyric poetry exhibits qualities of compression of language, restraint of emotion, and severity of diction that recall the virtues of the best classical poetry as Landor himself defined them. However, as he explained in his poem "On the Classick and Romantick," for Landor the "classical" designated not merely a set of authors or a time period, but an aesthetic style which reflected a broader vision of life—one that he insisted was not at odds with the values and priorities of what is generally thought of as "Romanticism." He asserted in the poem that not only his own romantic contemporaries but even peoples normally considered outside the classical inheritance—Tartar and Turk, Goth and Arab—could embody the classical virtues as fully as the Greeks and Romans. Indeed, though he himself was drawn to the stylistic ideals of classical poetry, Landor wrote verse that also expressed his own individualism, passion, refusal to conform, and antiauthoritarianism.[20] Stryer explores the process by which Landor adapts and recreates the values of classical civilization in order to bring them into engagement with the English present. Through close analysis of a representative group of poems, he traces Landor's achievement of what may variously seem a reconciliation of or a balancing of tensions between two imaginative poles: the universality, authority, and permanence often associated with the "classical" because of that civilization's presumed premodern elevation above transient modernity; and a stereotypical "romantic" emphasis on personal experience, occurring within the flux of time and conveyed through the poet's own lyric voice.

As one of our contributors, Herbert F. Tucker, writes, this is in fact why the epic and other classical forms of verse remained popular in Britain during the Romantic era. For the "entrenched belief that Romanticism was inherently suspicious of, even hostile to, traditional literary forms" and that as a result, there was "a radical generic breakdown" with the coming of "European Romanticism," is simply untrue. Rather, like Landor, the romantics' attitude toward convention and tradition was what Stuart Curran calls "Janus-visaged." Tucker argues that this renewed the contemporaneous possibilities for a genre like epic, even as it stretched the forms and conventions of the genre so that they might encompass new experiences and attitudes:

> By the 1780s literary minds in Britain had put behind them the grousing of crinkly Neoclassicism about epic's supersession by an inhospitable modernity. They had learned to believe that the sort of cultural work epic had always done remained to be done afresh under transitional circumstances that were not *ipso facto* different from the transitional circumstances that had prevailed in Virgil's time, and Homer's, and Moses'. The British reading classes were prepared to associate epic's cultural work with the advancing strength of a prosperous nation, to associate the national advance with the progress of civilization, and to receive with acclaim any complex narrative of elevated bearing that might enshrine these associations in a form suitable for transmission to posterity.[21]

Similarly, Christopher N. Phillips notes that "from the late seventeenth century, virtually all English dictionaries (including Johnson's and Webster's) . . . defined epic largely as an adjective. To the extent that the dictionaries recorded actual usage of the word, 'epic' as a concept seems to have behaved more as a mode than a genre; the expansiveness of the adjectival gave epic a penchant for acquiring new resonances and referents."[22] Consequently, "American literary engagements with epic form are myriad" during the years between the Revolution and the Civil War.[23] Whether traditional heroic poems or novels with epic trappings or non-fiction prose works that invoked the tradition to address matters broad in scope, "the epic impulse" was resilient. "Through the eighteenth and well into the nineteenth centuries . . . Americans just would not stop writing epics—not out of nostalgia or from missing the memo that the epic was dead, but because the epic tradition continued to have relevance on a personal level, as well as in regional, national, and international contexts."[24] Hence, if "to write an epic, or to engage with an epic via other genres, is to place oneself in a genealogy dominated by central ancestral figures, primarily Homer, Virgil, and Milton . . ."[25] it is also to think of those distinguished and dominant historical persons as being present to us now, as equals who empower us to emulate their example and come to terms with contemporary experience by way of the presence of their verse in our poetry and prose—and vice versa.

Much previous work on this subject has engaged issues of form and genre. For example, Stuart Curran's influential *Poetic Form and British Romanticism* describes how "the hegemony of neoclassical rules, with their simple-minded and impossible clarity, broke down in the eighteenth century and with it a facile means of taxonomy" regarding the literary genres disappeared too. For "genres have never depended upon rules per se, but rather" have been defined by "a conceptual syntax derived from earlier examples and applied to modern conditions." This syntax is applied not by "simple imitation but by a competition of values, a subversion of precursors," which can empower an author as well as create literary anxiety.[26] In the case of Romanticism, Curran shows how this model, in which a writer negotiates a relationship with previous poets and texts, enriches our understanding of the development of individual poetic genres, as well as of the romantics' attempt to foment revolution through other means by struggling with the presence of the literary past.[27] It also helps us see how generic boundaries broke down, most notably, between the epic and the novel, as the rich possibilities of the latter form emerged.[28] As Curran suggests, when the syntax created by the past practice of those writing within a genre rubs up against the situation, desires, and concerns of a modern author, this friction allowed writers to adapt past practices in order to address concerns that are not formal or generic but cultural and personal.

Christoph Irmscher's essay, "'Larger the shadows': Longfellow's Translation of Virgil's *Eclogue 1*," exemplifies this motive superbly. It takes up the subject of translation, traditionally a major concern in reception histories, but goes beyond that to personal and even environmental concerns. Praising Longfellow for many individual decisions as a translator, Irmscher sees his version of Virgil's first Eclogue as representative of that poet's campaign to create an American literature on the model of the literatures of Europe. Longfellow's effort to retain elements of his Virgilian source, hewing at times more literally to the Latin than other translators, marks him as a "foreignizer," both in particular and in general. Longfellow was also very aware of the history of pastoral poetry, and considered "the syntax" of the eclogue as a genre when he translated *Eclogue 1*. Yet, the resulting presence of Virgil's Latin at some distance from but also near to Longfellow's English reflects not just the choices of translation that he and others have historically made, nor the syntax of possibility for an English translation that they delimit. More importantly, the exercise of turning Virgil's Latin into English focused Longfellow's interest, at the end of his life, on two other areas of concern at some distance from literary matters.

The first is the issue of change, particularly the coming of old age, the loss of friends, and the poet's rising sadness at his own remaining years and impending demise. Virgil's use of "shade," "shadows," and "shades" (*umbra*) in this poem (as elsewhere in his poetry) drew Longfellow to the task of grappling with death and mortality. While this was a theme in Virgil perhaps less recognized in the nineteenth century than today, Longfellow clearly took its prominence in this eclogue as a reminder that pastoral was not an escapist form. *Eclogue 1* begins with Tityrus lying in the shade, at ease and enjoying life, and ends with advancing shades of night. The concerns of real life, nightfall, and mortality impinge, as everywhere in Virgil, on the world of love, pleasure, and eternal possibility that is the pastoral.[29] At the same time, the fact that Virgil's first Eclogue had as its original context the Roman Civil War and ensuing dispossession of those who had backed the losing side, also inflected Longfellow's choice of words in his translation. For Longfellow linked the loss of land by Meliboeus and the preservation of holdings by Tityrus, who had appealed to Rome, to the attempts he and others made in the Boston area to prevent the industrialization of the Brighton Marshes and to preserve the countryside generally. The fate of urban trees was on Longfellow's mind as he struggled to find the right botanical equivalents for terms used by Virgil; and the fragility of the green world, whether in the face of politics or economics, concerned him as he turned to the pastoral form at a time when he realized that his own days were numbered. Getting the translation right made Virgil's eclogue present for Longfellow; thereby allowing him to connect it with his own end-of-life concerns and efforts at natural preservation.

In "Changes of Address: Epic Invocation in Anglophone Romanticism," Herbert F. Tucker turns toward the ancient convention of invoking the epic muse and its reception among poets of the Romantic era on both sides of the Atlantic. Though some Enlightenment thinkers discredited invocation of a higher power, it survived well into the nineteenth century. Something about this manifestly incredible convention rescued it from oblivion, prolonged its life, and suited it to the performance of a set of tasks that helped define Romanticism as a paradoxically traditional orientation toward the modern. For one thing, the very presence of this topos at the start of an epic poem created, as Tucker explains, "a vacuum of power" within the epic machinery, "into which the Romantic imagination enthusiastically rushed," making "the invoking poet" the source of "motivation and direction to the Muse, instead" of the other way around. Consequently, in both Britain and America performances of the topos by poets, whether routine or surprisingly subtle, reflected the practical urgency of a revolutionary moment when the legitimacy and nature of political power was sharply at issue. For the invocation of a higher power at the start of a long poem was now really an assertion of individual authorial autonomy, the poet's right to replace tradition (including traditional sources of inspiration) and constitute an epic world of his own imagining, and place it before readers. And so, in an age that witnessed Thomas Paine assert in *Common Sense* (1776) that "we have it in our power to begin the world over again," and saw time recalibrated according to the French Revolution, to invoke divine authority as a poet now placed the craft of writing verse along charged coordinates whose vertical axis was a cosmopolitan tradition of classically learned verse, whose horizontal axis was an open publishing vista that entertained an expanding national readership, and whose zero point of axial intersection was the original and remaining mystery of poetic creation itself. The presence of the classical now comes almost full circle, telling us that revolution, in the arts as in politics, is now more enabled by ties to the past than, as with Gilpin's use of classical quotations, reassuringly thereby constrained.

The next seven chapters reveal how extensive the implications can be when the discussion of classical presences shifts from formal appropriation, where the syntax of the classical past of a genre is invoked vis-à-vis a concern or situation facing a romantic author, to issues that quickly escape such formal or generic points of origination. K. P. Van Anglen demonstrates, for example, that Henry David Thoreau, thoroughly familiar with Virgil's poetry, applies that familiarity in his early excursion, "A Walk to Wachusett," by citing the Roman poet a number of times—mostly from the *Eclogues* and *Georgics*. Like many of his contemporaries, Thoreau was educated at Harvard to regard the Virgilian *cursus honorum* as the relevant model for a literary career *par excellence*, a fact reflected in the Janus-like stance of "Wachusett" in which Thoreau concentrated on writing the prose equivalent of an eclogue, an "excursion" conveying his intimate, personal, and small-scale experience of nature. Yet, as Virgil had done, Thoreau kept looking beyond the generic boundaries of the pastoral to an inevitable epic engagement with nature. The fact that Thoreau invokes "Homer, Virgil, [and] Humboldt" as his literary forbears in "Wachusett" suggests, however, that while a formal, generic horizon for his concerns here is necessary, it is also insufficient for understanding what is going on in this piece. For "A Walk to Wachusett" is also his first stab at becoming a naturalist and a field observer; and so, in creating a *stemma* consisting of these three worthies, he is hinting that he will move from the eclogues of his early excursions (including his pastoral elegy for his brother: *A Week on the Concord and Merrimack Rivers*); to didactic georgics centered on the interaction of the human and the natural such as *Walden*, *The Maine Woods*, and *Cape Cod*; finally graduating to the great nature writings he left unfinished at his death, works that aspire to revise yet emulate the *Historia Naturalis* of Pliny the Elder, and that sum up the knowledge of Thoreau's culture concerning the most epic matter of them all: what Humboldt called *Kosmos*.

While the biographical trajectory just outlined seems to confirm the generic origins of Thoreau's prose and career goals in terms of the Virgilian precedent, his concerns go beyond the generic and the Virgilian, and even beyond the literary, to front the nature of education, the shape of the intellectual life, and the unity of reality. For Thoreau is also saying that Latin and Greek and the humanities in general, like physics, biology, and the other natural sciences, are all necessary for those who would give an account of the nature of things. Consequently, the intellectual life cannot be divided into competing and dispersed specializations, let alone polarized into "the scientific" versus "the literary"; rather, we are still called to seek the nature of cosmos as it constantly and empirically changes and evolves, yet also as it remains a living truth that unites all knowledge into a systemic whole.

Similarly, Margaret Fuller's extensive study of ancient and later European mythology, as well as her revisions of the stories and patterns she found there, participate in a negotiation with the past and with the generic syntax it provides for modern authors to speak to or write about their own situations. In particular, during the 1840s, she used her extensive knowledge of classical mythology to shape her writing. Beginning her career as a leading New England Transcendentalist, Fuller moved to New York and later to Europe, where she worked as a front-page columnist for Horace Greeley's *New-York Tribune*. Her first conversation class for Boston women was on the subject of mythology. Her comments in those discussions, as well as citations in essays later published in the *Dial*, reveal her deep knowledge of Hesiod, Ovid, Virgil, the Greek tragedians, Apuleius, Plutarch, and other ancient authors. Her essays and poems often use mythical models (such as Minerva, Diana, and Isis) to measure the contours of the self and the limits of human potential. Passages in *Woman in the Nineteenth Century* reveal her close identification with Cassandra, a misunderstood prophetess, and Iphigenia, Agamemnon's daughter sacrificed to obtain favorable winds for the war-fleet sailing to Troy. During Fuller's residence in New York, mythological references largely disappeared from her writing. But once she began her travels in Europe in 1846, classical mythology provided an expansive vehicle for capturing the turbulence of European revolution.

Yet, as Jeffrey Steele's "Pilgrimage and Epiphany: The Psychological and Political Dynamics of Margaret Fuller's Mythmaking" shows, the real question for Fuller was whether that mythological tradition was adequate for her to understand her experience, both as an individual and as a woman in the nineteenth century. Fuller's use of mythological figures was also shaped, therefore, by her profound identification with alchemical patterns drawn from the writings of Boehme, Swedenborg, Saint-Martin, Novalis, and Goethe. Articulating figures of aspiration, Fuller's syncretic mythical images, as they crystallized in the crucible of her imagination, projected idealized states of personal and social being. In a profound sense, Fuller was both a disseminator of classical traditions of mythology and a mythmaker in her own right. Myth, in her hands, was not a dead set of ancient narratives but rather an ongoing group of stories that she reinvigorated as she channeled, combined, and reframed mythical energies that meshed with her vision of personal transformation and social change. Adapting classical mythology so extensively as to create virtually her own mythopoetic syntax, she created myths that would empower her as a woman and console her for losses. In her development of a feminist mythology, she bears more comparison to Blake than to Emerson.

Some other occasions of classical literary influence would seem to fall more clearly on the side of strictly literary concerns. John McWilliams's "'In the face of the fire': Melville's Prometheus, Classical and Romantic Contexts" is the first thorough and systematic study to trace Melville's indebtedness to—and transformation of—characterizations of Prometheus taken from the works of Hesiod,

Aeschylus, Plato, Goethe, Byron, Mary Shelley, and Percy Shelley. Of the many literary analogues that contribute to assessing Captain Ahab's character, none are more revealing than the two extended references to Prometheus. Of particular importance is Melville's paradoxical interpretation of Ahab's Promethean quest for the essence of fire: fire is both the hidden, withheld knowledge of the gods and the self-consuming inner flame of a monomaniacal obsession. The divergent "classical" and "romantic" interpretations of Prometheus, both of them familiar to Melville from his wide reading, thus coalesce in an Ahab who with exultant despair seeks the fire he knows will consume him. Consequently, McWilliams provides perhaps the most thorough account to date of the imaginative and intellectual process by which a situation occurs in which the syntax of the past enables and yet is also almost completely changed by the experience and intentions of the author. The various versions of Prometheus and of his story are laid out in new detail and we see when and why Melville made the creative decisions that he did as he transformed the classical figure into an embodiment of his philosophical "yea-saying" and "nay-saying."

Jonathan Sachs's contribution, "Coleridge's Rome," renders problematic the assumption of the model of influence we are using here, that past practice and the present concerns of the writer are necessarily separate. His study takes as its starting point a series of essays by Samuel Taylor Coleridge that compares Napoleonic France with Rome under the Caesars. For Coleridge, what distinguishes France from Rome is the rapidity with which Napoleon has established his power, a rapidity that presages the speed of his future fall. But for Coleridge the seemingly increased speed of the present is not a product of the French Revolution. It instead follows the trajectory of print media and rapid communication. The meaning of Coleridge's sense of historical acceleration (a word that when applied to history was, at least in English, a recent coinage) is thus, in Sachs's account, brought into relief by the contrast between the speed of contemporary France and the slowness of imperial Rome. Sachs suggests that Coleridge's understanding of historical acceleration aligns him with more recent theorists like Reinhart Koselleck and Giovanni Arrighi, who insist that intensification and acceleration represent the defining qualities of modernity. In their insistence on the quickening of modernity, however, these theorists often overlook the role of slowness, here marked by Coleridge's understanding of Roman history, in determining speed. Coleridge's account of historical acceleration, Sachs shows, uses its long reach back to the classical past and its invocation of a classical exemplar, imperial Rome, and of a particular form of mediation, the arborially inspired book, to imagine a temporal framework in which speed and acceleration are enmeshed with patterns of slowness, especially the slowness that stands for Coleridge as a general sign of the classical. As such, he used his knowledge of classical history to order his experience of the French Revolution in a way that would comprehend both the resemblance of the present to the past while simultaneously recognizing that modernity has a sensibility decidedly unlike either that of the pre-modern or the ancient.

This appreciation for Coleridge's nuanced historical response finds a parallel in Edward Adams's sense of how history followed the precedent of literature. In line with the tendency of literary genres during the Romantic period to breach accustomed neoclassical boundaries yet not abandon broader classical definitions and forms entirely, Adams's "Gibbon, Virgil, and the Victorians: Appropriating the Matter of Rome and Renovating the Epic Career" finds that like the novel, historical prose could become the means by which authors pursued their epic ambitions to capture the *epos* of a culture. He begins by arguing that the deep narrative structure of *The Decline and Fall of the Roman Empire* is shaped by Gibbon's vaunting desire to emulate Virgil's *Aeneid* in the form of a modern, rational prose history—recasting Virgil's fallen Troy as the Roman Empire; Virgil's Rome as Western European civilization; and Virgil's Carthage as (at various times) Byzantium and the papacy (both, in Gibbon's view, tyrannous institutions that resisted the westward or progressive development of the *translatio imperii*). Adams then demonstrates how thoroughly Gibbon's success subsequently allowed his history to supplant Virgil's epic as the primary source for the matter of Rome in the eyes of major nineteenth- and twentieth-century historians and imaginative writers, from Macaulay and Michelet to G. M. Trevelyan, Proust, and Isaac Asimov. Gibbon's own career similarly replaced the Virgilian career or *cursus honorum* as a model for literate historians to emulate. This feat of literary displacement centered on Gibbon's pioneering autobiography, the *Memoirs of My Life* and, above all, its celebrated reiteration of his moment of enlightened inspiration and vocational discovery amidst the ruins of the Roman Capitol. Adams considers the implications of Gibbon's aggressive secularization of what had been a pagan, then a Christian vision of an eternal Virgilian and Roman achievement into a story of inevitable authorial and national decline. Here failure hounds even the greatest successes, and Edward Adams treats two of Gibbon's influential literary and historiographical heirs, Henry Adams and H. G. Wells.

Finally, James Engell sensed an absence in the overall plan of the volume. While "the classics" (i.e., Latin and Greek) were represented, and while Curran and many other scholars assume that "classical literature" is limited to these two languages, any consideration of what many in the eighteenth and early nineteenth centuries regarded as the other classic, Hebrew, was entirely absent. Indeed, a gap exists in our intellectual history, literary criticism, and poetic theory if we do not recognize Hebrew as a presence crucial to the development of literary and learned culture in the United States and Great Britain. The shaping power that Hebrew exerts on British and American poetry, politics, and culture from the sixteenth through the nineteenth centuries is enormous. It is responsible, Engell argues, for the greatest innovations in post-Renaissance English verse, for key developments in aesthetics, for persistent and fruitful arguments in political theory and practice, and for vital dimensions of British and American thought that cannot be accounted for in any other way. This shaping power—related to but not the same as the influence of biblical translations regarded as literature—has received sporadic attention, recently in studies of language, culture, and politics by scholars such as Shalom Goldman, Eric Nelson, Stephen Prickett, Eran Shalev, Sheila Spector, and Howard Weinbrot. Yet, Hebrew as the other classic has not obtained its rightful place in studies of literature in English, nor in what might be called Anglo-American literate culture.

In the hope of prompting greater recognition of its importance and impact, Engell details and explores the presence and recognition of the other classic in: British and American colleges and universities, Puritan Hebraists, the composer Handel, concepts of the sublime, the seminal criticism of Robert Lowth, the poets Milton, Dennis, Watts, Smart, Macpherson, Merrick, Blake, Wordsworth, Whitman, Longfellow, and Lazarus, in myths of national origin and identification, in writers such as Coleridge, De Quincey, Thoreau, Melville, Arnold, and Lowes, as well as in an appreciation of the stylistic and moral strength of Hebrew Scripture. Drawing on specialist studies and on his own readings of several overlooked texts, as well as overlooked aspects of familiar texts, Engell unfolds the larger sweep and modulations of the transformative and enduring presence of the other classic. Like feminist and African American critics who ask that the canon be broadened, Engell challenges the exclusions upon which discussion of the classical and its influence upon, and reception by, the romantics has been based. To see the importance of this neglected field one need only think of John Milton as a poet who knew Hebrew and who used his knowledge of the Hebrew Bible to revise the syntax of the epic. The same could be said of Bishop Lowth, Coleridge, and many others during the Romantic era broadly conceived. In the end, the presence of Hebrew as the other classic enlarges and redefines the nature of classical influences on the Romantic era.

Notes

1. It does not seek to compete with the admirable, on-going *Oxford History of Classical Reception in English Literature*, ed. David Hopkins and Charles Martindale (Oxford: Oxford University Press, 2012–). Volume 3 (1660–1790), ed. Hopkins and Martindale (2012), Volume 4 (1790–1880), ed. Norman Vance and Jennifer Wallace (2015), Volume 1 (800–1558), ed. Rita Copeland (2016), and Volume 2 (1558–1660), ed. Patrick Cheney and Philip Hardie (2015), have appeared so far. By examining specific engagements with the classics, essays in our volume supplement, sharpen, and in some cases make more accurate the narrative and studies of that *Oxford History*. The fact that the history of the classical presence in America from 1790–1880 is summarized in a single chapter (4:159–83) means that many important American authors, translations, and imitations go unremarked, and various significant transatlantic connections are ignored. (Most writers in North America read British authors. Reciprocally, many British authors read and often praised American writers such as Wheatley, Longfellow, Fuller, and Melville.) For example, the importance of the classics in shaping Henry David Thoreau's career, the breadth of his classical learning, his allusions to authors ranging from Homer and Virgil to Pliny the Elder, and his activity as a translator of Aeschylus, Pindar, and the *Anacreontea* are not mentioned in the *Oxford History*. The chapter on classical translation (4:57–78) does not discuss nineteenth-century American translations from Latin or Greek at all—in Thoreau's case failing to identify his metaphrastic translation style as a Yankee analogue to what F. W. Newman in 1856 called "the principle of the daguerreotype" followed by so many English Victorian translators (4:75–76). Similarly, essays in this volume concerning Gibbon's influence on later historians (replacing Virgil as a model both for their careers and for their histories), Coleridge's interest in time, the premodern, and the modern, and the account of Hebrew as a third classical tongue will supplement and perhaps

lead scholars to amend what one finds in the parallel sections of the *Oxford History*. The result should be a more exact sense of the "classical presence" in the Romantic era.

Another collection of general interest is *Romans and Romantics*, ed. Timothy Saunders (Oxford: Oxford University Press, 2012), comparative in scope. For learned introductions that treat the relation of British Romanticism to classical texts and scholarship, see Bruce Graver, "Classical Inheritances," *Romanticism: An Oxford Guide*, ed. Nicholas Roe (Oxford: Oxford University Press, 2005), 38–48; and Graver, "Romanticism," *A Companion to the Classical Tradition*, ed. Craig W. Kallendorf (Oxford: Blackwell, 2007), 72–86. Gilbert Highet, *The Classical Tradition: Greek and Roman Influences on Western Literature* (New York: Oxford University Press, 1949) remains broadly helpful, as does Douglas Bush, *Mythology and the Romantic Tradition in English Poetry* (Cambridge, MA: Harvard University Press, 1937).

2. *The Virgil Encyclopedia*, s.v. "classic and classicism"; *Oxford English Dictionary*, s.v. "classic."
3. *Virgil Encyclopedia*, s.v. "*auctoritas* (1–2)."
4. Ibid., s.v. "canon and canonization." See also Sir Frank Kermode, *The Classic: Literary Images of Permanence and Change* (New York: Viking Press, 1975), 27–28.
5. This statement in E[liakim and Robert S.] Littell, comp., *The Living Age* 86 (October–December 1864): 661, is taken from a book review appearing in a British periodical identified as *The Press*. Published in Boston, Littel's *Living Age* largely reprinted articles and reviews from British sources.
6. David Perkins, *Is Literary History Possible?* (Baltimore: Johns Hopkins University Press, 1992), 87. Chap. 5, "The Construction of English Romantic Poetry as a Literary Classification," is helpful (85–119).
7. Daniel Walker Howe, *The Unitarian Conscience: Harvard Moral Philosophy, 1805–1861* (1970. Rev. ed. Middletown, CT: Wesleyan University Press, 1988), 191, 198–99.
8. George Benjamin Woods, comp., *Poetry of the Victorian Period* (New York: Scott, Foresman, 1930), iv.
9. T. E. Hulme, "Romanticism and Classicism," in *Speculations: Essays on Humanism and the Philosophy of Art*, by T. E. Hulme, ed. Herbert Read (London: Kegan Paul, Trench, Trubner, 1924), 113–40, 113.
10. Kathleen Wheeler, "Classicism, Romanticism, and Pragmatism: The Sublime Irony of Oppositions," *Parallax* 4, no. 4 (1998): 5–20.
11. Edward Gibbon, *Memoirs of My Life*, ed. Georges A. Bonnard (London: Funk & Wagnalls, 1966), 248. For Burke's sense of classical tragedy in the American Revolution and the related classical studies of his son, see Gerald Chapman, "Burke's American Tragedy," in *Johnson*

and His Age, ed. James Engell (Cambridge, MA: Harvard University Press, 1984), 386–423, esp. 398–99 and nn.
12. Glenn W. Most, in "Virgil," *The Classical Tradition*, ed. Anthony Grafton, Glenn W. Most, and Salvatore Settis (Cambridge, MA: Belknap Press of Harvard University Press, 2010), 968, summarizes the *cursus honorum* and its pervasive influence on Western literary history:

> Beyond the influence exercised by his individual works, Virgil has also provided the Western literary tradition with its most compelling and durable model of a poetic career, one beginning with small, unambitious, personal works (the *Eclogues*), moving on to more difficult tasks of greater intellectual complexity and social significance (the *Georgics*), and culminating in a single massive work that subsumes all the earlier ones and provides an epic mirror for the destiny of a nation (the *Aeneid*). The influence exercised by this model can be traced as early as the 1st century CE.... For many centuries it continued to provide poets with a guideline for their own development and with suggestions for what kind of poem to write next, through the Middle Ages ... and the early modern period (when it fascinated such poets as Spenser, Milton, and Pope), and even into Romanticism (it stands behind William Wordsworth's, and the other English Romantic poets', dream of a career culminating in a single great philosophical epic) and the 20th century (Marcel Proust, James Joyce, and Robert Musil all began with smaller and more personal works before moving on to their larger epics).

This is not to say, of course, that Spenser and Milton either viewed Virgil or took his *cursus honorum* as the model for their own poetic careers in exactly the same way. E.g., Milton was wary of emulating classical texts and models—increasingly so as he aged; see Charles Martindale, "Milton's Classicism," in Hopkins and Martindale, *Oxford History of Classical Reception* 3:55–62.
13. Elena Theodorakopoulos, "Closure: the Book of Virgil," in *Cambridge Companion to Virgil*, ed. Charles Martindale (Cambridge: Cambridge University Press, 1997), 155–65.
14. *Virgil Encyclopedia*, s.v. "*aemulatio* and *imitatio*," discusses the renewed interest in this distinction in the eighteenth century in the wake of the popularity of Longinus's *On the Sublime*. See also Howard Weinbrot, "'An Ambition to Excell': The Aesthetics of Emulation in the Seventeenth and Eighteenth Centuries," *Huntington Library Quarterly* 48, no. 2 (Spring 1985): 121–39.
15. Penelope Wilson, "The Place of Classics in Education and Publishing," in Hopkins and Martindale, *Oxford History of Classical Reception* 3:30–31. Wilson, 3:31–52, outlines the details of this widening of access yet redirection of the purpose of studying the classics. As such, it is part of the broader coalescence of British national identity in the eighteenth century. See Linda Colley, *Britons: Forging the Nation, 1707–1837* (New Haven: Yale University Press, 1992) for an

overview of this process. Sir David Cannadine, *The Rise and Fall of Class in Britain* (New York: Columbia University Press, 1999), esp. 25–58, studies the role of social class in this transformation of self-understanding in the nations that made up the eighteenth-century transatlantic British world.
16. Carl J. Richard, *The Golden Age of the Classics in America: Greece, Rome, and the Antebellum United States* (Cambridge, MA: Harvard University Press, 2009), 1–82.
17. W. J. T. Mitchell, *Picture Theory: Essays on Verbal and Visual Representation* (Chicago: University of Chicago Press, 1994), 13–14. Mitchell develops the concept that pictures of any media and genre may offer a poetics or theory of images in *What Do Pictures Want?: The Lives and Loves of Images* (Chicago: University of Chicago Press, 2006).
18. John C. Shields, "Phillis Wheatley's Theoretics of the Imagination: An Untold Chapter in the History of Early American Literary Aesthetics," in *New Essays on Phillis Wheatley*, ed. John C. Shields and Eric D. Lamore (Knoxville: University of Tennessee Press, 2011), 337–70.
19. June Jordan, "The Difficult Miracle of Black Poetry in America: Something like a Sonnet for Phillis Wheatley," in *On Call: Political Essays* (Boston: South End Press, 1985), 88.
20. For instance, Landor himself began life by being expelled from both Rugby School and from Trinity College, Oxford on account of his rebelliousness and jacobinism.
21. Herbert F. Tucker, *Epic: Britain's Heroic Muse, 1790–1910* (Oxford: Oxford University Press, 2008), 48. The phrase "Janus-visaged" is from Stuart Curran, *Poetic Form and British Romanticism* (Oxford: Oxford University Press, 1986), 8.
22. Christopher N. Phillips, *Epic in American Culture, Settlement to Reconstruction* (Baltimore: Johns Hopkins University Press, 2012), 2–4.
23. Ibid., 6.
24. Ibid., 8.
25. Ibid., 6.
26. Curran, *Poetic Form*, 8.
27. Ibid., 8–9 and 22, respectively, reflect Curran's unwillingness to embrace wholly the Freudian dimensions of Harold Bloom's similar account of influence; and Curran's awareness of the complexity of the politics of Romanticism.
28. Whether the ambition to write epic was transferred from the long heroic poem to long prose fiction, and if so, why and to what extent it was transferred, has been much debated. Among many titles, see John P. McWilliams, Jr., *The American Epic: Transforming a Genre, 1770–1860* (Cambridge: Cambridge University Press, 1989); Phillips, *Epic in American Culture*; and Tucker, *Epic*.
29. Theodorakopoulos, "Closure," *Cambridge Companion to Virgil*, 162–64.

Bibliography

Bush, Douglas. *Mythology and the Romantic Tradition in English Poetry.* Cambridge, MA: Harvard University Press, 1937.

Cannadine, Sir David. *The Rise and Fall of Class in Britain.* New York: Columbia University Press, 1999.

Chapman, Gerald. "Burke's American Tragedy." In *Johnson and His Age,* edited by James Engell, 386–423. Cambridge, MA: Harvard University Press, 1984.

Colley, Linda. *Britons: Forging the Nation, 1707–1837.* New Haven: Yale University Press, 1992.

Curran, Stuart. *Poetic Form and British Romanticism.* Oxford: Oxford University Press, 1986.

Graver, Bruce. "Classical Inheritances." In *Romanticism: An Oxford Guide,* edited by Nicholas Roe. Oxford: Oxford University Press, 2005.

———. "Romanticism." In *A Companion to the Classical Tradition,* edited by Craig W. Kallendorf. Oxford: Blackwell, 2007.

Güthenke, Constanze. *Placing Modern Greece: The Dynamics of Romantic Hellenism, 1770–1840.* Oxford: Oxford University Press, 2008.

Highet, Gilbert. *The Classical Tradition: Greek and Roman Influences on Western Literature.* New York: Oxford University Press, 1949.

Hopkins, David, and Charles Martindale, eds. *The Oxford History of Classical Reception in English Literature.* 4 vols. to date. Oxford: Oxford University Press, 2012–.

———, eds. *The Oxford History of Classical Reception in English Literature: Volume 3 (1660–1790).* Oxford: Oxford University Press, 2012.

Hulme, T. E. "Romanticism and Classicism." In *Speculations: Essays of Humanism and the Philosophy of Art,* edited by Herbert Read, 113–40. London: Kegan Paul, Trench, Trubner, 1924.

Jordan, June. "The Difficult Miracle of Black Poetry in America: Something like a Sonnet for Phillis Wheatley." In *On Call: Political Essays,* 87–98. Boston: South End Press, 1985.

Kermode, Sir Frank. *The Classic: Literary Images of Permanence and Change.* New York: Viking Press, 1975.

Martindale, Charles. "Milton's Classicism." In *The Oxford History of Classical Reception in English Literature: Volume 3 (1660–1790),* edited by David Hopkins and Charles Martindale, 55–62. Oxford: Oxford University Press, 2012.

McWilliams, John P., Jr. *The American Epic: Transforming a Genre, 1770–1860.* Cambridge: Cambridge University Press, 1989.

Mitchell, W. J. T. *Picture Theory: Essays on Verbal and Visual Representation.* Chicago: University of Chicago Press, 1994.

———. *What Do Pictures Want?: The Lives and Loves of Image.* Chicago: University of Chicago Press, 2006.

Most, Glenn W. "Virgil." In *The Classical Tradition*, edited by Anthony Grafton, Glenn W. Most, and Salvatore Settis, 965–69. Cambridge, MA: Belknap Press of Harvard University Press, 2010.

Perkins, David. *Is Literary History Possible?* Baltimore: Johns Hopkins University Press, 1992.

Phillips, Christopher N. *Epic in American Culture: Settlement to Reconstruction*. Baltimore: Johns Hopkins University Press, 2012.

Richard, Carl J. *The Golden Age of the Classics in America: Greece, Rome, and the Antebellum United States*. Cambridge, MA: Harvard University Press, 2009.

Saunders, Timothy, ed. *Romans and Romantics*. Oxford: Oxford University Press, 2012.

Shields, John C. "Phillis Wheatley's Theoretics of the Imagination: An Untold Chapter in the History of Early American Literary Aesthetics." In *New Essays on Phillis Wheatley*, edited by John C. Shields and Eric D. Lamore, 337–70. Knoxville: University of Tennessee Press, 2011.

Theodorakopoulos, Elena. "Closure: the Book of Virgil." In *Cambridge Companion to Virgil*, edited by Charles Martindale, 155–65. Cambridge: Cambridge University Press, 1997.

Tucker, Herbert F. *Epic: Britain's Heroic Muse, 1790–1910*. Oxford: Oxford University Press, 2008.

Vance, Norman, and Jennifer Wallace, eds. *The Oxford History of Classical Reception in English Literature: Volume 4 (1790–1880)*. Oxford: Oxford University Press, 2015.

The Virgil Encyclopedia. Edited by Richard F. Thomas and Jan M. Ziolkowski. 3 vols. Oxford: Wiley-Blackwell, 2014.

Weinbrot, Howard. "'An Ambition to Excell': The Aesthetics of Emulation in the Seventeenth and Eighteenth Centuries." *Huntington Library Quarterly* 48, no. 2 (1985): 121–39.

Wheeler, Kathleen. "Classicism, Romanticism, and Pragmatism: The Sublime Irony of Oppositions." *Parallax* 4, no. 4 (1998): 5–20.

Wilson, Penelope. "The Place of Classics in Education and Publishing." In *The Oxford History of Classical Reception in English Literature: Volume 3 (1660–1790)*, edited by David Hopkins and Charles Martindale, 31–52. Oxford: Oxford University Press, 2012.

Woods, George Benjamin, comp. *Poetry of the Victorian Period*. New York: Scott, Foresman, 1930.

Part I

Classical Practice, Romantic Concerns, and Genre

Chapter 1

William Gilpin: A Classical Eye for the Picturesque
Margaret Doody

William Gilpin is an oddity among the aesthetic philosophers of the eighteenth century. He can scarcely be called a philosopher, even in the eighteenth century's broader sense, when placed beside Shaftesbury, Burke, or Kant. His works belong in a much more comfortable lower realm, of the travelogue and the light essay. Yet William Gilpin defined a set of principles and effects combined under the name of "the Picturesque." Developing his ideas fully in later middle age, he recreated a term that found a permanent footing. His "Picturesque" is both what we might call an aesthetic ideal and an ideological principle—or set of principles. In arriving at his own formulation Gilpin finds it necessary to avoid heavy-handed classical allusions of the sort the young Gilpin finds overtly expressed in the visual allegories of Stowe. Yet to endorse the value of his maturing notion of "the Picturesque" Gilpin must announce the qualifications of his mind in repeated (if somewhat unobtrusive) classical references. Such references, customarily untranslated, ascertain his masculinity and privileged authority as he develops an aesthetic unusually based on sensibility, and unusually wary of the Burkean and masculine Sublime.

Gilpin was born in Cumberland in 1724. His birthplace explains his unusually high praise for the superiority of northern scenery, though by the time his thought was fully unfurled, English tourists were already discovering the beauties of the Lake District. William's father and younger brother were both artists, but Gilpin went into the Church, with apparently all the seriousness of which the Augustan age is sometimes mistakenly thought incapable. Taking his B.A. in 1744 and his M.A. in 1748, he was ordained; most of his working life, however, was spent as master of a boy's school, not as a parish clergyman. He had leisure for writing and some travel. The middle years were productive, but his attention as a writer was focused on the lives of major English Protestant heroes: Latimer in 1755, Wycliffe in 1765, and Cranmer in 1784.

About the time he proceeded M.A., Gilpin undertook a modest excursion; like many other tourists he went to see the famous gardens at Stowe. This site, inevitably mentioned in the history of landscape gardening, offers the visitor an almost aggressively programmatic sequence of experiences, designed specifically to create certain forms of delight and moral-political response. Gilpin not only visited Stowe, he wrote a book about it, *A Dialogue upon the Gardens of the Right Honourable the Lord Viscount Cobham, at Stow [sic] in Buckinghamshire*, published anonymously in 1748. Gilpin's little book (more like a tract in size) uses the dialogue form so popular with English writers of the period, both in fiction and non-fiction, ultimately established as a philosophical mode from Plato through Shaftesbury. The visitor Polython is shown around by Callophilus. The latter, whose name proclaims him "a lover of beauty," is more of a booster and less discriminating than the visitor, whose name indicates a love of truth. Polypthon has doubts about the moral taste of some exhibits, like the temples of Venus and Bacchus, and thinks some of the forms irregular and rough. He is willing to praise most of the installations, but at times seems ready to hint a fault or hesitate dislike for Stowe's calculated effects. He makes claims for the beauty of northern scenery when it is not tamed like Stowe, and speaks up for spending money on use rather than for show—with backing from Pope.[1]

It is surprising to one who knows the later Gilpin to see how greatly impressed the young man is with Pope, who is a kind of second guide here. Pope's pleasure in the prospects of harmonizing diversity, combined with a refusal to yield his moral judgment entirely to the pleasures announced by the landscaper, reflect or embody Gilpin's stance. Gilpin's quotations in this little treatise are largely modern; there is little classical reference just where one might expect a great deal. Stowe itself is pushing its own versions of Cicero and Virgil, while also representing effects from Ovid, so Gilpin seems deliberately to hold back from recitation of these classical sources. Fresh out of college, he might have been readily tempted to do so—but he holds back. The most striking classical quotation is not something we would have expected. Polypthon is struck by the images of the three men whom Callophilus had neglected to notice.

Callophilus makes up for this lapse with apology and praise of "the Imperial Closet": "There, Sir, is a noble Triumvirate. *Titus, Trajan* and *Aurelius*, are Names which want not the Pomp of title to add a Lustre to them."[2]

To this, Polypthon replies with emphatic assent: "I wish you could persuade all the Kings in Europe to take them as Patterns. There is more Virtue and Public spirit in that single honest Sentiment, **Pro me: si merear, in me*, than for ought I know they could all together furnish out" (33). The asterisk points us to a footnote: "Trajan's Motto on his Sword." But the meaning is not explained. It was not Trajan's sword, but the sword he gave to the praetorian prefect, saying to him "For me; if I should merit it, in me." That is, that the prefect Suburanus should protect the emperor, but if Trajan deserves no better, or fails in virtue and public spirit, that sword should be turned against Trajan himself. For an emperor to recommend his own assassination creates strange constitutional puzzles—and a kind of suicidal impulse might be attributed to the speaker. There are difficulties in explaining the terse motto, and Gilpin leaves it unexplained, even fuzzy. But in this dialogic essay the young Gilpin is signaling his devotion to ancient public virtue, as well as indicating an inclination toward—and at moments antipathy to—the schematized attractions and concretized fictions of this place, which he allows Callophilus to voice more fully than the visitor.

The difficulty of coping with the eighteenth century's use of terms could be illustrated in one speech by Callophilus, as the two men observe Stowe's "Lake" and its environs:

> Not many years ago I remember it only a Marsh: it surprised me prodigiously when I first saw it floated in this manner with a Lake. Has not that Ruin a good Effect? The sound of the Cascade, the Shrubs half-concealing the ragged View, and those dancing Fawns and Satyrs, I assure you, raise very romantic ideas in my head.
>
> (*Dialogue upon the Gardens*, 4)

To which Polypthon assents:

> Yes, indeed, I think the Ruin a great Addition to the beauty of the Lake. There is something so vastly picturesque and pleasing to the imagination in such Objects, that they are a great Addition to any Landskip. And yet perhaps it would be hard to assign a reason, why we are more taken with Prospects of this ruinous kind, than with Views of Plenty and Prosperity in their greatest Perfection. (5)

Callophilus here comments first, if inadvertently, on the technology which has created an object which did not exist in Nature, which had wanted only a Marsh. The Ruin is acknowledged to be not a real ruin and that is precisely its virtue, for it has "a good effect." Yet the combination of artificiality creates a real experience. All this together with the Cascade and the shrubs and the statues of fawns and satyrs combine in the "romantic idea." The romantic, of course, is present in the Renaissance and in the eighteenth century. We have been doing a disservice to intellectual and artistic history in hiving off a period of fifty years or so as "the Romantic period," pretending that it supervened as a great surprise and novelty. Yet, even to one who thinks as I do, custom ensures that it must strike us as odd that classical imaginary beings could be sought for their "romantic" effect. The effect of the unreal is at the center of the appeal of Stowe. The "romantic" takes us out of ourselves and our realistic lives. The beautiful grounds of Stowe dissolve into imaginary scenery, a secondary importation, a private yet shared mental scene superimposed on the first order of reality. It is Polython who supplies the harder question—as it is hard to know exactly what pleases us. *Why* do we love the "ruinous kind" rather than "Views of Plenty and Prosperity"? What allows or entices us to perform this feat or operation on ourselves? This question will inspire the bulk of Gilpin's mature work.

The twenty-four-year old Gilpin is already trying to grapple with issues that are eventually not going to let him rest. After his long partnership with leaders of English Protestantism, he would eventually write a series of books on "the Picturesque," starting in 1782. In his "Picturesque" works Gilpin taught several generations of aspiring tourists how to see. They knew they were supposed to enjoy Nature, but Gilpin showed them exactly how to do it, how to cultivate, in his phrase, "the picturesque eye." His books are a set of "Observations"—a term with a visual emphasis. Gilpin's "Observations" are sets of intellectual remarks, intelligently combined with physical "observations" by the discerning walker (or discerning passenger in a carriage) of actual British landscapes and definable places. The external world, with its power over the mind through the senses, is emphasized, even as the mentally powerful observer retains a right of control as a reward of attentiveness.

Each of these books deals more or less systematically with a different region of Britain; the concept is based on tours Gilpin had taken in the early 1770s, a decade before his "Picturesque" works started to appear. He may always have felt twinges of guilt about writing these works; toward the end of his life he evidently implored his publishers to emphasize his religious writings: "I have figured so much lately as a picturesque man, that I should be glad to redeem my character as a clergyman."[3] Like all English travel books of the late Renaissance and Enlightenment, Gilpin's works are deeply indebted to the line struck out by William Camden in *Britannia* (first published 1607). This ambitious work by the Elizabethan geographer and historian is originally powered by a desire to restore the memory of what was wiped away in the dissolution of the monasteries. There was just time to recover memory of the religious sites that had been overthrown, taken over, and often destroyed, or nearly erased, forty years before. Beginning in the 1570s, Camden walked and rode about much of England in order to determine and record the sites of abbeys and priories as well as to describe terrain, communications, fertility, and fortifications. Camden's work, written and published in Latin, was originally intended for a European audience (including, of course, a large Catholic readership). It was rapidly translated into English by Philemon Holland.

The most notable revision and translation was undertaken in the late seventeenth century by Bishop Edmund Gibson in 1695. A strong Protestant, certainly without the Catholic leanings of the great and engaging Camden, Gibson still respected Camden's works and findings. Gibson's edition went into multiple reissues and amplifications. The 1722 revised edition was in time, for instance, to affect Defoe's *Tour* and Richardson's revision of it. To a not inconsiderable extent Gilpin adapts the modes of the observant Elizabethan traveler, moving from historical facts about ports and structures to lays of the land, legends, descriptions of its beauty, and poetry. Camden offers us Latin poems of his own. Gilpin unostentatiously offers us some scraps of English poetry of his own, in the guise of general quotation. For Latin works he turns to the classical writers. Gilpin is vying with Camden while fully benefiting from his editors and successors. Together they furnished a complex example of travel writing, enabling Gilpin to choose a new form and recreate it. He created an aesthetic travelogue all his own, though stemming from Camden's rich example—including Camden's struggle with Time. Camden contemplates ruins not distant in time or space, but nearby and nearly fresh, like scars on wounds. (The extensive adoption of Camden's tone and matter in John Denham's influential topographical poem "Cooper's Hill" is not, I think, generally recognized.)

William Gilpin's "Picturesque" is a mode of embodying time and the transient in aesthetic thought. His Picturesque is a happy combination of the Burkean Sublime with the Beautiful—with some extra ingredients added. Gilpin likes the ruined—the crumbling wall, the dead branch. Gilpin's Picturesque evokes and even tries to embody the element of Time. That the incomplete work we gaze upon is the reverse of timeless is part of its trembling appeal. Death is always near at hand to sweep away the past. As he says in the Preface to his early work on the Picturesque in 1786, an artist should feel free to add some touch of the timeworn *ad libitum*:

> Trees he may generally plant, or remove at pleasure. If a withered stump suits the form of his landscape better than the spreading oak . . . he may make the exchange.[4]

Above all, Gilpin loved the ruins of English ecclesiastical foundations, particularly abbeys. As living institutions he decries them. They fostered—so he repeatedly asserts—ignorance, superstition, idleness, and dependence. He repeats this theme in each of the works. His attack on Glastonbury Abbey in 1798 is the most thoroughgoing, but he begins with an assault on Tintern Abbey in the first of his "Picturesque" books, *Observations on the River Wye* (1782). The charities of such a place only encouraged laziness. So it is at Tintern:

> Among other things in this scene of desolation, the poverty and wretchedness of the inhabitants were remarkable. They occupy little huts, raised among the ruins of the monastery; and seem to have no employment, but begging: as if a place once devoted to indolence, could never again become the seat of industry.[5]

Catholicism encourages beggary. Abbeys are homes of indolence. These are axioms. Gilpin by no means abandoned his Protestantism in writing about the Picturesque. The Picturesque Man was always compelled to be the Protestant Man.

Indeed, in writing about the Picturesque, Gilpin is fulfilling his Protestant calling. He justifies not only the ways of God to Man, but the operations of Time and Change. And what delights and inspires him is not merely the cruel operation of Time, but the result of violent man-made revolution. The ravages of Time are at one with the human destruction of monuments of the past—which is not complete eradication but a kind of miraculous metamorphosis. The 1530s bequeathed to England the splendor of ruins. These priceless ruins he regards as an extra asset to the beauty of

England—something lacking in Europe (where, of course, the abbeys were not torn down):

> To these natural features, which are, in a great degree peculiar to the landscape of England, we may lastly add another, of the artificial kind—the ruins of abbeys; which, being naturalized to the soil, might indeed, without much impropriety, be classed among its natural beauties.[6]

So says Gilpin in *Observations, Relative Chiefly to Picturesque Beauty*, published in 1786, his most explicit manifesto. The young Jane Austen criticizes his view in her mocking account of Henry VIII:

> Nothing can be said in his vindication, but that his abolishing Religious Houses and leaving them to the ruinous depredations of time has been of infinite use to the landscape of England in general, which probably was a principal motive for his doing it. . . .

Austen suspects a Whig agenda veiled beneath Gilpin's raptures. The Picturesque has a political purpose. Later, she will make the young Tilneys of Northanger Abbey—direct beneficiaries of the dissolution of the monasteries—enthusiastic readers of Gilpin, and Henry Tilney a naïve expositor of the Picturesque. Austen's remark on Henry VIII's usefulness to the landscape in ruining the abbeys is a satiric exaggeration—not a distortion—of Gilpin's view, in which aggressiveness is shielded by aesthetic complacency.[7]

Gilpin nonetheless loves the abbeys in their new, fragmented decorative state. These monuments are not eradicated but transformed into beautifully mournful ghosts, memories of themselves that combine with sun and rain and land to create a flickering, beautiful, sad, wonderful experience. It is the essence of the Picturesque that it should not dwell on construction, or exhibit—or even propose as desirable—movement through revolution into another productive settled state. Transformation should remain a perpetual ideal, should find no objective or harbor. Gilpin despises without measure those who have modernized their abbeys and made them livable mansions—like the owner of Forde Abbey. He laments over this modernized abbey in Dorset. Once it was perfect, a picturesque ruin. But it has fallen:

> Now, alas! It wears another face. It has been in the hands of improvement. Its simplicity is gone; and miserable ravage has been made through every part. The ruin is patched up into an awkward dwelling; old parts

and new are blended together, to the mutual disgrace of both. The elegant cloister is still kept; but it is completely repaired, white-washed, and converted into a green-house. The hall too is modernized, and every other part. Sash windows glare over pointed arches, and Gothic walls are adorned with Indian paper.[8]

Gilpin generalizes upon the crude iniquity of those who desire to inflict such denigrating "improvement" upon a potentially inspiring edifice:

> When a man exercises his crude ideas in a few vulgar acres, it is of little consequence.... But when he lets loose his depraved taste, his absurd invention, and his graceless hands on such a subject as this, where art and nature cannot restore the havoc he makes, we consider such a deed under the same black character ... as we do sacrilege and blasphemy in matters of religion. (277–78)

Gilpin does not lament the "sacrilege and blasphemy" of the original assault or depredation. But he registers with horror the vulgarization that turns the sacredness of ruin itself into something commonplace and homelike. More sharply than in his youth, he not only prefers prospects of the "ruinous kind" but actively detests the introduction of "Plenty and Prosperity"—in all their banality. He would have despised General Tilney's Northanger—and what loathing Downton Abbey would have inspired in him! (Even without the ridiculous refabrication of fabulous Highclere.) Abbeys were a mistake of the past. If made useful and modern in the present they are detestable. Once forced to minister to carnal satisfaction, remnants of abbeys are an obscene vulgarity. But they have the happy posthumous opportunity of transformation into the perfect aesthetic object. An abbey is "Picturesque" *only* as its ruin. A ragged remnant of piety, with touches of incomplete lovely design, an empty container of run-out happiness—the ruin alone gives painful joy. It is an eternal yearning absence. It is not quite dead, but permanently frustrated in any endeavor to return to life among the living. It embodies transience. Thus it puzzles and torments while it fills the mind and heart. Ruins are magnificent. They are the sign of true art, for they are without utility, and spend their broken existence registering the work of time and change. As ruins—and *only* as ruins—English abbeys are perfect. They have reached, that is, the perfection for which they were apparently eternally designed.

A ruin is a sacred thing. Rooted for ages in the soil, assimilated to it, the ruin becomes, as it were, a part of it. We consider it almost as a work of nature, rather than of art, yet it retains the pathos of its human origin. Art cannot reach it. The *magnificence* of ruin was never attained by any modern attempt. Gilpin uses his quite versatile descriptive powers to convince his readers to enjoy both the barbarism of the Gothic, and its weakness and fall. His company is to feast delicately upon destruction. Famous poets wrote formerly of the ruins of Rome—but Gilpin evidently feels that he is the first truly to celebrate the beauty of the civilization of the Middle Ages in ruination. Gilpin is the anti-Camden.

In his mature writings, Gilpin entirely repudiates the former abbeys in their functional state in a manner that may win Protestant approval. Nevertheless, he knows he is unorthodox in challenging aesthetic tradition. His "Picturesque" does not have the intensity or exaltation, the glory or despair of the high Baroque. At first glance, the celebration of medieval ruins seems to have departed completely from Greco-Roman standards in favor of the "Gothic." Gilpin has to make sure that his reader sees that he has not forsaken the art and literature of high classical civilization. Indeed, that classical civilization may stand in triumphant counterpoint to the ideology of the medieval church. Medieval Catholic Christianity, in Gilpin's view, is too fond of feeding the poor and otherwise encouraging luxury and idleness. Classical works inspire strength and virtue. They provide a respectable intellectual backbone to the Whig position. In the earliest of his "Picturesque" books, Gilpin frequently includes quotations from Latin poetry, particularly though not only from Horace's *Ars Poetica*. Speaking of himself in the third person, Gilpin claims a right of fault-finding in looking upon settlements, mansions and landscaping:

> He hath without scruple therefore remarked freely upon them; and hath endeavoured to point out the many strange errors, and absurdities, to which an inattention to nature hath given birth:
> Quorum, velut aegri somnia, vanae
> Fingunter species: ac nec pes, nec caput uni
> Reddatur formae . . .[9]

Visions of a fever dream are not by-products of the imagination. Unrealistic and silly things should have fault found with them. In this reference to things fashioned as if in a fever dream, Gilpin includes the bastardized results of inattention, errors, and absurdities, like the modernized Forde Abbey. These he is free to find fault with. Horace's feverish image, which itself indicates flickering inner visions not totally unrelated to the transient gleam, captures the reader's attention—though not of course if the reader is incapable of reading Latin. Gilpin's books attracted numbers of female readers and others uneducated in Latin, the language of the rulers and thinkers, the language taught to upper-class boys. Gilpin both asserts his ruling-class masculinity and deviates from it in his pursuit of the strange and ruinous, the grotesquely deformed and the useless. His use of Latin poets serves, however, to offer an assurance that he is centrally sound, that he does not go in for the truly strange. Gilpin has to prove his credentials as a scholar and writer. Now, as not in the case of the *Dialogue* on Stowe, he really *needs* to call in the help of Virgil and Horace and others. The author must sustain credible authority, proving that he has a sound knowledge of real literature and real traditional aesthetics, and that his own developing concepts are not out of keeping with the great tradition. In the language of Horace and the others we can find the strong columns, the round domes, the proportions, and assertive civilized power from which the ecclesiastical foundations in their physical shape were wondrous but freakish departures. Classicism has won, and the Gothic is forever elegantly dying. Virgil and Horace are flags of an ultimate propriety, a return to high enlightened order, which we can count upon in all our lovely tours and observations. Perhaps.

Two pages after the quotation from *Ars Poetica* cited just above, we find another quotation from same work of Horace, as Gilpin talks about travel writing—and his own writing:

> if, tho' highly coloured, it keep within the
> Descriptas vices, operisque colores,
> it may be hoped, it will escape censure. (xx)

The Latin, not italicized, is given prominence by being set off. Gilpin is apparently quoting from memory—or wishes to create that effect. In order to make full sense of the allusion, the ideal reader should be able to recollect Horace's *Ars Poetica*: "if I cannot observe the turns of description and the color of poetic works, why should I be considered a Poet?" Through the quotation we can espy Gilpin's own literary ambition.

William Gilpin is undoubtedly self-conscious in pursuing his unusual and unorthodox interest in such a mixed mode as the Picturesque.

There is an element of nervousness at times in his summoning of classical authors. It is as if they are called in as character witnesses to support his new theoretical interest in the Picturesque eye. When we discuss the Picturesque we are likely to rehearse the eighteenth century's developing fondness for the effects of seventeenth-century painters like Claude Lorraine (tranquility, reflections in water, classical touches, pastoral legend) and Salvator Rosa (*banditti*, mountains, thunderclouds). But Gilpin is not really interested in attaching these painters or their traditions to his own discussion. He turns to a literal historical landscape in order to illustrate the full flickering of the mind.

Of course, it is of primary importance that Gilpin establish himself as simply in command of material. He must repeatedly show himself to be scholarly and knowledgeable. In *Observations on the Western Parts of England* (1798), he is inevitably called upon to deal with Salisbury Plain and Stonehenge. And he has a mighty predecessor in William Stukeley's *Stonehenge. A Temple Restor'd to the Ancient Druids* (1740). Stukeley (1687–1765) was a friend of Isaac Newton (whose memoir he wrote) and of Edmund Halley, who assisted him in calculating the relation of Stonehenge and its alignment to magnetic north. Stukeley's *Stonehenge*, a big illustrated work, had become the standard treatise on the subject, even though—or more probably, because—it is a very daring treatise going against orthodox chronologies and values. In claiming that the great ruins are of a temple of the Druids, Stukeley makes high claims for the Druids (and the ancient Britons all together). The ancient Britons were, in his view, a superior group, spiritually and intellectually, descended probably from Phoenicians, with their own religion and science. They stood in no need of importation from continental Europe. (And they did quite well without Christianity.) Stukeley's engaging treatise seems at times quite mad, and at other times ahead of its century and quite sane. His argument for the astronomical capabilities of Stonehenge has proven to have enduring popularity. His general view of Britons vs. Continentals is an extreme version of the "Norman yoke" argument, disputing even the claims of the Saxons.

William Gilpin does not want to become embroiled with William Stukeley. He refuses, in a masterly way, even to mention him in his own disquisition on Stonehenge—even while he is drawing on the same material regarding written sources. In *Observations on the Western Parts of England* he turns for himself to the ancient sources (already combed by Stukeley and others who had intently read and re-read Tacitus, Caesar, *et al.*). Gilpin also subtly turns a little more to the poets than to ancient prose writers in substantiating his claim to interpret the landscape of the area around Stonehenge with its ancient burial mounds or barrows.

> That they are mansions of the dead is undoubted; many of them having been opened, and found to cover the bones both of men and beasts; the latter of which were probably sacrificed at the funeral. We suppose also that some of them contained the promiscuous ashes of a multitude as Virgil describes them.
>
>   "Confusae ingentem caedis acervum,
> Nec numero, nec honore cremant. Tunc indique vasti
> Certatim crebris collucent ignibus agri.
> Tertia lux gelidam coelo dimoverat umbram;
> Moerentes altum cinerem, et confusa ruebant
> Ossa focis; tepidoque onerabant aggere terrae."[10]

Gilpin offers no translation of this sad picture of mass cremation and the confusion of remains transformed by fire (although he might easily have turned to Dryden to help out his unlettered readers).[11] Dryden picks up the sadness in Virgil's account of this heap of nameless dead, the common men who turn into a promiscuous heap of warm bones and ash buried in the earth. For Gilpin, "promiscuous ashes of a multitude" are an appropriate historical detritus with interesting results. All is as it should be. He continues in anthropological mode, surveying mankind from Greece to Guinea:

> Indeed this mode of burial, as the most honourable, seems to have been dictated by the voice of nature. We meet with it in Homer; we meet with it in Herodotus. The vestiges of it are found on the vast plains of Tartary; and even among the savages of Guinea. (85)

Gilpin goes on to argue that "these temples and cemeteries" are more antique than we are accustomed to allow. He cites Caesar's *Gallic Wars* as evidence:

> That chief, in the first book of his Commentaries, describing the place, which was . . . to be the scene of conference between him and Ariovistus, tells us, it was an extensive plain, in which was a large artificial mount. *Planities erat magna, et in ea tumulus terreus satis grandis.*

Gilpin argues in a learned manner for translating *terreus* as artificial. Here, he asserts, we are looking with Caesar at one of the ancient barrows:

> That Caesar's *tumulus* was intended also as a memorial for the dead, is probable.... We find Aeneas likewise haranguing his troops from a tomb of this kind:
> "Socios in caetum littore ab omni
> Advocat Aeneas, tumulique ex aggere fatur."[12] (86–87)

This is Gilpin the practical, somewhat aggressively sharpening his claws as a rhetorician of fact. He will not permit himself to be indebted—as he certainly is—to other scholars of his own century. Virgil is impressed into service as an historical supplement. The section on Stonehenge and environs in *Observations on the Western Parts of England* is not uninteresting, though served cold. We are safe from aesthetic disturbance.

The case is far otherwise elsewhere. Gilpin can call in Virgil to aid with startling poetic effect. In a later section of his tour in *Western Parts* the author deals with the region of Quantock and Bridgewater. This area is not exotic, though attractive and full of historical interest, as he acknowledges in describing the green flats of Sedgemoor where Monmouth was defeated (149). But it is in this section of *Western Parts* that Gilpin raises the stakes. He deals in an exciting and disconcerting manner on the effects of looking at landscape through obscuring and changeable mist.

We can recognize fully in this section that Gilpin challenges Edmund Burke. He is endeavoring to go beyond Burke on the Sublime, to find more subtle and more extraordinary effects than Burke acknowledges. Gilpin suddenly refers to a recent book (published 1790) which would appear to have nothing to do with the landscape of Western England. He alludes to an account of Captain John Meares in his *Voyages Made in the years 1788 and 1789, from China to the West Coast of America*. Gilpin summarizes and elaborates on Meares's narrated experience of being lost with his ship in a heavy sea mist off the unknown American coast. He can hear the dangerous boom of breakers on rocks without being able to discern where anything is. When the fog starts to lift, he finds himself in his small craft amongst gigantic snow-capped cliffs. Eventually he sees more and is able to save his life and ship: "Captain Meares now perceived the passage, through which he had been driven into this scene of horrors, and made his escape" (166).[13]

The site of Meares's ordeal is very far away, but the captain's straining to see through mist offers Gilpin a most satisfactory example and objective correlative:

> On reading such accounts as these in a picturesque light, one can hardly avoid making a few remarks on the grand effects which may often be produced by what may be called, *the scenery of vapour*. Nothing offers so extensive a field to the fancy in *invented* scenes; nothing subjects even the *compositions of nature* so much to the control and improvement of art. It admits the painter to participation with the poet in the use of the machinery of *uncertain forms*; to which both are indebted for their *sublimest images*. (166)

The remarkable phrase *"the scenery of vapour"* captures some of the various effects of Descartes, Locke, and Newton on the workings of sight as a working of the self. All "scenery" is in some sense a "*scenery of vapour*," a nebulous and shifting pact made between what we call "sense" and what we term "the mind."[14] Seeing itself is in great part invention, or construction—an important finding of seventeenth-century philosophers from Descartes to Newton. Art, then, is simply a more conscious pushing of the natural case. Not only the artist but even the ordinary sighted person is a "poet" in use of "the machinery of *uncertain forms*." The Sublime cannot exist in certainty—not at all.

> A *sublime image* is perhaps an incorrect phrase. The regions of sublimity are not peopled by *forms*, but *hints*; they are not enlightened by *sunshine*, but by *gleams* and *flashes*. The transient view of the summit of a cliff towering over the mast, filled the despairing seaman with more terror than if he had seen the whole rocky bay. It set his imagination at work. The ideas *of grace and beauty* are as much raised by leaving the image half immersed in obscurity, as the ideas of *terror*.

Gilpin admits but also defies Burke's "terror" which comes with grandeur. Gilpin emphasizes what Burke had certainly analyzed and stressed—the effect of uncertainty, loss of visual control. But Gilpin contradicts Burke in claiming that what is sauce for the Sublime is sauce also for the Beautiful. The transient gleam, the flash amid obscurity—these are also the territory of the Beautiful. The Sublime cannot claim solitary ownership of obscurity, or of momentary glimpses within the dark. But it takes a poet to demonstrate how this works.

Definition, which throws a light on philosophic truth, destroys at once the airy shapes of fiction. Virgil has given more beauty in three words,
> Lumenque juventae
> Purpureum—

than he could have done in the most labored description; as Grey [*sic*] likewise has in the two following lines, though some cold critic would probably ask for an explanation:
> O'er her warm cheek, and rising bosom move
> The bloom of young desire, and purple light of love.

It is by snatches only that you catch a glimpse of such beauties. Would you analyse them, the vision dissolves in the process; and disappears, like life pursued to its last retreat by the anatomist. You ruin the image by determining its form, and identifying its tints. (167)[15]

In calling on Virgil to substantiate his Salisbury Plain barrow, Gilpin uses the poet coldly, turning his poem into a lifeless explanatory footnote. It may be useful but it is not poetic. In this latter passage—which represents Gilpin at his very best—the use of Virgil is lively and effective. The bringing together of Thomas Gray (Gilpin's contemporary) and Virgil is most happy.[16] The modern poet's usage clearly derives from the classical predecessor who remains lively and current, a participant and not a dead letter. Unlike the ruins, Virgil is totally alive still. The flickering purple light is the gift of Venus. And Virgil can help to explain what is so wonderful about the ruined abbeys, the vision that dissolves in the process of seeing, the impossibility of reconstructing what flickers from the past, gleams and disappears, dissolving in our own minds.

Notes

1. This little work has been referred to by Alexander M. Ross in *The Imprint of the Picturesque in Nineteenth-Century Fiction* (Waterloo, ON: Wilfrid Laurier University Press, 1986), and by John Macarthur in *The Picturesque: Architecture, Disgust and Other Irregularities* (Abingdon: Routledge, 2007). Macarthur deals interestingly with attraction and repulsion in this early work of Gilpin.
2. *A Dialogue upon the Gardens of the right Honorable Lord Viscount Cobham, at Stowe in Buckinghamshire*, 2nd ed. (London: B. Seeley and J. and J. Rivington, 1749), 5–6.
3. Malcolm Andrews, *Oxford Dictionary of National Biography*, quoting Gilpin as cited in Andrews's own book, *The Search for the Picturesque: Landscape, Aesthetics and Tourism in Britain 1760–1800* (Stanford: Stanford University Press, 1990).

4. Gilpin, "Preface" to *Observations Relative Chiefly to Picturesque Beauty. Made in the year 1771, On several Parts of ENGLAND; Particularly the Mountains, and Lakes of Cumberland, and Westmoreland,* 2 vols. (London: R. Blamire, 1786), 1:xxviii.
5. Gilpin, *Observations on the River Wye and Several Parts of South Wales &c. Relative chiefly to Picturesque Beauty made in the Summer of the Year 1770* (London: R. Blamire, 1782), 35.
6. Gilpin, *Observations Relative Chiefly to Picturesque Beauty,* 1:12.
7. Jane Austen, "The History of England," in *Juvenilia,* ed. Peter Sabor (Cambridge: Cambridge University Press, 2006), 180.
8. Gilpin, *Observations on the Western Parts of England, Relative chiefly to Picturesque Beauty To which are added A few Remarks on the Picturesque Beauties of the Isle of Wight* (London: T. Cadell and W. Davies, 1798), 277–78.
9. Gilpin, "Preface" to *Observations Relative Chiefly to Picturesque Beauty,* 1:xviii. Quotation is from Horace, *Ars Poetica Ad Pisones* (sometimes called "The Epistle to the Pisos"), lines 7–9. "Like men in fever dreams they fashion vain species, of which neither foot not head will fit with any form."
10. Gilpin, *Observations on the Western Parts of England,* 85.
11. The quotation is from Virgil's *Aeneid,* Book XI, lines 207–12. Here is Dryden's rendition:

> The rest, unhonor'd, and without a name,
> Are cast a common heap to feed the flame.
> Trojans and Latians vie with like desires
> To make the field of battle shine with fires,
> And the promiscuous blaze to heav'n aspires.
> Now had the morning thrice renew'd the light,
> And thrice dispell'd the shadows of the night,
> When those who round the wasted fires remain
> Perform the last sad office to the slain.
> They rake the yet warm ashes from below;
> These, and the bones unburned, in earth bestow.
> These relics with their country rites they grace,
> And raise a mound of turf to mark the place.

12. Quotation from *Aeneid* Book V, lines 43–44. "Aeneas call'd the Trojan troops around, /And thus address'd them from a rising ground" (Dryden). Dryden's translation does nothing to help Gilpin's case.
13. Gilpin, *Observations on the Western Parts of England,* 166. Meares's own account is strikingly effective, yet Gilpin chooses not to quote but to paraphrase, heightening effects that he evidently thinks Meares is striving for. Gilpin gets rid of all references to native peoples and Russians inhabiting these parts. Meares's account can be found in "An Introductory Voyage of the Nootka," in *Voyages Made in the Years*

1788 and 1789, From China to the West Coast of America (London: Logographic Press, 1790), v–vi.
14. Gilpin's intense if delicate fascination with *"the scenery of vapour"* and the vaporishness of seeing expressed in 1798 could already have benefited from the works of Ann Radcliffe. As Jayne Lewis notes, "Her most popular romance, *The Mysteries of Udolpho*, opens onto a view of 'partial vapours' suffused with 'the blue tinge of air'" (*Air's Appearance: Literary Atmosphere in British Fiction, 1660–1794* [Chicago: University of Chicago Press, 2012], 192). Wordsworth's fondness for views observed through mists and vapors, an affection so decided in *The Prelude*, probably owes something considerable to Gilpin, but also to Radcliffe and others.
15. The Virgilian quotation comes from Book I of the *Aeneid*, lines 590–91. Aeneas, arriving in Carthage after a tiring journey, is transformed back into his natural beauty by the operation of Venus, his mother, and is thus bound to prove irresistible to Dido. A simple translation of the phrase quoted is "the purple light of youth" (or "the rosy light of youth"). It is unlikely that any critic with a classical education would be puzzled by Gray's phrase, where the poet is drawing on precisely the passage of the *Aeneid* from which Gilpin quotes.
16. The lines of Thomas Gray come from his *The Progress of Poesy* (1757), part I, section 3, lines 16–17.

Bibliography

Andrews, Malcolm. *The Search for the Picturesque: Landscape, Aesthetics and Tourism in Britain 1760–1800*. Stanford: Stanford University Press, 1990.

Austen, Jane. "History of England." In *Juvenilia*, edited by Peter Sabor. Cambridge: Cambridge University Press, 2006.

Gilpin, William. *A Dialogue upon the Gardens of the Right Honourable the Lord Viscount Cobham at Stow in Buckinghamshire*. 2nd ed. London: B. Seeley and J. and J. Rivington, 1749.

———. *Observations on the River Wye and Several Parts of South Wales &c. Relative Chiefly to Picturesque Beauty Made in the Summer of the Year 1770*. London: R Blamire, 1782.

———. *Observations Relative Chiefly to Picturesque Beauty Made in the Year 1771, on Several Parts of ENGLAND, Particularly the Mountains, and Lakes of Cumberland, and Westmoreland*. 2 vols. London: R. Blamire, 1786.

———. *Observations on the Western Parts of England, Relative chiefly to Picturesque Beauty. To Which Are Added a Few Remarks on the Picturesque Beauties of the Isle of Wight*. London: T. Cadell and W. Davies, 1798.

Lewis, Jayne Elizabeth. *Air's Appearance: Literary Atmosphere in British Fiction, 1660–1794*. Chicago: University of Chicago Press, 2012.

Macarthur, John. *The Picturesque: Architecture, Disgust and Other Irregularities*. Abingdon: Routledge, 2007.

Meares, John. *Voyages Made in the Years 1788 and 1789, from China to the West Coast of America*. London: Logographic Press, 1790.

Ross, Alexander M. *The Imprint of the Picturesque in Nineteenth-Century British Fiction*. Waterloo, ON: Wilfrid Laurier University Press, 1986.

Stukeley, William. *Stonehenge. A Temple Restor'd to the Ancient Druids*. London: W. Innys and R. Munby, 1740.

Chapter 2

Phillis Wheatley and the Political Work of Ekphrasis
Mary Louise Kete

For Phillis Wheatley, who was born in Africa during the early 1750s and died in Boston in 1784, the problem of ethos was particularly stark. During her lifetime, Boston seethed with arguments about political representation, taxation, and liberty.[1] Wheatley, a black, enslaved girl from Africa, had no standing from which to enter these arguments. She had no recognized ethos to speak by, for, or of her self on any topic because her society, quite unapologetically, didn't recognize her as having a self to represent. Amazingly, for so many reasons, Wheatley began composing and writing what increasingly looked like poetry (metered verse presenting topical or abstract subjects in forms inspired by contemporary and classical examples) even while it was almost unthinkable that she could be, somehow, a poet. What warrant could a slave offer to her readers to induce them to read her poems? I don't think anyone expected Wheatley herself to provide one. In 1773, for example, when the extraordinary effort was made to publish a collection of her works as *Poems on Various Subjects, Religious and Moral*, it was vouched for by her patrons. Her publisher, her master, a committee of Boston's worthies, and even Selina Hastings, Countess of Huntingdon, presented more than ample authorization for the volume in its elaborate front matter.[2] Nevertheless, in the proem Wheatley wrote for her volume, "To Maecenas," she took it upon herself to provide a personal warrant for the value of her poetry, and she did so by taking advantage of the radical potential of the classical mode of ekphrasis.[3]

"To Maecenas" is ekphrastic in both the broad sense of re-depicting and commenting upon one work of art by another, and the narrow sense of being a poem about an image. The ode re-depicts and comments upon some of the most famous literary works of the classical canon, while the poem as a whole contests, by re-depicting and commenting upon, the image of Phillis Wheatley created and authorized by her patrons.[4] In one sense, Wheatley is being quite old-fashioned by turning ekphrasis to the task of establishing the origin and nature of her own authority as a poet. For the classical rhetoricians, the interpretive description of what one has seen was understood as a powerful persuasive device. An ekphrasis not only places the subject of an orator "vividly before the eyes" of a listener, it could also establish or reinforce the authority of the speaker by revealing otherwise hidden aspects of one's character.[5] In the pages below I argue that Wheatley's ekphrasis serves to depict, and so reveal, aspects of her personal character obscured by her culture's insistence on mis-categorizing her on the basis of race and gender. But, further, I want to suggest that "To Maecenas" anticipates the more romantic use of ekphrasis as a means to interrogate the limits and possibilities of representation.[6] Reclaiming, through ekphrasis, the authority to represent her self and her world, she asserts the autonomy denied her by her culture and by the front matter of her book. In depicting what Gordon Wood might call the "revolutionary character" of the speaker of "To Maecenas," Wheatley posits that the freedom necessary as a predicate of the poetic ethos is not limited by race, gender, or the condition of slavery.[7] In this way, Wheatley's innovation underscores the inherently political potential of ekphrasis by using it to explore, and to claim, the necessary conditions of self-representation.

In the increasingly heated discourse of Boston during the 1760s, the meanings of terms such as "slavery," "liberty," and "representation" grew deeply entangled. The colonials complained that without the right to represent themselves in Parliament they were being enslaved. This meaning of slavery was taken from older, Roman concepts, but it was a definition beginning to be problematized by the modern practice of racialized slavery.[8] The question of whether, how, and why slaves such as the young girl whom John and Susanna Wheatley had bought in 1761 should be politically represented was not yet widely discussed, though it would be during the constitutional debates following the Revolution.[9] The question of whether the Wheatleys' slave could, much less should, represent her own self was even less of an issue. Her gender, her age, and especially her status as a black slave would suggest not: on these three different counts, Wheatley's self was not her own. Self-representation by a slave was a contradiction in terms. Slaves—like other property—were counted by and in the interest of their masters.[10] A slave like Phillis, well dressed and fed, educated, and allowed the leisure and resources to write down her verse, said much about the Wheatleys' wealth, politics, and religious beliefs.[11] As Harriet Beecher Stowe explained, under the condition of slavery, such "articles" as religion, character, or literary talent merely added to the value of the slave but then only, of course, if a prospective buyer valued such "articles."[12]

The Wheatleys' Phillis was, legally, just a particularly fancy "article" herself, and this is how she is depicted in the visual and verbal images offered as authenticating documents by the front matter to the first edition of her book. Framed this way, the verses in *Poems on Various Subjects, Religious and Moral* are presented as the prime illustrations of, and ancillary ornamentations to, the extraordinariness of Mr. Wheatley's slave: the fanciest thing about her was her talent for verse. Africans, slaves, and girls might be suitable objects of aesthetic or economic desire, but in the late eighteenth-century British world, no one expected them to create objects of beauty from their imagination. The introductory material, the front matter of the *Poems*, disposes the reader to "marvel," not as Countee Cullen would do, at God's seemingly perverse creation of a "poet black," then "bid him sing," but at the curiosity of the man-made "thing" that is "Phillis Wheatley, Negro Servant to Mr. John Wheatley, Boston."[13] The front matter was designed explicitly to solve the practical problem of transforming her verse into a book that readers would buy.[14] Wheatley and her patrons (inspired primarily by her mistress, Susanna Wheatley) had been unable to do this in provincial Boston, where an attempt to publish the collection failed. They then had turned to Archibald Bell of London to see this ambitious and unique project through. Vincent Carretta outlines, in *Biography of a Genius in Bondage*, how Bell assembled the variety of authenticating documents into a structure that might make Wheatley and her poems legible to readers and to warrant the investment of those readers' time and money.[15]

The Wheatleys were, in good part, responsible for much of the publisher's difficulty. Their Phillis was undoubtedly a commodity: she had been bought; she could be sold. It is clear, though, that the Wheatleys considered her a special kind of object: less functional than decorative, almost but not quite family. They had made her that way. The raw precociousness exhibited by the girl, whose age had been guessed at about seven when she was bought, was molded by religion and education, then polished to a state of verifiable erudition by the attention of mentors and by access to libraries. We don't really know what led the Wheatleys to foster their slave girl's intellect and spirituality by teaching her so much more than she would have needed in order to succeed as a household servant. Despite Carretta's comprehensive research into the lives of John and Susanna Wheatley, he has found no correspondence or other direct evidence concerning what the Wheatleys had in mind by treating their slave girl in such an unconventional manner.[16] Phillis had been bought as a companion for Susanna and her two children, and the Wheatleys' treatment of her could have been a deliberate extension or test of the egalitarian impulses of the new doctrines offered by evangelicals such as the Methodist Calvinist, George Whitefield. It could have been an indulgence for the children, or for their mother. It could have been love that led the Wheatleys to treat the delicate and sickly girl as they would want their own child to be treated in similar circumstances. In any case, their African, enslaved girl, under the skilled guidance of the whole family, became a paradigm or model for what a benevolent Christian upbringing could accomplish even for the least promising of objects.

Wheatley's precocity had manifested itself to her owners when, after less than two years in America, she was able to read even "the most difficult Parts of the Sacred Writings."[17] She was encouraged to join a church, was baptized, and when barely ten wrote a letter to the Mohegan minister Samson Occom (another protégé of Selina Hastings, Countess of Huntingdon). Christianity, as it did for her contemporaries the black Congregational minister Lemuel Haynes, the Pequot minister William Apess, and Occom himself, provided Wheatley some standing from which to speak and be heard. It is as a Christian, after all, that Wheatley addresses a countess as a fellow Christian and mourner upon the death of the Reverend George Whitefield. It is as a Christian that Wheatley reminds other "Christians" that "Negroes, black as Cain / May be refined and join the angelic train."[18] Part of the process of Christian refinement came through her study of the best of British literature, including translations of the Greek and Roman classics as well as contemporary essays, poetry, and sermons. But for the Wheatleys, as for Whitefield himself and the Countess of Huntingdon, Christianity was neither inconsistent with the legal fiction of her enslavement nor with the negative connotations associated with the physical fact of her blackness.[19] So compatible were these that Thomas Jefferson would, later, use Wheatley's Christianity as one of the arguments against granting her the ethos of a poet. Christianity and blackness were both indicative, to Jefferson, of an essentially slavish character, which was to say, to have no standing at all.

That her verse follows and even exceeds neoclassical standards of taste, and that it found at least some contemporary critical approval, posed a serious challenge to newly coalescing theories of racial inferiority that were being called upon to justify the racialized slavery undergirding much of the colonial economy and that of an expanding British empire.[20] The quality of her verse was excessively or even impossibly good.[21] Recognizing this, her publisher and other backers had to work hard to provide the kind of introductory material that would help readers negotiate the lack of congruence between the elite nature of her poetry and the supposedly debased nature of its enslaved writer. This was a transatlantic, collaborative effort involving a loose coalition of patrons composed of her owner and various prominent whites. Their aims may not always have been consistent or coherent, but all agreed that it was important that Phillis Wheatley's poems be available in print to a wide audience.[22] Bell's choice of front matter, part of the paratextual apparatus enclosing and presenting Wheatley's poems, was key to this effort. He provided her with the already conventional introduction of a poetess whose poems were "written originally for the Amusement of the Author." Yet this, apparently, did not seem quite adequate to the task of introducing an enslaved poet. Nor did the author's conventional "Dedication" to her patron the Countess of Huntingdon. So, in addition to providing the frontispiece image that had been suggested by the Countess, Bell also refers the reader to "her Master's Letter," which speaks "to the Disadvantages she has labored under." As if this were not enough, Bell also provided a statement from the "most respectable Characters in Boston, that none might have Ground for disputing their Original." All in all, the unusually long, eight-page introduction to the author comprised a frontispiece, a title page, an author's "Dedication to the Countess of Huntingdon," a "Preface" by the publisher, a "Letter" from the author's master, and an attestation "To the Publick" by Boston's worthies. Together, these transform Wheatley's collected poems into the book we know: *Poems on Various Subjects, Religious and Moral*. Together, they answer the question of how Phillis Wheatley could be both slave and author. This is the answer, as I'll discuss further on, that Wheatley tries hard to dispute in the course of her "To Maecenas."

It seems that Bell (and Wheatley's other supporters) anticipated that the main stumbling block for potential readers might be the conflict between two opposing, common figures or tropes: slave and poet. The first denies her a position from which to speak as a subject,

"Phillis Wheatley, Negro Servant to Mr. John Wheatley, of Boston." Her slavishness was triply marked by her gender, her color and her legal status. The latter, that of the poet (whose race, rank, and gender need not be marked because they are assumed to be, respectively, white, free, and male) stands for an unlimited power to represent the self and the world.[23] Read as a whole, the introduction of *Poems* addresses this as a problem of adjusting the ethos (character) of the reader and the ethos (character) of the author so that they better correspond. The reader needs, as the front matter of *Poems* suggests, to be able to imagine something for which there was no easy precedent: a black, African, enslaved, girl who writes verse.[24] Bell's challenge was to make the unseen visible without generating the kind of anxiety that would lead a reader to turn away rather than engage further. Emphasizing her enslavement, Bell meets this challenge by offering a series of three overlapping and redundant images that try to contain the threats posed by the incongruous fact of Phillis Wheatley's actual composition of the poems. The first image is presented by the frontispiece featuring an engraving, made at the behest of Selina Hastings, of a now lost portrait of Wheatley.[25] The other two images take the form of brief narrative descriptions of "PHILLIS," who "was brought from *Africa* to *America*," as her master put it in a letter to the publisher that goes on to explain:

> Without any Assistance from School Education, and by only what she was taught in the Family, she, in sixteen Months Time from her arrival, attained the English Language, to which she was an utter Stranger before, to such a degree, as to read any, the most difficult Parts of the Sacred Writings, to the great Astonishment of all who heard her.

The attestation "To the PUBLICK" in the final element of the front matter offers a slightly different version of this same story:

> PHILLIS, a young Negro Girl, who was but a few Years since, brought an uncultivated Barbarian from *Africa*, and has ever since been, and now is, under the Disadvantage of serving as a Slave in a Family in this Town. She has been examined by some of the best Judges, and is thought qualified to write them [her poems].

Each of these biographical anecdotes repeats and adds to what the frontispiece-portrait has already depicted. Together they repeat the image of Wheatley in different media (picture and words) and different genres (Preface, Letter, Attestation). This redundancy builds a multilayered, self-reflective picture of the Wheatleys' Phillis that stresses her status as a slave above her other attributes: her precocious intellect, her African origins, her youth, and even her Christianity. These other aspects—attributes or "articles," in Stowe's sense of the word—are subordinate to her status as a slave.

The ethos created by the multiple elements of the introduction seems designed to provide readers with a comfortable and familiarly sympathetic position to inhabit, if they choose, and from which they may be able to recognize what there is to be astonished by in *Poems on Various Subjects*. The introduction appeals to the reader's interest on the grounds of slavery, that the volume is worth reading *because* Wheatley is a slave. Directing the reader's attention to the image of the attractive and extraordinary slave at the center of this paratextual frame pushes the poetry aside until it becomes ancillary to the non-threatening pathos of this depiction. Framed this way, the verse which follows the front matter elaborates on, rather than challenges, the picture of John Wheatley's enslaved servant, Phillis. Figuring Wheatley as a suitable, if extraordinary, object of aesthetic appreciation, the introduction also constrains—almost, if not actually, silences—her ability to represent herself as the author of her own poetry.

Let me illustrate what I mean by paying close attention to the frontispiece page of the first edition, for it epitomizes what "To Maecenas" must work against. Representing Wheatley's body as a work of art, owned and represented by another, the frontispiece posits an ethos for slavery in words and images: the slave speaks by and through the authority of the owner. As is conventional, the verso of the first leaf following the unlabeled cover and the blank endpapers features the frontispiece, while the frontispiece faces the title page on the recto of the second leaf (Figure 2.1).

Like the rest of the front matter, the frontispiece is composed of heterogeneous elements: an engraved reproduction of a portrait of Wheatley (the frontispiece portrait) is set above the copyright date, the name and the street address of the "bookseller" and publisher. This is unusual, as other contemporary frontispiece portraits either have no writing outside the frame of the engraving (which indicates the assumption that the image is of the author whose name is found on the facing title page), or the frontispiece is labeled only by the author's name.[26] Most discussions of the frontispiece of *Poems* concentrate on the powerful depiction of the young black woman at the center of the engraving, and thus remove it from its context on the page within the engraving as a whole, and within the volume as a

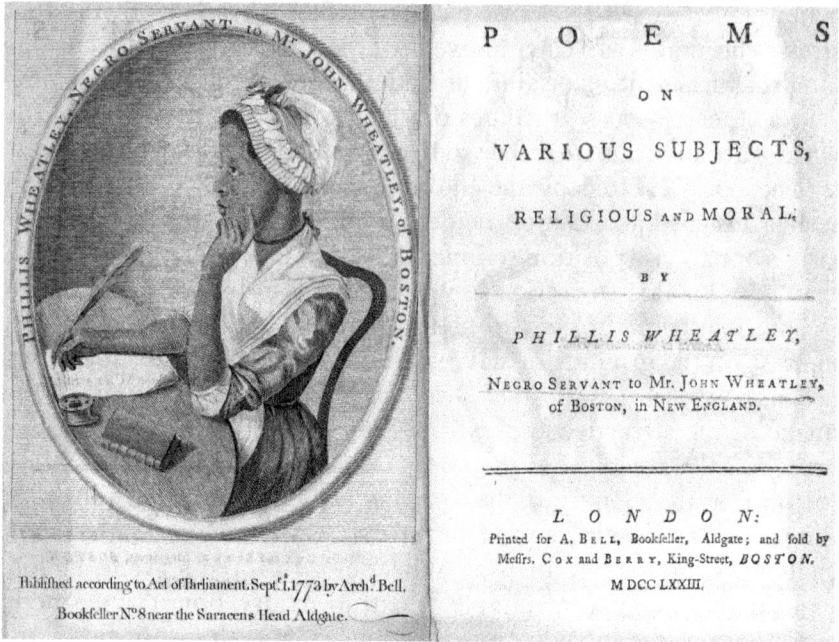

Figure 2.1 Frontispiece and Title Page, First Edition, Courtesy University of South Carolina, Irvin Department of Rare Books and Special Collections.

whole. Frequently, and not altogether unhelpfully, the picture is read for what can be learned about the historical Phillis. In other words, generally this image is read and judged as mimetic—an attempt to imitate or represent a supposedly extant reality.

The frontispiece as a whole may also be read as an instance of ekphrasis, for it re-depicts and comments upon an image of Phillis Wheatley that has been made, is owned, and is in the service of (i.e., represents) another. It is, to use Frederick Burwick's definition, a "mimesis of a mimesis."[27] What the reader sees on opening the book to the facing pages of the frontispiece and the title page are two slightly different iterations of the same figure, provided in two media: picture and words. The visual image of the frontispiece adds to and comments upon the title page, and vice versa. The female figure is dressed modestly, sitting at a table with all the resources needed for, and symbols of, creative writing: paper, book, pen, and ink. Why this particular picture might demand a comment or an interpretation arises from the, at least unexpected if not uncanny, dark shading of the figure's skin, as well as from the ribbon encircling the figure's neck.[28] The figure is designated, in this way, as both black and enslaved. Its setting, attitude, and accoutrements signal a class position not ordinarily imaginable for blacks on either side of the British Atlantic. The frontispiece also visually elaborates the information given by the title page: the Phillis Wheatley who wrote these poems, and who is the servant of Mr. John Wheatley of Boston, is black. It seems that neither a visual nor a verbal description of "Phillis Wheatley, Servant to Mr. John Wheatley, of Boston" would suffice by itself.

The engraving that occupies four fifths of the frontispiece is a rectangle formed by a solid black line within which a labeled oval frame surrounds an image of a young woman seated at an oval desk. Surrounding three sides of the rectangle is a thin border of blank page accentuating the difference between what is within (the engraving) and what is outside (the sheet of paper). The border demarcates the "made" or artificial aspect of the engraving that is composed of an assortment of lines, hatch work, images of objects, and words. The blank space also, however, integrates the rectangular image with the verbal statement printed in the lower fifth of the page into a visual whole. Read in this way, the engraving serves as the pictorial referent for what was "Published according to Act of parliament, Sept'r 1, 1773 by Arch'd Bell, Bookseller No. 8, near the Saracens Head Aldgate," in addition to providing an authorizing portrait of Phillis Wheatley. For what is being referred to, the work of art published by Bell, is the book that both contains and is represented by the engraved portrait. In this sense, then, the engraving is also picturing the words set above the double line on the facing title page: "*Poems on Various Subjects, Religious and Moral* by Phillis Wheatley, Negro Servant to Mr. John Wheatley of Boston, in New England." Below that double line, the publishing information given by the frontispiece is similarly repeated, and elaborated on, by the rendering of the publication date in roman numerals and the address where the book will be sold in Boston. The carefully labeled portrait of the frontispiece stands in for, and supplements, the title of the volume and vice versa. Becoming signs for each other, the difference between book and woman (thing and person) comes close to collapsing in this effort to gain and hold the reader's attention.

But what kind of attention? This series of frames disposes the reader toward the book by appealing to the pathos of this intriguing portrait. By drawing attention to themselves as artifices and to the artificiality of the image they contain, these frames also protect the reader from a potentially transgressive experience of emotional identification by redundantly demarcating the difference between the viewer (and potential reader) and the engraved figure (a work of art). The color and gender of the pictured figure are not the only unusual features of the frontispiece, for the *mise-en-scène* is extraordinarily dynamic for a frontispiece portrait of the time.[29] This dynamism—created by the contrasting directions of the hatch lines within the oval and the play of the orientation of the angles of the table, book, quill, ink pot, and the organic lines of the figure itself—is epitomized by the curl of the lower left-hand corner of the paper. The sheet of paper, like the thoughts of the figured woman, seems to have caught a breeze or, even, to be about to float off the table. However, multiple oval lines of various shades and thicknesses securely contain this energy. These ovals both form the frame around the image *and* depict a frame that bears a label for the object it encloses. While the term "servant" without the modifier "negro" could refer to a free or indentured worker, in the context of colonial New England, the term "negro servant" most often referred to enslaved workers. The unusual and masterly chiaroscuro of the engraving creates a sense of three-dimensionality, though not of realism, by stressing its own artifice. The balance, for example, of the heaviest shading within the oval against the heaviest shading outside of the oval reinforces the illusion that the engraving as a whole depicts something like a framed miniature which, like the page depicted within the oval, is separate and removable from the depicted background. Label, frame, and portrait together constitute the object being depicted within the larger rectangular space of the frontispiece engraving. This engraving, like the portrait it re-depicts, is not only a made object, it is also an owned and alienable object designed to serve the interests of John Wheatley, whose name, address, and status are prominently superimposed upon the oval-framed portrait. Each subsequent paratextual element overlays and repeats this initial representation with an additional verbal re-depiction of the authorizing image, not of an author, but of a work of art. The conundrum otherwise posed by the existence of Phillis Wheatley is solved, at least provisionally. As far as the front matter is concerned, the ethos of *Poems on Various Subjects, Religious and Moral*, like the ethos of "Phillis Wheatley, Negro Servant to Mr. John Wheatley, of Boston," lies safely with the owner and patrons of the historical writer, Phillis Wheatley.[30]

But Wheatley, apparently, was not satisfied. She didn't let this representation of the origin and authority of her poetry stand, but countered it with her own. Her adaptation of Horace's dedicatory ode,

"To Maecenas," is a tour-de-force demonstration of her own claim to the ethos of a poet:[31]

To Maecenas

MAECENAS, you, beneath the myrtle shade,
Read o'er what poets sung, and shepherds play'd.
What felt those poets but you feel the same?
Does not your soul possess the sacred flame?
Their noble strains your equal genius shares   5
In softer language, and diviner airs.
    While Homer paints, lo! circumfus'd in air,
Celestial Gods in mortal forms appear;
Swift as they move hear each recess rebound,
Heav'n quakes, earth trembles, and the shores resound.   10
Great Sire of verse, before my mortal eyes,
The lightnings blaze across the vaulted skies,
And, as the thunder shakes the heav'nly plains,
A deep felt horror thrills through all my veins.
When gentler strains demand thy graceful song,   15
The length'ning line moves languishing along.
When great Patroclus courts Achilles' aid,
The grateful tribute of my tears is paid;
Prone on the shore he feels the pangs of love,
And stern Pelides tend'rest passions move.   20
    Great Maro's strain in heav'nly numbers flows,
The Nine inspire, and all the bosom glows.
O could I rival thine and Virgil's page,
Or claim the Muses with the Mantuan Sage;
Soon the same beauties should my mind adorn,   25
And the same ardors in my soul should burn:
Then should my song in bolder notes arise,
And all my numbers pleasingly surprise;
But here I sit, and mourn a grov'ling mind,
That fain would mount, and ride upon the wind.   30
    Not you, my friend, these plaintive strains become,
Not you, whose bosom is the Muses home;
When they from tow'ring Helicon retire,
They fan in you the bright immortal fire,
But I less happy, cannot raise the song,   35
The fault'ring music dies upon my tongue.
    The happier Terence all the choir inspir'd,
His soul replenish'd, and his bosom fir'd;
But say, ye Muses, why this partial grace,
To one alone of Afric's sable race;   40

From age to age transmitting thus his name
With the finest glory in the rolls of fame?
    Thy virtues, great Maecenas! shall be sung
In praise of him, from whom those virtues sprung:
While blooming wreaths around thy temples spread,   45
I'll snatch a laurel from thine honour'd head,
While you indulgent smile upon the deed.
    As long as Thames in streams majestic flows,
Or Naiads in their oozy beds repose
While Phoebus reigns above the starry train   50
While bright Aurora purples o'er the main,
So long, great Sir, the muse thy praise shall sing,
So long thy praise shal' make Parnassus ring:
Then grant, Maecenas, thy paternal rays,
Hear me propitious, and defend my lays.[32]   55

Inserted at the last minute before publication, this proem looks both backward at the material that precedes it in the volume, and forward to the poems that follow.[33] Not unlike the publisher's introduction, "To Maecenas" might qualify as a parergon in the conventional sense of being extrinsic to the rest of Wheatley's poetry. Apparently, Wheatley *had* been satisfied with the collection of poems that had been sent ahead to London for publishing. But it can also be read, like the material in the front matter, as a parergon in Jacques Derrida's sense as "neither work (ergon) nor outside the work [*hors d'oeuvre*], neither inside nor outside, neither above nor below, it disconcerts any opposition but does not remain indeterminate and it *gives rise* to the work" by setting the terms by which a work of art can be read (Derrida's emphasis).[34] "To Maecenas" provides yet another introductory depiction of "Phillis Wheatley, Negro Servant to Mr. John Wheatley of Boston, in New England" in an attempt to "give rise to" a very different kind of work than that prefaced by Bell's front matter. It is extraneous not only because it was added at the last minute—it is an extra poem—and not only in its exceeding of neoclassical expectations, but also because it re-introduces Wheatley's readers to the rest of her poetry in terms that revise those already provided by the publisher.

As in the front matter, Wheatley focuses on the question of the authorizing agent, or ethos, animating the poetry. The front matter of *Poems*, as we have seen, contains an attestation by a committee of worthy Bostonians that Wheatley "is thought qualified" to have composed such classically informed verse. In her appropriation of the form and title of Horace's "To Maecenas," as well as in her multiple allusions to other classical authors and poems, she does indeed showcase an audacious familiarity (given her culture's assumptions about the abilities of girls, slaves, and Africans) with classical authors and their works.[35] Yet, in its self-conscious engagement with the question of poetic ethos and with its command of the mode of ekphrasis, "To Maecenas" demonstrates more than mere familiarity with the classical legacy. For, of course, the relation of the historical Maecenas to the historical authors, Virgil and Horace, was fundamentally different from Wheatley's relationship to her various patrons. Horace depended upon the wealthy, upper-class Maecenas, his "shield at once and glory of my life," for financial support, and he depended upon Maecenas for "the artist's meed, the ivy wreath" and the placement of his (Horace's) "name among that minstrel choir."[36] But though he might have depended upon Maecenas for the opportunity to be recognized as a poet, Horace did not depend upon his friend and patron for anything as fundamental as his freedom or his life. The freedom of Horace's character is inferred when the speaker compares his preferences and ambitions (for fame as a poet) to those whose ambitions lay in "Olympic strife," in the pleasures of the hunt, or in the merchant's pursuit of wealth.

One of Wheatley's ekphrastic objects is Horace's own famous poem "To Maecenas" and, more specifically, Horace's depiction there of his famous patron as well as Horace's notion of patronage. The Wheatleys of Boston did, in fact, also provide artistic patronage for her and so could have considered themselves addressed by this poem. But the Wheatleys were something else in addition to patrons: they "owned" the rights to their slave's body, her labor, any future children she might produce. Besides, Selina Hastings had as good a claim as John Wheatley to the ethos of patron and, in fact, the volume was dedicated to her. Neither, and both, fit the description of her Maecenas, who is addressed in singular and masculine forms. Unlike Horace, thus, Phillis goes out of the way to disrupt the connection between an historical person and the idealization of the patron of her poetry. In theorizing the role of the patron under the name of "Maecenas," Wheatley depicts a patron whose own authority is based neither on rank (Horace's Maecenas is, in contrast, "born of monarch's ancestors") nor on political power, but on the nature of the patron's response to poetry. He has read "o'er what poets sung, and shepherds play'd. / What felt those poets but you feel the same?" (2–3). Her Maecenas, who after all must be called forth from a "myrtle shade," seems strangely in need of the reassurance voiced by the rhetorical questions offered by the speaker: "Does not your soul possess the sacred flame? / Their noble strains your equal genius shares / In softer language and diviner airs" (5–6). To a great degree, here and throughout, Wheatley challenges the notion that patronage should or could determine the ethos of the artist. First, the nobility that allows Horace's Maecenas to offer such valuable patronage stems from his birth, rank, and political power, but here it is the poetry that is "noble" and ennobling. Second, the status differential between the figures of the poet and patron that Horace so carefully accentuates is leveled out by Wheatley: her speaker feels compelled to assure her Maecenas that he has the genius of a poet. Third, her poet denies Maecenas the chance to give her the laurels that would mark her entry in the "rolls of fame" by audaciously promising to "snatch a laurel from thine honour'd head." In her poem, it is the grace (or gift) of the Muses, rather than of the patron, that keeps the list "transmitting thus" the names of famous poets. In addition, although the poet asks that her Maecenas "defend my lays," the poet has already promised to sing of his "virtues" in "praise" that "shal' make Parnassus ring." In Wheatley's version, it is Maecenas who owes a debt to the poet, for it is the poet whose praise will keep Maecenas's name alive.

Wheatley's ekphrasis of Horace's depiction of his patron (and more generally, of the conventional personification of patronage under the name of Maecenas) is one of the key ways she exceeds the terms by which the front matter frames, defines, and confines her. Through this figure of what she regards as her perfect reader, she begins to express her theory of the conditions and consequences of successful verbal images.[37] The authority of her speaker's Maecenas is not intrinsically greater than that of the poets, but it is necessary for the production of great poetry and for the fame of the poets. Sharing the "equal genius" of the "noble strains" sung by the "poets" and played by the "shepherds" suggests that the kind of poetry that lasts "from age to age" results from the voluntary collaboration of a masterly reader (like Maecenas) with a masterly singer (like Homer). Like the poets with whom he feels the same, Maecenas's "soul" possesses "the sacred flame." In Wheatley's version, poets, patrons, and poetry are mutually constitutive and mutually free. The patron of her speaker is not a person, but a fiction in the form of a character, a character that can give poets the kind of perfect (because sympathetic, "indulgent," and "propitious") reception they need. Called out from the "myrtle shade," Wheatley's Maecenas registers the effect of Homer's epic on all the bodily senses; his ethos as a patron—his right to praise and be praised—rests on the profundity of his response to great poetry.

He sees, hears, and feels all that Homer had "circumfus'd in air." In contrast to the way that the front matter positions the reader vis-à-vis *Poems* (which positions the reader as superior to and essentially different, because free, from the poet), Wheatley offers a model of the perfect reader, or patron, as a sympathetic collaborator who may freely choose to join with the poet in a shared creative effort of the imagination.[38]

This characterization of Maecenas as a perfect reader sets the groundwork for Wheatley's ekphrastic treatment of the character, "Phillis Wheatley, Negro Servant to Mr. John Wheatley, Boston," presented by the front matter. John Shields has suggested that Wheatley's "theoretics of the imagination" is an important waystation leading to what James Engell calls the "culmination of a century of thought" about the relationship between sympathy and imagination by romantics such as Hazlitt or Keats.[39] Reading "On Imagination," another example from *Poems on Various Subjects*, Shields argues that Wheatley anticipates romantic arguments regarding the generative force of the imagination unlimited by the faculty of reason. If, as Shields suggests, "On Imagination" argues that it is possible for something entirely new, even revolutionary, to be imagined, "To Maecenas" describes how the imagination can permit what Engell calls the escape of the self from "its confines," even if those "confines" (as in the case of Wheatley) would deny that any free self exists.[40] Wheatley uses ekphrasis to replace the image her patrons have prescribed for her with a revolutionary new picture of a self—a self representation—who is free, black, and has all the agency of a poet.

One way that Wheatley marks the freedom of the poet depicted in her "To Maecenas" is in the description of the speaker's relationship to her addressee, Maecenas. Like his, the speaker's sympathetic response to Homer's verbal images is profound. Noting the difference between herself, who sees with "mortal eyes," and the long dead, great "sire of verse," the speaker nonetheless sees "the lightnings blaze across the vaulted skies," feels the shaking of the "heav'nly plains" with her body and emotional "horror" that "thrills through all" her veins in response to Homer's description. This self is moved not only by the content of Homer's images but also by his prosody. Wheatley illustrates the sensitivity and distinction of her speaker's perceptive abilities: she shares the depicted feelings of the characters and, like Maecenas, shares the feelings of the poet who has depicted them. She pays the "grateful tribute" of her tears to the combination of prosody and content in Homer's description of Achilles's grief. It isn't, Wheatley stresses, Homer's mimetic accuracy nor her speaker's familiarity with what he is describing that is at work, but rather a necessary combination of Homer's artistry and her own power of imagination. By analogy, the speaker of the poem shares the same kind of authority as Maecenas; feeling like and with the poets, she, like Maecenas, shares their genius and shares in the genius of their poetry. Claiming to share the ethos of a perfect reader, a patron to poets, Wheatley positions her speaker to supplant the example of Maecenas by becoming the patron to herself as poet.

Her ekphrasis of Horace's picture of Maecenas and her ekphrasis of a key description from the *Iliad* establish a personal ethos characterized by a particular quality of response to the artwork of others. These ekphrastics posit a freedom for the speaker that is as unquestionable as that of Maecenas, Homer, or Virgil. But "To Maeceneas" confronts the question of poetic ethos even more directly in the second half of the poem, where Wheatley depicts another, distinctly different, account of the speaker's authority as a poet. In comparing her speaker to the "happier Terence," Wheatley conspicuously tightens the connection between herself and the poet she depicts in "To Maecenas." Coming immediately after her description of the "fault'ring music that dies upon her tongue," Terence is "happier" in at least two senses. First, in contrast to the speaker's modest description of her own abilities, "all the choir inspir'd" her Roman predecessor, replenishing his soul and firing "his bosom" (36–38). The poetry of Terence doesn't falter: he is happier because he is a better poet. But Terence was also "happier" than the author because his early status as a slave did not preclude poetic aspirations, ability, or reputation. Wheatley comments upon the historical distance between her condition in the British Empire and Terence's in the Roman. For Terence, unlike herself, race and status were de-coupled. He could be a black African like her and be enslaved, but he could also be free and be a poet, too. For Terence, unlike Wheatley, was free to pursue happiness regardless of race.

Unlike Wheatley at the time of the composition of her proem, Terence had been legally freed by his master and had attained fame during his own lifetime. In asking the Muses why only one of "Afric's sable race" is found on the "rolls of fame," Wheatley's speaker begins to express the challenge that she has set herself, which is to pursue the kind of happiness that Terence had achieved. The attainment of this goal has not only personal consequences but also political ones; her poetry will, she hopes, increase the representation of black Africans in the "rolls of fame." While her "grov'ling mind," somewhat disingenuously referred to, is one obstacle (disingenuous, not least because her ekphrasis has already depicted a mind that is anything but groveling), her challenge to the Muses implies at least the possibility of racist prejudice on their part. Has there been a lack of black contenders for the attention of the Muses, or have the Muses refused their attention? The poems that follow "To Maecenas" will be their test. In "To Maecenas," the speaker and Terence share two essential qualities: they are poets and black Africans. What Wheatley emphatically does not stress is Terence's former status as a slave. She does not figure his enslavement as an essential attribute of his character; it does not shape or inform his poetic ethos, but she contends that his race and talents do. "To Maecenas" suggests that Wheatley's enslavement does not determine her poetic ethos either.

In the account given in "To Maecenas," Terence's character as a poet stems from the grace or gift of the muses delivered in the form of song. And so does the poetic character of the speaker of "To Maecenas," whose inspiration comes from the poetry of Homer, Virgil, and Horace. The speaker shares not only the ethos available to all free persons such as Maecenas, whose freedom is figured as collaboration with the poets, she also aspires to share the extraordinarily elite character of poets themselves. This poetic ethos, predicated on a free self, is depicted as an invention of the imagination. The essential freedom she shares with Maecenas—free to enter imaginatively into the notional reality of others, or not—is not something made or contingent. But the poetic status she aspires to share with the "Mantuan Sage," Homer, and Terence is something different, over and above, the status she shares with Maecenas and only exists in representation. The prosody of Homer invites the speaker to feel with and for his characters on the shores of Ilium (as Maecenas, or any free person, might), but this prosody also presents an extra opportunity for readers who are free to pursue the particular happiness of the poet: "O could I rival thine and Virgil's page, / Or claim the Muses with the Mantuan Sage" (23–24). The character of the poet is "extra," Wheatley suggests, built upon a foundational, free self. The truth of her character, misrepresented by the front matter, is that she is free; the warrant for her poems is that she is a poet.

If, like Wheatley's Maecenas, the speaker passively shares a "genius" with the poets as the perfect reader, then unlike Maecenas the speaker wishes to express this genius actively by inventing new works of art. The first and most important expression of that genius is to correct the misrepresentation of the authorizing agent of *Poems on Various Subjects*. Wheatley's actual patrons, "To Maecenas" suggests, mistake both themselves and her by depicting her as a characterless slave who needs them to speak for her. Though free, they are imperfect readers. Whether because of her age, gender, or race, and despite the impulses of their politics, religion, and affection, Wheatley's patrons cannot seem to imagine her as other than an owned self. But Wheatley can; and this ability to imagine her self in a revolutionary new way stems, as depicted in "To Maecenas," from active and voluntary engagement with the powerful verbal pictures created by the famous poets of the classical era. Her persona, like the speaker of Horace's ode, has chosen to aspire to the status of poet: her imagination "fain would mount, and ride upon the wind" (29). Words such as "fain" and "snatch" ("I'll snatch a laurel from thine honour'd head") depict the speaker as having and exerting the kind of agency denied by the spectacle of the enslaved Wheatley represented in the front matter. She re-imagines herself—through ekphrasis—into an aspiring, though faltering, poet whose authority rests on the power of her imagination. The authenticating force of this revised figure stems not from Wheatley's putative owner, nor from her religious status as a Christian, nor from the validation of her abilities by a committee of colonial worthies, but from her own encounters with classical poetry.[41] In depicting how the speaker of the poem came to dare to "snatch a laurel" that would mark her as a poet, "To Maecenas" offers a theory of poetry that insists upon the active and free agency of both reader and writer.[42] Although written a good forty years before John Keats used ekphrasis to depict the revolutionary, personal consequence of "First Looking Into Chapman's Homer," Wheatley, too, posits her claim to the authority of a poet upon her confrontation with the traces of the classical era. Depicting her response to the powerful verbal images of other poets, Wheatley makes an aesthetic argument (what makes a poet) while simultaneously advancing a political argument (what makes a person). In "To Maecenas," that is, the most important consequence for the reader of powerfully executed verbal images is the ability to imagine the self as free, and the most important sign of this freedom is the representation of that self. The confrontation with the poetry of Homer, Virgil, and Horace depicted in Wheatley's "To Maecenas" results in the recognition—if not the declaration—of the speaker's self as an autonomous subject rather than an object, as a person rather than as a thing.

Notes

1. For discussions of the pre-Revolutionary context of Wheatley's Boston, see Vincent Carretta, *Phillis Wheatley: Biography of a Genius in Bondage* (Athens: University of Georgia Press, 2011); Henry Louis Gates, Jr., *The Trials of Phillis Wheatley: America's First Black Poet and Her Encounters with the Founding Fathers* (New York: Basic Civitas Books, 2003); and especially John C. Shields, *Phillis Wheatley's Poetics of Liberation: Backgrounds and Contexts* (Knoxville: University of Tennessee Press, 2008). For discussions of Wheatley's cognizance of, and participation in, the political debates of her era, see also David Waldstreicher, "The Wheatleyan Moment," *Early American Studies: An Interdisciplinary Journal* 9, no. 3 (Fall 2011): 522–51, and Emily Greenwood, "The Politics of Classicism in the Poetry of Phillis Wheatley," in *Ancient Slavery and Abolition: From Hobbes to Hollywood*, ed. Edith Hall, Richard Alston, and Justine McConnell (Oxford: Oxford University Press, 2011), 153–80. Building on Greenwood, I argue for the innovative use of ekphrasis in what Greenwood describes as Wheatley's pursuit of *eleutherostomia* or the "right to speak freely" (155). In contrast to Greenwood, I see Wheatley aspiring to go beyond claiming the right to speak, to attempting to redefine the ontological status of her self through the re-description of the nature of her character.
2. Phillis Wheatley, *The Collected Works of Phillis Wheatley*, ed. John C. Shields (New York: Oxford University Press, 1988). All citations to *Poems on Various Subjects, Religious and Moral* are from this edition.
3. "To Maecenas" and "On Imagination" are beginning to compete for scholarly attention with the now canonical example of "On Being Brought from Africa to America." "To Maecenas" is at the heart of an argument over, as Greenwood puts it, "how Wheatley's classical poetics are embroiled in the politics of her slave status" (154). See also Karen Lerner Dovell, "The Interaction of the Classical Traditions and Politics in the Work of Phillis Wheatley," and Eric Ashley Hairston, "The Trojan Horse: Classics, Memory, Transformation, and Afric Ambition in *Poems on Various Subjects, Religious and Moral*," both in *New Essays on Phillis Wheatley*, ed. John C. Shields and Eric D. Lamore (Knoxville: University of Tennessee Press, 2011), 57–94. Like William Cook and James Tatum in *African American Writers and the Classical Tradition* (Chicago: University of Chicago Press, 2012), I too see "To Maecenas" as an explicit response to the front matter of *Poems*. While they see Wheatley as attempting to meet the claims made about her in the authenticating documents by displaying a mastery of neoclassical poetics, I read the poem as relating more antagonistically and dynamically to its textual context or paratext. Greenwood also argues that "To Maecenas" is part of an intentional intervention into the political

context, but she locates this force in Wheatley's deployment of classical, rather than neoclassical, poetics. Questions of taxonomy (whether to classify Wheatley's aesthetics as neoclassical, classical or romantic) aside, my argument joins Greenwood, Cook, and Tatum in seeing "To Maecenas" as Wheatley's attempt to define, at least, a voice for her self through engagement with the legacy of classical literature.
4. As W. J. T. Mitchell puts it in *Picture Theory: Essays on Verbal and Visual Representation* (Chicago: University of Chicago Press, 1994), the "minority and obscurity of ekphrasis has not, of course, prevented the formation of an enormous literature on the subject that traces it back to the legendary 'Shield of Achilles' in the *Iliad*, locates its theoretical recognition in ancient poetics and rhetoric, and finds instances of it in everything from oral narrative to postmodern poetry" (152). Whether understood broadly as a mode that may operate in various media or narrowly as a specific genre of poems about painting, definitions of ekphrasis defer to the original use of the term to refer to the rhetorical trope of speaking forth (*ex*—out, *phrazein*—speaking) what is seen. Mitchell's work on ekphrasis lays the groundwork for understanding the political implications of the poetics of ekphrasis as he returns attention to the affects of ekphrasis: fear, hope, or indifference. My analysis is also indebted to Barbara K. Fischer, who in *Museum Mediations: Reframing Ekphrasis in Contemporary American Poetry* (New York: Routledge, 2006) locates the political force of ekphrasis in its ability to let "poets use ekphrasis to allow for an interplay of complicity and provocation" (3). In contrast to Mitchell and Fischer, though, I locate the political force of ekphrasis in the way that the mode shapes and reshapes the persona of the speaker and thus revises the ontological status occupied by the speaker. I am indebted to Elizabeth B. Bearden, *The Emblematics of the Self: Ekphrasis in Renaissance Imitations of Greek Romance* (Toronto: University of Toronto Press, 2012) and to Ruth Webb, *Ekphrasis, Imagination and Persuasion in Ancient Rhetorical Theory and Practice* (Burlington, VT: Ashgate, 2009) for a full discussion of the early association between ethos and ekphrasis. For overviews of the poetics of ekphrasis, see Murray Krieger, *Ekphrasis: The Illusion of the Natural Sign* (Baltimore: Johns Hopkins University Press, 1992); John Hollander, *The Gazer's Spirit: Poems Speaking to Silent Works of Art* (Chicago: University of Chicago Press, 1995); James A. W. Heffernan, *The Museum of Words: The Poetics of Ekphrasis from Homer to Ashbery* (Chicago: University of Chicago Press, 1993); Andrew S. Becker, *The Shield of Achilles and the Poetics of Ekphrasis* (Lanham, MD: Rowman and Littlefield, 1995); and, of course, Jean H. Hagstrum's field-changing study, *The Sister Arts: The Tradition of Literary Pictorialism and English Poetry from Dryden to Gray* (Chicago: University of Chicago Press, 1958).
5. Webb, *Ekphrasis, Imagination and Persuasion*, 1, and Bearden, *Emblematics of the Self*, 36.

6. The ekphrases of the British romantic poets have had a privileged place in the canon of literary ekphrasis. As Frederick Burwick explains in *Mimesis and its Romantic Reflections* (University Park: Penn State University Press, 2001), "the province and techniques of mimesis were being redefined in romantic literature. Self-awareness, with its alert attention to the subjective apprehension of external reality, involved an attendant concern with the representation of the interior processes of perception" (11). For the romantics, ekphrasis, which Burwick defines as a "mimesis of a mimesis" (13), was ready-made to perform this essentially self-reflective and theoretical work. See also Paul de Man, *The Rhetoric of Romanticism* (New York: Columbia University Press, 1984) and James Engell, *The Creative Imagination: Enlightenment to Romanticism* (Cambridge, MA: Harvard University Press, 1981) for discussions of the romantics' concern with the meaning, limits, and origin of representations.
7. Gordon S. Wood, *Revolutionary Characters: What Made the Founders Different* (New York: Penguin, 2006), 11. What made the founders different, according to Wood, was that their conception of personal "character" was "revolutionary" in two senses. As character was understood to be a social construction, one's individual character was not an essential, given, and unchangeable aspect of the self but was subject to change, improvement, even revolution. In turn, the type of character or moral disposition aspired to by the founders, Wood argues, revolutionized or changed the political culture in ways they couldn't anticipate.
8. The framework for unpacking the protean relationships among the concepts of liberty, slavery, and representation in late eighteenth-century thought and practice was established by Bernard Bailyn, *The Ideological Origins of the American Revolution* (Cambridge, MA: Belknap Press of Harvard University Press, 1967), later expanded by Orlando Patterson, *Slavery and Social Death: A Comparative Study* (Cambridge, MA: Harvard University Press, 1982) and Gary B. Nash, *Race and Revolution* (Madison, NJ: Madison House, 1990). See also Patricia Bradley, *Slavery, Propaganda, and the American Revolution* (Jackson: University Press of Mississippi, 1998) and Wood, *Revolutionary Characters*.
9. For discussions of the debate about the political representation of blacks and enslaved people, see Hannis Taylor's classic *The Origin and Growth of the American Constitution: An Historical Treatise* (Boston: Houghton Mifflin, 1911), and more recently, Gary Wills, *"Negro President": Jefferson and the Slave Power* (Boston: Houghton Mifflin, 2003). There seems some confusion over the spelling of the name of Phillis Wheatley's mistress, Susanna or Susannah. I follow Carretta's usage and drop the final "h."
10. In 1641 Massachusetts was the first colony to legalize slavery but, according to many sources, it was also the first state to abolish it when

a 1783 judicial decision ruled that a passage in the state constitution of 1780, which included a Declaration of Rights, effectively prohibited it.
11. See Carretta and Bradley for discussions of the prestige value of black slaves in New England.
12. Harriet Beecher Stowe, *Uncle Tom's Cabin, or, Life Among the Lowly*, ed. Elizabeth Ammons (New York: W. W. Norton, 2nd ed., 1996). Although better known for her deployment of sentiment in *Uncle Tom's Cabin*, Stowe's novel opens in the mode of irony with a chapter, entitled "A Man of Humanity," in which the value of a slave's Christianity is debated by two men, slave seller and slave buyer, who believe themselves to be men of humanity. Stowe uses irony to highlight how the slave system depends upon the mis-recognition and/or mis-classification of the nature of humanity and of the nature of the self and other.
13. Countee Cullen, "Yet Do I Marvel," in *My Soul's High Song: The Collected Writings of Countee Cullen, the Voice of the Harlem Renaissance*, ed. Gerald Lyn Early (New York: Doubleday, 1991), 79.
14. See chaps. 4 and 5 of Carretta, *Biography*, for a detailed publication history of *Poems*. The model I use here for discussing the function of this material draws on both Gérard Genette, *Paratext: Thresholds of Interpretation* (Cambridge: Cambridge University Press, 1997), and Jacques Derrida, *The Truth in Painting*, trans. Geoff Bennington and Ian McLeod (Chicago: University of Chicago Press, 1987).
15. Carretta, *Biography*, 94.
16. See chap. 1 of Carretta's *Biography* for a description of the unconventional and not wholly coherent way that the Wheatleys treated Phillis. Carretta refers to a letter written by Mrs. Wheatley in which it is clear that though she considered that Phillis belonged on a different and superior plane to her other enslaved black servants, she nevertheless worried that Phillis would forget this station when in England.
17. From "LETTER sent by the Author's Master to the Publisher."
18. "On Being Brought From Africa to America."
19. George Whitefield (1714–70), one of the founders of Methodism, devoted much of his life to evangelizing the North American colonies. Famous and controversial for advocating the spiritual salvation of slaves, he nevertheless owned slaves himself. See Thomas Kidd, *George Whitefield: America's Spiritual Founding Father* (New Haven: Yale University Press, 2014), and Carretta, *Biography*, 33.
20. See James Walvin, *Black Ivory: Slavery in the British Empire* (Oxford: Blackwell, 2nd ed., 2001), and Kenneth Morgan, *Slavery and the British Empire: from Africa to America* (Oxford: Oxford University Press, 2007).
21. In reviewing contemporary responses to Wheatley's poems, Carretta finds both negative and positive reviews, but it seems that the latter outweighed the former (108). See also Shields in *Phillis Wheatley and the Romantics* for discussion of the circulation and consequence of Wheatley's poetry among European philosophers of the period.

22. This was particularly important to Selina Hastings, Countess of Huntingdon, who had a long involvement fostering both the Methodist reform movement within the Church of England, and the careers of such Native American and African writers as Ukawsaw Gronniosaw, Olaudah Equiano, and Samson Occom.
23. As an unmarried servant girl, of whatever race or status, Phillis would be considered "covered" in political and economic terms by her master and head of the family, John Wheatley. In *Slavery and Social Death*, Patterson describes how the racialized slave system, organized by the eighteenth century, legally and conceptually figured African slaves as the opposite of persons. What he calls the conceptually "nil condition" of slavery denies the slave a self to protect or to express.
24. Bell's effort, which stands in for the efforts of both Wheatley and her various patrons, needs to be seen in the contemporary argument about racial classification and political theory, especially as Shields points out in *Phillis Wheatley and the Romantics*.
25. Carretta emphasizes how "revolutionary" a "frontispiece depicting an eighteenth-century black woman capable of writing poetry" was by detailing how rare it was for any living authors to be represented in frontispiece-portraits, much less black authors (99–102).
26. See Janine Barchas, *Graphic Design, Print Culture, and the Eighteenth-Century Novel* (Cambridge: Cambridge University Press, 2003), 21–22, and Carretta, *Biography*, 99–100.
27. Burwick, *Mimesis*, 13.
28. Carretta, *Biography*, 101.
29. Barchas, *Graphic Design*, 22.
30. The continuing power of this frame can be seen in many of the readings of Wheatley that date from the initial attempt to recover her work in the 1980s and also in the peculiar persistence of the imagined scene of her interrogation by the Boston worthies who testified to their belief in her ability to have written the poems. Alice Walker first fleshes out this scene in her provocative 1983 essay, "In Search of Our Mother's Gardens," as a means of coming to terms with what seems like the accommodationist betrayal of poems such as "On Being Brought from Africa to America." See Walker, *In Search of Our Mother's Gardens: Womanist Prose* (Orlando: Harcourt, 2004), 236. A major exception to this early trend was June Jordan, "The Difficult Miracle of Black Poetry in America: Something like a Sonnet for Phillis Wheatley," in *On Call: Political Essays* (Boston: South End Press, 1985), 87–98. My essay explores how it was, as Jordan put it, that Wheatley "created herself a poet, notwithstanding and in despite of everything around her" (88). The imagined nature of this scene gets forgotten despite, as Carretta notes, the unlikeliness of it ever having occurred. This frame shapes the prevailing reading of Wheatley provided in the headnotes of, for example, the *Norton Anthology of African American Literature*, and it is most fully expressed by Gates, Jr., *The Trials of Phillis Wheatley*.

See Joanna Brooks, "Our Phillis, Ourselves," *American Literature* 82, no. 1 (2010): 1–28, for a full discussion of the continuing effect of the vividness of what Gates describes as the "primal scene" of the African American literary tradition. See also Shields, *Poetics of Liberation*, for a full attempt to revise our understanding of Wheatley based more upon what she does in her poetry than how she was depicted by her contemporaries.

31. My argument is substantially different from Cook and Tatum's, who also see the poem as an "implicit response" to "the claims those documents make for her art," but read this response as a confirmation of those claims (*African American Writers and the Classical Tradition*, 13). My argument locates Wheatley's anxiety not in the fear of being inadequate to the claims being made on and for her behalf, but in the fear of being complicit in the limits imposed upon her self by the front matter.
32. Wheatley, *Poems*, 9. Parenthetical references to passages in this poem are to line numbers.
33. Cook and Tatum, *African American Writers and the Classical Tradition*, 13.
34. Derrida, *The Truth*, 9.
35. In addition to Cook and Tatum, see Cynthia J. Smith, "'To Maecenas': Phillis Wheatley's Invocation of an Idealized Reader," *Black American Literature Forum* 23 (1989): 579–92; John C. Shields, "Phillis Wheatley's Use of Classicism," *American Literature* 52, no. 1 (1980): 97–111, and Patrick Mosely, "Empowerment Through Classicism in Phillis Wheatley's 'Ode to Neptune,'" in *New Essays on Phillis Wheatley*, ed. Shields and Lamore, 95–110.
36. Cook and Tatum (*African American Writers and the Classical Tradition*, 19) remind us that Horace's father had been a freedman and thus would offer a model to Wheatley of American upward mobility or the possibility to reinvent the self that is not limited by skin color.
37. See Cook and Tatum for discussions of Wheatley's use of ekphrasis here. In contrast, I suggest that Wheatley's use of ekphrasis is more consistent with the general argument that Shields makes regarding her anticipation of the values and aesthetics of the romantics. See Shields, *Phillis Wheatley and the Romantics*, and his more recent *Poetics of Liberation*.
38. Here I agree with Greenwood and Smith, who also see Wheatley's description of the character Maecenas as part of what Greenwood calls an "equalizing strategy" ("The Politics of Classicism," 169).
39. Engell, *The Creative Imagination*.
40. According to Engell the imagination works through the power of sympathy to permit "the self to escape its own conditions, to identify with other people, to perceive things in a new way, and to develop an aesthetic appreciation of the world that coalesces both the subjective self and the objective other" (*The Creative Imagination*, 143–44).

41. Jordan, "The Difficult Miracle," 88.
42. Mitchell, *Picture Theory*. Like Mitchell, I see ekphrasis as a mode of poetics, one that allows authors to "picture" (work out through depiction) their theories about pictures. I am particularly interested in the way that ekphrasis, with its emphasis on the consequence of a confrontation with another's work of art, allows for the theorization of ethos. Mitchell elaborates his earlier theory in *The Lives and Loves of Images* (Chicago: University of Chicago Press, 2005). This is another way in which, as Shields has argued, Wheatley's poetics anticipates that of the Romantics, for her understanding of the primacy of the imagination complicates, if not argues against, the conventional classification of Wheatley as a neoclassical poet.

Bibliography

Bailyn, Bernard. *The Ideological Origins of the American Revolution*. Cambridge, MA: The Belknap Press of Harvard University Press, 1967.

Barchas, Janine. *Graphic Design, Print Culture, and the Eighteenth-Century Novel*. Cambridge: Cambridge University Press, 2003.

Bearden, Elizabeth. *The Emblematics of the Self: Ekphrasis in Renaissance Imitations of Greek Romance*. Toronto: University of Toronto Press, 2012.

Becker, Andrew. *The Shield of Achilles and the Poetics of Ekphrasis*. Lanham, MD: Rowman and Littlefield, 1995.

Bradley, Patricia. *Slavery, Propaganda and the American Revolution*. Jackson: University Press of Mississippi, 1998.

Brooks, Joanna. "Our Phillis, Ourselves." *American Literature* 82, no. 1 (2010): 1–28.

Burwick, Frederick. *Mimesis and its Romantic Reflections*. University Park: Penn State University Press, 2001.

Carretta, Vincent. *Phillis Wheatley: Biography of a Genius in Bondage*. Athens, GA: University of Georgia Press, 2011.

Cook, William, and James Tatum. *African American Writers and Classical Tradition*. Chicago: University of Chicago Press, 2010.

Cullen, Countee. *My Soul's High Song: The Collected Writings of Countee Cullen, the Voice of the Harlem Renaissance*. Edited by Gerald Early. New York: Doubleday Anchor Books, 1991.

de Man, Paul. *The Rhetoric of Romanticism*. New York: Columbia University Press, 1984.

Derrida, Jacques. *The Truth in Painting*. Translated by Geoff Bennington and Ian McLeod. Chicago and London: University of Chicago Press, 1987.

Dovell, Karen L. "The Interaction of the Classical Traditions and Politics in the Work of Phillis Wheatley." In *New Essays on Phillis Wheatley*, edited by John C. Shields and Eric D. Lamore. Knoxville: University of Tennessee Press, 2011.

Engell, James. *The Creative Imagination: Enlightenment to Romanticism.* Cambridge, MA: Harvard University Press, 1981.

Fischer, Barbara K. *Museum Mediations: Reframing Ekphrasis in Contemporary American Poetry.* New York: Routledge, 2006.

Gates, Henry Louis, Jr. *The Trials of Phillis Wheatley: America's First Black Poet and her Encounters with the Founding Fathers.* New York: Basic Civitas Books, 2003.

Gennette, Gérard. *Paratext: Thresholds of Interpretation.* Cambridge: Cambridge University Press, 1997.

Greenwood, Emily. "The Politics of Classicism in the Poetry of Phillis Wheatley." In *Ancient Slavery and Abolition: From Hobbes to Hollywood*, edited by Edith Hall, Richard Alston, and Justine McConnell. Oxford: Oxford University Press, 2011.

Hagstrum, Jean H. *The Sister Arts: The Tradition of Literary Pictorialism and English Poetry From Dryden to Gray.* Chicago: University of Chicago Press, 1958.

Hairston, Eric Ashley. "The Trojan Horse: Classics, Memory, Transformation and African Ambition in *Poems on Various Subjects, Religious and Moral*." In *New Essays on Phillis Wheatley*, edited by John C. Shields and Eric D. Lamore. Knoxville: University of Tennessee Press, 2011.

Heffernan, James. *The Museum of Words: The Poetics of Ekphrasis from Homer to Ashbery.* Chicago: University of Chicago Press, 1993.

Hollander, John. *The Gazer's Spirit: Poems Speaking to Silent Works of Art.* Chicago: University of Chicago Press, 1995.

Jordan, June. "The Difficult Miracle of Black Poetry in America: Something like a Sonnet for Phillis Wheatley." In *On Call: Political Essays*, 87–98. Boston: South End Press, 1985.

Kidd, Thomas. *George Whitefield: America's Spiritual Founding Father.* New Haven: Yale University Press, 2014.

Krieger, Murray. *Ekphrasis: Illusion of the Natural Sign.* Baltimore: Johns Hopkins University Press, 1992.

Mitchell, W. J. T. *Picture Theory: Essays on Verbal and Visual Representation.* Chicago: University of Chicago Press, 1994.

———. *What Do Pictures Want?: The Lives and Loves of Images.* Chicago: University of Chicago Press, 2005.

Morgan, Kenneth. *Slavery and the Britsih Empire from Africa to America.* Oxford: Oxford University Press, 2007.

Mosely, Patrick. "Empowerment Through Classicism in Phillis Wheatley's 'Ode to Neptune.'" In *New Essays on Phillis Wheatley*, edited by John C. Shields and Eric D. Lamore. Knoxville: University of Tennessee Press, 2011.

Nash, Gary B. *Race and Revolution.* Madison, NJ: Madison House, 1990.

Patterson, Orlando. *Slavery and Social Death*. Cambridge, MA: Harvard University Press, 1985.
Shields, John C. *Phillis Wheatley and the Romantics*. Knoxville: University of Tennessee Press, 2010.
———. *Phillis Wheatley's Poetics of Liberation: Backgrounds and Contexts*. Knoxville: University of Tennessee Press, 2008.
———. "Phillis Wheatley's Theoretics of the Imagination: An Untold Chapter in the History of Early American Literary Aesthetics." In *New Essays on Phillis Wheatley*, edited by John C. Shields and Eric D. Lamore. Knoxville: University of Tennessee Press, 2011.
———. "Phillis Wheatley's Use of Classicism." *American Literature* 52, no. 1 (1980): 97–111.
Shields, John C., and Eric D. Lamore, eds. *New Essays on Phillis Wheatley*. Knoxville: University of Tennessee Press, 2011.
Smith, Cynthia J. "'To Maecenas': Phillis Wheatley's Invocation of an Idealized Reader." *Black American Literature Forum* 23 (1989): 579–92.
Stowe, Harriet Beecher. *Uncle Tom's Cabin, or, Life Among the Lowly*. Edited by Elizabeth Ammons. New York: W. W. Norton, 2010.
Taylor, Hannis. *The Origin and Growth of the American Constitution: An Historical Treatise*. Boston: Houghton Mifflin, 1911.
Waldstreicher, David. "The Wheatleyan Moment." *Early American Studies: An Interdisciplinary Journal* 9, no. 3 (Fall 2011): 522–51.
Walker, Alice. "In Search of Our Mother's Gardens." In *In Search of Our Mother's Gardens: Womanist Prose*. Orlando: Harcourt, 2004.
Walvin, James. *Black Ivory: Slavery in the British Empire*. 2nd ed. Oxford: Blackwell, 2001.
Webb, Ruth. *Ekphrasis, Imagination and Persuasion in Ancient Rhetorical Theory and Practice*. Burlington, VT: Ashgate Press, 2009.
Wheatley, Phillis. *The Collected Works of Phillis Wheatley*. Edited by John C. Shields. New York: Oxford University Press, 1988.
Wills, Gary. *"Negro President": Jefferson and the Slave Power*. Boston: Houghton Mifflin, 2003.
Wood, Gordon S. *Revolutionary Characters: What Made the Founders Different*. New York: Penguin Press, 2006.

Chapter 3

"Past ruin'd Ilion": The Classical Ideal and the Romantic Voice in Landor's Poetry
Steven Stryer

Over the course of a literary career that spanned eight decades between the appearance of his first volume in 1795 and his death in 1864, Walter Savage Landor repeatedly emphasized his isolation within his own age, declaring that "I claim no place in the world of letters; I am alone; and will be alone, as long as I live, and after."[1] In the epigrammatic poem "With An Album," published in 1846, he echoed and extended the opening line of Horace's *Ode* III.1 ("Odi profanum vulgus et arceo") in order to define his own poetry against the qualities of more widely read contemporary verse: "I know not whether I am proud, / But this I know, I hate the crowd: / Therefore pray let me disengage / My verses from the motley page, / Where others far more sure to please / Pour out their choral song with ease. / And yet perhaps, if some should tire / With too much froth or too much fire, / There is an ear that may incline / Even to words so dull as mine" (15:224; ll. 1–10). By his own account, Landor's work is neither facile nor readily pleasing. Instead it achieves its effects—not on "the crowd" but on a single worthy listener ("an ear that may incline")—through the restraint, control, and verbal difficulty which are implicitly opposed to the excesses of insubstantial "froth" and passionate "fire" among his contemporaries. Landor eschews their "choral song" for the individuality of his own voice, and the pride which he takes in his position apart from "the crowd" is not obscured by the self-conscious modesty of the final line.

But as much as Landor insisted on his separation from the readers and writers of his own time, he was equally adamant about those with whom he did claim a place, and by whose standards he measured his own achievement: the poets of ancient Greece and Rome. Landor often connected the two points, linking his lack of popularity with his dedication to the art and ideals of classical antiquity. For instance, in writing to his biographer John Forster in 1838 about the reception of his works by the reading public, he explained that "I found my company in a hothouse warmed with steam, and conducted them to my dining-room through a cold corridor with nothing but a few old statues in it from one end to the other, and they could not read the Greek names on the plinth, which made them hate the features above it." He then concluded with a wish: "God grant I may never be popular in any way, if I must pay the price of self-esteem for it."[2] In order to describe the kind of audience that he did seek and expect, Landor later modified this metaphorical comparison of his works to a dining room and his readers to guests, replacing the earlier company of disgruntled visitors with a gathering of worthy admirers in order to predict that "I shall dine late; but the dining-room will be well lighted, the guests few and select." Landor repeated this assertion on two different occasions during the last years of his life. In the midst of an imagined dialogue between himself and Archdeacon Hare that appeared in 1853, he uttered the statement in his own character, immediately following his confident declaration that "I have publisht [sic] five volumes of *Imaginary Conversations*: cut the worst of them thro the middle, and there will remain in this decimal fraction quite enough to satisfy my appetite for fame" (6:37). Several years earlier, in a letter of April 1850, the same image of a dining room with "few and select" guests is preceded by Landor's equally confident claim that "I shall have as many readers as I desire to have in other times than ours," and then is followed by the qualification that "I neither am, nor ever shall be, popular. Such never was my ambition."[3]

In each of these passages where he makes use of the dining-room metaphor, Landor goes on to align himself with the classical past, which is both the source and the fullest embodiment of his literary ideal. In the *Imaginary Conversation* with Archdeacon Hare, Landor grounds his claim to enduring fame on his ability to capture the authentic voice of antiquity rather than adapting it to modern English forms and manners: "In this age of discovery it may haply be discovered, who first among our Cisalpine nations led Greek to converse like Greek, Roman like Roman, in poetry or prose." By contrast, earlier "Gentlemen of fashion" have merely "patronized them occasionally, have taken them under the arm, have recommended their own tailor, their own perfumer, and have lighted a cigar for them from their own at the door of the *Traveler's* [sic] or *Athenaeum*: there they parted" (6:37). In the other instance of the dining-room metaphor, within the

1850 letter, Landor specifies the poetic qualities inherent in his classical ideal. Landor makes clear that he is not a mere imitator of any particular classical author's style: "I resemble none of the ancients, and still less the moderns." Yet the characteristics through which Landor defines his own works are once again those of the ancients, contrasted here with the defects of the moderns:

> I am obscure; this is too certain; everybody says it. But are Pindar and Aeschylus less so? I am unable to guess what proportion of their poetry the best poets have cancelled. Wordsworth and Byron, and most now living, leave no traces of erasure: I wish they had. I have rejected quite as much as I have admitted, and some of it quite as good. Order and proportion always were my objects. My real strength, I believe, lies in the dramatic, and I think I could have composed a drama suitable for the stage, if I had willed it: but intricacy, called plot, undermines the solid structure of well-ordered poetry. There is nothing of it in the *Iliad*, or in Aeschylus; once only in Sophocles is there much of it. The Spaniards are known for little else; and they brought over to England these instruments of mental torture in their poetical Armada.

Each of the qualities on which Landor prides himself—"order and proportion," avoidance of that "intricacy, called plot," merciless compression of one's own verse to eliminate whatever is extraneous, even at the price of obscurity—is justified by an appeal to the authority of classical Greek precedent. Following this passage, the whole paragraph culminates in the dining-room metaphor and the assertion that "I neither am, nor ever shall be, popular"—which in turn is followed by an even more sweeping alignment of Landor, in his deliberate shunning of popularity, with the values of classical civilization and against those of contemporary (and future) English taste: "Thousands of people, for centuries to come, will look up at the statues of the Duke of York, George III, Canning, Pitt, and others of that description; but in no centuries to come will fifty in any one generation feast their eyes in silent veneration on the marbles from the Parthenon."[4] The small group of onlookers who will venerate the Elgin Marbles rather than gape at the statues of British rulers and politicians overlaps, in Landor's mind, with the "few and select" readers with whom he hopes to dine, as he joins himself imaginatively with all the other devotees of the classical ideal past and present.

Many of Landor's most fervent admirers have echoed the claims which he makes for himself as an inheritor of this classical ideal. Swinburne, in his "Song for the Centenary of Walter Savage Landor," evoked the elder poet's fusion of Greek, Roman, and modern when he described how "through the trumpet of a child of Rome / Rang the pure music of the flutes of Greece. / As though some northern hand / Reft from the Latin land / A spoil more costly than the Colchian fleece / To clothe with golden sound . . . / The naked north-wind's cloudiest clime"; Elizabeth Barrett Browning singled him out as the living writer "in whose hands the ashes of antiquity burn again" and "the most unconventional in thought and word, the most classical because the freest from mere classicalism"; while the Countess of Blessington declared that Landor "reads of the ancients, thinks, lives with, and dreams of them; has imbued his thoughts with their lofty aspirations, and noble contempt of what is unworthy . . . ."[5] Such praise may seem extravagant, but even a brief survey of the facts of Landor's career helps to support it by revealing the extent of his devotion to the classical world. His education at Rugby between the ages of eight and sixteen consisted almost entirely of reading in Greek and Roman authors, as well as Latin verse and prose composition. During the subsequent year that he spent studying with a private tutor before his entrance into Oxford, Landor widened his reading in Latin literature to encompass the Latin works of British poets and deepened his knowledge of Greek writers such as Sophocles and Pindar.[6] The most significant classical influences on his own works included these two poets as well as Homer, Aeschylus, Theocritus, Sappho, Lucretius, Lucian, Catullus, and Ovid.[7]

The subjects and genres of Landor's works define them as a series of extended acts of engagement with the classical inheritance. In addition to his volume of prose *Imaginary Conversations of Greeks and Romans* (1853), these works include essays in English on Catullus and Theocritus (1842) and in Latin on the literary use of the Latin language by modern writers (1795, 1815, 1820, and 1847), as well as a book-length epistolary recreation of classical Athens, *Pericles and Aspasia* (1836). His first major poetic projects were the classically inspired heroic fragments *The Phocaeans* (1802) and *Crysaor* (1802) and the seven-book epic *Gebir*, which he composed simultaneously in both English and Latin versions (published in 1798 and 1803, respectively); as Joseph Kestner has argued, *Gebir* is grounded not only in the broader category of classical epic but in the genre of the epyllion or little epic, as practiced by Catullus and reflected within "the nearly dazzling 'miniaturizing' effects of diminutives, frequent elision, and syncope" in both the English and Latin texts of Landor's poem.[8] Late in his long life, Landor completed another classical project in the *Hellenics* (1846, with revised and expanded versions appearing in 1847 and 1859), a group of "heroic idylls" in the manner of Theocritus that treat subjects from classical mythology; many of the *Hellenics* began life as Latin narrative poems which were then translated and adapted into English versions. In his "Apology for the *Hellenics*" Landor expressed the full audacity of his ambition: "None had yet tried to make men speak / In English as they would in Greek" (15:240; ll. 1–2). Landor made surprisingly few direct translations from Greek and Latin literature, preferring to adapt, reshape, and reimagine the classical inheritance on his own terms.[9] But he also spoke extensively in Latin himself, publishing a body of several hundred shorter Latin poems which constitutes the last major corpus of Latin works by an English poet. As Andrea Kelly has demonstrated, Landor's Latin lyrics support his claims to literary independence by transcending mere imitation of classical authors and forms to attain a distinctive individuality of voice on both political and personal topics.[10] Indeed, for all his confidence in the value of his own poetic achievement in English, Landor was always more sure of his genius in Latin, writing to Wordsworth in 1822 that "In english [*sic*] I could not compose a work so delightful to me as several of yours and Southeys [*sic*], but I can write without much difficulty a latin [*sic*] poem which shall please me very far above any of the last eighteen hundred years . . . ."[11]

But while the extent of Landor's absorption of classical literature has been widely agreed on, its particular implications for the meanings of individual poems have been harder to define. Critics have usually resorted to impressionistic descriptions of Landor's style which take their cues from his own remarks about his poetry: they cite his "classical regularity of language and . . . classical composure and restraint of style," his "Greek ideals" of "[o]rder, proportion, harmony, cadence, simplicity," and his ability to attain "those qualities generally agreed upon as classical: purity, conciseness, clarity, objectivity, graceful simplicity, dignity."[12] This tendency to loose stylistic generalization has been particularly true of critical remarks on the shorter lyric poems written in the poet's own voice, the ones that most frequently represent him in modern anthologies and that (unlike the heroic poems and the idylls) seem to have obvious affinities with the romanticism of his age because of their emphasis on the poet's own emotions and experiences. The longer poems have been intriguingly approached as "a series of sculptured tableaux" that reflect the characteristic gestures and poses of Greek sculpture;[13] but discussions of the classical aspects of the shorter poems have largely been limited to observations such as Ernest de Selincourt's view that "Landor's lyrics are distinguished by that perfect symmetry of form, that limpidity of diction, that rejection of all extraneous ornament, which is the ideal of the best classic epigram," or George Saintsbury's remark that Landor "assimilated the nature of the ancient epigram— its singular pellucidity, and the closeness and cleanness of form which accompanies pellucidity naturally enough."[14] Such comments in turn restate the poet's claims about his own classical style, such as the note to one of his *Poems from the Arabic and Persian* (1800) explaining that "This poem resembles not those ridiculous quibbles which the English in particular call Epigrams, but rather, abating some little for *orientalism*, those exquisite *eidyllia*, those carvings as it were in ivory or on gems, which are modestly called Epigrams by the Greeks" (15:434). Similarly, the more recent observation by John Buxton that Landor's shorter lyrics are written "in the tradition of the epigrams of the *Greek Anthology*, with an elegant and compendious simplicity" achieved through avoidance of metaphor and color, expands on the poet's own statement in the 1859 preface to the *Hellenics* that the poetry in the volume differed from most contemporary verse in being "diaphanous" rather than "prismatic," so that it "leaves to the clear vision a wide expanse of varied scenery" and "they who look into it may see through" (14:353).[15] Even the most sensitive modern interpreter of Landor's poems, Robert Pinsky, defines his subject's classical achievement entirely in stylistic terms by arguing that "Landor's peculiar successes and failings ... are stylistic," that "the lovely, distinctive way of writing which is often described as Landor's 'classical style' ... arises in fact from a particular method, or attitude toward poem writing," and that this method is "to revitalize, through profound energies of understanding and a cleanly exactitude of style, an already established situation or observation." In Pinsky's view, "The tone, the precise psychological effect of the style, embodies Landor's creative effort. The style is his proof that he has wrested a device—the commonplace—to the condition of a statement."[16]

Landor himself, however, for all his own emphasis on the stylistic and tonal aspects of his classicism, was never content to limit his classical ideal to a manner of writing alone, or even to the larger aesthetic vision that a style implies. Instead he always maintained that this ideal encompassed humane values that extend across all times and all places. In the "Apology for *Gebir*" (1854) that he published more than fifty years after his epic, Landor rejected any binary opposition between the ancient and the modern, the Greco-Roman and the English. In response to the imagined question "'Do heroes of old times surpass / Brown, Cambridge, Somerset, Dundas?'" Landor answered with a defense of the classical that emphasizes its embodiment of enduring human concerns: "No, no: but let me ask in turn / Whether, whene'er Corinthian urn / With ivied Faun upon the rim / Invites, I may not gaze on him? / I love all beauty . . . . / I love old places and their climes, / Nor quit the syrinx for the chimes. / Manners have changed; but hearts are yet / The same, and will be while they beat" (15:231–32; ll. 49–50, 53–57, 71–74). Similarly, in the 1853 poem "To Shelley," Landor immediately retreated from his initial exaltation of the classical over the modern and the English—"He who beholds the skies of Italy / Sees ancient Rome reflected, sees beyond, / Into more glorious Hellas, nurse of Gods / And godlike men: dwarfs people other lands"—with an apologetic self-correction: "Frown not, maternal England! thy weak child / Kneels at thy feet and owns in shame a lie" (15:179; ll. 13–18). In another poem from the same year, Landor reconciled the ancient inheritance with contemporary achievement by imaginatively situating present-day writers alongside their Greek predecessors within a pagan temple, so that the English present is drawn physically into a structure metaphorically embodying the classical past: "On old Greek idols I may fix my eyes / Oftener, and bring them larger sacrifice, / Yet on the altar where are worshipt ours / I light my taper and lay down my flowers" (15:227; ll. 3–6).

Landor's response to the literary movement that dominated his own lifetime reflects his desire to draw together past and present through a commitment to transcendent values that span the centuries. In spite of his willingness to define himself in opposition to contemporary taste in other contexts, Landor did not reject the romantic in favor of the classical, but rather sought to hold the two in a dynamic balance with each other. In his most detailed consideration of the relationship between classical values and those of Romanticism, Landor insisted that the classical ideal could be fully achieved by the most romantic of poets. "To the Author of *Festus*: on the Classick and Romantick" (1849) asserts that not only his own romantic contemporaries but even peoples normally considered to lie outside the classical inheritance could embody the classical virtues as fully as the Greeks and Romans themselves: "We talk of schools . . unscholarly; of schools. / Part the romantick from the classical. / The classical like the heroick age / Is past; but Poetry may reassume / That glorious name with Tartar and with Turk, / With Goth or Arab, Sheik or Paladin, / And not with Roman and with Greek alone" (15:163–66; ll. 35–41). The real distinction, Landor urges, is not between "romantic" and "classical" as two opposed poetic schools, but between those poems that exemplify the classical virtues of clarity, proportion, restraint, and directness and those that do not: "In every poem train the leading shoot; / Break off the suckers. Thought erases thought, / As numerous sheep erase each other's print / When spungy moss they press or sterile sand. / Blades thickly sown want nutriment and droop, / Altho' the seed be sound, and rich the soil. / Thus healthy-born ideas, bedded close, / By dreaming fondness, perish overlaid" (ll. 27–34). In order to make clear the relevance of this ideal to his own time and country, Landor goes on to list a series of English poets, including several of his own romantic contemporaries, who are classical because of the inherent qualities in their works rather than their place or time of origin—"The name is graven on the workmanship" (l. 42). "Classick" becomes exclusively a term of praise, denoting the achievement of particular virtues by his fellow nineteenth-century poets that raise them to the level of the exemplary ancients. The trumpet blast of Walter Scott's *Marmion* "never shook / The walls of God-built Ilion; yet what shout / Of the Achaians swells the heart so high?" (ll. 43–45). Wordsworth, "in sonnet, is a classick too," though he falls short in the major classical poetic genres—"Too weak for ode or epick, and his gait / Somewhat too rural for the tragick pall"; nevertheless, "Large lumps of precious metal lie engulpht / In gravelly beds, whence you must delve them out" (ll. 73, 83–84, 79–80). And Landor's close friend Southey was "Classick in every feature"—"none who ruled around / Held in such order such a wide domain . . / But often too indulgent, too profuse" (ll. 88–91).

At this point in the poem, the terms of the discussion broaden out from the purely stylistic ones of the poetic survey to underlying qualities of the Greek character. The shift is accomplished through the vivid description of figures from classical mythology, beginning with the Muses and their self-discipline: "Abstemious were the Greeks; they never strove / To look so fierce: their muses were sedate, / Never obstreperous: you heard no breath / Outside the flute; each sound ran clear within" (ll. 95–98). The imagery with which Landor concludes this poem portrays a dynamic tension between the classical virtues of order and control and the characteristic romantic emphasis on subjective emotion and private experience. Such a dynamic interplay contradicts the position of those critics who have suggested that the "classical" qualities of Landor's poems are at odds with the supposedly "romantic" qualities of his character. J. A. K. Thomson, for instance, describes Landor as both "the most classical author in the language" and "less classical than he thought himself, for in temper he is almost extravagantly romantic"; while Elizabeth Nitchie argues that Landor is set apart from the major romantics because his poetry avoids the expression of "subjective" feeling in favor of a "manner of looking at life . . . which was essentially Greek and therefore objective, for the Greeks regarded the problems of existence in a singularly impersonal fashion."[17] According to Landor's own account at the end of "To the Author of *Festus*," however, the classical does not exclude the chaos of feeling but channels and controls it: "The Fauns might dance, might clap their hands, might shout, / Might revel and run riotous; the Nymphs / Furtively glanced, and fear'd, or seem'd to fear: / Descended on the lightest of light wings, / The strong tho' graceful Hermes mused awhile, / And now with his own lyre and now with voice / Tempered the strain; Apollo calmly smiled" (ll. 99–105). The typically romantic expression of subjective, personal, and transient feeling occurs here in the frenzy of the Fauns and the fear of the Nymphs; but this passion is then subsumed beneath the grace and calm of Hermes and Apollo, which bring order and control to the earlier display of emotion. Unrestrained feeling and self-discipline exist in an ongoing balance, each reacting to the other and revealing its own nature through the contrast.

The emotions here, of course, are still those attributed to characters drawn from classical mythology rather than those experienced by the poet personally and expressed in his own lyric voice. In order to examine further the interplay between Landor's romanticism and his classicism as complementary visions of life, I would now like to consider how Landor in the short lyric poems makes use of references and allusions to the classical past—with all their implications of generality, permanence, and authority—in order to give expression to his own personal, subjective emotions in the transient present. Robert Pinsky has described how Landor as a romantic poet seeks to achieve a personal revitalization of traditional literary forms, sentiments, and commonplaces—"tones, exact qualities of response to generalized, and therefore familiar experience," as he "struggles for clarification and definition within this commonality"; in the process he attains in his short lyrics "an emotional balance between a particular, real situation and a general, artificial one" through his "precise balancing of the formal donnée with personal emotion," and his "response to the relationship between an absolutely particular perception and the contrasting absolute of time."[18] I am interested in a related but distinct kind of balance, one achieved through the overt references to classical civilization in Landor's personal lyrics rather than through manipulation of tone and form. This approach allows us to expand the discussion of Landor's classicism and romanticism beyond its usual limitation to questions of style, in order to show how Landor brings the values of the classical and the romantic into tension, engagement, and alignment with each other.[19] For instance, in one short poem mourning the death of an infant, the effect of the classical allusion in the first stanza is to make the expression of individual emotion in the second stanza all the more poignant. The opening lines evoke classical elegy through their formulaic reference to a funerary urn inscribed with the fate of the dead child: "Child of a day, thou knowest not / The tears that overflow thy urn, / The gushing eyes that read thy lot, / Nor, if thou knewest, couldst return!" (16:74; ll. 1–4). But in the second stanza, Landor progresses from the generic classical image of the urn to the still generic but Christian and modern reference to "the pure and blest," and then finally to the overwhelming personal grief of the child's mother, who becomes the focus of the poem's last words after being introduced as the vehicle of a simile in line 6: "And why the wish! the pure and blest / Watch like thy mother o'er thy sleep. / O peaceful night! O envied rest! / Thou wilt not ever see her weep" (ll. 5–8). The overarching movement in the poem is from the classical and generalized or impersonal to the modern and personal, with the typically romantic emphasis on the private experience of grief emerging in the final line.

One particular group of Landor's shorter lyric poems, those written to and about his beloved Ianthe, serves as a case study in how he shifts and balances between these two imaginative poles. The Ianthe poems, which appeared over the course of more than fifty years beginning in 1806, are by turns (and often simultaneously) both profoundly classical and deeply romantic, reaching for the transcendence of time and space inherent in the former while remaining grounded in the personal—even autobiographical—experiences that characterize the latter. They extend over forty-three pages of short lyrics and epigrams in the standard Wheeler edition of Landor's poetry, and include poems published by Landor under the heading "Ianthe" within his lifetime, as well as others in which she is named or which he elsewhere describes as connected to her.[20] Landor's decision to address a large body of poetry to a mistress with a classically inspired pseudonym (derived from the Greek word for violet) is itself one that hearkens back to the practice of the Latin love elegists—Catullus's Lesbia, Propertius's Cynthia, Tibullus's Delia, or Ovid's Corinna; Landor likely came across the name in the story of Iphis and Ianthe within Book IX of Ovid's *Metamorphoses*.[21] The biographical inspiration for this revival of a classical convention was his lifelong love for Jane Sophia Swift (the object of his devotion despite her marriages to two other men), whose name he modified to "Ianthe." This decision to substitute a classical name so close to the English "Jane" itself reflects a mediation between Landor's own autobiographical experiences and the literary conventions of Roman antiquity: the personal is being elevated to a classical generality of meaning through the medium of art. Landor draws attention to this act of mediation within one of the poems, as he playfully shows his subject herself urging it: "'Cannot you make my name of Jane / Sound pleasanter? Now try again,' / Said she. At once I thought about / The matter, and at last cut out / A letter from Greek alphabet, / And had it, as I thought, well set; / 'Twas then 'Ianthe'" (15:404; ll. 1–7). The language of craftsmanship here in Landor's "cutting" and "setting" is also classical, recalling his earlier comparison of one of his poems to "those exquisite *eidyllia*, those carvings as it were in ivory or on gems, which are modestly called Epigrams by the Greeks."

The same idea of universality and permanence achieved through classical craftsmanship occurs again in one of the most widely anthologized of the Ianthe poems, where Landor reworks a conceit from Sonnet 75 of Spenser's *Amoretti* (which in turn looks back to Horace's boast at the beginning of *Odes* III.30, "Exegi monumentum *aere perennius*"): "Well I remember how you smiled / To see me write your name upon / The soft sea-sand . . . / 'O! what a child! / You think you're writing upon stone!' / I have since written what no tide / Shall ever wash away, what men / Unborn shall read o'er ocean wide / And find Ianthe's name agen" (15:402; ll. 1–8). As in "Child of a day," the classical here evokes the universal and the timeless, set against the transience of the poet's private experiences and emotions; but where "Child of a day" moves from the generic classical urn to the individual grief of the mother, "Well I remember how you smiled" moves in the opposite direction, from the humble private memory of a whimsical moment in Landor's own life (ll. 1–4) to the immortality of poetry (ll. 5–8), which is elevated beyond the limitations of time and space ("what men / Unborn shall read o'er ocean wide"). The permanence which Landor boasts of for his own poetry is underscored through the attention drawn to "Ianthe's name" in the final line; its Greek resonance contrasts with the extremely simple, Anglo-Saxon and largely monosyllabic diction of the poem as a whole. The immortalization of Ianthe achieved in this poem has those qualities of chiseled permanence—"writing upon stone" or "carvings . . . in ivory or on gems"—which the playful personal act of writing the beloved's name in the sand (and by extension the remembered experience itself) does not have. The classical qualities of art here both incorporate and subsume the initial romantic emphasis on the subjective memory of private experience.

Transient personal experience is once again elevated to a classical permanence via the medium of the poet's classicizing art in another of Landor's most anthologized poems, "Past ruin'd Ilion Helen lives." Here again as in "Child of a day," the movement is from classical generality and timelessness to romantic particularity and immediacy, as the poem opens with two mythological women who have been immortalized by the Greek epic and dramatic poets: "Past ruin'd Ilion Helen lives, / Alcestis rises from the shades; / Verse calls them forth; 'tis verse that gives / Immortal youth to mortal maids" (15:376; ll. 1–4). It then shifts to the present and the personal, as Landor promises to bestow the same immortality on his own classically named mistress:

> Soon shall Oblivion's deepening veil
> Hide all the peopled hills you see,
> The gay, the proud, while lovers hail
> In distant ages you and me.
>
> The tear for fading beauty check,
> For passing glory cease to sigh;
> One form shall rise above the wreck,
> One name, Ianthe, shall not die. (ll. 5–12)

As Ernest Dilworth comments, in this three-stanza poem "we go, in three steps, from general and impersonal immortality, to personal but anonymous, and finally to personal and named—though the very name, in its classical impersonality, takes us back to the beginning."[22] Landor's boast, in all its romantic emphasis on the personal and particular, emerges out of and gains authority from its association with the classical and general.

For convenience of analysis, the Ianthe poems may be divided into three broad categories according to the role played by classical references within them. (These references are generally drawn from classical mythology, the source for so many of Landor's longer verse and prose reimaginings of antiquity.) The first category includes those lyrics whose classical references are the most sustained and developed, forming extended conceits around which the poem as a whole pivots. The second category consists of poems which allude briefly but explicitly to the classical world in a single phrase or image that ripples outward to shape the larger meaning of the work. The third and largest category comprises those poems whose offhand or submerged references to classical antiquity do not seem (as in the case of the first two categories) the product of conscious authorial decisions; instead, these references serve to reveal how thoroughly embedded the classical idiom is in Landor's verse style, and therefore how deeply it pervades his mind even when he is treating the most personal of subjects. In all three cases, the classical references are all the more noticeable for the generally (in Saintsbury's phrase) "pellucid" nature of Landor's verse, which allows these allusive moments to stand out sharply against the transparent backdrop of the poems in which they occur.

The distinctions among the three categories are largely a matter of degree: poems within the first group, for example, are marked by the lengths to which they will go in developing a phrase or image that might otherwise seem only a half-conscious echo of ancient Greece or Rome. For instance, in the first two lines of one short lyric consisting of five heroic couplets, the personified "Loves" seem merely a convenient circumlocution for describing Landor's emotional state (a practice in keeping with the romantics' association of the heroic couplet with eighteenth-century "poetic diction"), rather than an actual evocation of classical deities: "The Loves who many years held all my mind, / A charge so troublesome at last resign'd" (15:394; ll. 1–2). But the succeeding couplet then unexpectedly literalizes the image by moving from abstract "Loves" symbolic of Landor's devotion to winged deities who actually guard his person—and who then abandon him, leaving physical traces of themselves among his belongings: "Among my books a feather here and there / Tells what the inmates of my study were" (ll. 3–4). The development from an initially abstract reference to the concept of love to the literal envisioning of a Cupid-like deity is a technique that Landor employs again in another poem addressed to Ianthe, here through the physical details of a feather, a torch, and a pagan temple: "You see the worst of love, but not the best, / Nor will you know him till he comes your guest. / Tho' yearly drops some feather from his sides, / In the heart's temple his pure torch abides" (15:387; ll. 1–4).

Elsewhere, in "Written at Malvern," the classical nature of abstractions introduced in the first three lines is similarly only revealed later in the poem. Landor progresses from a personal plea addressed to these faintly personified abstractions—"Come back, ye Smiles, that late forsook / Each breezy path and ferny nook. / Come Laughter" (15:368; ll. 1–3)—to the fuller personification of these powers as "Sweet children of celestial breed" (l. 9)—to the explicit association of them with the classical pantheon, as the offspring of the gods of satire and love: "Laughter, though Momus gave thee birth, / And said—'my darling, stay on earth.' / Smiles, though from Venus you arise, / And live for ever in the skies" (ll. 11–14). The poem then returns once again to the personal in lines that are made all the more powerful by the weight of classical divinity that Landor now commands to serve his beloved: "I order that not one descend / But first alights upon my friend. / When one upon her cheek appears, / A thousand spring to life from hers" (ll. 15–18). The final couplet of the poem underscores this praise of Ianthe with the image of her triumphing even over the personified figure of Death, who is imagined with a classical funerary urn: "Death smites his disappointed urn, / And beauty, health, and joy, return" (ll. 19–20). Likewise, at the end of "The Loves who many years held all my mind," the classical, after being made literal through the conceit of winged deities, is then drawn into contact with the present when their discarded feathers unexpectedly appear as bookmarks: "Strong for no wrestle, ready for no race, / They only serve to mark the left-off place" (ll. 5–6). The intensely personal nature of Landor's experience of love (whether as a lover, a poet writing about love, or both is left ambiguous) is conveyed here through the references to his books and study—objects autobiographically specific to him as an author; the passing of this experience is then dignified and elevated to a level of general, permanent truth through the association with classical mythology. The romantic and the classical converge, resulting in a poem that avoids the excesses of both consumingly personal and exclusively abstract or general treatments of the theme. The final couplets extend this synthesis of the personal with the general by portraying the Loves as frequenting and avoiding generic scenes from nature that metaphorically represent the past and present periods of Landor's own life: "'Twas theirs to dip in the tempestuous waves, / 'Twas theirs to loiter in cool summer caves; / But in the desert where no herb is green / Not one, the latest of the flight, is seen" (ll. 7–10).

The technique of moving from the present and personal to the classical and generalized via the extended literalizing of an apparently offhand figure of speech is one that Landor employs elsewhere in the Ianthe poems of the first category. One poem addressed to Ianthe follows the emotional immediacy of his opening plea to her—"Beloved the last! beloved the most! / With willing arms and brow benign / Receive a bosom tempest-tost, / And bid it ever beat to thine" (15:386–87; ll. 1–4)—with an extended tale situated in the world of classical myth. This tale begins by bringing to life the dead metaphor latent in "tempest-tost": "The Nereid maids, in days of yore, / Saw the lost pilot loose the helm, / Saw the wreck blacken all the shore, / And every wave some head o'erwhelm" (ll. 5–8). The poem goes on to relate the regrets of one of the Nereids ("the youngest of the train" [l. 9]); she laments her failure out of fear to aid "A minstrel from the billowy main" (l. 11)—analogous to Landor as poet—whose lifeless corpse has been "Borne breathless near her coral grot" (l. 12). The terms of her lament point back to Landor's own plight as both poet and lover, while also offering an implicit warning to Ianthe in support of the plea in the opening stanza: "'Ah me!' she cried, 'I come too late! / Rather than not have sooth'd his woes, / I would, but may not, share his fate.' / She rais'd his hand. 'What hand like this / Could reach the heart athwart the lyre! / What lips like these return my kiss, / Or breathe, incessant, soft desire!'" (ll. 14–20). The description of the drowned poet's situation, as well as some of the poem's language, echo Milton's *Lycidas*; but Landor's lyric is notably devoid of the Christian consolation that emerges at the conclusion of Milton's elegy. Instead, the classical episode here illustrates the poet's personal predicament and in the process elevates and dignifies it by providing a parallel that is remote in place and time, while also displacing private emotion into external action.

By contrast, in another poem which juxtaposes the classical Nereids and the poet's love for Ianthe, the personal, instead of being elevated by association with the classical, exists in competition with it. Landor addresses the poem to a "Darling Shell" (15:376–77; l. 1), which he exalts because it belongs to Ianthe, even though it lacks the classical pedigree of other inhabitants and objects of the ocean: "Whether thou hast tuned the dance / To the maids of ocean / Know I not .. but Ignorance / Never hurts devotion"; "This I know, Ianthe's Shell, / I must ever love thee well, / Tho' too little to resound / While the Nereids dance around"; "That which into Cyprus bore / Venus from her native sea, / (Pride of shells!) was never more / Dear to her than thou to me" (ll. 5–8, 9–12, 21–24). Landor here asserts the claims of the humble and personal alongside those of the classical, rather than seeking to imbue the personal with the elevation of the classical. Elsewhere he goes even further in this direction by suggesting the superiority of his beloved to the most celebrated woman of classical myth, as he brings the mythological Helen into juxtaposition with his own Ianthe in order to underscore their very different reactions to the shared human experience of aging. This Helen is not the timeless classical beauty immortalized through the power of verse in "Past ruin'd Ilion Helen lives," but a mortal woman grieving at her own decline: "When Helen first saw wrinkles in her face . . . / She threw herself upon her couch, and wept: / On this side hung her head, and over that / Listlessly she let fall the faithless brass / That made the men as faithless" (15:380; ll. 1, 4–7). Indeed, it is Ianthe here who reacts more admirably than her classical antecedent, demonstrating an equanimity and good humor that Helen lacks: "But when you / Found them, or fancied them, and would not hear / That they were only vestiges of smiles, / Or the impression of some amorous hair . . . / Upon a skin so soft . . *No, no,* you said, / *Sure, they are coming, yes, are come, are here* . . / *Well, and what matters it . . while you are too!*" (ll. 7–10, 13–15).

The second category of Ianthe poems, those which allude briefly but explicitly to the classical world, achieves a similar effect of juxtaposing the personal and the classical in more measured ways. Often the classical reference comes at the beginning of the poem, and sets a tone or establishes a frame of reference for everything that follows. For instance, the opening statement "I sadden while I view again / Smiles that for me the Graces wreathed" (15:377; ll. 1–2) imparts a classical nobility and permanence to the bittersweet memory of love that it introduces: "Sure my last kiss those lips retain / And breathe the very vow they breathed" (ll. 3–4). This image then leads up to the revelation in the third stanza that Landor is gazing on a picture of Ianthe—not the woman herself—as he writes the poem, remembers her parting vow that "At peace, in sorrow, far or near, / Constant and fond she still would be," and promises to maintain his own constancy to her: "yet shalt thou night and day, / Sweet image, to this heart be prest" (ll. 5–6, 11–12). Similarly, at the beginning of "Memory," a poem published just a year before Landor's death, the poignant memory of the dead Ianthe is introduced by a reference to the classical Muses. The conceit here is not maintained deep into the poem as it would be in poems of the first category, but its brief appearance serves to underscore the contrast between the timelessness of antiquity and Landor's own time-bound frailty, as he lives on deprived of all but the memory of Ianthe: "The mother of the Muses, we are taught, / Is Memory: she has left me; they remain, / And shake my shoulder, urging me to sing / About the summer days, my loves of old. / *Alas! alas!* is all I can reply. / Memory has left with me that name alone, / Harmonious name, which other bards may sing, / But her bright image in my darkest hour / Comes back, in vain comes back, call'd or uncall'd" (15:403; ll. 1–9). The poem proceeds from its impersonal opening invocation of classical myth to a deeply personal account of Landor's memories of Ianthe, followed by all the friends and acquaintances whose names he has forgotten, in a haunting depiction of the experience of mental decay.

Elsewhere the classical references in this second category occur later within the poems, retrospectively shaping the implications of what has come before them. For example, "To Ianthe" consists entirely of straightforward personal reflections and questions for the first nine lines, which are focused entirely on the relationship of the poet and his beloved: "We once were happier; true; but were / Our happiest hours devoid of care? / Remains there nothing like the past, / But calmer and less overcast / By clouds no effort could dispell, / And hopes we neither dared to tell? / I wish that hand were earlier free / Which Love should have preserv'd for me" (15:402; ll. 1–8). But the poem then concludes with a striking reference to the classical Fates, which suggests a view of this relationship as determined by factors beyond the control of the two lovers. The personal and immediate experience captured within the earlier lines is now subject to impersonal forces as remote as classical antiquity itself: "Content, if sad, I must be now / With what the sparing Fates allow, / And feel, tho' once the hope seem'd vain, / There may be love that feels no pain" (ll. 9–12). Or the single classical reference can occur at a significant moment in the middle of the poem, as when, in the midst of a description of Clifton, Landor places the classical Naiads alongside the actual modern-day pleasures of the rural seashore. The effect is to align present and classical past, autobiographical experience and mythological fantasy, in order to situate all of human experience on a single timeless plane: "Pleasant I've thought it, to pursue the row'r, / While light and darkness seiz'd the changeful oar; / The frolic Naiads drawing from below / A net of silver round the black canoe. / Now, the last lonely solace let it be / To watch pale evening brood o'er land and sea" (15:372; ll. 7–12).

The third and final category of Ianthe poems offers an appropriate place to conclude this discussion of Landor's classical ideal. For it shows Landor operating in a classical idiom that exists below the level of self-conscious allusion or explicit invocation of classical mythology. Such instances are revealing because they are so pervasive: in poems on the most personal of experiences, describing the most private memories, feelings, and longings, he nevertheless instinctively draws upon a vocabulary that points back (if only by half-conscious implication) to ancient Greece and Rome. Such instances can be as slight and occasional as the echo of a Homeric phrase when he ends a poem with "That winged word" (15:391; l. 12). Or they can accumulate within a recurring pattern, as in Landor's frequent references to the pagan concept of Fate (as opposed to the more explicitly classical allusion to the Fates as divinities noted above). In these instances, the context in which the word occurs calls up a very different world from that of nineteenth-century Christian Europe. The seemingly offhand reference to prophecy, for example, has this effect when the poet observes that "Whether I shall or not / Draw from Fate's hand that lot / I'd give a prophet all I'm worth to say" (15:386; ll. 5–7): the terms in which Landor thinks when reflecting on his own predicament here—including the apparent allusion to the ancient practice of divining the future through the drawing of lots ("sortes")—are unmistakably classical. So too when Landor, after predicting his eventual decline into old age and the fading of Ianthe's devotion to him, invokes the classical conception of "Malignant Fate" to declare: "It must be so, Ianthe! but to think / Malignant Fate should also threaten *you*, / Would make my heart, now vainly buoyant, sink: / Believe it not: 'tis what I'll never do" (15:388; ll. 5–8).

Elsewhere it is the vague references to multiple deities overseeing the lives of human beings from their own remote abodes that recall the Greco-Roman pantheon rather than the Christian God: for instance when Landor, worrying that Ianthe may be unfaithful to him while she is absent, pleads, "mighty powers! assert your just controul, / Alarm her thoughtless breast; / Breathe soft suspicion o'er her yielding soul—/ But never break its rest" (15:373; ll. 5–8); or when, wishing health, pleasure, and wit to return to the suffering Ianthe, whose "nights are restlessness, her days are pain" (15:367; l. 2), Landor implores, "Grant me, O grant this wish, ye heavenly powers, / All other gifts, all other hopes, restrain" (ll. 7–8). A similarly half-conscious echo of classical notions of divinity can be heard when Landor begins another poem about a remembered encounter with Ianthe with a curiously roundabout figure of speech that seems to recall the Greek conception of the Hours as goddesses: "Along this coast I led the vacant Hours / To the lone sunshine on the uneven strand" (15:390; ll. 1–2). Even Landor's manner of vividly personifying abstractions suggests his absorption of an older pagan view of the divine, as he shows the abstract concept acting with invisible agency in the physical world: "There even Memory should sit / Absorbed, and almost doubting it" (15:388; ll. 19–20); "'for Memory / Where you but once have been must ever be, / And at your voice Pride from his throne must rise'" (15:395; ll. 4–6); "No longer to these eyes / Love shows the place he flew from; there, bereft / Of motion, Grief is left" (15:394; ll. 4–6).

Such echoes and adaptations of the classical ethos do not shape the meaning and tone of the poems in which they occur to the same extent as the more extended or more explicit references in the first two categories. But they do demonstrate just how deeply permeated Landor's body of work is by the attitudes and idioms of classical antiquity, even when he is writing about times, places, and experiences as far removed as possible from ancient Greece and Rome. Throughout the Ianthe poems, in ways both large and small, Landor sought to achieve the romantic expression of his own personal experiences through reference to the universality, authority, and permanence that he associated with the classical world because of its distance from the transient present. In doing so, Landor fulfilled his lifelong ambition of embodying the classical ideal within an age that seemed to be drifting away from it. By bringing the romantic into juxtaposition with the classical and expressing his own vision of life through the tension between and the reconciliation of the two, the poet achieved his confident prediction for his literary fate: "I shall dine late; but the dining-room will be well lighted, the guests few and select."

Notes

1. T. Earle Welby and Stephen Wheeler, eds., *The Complete Works of Walter Savage Landor*, 16 vols. (New York: Barnes & Noble, 1969), 12:137 ("To Lord Brougham on the Neglect of Southey" [1850]). All parenthetical citations refer to this edition. The unusual two ellipsis points (..) contained in certain verses quoted from Landor are from the original printed text.
2. John Forster, *Walter Savage Landor: A Biography*, 2 vols. (London: Chapman and Hall, 1869), 2:345.
3. Ibid., 2:531.
4. Ibid., 2:530–31.
5. Algernon Charles Swinburne, *The Poems of Algernon Charles Swinburne*, 6 vols. (London: Chatto & Windus, 1904), 5:17; Frederic G. Kenyon, ed., *The Letters of Elizabeth Barrett Browning*, 2 vols. (New York: Macmillan, 1899), 1:47; Forster, *Walter Savage Landor*, 2:298; Marguerite Gardiner, Countess of Blessington, *The Idler in Italy*, 2nd ed., 2 vols. (London: Henry Colburn, 1839), 2:311–12.
6. R. H. Super, *Walter Savage Landor: A Biography* (New York: New York University Press, 1954), 3, 6, 9, 14. On Landor's classical education see also Ruth Ingersoll Goldmark, *Studies in the Influence of the Classics on English Literature* (New York: Columbia University Press, 1918), 44–52.

7. See Andrea Kelly, "The Latin Poetry of Walter Savage Landor," in *The Latin Poetry of English Poets*, ed. J. W. Binns (London: Routledge & Kegan Paul, 1974), 157; Ann Gossman, "Landor and the 'Higher Fountains,'" *The Classical Journal* 50 (1955): 304–6; David M. Robinson, "Landor's Knowledge of the Classics," *The Classical Journal* 51 (1955): 25–26; and Stanley T. Williams, "Walter Savage Landor as a Critic of Literature," *PMLA* 38 (1923): 914–17 (which compiles Landor's comments on various Greek and Roman writers). For the formative influence of Catullus on Landor's epigrammatic poems, with their shared qualities of "precision of expression," "metrical variation," and "delicacy of language" (37), see R. H. Super, "Landor and Catullus," *The Wordsworth Circle* 7 (1976): 31–37; for Landor's engagement with Catullus in his own Latin poetry, see Henry Stead, *A Cockney Catullus: The Reception of Catullus in Romantic Britain, 1795–1821* (Oxford: Oxford University Press, 2016), 154–65. On Landor's more mixed assessments of Horace and Virgil see, respectively, A. LaVonne Ruoff, "Walter Savage Landor's Criticism of Horace: The Odes and Epodes," *Arion* 9 (1970): 188–204, and Elizabeth Nitchie, *Vergil and the English Poets* (New York: Columbia University Press, 1919), 200–11.
8. Joseph Kestner, "The Genre of Landor's *Gebir*: 'Eminences Excessively Bright,'" *The Wordsworth Circle* 5 (1974): 46. On the frequent stylistic obscurity which results from Landor's cultivation of a Latinate verbal compression in the English poem, see Pierre Vitoux, "*Gebir* as an Heroic Poem," *The Wordsworth Circle* 7 (1976): 51–52.
9. Vivian Mercier, "The Future of Landor Criticism," in *Some British Romantics: A Collection of Essays*, ed. James V. Logan, John E. Jordon, and Northrop Frye (Columbus: Ohio State University Press, 1966), 62.
10. See Kelly, "The Latin Poetry of Walter Savage Landor," 150–93; cf. also Leicester Bradner, *Musae Anglicanae: A History of Anglo-Latin Poetry, 1500–1925* (New York: Modern Language Association, 1940), 315–25.
11. R. H. Super, "Landor's Letters to Wordsworth and Coleridge," *Modern Philology* 55 (1957): 76.
12. Sidney Colvin, *Landor* (London: Macmillan, 1888), 201; Goldmark, *Studies in the Influence of the Classics*, 55; Gossman, "Landor and the 'Higher Fountains,'" 303.
13. Mercier, "The Future of Landor Criticism," 60. See also Stephen A. Larrabee, *English Bards and Grecian Marbles: The Relationship Between Sculpture and Poetry Especially in the Romantic Period* (New York: Columbia University Press, 1943), 233–51.
14. Ernest de Selincourt, "Classicism and Romanticism in the Poetry of Walter Savage Landor," in *Vorträge 1930/1931: England und die Antike*, ed. Fritz Saxl (Leipzig: B. G. Teubner, 1932), 247; George Saintsbury, *A History of English Prosody from the Twelfth Century to the Present Day*, 3 vols. (London: Macmillan, 1906–10), 3:88.

15. John Buxton, *The Grecian Taste: Literature in the Age of Neo-Classicism 1740–1820* (London: Macmillan, 1978), 106, 112, 116.
16. Robert Pinsky, *Landor's Poetry* (Chicago: University of Chicago Press, 1968), 26, 30.
17. J. A. K. Thomson, *The Classical Background of English Literature* (London: Allen & Unwin, 1948), 226; Elizabeth Nitchie, "The Classicism of Walter Savage Landor," *The Classical Journal* 14 (1918): 157.
18. Pinsky, *Landor's Poetry*, 32, 92, 38, 96.
19. Adam Roberts recently has proposed another critical framework for treating the balance between classical and Romantic elements in Landor's works, one that proceeds along very different lines from my own by arguing that "the Latinate *polish* of Landor's poetry is . . . the formal embodiment of the most fascinating and far-reaching engagement with questions of cleanness in literature," extending to "ethical, sexual, political, classical, formal, and stylistic matters" (2), and that "there is something characteristically, even crucially, Romantic about the way he navigates cleanness and uncleanness in his work" (184): see Adam Roberts, *Landor's Cleanness: A Study of Walter Savage Landor* (Oxford: Oxford University Press, 2014). Cf. also Adam Roberts, "Walter Savage Landor and the Classics," in *The Oxford History of Classical Reception in English Literature, Vol. 4 (1790–1880)*, ed. Norman Vance and Jennifer Wallace (Oxford: Oxford University Press, 2015), 365–84.
20. Welby and Wheeler, *Complete Works*, 15:367.
21. Allan D. Burns, "Landor, Ianthe, and the 'Other Bards,'" *English Language Notes* 37 (1999): 57.
22. Ernest Dilworth, *Walter Savage Landor* (New York: Twayne, 1971), 78–79.

Bibliography

Bradner, Leicester. *Musae Anglicanae: A History of Anglo-Latin Poetry, 1500–1925*. New York: Modern Language Association, 1940.

Burns, Allan D. "Landor, Ianthe, and the 'Other Bards.'" *English Language Notes* 37 (1999): 56–64.

Buxton, John. *The Grecian Taste: Literature in the Age of Neo-Classicism 1740–1820*. London: Macmillan, 1978.

Colvin, Sidney. *Landor*. London: Macmillan, 1888.

de Selincourt, Ernest. "Classicism and Romanticism in the Poetry of Walter Savage Landor." In *Vorträge 1930/1931: England und die Antike*, edited by Fritz Saxl, 230–50. Leipzig: B. G. Teubner, 1932.

Dilworth, Ernest. *Walter Savage Landor*. New York: Twayne, 1971.

Forster, John. *Walter Savage Landor: A Biography*. 2 vols. London: Chapman and Hall, 1869.
Gardiner, Marguerite, Countess of Blessington. *The Idler in Italy*. 2nd ed. 2 vols. London: Henry Colburn, 1839.
Goldmark, Ruth Ingersoll. *Studies in the Influence of the Classics on English Literature*. New York: Columbia University Press, 1918.
Gossman, Ann. "Landor and the 'Higher Fountains.'" *The Classical Journal* 50 (1955): 303–7.
Kelly, Andrea. "The Latin Poetry of Walter Savage Landor." In *The Latin Poetry of English Poets*, edited by J. W. Binns, 150–93. London: Routledge & Kegan Paul, 1974.
Kenyon, Frederic G., ed. *The Letters of Elizabeth Barrett Browning*. 2 vols. New York: Macmillan, 1899.
Kestner, Joseph. "The Genre of Landor's *Gebir*: 'Eminences Excessively Bright.'" *The Wordsworth Circle* 5 (1974): 41–49.
Larrabee, Stephen A. *English Bards and Grecian Marbles: The Relationship Between Sculpture and Poetry Especially in the Romantic Period*. New York: Columbia University Press, 1943.
Mercier, Vivian. "The Future of Landor Criticism." In *Some British Romantics: A Collection of Essays*, edited by James V. Logan, John E. Jordon, and Northrop Frye, 43–85. Columbus: Ohio State University Press, 1966.
Nitchie, Elizabeth. "The Classicism of Walter Savage Landor." *The Classical Journal* 14 (1918): 147–66.
———. *Vergil and the English Poets*. New York: Columbia University Press, 1919.
Pinsky, Robert. *Landor's Poetry*. Chicago: University of Chicago Press, 1968.
Roberts, Adam. *Landor's Cleanness: A Study of Walter Savage Landor*. Oxford: Oxford University Press, 2014.
———. "Walter Savage Landor and the Classics." In *The Oxford History of Classical Reception in English Literature: Volume 4 (1790–1880)*, edited by Norman Vance and Jennifer Wallace, 365–84. Oxford: Oxford University Press, 2015.
Robinson, David M. "Landor's Knowledge of the Classics." *The Classical Journal* 51 (1955): 25–26.
Ruoff, A. LaVonne. "Walter Savage Landor's Criticism of Horace: The Odes and Epodes." *Arion* 9 (1970): 188–204.
Saintsbury, George. *A History of English Prosody from the Twelfth Century to the Present Day*. 3 vols. London: Macmillan, 1906–10.
Stead, Henry. *A Cockney Catullus: The Reception of Catullus in Romantic Britain, 1795–1821*. Oxford: Oxford University Press, 2016.
Super, R. H. "Landor and Catullus." *The Wordsworth Circle* 7 (1976): 31–37.

———. "Landor's Letters to Wordsworth and Coleridge." *Modern Philology* 55 (1957): 73–83.

———. *Walter Savage Landor: A Biography*. New York: New York University Press, 1954.

Swinburne, Algernon Charles. *The Poems of Algernon Charles Swinburne*. 6 vols. London: Chatto & Windus, 1904.

Thomson, J. A. K. *The Classical Background of English Literature*. London: Allen & Unwin, 1948.

Vitoux, Pierre. "*Gebir* as an Heroic Poem." *The Wordsworth Circle* 7 (1976): 51–57.

Welby, T. Earle, and Stephen Wheeler, eds. *The Complete Works of Walter Savage Landor*. 16 vols. New York: Barnes & Noble, 1969.

Williams, Stanley T. "Walter Savage Landor as a Critic of Literature." *PMLA* 38 (1923): 906–28.

Chapter 4

"Larger the shadows": Longfellow's Translation of Virgil's *Eclogue 1*
Christoph Irmscher

On November 29, 1870, Longfellow wrote in his journal: "Everett's Lecture on Virgil. Excellent. Rain in the afternoon.—Evening tried to render the First Eclogue into English hexameters; but did not write it down."[1] It seems remarkable that Longfellow—an inveterate note-taker and proud owner of a sizable collection of pencils—would not have recorded his effort.[2] Is it possible that he committed his translation—or parts of it—to memory? If he didn't write anything down at the time, he did so later.[3] He included "Virgil's First Eclogue" in *Kéramos and Other Poems* in 1878, along with another Latin translation, "Ovid in Exile" (from Ovid's *Tristia*), the two first entries in a whole section of translated poetry which also contained seven sonnets and a canzone by Michelangelo, as well as other translations from less prominent French and German authors. The structure of the new volume echoes that of earlier collections, notably his first book of poetry, *Voices of the Night* (1839), which featured twenty-three translated poems and only seventeen original ones.[4]

Latin was not among the languages represented in *Voices of the Night*, for obvious reasons. He never tried his hand at blank verse renderings of Homer, as William Cullen Bryant did, and he never sought to reinvigorate, as Thoreau did, his "fallen English" by returning to Pindar's Odes.[5] To be sure, literary translation was part and parcel of Longfellow's poetics, which presented a powerful alternative to the more familiar nationalistic conceptions of U.S. American literature that have for too long dominated our view of the nineteenth-century canon. With a few exceptions (Anglo-Saxon being one of them), Longfellow's advocacy for a "cosmopolitan" American literature—one that made use of all the literary traditions and languages present in a nation of immigrants, while also respecting indigenous traditions—depended on the appreciation of *living* languages, languages still spoken around him, whether in the fish markets of Boston or by his Ojibwa visitor, Kah-ge-ga-gah-bowh, better known as George Copway. It helped that Longfellow spoke nine languages fluently and was able to read, by a conservative estimate, eight more.[6]

But we also know that he was an avid student of the classics. He was only seven years old when he was reported to have "gone half through his Latin Grammar," surpassing "several boys twice as old as he."[7] The story goes that at the Bowdoin Commencement twelve years later, Longfellow's elegant translation of an Horatian ode (we don't know which one) had such a powerful effect on one of the college trustees that he proposed Longfellow's name for the newly created Professorship of Modern Languages—which, if true, would reveal a remarkable misunderstanding of what the subject of this position was intended to be.[8] Throughout his life, Longfellow would pepper his letters with Latin quotations, especially when he was writing to George Washington Greene, his classically trained friend.[9] Thanks to Dante's *Divina Commedia*, Virgil was a familiar presence in Longfellow's literary world. In the *Divina Commedia*, Virgil acts as Dante's mentor and guide, and as Longfellow immersed himself in the project of translating Dante's masterwork and increasingly identified with Dante, Virgil began to assume some of that role for him too.[10]

Thus, while the classics might not have been paramount in his efforts to reinvent American literature as a "composite" of the living languages making up the tapestry of American culture, they provided the solid foundation on which his work rested, the way Virgil had enabled Dante to create the epic that Longfellow knew would help modern Italy find its political and cultural identity.[11] Longfellow, too, had tried to be a Dante of sorts for his nation by giving it two extremely popular poems with epic ambitions, *Evangeline: A Tale of Acadie* (1847) and *A Song of Hiawatha* (1855). But Longfellow was, at heart, a poet of the everyday rather than of epic grandeur. As we know from the thousands of letters his fans wrote him, his readers loved him best when he wrote about mundane experiences, the rain that must fall into everyone's life, the courage that is required when we must be "up and doing," the consolations of the night when sleep relieves us from the cares of the day. By 1870, with his Dante translation finished, Longfellow had returned to his earlier preoccupations, and Professor Everett's comments on Virgil's lesser-known *Eclogues*, delivered for a general audience, came at just the right time, for reasons that were at least as personal as they were scholarly or literary. Virgil's first Eclogue is a poem about change and in translating it, Longfellow, whose commitment to "green spaces" is only now being recognized, responded to changes both in himself and around him as well as in his immediate environment.[12] Cheerfully inverting the Virgilian *rota*, the hierarchy of Virgil's works familiar since the Middle Ages, Longfellow in the 1870s went from the grand to the plain, from the end to the beginning.[13] This essay, too, will be focused less on the grand than on the plain, more on microhistory, if you will, than on macrohistory. But in doing so, it will offer us a compelling illustration of how the classics had seeped into the fabric of everyday life.

The "Everett" mentioned in Longfellow's journal entry of November 29, 1870 was William Everett, Harvard class of 1859 and youngest son of Edward Everett, Longfellow's former academic superior and president of Harvard from 1846–49 (and not a Longfellow favorite in that role), as well as governor of Massachusetts and U.S. Secretary of State. Fortunately, "young Everett," as Longfellow called William, was quite different from the old man. He was witty, passionate, eccentric. A friend, looking back in 1910, considered him a "live wire" and offered a memorable description of Everett's style as a lecturer: "His body, which was frail and spare, seemed pathetically insufficient for the force and volume of the current that throbbed and hurried through him. Tingling with excitement, his whole frame quivering with emotion, he would fling his text out from the pulpit or his challenge from the platform at some political assembly, and from that time on till he had sunk back, spent and partially exhausted, there was no opportunity for drowsiness or wandering attention."[14] William Everett was a multi-talent—preacher, novelist, historian, man of letters, scholar, and teacher-reformer. In 1870, he had just been appointed Tutor in Latin at Harvard, soon to be upgraded to Assistant Professor. He didn't stay, though. In 1877, after resigning from Harvard, he became Head Master of the Adams Academy in Quincy, Massachusetts, a somewhat surprising move that seems to have been intended to get him away from the persistently powerful influence of his late father, who had been Professor of Greek at Harvard.

William Everett possessed a famously capacious memory—among other things, he was known to have memorized the entire *Aeneid*. When prompted, he could rattle off the names of all the presidents of the United States, along with the members of their cabinets.[15] Above all, he regarded the classics highly. In one of his novels for boys, *Changing Base*, the young protagonist helps another boy struggling with the *Aeneid* to translate a particularly difficult passage. Not surprisingly, the boy sees the light. He had, he declares, until that time never "associated Virgil with fun."[16]

In the fall of 1870, Everett was giving a series of "university lectures," open to the public, on "Virgil's Place in Literature."[17] There is no transcript of this course, and Everett's papers—collected at Harvard's Houghton Library, the Massachusetts Historical Society, and the Library of Congress, among other institutions—do not seem to contain drafts for what must have been a momentous occasion for the young lecturer. It seems likely, though, that Everett, passionate devotee of the *Aeneid*, didn't spend much time on Virgil's first authenticated work of poetry. For the *Eclogues*, circulated when Virgil was about the same age as our lecturer in 1870, did not particularly appeal to him. In fact, some of the funniest pages that Everett wrote—though much later in life—dealt with the idea of pastoral poetry and the vogue for the kind of writing that Virgil had triggered. In *Dante and the Italian Poets*, published in 1904 but intended as a summary of ideas Everett had been pursuing for some time, he offered a description of the concept behind these poetic scenes from bucolic life, which had originated with Virgil and had contaminated writers ever after: "The fundamental idea is that somewhere in the world ... there lives a shepherd people whose chief occupation is tending flocks and herds, but who also carry on all the ordinary farming and household operations, varied by a good deal of hunting of the most ferocious wild beasts, bears, and boars, who never seem to get exterminated." The men and women who appear in pastoral poems reminded Everett of the "giants and fairies of romance."[18]

In short, pastoral writing seemed not conducive to literary greatness: Virgil was no Theocritus, the Greek poet he was imitating in the *Eclogues*. Pastoral verse produces "sweet" and "limpid" little poems that seem intended to give city-dwellers precisely what they want. "Unsurpassed for charm of verse and gracefulness of thought," the *Eclogues* "were the first productions of a very young poet" who never intended to give us a portrait of an actually existing society. Annoyingly content with their lot, the heroes of pastoral poetry as popularized by Virgil never seem to consider emigrating or improving their situation. The weather is always fine, the gods always worshipped, the purest Roman Latin spoken, and there's always enough to eat, for both sheep and men: "Nobody ever goes to the war, or pays taxes, or has his house burned, or finds living uphill work, or dies of anything but old age or a wound from boar's tusk."[19] And the landscapes—the rivers, the mountains, the plains and forests—all look alike. Pastoral poems are sketches "in black and white," and farming, in these texts, is nothing but a fiction: "Any one who knows what real farming is ... also knows that this Arcadian innocence and serenity are as far removed from it as possible."[20] This is not to say that there weren't some spots in the world where people do engage in agricultural occupations without paying attention to what is happening in the world at large. But they have faults and vices too, and they are morally not better than their fellow human beings in the great cities. And now Everett reveals the source of his annoyance with pastoral literature. Real people were prejudiced, superstitious, and slow to learn, but when one looked at pastoral literature—and he had a specific work in mind—one found instead calm rectitude, serene acceptance of duty, "however hard," and self-denial, "however charming." He had a specific poem in mind: *Evangeline*. Almost imperceptibly, William Everett has transitioned from Virgil to Longfellow. Forced to choose between the poet Longfellow and the historian Parkman, he would always elect the latter: "Parkman's History indicates that the dwellers by the Basin of Minas had a goodly admixture of the fox among their lamb-like qualities."[21]

We don't know if Everett mentioned Longfellow's *Evangeline* on that November evening in 1870 at Harvard College. Yet, given Everett's later remarks on the *Eclogues*, it seems likely that whatever he said about the Latin poems would have allowed Longfellow to make a connection between Virgil and his own interests, which were, as we shall see, not limited to the pastoral sections of *Evangeline*. The first Eclogue is a dialogue between an older man, Tityrus, who has recently traveled to buy his freedom from Octavian and to ensure that he can continue to enjoy his rural existence, and a younger visitor, Meliboeus, who has been expelled from his farm and is contemplating a dismal existence in prolonged exile. Their conversation reflects the situation in Mantua, Virgil's hometown, after the Battle of Philippi, in which the forces of Mark Antony and Octavian (later Augustus) defeated the forces controlled by Marcus Junius Brutus and Gaius Cassius Longinus, the assassins of Julius Caesar. To show his gratitude, Octavian disowned the farmers of Mantua and distributed their land among his soldiers (by some accounts, 50,000 of them). Virgil, who had also been disowned, sought relief during a visit to Rome—successfully so, though he never actually took possession of his land.

Scholars have suggested that both sides of the dialogue are influenced by Virgil's own experiences: while the older Tityrus represents Virgil after the Emperor has forgiven him, Meliboeus embodies his younger, former self, deprived of his rightful property. But even the latter is not a political rebel, and instead casts what has happened to him in terms of a natural disaster. In a series of responses to Tityrus, who somewhat smugly lists all the things he has done and will do to appease his ruler (Octavian will be his god forever, will receive lambs from his flocks, and he will revere him forever), Meliboeus sees destruction everywhere. After crows and trees hit by lightning have foretold disaster, he has indeed lost everything. The offspring of his last goat, delivered on rocky ground, ended up dead. He now envisions his farm—which wasn't lavish to begin with—and all the results of his hard work in the possession of an "impious" soldier. Meliboeus considers emigrating—something that Everett says the shepherds in the pastoral tradition never do—to Africa, Scythia, or perhaps even Britain, separated as it is from all the world (*"penitus toto . . . orbe"*) by an ocean. Tityrus ends the poem by inviting Meliboeus to stay with him and to seize the day. Be merry while the food—ripe chestnuts and copious amounts of cheese—lasts.

Even this rough summary shows the inadequacy of Everett's characterization of Virgil's poems. There's a lot of trouble on the horizon in this poem, and it is an open question whether Tityrus—an old, simple-minded man with a grizzled beard—can really help Meliboeus, who emerges as a much more complex character than his friend. Throughout the poem, Meliboeus is torn between despair and a touching desire to celebrate Tityrus's situation—a desire that he says, not unconvincingly, is free of envy (*"Non . . . invideo"*).

In 1878, when Longfellow added his translation of *Eclogue 1* to *Kéramos*, he was not sure that it was entirely successful. He thought it sounded like the work of a "school-boy."[22] But what some might regard as the rough spots in the poem in fact reflect well his intentions as a translator. Comparisons with the translations of the *Eclogues* Longfellow owned—Joseph Trapp's 1735 *Works of Virgil*, George Mackie's 1847 *Eclogues of Virgil*, and an 1870 edition of Joseph Davidson's prose version—as well as with other translations he was likely to have known (such as John Dryden's or Francis Wrangham's)—shed light on the complex decisions Longfellow made as he worked his way through Virgil's Latin text.[23] I am also adding a modern translator, David Ferry, to the mix, because his decisions shed additional light on the appropriateness of Longfellow's choices.

Longfellow's Dante translation had firmly established him as a "foreignizer"—as a translator who wanted to remind his readers that they were reading not a poem originally written in English, but imported from a language not their own.[24] George Ticknor, Longfellow's predecessor at Harvard, told him that he would always read his translation "with the original ringing in my ears," a remark Ticknor had not intended to be entirely flattering.[25] In "First Eclogue," Longfellow's choice to replicate Virgil's dactylic hexameters in modern English requires multiple adjustments in syntax or in the number of syllables per line, and sometimes yields lines that are less than smooth. An obvious means of "foreignization" is Longfellow's preference for English words that sound like their Lain counterparts. Thus we get "resound" for "*resonare*"; "imbue" for "*imbuet*"; "permit" for "*permisit*"; "predict" for "*praedicere*"; "gravid" for "*gravis*"; and "susurrus" for "*susurro*," to name just a few examples. Where he cannot imitate the sound of the original, he departs from it only to achieve a comparable effect, though with less expected means. For example, when Tityrus compares Rome to cypresses that tower over the "*lenta . . . viburna*," Dryden laconically translates the latter phrase as "the shrubs" and Trapp as "the undergroves." Others offer more botanically concrete but also confusing phrases, such as "the osier's shoot" (Wrangham) or "the way-faring trees" (Mackie).[26] Inspired perhaps by Davidson's more literal "the limber trees," Longfellow opts for an extravagant-sounding, yet accurate adjective:

> *Verum haec tantum alias inter caput extulit urbes,*
> *Quantum lenta solent inter viburna cupressi.* (Conington 1–2)
>
> But this among other cities its head hath far exalted
> As the cypresses do among the lissome viburnums.[27]

Virgil gives the reader a beautiful image of Rome as dwarfing other, lesser cities the way cypresses would a bunch of shrubs. "Lissome" indeed means "supple" and "limber" and therefore works as a translation for "*lenta*." The adjective has an added advantage; it draws attention to the s-alliteration prominent in the Latin original, which transfers the reader into a sylvan setting, with cypresses standing tall while other trees bend down with the force of the wind. Compare with this David Ferry's modern translation of the same lines:

> But Rome is as much taller than other cities
> As cypress trees taller than the little viburnums below them.[28]

Not only does Ferry sacrifice Virgil's metaphor of the city holding its head high (which contrasts nicely with Tityrus's compliant meekness), he also loses much of the music of Virgil's lines. That this doesn't make the text necessarily more comprehensible becomes evident in the piling up of conjunctions ("as . . . than"; "as . . . than") that muddles rather than clarifies the image.

Music is the topic of the very first exchange between Meliboeus and Tityrus. We see—as Meliboeus does when he encounters him—Tityrus under the shade tree playing his flute. Shades, trees, and covers play a role throughout the poem.

> *Tityre, tu patulae recubans sub tegmine fagi*
> (Conington 1)

> Tityrus, thou in the shade of a spreading beech tree reclining
> Meditatest, with slender pipe, the muse of the woodlands.
> (*Kéramos*, 101)

Longfellow actively ignores the advice given in one of the most widely available annotated editions of Virgil's works at the time, the Reverend J. G. Cooper's *Publii Virgilii Maronis Opera*, to translate "*meditaris*" as "you practice or exercise" and "*sylvestrem musam*" as "pastoral song."[29] Other translators too choose "woodland lay" (Davidson) or "sylvan melodies" (Wrangham) and have Tityrus "practise" or "pour" or, in Trapp's case, "warble" his music.[30] Longfellow's translation salvages Virgil's m-alliteration. The interruption caused by the anticipatory clause "with slender pipe" recreates the (to English ears) strange syntax of the Latin, in which the adverbial phrase (the ablative "*tenui . . . avena*") is separated by object and verb. Longfellow might have received the idea from Dryden, though the latter's much freer rendition, determined not by considerations of sound but by the wish to evoke the power of the Muse familiar to his readers, would not have appealed to him: "Beneath the shade which beechen bough diffuse, / You, Tityrus, entertain your sylvan Muse."[31] To show Tityrus "meditating" while Meliboeus is worried about how to make a living without his farm is exactly what Longfellow had intended. The world Virgil evokes is not, as William Everett thought, free of tragedy.

David Ferry, for one, takes his inspiration from Longfellow and attempts to improve on it: "Tityrus, there you lie in your beech-tree shade, / Brooding over your music for your muse."[32] Arguably, this changes the meaning of the poem. Tityrus is by no means the brooding type but someone to whom the gods have been good, who lives in a peaceful world from which Meliboeus seems forever barred. In fact, Longfellow's choice to render "*avena*" as "pipe" (perhaps inspired by Cooper, who suggests "oat-straw pipe"³³) conjures an image of absolute repose immediately comprehensible to the contemplators among his nineteenth-century readers, although they, like Longfellow himself, would have had a different pipe in mind (see Figure 4.1). That Longfellow—whose sense of humor is rarely recognized—can do so without violating either the letter or the meaning of Virgil's poem is remarkable and puts modernizing attempts like Ferry's translation into perspective.

Figure 4.1 Henry Wadsworth Longfellow, "Mr. Peter Quince takes some repose after breakfast." Undated. Longfellow Papers, Houghton Library, Harvard University, MS Am 1340 (163).

Tityrus's subsequent response dispels any idea that the purpose of his playing might be other than entertainment:

O Meliboee, deus nobis haec otia fecit—
Namque erit ille mihi semper deus, illius aram
Saepe tener nostris ab ovilibus imbuet agnus—:
Ille meas errare boves, ut cernis, et ipsum
Ludere, quae vellem, calamo permisit agresti.

(Conington 2)

O Meliboeus, a god for us this leisure created,
For he will be unto me a god forever; his altar
Oftentimes shall imbue a tender lamb from our sheepfolds.
He, my heifers to wander at large, and myself, as thou seest,
On my rustic reed to play what I will, hath permitted.

(Kéramos 101–2)

Tityrus responds to Meliboeus by celebrating, somewhat annoyingly, the glorious leisure that has been granted to him. In fact, he sounds like a character out of William Everett's ironic script on how to write (or not to write) a pastoral poem. Praising Octavian's benevolence, Tityrus vows everlasting loyalty to him: "*erit ille mihi semper deus*" or, in Longfellow's translation, "he will be unto me a god forever," an echo perhaps of "God is unto us a God of deliverance" (Psalm 68:8). Contemporary readers would have recognized the biblical echo, but not without also noticing the crucial difference ("unto *me*"), which highlights Tityrus's self-centeredness. Neither Dryden nor Wrangham have "unto me" in their translations, while Mackie comes up with a rather stilted solution: "Aye, a God I'll deem him." Dryden, opting for elegant variation and also constrained by his blank verse, loses the repetition of "*deus*" that lends an air of self-persuasion to the aging Tityrus's pledge: "These blessings, friend, a Deity bestow'd / For never can I deem him less than God."[34] In varying degrees, all these translations ascribe some sort of agency to Tityrus that is not present in the original ("I'll deem him"; "can I deem him"). Trapp breaks the line in two: "For to Me a God / He shall be ever." The simplest version, unencumbered by the requirements of verse, comes from the pen of Davidson, who has Tityrus declare: "For to me he shall always be a god."[35] Longfellow's translation takes its cue from Trapp and Davidson but adds an ironic twist. The internal rhyme ("For *he* will *be* unto *me*") approximates Virgil's double assonance of short and long "i" ("er*i*t *i*lle m*i*h*i*") and creates a phonetic equivalent for the fusion of "he" and "I" achieved by Virgil's syntactic positioning, which has "*ille*" (the Emperor) join "*mihi*" (Tityrus) in a kind of syntactic mock embrace.

To Meliboeus it must seem that Tityrus protests too much, and indeed in the response that follows Meliboeus wants to know who this benevolent, leisure-granting god might be (although it stands to reason that he already knows the answer): "*iste deus qui sit, da, Tityre, nobis.*" Seen in the cold light of day, this wonderful "god's" spectacular gift to Tityrus doesn't amount to much: it consists in free roaming rights for his cattle and the permission to play little tunes on his homemade reed. And how exactly, absent that permission, would Octavian in distant Rome have enforced Tityrus's compliance? It seems little privilege. And yet, as Meliboeus knows, he doesn't even have those benefits left to him.

As Longfellow would have known, Virgil's "*calamus agrestis,*" the sweet-smelling calamus plant, was an important motif in his poetic antagonist Walt Whitman's 1860 edition of *Leaves of Grass*, where it serves as a symbol of male camaraderie or homoerotic adhesiveness: "Oh this shall henceforth be the token of comrades, this calamus-root shall, / Interchange it, youths, with each other! let none render it back."[36] In Virgil, the calamus root separates the two men—while Tityrus, God's faithful servant, gets to play, Meliboeus does not.

Longfellow departs slightly from Virgil in order to emphasize a point that he sees Virgil making—that Tityrus's so-called freedom is entirely at the bidding of Octavian, and that what his heifers and what he (a juxtaposition!) are allowed to do is controlled by the emperor alone. The second sentence of the stanza begins with "He" (as it does in Virgil, with "*ille*") and ends with "permitted." The "*ipsum*" in Virgil refers to the song Tityrus plays. But by replacing it with "myself" Longfellow saves both the emphasis the pronoun adds to the line (difficult to recover in English) and reinforces the central point of the second stanza—and one that must by now be evident to Meliboeus: Tityrus is what he is only because Octavian allows it. Ferry's rendering, with its entirely unironic celebration of the pleasure of Tityrus and his cattle, pushes the poem in a direction that Longfellow would argue Virgil might not have intended:

> Because of him, as you can see, my cattle
> Can browse in the fields as they please, and as I please,
> I idly play upon my slender root.[37]

While Tityrus makes idle music, Meliboeus, dispossessed of his "verdurous cabin" ("*viridi . . . antro*"), can no longer sing. In one of the most dramatic moments in the poem, he articulates his predicament in the starkest terms. Octavian's punishing redistribution of property means that he can be neither a shepherd nor a musician:

> *Carmina nulla canam; non me pascente, capellae*
> *florentem cytisum et salices carpetis amaras.*
>
> (Conington 3)

These beautiful lines, in expressing what the exiled Meliboeus can no longer do, paint a vision of how delicious it would be if he still could. But things being as they are, he won't be able to chant his verse while watching his goats. Since he cannot recreate the dominant c-alliteration of the original, Longfellow offers a substitute—the s or sh-sounds in the first line and b-alliterations in the stanza's final line—even though this requires him to substitute one plant (*laburnum*) for the original one (*cytisus*).

> Songs no more shall I sing; not with me, ye goats, as your shepherd
> Shall ye browse on the bitter willow or blooming laburnum.
>
> (*Kéramos* 109)

Mackie proposes "Ne'er shall I sing" for "*Carmina nulla canam*," while Davidson diminishes the source of Meliboeus's pain when, like Trapp before him, he reduces his unsung songs to "carols" ("No carols shall I sing").[38] Meliboeus is a poet who, deprived of his land, has also lost his voice, and Longfellow's incantatory version of these first three words underlines his predicament, as does the faithfully recreated medial caesura.

In the final scene of the poem, Tityrus confirms the pleasures, shallow as they may be, of his current life.

> T. *Hic tamem hanc mecum poteris requiescere noctem*
> *Fronde super viridi. Sunt nobis mitia poma,*
> *Castanea molles, et pressi copia lactis.*
> *Et iam summa procul villarum culmina fumant,*
> *Majoresque cadunt altis de montibus umbrae.*
>
> (Conington 3)

> Nevertheless, this night together with me canst thou rest thee
> Here on the verdant leaves; for us there are mellowing apples,
> Chestnuts soft to the touch, and clouted cream in abundance!
> And the high roofs now of the villages smoke in the distance;
> And from the lofty mountains are falling larger the shadows.
>
> (*Kéramos* 110)

This is a scene Longfellow had recreated multiple times in his own poetry, too, notably in "The Day is Done" (1844), where the speaker sees the lights of the "village / Gleam through the rain and the mist," while the sun is setting and the poet "long[s] for rest."[39] In Longfellow's capable hands, "*fronde . . . viridi*" ("on green foliage") turns into "verdant leaves," with "verdant" (taken from Trapp) echoing "*viridi.*" The dense phrase "*copia pressi lactis*" (which Mackie, for example, renders as "of curds an ample hoard" and Dryden as "curds and cream"), here refashions as "clouted cream in abundance."[40] Longfellow did need the association of "clotting"—not only because it captures the violence—or literally, pressure—inherent in "*pressi . . . lactis*," but also because it helps him put in proper perspective the ending of the poem, where darkness falls on Tityrus's little grove of sylvan delight. The "*maiores . . . umbrae,*" Trapp's "longer" shades, loom "larger" in Longfellow's verse. Darkness in Longfellow is not just long but large—a physical threat that resides in the low-frequency vowels of Longfellow's last line. When you seize the day, night is part of the deal. *Pace* William Everett, death is always present at the edges of the pastoral. And it is—though in a very different sense from what Everett suspected—the death of poetry. For this is Meliboeus's fear: "*Carmina nulla canam.*"

The shadows had been lengthening for Longfellow too. He turned sixty-three on March 26, 1870. His father, long dead, had warned him early on that a literary life was not a viable career. But Longfellow, the first and, until Seamus Heaney, the last to resign from a Harvard University professorship because he could make a living as a poet, had proved him wrong. He had rolled the stone over the hill, as it were. If only there weren't all the visitors—the crazy women, disheveled poets, businessmen in trouble, and now, increasingly, the tourists. "I like him much better than his poems," observed Longfellow after a particularly irritating would-be writer had taken up eons of his time (March 2, 1870). Sometimes it seemed that his entire life was being swallowed up by "external annoyances," as he noted in his journal on the second day of the new year. "I stay at home and read" (January 1, 1870). Too much of his time was spent answering mail from complete strangers, too little in writing new things. He did enjoy the company of those guests he had actually asked to come, and he took the time to write out little invitations, sometimes in French, as in this note to James Russell Lowell: "N'arrivez pas trop tard."[41] He read Plautus in translation ("am rather tired of Pimps,

Parasites and debauchery in general," April 1, 1870) and began to collect more translations for a new edition of his expansive collection of translated poetry, *Poets and Poetry of Europe*. But his work had come to a standstill. Indeed, he wondered "whether I shall ever write anything more"—a question that assumed more urgency as the unproductive days went by (March 5, 1870).

More and more, despite what this fantasy did to his writing, he found himself wishing that the "domestic planetary system . . . move on in its ordinary course, and keep time with the old clock in the corner."[42] And he would get upset when the universe did not comply. The death of Charles Dickens on June 14, for example, shocked Longfellow greatly. If a literary giant like Dickens, so full of life just days ago, could die so suddenly, what then would happen to him? When he left for his summer stay in the family cottage at Nahant, Longfellow was even less inclined to work. Things were mostly unchanged there, he noted.[43] After weeks of idleness, his dreams wreaked havoc on him, lingering on into his daytime hours so that he wasn't sure if he was awake or not, as he joked in a letter to his friend James Fields.[44] He missed his friends, especially Louis Agassiz, laid low by illness and recuperating in the White Mountains. "I am afraid! I am afraid," he wrote to Charles Eliot Norton.[45] In Longfellow's lighter moments, it did seem pleasant to admire the beauty of the world and not feel compelled to "attempt to describe it, even in verse" (September 8, 1870). He was Tityrus, reclining in the shade, warbling inconsequential little tunes on his reed, keeping the shadows at bay, for now.

But he was also Meliboeus, haunted by nightmares of the impending loss of his semi-rural *locus amoenus*. In a recent plea for the environmental significance of the pastoral that seems as if written against Everett's contention that the landscapes in pastoral poetry are mere scenery, Ken Hiltner points out the central irony that the natural backdrop of Virgil's poem matters to Meliboeus, even though he has lost it, while it "fails to make its appearance to Tityrus, who still has possession of it."[46] It seems that Longfellow—deemed by Charles Calhoun an "environmentalist before his time"[47]—had already spotted this irony. The poet's last decade was indeed marked by an increasing commitment to protect what was left of nature around him—and by getting the Tityrus in him to recognize what Longfellow-Meliboeus already realized.

In 1868, Longfellow heard that several Brighton butchers had joined forces and were about to start building a gigantic, industrial-style slaughterhouse or *abattoir* on the marshland flats on the other side of the Charles River, across from the old Cambridge gas works.[48] The Brighton Meadows, which ran for nearly a mile along the Charles River and which Longfellow could see easily from his windows on Brattle Street, were to be no more, transformed out of existence by the barbarians whom Meliboeus envisions in possession of his fields. Longfellow would have appreciated the grim irony of the situation: the projected slaughterhouse would have been the institutionalized, perverted opposite of the shepherd's caring for his flock that is so essential to the pastoral tradition. He rallied the troops. All of the Longfellow children, even the perennially destitute Charley in Paris, contributed $500 toward the purchase of the flats, and Longfellow also convinced his relatives and neighbors (from Thomas Gold Appleton to W. L. Whitney) to contribute twice that amount. He made up the rest required to purchase the land.[49] The grand total, which Longfellow's makeshift committee bought from an individual named Captain Edmund Rice, was over $12,000.[50] On July 4, 1870, a date that he had picked with deliberation, he transferred the deed to the President and Fellows of Harvard College, giving them some seventy acres of land, along with a check for a still active mortgage whose debtor had refused to relinquish it.[51] Some people suspected Longfellow of being interested in the land for his own enrichment, and an irate member of the state legislature denounced Longfellow as a land speculator. Longfellow did not protest too vigorously: "My vulnerable point was not this, but another; namely that I wanted to keep the land open in front of my own house" (to Charles Eliot Norton, September 8, 1870).[52]

Yet Longfellow, in spite of his preservationist efforts, had no interest in playing at being Romans. For him, Virgil's poem, rather than offering the escapist faux paradise Everett found in the *Eclogues*, offered a real opportunity to clarify issues that pursued him in his own life—whether to conform or to lament and ultimately to confront. It is true that, unlike Meliboeus, Longfellow did not depend on the land for his livelihood. Nevertheless, he could relate to the strong sense of nostalgia for a peaceful "verdurous cabin" expressed by Meliboeus. His hope was that the Meadows might be used for "walks and gardens" and be "kept open forever" (to Charley Longfellow, Christmas, 1869).[53] That was not to be the case: Harvard built its athletic facilities, including the 1903 Harvard Stadium (see Figure 4.2).

Figure 4.2 Leslie Jones (1866–1967), Roman Chariot on the Charles River Speedway, with Harvard Stadium in the Background. Courtesy of the Boston Public Library, Leslie Jones Collection.

The photograph also shows what the Boston Metropolitan Park Commission had done with the rest of the marsh: in 1898, it became the Charles River Speedway, built expressly for horse and bicycle races and thus for mass entertainment events, not what Longfellow had in mind with his generous preservationist gift of 1870. "A continuous chain of pleasure-grounds," jubilated *Harper's Weekly* in 1898.[54] A photograph taken long after the Speedway was completed shows a driver dressed up as a Roman in a faux Roman chariot, with the Harvard Stadium in the background looking like a scaled-down version of the Roman coliseum.

The Brighton Meadows were not the only environmental problem Longfellow was worried about in 1870. Just a week before the Everett lecture, Longfellow had noticed, to his dismay, the trees that had been removed on Mount Auburn so that a new road could be built: "Trees cut down; the beautiful irregularities of the ground leveled; and nothing to be seen but granite, granite, granite!" (November 13, 1870). Longfellow also deeply resented a proposed "widening" of Brattle Street, "which will . . . be the destruction of a vast number of trees" (November 13, 1870), and forced himself to attend public meetings over the issue.[55] He was not successful. One of the most prominent victims of the expansion, when it took place, was the famous chestnut tree featured in Longfellow's "The Village Blacksmith" (1840). A chair was made from the wood of the tree and presented to Longfellow on his seventy-second birthday, as a gift from the children of Cambridge. Longfellow wrote a poem, "From My Arm-Chair," usually regarded as a prime example of literary sentimentalism. Note, however, that he does not forget to mention, even in this slight *vers d'occasion*, that the throne on which he sits is made from the "dead wood" of a tree that was his only because he had written a "song" about it.[56]

If we keep in mind Longfellow's fight for the preservation of trees and green spaces in Cambridge, a fight going on during the very month that Everett explained Virgil to his students at Harvard University, Longfellow's interest in the first Eclogue makes even more sense. It is certainly possible that Longfellow, rereading the first Eclogue, felt himself transported twenty years back in time, remembering the pastoral chapters of his most popular poem, *Evangeline*: "Thus dwelt together in love these simple Acadian farmers. . . ."[57] But it seems more likely that he was primarily commenting on his present life in Cambridge, a life too comfortable even by his own standards. For a moment at least, the thought of the trees that were about to be hacked down yanked him out of his literary concerns. Longfellow's preoccupation with Virgil's first Eclogue thus shows us that, despite his interest in "foreignization" (i.e., reminding readers that they were reading a translation), a translated poem, to him, was also a medium of self-reflection. The foreign and the domestic, for Longfellow, were not opposed—hence his conception of American literature as a "composite" made up of different national traditions, "embracing French, Spanish, Irish, English, Scotch and German peculiarities."[58]

In Roman culture, there was no difference between a poet and a translator (Carvalho 3). Poetry was always in some way translation—Virgil's *Eclogues*, in many ways, would have been unthinkable without Theocritus's model.[59] By the same token, translation was poetry, too. And so Virgil's eclogue spoke to Longfellow in very personal terms. Longfellow was both Tityrus and Meliboeus: drawn to the idle life his success had allowed him, yet also permanently exiled from it, an American writer dreaming of other places as urban encroachment upon the country occurred even at his very doorstep. While his desire for stability kept him chained to his lavish house on Brattle Street and his summer retreat at Nahant, his mind kept on traveling restlessly. In 1876 he began editing his *Poems of Places*, the largest poetry anthology ever compiled in American literature, with volumes devoted to Africa, Oceanica, and Japan, as well as to England, Italy, Spain, France, Ireland, Scotland, and different regions of the United States. Closer to home, he knew that the Brighton Meadows weren't going to last. In 1876, in *The Masque of Pandora*, Longfellow published one of his most haunting works, the pastoral elegy "Three Friends." The poem recalls three of his closest friends who had died over the course of the last few years: the publisher James Fields, the scientist Louis Agassiz, and the man he was closest to in the world, the senator and abolitionist Charles Sumner. Opening his doors to the warm summer air and the scent of the lilacs outside, looking at his beloved Brighton Meadows across the river, at the "dreamy haze" that hung over them "like a fate" (note the indefinite article), he felt as if the Charles River, for a moment, had halted its course, waiting, along with the poet, for something that both knew would never happen: "Something is gone from nature since they died."[60]

Notes

1. See Longfellow, Journal, 1 January 1870–16 November 1873, Longfellow Papers, Houghton Library, Harvard University, MS Am 1340 (213). Subsequent quotations from this journal are referenced parenthetically by dates in the text.
2. See Fig. 35 in Christoph Irmscher, *Public Poet, Private Man: Henry Wadsworth Longfellow at 200* (Amherst: University of Massachusetts Press, 2009), 107.
3. Longfellow quotes from his translation in a letter to James Fields on September 9, 1877, proof that the translation was essentially done before he published it in *Kéramos*. Asking Fields to hurry back from his summer cottage in Manchester, MA, he assures him that "Thee, the very fountains, the very copses are calling" (*Eclogues* I:38–39)—a reference to the Boston Common (*The Letters of Henry Wadsworth Longfellow*, ed. Andrew Hilen, 6 vols. [Cambridge, MA: Belknap Press of Harvard University Press, 1966–82], 6:298). He uses the same quotation to tell James Russell Lowell, now the U.S. Minister in Spain, how much the trees of Elmwood (Lowell's Cambridge residence) seemed to be missing him (January 6, 1878; Longfellow, *Letters*, 6:326).

4. Longfellow, *Voices of the Night* (Cambridge: Owen, 1839).
5. K. P. Van Anglen, "Greek and Roman Classics," in *The Oxford Handbook of Transcendentalism*, ed. Joel Myerson, Sandra Harbert Petrulionis, and Laura Dassow Walls (New York: Oxford University Press, 2010), 3–8.
6. Irmscher, *Public Poet, Private Man*, 153.
7. See Samuel Longfellow, *Life of Henry Wadsworth Longfellow, with Extracts from His Journals and Correspondence*, 3 vols. (Boston: Houghton Mifflin and Company, 1891), 1:17.
8. Ibid., 1:67–68.
9. See John Paul Pritchard, "The Horatian Influence Upon Longfellow," *American Literature* 4, no. 1 (1932): 22–38.
10. See Irmscher, "Reading for Our Delight," *Dante Studies* 78 (2010): 45–65.
11. On Longfellow's conception of a "composite" American literature, see my *Longfellow Redux* (Urbana, Champaign: University of Illinois Press, 2006), 198–99. A special copy of the first volume of Longfellow's translation of the *Divine Comedy* was presented to the Italian government in 1865 (Irmscher, *Public Poet, Private Man*, 162).
12. The "green" Longfellow was first explored in Lloyd Willis, *Environmental Evasion: The Literary, Critical, and Cultural Politics of "Nature's Nation"* (Albany, NY: SUNY Press, 2012).
13. See Ernst Robert Curtius, *European Literature and the Latin Middle Ages*, trans. R. W. Trask (London: Henley, 1953), 201n35, 232.
14. Paul Revere Frothingham, "William Everett, '86," *Harvard Graduates' Magazine* 18 (1910): 657–63, at 658.
15. One of Everett's problems was that he could not stick to a single thing—rather than being content with being a scholar and a school principal, he also became a lawyer, a preacher and, finally, a congressman. As Frothingham saw it, his temperament warred against his talents: "I see things in their general aspect" (Frothingham, "Everett," 662).
16. Everett, *Changing Base: Or What Edward Rice Learned at School* (Boston: Lee and Shepard, 1869), 202.
17. See the note in *The Boston Recorder*, September 22, 1870, 297: "All competent adults, male and female" were invited to attend, as long as they paid a fee of ten dollars.
18. Everett, *Dante and the Italian Poets, Accompanied by Verse Translations* (New York: Scribner's Sons, 1904), 124.
19. Ibid., 131, 128, 125.
20. Ibid., 125–26.
21. Ibid., 126.
22. Longfellow to George Washington Greene, February 24, 1878; Longfellow, *Letters*, 6:341–42. Robert L. Gale, misunderstanding Longfellow's method as a translator, takes this remark as his cue to complain about his "awkward unsyntactical hexameters" (*A Henry Wadsworth Longfellow Companion* [Westport, CT: Greenwood, 2003], 279).

23. All these editions are in Longfellow's library at the Longfellow House–George Washington's Headquarters National Historic Site on Brattle Street, Cambridge, MA. I have consulted George Mackie, trans., *The Eclogues of Virgil* (Quebec: Stanley, 1847) (LONG 2712); Joseph Davidson, trans., *Works of Virgil* (London: Clowes & Son, 1870) (first published in 1813; LONG 10337); and Joseph Trapp, trans., *The Works of Virgil: Translated Into English Blank Verse, With Large Explanatory Notes, and Critical Observations*, 2nd ed. (London: J. Brotherton, et al., 1735) (LONG 25996, 25998). The Trapp translation belonged to Stephen Longfellow (either Longfellow's great or great-great grandfather). On the flyleaf appears the penciled date "1869," possibly in Longfellow's hand. Quotations from Virgil are from Longfellow's own edition by John Conington (*Publi Vergili Maronis Opera* [New York: Harper, 1868]) and are referenced in the text as "Conington." Interestingly, Longfellow's library also contains an Armenian translation of the *Aeneid* (LONG 2890), published at the Convent of San Giorgio (Venice), with an inked inscription in Longfellow's hand, acknowledging it to be a gift from the Boston dentist, poet, and Dante translator Thomas William Parsons (1819–92): "Henry W. Longfellow / from T. W. Parsons / June 1849." Thanks to David Daly, Curator of the Longfellow House–George Washington's Headquarters National Historic Site.
24. Irmscher, *Longfellow Redux*, 268–73.
25. Ticknor to Longfellow, June 1, 1867, in Samuel Longfellow, *Life*, 3:90–91.
26. *Dryden's Virgil*, vol. I, in *Works of the English Poets, with Prefaces Biographical and Critical, by Samuel Johnson*, vol. 17 (London: Cornish, 1779), 23; Francis Wrangham et al., *Virgil: The Eclogues Translated by Wrangham, the Georgics by Sotheby, and the Aeneid by Dryden*, vol. 1 (London: Colburn and Richard Bentley, 1830), 5; Mackie, *Eclogues*, 4.
27. Longfellow, *Kéramos and Other Poems* (Boston: Houghton, Osgood, and Company, 1878), 103. Hereafter cited in the text as *Kéramos*.
28. David Ferry, trans., *The Eclogues of Virgil: A Translation* (New York: Farrar, Straus, 2009), 5.
29. J. G. Cooper, ed., *Publii Virgilii Maronis Opera; or, The Works of Virgil, with Copious Notes, Methological, Biographical, Historical, Geographical, Philosophical, Critical, and Explanatory, in English* (New York: N. & J. White, 1833), 4n14. A later verse in Longfellow's translation ("Never did my right hand return home heavy with money") is identical with a translation Cooper proposes in one of his annotations, which (along with the book's wide distribution) suggests that Longfellow consulted it (see Cooper 5n36).
30. Davidson, *Works of Virgil*, 2; Wrangham, *Virgil*, 3; Trapp, *Works of Virgil*, 3.
31. *Dryden's Virgil*, 21.
32. Ferry, *Eclogues*, 3.

33. Cooper, *Publii Virgilii Maronis Opera*, 14n2.
34. *Dryden's Virgil*, 22; Mackie, *Eclogues*, 3.
35. Trapp, *Works*, 3; Davidson, *Works*, 1.
36. Whitman, *Leaves of Grass and Other Writings*, ed. Michael Moon (New York: Norton, 2002), 102.
37. Ferry, *Eclogues*, 3.
38. Mackie, *Eclogues*, 6; Davidson, *Works*, 4; Trapp, *Works*, 12.
39. *The Complete Poetical Works of Henry Wadsworth Longfellow*, ed. Horace Scudder (Boston: Houghton, Mifflin and Company, 1895), 64–65.
40. Trapp, *Works*, 12; *Dryden's Virgil*, 52; Mackie, *Eclogues*, 6.
41. Longfellow to James Russell Lowell, February 28, 1870; Samuel Longfellow, *Life*, 3:144.
42. Longfellow to James T. Fields, April 20, 1870; *Life*, 3:148.
43. Longfellow to Greene, July 10, 1870; *Letters*, 5:364.
44. July 29, 1870; *Letters*, 5:367.
45. Longfellow, *Letters*, 5:372.
46. Ken Hiltner, *What Else is Pastoral? Renaissance Literature and the Environment* (Ithaca: Cornell University Press, 2011), 41–42. Hiltner's argument is directed against the notion of the pastoral as a simplification of complex matters, advocated by, among others, William Empson (*Some Versions of Pastoral* [1935], [New York: New Directions, 1974]) and Paul Alpers (*What is Pastoral?* [Chicago: University of Chicago Press, 1996]).
47. Charles C. Calhoun, *Longfellow: A Rediscovered Life* (Boston: Beacon, 2005), 233.
48. See William P. Marchione, *Allston-Brighton in Transition: From Cattle Train to Streetcar Suburb* (Charleston, SC: The History Press, 2007), 144.
49. See the draft list of subscribers (which also includes the amount donated) in the archives of the Longfellow House–George Washington's Headquarters National Historic Site.
50. See "Important Purchase in Connection with Harvard College," *The Boston Daily Journal*, March 28, 1870.
51. Longfellow, *Letters*, 5:362–63.
52. Ibid., 5:372–73.
53. Ibid., 5:311.
54. "Greater Boston Speedway," *Harper's Weekly* (February 26, 1889), 285.
55. On November 15, 1870, Longfellow "saw the Committee on the widening Brattle Street" and, to his dismay, found them "determined upon it." No protest would, he felt, be "of any avail." On November 30, the day after he translated Virgil's first Eclogue, he went to a meeting "of Mayor and Aldermen of City Hall" concerning the proposed project.
56. Longfellow, *Poetical Works*, 343.
57. Longfellow, *Poetical Works*, 72.

58. Longfellow's journal, January 6, 1847, quoted in Irmscher, *Public Poet*, 203.
59. See Raimundo Carvalho, "Virgil's *Eclogues*: An Experience of Poetic Translation," *REEL: Revista Eletrônica de Estudos Literários* 2, no. 2 (2006): 1–18, 3, accessed April 27, 2017, http://periodicos.ufes.br/reel/article/view/3440/2695.
60. Longfellow, *The Masque of Pandora and Other Poems* (Boston: Osgood and Company, 1876), 133.

Bibliography

Alpers, Paul. *What is Pastoral?* Chicago: University of Chicago Press, 1996.
Calhoun, Charles C. *Longfellow: A Rediscovered Life*. Boston: Beacon, 2005.
Carvalho, Raimundo. "Virgil's *Eclogues*: An Experience of Poetic Translation." *REEL: Revista Eletrônica de Estudos Literários* 2, no. 2 (2006): 1–18. Accessed April 27, 2017. http://periodicos.ufes.br/reel/article/view/3440/2695.
Conington, John, ed. *Publi Vergili Maronis Opera*. New York: Harper, 1868.
Cooper, J. G., ed. *Publii Virgilii Maronis Opera; or, The Works of Virgil, with Copious Notes, Methological, Biographical, Historical, Geographical, Philosophical, Critical, and Explanatory, in English*. New York: N. & J. White, 1833.
Curtius, Ernst Robert. *European Literature and the Latin Middle Ages*. Translated by R. W. Trask. London: Henley, 1953.
Davidson, Joseph, trans. *Works of Virgil*. 1813. Reprint, London: Clowes & Son, 1870.
Dryden, John. *Dryden's Virgil*, vol. I. *Works of the English Poets, with Prefaces Biographical and Critical, by Samuel Johnson*, vol. 17. London: Cornish, 1779.
Empson, William. *Some Versions of Pastoral*. 1935. Reprint, New York: New Directions, 1974.
Everett, William. *Changing Base: Or What Edward Rice Learned at School*. Boston: Lee and Shepard, 1869.
———. *Dante and the Italian Poets, Accompanied by Verse Translations*. New York: Scribner's Sons, 1904.
Ferry, David, trans. *The Eclogues of Virgil: A Translation*. New York: Farrar, Straus, 2009.
Frothingham, Paul Revere. "William Everett, '86." *Harvard Graduates' Magazine* 18 (1910): 657–63.
Gale, Robert L. *A Henry Wadsworth Longfellow Companion*. Westport, CT: Greenwood, 2003.
"Greater Boston Speedway," *Harper's Weekly* (February 26, 1889), 285.
Hiltner, Ken. *What Else is Pastoral? Renaissance Literature and the Environment*. Ithaca: Cornell University Press, 2011.

"Important Purchase in Connection with Harvard College." *The Boston Daily Journal*, March 28, 1870.

Irmscher, Christoph. *Longfellow Redux*. 2006. Revised edition, Urbana: University of Illinois Press, 2008.

———. *Public Poet, Private Man: Henry Wadsworth Longfellow at 200*. Amherst: University of Massachusetts Press, 2009.

———. "Reading for Our Delight." *Dante Studies* 78 (2010): 45–65.

Longfellow, Henry Wadsworth. *The Complete Poetical Works of Henry Wadsworth Longfellow*. Edited by Horace Scudder. Boston: Houghton, Mifflin and Company, 1895.

———. Journal, 1 January 1870–16 November 1873. AMs. Longfellow Papers. Houghton Library, Harvard University, MS Am 1340 (213).

———. *Kéramos and Other Poems*. Boston: Houghton, Osgood, and Company, 1878.

———. *The Letters of Henry Wadsworth Longfellow*. 6 vols. Edited by Andrew Hilen. Cambridge, MA: Belknap Press of Harvard University Press, 1966–82.

———. *The Masque of Pandora and Other Poems*. Boston: Osgood and Company, 1876.

———. *Voices of the Night*. Cambridge: Owen, 1839.

Longfellow, Samuel. *Life of Henry Wadsworth Longfellow, with Extracts from His Journals and Correspondence*. 3 vols. Boston: Houghton Mifflin, 1891.

Mackie, George. *The Eclogues of Virgil*. Quebec: Stanley, 1847.

Marchione, William P. *Allston-Brighton in Transition: From Cattle Train to Streetcar Suburb*. Charleston, SC: The History Press, 2007.

Pearl, Matthew. *The Dante Club*. New York: Random House, 2003.

Pritchard, John Paul. "The Horatian Influence Upon Longfellow." *American Literature* 4, no. 1 (1982): 22–38.

Trapp, Joseph, trans. *The Works of Virgil: Translated Into English Blank Verse. With Large Explanatory Notes, and Critical Observations*. 2nd ed. London: J. Brotherton, et al., 1735.

Van Anglen, K. P. "Greek and Roman Classics." In *The Oxford Handbook of Transcendentalism*, edited by Joel Myerson, Sandra Harbert Petrulionis, and Laura Dassow Walls (New York: Oxford University Press, 2010) 3–8.

Whitman, Walt. *Leaves of Grass and Other Writings*. Edited by Michael Moon. New York: Norton, 2002.

Willis, Lloyd. *Environmental Evasion: The Literary, Critical, and Cultural Politics of "Nature's Nation."* Albany: SUNY Press, 2012.

Wrangham, Francis, William Sotheby, and John Dryden, trans. *Virgil: The Eclogues Translated by Wrangham, the Georgics by Sotheby, and the Aeneid by Dryden*, vol. 1. London: Colburn and Richard Bentley, 1830.

Chapter 5

Changes of Address: Epic Invocation in Anglophone Romanticism
Herbert F. Tucker

Calling on the Muse at the start of an epic poem is an archaic custom that, were intellectual history logical, the protocols of the Enlightenment ought to have called off for good. They didn't, though, and the convention of epic invocation persisted with vigor well into the nineteenth century. Decades before 1700 it was quite clear to René Le Bossu, doyen of neoclassical epic theory, that the generic machinery of deities and demons, angels and extramundane go-betweens, possessed only an allegorical significance, and that the Muse in particular was an allegory for poetic genius—a personification, in other words, of the very power that conceives her.[1] While this last, recursive point may seem peculiarly modern, its modernity was not beyond reach for the young Voltaire: witness the irony that smiles across the opening of his *Henriade* (1723), where the epic bard, having invoked "sévère vérité," then seeks that alpha Muse's permission to recruit "la fable" as historiographical *dame de chambre*: a prudent if belated collateral move, since it is imaginative fabling that makes invocation, even of Truth herself, possible to begin with.[2] Philosophic Voltaire thus amused the neoclassical reader with a paradox to which more earnestly bemused anglophone epoists of the Romantic era would inventively return. Something about the manifestly incredible convention of invocation rescued it from discredit, prolonged its life, and suited it to the performance of a set of tasks that helped define poetic Romanticism as a traditionally grounded orientation toward the modern.

The first such romantic task, especially given the comparatively fallow because merely academic status of verse epic across the middle of the eighteenth century, was simply to get the rusty genre up and running. How to bootstrap epic, to turn the key in the generic ignition before engaging the transmission of the tale, formed a potentially daunting problem, to which the solution offered by invocation was tautologically, which is not quite to say trivially, foolproof. "Sing, O Muse": to say as much, with Homer, was to have begun the song, no matter what matter might follow; here was one petitionary prayer that was always already granted. Much the same advantage attached to the closely allied if technically non-invocative declaration "I sing" that had been installed into the canon by Virgil's *Arma virumque cano*. Whatever the ensuing admixture of fable with truth might prove to be, that performative illocution was *ipso facto* the case. And, once its self-evident truth had been taken in poetic stride, the indispensable business of beginning was under way, launched on the afflatus of a prevenient inspiration that even the clumsiest hobbyist found included in the box of epic conventions, just as it came off the library shelf.

The axiomatic givenness and cheap availability of such preliminary conventioneering can blind us to invocation's uncanny interrogation of certain standard epic premises that come with it. For the device engages a curious "paratextual" temporality, as Gérard Genette would have it, that entrains confusions of priority and authority.[3] Its inspirational bellows worked by creating within the epic machinery a vacuum of power, into which the romantic imagination enthusiastically rushed, often in the process shaping the rugged hereditary topos into a trope surprisingly subtle and plastic. Everybody agrees that the Muse motivates and directs the poet's epic narrative; by some accounts, preeminently Milton's, she even dictates it. But invocation reverses this chain of command: the invoking poet, prompting the prompter, imparts motivation and direction to the Muse instead. What this conspicuously staged reversal of priorities may imply about agency and authority is an intriguing theoretical question for the poetics of any epoch.[4] But it is in form a kind of question that took on practical urgency during the revolutionary years before 1800, on both sides of the Atlantic, when the power to constitute and to govern was sharply at issue. Who comes first? Who calls the shots? *Says who?* Poets "hail" the Muse, but that verb is as ambiguous in her case as in a taxi driver's: maybe it names a serendipitous greeting by the way, maybe an exasperated summons from afar. When, as not seldom occurs, the Muse is exhorted to awaken and arise in order that she may furnish lift and support—when the poet expressly undertakes to be overtaken—it is hard to know by what reserve of battery power the poet's voice has been raised to the requisite pitch of alarm or, after the Muse is properly roused to her task of tale-conveyance, just who is propping or topping whom.

A single line from *Don Juan* brings these paradoxical issues into focus:

Hail, Muse! *et cetera*.—We left Juan sleeping. . . .

(3.1)[5]

The perennially startling insouciance of these first words from Byron's second installment (1821) in an unstoppable serial epic both disrupts and affirms the continuity of a narrative that they carry directly forward from where canto 2 left things in 1819. The last four words resume an idyll without events—literally so for the first dozen stanzas of this new canto, which are all chatty authorial digression that leave Haidée and Juan sleeping still, somewhere off-page, in suspended narrative animation. In contrast the first four words—macaronic, ejaculatory, nondeclarative, punchily punctuated—constitute a metanarrative disclosure of *Don Juan*'s entire modus operandi: radical miscellaneity of matter, superintended by the bravura performance of mercurially labile attitudes toward that matter. "*Et cetera*" flippantly signifies on one hand the tiresome machinery of a traditional epic invocation with which Byron can't be bothered. On the other hand it denotes with some etymological nicety the *heter*ogeneous epic universe into which this fresh beginning reinducts us. Nothing in the world is alien to that ample *cetera*, as there is nothing in the world which its improvisatory mode cannot contain; for the Muse in requisition/recognition here is entirely *ex tempore*, aloft on the whims of caprice and the chances of rhyme. In this far from frivolous sense the deferred invocation Byron did not write out, and so did not delimit, expands to swallow his whole poem. *Cetera* includes everything. And the romantic implication here realized—that the true Muse says it all, that the epic cosmos is a vitally, incessantly *imagined* one—is a corollary which, by a logic inherent to the convention, shadows not only this but any epic that has invoked her.

To coordinate the initialization of the operating system with the software of narrative was a problem for which romantic-era poets designed a variety of patches, which we shall presently return to sample. First, though, let's honor the curiosity with which the poets tried (essayed and assayed) the initiatory rite itself—both because that curiosity can be infectious even today and because it expresses certain aspects of autopoesis whose isolated cultivation represents one of Romanticism's distinguishing traits. Take as benchmarks a pair of opening blank-verse triplets from early-period epics that honor, respectively, classical and British antiquities:

> The Persians vanquish'd, Greece from bondage sav'd,
> The death of great Leonidas aveng'd
> By Attic virtues—celebrate, O Muse!

> Of Donald's warlike deeds, the hardy Lord
> Of Scotia's Western Isles, by fame forgot
> And Gaelic bards, assist me, Muse, to sing!

Richard Glover (1787) and George Skene (1796) each get a lot done in just three lines.[6] A syntactic inversion that puts the proposition of theme before the invocation proper gives the latter a climactic boost and also, as was just discussed, lets the poem hit the ground running. Glover manages besides, à la Virgil, to remind readers of the *Athenaid* about his hereby sequelized previous writing (the 1737 epic *Leonidas*, enlarged in 1779 to twelve books), while Skene conversely indicates what's not there, making it known that what the Muse assists him to remember will repair a national amnesia: *aletheia*, the unforgotten, will be his epic truth. Such compression as this was hard to beat on its own terms, though Joseph Cottle in 1800 showed it could be done by a single line—"Alfred victorious o'er the Danes, I sing," while a couple of years before him Landor had swept the stakes in lapidary plainness by dispatching his business in a mere hemistich: "I sing the fates of Gebir."[7] Thrift on this scale could be underbid only by skipping the invocation altogether, which admittedly is what numerous romantic-era epic poets did. Works as diverse as Helen Maria Williams's *Peru* (1786), Robert Southey's ethnopoetic anthology of epics from *Thalaba* (1801) and *Madoc* (1805) forward, Cottle's *Fall of Cambria* (1808) and James Montgomery's *The World before the Flood* (1813), for example, all dispensed with the convention. That choice places them beyond our further notice here, except in demonstrating that invocation was, like virtually all epic conventions by 1800, an option and not a mandate.

Those poets who exercised the option did so for a purpose, which many of them flourished in fond vows of preferential allegiance. Milton's prestigious credentials as spotless puritan and persevering republican enlisted from two different romantic-era camps adherents to his policy of what I'll call *abvocation*: rejecting the Greco-Roman Muse in favor of an inspiration more doctrinally or politically correct. Pious epoists' direct imitations of the Miltonic petition to the

Holy Spirit, bypassing Parnassus for Zion's sake, span the romantic decades, from William Roberts in *Judah Restored* (1774) and Richard Cumberland in *Calvary* (1792) to Charles Hoyle in *Exodus* (1807) and Robert Pollok in *The Course of Time* (1827). Even a decidedly non-biblical epic like Alexis Eustaphieve's *Demetrius: The Hero of the Don* (1818) traces the familiar abvocative pattern, forsaking pagan inspiration in favor of divine. This may be because for American bards a path to celebrating secular, political heroism had been well worn by a developing Revolutionary poetic, tentatively hazarded by Nathaniel Tucker's *America Delivered* as early as 1782, and fully established in Joel Barlow's sumptuous *Columbiad* of 1807.[8] Here the invocatory preference went to allegories of Liberty, which by common consent entailed liberation from the Old World's siren song. Impassioned denunciation of an effete servility sufficed to let James Paulding, in *The Backwoodsman* (1818), not so much renounce the "neglected Muse" (1.17–38) as reclaim her on Western terms; but Paulding's was an eccentric, frontier maneuver.[9] The early nineteenth-century *locus classicus* remains Barlow's invocation, "Almighty Freedom! give my venturous song / The force, the charm that to thy voice belong" (1.23–24), premissed as it is on his abjuring superseded fealties: "I bend no suppliant knee, / Invoke no miracle, no Muse but thee" (1.29–30).[10]

Epic invocation thus served early as a literary badge of American exceptionalism. Yet it is unclear whether poets in the United States realized how freely the Muse of Freedom was being concurrently approached by their counterparts in the United Kingdom, where across the Channel a Revolution much closer to hand polarized national identity for decades. Radical and conservative bards called on her alike, albeit with different understandings and agendas promoting, respectively, liberty's extension and defense. Thus Southey's francophile *Joan of Arc* (1796) skirted traditional invocation, but ended its proposition all the same with the line "I sing: nor wilt thou FREEDOM scorn the song" (1.6). In due course King George's laureate Henry James Pye launched the royalist *Alfred* (1801) by addressing the "Guardian and glory of the British isles, / Immortal Freedom!" (1.5–6); William Walker upheld a Swedish patriot hero in *Gustavus Vasa* (1813) by invoking "Celestial Liberty!" (1.5); and, to close our epicycling survey of epic independencies, the British Dissenter Charles Smith kept the old Miltonic faith by undertaking his Exodus epic *The Mosiad* in 1815 with a claim upon "FREEDOM my theme, and LIBERTY my muse!" (1.6).[11] Last refinements of what shapes up during the Romantic period as *British* exceptionalism came when epic poets after Waterloo dropped the rhetoric of liberty in favor of ordinary patriotism—retaining, however, the express repudiation of classicism as an ideology too internationally oriented for their purpose. Henry Hart Milman's *Samor, Lord of the Bright City* (1818) and William Lisle Bowles's *The Grave of the Last Saxon* (1822) both nourish myths of old England on aggressively staked native soil. The former declines to "invoke, / Or Nymph, or Muse," in confident reliance that ancient Glow-cester (the "bright city" of his title) keeps her glow, and that the "Land of my birth, oh Britain!" will "Burn in my heart, and give to thought and word / The aspiring and the radiant hue of fire" (1.1–26). Bowles devotes an introductory canto to summoning "Ye blue Italian skies," "Etruscan shades" (31–34), and "thou wond'rous WESTERN WORLD" (41), only to banish these tourist indulgences as "themes of other song" (39) now forsworn in the name of "One patriot theme, one ancient British song" (60).[12]

Cultural and national politics aside, all this picking and choosing amongst Muses answered to a hunger more widely and perhaps deeply felt: the sharp taste romantic poets cultivated for savoring the sources of their own inspiration. They can seem magnetized, sometimes transfixed, by the intrinsic appeal of appealing. Such *metavocation*, as it were, calls out the poet's calling, calls it in a sense out of nowhere but in another sense out of poetry's situation circa 1800: along charged coordinates whose vertical axis was a classically learned, cosmopolitan tradition of scholarly verse, whose horizontal axis was an open vista of contemporary publishing that entertained an expanding audience of more widely leisured, nationally identified readers, and whose zero point of axial intersection was the original mystery of poetic creation. The Muse descends through a poetic history that epoists long to join, in order that the poem may go forth among a public they long to reach. Some poets find the challenge of an invocatory beginning so absorbing that they dwell on it, draw it out, indeed make it harder than it seems they ought to, with the aim of prolonging its exquisite performativity. Take, for example, Walter Scott, the most transatlantically influential writer of the nineteenth century, who begins *The Lady of the Lake* (1810) by approaching his "Enchantress" Muse formally in Spenserians and metonymically by way of her instrument, the "Harp of the North!" (1), "O minstrel Harp" (6).[13] This attention-fixing doubled address gives way before long to the fixated stammer of sheer verbal iteration: "O wake once more!" (19, again verbatim 21); "Then silent be no more! Enchantress, wake again!" (27). Repetition underscores urgency, to be sure, via the performance of a rote anxiety over the superannuation of a literary mode—an anxiety quite superfluous in view of Scott's phenomenal sales from 1805 forward. Yet, where what gets repeated is the expression of a will to repeat ("once more," "again"), we may hail in the poet's greeting a self-pleasing dalliance with invocation's instrumentality as such.

One year previously, Margaret Holford's *Wallace* (1809) had ventured into Scott's new epic subgenre of metrical romance by opening canto 1 with an abvocative double sonnet. The first half practices, by repetitive drill, a romantic apophasis disowning the Muses: "Wake not for me, ye Maids of Helicon!" (1, again verbatim 14).[14] Having stoppered in slumbrous quarantine the classic perfumes of Hellenism, Holford stakes a counter-claim on the windy sublimity of Gothic sternness, the apostrophized "Dark Spirit of the northern lay" (15):

> Spirit of northern song!—Awake! descend;
> Bend from thy misty throne—dark spirit bend!
>
> (27–28)

Both Holford's invocations, the supine lullaby and the erect wake-up call, trade in verbal repetition heavily enough to communicate something of the fascinated arrest that reposes within incantation itself, over and above its indifferently credited efficacy as "magic numbers" (3) or, in Scott's parallel phrase, the Muse's "wizard note" (26).[15]

When William Gilbank effused with a like insistence during his invocation to *The Day of Pentecost* (1789), the mode of biblical epic differed sharply from that of Scott and Holford, but the effect of discursive suspension was much the same: "Deign then, oh deign, proceeding Spirit, deign / T' instruct my trembling soul" (1.70–71).[16] Nearly aphasic verbatim unction before the Holy Ghost oils the temporarily seized-up machinery of rapturous address, in a miniaturized line-long version of the histrionic interference effect whereby Gilbank has absent-mindedly contrived to forget his invocation until fifty-plus lines into book 1. A no less obscure contemporary stumbled on something of the kind by enlisting the ambiguous inertia of a Miltonically classicizing syntax. The poet was Henry Murphy, his transatlantic theme the recent British *Conquest of Quebec* (1790), his ad-hoc inspiration the metaleptic versatility of an absolutized past participle most germane to our purpose:

> But first, oh heavenly Maid, whose boundless eye
> Sees, at once glance, thro' all eternity,
> Invok'd, proclaim, what cause, what hand divine
> In Pitt's great soul, inspir'd the vast design.
>
> (1.17–20)[17]

The eruption of "first" into a seventeenth line is a sort of oddity to which readers of epic are probably inured, yet whose strangeness our topic has a way of reviving. But this time-lag is nothing compared to the way "Invok'd" performs the temporal ambiguity we have been tracing within romantic epic originations. In view of the first line quoted, the punctual sense of the participle seems to be "now that you have been invoked"; yet its very redundancy in that view elicits a second reading, the hoveringly hypothetical condition "when and if you should be invoked." The one corresponds to the Canadian news from yesterday that Murphy has taken as his historical subject, the other to the *species aeternitatis* that, as he contacts the Muse, he for a moment shares with her. The reluctant iambic forward trudge of line 19—a prosodic fixation akin to Gilbank's dogged reiteration of "deign" and Scott's "once more"—performs the poet's will to dig in and linger with the Muse, right here at the threshold of his narrative, in that space of invocation where all is potential, the Muse's presence something presently to take place in a Wordsworthian world not realized, a something ever more about to be.

To describe how inspiration felt was one eligible way of vouching for its authenticity, and an inventory of affect formed part of the romantic invocatory repertoire. Women poets, cold-shouldered by the overwhelmingly masculinist generic tradition, sought grounding and traction in the Sensibility tradition instead; and they were especially forthright about the feelings that attended a call from, or on, the Muse. Hannah Cowley indeed puts feeling first and lets (re)cognition follow:

> I greet thee freely, whatsoe'er thou art
> My Mind exciting as thou thrill'st my Heart!
> Is it THE MUSE whose Influence I greet,
> Whose cheering Influence makes lone hours so sweet?
> Art Thou the Muse? Ah no! for Fiction she—
> Celestial TRUTH! I seize the Theme from Thee.
> (*The Siege of Acre* [1801], 1.1–6)[18]

Open-hearted fidelity to her own veridical sensations lets Cowley open-mindedly sift the fictional from the true Muse, who could alone excite thrills so lone and sweet as she has enjoyed. In her instant epic about a late campaign in Britain's ongoing war with Napoleon, she issues a license to feel "freely" by recourse to a plot based, as we still say at the movies, on a true story. When Margaret Holford returned to the epic lists, it was with full recognizance of a Muse likewise hailed by strong and intimate touch:

> Oh, I do feel thee now! oh, once again
> Warm gleams of rapture burst upon my brain!
> Quick heaves my lab'ring breast, and to my eyes
> Lo! what strange forms in long succession rise!
> Oh, Muse belov'd, I know thee now!
> I feel thee glowing in my soul,
> I feel thy beam upon my brow,
> I feel thee thro' each artery roll
> Tumultuous, fierce, and bright—impatient of controul!
> (*Margaret of Anjou* [1816], 1.1–9)[19]

The priority of "I feel thee now" to "I know thee now" is not just textual. Nor is it just sensational: more important than the Muse's spectacular *éclat* is the fact that this advent is a *return*. Holford knows the Muse now because she has known her before, known her, in fact, from the visitation we saw invoked just a page ago in her *Wallace* epic of 1809, as the poet goes straight on to affirm: "Oh, thou art she who led me forth / Mid the cold mountains of the north" (1.14–15). The continuity between sequel and maiden effort serves to validate Holford's bold choice, this time around, of a female hero: Margaret d'Anjou, her queenly namesake and, not coincidentally, her match in emotional dynamism.

Such a melodramatically subjective encounter with the Muse framed a romantic epic topos out of heterogeneous parts: on one side the Sapphic, lyric enumeration of bodily sense data; on the other an autobiographical self-assessment that, deriving from the Virgilian *Ego ille* progression between pastoral and epic, was further ratified for anglophone poets by the examples of Spenser and Milton. Cumberland's *Calvary* (1792) thus taps a vein of personal melancholy suited to his theme, first visiting the "sad haunt" of the crucifixion to solicit its "mournful echoes to my deep-ton'd harp" (1.3–4), and then in an abvocatory reprise four books later preferring the gospel evangelists as guides over the "idly babbling" Muses of "the Parnassian Mount" (5.7–8).[20] When Cumberland proceeds to assert that this renunciation of accessory baggage "fits a bard / Far onward in the wint'ry track of age," "a pilgrim gray with years" (5.27–31), he is not so diminished by the Miltonic footprint he treads in as to forfeit a genuine austerity of his own, forged on the anvil of hard times. That the feeling of sensory retrenchment may itself be strongly felt is a principle that put spring in the step of Bowles a decade later:

> Awake a louder and a loftier strain!
> Beloved Harp, whose tones have oft beguil'd
> My solitary sorrows.
>
> (*The Spirit of Discovery* [1804], 1.1–3)[21]

A "strain" of epic song, yes; but before it can be that, a strain of hopeful emotion, grounded for contrast in the context of a disregarded poetic career:

> But I had hope that one day I might wake
> Thy strings to higher utterance; and now
> Bidding adieu to glens, and woods, and streams,
> And turning where, magnificent and vast,
> Main Ocean bursts upon my sight, I strike,—
> Rapt in the theme on which I long have mus'd,—
> Strike the loud lyre, and as the blue waves rock,
> Swell to their solemn roar the deep'ning chords.
>
> (1.16–23)

As with Scott above, the harp stands metonymic proxy for the Muse, who emerges, moreover, in this compound invocation in verbal not nominal form, rather an experience than a person—an effect stressed by that dashed-in intervention of line 21. Bowles adduces in effect, as collateral securing the reader's attention, a life's long-musing tendance of his art under duress. Further invocations address Camoens and the river Thames in lines that follow, triangulating Bowles's position as a naval epoist in the offing; but the real interest of this induction inheres in the redundant overlap between the apostrophic solicitation of the first quoted passage and the declarative self-advertisement of the second, which performs in the "higher utterance" of its "loud lyre" precisely the "louder and loftier strain" petitioned for earlier.

No epoist was fonder of hovering at the genre's incantatory threshold than the American Richard Emmons. His 1827 *Fredoniad*, finding it understandably tedious to stick for forty cantos to the War of 1812, returned to ground zero no fewer than six times for the renovating virtue of a top-up with the Muse, whose shape-shifting from canto to canto—now God's "supernal Power" (1.7), now "th' inspiring Genius" of "Poesy" (3.13–23), now the "Spirit of

Ocean" (6.8)—shows how for Emmons petitionary intercourse itself outweighed all questions about the nature or reality of the being he invoked.[22] Already in the first canto his piggybackingly syncretic prayer that almighty God should "Inspire my Muse!" (1.29) takes a doctrinally scrupulous reader's breath away. By canto 11 we no longer know who the "ethereal Muse" may be, nor does the poet himself seem to care.[23] What he does know is a craving to sense her intimately:

> O let me feel thee through each vein of life,
> That I may madden in the maddening strife.
>
> O for a spark that Homer did inspire,
> That I may burn, and feel myself on fire!
> Virgilian sweetness to my verse impart,
> To charm with beauty, and dissolve the heart.
>
> (11.7–12)

Insanity, conflagration, dissolution: the sublime energy of sense-as-feeling is bent on extinguishing sense-as-meaning. Just possibly "maddening strife" spares a thought for the epic matter of international warfare at hand, but it hardly holds a candle to the ardor of Emmons's identity-exhausting Muse, which in the third line quoted makes it impossible to say whether her spark has inspired Homer or has been inspired by him. Where "feel thee" proves equivalent to "feel myself," the striving narcissism of romantic invocation has played itself out to a point of no return.

That may be why one of the last, and best-selling, epics produced during the period, having acknowledged the self-regarding personal "strain" within the evolving genre, strictly disdained to succumb. This was Pollok's apocalyptic *The Course of Time* (1827):

> The muse, that soft and sickly wooes the ear
> Of love, or chanting loud in windy rhyme
> Of fabled hero, raves through gaudy tale
> Not overfraught with sense, I ask not; such
> A strain befits not argument so high.
>
> (1.13–17)[24]

Pollok's one Muse, hailed in the first words of the poem as "Eternal Spirit! God of truth! to whom / All things seem as they are" (1.1–2), is all strong sense, all the time ("sense" in the sense of true meaning, that is, and not the felt distractions of sensuous seeming in a "gaudy tale"). From the absolute eschatological vantage to which Pollok stakes his claim, where no human frailty blurs the formulaic channeling of doubt-proof divine inspiration, any stressful "strain" is inconceivable. Yet it remains, for all that, imaginable: a paradox on which the legibility, such as it is, of *The Course of Time* utterly depends, and which with a fetching inconsistency this invocation acknowledges toward its close: "Hold my right hand, Almighty!" (1.22). That this disembodied, immaterialist, postmillennial epic of last things needs manual labor to build it aright constitutes its one saving grace.

It was the handiest of the romantics who made, all told, the period's most artisanal epics; and this is so even when we set Blake's engraving and printing aside and confine ourselves to the ceremonious words he wrote at the head of an epic text. The first book of *Milton* (1804) opens by directing the "Daughters of Beulah! Muses who inspire the Poets Song" to "Record the journey of immortal Milton" (1.1–2).[25] Beulah is Parnassus biblicized, and the hero's journey will be a mental traveler's odyssey that revisits, and correctively reclaims, an imaginative paradise inadvertently lost. But before this action can be set in motion ("what mov'd Milton," 1.2.16), something else must move first, limned along the living chart that is the author's body. The verb "Record" means to have by heart, a trope whose corporeal literality Blake unwaveringly exalted over mere museal-archival memory—an allegiance that Milton's great anagnorisis will soon confirm in contrasting "the daughters of memory" with "the daughters of inspiration" (1.14.29). Blake's invocation to the embodied recording angels who are his Muses accordingly takes as its sphere of operation his own physical frame:

> Come into my hand
> By your mild power; descending down the Nerves of my right arm
> From out the Portals of my Brain, where by your ministry
> The Eternal Great Humanity Divine, planted his Paradise,
> And in it caus'd the Spectres of the Dead to take sweet forms
> In likeness of himself.
>
> (1.2.5–10)

The epic descent from heaven emerges here as generic machinery radically *organized*, into the neuroskeletal system Blake's nouns specify, and also the cardiopulmonary one engaged by the prosodic pulse of his fourteeners and the punctuated breathings of his clauses. Epic history, animated as those re-formed "Spectres of the Dead," is made prophetically current, galvanized into contemporaneity by imagination's sympathetic ministration. Such is the mercy of eternity that clocks the Muses' paratextual temporality in this induction, very much as it will the redemptive nonviolent heroism of Milton in the action to come. Compared to a feelingful epoist like Holford or Emmons, Blake pays little mind at this initial juncture to sensation as such, downplays it even with the bland modifiers "mild" and "sweet." He aims rather to establish the sensate body as the theater of an epic action whose pivot will be such a change of mind, or of heart, as makes the distinction between mind and heart a matter of indifference.

Here goes, says the invoking poet or, as Whitman would call him at mid-century, "the outsetting bard."[26] But then where is *here*? To what if any referential place does our commonplace invocatory topos belong? And what becomes of it once the enginery of narrative gets going and transmits the story that it is an outsetting epic bard's business to set out? "Hither, O Epic Muse, fresh laurels bring": thus James Ogden in *The Revolution* (1790).[27] What could the poet do to ventilate that laureate space, secure the hithering supply of laurels against withering, keep invention fresh? In some such shape did the romantic mind tend to pose the question of how the Muse's inspiration could not just sustain the long burden of an epic tale, but survive it.

Poets conspicuously worried by this question arrived at two complementary answers. One answer, generic secession, lies outside the purview of this essay, but it exerted an immense influence on literary history. When the American poet Elizabeth Graeme excerpted an "Invocation to Wisdom" (1768)[28] from her unpublished verse translation of Fénelon's *Télémaque*, she set a fashion that was to be pursued with fidelity by sister poets coping with the gender prejudice that attached to the writing of epic across the period, and across the ocean, including Phillis Wheatley's "To Maecenas" and "Niobe in Distress" (1773), Sara Lee Pike's "Introduction" to *Israel* (1795), Mary Tighe's proem to *Psyche* (1805), and Eleanor Porden's royal ode prefatory to *Coeur de Lion* (1822). The fashion likewise recommended itself to male poets, such as John Thelwall in *The Hope of Albion* (1801) or Anthony Hunn in *Sin and Redemption* (1812), when for public approval (usually, alas, withheld) they floated specimen epics that boasted an invocation or two; Hunn, amazingly, frames his address as an evasive action or temperance tract, abvocing not a false power he disdains but the very power he invokes as true: "DESIST—desist, Controller of the mind, / To fill my breast"; "Pray, mollify thy fire" (1.1–2, 25).[29] Hedged or sequestered invocation also appealed to such canonical figures as Wordsworth, when he prefaced *The Excursion* (1814) with a detached "Prospectus" to the unfinished *Recluse* that, although strictly speaking it forms part of no epic poem, now probably ranks as the signature invocation from our period; and Keats, whose 1818 "Ode to May: Fragment" points ahead to the (uninvocated) epic drafts of *Hyperion*.[30] In each case just cited, and numerous others besides, invocation served as a crossroads where the poet's imagination of an elite filial relation to epic precursors merged with the vocational ideal of a spokesman's role abroad in the public sphere, where odes rang out and prospectuses tested the waters.

If the romantic calving of odes from epics is a story distinct from ours here, it is harder to disregard the claim of its generic complement, namely the embedding of invocatory verses within an episode of the action an epic narrates. As it happens, both Wordsworth and Keats tried their hands at this option too, the latter's being the more classically elaborated. *Hyperion* (composed 1818) seized on the liminality of epic invocation and reversed it into a scene of instruction—the god Apollo's no less, by tuition of the Muses' mother Mnemosyne no less (3.42–136)—in an apotheosis of the vital-signs-indulgent mode of invocatory sensibility we have just been discussing. Keats's experiment, rather than initiate an epic, brought it crashing to a halt, as if learning the hard way that invocation constituted, in germ and pre-emptively, the whole story that modern poetry had to tell.[31] One could hardly look for a wryer twist on the *Here goes* motif: when narrative was over and gone, here came invocation to stay—and, incidentally, to incubate the great odes of Keats that lay just around the corner of 1819.

As for Wordsworth, he more faithfully embedded his invocation at a beginning: the first forty-five lines of *The Prelude* (1805), while they don't petition the "gentle breeze" (1.1) of inspirational "blessing" as if it were a Muse outright, do apostrophically acknowledge beyond doubt that this is what it is: "O welcome messenger! O welcome friend" (1.5).[32] But then comes the poet's twist: he steps back and, by way of an address to Coleridge the "friend" (1.55), incorporates the invocatory passage into the story by retroactively disclosing that it is a quotation of something Wordsworth once exclaimed to himself. Not Mnemosyne but Memory itself is here the Muse, Wordsworth's own memory to be precise, by which *The Prelude* will show the mind to have been, and still to be, reflexively yet Muse-like "nourished and invisibly repaired" (11.265). This back-and-fill operation was structurally anticipated a few years earlier by Joseph Sympson in *Science Revived, or The Vision of Alfred* (1802), where the extended introductory address to "Science" is revealed, after the fact only, to have been spoken by King Alfred within a narrative that has thus been stealth-launched under cover of invocation. Suspicion that these set-pieces were independently composed, then belatedly slotted into the longer work, receives encouragement from the instance of James Hogg, who freely confessed to having "popped" into the last book of *Queen Hynde* (1825), as a hundred-line invocation to "my loved muse, my Fairy Queen" (6.44), a recently published lyric of his that archly begins, "No muse was ever invoked by me, / But an uncouth harp of olden key" (6.1–2)—a claim doubly mischievous, of course, in the light of its publication history.[33]

Smuggling invocation into an epic poem, like quarrying it out of one, looks to the generic purist like an abdication of the duties of unification that theorists of epic since Aristotle have entailed on its practitioners. The switchpoint of invocation ought, in theory, to be a synapse that puts poetic power and heroic virtue into communication with each other, a point at which form melds with method, frame with content, and the aesthetic, ethical, and cultural dimensions of the work converge. Admittedly few epics from any period meet this high standard of integration, but the ideal it elevates is salutary; and, during the Romantic era, it prompted a variety of poets negotiating the handoff between invocation and narration to forge intriguing linkages of parallel or correspondence. Walker's *Gustavus Vasa* establishes right away that its warrior king has been "impell'd" by the very same "Celestial Liberty" the poet names as Muse; Walker in the process hitches an economical ride to greatness ("Me too assist": 1.5–11) on the coat-tails of heroic analogy. Ogden's 1790 *Revolution*—which treated not France's revolution or America's, but England's a hundred years before them—having called on the Muse, inaugurates its plot with a political echo of that poetic summons: "At freedom's call the Prince of Orange came, / The rights of English subjects to reclaim; / Worthy to fill the abdicated throne" (1.7–9). May not some portion of the hero's worth redound to an author who, eyeing the king of poetic kinds, offers to reclaim in his own way the rights of an "English subject" for epic poetry? When Richard Cumberland and Richard Bland Burges, in their jointly composed *Exodiad* (1807), invoked the "heavenly Muse" to "prop these mortal powers, / Which but for thy sustaining aid must sink" (1.7–8), they borrowed a buttressing technique (as they did the phrase "heavenly Muse") from Milton.[34] Their vertical image also anticipates the diegetic insider's discovery that the story will commence on the safe side of the Israelites' Red Sea crossing, whence Pharaoh's bathetic fate—"In whose profound abyss / He and his thousands were for ever sunk" (1.24–25)—contrasts the bards' figural assurance of being preveniently saved and uplifted.

That plenary inspiration might engross the full text was, indeed, the romantic ideal; and at least three major period epics we have glanced at (*Milton, The Prelude, Don Juan*) made good on the proposition in ways whose idiosyncratic diversity remains the best authenticating warrant of their creative originality. The proposition itself remained available, nevertheless, to any comer who stood ready to put it into practice. The most charming of these was the pre-teen author of a *Battle of Marathon* that her indulgent father privately published in 1820. There Elizabeth Barrett [Browning], her daddy's Minervan girl in name and not just that, took the invocational plunge ("The war of Greece with Persia's haughty King, / No vulgar strain, eternal Goddess, sing!" [1.1–2]) in terms soon afterward parroted, within the epic action, by her identically inspired boy-hero Aristides: "No madness mine, for mark, oh favored Greeks! / That by my mouth the martial Goddess speaks" (1.41–42).[35] Not vulgar nor mad, but high and true, the protagonist's awesome mission dovetails in flawless innocence with the poet's. That the narrative result is unbearably predictable is no great fault in so precocious an achievement. It does, however, outline with diagrammatic clarity a disaster that awaited epoists by the dozen who should have known better but were seduced all the same by inspirationism into launching their flotilla of derelict hulks, with which our focus here on gleaming bowsprits and brave figureheads has spared us the labor of grappling.[36] Taken seriously, the romantic ideology of creative originality exacted a far more thorough imagination of the epic whole—more inventiveness in concept and execution, shape and detail—than the mere stamina of naked ambition could sustain. A minor and a major example of successful follow-through, at least as the occasion of epic invocation lets us glimpse it, will round off our exploration of the topic here.

When William Sotheby devoted an heroic poem to the doomed King Saul, he broke a rule of epic theory requiring that protagonists be paragons, models of the virtue that the rehearsal of their deeds was designed to impart. In fact, every great epic had bent this rule, sometimes pretty hard; but the fact had not registered within neoclassical epic theory, whose theoretic deficiency had littered the eighteenth century with impeccably principled, imaginatively stillborn fossils of the genre. With *Saul* (1807) Sotheby helped revive epic's tragic potentiality; and one sign of his conscious participation in the unfrequented tradition is the arresting, disjunctive invocation with which the poem began:

> Yet . . . . if not fled for ever . . . . ever fled,
> Celestial spirit of Poesy! whose voice,
> Temper'd to touch of prophet harps, redeem'd
> The soul from sin's dire thraldom; yet, invok'd,
> Gracious descend; and to my fervent pray'r
> Vouchsafe due inspiration while I strike,
> Vent'rous, the sacred lyre: and shape in song,
> Following the maze of frenzy's changeful moods,
> The troubled image of a mind distraught
> With guilt-avenging horror.
>   Saul I sing
> Smitten of God.
>
>   (1.1.1–11)[37]

This passage resumes signal features canvassed in our foregoing pages, among them the stammering trepidation of stuck diction, the ground of bodily feeling ("touch," "strike," "Smitten") and the generically fraught, ambiguously tentative participle "invok'd," which makes the "due" that comes after it mean at once arrived and awaited, pending and paid. Sotheby enlists these features to express a remarkably forthright dubiety concerning the Muse's survival and accessibility under a modern epic dispensation, which affect is linked in turn to an apprehension of mental unease verging on disease—and thereby on the burden of madness that will afflict the royal hero in the story to come. Out of phase with the "Celestial spirit" from which each seeks validation, both poet and monarch come before us in discord with themselves, yet so attuned to each another in obscurely participated guilt that the final sentence—Sotheby's spare transition from invocation to story—represents singer, sung, and song as equivalently, ambivalently "Smitten."

After such knowledge, what forgiveness? Little enough, in the slender hope of redemption that Sotheby's invocation tucks into the past tense of a relative clause describing a Muse that may or may not be "fled for ever." And yet just enough: enough to underwrite a steady look at "The troubled image of a mind distraught," regarded *ab extra* from a vantage of sympathetic understanding, outside the internally clueless "maze" of neurotic self-absorption. Absent such a standpoint, and the forgiveness that enables it, what knowledge? For that matter, what story? This is the question behind Blake's final epic accomplishment, *Jerusalem* (1820), whose special gift to our project here is the way it figures the romantic identification of poet with Muse with hero in the utterly fluid to-and-fro of an initiatory segue between invocation and tale:

> Of the Sleep of Ulro! and of the passage through
> Eternal Death! and of the awaking to Eternal Life
>
> This theme calls me in sleep night after night, & ev'ry morn
> Awakes me at sun-rise, then I see the Saviour over me
> Spreading his beams of love, & dictating the words of this mild song.
>
> Awake! awake O sleeper of the land of shadows, wake! expand!
> I am in you and you in me, mutual in love divine:
> Fibres of love from man to man thro Albions pleasant land. . . .
> I am not a God afar off, I am a brother and friend;
> Within your bosoms I reside, and you reside in me:
> Lo! we are One; forgiving all Evil; Not seeking recompense!
> Ye are my members O ye sleepers of Beulah, land of shades!
>   (1.1–8, 18–21)[38]

"I am in you and you in me" puts into a nutshell what was at once Blake's artistic practice and his epic ethos. It was also a proclamation of what, as we have seen, other romantic invocations again and again verged on saying. The epic-engendering difficulty of this gnomic disclosure attaches not to saying it, though, but to hearing it; and it is to this difficulty that Blake devotes a set of preliminary disorienting tactics that keep tripping us into renewed receptivity.

Having the Muse invoke the poet, rather than the other way round, is an unusual move; but it is not an unprecedented one within the charged field of romantic inspirationism we have been traversing. Still, Blake's unremitting wake-up call—forms of "awake" occur five times in these dozen lines—solicits us with noisier syntactic disturbance than we have encountered thus far. Clearly some "mild song" is dictated to the poet by the Muse who is his "Saviour," but the deictic modifier "this" that precedes it is ambiguous. "This" reaches both forward, if we take the ensuing full stop as a colon, to lines 6–21, whose quoted vocal refraction of the "beams of love" it introduces; and backward, across the under-punctuated prior lines, to join hands with "This theme" (3) and so indicate lines 1–2. That two-line grammatical fragment reads as a haunting snatch of song, something as it were overheard but insufficiently grasped. The Miltonically echoic preposition "Of" debuts a syntactical dependency that, begging pardon in its own mute way, relies by default on the forgiveness of *Jerusalem* as a whole. The interpenetration of proposition and invocation with narration persists besides into the lines that follow, which do a volte-face on the Saviour's words, conscripting them out of invocation and impressing them straight into the story. There the benighted hero Albion is about to hear and submit them to a severe interpretive reduction (1.22–31), from which it will take him the rest of this long epic to recover.

"Within your bosoms I reside," "Ye are my members." What Blake's invocation keeps saying elaborates with special insistence a message that has been generally implicit in the Romantic-era invocation as we have considered it. Epic's age-old claim to tell a people their own story, with a plot that embodies and a heroism that enacts values their culture lives by, found romantic voice by declaring an independence that, while vested in the exemplary creative freedom of the poet, was at the same time shared among the poet's readership as their collective right. Thus the invocation to *Jerusalem* not only affirms the gospel of universal mutual participation in epic song but executively confirms it, too, by the equivalence among its numerous grammatical persons and by the topological fungibility whereby quotation and frame, inside and outside, keep swapping places. The "passage" of Blake's opening verses, whether enjambed like lines 1–4 or end-stopped like the rest, enacts a continual, "Eternal" passage between the death of the letter and the life of spirited recitation. Summons and story, poet and Muse, hero and reader, awaken from themselves and into one another's bosom, and one another's voice, for as long as may be necessary to receive that forgiving re-membership which is Blake's final name for memory and inspiration alike.

Notes

1. René Le Bossu, *Traité du Poème Epique* (1675), vol. 5. chap. 5, vol. 2. chap. 4, in *Le Bossu and Voltaire on the Epic*, ed. Stuart Curran (Gainesville: Scholars Press, 1970).
2. Voltaire, *La Henriade de M. de Voltaire* (London: n.p., 1728), 1.7–20. The discrimination of truth from fable remained alive among poets, we shall see, during Romantic decades. William Preston's edition of the *Argonautica* of Apollonius Rhodius disdains epic invocation as the

poet's bold-faced apology for telling lies: *The Argonautics* (London: Whittingham and Rowland, 1811), 4:885.
3. See Gérard Genette, *Seuils* (Paris: Editions de Seuil, 1987), trans. Jane E. Lewin as *Paratexts: Thresholds of Interpretation* (Cambridge: Cambridge University Press, 1997). For Genette the epic invocation derives from a paratextual "prehistory" that ran from antiquity (Homer) through the Middle Ages (Tasso), "when for obvious reasons the prefatorial function is taken on by the opening lines or pages," which constitute an "incorporated preface" (163–64).
4. This durable generic wrinkle is explored with learning and subtlety by A. D. Nuttall, *Openings: Narrative Beginnings from the Epic to the Novel* (Oxford: Clarendon Press, 1992). "Why did Homer, as his sole contribution to the *Iliad* (for everything after the first paragraph is from the Muse) *tell* the Muse where to begin, instead of being told by her?" (22). See especially chap. 1, "The Beginning of the *Aeneid*" (1–32).
5. George Gordon, Lord Byron, *Complete Poetical Works*, ed. Jerome J. McGann, vol. 5 (Oxford: Clarendon Press, 1986).
6. Richard Glover, *The Athenaid, A Poem* (London: Cadell, 1787); George Skene, *Donald Bane: An Heroic Poem* (London: Robinson, 1796).
7. Joseph Cottle, *Alfred: An Epic Poem* (Newburyport: Allen, 1814), 1.1; Walter Savage Landor, *Gebir: A Poem in Seven Books* (London: Rivingtons, 1798), 1.1.
8. On Tucker's unpublished epic draft see John P. McWilliams, Jr., *The American Epic: Transforming a Genre, 1770–1860* (Cambridge: Cambridge University Press, 1989), 31–33. In the invocation quoted there, syntax comes to grief through Tucker's (phobic?) omission of the one word Romantically needful: *inspire*.
9. James Paulding, *The Backwoodsman: A Poem* (Philadelphia: Thomas, 1818).
10. Joel Barlow, *The Columbiad: A Poem* (Washington: Milligan, 1825). For discussion of Barlow's harbingers and cohort, see McWilliams, *American Epic*, 15–66. This important critic's claim that, through the American restriction of epic machinery "to occasional personifications and place gods, all events become traceable to human or environmental causes" (58) regrettably irons into mere conventionality what a careful look at actualizations of the convention often reveal to be more various and interesting than that.
11. Robert Southey, *Joan of Arc* (London: Cadell and Davies, 1796); James Pye, *Alfred: An Epic Poem* (London: Suttaby, 1801); William Walker, *Gustavus Vasa and Other Poems* (London: Longman, 1813); Charles Smith, *The Mosiad, or Israel Delivered: A Sacred Poem* (London: Nicol, 1815).
12. Henry Hart Milman, *Samor, Lord of the Bright City: An Heroic Poem* (New York: Wiley, 1818); William Lisle Bowles, *The Grave of the*

Last Saxon; or, The Legend of the Curfew: A Poem (London: Hurst, Robinson, 1822).

13. Sir Walter Scott, *The Lady of the Lake* (1810), in *Poetical Works*, ed. J. Logie Robertson (London: Oxford University Press, 1904).
14. Margaret Holford, *Wallace; or, The Fight of Falkirk: A Metrical Romance* (London: Longman, 1809).
15. On invocation's seldom very remote magical connotations, see Thomas M. Greene, "Poetry as Invocation" (1993), reprinted in *Poetry, Signs, and Magic* (Newark: University of Delaware Press, 2005), 43–61.
16. William Gilbank, *The Day of Pentecost, or Man Restored* (London: Reynell, 1789).
17. Henry Murphy, *The Conquest of Quebec: An Epic Poem* (Dublin: Porter, 1790).
18. Hannah Cowley, *The Siege of Acre: A Poem* (London: Wilkie and Robinson, 1810).
19. Margaret Holford, *Margaret of Anjou: A Poem* (Philadelphia: Carey, 1816).
20. Richard Cumberland, *Calvary; or The Death of Christ: A Poem* (London: Dilly, 1792).
21. William Lisle Bowles, *The Spirit of Discovery; or, The Conquest of Ocean: A Poem* (Bath: Cruttwell, 1804).
22. Richard Emmons, *The Fredoniad; or, Independence Preserved: An Epic Poem* (Philadelphia: Emmons, 1830).
23. In this respect Emmons displays an agnosticism that typifies one class of epic that dates from the years of decompression after Napoleon—or, by a more literary reckoning, after Byron. Witness the entirely sober-sided Edwin Atherstone's *The Fall of Nineveh: A Poem* (London: Baldwin and Cradock, 1828): "So thou, Great Spirit, whatsoe'er thy name, / Muse, Inspiration, or Divinity" (1.19–20); the ensuing question "Yet how should I invoke thee?" (1.26) distinguishes Atherstone's scruples from those of Milton, which they superficially recall, as from the diplomatically distributive eclecticism of earlier invocations like Thomas Northmore's to *Washington, or Liberty Restored: A Poem* (London: Taylor, 1809), Charlotte Dixon's to *The Mount of Olives, or The Resurrection and Ascension* (London: Adland, 1814), or those by Thelwall, Cowley, and Bowles discussed elsewhere in this essay. Atherstone's dubiety is more closely anticipated by the oddly conditional invocation found in Murphy ("if thy voice can reach the mournful theme" [1.9]) and in Richard Wharton's 1812 *Roncesvalles* ("If aught divine e'er fanned a Poet's flame" [1.7]). The other major class of 1820s epic, the apocalyptic (as in Pollok, treated *infra*), categorically proscribed doubt on this as on all topics.
24. Robert Pollok, *The Course of Time* (Amherst: Adams, 1828).
25. William Blake, *Milton: A Poem*, in *The Poetry and Prose of William Blake*, ed. David V. Erdman (Garden City, NY: Doubleday, 1970).

26. Walt Whitman, "Out of the Cradle Endlessly Rocking" (1859, revised 1871) in *The Complete Poems*, ed. Francis Murphy (Harmondsworth: Penguin, 1975), l.143.
27. James Ogden, *The Revolution: An Epic Poem* (London: Johnson, 1790).
28. See the discussion in Christopher N. Phillips, *Epic in American Culture: Settlement to Reconstruction* (Baltimore: Johns Hopkins University Press, 2012), 24–27.
29. John Thelwall, "Specimens of *The Hope of Albion; or, Edwin of Northumbria: An Epic Poem*," in *Poems Written Chiefly in Retirement* (Hereford: Parker, 1801); Anthony Hunn, *Sin and Redemption: A Religious Poem* (Lexington: Worsley, 1812).
30. Part of the greatness of Wordsworth's "Prospectus" comes from the extremity to which it presses the question of creative origins that haunts Romantic epic invocation. As Leslie Brisman puts it in *Romantic Origins* (Ithaca and London: Cornell University Press, 1978), 342, the text "could be described as Wordsworth's most prestigious effort to confront the origin of his unique poetic voice, or as an ultimate proof against autogenesis because even in self-created myths the poet needs to hypothesize voice as being given to him."
31. John Keats, "Hyperion: A Fragment" (written 1818, published 1820), in *The Complete Poems*, ed. John Barnard (Harmondsworth: Penguin, 1973). The longer Keats worked on the matter of *Hyperion*, the further back he delved into narrative's preconditions, which furnish the internally replicative topic of *The Fall of Hyperion*, a text that needs no invocation because it is preoccupied entirely by what traditional invocation compresses and implies: the story of the poet's encounter with the Muse. See Brisman, *Romantic Origins*, 94: "one comes to see the later poem gaining anteriority and dramatizing the begetting of *Hyperion*." When Keats's chief American heir, the compulsive apostrophizer Whitman, finally wrote a poem invoking the Muse by name in "Song of the Exposition" (1871), his doing so forestalled all exposition in the storytelling sense: "Once his invocation has been completed, Whitman can find no narrative" (McWilliams, *American Epic*, 231). Characteristically, when Whitman's "Inscriptions" invoke the Muse, as James E. Miller, Jr., remarks in *The American Quest for a Supreme Fiction: Whitman's Legacy in the Personal Epic* (Chicago and London: University of Chicago Press, 1979), 33, "then he tells her what *he* is going to do, what is good for *her*."
32. William Wordsworth, *The Prelude: A Parallel Text*, ed. J. C. Maxwell (Harmondsworth: Penguin, 1972). Wordsworth's first epic, substantially complete by 1805 but unpublished, underwent significant revision before appearing posthumously in 1850. This poem's structured logic of fractal anticipation has been remarked often, and resiliently, by students of our larger topic. See Edward Said, *Beginnings: Intention*

and *Method* (New York: Basic Books, 1975), 44: "what was initially intended to be the beginning became the work itself"; for Nuttall, *The Prelude* "is exactly what its name tells us: all proem, all exordium" (*Narrative Openings*, 115).

33. Hogg's letter to Alaric Watts is quoted in *Queen Hynde*, ed. Suzanne Gilbert and Douglas S. Mack (Edinburgh: Edinburgh University Press, 1998), 270.
34. Richard Cumberland and Richard Bland Burges, *The Exodiad: A Poem* (London: Lackington, Allen, 1807).
35. Elizabeth Barrett [Browning], *The Battle of Marathon* (1820), in *The Poetical Works of Elizabeth Barrett Browning*, ed. Harriet Waters Preston and Ruth M. Adams (Boston: Houghton Mifflin, 1974).
36. Exercise contributing to that labor may be taken in chaps. 2–6 of my *Epic: Britain's Heroic Muse 1790–1910* (Oxford: Oxford University Press, 2008).
37. William Sotheby, *Saul: A Poem* (Boston: West, 1807).
38. William Blake, *Jerusalem: The Emanation of the Giant Albion*, ed. Morton D. Paley (Princeton: Princeton University Press, 1991).

Bibliography

Apollonius Rhodius. *The Argonautics*. Edited by William Preston. 4 vols. London: Whittingham and Rowland, 1811.

Atherstone, Edwin. *The Fall of Nineveh: A Poem*. London: Baldwin and Cradock, 1828.

Barlow, Joel. *The Columbiad: A Poem*. Washington: Milligan, 1825. Accessed April 27, 2017. http://collections.chadwyck.com/.

Blake, William. *Jerusalem: The Emanation of the Giant Albion*. Edited by Morton D. Paley. Princeton: Princeton University Press, 1991.

———. *The Poetry and Prose of William Blake*. Edited by David V. Erdman. 4th ed. Garden City, NY: Doubleday, 1970.

Bowles, W. L. *The Grave of the Last Saxon; or, The Legend of the Curfew: A Poem*. London: Hurst, Robinson, 1822. Accessed April 27, 2017. http://tinyurl.galegroup.com/tinyurl/Bx2v7.

———. *The Spirit of Discovery; or, The Conquest of Ocean: A Poem*. Bath: Cruttwell, 1804. Accessed April 27, 2017. http://hdl.handle.net/2027/uc2.ark:/13960/t8rb70m1g.

Brisman, Leslie. *Romantic Origins*. Ithaca and London: Cornell University Press, 1978.

Browning, Elizabeth Barrett. *The Poetical Works of Elizabeth Barrett Browning*. Edited by Harriet Waters Preston and Ruth M. Adams. Boston: Houghton Mifflin, 1974.

Byron, George Gordon. *The Complete Poetical Works*. Edited by Jerome J. McGann. vol. 5. Oxford: Clarendon Press, 1986.

Cottle, Joseph. *Alfred: An Epic Poem.* Newburyport: Allen, 1814.
Cowley, [Hannah] Mrs. *The Siege of Acre: A Poem.* London: Wilkie and Robinson, 1810. Accessed April 27, 2017. http://hdl.handle.net/2027/njp.32101066458447.
Cumberland, Richard. *Calvary; or The Death of Christ: A Poem.* London: Dilly, 1792. Accessed April 27, 2017. http://hdl.handle.net/2027/nyp.33433000180145.
Cumberland, Richard, and Richard Bland Burges. *The Exodiad: A Poem.* London: Lackington, Allen, 1807.
Dixon, Charlotte. *The Mount of Olives, or The Resurrection and Ascension.* London: Adland, 1814.
Emmons, Richard. *The Fredoniad; or, Independence Preserved: An Epic Poem.* Philadelphia: Emmons, 1830. Accessed April 27, 2017. http://books.google.com/.
Genette, Gérard. *Seuils* (1987). Translated by Jane E. Lewin as *Paratexts: Thresholds of Interpretation.* Cambridge: Cambridge University Press, 1997.
Gilbank, William. *The Day of Pentecost, or Man Restored.* London: Reynell, 1789.
Glover, Richard. *The Athenaid, A Poem.* London: Cadell, 1787. http://find.galegroup.com/ecco/.
Greene, Thomas M. *Poetry, Signs, and Magic.* Newark: University of Delaware Press, 2005.
Hogg, James. *Queen Hynde.* Edited by Suzanne Gilbert and Douglas S. Mack. Edinburgh: Edinburgh University Press, 1998.
[Holford] Hodson, Margaret. *Margaret of Anjou: A Poem.* Philadelphia: Carey, 1816. http://textbase.wwp.brown.edu/WWO/.
———. *Wallace; or, The Fight of Falkirk: A Metrical Romance.* London: Longman, Hurst, Rees, Orme, and Brown, 1809. Accessed April 27, 2017. http://hdl.handle.net/2027/uc2.ark:/13960/t8pc2xt15.
Hunn, Anthony. *Sin and Redemption: A Religious Poem.* Lexington: Worsley, 1812.
Keats, John. *The Complete Poems.* Edited by John Barnard. Harmondsworth: Penguin, 1973.
Landor, Walter Savage. *Gebir: A Poem in Seven Books.* London: Rivingtons, 1798.
Le Bossu and Voltaire on the Epic. Edited by Stuart Curran. Gainesville: Scholars Press, 1970.
McWilliams, John P., Jr. *The American Epic: Transforming a Genre, 1770–1860.* Cambridge: Cambridge University Press, 1989.
Miller, James E., Jr. *The American Quest for a Supreme Fiction: Whitman's Legacy in the Personal Epic.* Chicago and London: University of Chicago Press, 1979.
Milman, H. H. *Samor, Lord of the Bright City: An Heroic Poem.* New York: Wiley, 1818. Accessed April 27, 2017. http://hdl.handle.net/2027/mdp.39015063945177.

Murphy, Henry. *The Conquest of Quebec: An Epic Poem*. Dublin: Porter, 1790. http://find.galegroup.com/ecco/.

Nuttall, A. D. *Openings: Narrative Beginnings from the Epic to the Novel*. Oxford: Clarendon Press, 1992.

Ogden, James. *The Revolution: An Epic Poem*. London: Johnson, 1790.

Paulding, J. K. *The Backwoodsman: A Poem*. Philadelphia: Thomas, 1818.

Phillips, Christopher N. *Epic in American Culture: Settlement to Reconstruction*. Baltimore: The Johns Hopkins University Press, 2012.

Pollok, Robert. *The Course of Time*. Amherst: Adams, 1828. Accessed April 27, 2017. http://hdl.handle.net/2027/njp.32101065701656.

Pye, Henry James. *Alfred: An Epic Poem*. London: Suttaby, 1801.

Said, Edward. *Beginnings: Intention and Method*. New York: Basic Books, 1975.

Scott, Walter. *Poetical Works*. Edited by J. Logie Robertson. London: Oxford University Press, 1904.

Skene, George. *Donald Bane: An Heroic Poem*. London: Robinson, 1796. http://find.galegroup.com/ecco/.

Smith, Charles. *The Mosiad, or Israel Delivered: A Sacred Poem*. London: Nicol, 1815.

Sotheby, William. *Saul: A Poem*. Boston: West, 1807.

Southey, Robert. *Joan of Arc: An Epic Poem*. London: Cadell and Davies, 1796.

Thelwall, John. "Specimens of *The Hope of Albion; or, Edwin of Northumbria: An Epic Poem*." In *Poems Written Chiefly in Retirement*. Hereford: Parker, 1801.

Tucker, Herbert F. *Epic: Britain's Heroic Muse 1790–1910*. Oxford: Oxford University Press, 2008.

Voltaire. *La Henriade de M. de Voltaire*. London: n.p., 1728.

Walker, W. S. *Gustavus Vasa and Other Poems*. London: Longman, Hurst, Rees, Orme, and Brown, 1813. Accessed April 27, 2017. http://hdl.handle.net/2027/uc2.ark:/13960/t18k7852k.

Whitman, Walt. *The Complete Poems*. Edited by Francis Murphy. Harmondsworth: Penguin, 1975.

Wordsworth, William. *The Prelude: A Parallel Text*. Edited by J. C. Maxwell. Harmondsworth: Penguin, 1972.

Part II

Wider Romantic Engagements with the Classical World

Chapter 6

Thoreau's Epic Ambitions: "A Walk to Wachusett" and the Persistence of the Classics in an Age of Science
K. P. Van Anglen

Since the 1970s, scholars of Henry David Thoreau have taken a renewed interest in the last dozen years or so of his life, seeing it as a period principally marked by his devotion of time and intellectual effort to understanding the natural world. They have in many ways been right to do so, of course, since after about 1849, Thoreau increasingly came under the influence of Darwin and Alexander von Humboldt; his commitment of time and energy to field work and observation grew as well; and both his later *Journal* and the nature writings he left unfinished at his death more and more focus on nature as a system of which we are observers and yet a part. It would be wrong, however, to conclude from this that Thoreau's biography can be neatly divided into an earlier, chiefly literary or philosophical period, and a final, more "scientific" one. For one thing, Thoreau's commitment to political, social, and personal reform (e.g., with regard to abolition) actually grew during the 1850s and 1860s alongside his increased engagement with the natural world. Thoreau's writing about nature was, moreover, often affected both stylistically and substantively by his political and social concerns, as also by his awareness of his double stance, as both a writer about and recorder of natural phenomena, of which he himself was one. For example, his comments on the advocates of the Free Soil movement not only correct their tendency toward misreading the landscape in political terms, they also bespeak Thoreau's own range of reference in writing about nature and in observing phenomena. This illustrates the persistence—indeed, flourishing—of intellectual *foci* in his later works other than natural science. For Thoreau was interested neither in pursuing a strategy of polarization between opposing thematic interests nor in declaring any one of them his predominant or ultimate area of concern. What we find, instead, is the recurrent revelation that Thoreau's "central strategy" is that of "doubleness or paradox ... a persistent habit of non-binary thought, a continual recognition of the ways in which 'the universe is wider than our views of it.'" This led him to reject "*any* one-sided or absolute statement" as a betrayal of "the wildness of actual experience. . . . Thoreau's lifelong response to a world of irreducible wildness and complexity was to push at the bounds of language, logic, and custom to attain closer contact with the real, in all of its unexpected and untheorizable" forms, wherever they might be encountered.[1]

In taking this stance toward experience, Thoreau was responding to one of the great tectonic shifts in intellectual history. As Sir Isaiah Berlin famously noted, before the eighteenth century nearly all Western intellectuals (Machiavelli being a prominent exception) held to "a Platonic ideal: in the first place, that, as in the sciences, all genuine questions must have one true answer and one only, all the rest being necessarily errors; in the second place, that there must be a dependable path towards the discovery of these truths; in the third place, that the true answers, when found, must necessarily be compatible with one another and form a single whole, for one truth cannot be incompatible with another—that we knew *a priori*." Later, in the eighteenth century, many Enlightenment thinkers still assumed this Platonic ideal, e.g., applying rational and empirical techniques first developed in understanding mathematics and nature to "the realm of human affairs" in the *a priori* faith that all experience and knowledge was part of "a great harmonious system" that could be found by the use of logic, empirical observation, and reason.[2] One corollary of this was that whatever their field, scholars were thought to be engaged in a common effort to understand and to describe this universal truth. Consequently, there was little difference between the natural philosopher and the man of letters; one could, indeed, like Dr. Franklin of Philadelphia, combine these and many other roles in a single career.

At the same time, however, other intellectuals during the Age of Reason (e.g., Giambattista Vico and Johann Gottfried Herder) took a different view. They maintained that societies and cultures and languages and species and intellectual fields of endeavor were all various, unique, ever-changing, and historically contingent.[3] They therefore proposed an alternative, pluralistic view of human knowledge and of reality to replace the older Platonic ideal. It was this second model (along with its implications for intellectual specialization) that was in the ascendant as Thoreau began his career, yet it had not yet wholly triumphed over either the belief that "a great harmonious system" lay within our intellectual grasp, if only we could find the right means of discovering it, or that such an explanation would, as in Hegel and Marx, eventually emerge from the processes of history. Thoreau was intellectually drawn to writers like Darwin and Humboldt, who tried to compromise between these two positions, by uniting the study of the empirical and the individual with the concept of the cosmos as a comprehensive and holistic but provisional, empirically-driven, and evolving model. It is also why he did not fall into the intellectual specialization that was beginning to occur during his own lifetime, but instead combined many roles and pursued many interests throughout his life, including those of the classical scholar and the natural historian. All of which explains why a somewhat neglected early text by Thoreau, "A Walk to Wachusett," is far more significant than it at first seems to be; for it suggests that throughout his life he used the most traditional model of the poetic calling, the Virgilian *cursus honorum*, to pursue his new Humboldtian ambitions.

As David M. Robinson has argued, Henry David Thoreau wrote "A Walk to Wachusett" (1843) in response to "a crisis of vocation" that "simmered throughout his early and middle twenties."[4] Uninterested either in the family pencil-making business or in the professions traditionally pursued by Harvard graduates, he had for a time tried school teaching.[5] But by 1842 this option too seemed forestalled. He still sought what Robinson calls "a task and a place in society that would be both socially useful and personally fulfilling," a solution to what was both an "identity crisis" and a vocational search.[6] In the end, Thoreau resolved this search for "a suitable place and a suitable vocational task in the world"[7] by redefining his ambitions. Eventually, he came to see that his moral purpose and his literary needs were alike fulfilled by "studying" the details of "what we now call ecology, the interactions of whole systems of life within a particular place."[8]

He also discovered a literary form to express this interactive view of nature: the idiosyncratic Transcendentalist combination of philosophical reflection, travelogue, and nature essay known as the "excursion." As Lawrence Buell defined it, "like the conversation, the sermon, and the essay, the excursion is also a potentially encyclopedic form. Though somewhat more controlled by the obligation to describe a particular setting, it tends to become, in effect, an account of the whole universe as it appears to the speaker . . . ."[9] This is why "the bulk of what Thoreau wrote for publication was" what Robert Sattelmeyer calls "either travel narration or a closely related form of narration . . . that was based upon traveling by foot and that he usually called the excursion."[10] For as a form, this sort of travel writing allowed him to describe places both near and far from Concord, as well as the structure of the cosmos as it gradually emerged from his local, empirical observations.

"A Walk to Wachusett" marks the moment, then, when Thoreau seems both to tilt toward the natural world as his subject matter and toward the prose genre in which he often later wrote about it. Many scholars have made this point. Sherman Paul, for instance, characterizes "Wachusett" and another early excursion, "A Winter Walk," as follows: "though the experiences recorded in these essays were brief, the method Thoreau used in them was essentially that of his best work. Indeed, the method and materials of Thoreau's work remained fairly constant . . . . 'A Walk to Wachusett' and 'A Winter Walk,' with their espousal of nature, were the earlier versions of 'Walking,' in which nearly two decades of experience prompted Thoreau to make 'an extreme statement' in nature's behalf."[11] Similarly, Stephen Adams and Donald Ross, Jr. remind us that while Thoreau's "*Journal*, poetry, and essays from 1834 to 1846 reveal the influence of his schooling by men rooted in neoclassicism and the eighteenth century,"[12] the "greater control" they find in "A Walk to Wachusett" results from his "having discovered the 'excursion' structure that would inform his major writings." Indeed, Adams and Ross regard "Wachusett" as a kind of "miniature *Week on the Concord and Merrimack Rivers*."[13]

Laura Dassow Walls goes further in her highly acclaimed *The Passage to Cosmos: Alexander von Humboldt and the Shaping of America*, writing that in "Wachusett" Thoreau reveals a new role model, a new calling, and the version of *Naturphilosophie* he would practice the rest of his life. She cites, for instance, the first paragraph of the excursion:

The needles of the pine,
All to the west incline.

CONCORD, July19, 1842

Summer and winter our eyes had rested on the dim outline of the mountains in our horizon, to which distance and indistinctness lent a grandeur not their own, so that they served equally to interpret all the allusions of poets and travellers; whether with Homer, on a spring morning, we sat down on the many-peaked Olympus, or, with Virgil, and his compeers, roamed the Etrurian and Thessalian hills, or with Humboldt measured the more modern Andes and Teneriffe. Thus we spoke our mind to them, standing on the Concord cliffs.—[14]

Then, having just praised Coleridge by quoting a scholar who claims "that his [Coleridge's] 'entire life occurred in what might be aptly named the "Age of Humboldt,"'" Walls adds:

> So did the entire life of Henry David Thoreau. . . . Thoreau was fascinated by the reports of explorers, and it was probably in Emerson's library that he first picked up McGillivray's biography of Humboldt. In one of his earliest essays, "A Walk to Wachusett" of 1842, Thoreau looks longingly at the mountains of his Concord horizon and imagines himself "with Humboldt, measur[ing] the more modern Andes and Teneriffe," step by step across the landscape. What follows is his own exploring expedition, albeit only to the top of a local landmark. Already Thoreau is casting himself as the traveler who stays home, seeing the familiar and the local with the intensity of the visitor who in his passage comprehends the local in its planetary relations. In his passage to Walden Pond, a journey of barely two miles that took him over two years to complete, Thoreau entertained passersby between rambles in the woods and supply runs home. He also wrote his first book, a travel narrative of the river excursion with his best friend and elder brother, John when John was still alive, and the Thoreau we know, the lonely man who walked the face of the planet, was not yet born.[15]

In what is arguably Thoreau's first public reference to the German writer, the hills on the horizon remind him of a similar stage in Humboldt's life, when the geographer explored South America and the Canary Islands, gaining insight into the facts and methods of natural history and observation from which he would later construct his model of everything. In addition, it is a moment that opens up what Walls considers the central feature of Thoreau's intellectual development: his evolution from "'rational holism'" (the position of Emerson and Goethe, who "conceived the mechanico-organic whole" of nature "as a divine or transcendent unity fully comprehended only through thought") to "'empirical holism'" (an "emergent alternative" advanced by Humboldt and Darwin), which stressed "that the whole could be understood only by studying the interconnectedness of its consistent and individual parts." Furthermore, since Thoreau's interest began with his observations of "particularized nature," and since from about 1842 he combined "transcendentalism with empiricism," the intellectual shift initially seen here at the start of "Wachusett" marks a biographical *telos* (or at least as close to one as one can have in a modern biography) as well as a *terminus*. Walls sees the increasingly empirical *Journal* from 1849 on, and other late writings like those published in *Faith in a Seed*, as evidence that in his last years Thoreau wrote "as a Humboldtian empirical naturalist" seeking to advance "an alternative tradition of romantic science and literature" that looked ahead "toward ecological approaches to nature."[16] Likewise, he spent much of his final decade exploring how we become "players in that range of processes and actions by which human beings tie themselves morally, epistemologically, and ontologically together with their nonhuman neighbors," an anti-Cartesian endeavor that makes us aware of our situation in our environment.[17]

For Walls, "the dim outline of the mountains in our horizon, to which distance and indistinctness lent a grandeur not their own," is therefore, symbolically, the key to interpreting "all the allusions of poets and travellers alike."[18] Yet she makes no reference to Homer and Virgil, the first two members of Thoreau's triad in the passage just quoted. In later correspondence with me, Walls justified her exclusive focus on Humboldt here by arguing that in the book in which it appeared, her aim had been to make the case for Alexander von Humboldt's influence on Thoreau in particular, and on early nineteenth-century American thought in general. Given this overarching purpose, Walls's exclusion of any treatment of Homer or Virgil seemed to her to be merely a matter of avoiding a digression. Furthermore, elsewhere in this first book, she admits that, of course, Thoreau knew "that certain modern scientists—such as Humboldt and Lyell—explicitly placed their work in a tradition which honored and embraced classical and Oriental thought.... Humboldt" thus, in fact, "contributed a program for connection, not estrangement," between traditional humanistic learning and emerging natural science, one "which came with the highest endorsements: Greek and Hindu classics, even Goethe himself. In Humboldt, Thoreau found the catalyst for" forging such a connection, for "which he was so manifestly ready."[19]

This explanation is entirely satisfactory, given what Walls was trying to do. The fact remains, however, that she mentions Humboldt a lot—and Homer and Virgil only once each, and that in passing. Yet Thoreau clearly meant all three to share the limelight here, to an equal degree. He spent just as much time imagining himself "with

Homer, on a spring morning," sitting "down on the many-peaked Olympus," or "with Virgil, and his compeers," roaming "the Etrurian and Thessalian hills," as he did dreaming of exploring Teneriffe with Humboldt. Homer, Virgil, and Humboldt are each given equal billing; indeed, the two ancient poets collectively get more space than does the modern natural scientist. This suggests that there is another way of reading this passage, one that proclaims the essential unity of the literary and the scientific, and of the ancient and the modern, without privileging either polarity. Similarly, Humboldt is not about the business of preventing a disconnection from occurring or reconciling an estrangement between science and the arts. Rather, Thoreau construes all three authors as members of the same undivided line of thinkers who, generation after generation, have aimed at achieving a comprehensive vision of reality in its totality. In particular, Virgil's presence as the middle partner in Thoreau's literary *stemma* reminds us that the Roman writer's career was the *locus classicus* of the notion that poets progress toward this goal via a literary *cursus honorum*, the stages of which are the pastoral, the georgic, and the epic. Glenn W. Most describes this traditional and most widespread formulation of how writers ought to be trained and prepared for greatness:

> Beyond the influence exercised by his individual works, Virgil has also provided the Western literary tradition with its most compelling and durable model of a poetic career, one beginning with small, unambitious, personal works (the *Eclogues*), moving on to more difficult tasks of greater intellectual complexity and social significance (the *Georgics*), and culminating in a single massive work that subsumes all the earlier ones and provides an epic mirror for the destiny of a nation (the *Aeneid*). The influence exercised by this model can be traced as early as the 1st century CE.... For many centuries it continued to provide poets with a guideline for their own development and with suggestions for what kind of poem to write next, through the Middle Ages ... and the early modern period (when it fascinated such poets as Spenser, Milton, and Pope), and even into Romanticism (it stands behind William Wordsworth's, and the other English Romantic poets', dream of a career culminating in a single great philosophical epic) and the 20th century....[20]

The sequence found here in "Wachusett," "Homer, Virgil, Humboldt" (rather than "Homer, Virgil, Milton" or "Homer, Virgil, Dante") is therefore deliberately provocative, but in an unexpected way. It is not an announcement by Thoreau that he is abandoning the classical past for the scientific future, let alone endorsing the Whiggish view of intellectual history implicit in that polarity. Thoreau is not abandoning the hieratic, prophetic tradition of Western poetry, let alone its visionary aims, or his faith in the Virgilian *cursus honorum* as a means by which such poetic greatness may be attained. Rather, Humboldt's presence on Thoreau's list implies that—understood rightly—prose nature writing can also, in turn, be pastoral or georgic or epic in subject matter, scope, and ambition. Thoreau too can hope to achieve a place among the visionary company by using non-fiction prose to reveal the essential and unsundered unity of the literary and the observational, the transcendental and empirical. In line with the "revolutionary traditionalism" characteristic of so much Romanticism, "A Walk to Wachusett" thus marks Thoreau's first step in fulfilling an old calling in a new way. He aspires to be a *vates* or poet-priest, one (as Milton says) "smit with the love of sacred song," only now a *vates* called to undertake the most epic task of them all: that of singing not the Fall of Troy or the matter of Rome or the "rising glory of America," but that of the nature and existence of the eternal yet ever-changing cosmos itself.[21]

This is why there is the reference here as well to the related concepts of the "translation of empire" (*translatio imperii*) and the "translation of the arts" (*translatio studii*), in the lines with which the excursion begins: "The needles of the pine, / All to the west incline." For Virgil (as for Dante, Spenser, and Milton), the pastoral is not an escapist form. Even in *Eclogue 1*, after celebrating the carefree realm of love and laughter and youth, the shadows of nightfall and mortality approach, encroaching at the end on the garden and the shepherds' songs. Likewise, from their very first line, Virgil's *Eclogues* pitch back and forth, admitting and then resisting the themes of the pastoral and those of the epic: love and pleasure and the individual experience of nature against the power of death, the inevitability of loss, and the injustice of politics and war, the rise and fall of empires, and the collective need for order. (A fact lost neither on those who had for decades asked what the implications were of Bishop Berkeley's assertion that now "westward the course of empire takes its way," to America;[22] nor on Humboldt himself, since he had used Teneriffe and the Andes to speak about the origins of European colonialism as well as the structure of nature.)[23] As one critic has recently argued, from the time of the "Virgilian *Vitae*" in classical antiquity to the end of the nineteenth century, scholars of Virgil have tended to "impose on the poet's life a strong pattern of linear development, a teleology which constructs the *Aeneid* as the simultaneous closure—ideological and narrative—of Virgil's life and his writings. Within this pattern, which distinguishes Virgil from his contemporaries and makes of him a paradigm for his successors, the *Eclogues*, the *Georgics*, and the *Aeneid* become part of one text, which we might call 'the Book of Virgil,' or . . . 'the poetic career'" of Virgil. For Virgil implies that the breadth of his biographical experience links "the heroic epic with its bucolic and didactic predecessors" in a hierarchy of genres that parallels the hierarchy found in society. It is in this sense that "the texts of Virgil come to stand for all possible forms of human life and expression."[24]

Thoreau's exposure to the *cursus honorum* began early on. His instructors at Harvard assumed the existence of a canon of great poets who were to be studied and emulated. Not least among these was Virgil. This is, in part, why Thoreau was required to read all of his verse for the Harvard entrance examination,[25] and then, after matriculating, as part of "the regular classical course,"[26] to read him all again.[27] For even the more up-to-date and pedagogically effective members of Harvard's culturally conservative faculty took the view that Virgil—though he lost prestige relative to Homer in Europe throughout Thoreau's lifetime—remained important because of his place in the literary canon and the extent of his influence over the centuries. For example, both Boylston Professor of Rhetoric and Oratory Edward Tyrell Channing's classes and informal discussions emphasized Virgil's poetic achievements, and the resulting extent of his literary influence. In this respect, he was only surpassed among the ancients by Homer. Similarly, C. C. Felton, Eliot Professor of Greek, who also taught Thoreau, defined the example and influence of the poets of classical antiquity as being fundamentally moral in nature. Reading Virgil and Homer built character; this alone justified leaving the classics at the center of the College curriculum: for "the study of antiquity has a noble power to elevate the mind above the low passions of the present, by fixing its contemplations on the great and immortal spirits of the past." In the end, furthermore, this didactic side of Felton's thought predominated, outweighing his somewhat more typical early nineteenth-century views, e.g., his belief that "students should widen their interest beyond the purely linguistic, and become aware of 'the whole life of the people whose language was studied.'" In particular, Felton, who in 1834 published an annotated English edition of Friedrich August Wolf's text of the *Iliad*, taught his students to follow Wolf and to regard Greek literature, especially Homer, "in the light of contemporary European classical scholarship," which was "openly primitivist in orientation and partook of the Hellenism so widespread" during the Romantic period. The criticism Thoreau read in college by Friedrich von Schlegel and Henry Nelson Coleridge (nephew and son-in-law of the poet)—which Thoreau himself in turn wrote about in essays for Channing—likewise emphasized the "primitive." For it was "thanks to" F. A. Wolf, whose *Prolegomena to Homer* (1795) had revived the Homeric Question, that the portrait of "Homer the oral bard was reinstated in the scholarship of a period drawn to the notion that the voice of nature (or more often of the *Volk* or *ethnos*) was to be heard in 'primitive' poetry. All these developments, however, Wolf's contribution included, still found room for a Homer who—at least potentially—had a biography." Homer, like Virgil, was, therefore, still more than anything else, a poet to be emulated, and while Coleridge's *Greek Classic Poets* summarized the scholarship of the day on the Homeric Question, it was written for the didactic purpose of enabling students "to form a more just and liberal judgment of the characters and merits of the Greek Poets."[28] When combined with his training in modern foreign languages, which introduced him to writers from Dante and Ariosto to Goethe, as well as with his reading in the classic English poets (especially Spenser and Milton), by the time he graduated Thoreau had a high view of the literary calling and yet too, a deferential view toward the poetic achievements of the past. This did not lessen his own ambition to be the equal of these great authors, however. Indeed, "when Emerson delivered his rousing call for a new age in American letters" in the "American Scholar," which he read to "Thoreau's graduating class in the summer of 1837, its effect on Thoreau must have been" to confirm and corroborate his current course of action, since "he was already preparing himself to carry out the duties of Emerson's scholar, especially that of 'preserving and communicating . . . melodious verse.'"[29]

Moreover, his undergraduate writings openly invoke the *cursus honorum* and allied concepts. For instance, a January 1837 essay written for Channing describes Milton's "L'Allegro" and "Il Penseroso" as welcome relief from the political and religious controversies of the poet's later years. Thoreau in particular mentions Milton's vatic calling and the Virgil-like teleology of his career toward epic when he characterizes these two poems, in an allusion to the invocation of the Holy Spirit in *Paradise Lost*, Book 1, as "the flights of one who," even as a youth, "was contemplating to soar 'Above the Aonian mount', a heavenward and unattempted course."[30] Similarly, in another undergraduate essay on "Sublimity," Thoreau describes Milton's prophetic powers, saying that scenes like the battle in Heaven in *Paradise Lost* illustrate "the sublimest efforts of the poet and the painter. The trump which shall awake the dead is the creation of poetry . . . ."[31] Then, "three days after commencement he summarized and recorded his approval of the poet-prophet concept by quoting in his commonplace book part of the closing passage of Sidney's *Defense of Poesy*." Sidney not only defines the poet as a *vates* and a seer, he recommends "the reading of Virgil for the making of an 'honest man' and the reading of Homer and Hesiod for the discovery of mythological truth," which may embody all knowledge.[32]

After 1837, Thoreau developed these undergraduate interests.[33] For example, we see him, at a time when his interest in Virgil seems to have peaked, repeatedly taking up two positions of great relevance to "A Walk to Wachusett." First, he adopts the classic stance of a writer placing himself within the tradition of the *cursus honorum*, admitting his indebtedness to predecessors like Homer and Virgil, yet also claiming equality with them—including the right to adapt the tradition (e.g., by adding Humboldt to his pantheon of the great and the good). As Paul Alpers puts it, ". . . a conventional song is a song sung for you . . . and that you in turn sing or sing back: this is the particular emphasis or inflection of Virgilian pastoral;" for "in pastoral poetry, the model for close imitation is the singing contest, in which the challenge for the second singer is to accept the terms set by the first singer and at the same time establish his own images or voice or claims. Virgil takes up Theocritus as one shepherd answers another, by giving his own version of the song in his predecessor's poem." Dante and Spenser and Milton do the same vis-à-vis their predecessors, and in "Wachusett," albeit now in prose, Thoreau follows their example.[34]

One of his first *Dial essays*, "Dark Ages," conventionally applauds the art and poetry of antiquity but then declares that we have equal opportunity today to see and to do great things:

> What is near to the heart of this generation is fair and bright still. Greece lies outspread fair and sun-shiny in floods of light, for there is the sun and day-light in her literature and art. Homer does not allow us to forget that the sun shone—nor Phidias, nor the Parthenon. . . . There has always been the same amount of light in the world. . . . Always the laws of light are the same, but the modes and degrees of seeing vary. The gods are partial to no era, but steadily shines their light in the heavens, while the eye of the beholder is turned to stone. There is but the eye and the sun from the first. The ages have not added a new ray to the one, nor altered a fibre of the other.[35]

"Homer, Ossian, Chaucer" (1843) declares the *Iliad* among "the wisest" of books, one unequalled in modern times. Yet Thoreau ends the passage urging his own generation to try to do better anyway: "The mythological system of the ancients, and it is still the only mythology of the moderns, the poem of mankind . . . seems to point to a time when a mightier genius inhabited the earth. But man is the great poet, and not Homer nor Shakspeare; and our language itself, and the common arts of life are his work. Poetry is so universally true and independent of experience, that it does not need any particular biography to illustrate it . . . ."[36]

Likewise, Thoreau virtually begins his *Journal* praising Virgil for the last three lines of *Eclogue 6*. Significantly, this eclogue is all about the generic choices that both Thoreau and Virgil had to make early in their careers. It opens with Virgil's description of how his muse had ordered him to abandon his early attempts at writing an epic and to write pastoral instead;[37] and it ends with his seeming obedience to that command, as he drives his sheep back into the fold, the very portrait of the shepherd/poet. Yet the rest of *Eclogue 6* in fact either combines the two genres or presents us with pastoral poetry that is reminiscent of epic. In terms of form and style, for instance, Michael C. J. Putnam claims that here Virgil creates "a new union between Callimachus and Theocritus, between narrative poetry and customary pastoral procedure."[38] Furthermore, lines 12–83 not only closely resemble the *Aeneid*, they include a vatic poet *manqué* (Silenus, drunk with wine rather than with the muses' inspiration, yet cognizant still of both past and future);[39] a Hesiod-like epic catalogue on the creation and nature of the cosmos, which also owes something to "Apollonius [of Rhodes's] song of Orpheus"; and an *epyllion* [or short epic episode] on the story of Pasiphae and the bull.[40]

As this list suggests, by quoting this eclogue near the start of his *Journal*, Thoreau announces that he is aware of the *cursus honorum* and the choices earlier poets had made as they set out along that path, as well as of the subject matter (the cosmos) of his own prose epic to come. Moreover, Thoreau's *Journal* regularly mixes deference with self-assertion vis-à-vis past poetic masters. Two days later, for instance, in an entry later reworked into "Wachusett," he claims imaginative equality with Virgil due to their common human experience: "I would read Virgil, if only that I might be reminded of the identity of human nature in all ages. I take satisfaction in 'jam laeto turgent in palmite gemmae,' or 'Strata jacent passim sua quaeque sub arbore poma.' It was the same world, and the same men inhabited it."⁴¹ Similarly, he praises ancient Greece (February 16, 1838) as follows:

> In imagination I hie me to Greece as to enchanted ground. No storms vex her coasts—no clouds encircle her Helicon or Olympus—no tempests sweep the peaceful Tempe—or ruffle the bosom of the placid Aegean; but always the beams of the summer's sun gleam along the entablature of the Acropolis—or are reflected through the mellow atmosphere from a thousand consecrated groves and fountains. Always her sea-girt isles are dallying with their zephyr gusts—and the low of kine is heard along the meads—and the landscape sleeps—valley—and hill—and woodland—a dreamy sleep. Each of her sons—created a new heaven and a new earth for Greece.⁴²

And he can then declare (January 29, 1840) that we must stand in awe of Homer, and Aeschylus, and the rest: "The Greeks were stern but simple children in their literature. We have gained nothing by the few ages which we have the start of them. This universal wondering at those old men is as if a matured person should discover that the aspirations of his youth argued a diviner life than the contained wisdom of his manhood." But in the end, Thoreau believes that anyone can look at human experience with "the common eye" and give it expression. "The Greeks had no transcendent geniuses like Milton and Shakespear—whose merit only posterity could fully appreciate. The social condition of genius is the same in all ages. Aeschylus was undoubtedly alone and without sympathy in his simple reverence for the mystery of the universe."⁴³

This applies to Virgil too. For example, on November 14, 1841, Thoreau describes his reaction to reading Gavin Douglas's translation of the *Aeneid* into sixteenth-century Scots, asserting that what "restores and humanizes antiquity" is the realization that the great writers of the past lack visionary priority over us: for "the heavens stood over the heads of our ancestors as near—as to us.—Any living word in these books abolishes the difference of time."⁴⁴ They lack such priority not only because of the commonality of human experience, but also because reading a true poem, like Homer's *Iliad*, restores us to our basic humanity and so, primitive clarity of insight: "we read him with a rare sense of freedom and irresponsibleness, as though we trod on native ground, and were autochthones of the soil."⁴⁵

Thoreau also adopted another stance relevant to "Wachusett": he repeatedly names nature and the reporting of facts (especially about nature) as his own goal and that of the writers he admires. One can see this second theme in Thoreau's Harvard writings. For example, his review for Channing of H. N. Coleridge's book approvingly notes that "Shakspeare is justly styled the 'poet of nature'—here is the secret of his popularity—his was no ideal standard—man was his hobby. It was one of the characteristics of his genius that it adapted itself to the reality of things, and was on familiar terms with our feelings."[46] Later, after graduation, in "Homer, Ossian, Chaucer," he says that Homer ". . . is as serene as nature, and we can hardly detect the enthusiasm of the bard. It is as if nature spoke."[47] It is the descriptiveness of great literature that Thoreau prizes. Consider Goethe's *Die Italienische Reise*, whose style he describes in a December 8, 1837 *Journal* passage as follows:

> He is generally satisfied with giving an exact description of objects as they appear to him, and his genius is exhibited in the points he seizes upon and illustrates. His description of Venice and her environs as seen from the Marcusthurm, is that of an unconcerned spectator, whose object is faithfully to describe what he sees, and that too, for the most part, in the order in which he saw it. It is this trait which is chiefly to be prized in the book—even the reflections of the author do not interfere with his descriptions.[48]

Only eight days later, he famously outlines the "empirical holism" of Humboldt's methodology by asserting that "The fact will someday flower out into a truth. The season will mature and fructify what the understanding had cultivated."[49] But then, on March 5, 1838, in a long passage, he also applies the same principal to the style of Homer's epic poetry, which he says is ever grounded in being "humanly observant" of the facts and letting the "very truth" of things arise out of those facts.[50] Thoreau returns to this aspect of Homer later, at greater length, in his *Journal* during September and October of 1838, writing in similar fashion.[51] His view in general is that "books are to be attended to as new sounds merely. . . . They are but a new note in the forest. . . . Let me but put my ear close, and hear the sough of this book—that I may know if any inspiration yet haunts it."[52]

Thus, writing in a new bucolic prose centered on his own experience of nature, Thoreau felt that he could equal the achievement of earlier masters in verse like Virgil. He also felt empowered by yet another factor. For he did not share the "entrenched belief [of some modern scholars] that Romanticism was inherently suspicious of, even hostile to, traditional literary forms" and that as a result, there was "a radical generic breakdown in European Romanticism." Rather, his attitude toward convention and tradition was what Stuart Curran calls "Janus-visaged."[53] Thoreau felt the force of convention and formal tradition, yet also felt permitted to experiment and adapt his writing to new circumstances—a double perspective that he found empowering.

This stance was in keeping with the spirit of his age. In the case of the epic, for instance, Herbert F. Tucker argues that:

> By the 1780s literary minds in Britain had put behind them the grousing of crinkly Neoclassicism about epic's supersession by an inhospitable modernity. They had learned to believe that the sort of cultural work epic had always done remained to be done afresh under transitional circumstances that were not *ipso facto* different from the transitional circumstances that had prevailed in Virgil's time, and Homer's, and Moses'. The British reading classes were prepared to associate epic's cultural work with the advancing strength of a prosperous nation, to associate the national advance with the progress of civilization, and to receive with acclaim any complex narrative of elevated bearing that might enshrine these associations in a form suitable for transmission to posterity.[54]

Moreover, Christopher N. Phillips notes that "from the late seventeenth century, virtually all English dictionaries (including Johnson's and Webster's) ... defined epic largely as an adjective. To the extent that the dictionaries recorded actual usage of the word, 'epic' as a concept seems to have behaved more as a mode than a genre; the expansiveness of the adjectival gave epic a penchant for acquiring new resonances and referents."[55] "American literary engagements with epic form are myriad" during the years between the Revolution and the Civil War.[56] Whether traditional heroic poems or novels with epic trappings or non-fiction prose works that invoked the tradition to address matters broad in scope, "the epic impulse" was resilient. "Through the eighteenth and well into the nineteenth centuries ... Americans just would not stop writing epics—not out of nostalgia or from missing the memo that the epic was dead, but because the epic tradition continued to have relevance on a personal level, as well as in regional, national, and international contexts."[57]

Likewise, if "to write an epic, or to engage with an epic via other genres, is to place oneself in a genealogy dominated by central ancestral figures, primarily Homer, Virgil, and Milton . . . ",[58] then the same is true of the first stage in the *cursus honorum*, the pastoral. Michael McKeon affirms that "pastoral poetry didn't really die in 1800. Both the romantic poets and their heirs continue to write not only poetry they are content to call 'pastorals' but also poetry that lacks the name yet bears the deep imprint of pastoral preoccupation—preoccupation with the dream of a direct apprehension of nature as well as with the inevitability of nature's imaginative construction."[59] As we have seen, this revolutionary traditionalism involved being turned in two directions at once: toward the tradition and its conventions, and toward one's own concerns and ambitions.[60] Similarly, Curran points out that the temporal and geographic space in which the pastoral scene is itself set also forces pastoral poets to be "Janus-visaged": "The golden age is a cultural memory enshrined in a pastoral longing that acknowledges the irrecoverability of the past, the inevitability of its defeat, the inability to enclose the garden. At the same time, the pastoral paradigm through its very vulnerability counters its multitude of threats, minimizing their ultimate power, even subsuming them within the unending principle of life."[61] In the case of Virgil and those who (from Ovid on) have felt drawn to follow him along the *cursus honorum*, the double perspective of pastoral can still be found, despite the fact that "the sense of a totalising teleology within [his] *oeuvre* is stronger here than in any other ancient poet." For as Elena Theodorakopoulos observes, "the linear and teleological impulse" in which Virgil's life and his three main texts all seem to point toward the "generic and political climax" of the foundation of the Roman Empire foretold by the *Aeneid* is also "often fought against throughout the three texts, especially in the *Georgics* and in the *Aeneid*. Both of these texts ostensibly celebrate the achievements of Octavian/Augustus; both therefore ostensibly share a sense of ideological closure. Yet recent interpretations have shown that neither text has to be read as ultimately committing itself to empire. The *Aeneid* in particular struggles violently against the linear and seemingly inevitable triumph of epic teleology," instead, at times reasserting the alternative perspective of the *Eclogues*, "an Italian landscape which is not yet part of the public world of epic," even as that landscape is threatened from without by the forces of civil war and political ambition.[62]

In "A Walk to Wachusett" Thoreau takes up a "Janus-visaged" stance toward each of these three questions as they presented themselves to him at the beginning of his career. As one newly entered into the vatic tradition of the *cursus honorum*, he offers deference toward his predecessors (Homer, Virgil, Humboldt, and the rest) even as he proclaims his equality with and independence from them. Likewise, he hints at the eventual subject of his literary and scientific efforts—a portrait of the cosmos that will emerge out of his own experience—but for now, he postpones fulfilling that epic ambition to pursue writing on a more pastoral scale, pieces like this excursion that are (as Glenn W. Most terms them) "small, unambitious, [and] personal." This illustrates both the methodology of Humboldt's "empirical holism" that Thoreau was beginning to explore, and his understanding of the literary tradition of the *cursus honorum* and how it might be adapted to serve new needs and apprehend new intellectual concepts. Finally, in writing a "Janus-visaged" excursion Thoreau hints broadly at what his stance will be toward his traditional role as a prophetic poet and his new one as a student of the cosmos.

Thoreau begins by appending a poem to the end of the first paragraph of "A Walk to Wachusett" addressed to Homer's "Olympus," Virgil's "Etrurian and Thessalian hills," and Humboldt's "more modern Andes and Teneriffe," as well as to "Monadnock, and the Peterboro' hills" on his own horizon, looking out from "the Concord cliffs." Since mountaintops are traditionally places of inspiration and vision, and of decision and dedication, this implicitly asserts Thoreau's participation in the vatic tradition as an equal to, not a subordinate of, Homer, Virgil, and Humboldt. So too does his proclamation of the "frontier strength" of this (his own) visionary landscape, which like Olympus and the other peaks, stands its ground, encircling him "with grand content" (lines 1–2).[63] Thoreau then deploys an epic simile for these ever-searching mountains borrowed from *Paradise Lost*:

> As when far off from sea a fleet descried
> Hangs in the clouds, by equinoctial winds
> Close sailing from Bengala, or the isles
> Of Ternate and Tidore, whence merchants bring
> Their spicy drugs: they on the trading flood
> Through the wide Ethiopean to the Cape
> Ply stemming nightly toward the pole. So seemed
> Far off the flying fiend.
>
> (*Paradise Lost* 2.636–43)[64]

> Like some vast fleet,
> Sailing through rain and sleet,
> Through winter's cold and summer's heat;
> Still holding on, upon your high emprise,
> Until ye find a shore amid the skies;
> Not skulking close to land,
> With cargo contraband,
> For they who sent a venture out by ye
> Have set the sun to see
> Their honesty.
> Ships of the line, each one,
> Ye to the westward run,
> Always before the gale,
> Under a press of sail,
> With weight of metal all untold.
>
> (lines 6–20)

In creating this simile, which describes Satan[65] as he voyages past Sin and Death, amidst Chaos and Old Night, in search of Eden and revenge, Milton had done two things: first, he had invoked the general practice in epic poems of reworking epic similes used by one's predecessors;[66] and second, he was in particular "thinking of Aeneas' storm-tossed voyage from Troy" at the start of Virgil's *Aeneid*. However, Milton did so not in order to affirm empire and authority but to give voice to his own seventeenth-century republican "hostility to human aspirations to imperial dominion." If we credit authorial intention at all here, "the only searcher after an empire" in *Paradise Lost* "is the devil himself,"[67] and as Sir William Empson notes, there is also a mirage-like quality to Milton's deployment of multiple perspectives in the simile.[68] This critique of empire is one, furthermore, as we have seen, that Virgil himself makes recessively throughout his poetry, notwithstanding his dominant commitment to order and *imperium*.

Thoreau, in then—perhaps at the suggestion of Wordsworth[69]—further recycling the simile from Milton, and in connecting it with Virgil, is once more in dialogue with the literary tradition. But he is also telling us something about his own intended epic subject matter and why he will not pursue it now. As Thoreau goes on to say, he only "seem[s] to feel" the mountains' inspiration (line 21); at most, the peaks before him represent "unappropriated strength" and "unhewn primeval timber" that may "one day" be "fit for the stanchions of a world / Which through the seas of space is hurled" (lines 29–35). We may imagine that this walking tour to Wachusett will lead to a vision of the nature of the cosmos, emerging out of the pastoral dream of an almost lost golden age:

> I fancy even
> Through your defiles windeth the way to heaven:
> And yonder still, in spite of history's page,
> Linger the golden and the silver age;
> Upon the laboring gale
> The news of future centuries is brought,
> And of new dynasties of thought,
> From your remotest vale.
>
> (lines 50–57)

Of that possibility, Mount Wachusett (lines 58 ff.) is a solitary reminder and embodiment, its "far blue eye / A remnant of the sky," and symbol of the "rational holism" of Emerson and Goethe; but Thoreau's sight of it is by now partial, interrupted by other truths; and his assertion of kinship with nature in the poem is more a *desideratum* than an actual achievement. The pull of the epic and its ideology, strong in the *cursus honorum* model, pushes Thoreau toward closure with regard to his own high theme, the nature of the cosmos, but it is an impulse that he feels must be resisted, at least in this excursion. To be sure, Thoreau confesses that he and his companion "at length, like Rasselas, and other inhabitants of happy valleys," impelled by the hunger of the imagination, "resolved to scale the blue wall which bound the western horizon, though not without misgivings, that thereafter no visible fairy land would exist for us." They do begin their walk to Wachusett with hopes of romantic visionary experiences amidst the mountains. But we also know how Johnson's tale ends: having experienced much and traveled far, Imlac and his companions decide to return to the happy valley. And so, Thoreau reassures us that "we will not leap at once to our journey's end, though near, but imitate Homer, who conducts his reader over the plain, and along the resounding sea, though it be but to the tent of Achilles." Following Johnson's example, Thoreau puts his faith in coming to terms with empirical reality and human nature, proclaiming: "in the spaces of thought are the reaches of land and water, where men come and go. The landscape lies far and fair within"—here, and not on the visionary peaks—"and the deepest thinker is the farthest travelled."[70]

This is why the next part of the excursion opens describing in detail the sensations and experiences of the pair on the first morning of their journey, with no mention of their goal of climbing Mount

Wachusett. Thoreau wants to engage as many of his senses as possible (to hear the "lowing of kine" and see the hop fields, and the mower at his work, etc.), in order to assert the claims of studying the local as the way of seeing the universal, of focusing on experience in order to let insight and understanding emerge: "So soon did we, wayfarers, begin to learn that man's life is rounded with the same few facts, the same simple relations everywhere, and it is vain to travel to find it new."[71] Later the same day, having reached "the highlands," with Wachusett before them, they rest and read, not Humboldt's biography, but Virgil's *Aeneid*. However, they only get as far as Book 1, line 7 ("—atque altæ mœnia Romæ /—and the walls of high Rome"). Significantly, the lesson they draw is how relevant Virgil remains in the nineteenth century, not because of Rome, empire, war, or heroic perseverance—the themes behind the first seven lines of Virgil's epic—but because of "the identity of human life in all ages."

Thoreau declares, "we are both the children of a late age, and live equally under the reign of Jupiter." He then illustrates this by quoting *Georgics* 1.131–35 in English: "He shook honey from the leaves, and removed fire, / And stayed the wine, everywhere flowing in rivers, / That experience, by meditating, might invent various arts / By degrees, and seek the blade of corn in furrows, / And strike out hidden fire from the veins of the flint."[72] Though it run athwart what some modern scholars say about this part of the first *Georgic*,[73] Thoreau's aim here is to show that Virgil's human experience was like our own, and that this is what makes him valuable even today. By contrast, if Roman history and myth be not confirmed by our personal experience; if "the very children in the school we had that morning passed, had gone through her wars, and recited her alarms, ere they had heard of the wars of neighboring Lancaster," then we will be trapped by history, unable to see any pattern emerge or to apply any lessons it may teach. In such a case, "the old world stands serenely behind the new, as one mountain yonder towers behind another, more dim and distant. Rome imposes her story," giving us no space to write our own tales based upon our own experience. "The roving eye still rests inevitably on her hills," not on the more immediate Concord cliffs, "and she still holds up the skirts of the sky on that side, and makes the past remote."[74]

Indeed, the rest of the excursion suggests that though Thoreau and his companion are on a visionary quest up a sacred mountainside, the actual landscape through which they travel and the journey as they experience it constantly separate themselves from the literary conventions of such ascents. As Adams and Ross suggest:

> "A Walk to Wachusett" at first seems a miniature *Week on the Concord and Merrimack Rivers* . . . . the narrator here is a "pilgrim" (*Excursions* 34), the goal of whose journey is a mountaintop associated with heaven and with gods (37, 39). Before ascending the mountain, he consumes a sacrificial meal of raspberries and spring water, "thus propitiating the mountain gods, by a sacrifice of their own fruits" (37). Once on top of the mountain, though, the pilgrim does not hint at a mystical experience or even a sensuous one but, logocentrically and anticlimactically, reads Virgil and Wordsworth and surveys the geography visible from the summit (38–39). He does not encounter a Spirit that pervades the mountains but instead meditates rather conventionally on "the hand which moulded their opposite slopes, making one to balance the other" (42)—another version of the Enlightenment's rational God. The journey remains in the eighteenth-century tradition, as suggested by the reference to *Rasselas* at the start (31), and by the moral about the elevated life tacked on at the end (45–46). . . . this essay is not very romantic . . . .[75]

While one might disagree with aspects of this characterization, Adams and Ross rightly argue that the literary language Thoreau deploys here is inadequate for describing his actual experience. Someday, Wachusett *may* be a sacred site, a visionary *locus*, a place of inspiration: "Who knows but this hill may one day be a Helvellyn, or even a Parnassus, and the Muses haunt here, and other Homers frequent the neighboring plains." But today, on Thoreau's trip up the hill, "our eyes rested on no painted ceiling, nor carpeted hall, but on skies of nature's painting, and hills and forests of her embroidery." Thoreau is saying that in this excursion he must at least postpone his epic ambitions to comprehend the cosmos and focus on nature as he experiences it, here and now, in all of its particularity. Mount Wachusett must first be regarded as what it "is, in fact, the observatory of the state,"[76] a place where we will be able to observe and experience phenomena, from birds, to clouds, to the stars, out of which a view of the whole may someday provisionally emerge. This is why the last five or six pages of the excursion leave the language of classical, Miltonic, and romantic poetry behind and describe the natural world and New England's own history as they are and in detail, in all their variety.

At the same time, though, we must remember that, here as elsewhere, the pressure of the *cursus honorum* pulls writers toward a kind of ideological and formal closure. This is why when evening comes, Thoreau and his fellow traveler remember Virgil again; but now, it is the very humane last two lines of *Eclogue 1*:

> Et jam summa procul villarum culmina fumant,
> Majoresque cadunt altis de montibus umbræ.
>
> And now the tops of the villas smoke afar off,
> And the shadows fall longer from the high mountains.[77]

These lines have domestic rather than imperial or triumphal associations, and they follow an act of kindness by Tityrus, secure in his lands, toward the homeless political exile, Meliboeus. Moreover, the end of this eclogue subverts the celebration of order and empire as the necessary compensations for the loss of pastoral innocence that Virgil elsewhere promotes, and that are at the core of all three genres in the *cursus honorum*. As Wendell Clausen says, "Virgil's sympathies are usually engaged on the side of defeat and loss; and here, in a poem praising Octavian, it is rather the dispossessed Meliboeus than the complacent Tityrus who more nearly represents Virgil. Yet Tityrus is not without compassion. What little he can he does."[78] Likewise, Theodorakopoulos argues, in these lines Virgil—though ever "Janus-visaged" and "not entirely committed to the model of progress" toward Augustan rule he elsewhere proclaims—also makes sure that we experience both "the death of an ideal 'Arcadian' Italy and the darkness which puts an end to all singing." By the end of the first Eclogue, the leisurely "shade" under which Tityrus lies at the beginning "(*Ecl. 1.* 4, *lentus in umbra*)" becomes transformed from being a symbol of "peaceful enclosure or shelter into" one that represents the "menacing darkness which envelops the landscape completely in *Ecl. 1.* 83 *maioresque cadunt altis de montibus umbrae* ('larger now the shadows are falling from the high mountains'). It contains also the destruction of pastoral innocence and the compensation offered by Rome and civilization." The first Eclogue ends not "with the triumph of epic and empire," but the loss of innocence, "exile and the end of poetry," silence and the shadows of the grave—"a shading toward dark that is universal." Because "all of Virgil's endings tend to look back to the final line of the First Eclogue, . . . Eclogue 1 is the beginning of the end, and the shadows that fall from its closure reach out over the entire corpus of Virgil's poetry."[79]

Thoreau's renunciation of epic ambition here is temporary, not absolute. He is as drawn as ever to the task of understanding the cosmos as it emerges out of "human life—now climbing the hills, now descending into the vales. From the summits he beholds the heavens and the horizon, from the vales he looks up to the heights again. He is treading his old lessons still, and though he may be very weary and travel-worn, it is yet sincere experience."[80] "Tomorrow," he seems to say (like Milton at the end of "Lycidas") he will "to fresh woods and pastures new," but not until he has prepared the ground, and learned the trades of being both a naturalist and a writer. As this suggests, Thoreau's texts have a complex intellectual heritage. "A Walk to Wachusett" reveals both a deep commitment to classical studies and excitement over his first encounter with Humboldt.[81] Moreover, in general, Thoreau like Darwin illustrates a tendency in mid-nineteenth-century nature writing "to resist" what Noah Heringman calls the "constraints of specialization that were just beginning to form in the early industrial era." "'Scientists themselves in their texts drew openly upon literary, historical and philosophical material as part of their argument,'" and "the disciplinary boundaries between literature and science" were "neither textually nor institutionally as solid as they may seem to be today."[82]

It is, therefore, not a matter of Thoreau after a certain point becoming a scientist and letting go of his other intellectual commitments. His interest in classical antiquity, for example, never faded, even as he became more engaged in scientific observation and speculation. In fact, though it is beyond the scope of this essay to discuss it in detail, the *cursus honorum* provides an outline to his subsequent career, with "Wachusett" and the other early excursions constituting his pastoral phase (punctuated by *A Week on the Concord and Merrimack Rivers*, his pastoral elegy for his brother, John); *Walden*, *The Maine Woods*, and *Cape Cod* then constitute a more didactic, georgic period; until, finally, the late *Journal* and writings like those found in *Faith in a Seed* mark his attempt at creating a comprehensive model of the universe on an epic scale. (The order and ways in which authors received the *cursus honorum* and applied it to their own careers is various and flexible.) In all three stages, the evidence suggests that Thoreau's new orientation toward what today we would call science did not efface his other interests; instead, it swept them up and arrayed them along a new front, now unified toward a new purpose. It was in a very literal sense, therefore, that he could list his occupation as "'literary and scientific'" on a questionnaire sent to him in 1853 by the American Association for the Advancement of Science.[83]

For example, William Batstone writes that "most interpreters have agreed that" in Virgil's *Georgics* "'didacticism about agriculture proves metaphor for didacticism about man.'"[84] Thoreau's *Walden* has similarly strong georgic elements,[85] but it uses didacticism about his personal experience of "life in the woods" as a metaphor for approaching life more generally. In line with this, the principal series of references to Homer in *Walden* occur in the "Reading" chapter. At first glance they may sound like a repetition of conservative early nineteenth-century defenses of the classical curriculum. "The reader," we are reassured, "may read Homer or Æschylus in the Greek without danger of dissipation or luxuriousness, for it implies that he in some measure emulate their heroes, and consecrate morning hours to their pages." Yet this restatement of the notion that the classics provide fit models on which to pattern our daily lives is quickly turned by Thoreau into a statement about their language, which has the transformative potency of "Nature" herself, and calls the reader "to read true books in a true spirit."[86] As such, it is part of his didactic call in *Walden* to reform the language, pressing it into more ancient and primitive and natural and spiritually potent shapes, so that we may come to see things as they are:

> Those who have not learned to read the ancient classics in the language in which they were written must have a very imperfect knowledge of the history of the human race; for it is remarkable that no transcript of them has ever been made into any modern tongue, unless our civilization itself may be regarded as such a transcript. Homer has never yet been printed in English, nor Æschylus, nor Virgil even,—works as refined, as solidly done, and as beautiful almost as the morning itself.... That age will be rich indeed when those relics which we call Classics, and the still older and more than classic but even less known Scriptures of the nations, shall have still further accumulated, when the Vaticans shall be filled with Vedas and Zendavestas and Bibles, with Homers and Dantes and Shakespeares, and all the centuries to come shall have successively deposited their trophies in the forum of the world. By such a pile we may hope to scale heaven at last.[87]

Thoreau, who, as Ethel Seybold long ago remarked, took "delight in the material simplicity of Homeric life," recommends that we study Homer and study nature in order "to realize" that simplicity for ourselves, allowing "the Homeric philosophy [to] spread out into" our "whole life."[88] Likewise, in his last works and late *Journal*, Thoreau turned to issues on a more universal scale, addressing the *epos* of the cosmos. It is appropriate, therefore, that the first thing one encounters in "The Dispersion of Seeds" is not a citation from Charles Darwin—that waits till page 3 of Thoreau's book—but a quotation from Pliny the Elder, telling us "that some trees bear no seed." "'The only ones,' says he, 'among the trees that bear nothing whatever, not so much as any seed even, are the tamarisk, which is used only for making brooms, the poplar, the Atinian elm [*Ulmus campestris* rarely does in England], and the alaternus'; and he adds that 'these trees are regarded as sinister [or unhappy, infelices] and are considered inauspicious.'" If this quotation had stood alone, one might think that Thoreau was invoking the *auctoritas* of a classical author. But he precedes it with a phrase dismissive of the Roman author's opinion, declaring that it merely "embodies the natural science of his time." This implies that *all* knowledge (including ours) is contingent and that intellectual developments and historical change may undermine all claims. "Facts" are by-products of experience, and Pliny in this case neither observed closely enough nor drew the right conclusions from his observations.[89]

"The Dispersion of Seeds," for instance, thus opens by implicitly affirming that Thoreau's text is one written in accord with the values of the Enlightenment, preferring experience and reason over blind tradition and authority. It affirms the values that, along with developments in the history of science paved the way in the broadest sense for Charles Darwin's *Origin of Species*, which is quoted shortly afterwards. Yet significantly, in its "Janus-visaged" way, the presence of this quotation at the start of Thoreau's manuscript also asserts that Thoreau and Humboldt and Darwin are only the latest in a long line of those who have attempted to write encyclopedic accounts pulling together all their culture's knowledge about the world. (Today one might add Hawking, or Watson and Crick, or E. O. Wilson.) Pliny's *Historia Naturalis* is just such an epic account of the cosmos. As Trevor Murphy puts it, "it is crucial in this connection to recognize the essentially undidactic nature of the *Natural History*. Though it claims to transmit *encyclios paideia*" ["the totality of human knowledge," or what we would today call general education], it teaches nothing, and unlike "the great majority of other Roman technical writings," "it makes no claims to instruct any individual in any career or course of self-improvement." At the same time, however, ". . . it is very much concerned to put the natural world at the reader's disposal."⁹⁰ "'*Learned*, comprehensive, as full of variety as nature herself,'" it tried, as best it could under ancient conditions, to apply the test of observation to the study of nature and to discover patterns of relationships arising from that. Later, as one enters the seventeenth century, despite "an increasing tendency to question Pliny's authority as a scientific source, the *Historia Naturalis*' classification of material into a universal system foreshadowed the great classificatory systems of the eighteenth century naturalists such as Buffon and Linnaeus."⁹¹ And so, Thoreau, "Janus-visaged" as ever, begins by acknowledging his indebtedness to Pliny even as he disagrees with this ancient source.

Moreover, Pliny's work exhibits an imperial subtext and a Virgilian connection. His natural history explicitly endorsed "Virgil's belief concerning the imperial mission" of his poetry; therefore, "Pliny's is a nationalistic encyclopedia, just as the *Aeneid* and the *Georgics* are national poems." In particular, "early in the third book (38) . . . Pliny wrote "a passionate *laudatio Italiae*, which has much in common with Virgil's encomium in the second *Georgic* (136 ff.) and with the verses in the sixth [book of the] *Aeneid* (851 ff.) proclaiming the mission of Rome." Pliny's emulation of "the mystical sense of the Roman destiny" and "love of Italy" which comprise the emotional component of Virgil's ideology of *imperium* throughout his *cursus honorum*⁹² is all the more striking when one remembers that elsewhere he is all too ready to criticize Virgil for mistakes as an observer and scientist. As this suggests, Thoreau was writing a modern scientific account of the dispersion of seeds that also invoked the *cursus honorum*. He regarded literature as a record of human experience equal to the natural sciences and so, relevant to his task as a scientist. Thoreau does not toss his classical learning into the dustbin of intellectual history. Pliny makes other appearances later in the text, usually because they are confirmed by Thoreau's empirical observation.

It is as if the classics and the humanist project in education stretching back to Tudor times gets a new lease on life. It is now subsumed in the process of observing and gathering data about natural phenomena, finding patterns, and drawing conclusions, activities that dominate "Dispersion of Seeds." Pliny, not Homer or Virgil or Milton, is the author quoted now. It is not the search for primitive historic origins and linguistic purity but the facts about seeds and rebirth through the natural cycle that represent Thoreau's goal. Yet—and it is a supremely vital "yet"—classical studies live on, working in tandem with biology and ecology to define Thoreau's intellectual purpose and methods in a complex way. Rather than acquiescing in the fragmentation of knowledge into separate disciplines that was going on all around him, Thoreau, like Pliny the Elder, makes a plea here for *encyclios paideia*, what Mary Beagon calls "a non-specialized but wide-ranging knowledge which, as it were, makes its pupils properly educated and decent citizens. . . . a general education preliminary to more specialized studies." His model would have been familiar to any of the writers of the great tradition, for it was nothing less than the vision that inspired Sidney and Milton and Wordsworth: ". . . the idea of the educated man, who is neither an intellectual expert nor a specialist," but "a cultivated man of action."[93]

Bronson Alcott said as much about his friend, Henry Thoreau, as the latter lay dying in 1862. Writing in the *Atlantic Monthly*, he claimed that Thoreau had "the profoundest passion for" nature "of any one living; and had the human sentiment been as tender from the first, and as pervading, we might have had pastorals of which Virgil and Theocritus would have envied him the authorship, had they chanced to be his contemporaries. As it is, he has come nearer the antique spirit than any of our native poets, and touched the fields and groves and streams of his native town with a classic interest that shall not fade." In his love of nature and close observation of its smallest details, he belongs "to the Homeric age,—is older than pastures and gardens, as if he were of the race of heroes, and one with the elements. . . . the native New- Englander . . . an indigenous American, untouched by the Old Country, unless he came down from Thor, the Northman; as yet unfathered by any, and a non-descript in the books of natural history," he made "possible and actual the virtues of Sparta and the Stoics. . . . Plutarch would have made him immortal in his pages, had he lived before his day. . . . Perhaps we have had no eyes like his since Pliny's time. . . . Seldom has a head circumscribed so much of the sense of Cosmos as this footed intelligence. . . . Nature, poetry, life,—not politics, not strict science, not society as it is,—are his preferred themes. . . . When he goes hence, then Pan is dead, and Nature ailing throughout."[94]

Notes

1. Kristen Case and K. P. Van Anglen, Introduction, in *Thoreau at Two Hundred: Essays and Reassessments*, ed. Case and Van Anglen (Cambridge: Cambridge University Press, 2016), 2–3. Thoreau's famous declaration about the universe is quoted from Henry D. Thoreau, *Walden*, ed. J. Lyndon Shanley, *The Writings of Henry D. Thoreau*,

ed. William L. Howarth (Princeton: Princeton University Press, 1971), 100–1. Quotations from the Princeton Edition of Thoreau retain the wording and spelling of that edition. Latin and Greek texts that Thoreau read sometimes differ from modern editions. For a discussion of Thoreau and Free Soil in the terms mentioned, see James S. Finley, "A Free Soiler in His Own Broad Sense: Henry David Thoreau and the Free Soil Movement," in Case and Van Anglen, *Thoreau at Two Hundred*, 31–44.
2. Sir Isaiah Berlin, "The Pursuit of the Ideal," in *The Crooked Timber of Humanity: Chapters in the History of Ideas*, ed. Henry Hardy (New York: Knopf, 1991), 5–6.
3. Ibid., 8–14.
4. David M. Robinson, *Natural Life: Thoreau's Worldly Transcendentalism* (Ithaca: Cornell University Press, 2004), 2.
5. Robert Sattelmeyer, *Thoreau's Reading: A Study in Intellectual History with Bibliographical Catalogue* (Princeton: Princeton University Press, 1988), 25.
6. Robinson, *Natural Life*, 29.
7. Ibid., 18.
8. Ibid., 5.
9. Lawrence Buell, *Literary Transcendentalism: Style and Vision in the American Renaissance* (Ithaca: Cornell University Press, 1973), 188.
10. Sattelmeyer, *Thoreau's Reading*, 48, which goes on to describe Thoreau's early interest in travel writing, as does John Aldrich Christie, *Thoreau as World Traveler* (New York: Columbia University Press and the American Geographical Society, 1965).
11. Sherman Paul, *The Shores of America: Thoreau's Inward Exploration* (Urbana: University of Illinois Press, 1958), 157.
12. Stephen Adams and Donald Ross, Jr., *Revising Mythologies: The Composition of Thoreau's Major Works* (Charlottesville: University Press of Virginia, 1988), 6–7.
13. Ibid., 28–29.
14. Henry David Thoreau, "A Walk to Wachusett," in *Excursions*, ed. Joseph J. Moldenhauer, *The Writings of Henry D. Thoreau*, ed. Elizabeth Hall Witherell (Princeton: Princeton University Press, 2007), 29.
15. Laura Dassow Walls, *The Passage to Cosmos: Alexander von Humboldt and the Shaping of America* (Chicago: University of Chicago Press, 2009), 261–62.
16. Laura Dassow Walls, *Seeing New Worlds: Henry David Thoreau and Nineteenth-Century Natural Science* (Madison: University of Wisconsin Press, 1995), 4–5. Joel Porte, *Thoreau and Emerson: Transcendentalists in Conflict* (Middletown, CT: Wesleyan University Press, 1965) treats Thoreau's empiricism in a more philosophical context.
17. Laura Dassow Walls, "Science and Technology," in *The Oxford Handbook of Transcendentalism*, ed. Joel Myerson, Sandra Harbert

Petrulionis, and Laura Dassow Walls (Oxford: Oxford University Press, 2010), 579.
18. Discussed in Walls, *Passage to Cosmos*, 262.
19. Walls, *Seeing New Worlds*, 120. Walls discussed her reasons for focusing exclusively on Humboldt in an email response to an early draft of this essay.
20. Glenn W. Most, "Virgil," in *The Classical Tradition*, ed. Anthony Grafton, Glenn W. Most, and Salvatore Settis (Cambridge, MA: Belknap Press of Harvard University Press, 2010), 968.
21. One passage in *Paradise Lost* in which Milton frames his vaunting, vatic ambitions is his invocation of the Holy Spirit at the beginning of Book 3.1–55. His magisterial control of perspective here flows from his technical mastery of the "Janus-visaged" stance [see below, n30] from which he writes. He begins by looking backward toward the classical past, trying to imitate one of the conventions of the Homeric and Virgilian epic: the invocation of a higher power to aid the poet in telling his tale. Yet this deference toward antiquity and classical tradition is short-lived. For Milton must turn to face the fact that as a Christian, he did not believe in the Muses. He then innovates, replacing the Muses with the Holy Spirit as the source of his inspiration. Simultaneously, he also remakes the epic invocation into a different form, one perhaps more appropriate to its author's reformed sensibilities: the lyric voice of the faithful Christian at prayer, struggling to follow God's commands and seeking help to fulfill his vocation as a poet. It is a position that is "Janus-visaged" in that the poet looks back to the literary past and then looks forward to individual, interior spiritual experience as the source of poetic inspiration. It is also a position typical of John Milton's "revolutionary traditionalism" as well as that later on of the romantics, and other nineteenth-century writers who patterned their careers after Virgil.
22. The history and development of the ancient concept of the *translatio*, in which nations become the seat of and then lose control over empire and civilization through a cyclic pattern of rise and fall that drives the geographical *locus* of world power and high culture ever westward, is described in detail in *The First Decline and Fall* (Cambridge: Cambridge University Press, 2003), vol. 3 of *Barbarism and Religion*, J. G. A. Pocock's recently completed, six-volume commentary on Edward Gibbon's *Decline and Fall of the Roman Empire*. While Humboldt, as Walls claims, may well have encouraged this idea's popularity in America, and to a degree tied it in the popular mind to the concept of manifest destiny (*Seeing New Worlds*, 105), it was, in fact, already widely disseminated in the new world from about 1765 on; see Ernest Lee Tuveson, *Redeemer Nation: The Idea of America's Millennial Role* (Chicago: University of Chicago Press, 1968), 94–95. By the 1840s, furthermore, regardless of Humboldt's influence, various

ideological configurations of the *translatio* were common in American political thought, fiction, literary criticism, and art, from James Fenimore Cooper's *Leatherstocking Tales* and *The Crater* to Thomas Coles's *Course of Empire* paintings; for instances of this see J. G. A. Pocock, *The Machiavellian Moment: Florentine Political Thought and the Atlantic Republican Tradition* (Princeton: Princeton University Press, 1975); John P. McWilliams, Jr., *Political Justice in a Republic: James Fenimore Cooper's America* (Berkeley: University of California Press, 1972); K. P. Van Anglen, "Before Longfellow: Dante and the Polarization of New England," *Dante Studies* 119 (2001): 155–86; William L. Vance, *America's Rome*, 2 vols. (New Haven: Yale University Press, 1989), esp. 1:1–113; and Barbara Novak, *Nature and Culture: American Landscape and Painting, 1825–1875*, rev. ed. (Oxford: Oxford University Press, 1995), esp. 3–20. Thoreau famously slightly misquotes Berkeley in "Walking"; see Thoreau, "Walking," *Excursions*, 575 (Textual Note to 201.2).

23. As Walls shows in many places in *Passage to Cosmos*, the old charge that Humboldt was an apologist for imperialism and colonial expansion is far off the mark.
24. Elena Theodorakopoulos, "Closure: the Book of Virgil," in *Cambridge Companion to Virgil*, ed. Charles Martindale (Cambridge: Cambridge University Press, 1997), 155.
25. Sattelmeyer, *Thoreau's Reading*, 3.
26. Ethel Seybold, *Thoreau, the Quest, and the Classics* (New Haven: Yale University Press, 1951), 23.
27. Discussed ibid., 22–26; and by Sattelmeyer, *Thoreau's Reading*, 7–9.
28. Descriptions of the formative influence on Thoreau of faculty members like Channing, Felton, and the German-educated George Ticknor and Henry Wadsworth Longfellow (albeit only briefly in the last case, since Longfellow's first term at Harvard was Thoreau's last), as well as of the romantic philhellenic scholarship he was exposed to in H. N. Coleridge and Schlegel include Sattelmeyer, *Thoreau's Reading*, 8–9; Robert D. Richardson, Jr., *Henry Thoreau: A Life of the Mind* (Berkeley: University of California Press, 1986), 13–14; and Henry D. Thoreau, *Translations*, ed. K. P. Van Anglen, *The Writings of Henry D. Thoreau*, ed. Elizabeth Hall Witherell (Princeton: Princeton University Press, 1986), 184–87. Sattelmeyer, *Thoreau's Reading*, 203, lists Felton's edition of F. A. Wolf's text of the *Iliad* (1834). Thoreau wrote his review of Henry Nelson Coleridge's book in 1836 for Channing; see Henry David Thoreau, "The Greek Classic Poets," *Early Essays and Miscellanies*, ed. Joseph J. Moldenhauer and Edwin Moser with Alexander C. Kern, *The Writings of Henry D. Thoreau*, ed. William L. Howarth (Princeton: Princeton University Press, 1975), 50–58. Robert Fowler, "The Homeric Question," in *The Cambridge Companion to Homer*, ed. Robert Fowler (Cambridge: Cambridge University Press,

2004), 220–32, summarizes the history and opposing positions in the controversy over the authorship and composition of the texts traditionally claimed for "Homer"; as does Robert Lamberton, "Homer," in Grafton et al., *Classical Tradition*, 449–52. Lamberton summarizes the state of the Question during Thoreau's lifetime (see passage quoted above, 450).
29. Sattelmeyer, *Thoreau's Reading*, 14–15.
30. Henry David Thoreau, "'L'Allegro' & 'Il Penseroso,'" in *Early Essays*, 78; British punctuation follows source. Thoreau quotes part of the opening invocation in Book 1 of *Paradise Lost*, lines 15–16. It is a most "Janus-visaged" part of Milton's poem, because it both replicates the formal conventions of the traditional epic and announces that it will surpass Homer, Virgil, et al. due to its openly Christian subject matter. "The Aonian mount" refers to Helicon, home of the muses; "unattempted" is taken from the next line, "Things unattempted yet in prose or rhyme," which in turn translates "Ariosto's boast in *Orlando Furioso* 1.2: *Cosa non detta in prose mai, né in rima*"; see John Milton, *Paradise Lost*, ed. Alistair Fowler (London: Longman's, 1968), 43, nn 1.15 and 1.16.
31. Henry David Thoreau, "Sublimity," *Early Essays*, 95.
32. Seybold, *Thoreau*, 27–28. Sidney's treatise is also known as *An Apologie for Poetry*.
33. Sattelmeyer, *Thoreau's Reading*, 26.
34. Paul Alpers, *What Is Pastoral?* (Chicago: University of Chicago Press, 1996), 85–86. This stance is sometimes openly stated, as it is in Dante's "Inferno," Canto 4, or it can be declared surreptitiously through the creation of a rich texture of allusion and revision (e.g., see the treatment of Virgil's *Eclogue 6* in Charles Martindale's "Green Politics: the Eclogues" in Martindale, *Cambridge Companion to Virgil*, 111–15).
35. Henry D. Thoreau, "T. Pomponious Atticus as an Example," in *Early Essays*, 145–46; British spelling of "fibre" follows source.
36. Henry D. Thoreau, "Homer. Ossian. Chaucer.," in *Early Essays*, 156–57. Like Emerson, Thoreau here and elsewhere sometimes uses variant spellings of "Shakespeare."
37. Brooks Otis, *Virgil: A Study in Civilized Poetry* (Oxford: Clarendon Press, 1963), 33 writes that "Virgil had originally . . . thought of writing a Roman epic (*res Romanae*) but gave up the attempt and turned instead to the *Bucolics*" (i.e., the *Eclogues*).
38. Michael C. J. Putnam, *Virgil's Pastoral Art: Studies in the Eclogues* (Princeton: Princeton University Press, 1970), 196. Thoreau could not, of course, have known that the opposition here for Virgil was specifically between "Callimachus' rejection of epic" and Theocritus's embrace of pastoral, because Callimachus's prefatory Aetia fragment 1 Pf. was only unearthed at Oxyrhincus and published by A. S. Hunt (P. Oxy. XVII 2079) in 1927; but his training in rhetoric and Greek

poetry certainly allowed him to see the difference between the conventions of narrative and pastoral verse; see Wendell Clausen, *A Commentary on Virgil: Eclogues* (Oxford: Clarendon Press, 1994), 174–75 and esp. 174n1.

39. Putnam, *Virgil's Pastoral Art*, 201 (paraphrase).
40. Clausen, *Commentary*, 175–77 discusses Silenus's paradoxical characterization. Otis, *Virgil*, 125–43 and ibid., 195–221 detail how this portion of *Eclogue 6* resembles the *Aeneid*.
41. Henry D. Thoreau, *Journal, Volume 1: 1837–1844*, ed. Elizabeth Hall Witherell et al., *The Writings of Henry D. Thoreau*, ed. Elizabeth Hall Witherell (Princeton: Princeton University Press, 1981), 13–14. Perhaps the reason Thoreau takes such satisfaction in these two lines (48, 54) from *Eclogue 7* is that they are part of a singing contest between Corydon and Thyrsis centered on a description of the four seasons and the power of love as manifested in nature that is itself a kind of miniature but complete description of the cosmos.
42. Thoreau, *Journal 1*, 29.
43. Ibid., 106–7; variant spelling of "Shakespeare" follows source.
44. Ibid., 343. See Eric A. Havelock, "*The Aeneid* and Its Translators," *Hudson Review* 27, no. 3 (1974): 338–70.
45. Thoreau, *Journal 1*, 332.
46. Henry David Thoreau, "Writer's Nationality," in *Early Essays*, 71; variant spelling of "Shakespeare" follows source.
47. Thoreau, "Homer. Ossian. Chaucer.," in *Early Essays*, 154–55.
48. Thoreau, *Journal 1*, 16.
49. Ibid., 19.
50. Ibid., 33–34.
51. Ibid., 55–58.
52. Ibid., 310.
53. Stuart Curran, *Poetic Form and British Romanticism* (Oxford: Oxford University Press, 1986), 4–5, 28. Coleridge, Byron, Hazlitt, Shelley, and even Wordsworth all exemplify this. Erasmus Darwin, a lesser but highly influential poet, tried to fuse science and poetry.
54. Herbert F. Tucker, *Epic: Britain's Heroic Muse, 1790–1910* (Oxford: Oxford University Press, 2008), 48.
55. Christopher N. Phillips, *Epic in American Culture, Settlement to Reconstruction* (Baltimore: Johns Hopkins University Press, 2012), 2–4.
56. Ibid., 6.
57. Ibid., 8.
58. Ibid., 6.
59. Michael McKeon, "The Pastoral Revolution," in Kevin Sharpe and Steven N. Zwicker, eds., *Refiguring Revolutions: Aesthetics and Politics from the English Revolution to the Romantic Revolution* (Berkeley: University of California Press, 1998), 289.

60. Failure to see that among the Romantics, including Thoreau, innovation and breaking with the past are among the most traditional expectations placed on a poet who follows the *cursus honorum* is at the heart of the critical misapprehensions behind Robert Klevay's argument in "The Reader and the Classics in Thoreau's *Walden*," *The Concord Saunterer: A Journal of Thoreau Studies*, n.s., 19–20 (2011/2012): 192–222.
61. Curran, *Poetic Form*, 89.
62. Theodorakopoulos, "Closure," 156–57. Twentieth-century perspectives on Virgil consider his ideological commitments to have been more divided; see Theodore Ziolkowski, *Virgil and the Moderns* (Princeton: Princeton University Press, 1983). Annabel Patterson, *Pastoral and Ideology: Virgil to Valéry* (Berkeley: University of California Press, 1987), 8, lists the ideologies that compete with Virgil's celebration of empire and authority in the *Eclogues*.
63. Thoreau, "Wachusett," 29–31.
64. Milton, *Paradise Lost*, 119–20.
65. The complicated association between visionary romantic experiences atop mountains and Satan's transgressive journey in Book 2 of *Paradise Lost* is taken up again by Thoreau in recounting his own climb up Mount Ktaadn [Thoreau's spelling] in *The Maine Woods*; see K. P. Van Anglen, *The New England Milton: Literary Reception and Cultural Authority in the Early Republic* (University Park: Pennsylvania State University Press, 1993), 217–23.
66. Although it does not specifically discuss this simile in a comparativist context, a classic study of the epic simile from Homer to the Romantics is Sir Christopher Ricks, *Milton's Grand Style* (Oxford: Oxford University Press, 1963), esp. 118 ff.
67. Colin Burrow, "Virgils, from Dante to Milton," in Martindale, *Cambridge Companion to Virgil*, 87–89. Thoreau also has in mind various similes used to describe "the wanderings of Odysseus"; see Penelope Wilson, "Homer and English Epic," in Fowler, *Cambridge Companion to Homer*, 278–80.
68. Sir William Empson, *Some Varieties of Pastoral* (London: Chatto and Windus, 1950), 171.
69. In the *Preface* to his *Poems* (1815), Wordsworth connects this passage in *Paradise Lost* to a similar use of the image of "hanging" in Virgil's *Eclogue 1* in order to illustrate the higher power of the imagination. The passage is found in the Wordsworth edition Thoreau owned: the 1839 Boston reimpression published by James Monroe and Company in Boston of *The Complete Poetical Works*, ed. Henry Reed (Philadelphia: Kay, 1837), xi–xii. Sattelmeyer, *Thoreau's Reading*, 294, is not clear on this point; instead, see Joseph J. Moldenhauer, "*Walden* and Wordsworth's Guide to the English Lake District," in *Studies in the American Renaissance: 1990*, ed. Joel A. Myerson (Charlottesville: University Press of Virginia, 1990), 261–62.

70. Thoreau, "Wachusett," 31; British spelling of "travelled" follows source.
71. Ibid., 31–33.
72. Ibid., 33–34.
73. For example, William Batstone, "Virgilian *Didaxis*: Value and Meaning in the *Georgics*," in Martindale, *Cambridge Companion to Virgil*, 137–38, argues that the long, paradoxical, contradictory *theodicy* of which this is a part is typical of so much of what one finds in Virgil due to its Janus-visaged ambivalence. On the one hand, "the Jovian dispensation had promised *artes*" as compensation for our lost innocence, "and *artes* we got: navigation, astrology, hunting, fishing, and tools. But as the Jovian age moves forward toward the present, *labor* itself expands its scope and ethical implications" till we realize that we have lost almost as much as we have gained.
74. Thoreau, "Wachusett," 34.
75. Adams and Ross, *Revising Mythologies*, 29. For the sake of uniformity, the parenthetical page references provided by Adams and Ross to "A Walk to Wachusett" here have been changed to refer to the Princeton Edition, as has, in one case, the punctuation of a quotation. It should be noted that as he comes down the mountain, Thoreau uses the phrase "*gellidæ valles*" in a sentence that separates his experience on Wachusett even more from the literary conventions in play here (*Excursions*, 35). As Jeffrey S. Cramer points out in his recent edition of this excursion, this phrase is a quotation from Claudian's *De Consulatu Stilichonis* 1:131; see Henry David Thoreau, *Essays: A Fully Annotated Edition*, ed. Jeffrey S. Cramer (New Haven: Yale University Press, 2013), 52. However, the appearance of this phrase in Claudian is in a very different context, and so, despite Thoreau's quotation from another work by this late antique author in his *Journal* in 1841 (*Journal 1*, 310) and his allusion to that work at one point in "Excursion to Canada" (*Excursions*, 98), one is tempted to look elsewhere, especially as in all three cases the specific edition of Claudian or anthology containing excerpts of him from which Thoreau quoted is still unknown. Given Thoreau's orientation toward Virgil in "Wachusett," an allusion to *Georgics* 2.488 putting the phrase back into the nominative is also possible here, especially given the relevance of Virgil's Lucretian sentiments in line 490: "Happy is he who knows the causes of things . . . ."
76. Thoreau, "Wachusett," 41.
77. Ibid., 39.
78. Clausen, *Commentary*, 32–33.
79. Theodorakopoulos, "Closure," 162–64.
80. Thoreau, "Wachusett," 45.
81. Similarly, "Natural History of Massachusetts" reflects Thoreau's discovery of empirical science yet also his rootedness in Linnaeanism and in older notions of elite cultural authority. See K. P. Van Anglen, "True

Pulpit Power: 'Natural History of Massachusetts' and the Problem of Cultural Authority," in Myerson, *Studies in the American Renaissance*, 119–47.

82. Noah Heringman, ed., *Romantic Science: The Literary Forms of Natural History*, SUNY Studies in the Long Nineteenth Century, ed. Pamela K. Gilbert (Albany: State University of New York Press, 1998), 4. Heringman quotes Gillian Beer, *Darwin's Plots: Evolutionary Narrative in Darwin, George Eliot, and Nineteenth-Century Fiction* (London: Routledge, 1983), 7.

83. The questionnaire was sent to Thoreau along with a request that he renew his membership in the AAAS. He demurred. While Laura Walls thinks that this had to do with the nature of Thoreau's scientific views, which were in "the tradition of empirical holism" associated with S. F. Baird, Asa Gray, and Humboldt himself, "not the idealist/positivist science being institutionalized in America by [Louis] Agassiz" (*Seeing New Worlds*, 146–47); I think that Thoreau was pointing out a more basic complexity in his career identity; cf. Laura Dassow Walls, "'The Value of Mutual Intelligence:' Science, Poetry, and Thoreau's Cosmos," in Case and Van Anglen, *Thoreau at Two Hundred*, 188–90.

84. Batstone, "Virgilian *Didaxis*," 125; he quotes A. J. Boyle, *Virgil's Ascraean Song: Ramus Essays on the* Georgics (Berwick, Australia: Aureal Publications, 1979), 37.

85. Brilliantly evoked by Laura Dassow Walls in her 2011 Annual Address to the Thoreau Society entitled, "Henry David Thoreau: Writing the Cosmos," *The Concord Saunterer: A Journal of Thoreau Studies*, n.s., 19–20 (2011/2012): 1–21.

86. Thoreau, *Walden*, 100–1. Paul Giles, "American Literature and Classical Consciousness," in *The Oxford History of Classical Reception in English Literature, Vol. 4 (1790–1880)*, ed. Norman Vance and Jennifer Wallace, says that Thoreau here sounds "for all the world like the most conventional kind of Oxbridge tutor," commending "the reading of the classics as a cleansing operation, a way of regenerating the spirit by stripping away everything that is superfluous." He concludes that Thoreau's appreciation of the Classics stemmed from his Victorian elitism and prudery combined with his proleptic adherence to the principles of the New Criticism (4:171–72). While there is more truth to each of these characterizations than many Thoreauvians would like to admit, Thoreau's interest in classical texts as examples of the redemptive and transformative power of primitive language and vision seems more relevant here.

87. Thoreau, *Walden*, 103–4.

88. Seybold, *Thoreau*, 50–51.

89. Henry D. Thoreau, "The Dispersion of Seeds," in *Faith in a Seed*, ed. Bradley P. Dean (Washington, DC and Covello, CA: Shearwater Books, 1993), 23–24.

90. Trevor Murphy, *Pliny the Elder's* Natural History: *the Empire in the Encyclopedia* (Oxford: Oxford University Press, 2004), 211–12; translation of Greek phrase used by Pliny in his preface to the *Historia Naturalis* is from Murphy 33.
91. Mary Beagon, "Pliny the Elder," in Grafton et al., *Classical Tradition*, 744–45; at the beginning of the quotation here, she cites Pliny the Younger's tribute to his uncle's great work (Letters 3.5).
92. Richard T. Bruère, "Pliny the Elder and Virgil," *Classical Philology* 51, no. 4 (1956): 229–30.
93. Mary Beagon, *Roman Nature: the Thought of the Elder Pliny*, Oxford Classical Monographs (Oxford: Oxford University Press, 1992), 12–13.
94. A. Bronson Alcott, "The Forester," *The Atlantic Monthly* 9 (1862): 443–45.

Bibliography

Adams, Stephen, and Donald Ross, Jr. *Revising Mythologies: The Composition of Thoreau's Major Works*. Charlottesville: University Press of Virginia, 1988.

Alcott, A. Bronson. "The Forester." *The Atlantic Monthly* 9 (1862): 443–45.

Alpers, Paul. *What Is Pastoral?* Chicago: University of Chicago Press, 1996.

Batstone, William. "Virgilian *Didaxis*: Value and Meaning in the *Georgics*." In *Cambridge Companion to Virgil*, edited by Charles Martindale, 125–44. Cambridge: Cambridge University Press, 1997.

Beagon, Mary. "Pliny the Elder." In *The Classical Tradition*, edited by Antony Grafton, Glenn W. Most, and Salvatore Settis. Cambridge, MA: Belknap Press of Harvard University Press, 2010.

———. *Roman Nature: the Thought of the Elder Pliny*. Oxford Classical Monographs. Oxford: Oxford University Press, 1992.

Beer, Gillian. *Darwin's Plots: Evolutionary Narrative in Darwin, George Eliot, and Nineteenth-Century Fiction*. London: Routledge, 1983.

Berlin, Sir Isaiah. "The Pursuit of the Ideal." *The Crooked Timber of Humanity: Chapters in the History of Ideas*, edited by Henry Hardy, 1–19. New York: Knopf, 1991.

Boyle, A. J. *Virgil's Ascraean Song: Ramus Essays on the Georgics*. Berwick, VIC, Australia: Aureal Publications, 1979.

Bruère, Richard T. "Pliny the Elder and Virgil." *Classical Philology* 51, no. 4 (1956): 229–30.

Buell, Lawrence. *Literary Transcendentalism: Style and Vision in the American Renaissance*. Ithaca: Cornell University Press, 1973.

Burrow, Colin. "Virgils, from Dante to Milton." In *Cambridge Companion to Virgil*, edited by Charles Martindale, 79–90. Cambridge: Cambridge University Press, 1997.

Case, Kristen, and K. P. Van Anglen, "Introduction". In *Thoreau at Two Hundred: Essays and Reassessments*, edited by Kristen Case and K. P. Van Anglen, 1–13. Cambridge: Cambridge University Press, 2016.
Christie, John Aldrich. *Thoreau as World Traveler.* New York: Columbia University Press and the American Geographical Society, 1965.
Clausen, Wendell. *A Commentary on Virgil: Eclogues*. Oxford: Clarendon Press, 1994.
Curran, Stuart. *Poetic Form and British Romanticism*. Oxford: Oxford University Press, 1986.
Empson, Sir William. *Some Varieties of Pastoral*. London: Chatto and Windus, 1950.
Finley, James S. "A Free Soiler in His Own Broad Sense: Henry David Thoreau and the Free Soil Movement." In *Thoreau at Two Hundred*, edited by Kristen Case and K. P. Van Anglen, 31–44. Cambridge: Cambridge University Press, 2016.
Fowler, Robert, ed. *Cambridge Companion to Homer*. Cambridge: Cambridge University Press, 2004.
———. "The Homeric Question." In *Cambridge Companion to Homer*, edited by Robert Fowler, 220–32. Cambridge: Cambridge University Press, 2004.
Giles, Paul. "American Literature and Classical Consciousness." In *The Oxford History of Classical Reception: Volume 4 (1790–1880)*, edited by Norman Vance and Jennifer Wallace, 159–83. Oxford: Oxford University Press, 2015.
Grafton, Antony, Glenn W. Most, and Salvatore Settis, eds. *The Classical Tradition*. Cambridge, MA: Belknap Press of Harvard University Press, 2010.
Gruber, Christian P. "The Education of Henry Thoreau, Harvard 1833–1837." Ph.D. Dissertation, Princeton University, 1953.
Havelock, Eric A. "*The Aeneid* and Its Translators." *Hudson Review* 27, no. 3 (1974): 338–70.
Heringman, Noah, ed. *Romantic Science: The Literary Forms of Natural Science*. SUNY Studies in the Long Nineteenth Century, edited by Pamela K. Gilbert. Albany: State University of New York Press, 1998.
Jackson, Virginia. *Dickinson's Misery: A Theory of Lyric Reading*. Princeton: Princeton University Press, 2005.
Klevay, Robert. "The Reader and the Classics in Thoreau's *Walden*." *The Concord Saunterer: A Journal of Thoreau Studies* 19–20 n.s. (2011/2012): 192–222.
Lamberton, Robert. "Homer." In *The Classical Tradition*, edited by Antony Grafton, Glenn W. Most, and Salvatore Settis, 449–52. Cambridge, MA: Belknap Press of Harvard University Press, 2010.
Martindale, Charles, ed. *Cambridge Companion to Virgil*. Cambridge: Cambridge University Press, 1997.

———. "Green Politics: the *Eclogues.*" In *Cambridge Companion to Virgil*, edited by Charles Martindale, 107–24. Cambridge: Cambridge University Press, 1997.

McKeon, Michael. "The Pastoral Revolution." In *Refiguring Revolutions: Aesthetics and Politics from the English Revolution to the Romantic Revolution*, edited by Kevin Sharpe and Steven N. Zwicker, 267–89. Berkeley: University of California Press, 1998.

McWilliams, John P., Jr. *Political Justice in a Republic: James Fenimore Cooper's America*. Berkeley: University of California Press, 1972.

Milton, John. *Paradise Lost*. Edited by Alistair Fowler. London: Longman, 1968.

Moldenhauer, Joseph J. "*Walden* and Wordsworth's Guide to the English Lake District." In *Studies in the American Renaissance: 1990*, edited by Joel A. Myerson, 261–92. Charlottesville: University Press of Virginia, 1990.

Most, Glenn W. "Virgil." In *The Classical Tradition*, edited by Antony Grafton, Glenn W. Most, and Salvatore Settis, 965–69. Cambridge, MA: Belknap Press of Harvard University Press, 2010.

Murphy, Trevor. *Pliny the Elder's* Natural History: *the Empire in the Encyclopedia*. Oxford: Oxford University Press, 2004.

Novak, Barbara. *Nature and Culture: American Landscape and Painting, 1825–1875*, rev. ed. Oxford: Oxford University Press, 1995.

Otis, Brooks. *Virgil: A Study in Civilized Poetry*. Oxford: Clarendon Press, 1963.

Patterson, Annabel. *Pastoral and Ideology: Virgil to Valéry*. Berkeley: University of California Press, 1987.

Paul, Sherman. *The Shores of America: Thoreau's Inward Exploration*. Urbana: University of Illinois Press, 1958.

Phillips, Christopher N. *Epic in American Culture: Settlement to Reconstruction*. Baltimore: Johns Hopkins University Press, 2012.

Pocock, J. G. A. *The First Decline and Fall*. vol. 3 of *Barbarism and Religion*. Cambridge: Cambridge University Press, 2003.

———. *The Machiavellian Moment: Florentine Political Thought and the Atlantic Republican Tradition*. Princeton: Princeton University Press, 1975.

Porte, Joel. *Thoreau and Emerson: Transcendentalists in Conflict*. Middletown, CT: Wesleyan University Press, 1965.

Putnam, Michael C. J. *Virgil's Pastoral Art: Studies in the* Eclogues. Princeton: Princeton University Press, 1970.

Richardson, Robert D., Jr. *Henry David Thoreau: A Life of the Mind*. Berkeley: University of California Press, 1986.

Ricks, Sir Christopher. *Milton's Grand Style*. Oxford: Oxford University Press, 1963.

Robinson, David M. *Natural Life: Thoreau's Worldly Transcendentalism*. Ithaca: Cornell University Press, 2004.

Sattelmeyer, Robert. *Thoreau's Reading: A Study in Intellectual History with Bibliographical Catalogue*. Princeton: Princeton University Press, 1988.

Seybold, Ethel. *Thoreau, the Quest, and the Classics*. New Haven: Yale University Press, 1951.

Theodorakopoulos, Elena. "Closure: the Book of Virgil." In *Cambridge Companion to Virgil*, edited by Charles Martindale, 155–65. Cambridge: Cambridge University Press, 1997.

Thoreau, Henry D. "The Dispersion of Seeds." In *Faith in a Seed*, edited by Bradley P. Dean, 23–210. Washington, DC and Covello, CA: Shearwater Books, 1993.

———. *Early Essays and Miscellanies*. Edited by Joseph J. Moldenhauer and Edwin Moser, with Alexander E. Kern. *The Writings of Henry D. Thoreau*, edited by William L. Howarth. Princeton: Princeton University Press, 1975.

———. *Essays: A Fully Annotated Edition*, edited by Jeffrey S. Cramer. New Haven: Yale University Press, 2013.

———. *Journal, Volume 1: 1837–1844*, edited by Elizabeth Hall Witherell et al. *The Writings of Henry D. Thoreau*, edited by Elizabeth Hall Witherell. Princeton: Princeton University Press, 1981.

———. *Translations*. Edited by K. P. Van Anglen. *The Writings of Henry D. Thoreau*, edited by Elizabeth Hall Witherell. Princeton: Princeton University Press, 1986.

———. *Walden*. Edited by J. Lyndon Shanley. *The Writings of Henry D. Thoreau*, edited by William L. Howarth. Princeton: Princeton University Press, 1971.

Tucker, Herbert F. *Epic: Britain's Heroic Muse, 1790–1910*. Oxford: Oxford University Press, 2008.

Tuveson, Ernest Lee. *Redeemer Nation: The Idea of America's Millennial Role*. Chicago: University of Chicago Press, 1968.

Van Anglen, K. P. "Before Longfellow: Dante and the Polarization of New England." *Dante Studies* 119 (2001): 155–86.

———. *The New England Milton: Literary Reception and Cultural Authority in the Early Republic*. University Park: Pennsylvania State University Press, 1993.

———. "True Pulpit Power: 'Natural History of Massachusetts' and the Problem of Cultural Authority." In *Studies in the American Renaissance: 1990*, edited by Joel A. Myerson, 119–47. Charlottesville: University Press of Virginia, 1990.

Vance, William L. *America's Rome*. 2 vols. New Haven: Yale University Press, 1989.

Walls, Laura Dassow. *Emerson's Life in Science: The Culture of Truth*. Ithaca: Cornell University Press, 2003.

———. "Henry David Thoreau: Writing the Cosmos." *The Concord Saunterer: A Journal of Thoreau Studies*. 19–20 n.s. (2011/2012): 1–21.

———. *The Passage to Cosmos: Alexander von Humboldt and the Shaping of America*. Chicago: University of Chicago Press, 2009.

———. "Science and Technology." In *Oxford Handbook of Transcendentalism*, edited by Joel Myerson, Sandra Harbert Petrulionis, and Laura Dassow Walls, 572–82. Oxford: Oxford University Press, 2010.

———. *Seeing New Worlds: Henry David Thoreau and Nineteenth-Century Natural Science*. Madison: University of Wisconsin Press, 1995.

Wilson, Penelope. "Homer and English Epic." In *Cambridge Companion to Homer*, edited by Robert Fowler, 272–86. Cambridge: Cambridge University Press, 2004.

Wordsworth, William. *The Complete Poetical Works*. Edited by Henry Reed. Philadelphia: Kay, 1837. Reprinted Boston: James Monroe, 1839.

Ziolkowski, Theodore. *Virgil and the Moderns*. Princeton: Princeton University Press, 1983.

Chapter 7

Pilgrimage and Epiphany: The Psychological and Political Dynamics of Margaret Fuller's Mythmaking
Jeffrey Steele

During the 1840s, Margaret Fuller used her extensive knowledge of classical mythology to shape her understanding of the self, society, and social change. Beginning her literary career as a leading member of the Transcendentalist circle in New England, Fuller later moved to New York and then to Europe, as she expanded her literary horizons as a front-page columnist for Horace Greeley's *New-York Tribune*. In New England, part of Fuller's first conversation class for Boston women was devoted to the subject of mythology. Her comments in those discussions, as well as citations in essays later published in the *Dial*, reveal her extensive knowledge of Hesiod, Ovid, Virgil, the Greek tragedians, Apuleius, Plutarch, and other ancient authors. In many of her essays and in her poetry, Fuller used mythical models (such as Minerva, Diana, and Isis) to measure the contours of the self and the limits of human potential. Passages in *Woman in the Nineteenth Century* reveal that she identified closely with the figures of Cassandra (a misunderstood prophetess) and Iphigenia (Agamemnon's daughter, who was sacrificed to obtain favorable winds for the war-fleet sailing to Troy). Throughout her career, Fuller's use of mythological figures was also shaped by her profound identification with alchemical patterns that she found in the mystical writings of Jacob Boehme, Novalis, Goethe, and others. Articulating figures of aspiration, Fuller's syncretic mythical images projected idealized states of personal and social being, as they crystallized in the crucible of her imagination. In a profound sense, Fuller was both a disseminator of the classical mythic tradition and a mythmaker in her own right. Myth, in her hands, is not a dead set of ancient narratives but rather an ongoing tradition that she reinvigorates, as she channels, combines, and reframes mythical energies that mesh with her vision of personal and cultural transformation.

In order to change the conditions of being it is necessary to reconfigure the cultural imaginary, which defines the limits of the self and of human potential. Fuller encountered a new image of selfhood in Emerson's concept of "self-reliance." Like Emerson, she firmly believed that the self's independence was firmly anchored in the direct intuition of inner creative power, which Emerson in his essay "Self-Reliance" characterized as the "god . . . within." As William Henry Channing put it in his *Memoirs*, "Transcendentalism was an assertion . . . of the immanence of Divinity in instinct," and an "exalting conception of the godlike nature of the human spirit" (M 2:12–13). Intuiting the divine forces lying in the depths of the psyche, both Emerson and Fuller believed that one gained the capacity to authorize oneself, sidestepping individuals and institutions that had lost the impulse to grow and change. Such independence, Fuller asserted throughout *Woman in the Nineteenth Century*, was of preeminent importance for women, who needed to realize that they, as well as men, were "in themselves the possessors of . . . immortal souls" and could escape the "precepts" of "guardians" that had "impeded" their minds with "doubts" (EMF 272–73). Achieving "self-reliance" or "self-dependence," Fuller affirmed, women would no longer "learn their rule from without" but, instead, "unfold it from within" (262). But as we shall see, Fuller had to learn how to *feminize* the idea of "self-reliance" before she could make it completely her own. In the process, she transposed Emerson's most famous concept into a different key, using a tonal range that he at times had difficulty hearing. As Fuller adapted the concept of self-reliance and made it her own, she found an important clue in classical mythology, where powerful images of womanhood supplemented Emerson's limited vocabulary of female transformation.

Fuller's multifaceted engagement with mythology is evident as early as her 1839–40 Conversations, which supplied the building blocks for her mythic explorations over the next five years. Initially, in her discussions, Fuller used the study of myth as an intellectual tool that allowed her to address questions of culture, aesthetics, and sexual politics. Most notably, she used the opening classes of her first set of Conversations to generate a new psychological vocabulary. In a November 1839 description of her class, she linked different classical deities to different psychological faculties: Jupiter representing "the will"; Mercury, "the Understanding"; and Apollo, "genius" (L 2:102). In the record left by Elizabeth Peabody, Fuller interprets classical mythology in psychological terms. "Other forms of the mythology—as Jupiter—Juno—Apollo—&c.," she asserts, "are great instincts—or ideas—or facts of the internal constitution separated & personified." The "fables & forms of Gods," she added, "were the reverence for & idealization of the universal sentiments of religion—aspiration—intellectual action of a people whose political & aesthetic life had become immortal."[1] Ensuing conversations focused on Apollo and "the history of Genius," Venus, the narrative of Cupid and Psyche, and both the practical and creative power of Minerva.[2]

Judging from the fullness of Elizabeth Peabody's account, Fuller paid special attention to the narrative of Cupid and Psyche found in Apuleius's *The Metamorphosis, or Golden Ass*. Rescued from the envy of Venus (because of Psyche's great beauty) and from a sacrificial death, Psyche (in Fuller's summary) is carried "into a palace among the mountains," where she "was visited nightly by Cupid . . . who became her husband on the condition that she should never ask his name or explore his person." But one night, after having been incited to curiosity by her malicious sisters, Psyche is "induced to examine him while sleeping by the light of a lamp—But bending over him in extacy [sic] at his beauty she spilled a drop of boiling oil on his shoulder & he awoke & flew away from her."[3] Psyche then spends the remainder of her time on earth searching for her lost husband, until finally she is made immortal and reunited with her lost love, Cupid. Fuller and her friends read this myth as a spiritual allegory of loss and recovery, which showed how we are "tempted away from our own deepest spiritual affections."[4] In the words of the translator Thomas Taylor (whose works were well known to Fuller), this "fable" was "designed to represent the lapse of the soul from the intelligible world to the earth."[5] Such an interpretation resonated nicely with the Gnostic mythology of spiritual descent into a world of matter that Fuller was learning from Bronson Alcott. But even more important, it imagined the recovery of divine power as a pilgrimage in search of the missing beloved. As Meg McGavran Murray perceptively notes in her recent biography, Fuller imagined herself as engaged in a "lifelong quest for self-insight and love."[6] In October 1840, for example, she wrote to her confidant William Henry Channing that she was "a poor wandering pilgrim" (L 2:173). Given her identification with mythological narratives of pilgrimage, Fuller would have greeted with approbation Channing's reflection that "Transcendentalism, as viewed by its disciples, was a pilgrimage from the idolatrous world of creeds and rituals to the temple of the living God in the soul" (M 2:13). But she supplemented Channing's Christian emphasis with a pantheon of classical deities. As Caroline Healey Dall records, Fuller said "that when she [w]as first old enough to think about Christianity, she cried out for her dear old Greek gods. Its [Christianity's] spirituality seemed nakedness."[7]

The figure of pilgrimage oriented many of the classical myths that most attracted Fuller. She knew well the account of Isis searching for her lost consort Osiris and the narrative of Demeter searching for Persephone—the basis of the two most prominent Hellenistic mystery religions: the cult of Isis and the Eleusinian Mysteries. We know from Dall's transcript of Fuller's 1841 Conversation class that Fuller had begun to link these myths to each other, at the same time that she interpreted them syncretically as different dimensions of a central classical "goddess." "Ceres, Persephone, and Isis, as well as Rhea, Diana, and so on," Dall records Fuller as observing,

> seem to be only modifications of one enfolding idea—a goddess accepted by all nations, and not peculiar to Greece. The pilgrimages of the more prominent of these goddesses, Ceres [Demeter] and Isis, seem to indicate the life which loses what is dear in childhood, to seek in weary pain for what after all can be but half regained. Ceres regained her daughter, but for half the year. Isis found her husband, but dismembered.[8]

In her reading notes on mythology, Fuller stressed the resemblances that she perceived between different female divinities. She noted, for example, the "Various apparitions and aspects of the Magna Dea," and found in the "whole history of Ceres . . . the Isis, the Magna Dea, the feminine principle, par excellence, of all the divinest dynasty."[9] Fuller's syncretic reading of classical goddess myths accords with recent interpretations of Hellenistic myths. In Apuleius's *The Golden Ass*, Luther H. Martin observes, the final reunion of Psyche with Cupid parallels the larger frame narrative that culminates in the transformative reunion of Lucius with the goddess Isis. Both moments of epiphany "effect a transformation of existence by offering a religious alternative to a dangerous and chaotic world" ruled by Fortuna.[10] These mythic narratives, along with the mystery cults associated with them, center on the narratives of pilgrimage in which "transformed deities are represented as wanderers whose journeys lead them from an existence of humanlike suffering to a transformed existence as celestial saviors."[11]

We know from evidence in Fuller's writing that she tended to read such myths creatively, as she synthesized them into her own mythic narratives. For example, she combined the myths of Orpheus and Demeter (searching in the Underworld, respectively, for Eurydice and Persephone) in her poem included in *Woman in the Nineteenth Century*. "Each Orpheus must to the depths descend /," Fuller writes, ". . . Must make the sad Persephone his friend, / And buried love to second life arise." More radically, she reversed the gender roles in the myth of Orpheus and Eurydice. In the classical myth, Orpheus (like Demeter searching for Persephone) journeys to the underworld to rescue his wife Eurydice. But in her version, Fuller makes Eurydice the hero and Orpheus the victim needing rescue. "Meanwhile not a few believe," she observes, "that the time has come when Eurydice is to call for an Orpheus, rather than Orpheus for Eurydice" (EMF 252). As Fuller was to discover during the year and a half following her 1839–40 Conversations, such narratives of loss and recovery would hold a special resonance for her, as she began to transcend a painful series of emotional losses by constructing a powerful mythology of pilgrimage and epiphany. Like Psyche, Demeter, Isis, and Orpheus (later recast as "Eurydice"), she needed to recover from the depths of the psyche the divine "child that is lost," "a love that cannot be crucified" (EMF 250). Myths of the lost child (Persephone), the consort (Osiris), and the spouse (Cupid, Eurydice) blended together in the crucible of Fuller's imagination.

Fuller first learned how to represent her *own* mythic vision of self-reliance during the remarkable spiritual crisis that she passed through during the fall and winter of 1840–41, a period that she later identified as the "era of illumination in my mental life" (L 3:55). Experiencing a profound crisis precipitated by her sense of abandonment by her closest friends, she used her knowledge of myth to navigate the turbulent emotional and spiritual currents of her life. In October 1840, within days of the anniversary date of her father's death five years earlier, two of Fuller's most intimate friends, Samuel Gray Ward and Anna Barker, married each other. It is clear from Fuller's letters and journals that she was deeply involved with both individuals; she had earlier hoped for a proposal of marriage from Ward and was in love with Anna Barker. As the date of the Ward-Barker wedding approached, Fuller's intense feelings of abandonment were amplified by the approaching anniversary of her father's death. At this crucial moment, Fuller turned to her three closest friends, Caroline Sturgis, Ralph Waldo Emerson, and William Henry Channing, in the hope that they might help her sort out her momentous emotional reaction to the changes that were taking place in both her social life and her psyche. But as we know from Fuller's anguished letters, each one of them could only follow Fuller part way into the complicated psychological and mythical terrain that she had begun exploring. Forced by social circumstances into an unexpected isolation, Fuller began to map out her own pathway through the tangled labyrinth of her psychic being. What none of her friends completely understood was that this crisis was the moment when Fuller finally constructed for herself an effective model of self-reliance—one that she feminized by connecting it to the imaginative energy of powerful, woman-centered myths.

Following partly the footsteps of Emerson, Fuller looked for clues in the spiritual traditions of classical mythology, Platonic philosophy, European mysticism, and romantic literature. But she added to the equation an intense interest in the Western esoteric tradition found in Rosicrucianism, alchemy, and mystics such as Jacob Boehme. In addition, Fuller's reading for her first Conversation series on "Mythology" the previous year had exposed her to the great Goddess images of antiquity: for example, Greek and Roman images of Athena, Hera, and Diana. She encountered the exalted portrait of the goddess Isis at the end of Apuleius's *The Golden Ass* (a passage that Fuller later included as the first appendix to *Woman in the Nineteenth Century*), as well as the powerful myth of Demeter searching for her lost daughter Persephone. In a profound act of mythmaking, Fuller blended together symbols derived from these materials. Her guides in this process were German romantics such as Novalis and, especially, Johann Wolfgang Goethe, whose works contain profound references to the daemonic, alchemy, and the Rosicrucian mysteries. With the possible exception of Bronson Alcott, noted for his own mystical tendencies, no other American writer had read this particular combination of esoteric and mythical materials.[12] Although he knew many of Fuller's favorite authors (for example, Goethe and Plato), Emerson lacked Fuller's enthusiasm for such alternative spiritual traditions. It seems never to have occurred to him that Fuller might develop a competing model of self-reliance. As a result, he was unable to connect completely with the profound spiritual and literary growth that Fuller experienced in 1840 and 1841.

Much of the imaginative and emotional tension in Emerson's response lay in Fuller's unconventional approach to a spiritual problem that he thought he had already solved. The goal of Fuller's mythmaking was the same as Emerson's: to stabilize images of the inner divine power authorizing self-reliance. Like her fellow Transcendentalists,

Robert D. Richardson observes, "she was intensely interested in the idea that humanity has the seeds of divinity within itself . . . in short, that men and women can become as gods and goddesses."[13] Fuller's letters during this period reveal her use of mythical figures as such avatars of enlarged being. These figures enabled her to *generalize* the changes taking place in her being, by attaching them to mythic narratives and symbols that she hoped to communicate to others. Emerson, of course, also multiplied the terms he used to evoke his sense of the divine depths of the self, but he stopped far short of imagining them in female terms as the changing faces of an inner Goddess. Radically revising her friend's vision of the self's potential, Fuller challenged him to connect his thinking to mythical and esoteric sources that lay far outside his comfort level. The two of them, Emerson reflected in a letter to Fuller, spoke different languages and met as representatives of "foreign states, one maritime, one inland, whose trade & laws are essentially unlike."[14] Emerson's reluctance to learn Fuller's mythic language is painfully evident in the posthumous *Memoirs of Margaret Fuller Ossoli*. "[T]here was somewhat a little pagan about her," he snidely observes (M 1:219). She was "self-deceived by her own phantasms," he comments elsewhere. "In our noble Margaret," he continues, "her personal feeling colors all her judgment of persons, of books, of pictures, and even of the laws of the world. . . . This mere feeling exaggerates a host of trifles into a dazzling mythology" (M 1:279). What such comments reveal is that, in Emerson's case, Fuller's interest in Mediterranean mystery religions, alchemy, and mysticism largely fell on deaf ears.

Ironically, Fuller was taking Emerson's key idea—that it is necessary to follow the "gleams" of illumination into the depths of the self—and applying to it an intense imaginative and emotional pressure that pushed Emerson's imagery even further into a subterranean realm of psychic exploration. But despite Emerson's obvious distaste for Fuller's mystical bent, he possessed the intellectual integrity to acknowledge the importance to Fuller of her mythological and mystical impulses, which "gave a religious dignity to her thought" (M 1:309). Even though he lacked Fuller's imaginative investment, Emerson recorded the contours of her mythical language. Describing the iconography of her letters in the *Memoirs*, he observes: "Whole sheets of warm, florid writing are here, in which the eye is caught by 'sapphire,' 'heliotrope,' 'dragon,' 'aloes,' 'Magna Dea,' . . . 'stars,' and 'purgatory' . . ." (M 1:279). Given Emerson's own confessed inability to connect this imagery with any "universal experience" (that is, with emblems of patriarchal authority), he tends to dismiss it as so much mystical gibberish. However, the modern reader—exposed to a wide range of mythical and theological texts—should not be as quick to pass judgment. Most people acquainted with mythical narratives recognize the significance of the "dragon"—the hero's most formidable antagonist. As many scholars now recognize, references to flowers such as the "heliotrope" were part of the nineteenth-century language of flowers, a complex semiotic code in which flowers were linked to different sentiments. The "Magna Dea" (literally, the Great Mother Goddess) refers to the female divinities of classical antiquity—a profound site of feminist mythmaking since the nineteenth century, if not earlier. For example, it is striking that within twenty years of Fuller's death, her *male* acquaintance Thomas Wentworth Higginson published an essay on the feminist theological significance of goddesses in the 1869 *Atlantic Monthly*.[15] Finally, the reference to "sapphire" evokes both the semiotic code of talismanic gems and—more profoundly—the alchemical language used since the Middle Ages to describe processes of spiritual transformation. Fuller encountered such symbols in the works of Jacob Boehme, Goethe, and even in the writings of her friend Nathaniel Hawthorne.

During her spiritual crisis of 1840–41, Fuller had begun to meld all of this material together into her own distinctive mythology. In contrast to Emerson's skepticism, she insisted that her involvement in mythical landscapes was not a form of escapism. "The way," she asserted in one of her letters, "is not . . . to live in a trance; nor yet in a whirl" (L 2:40). Instead, she saw mythmaking as a way to transform consciousness. She wanted, she continues, "the Attic honey on the lip, the Greek fire in the eye" (L 2:41). By consuming the "honey" of Greek (and Roman) mythology, Fuller intuited, her awareness might be transformed into a new, exalted mode of insight. One finds Fuller's defense of mythmaking too in her "Autobiographical Romance," begun in 1840, a text that demonstrates her growing facility at using mythological references to explore her inner life. Critiquing her father's rigid and imperious educational practices, for example, Fuller links them to the classical image of Roman will, "commanding nature too sternly to be inspired by it" (EMF 29). Exhibiting the "dignity of a fixed purpose," Timothy Fuller (one of the most powerful Congressmen of his era) acted as if he had been "suckled by [the] wolf." Like Romulus and Remus, the legendary founders of Rome, he was nourished on the milk of male will and masculine aggression, not "the Greek honey" (20) that opened up Fuller's imaginary vistas. Her father's stern instruction, she reflects, repressed her inner life, covering over her feelings and imagination, which "sank deep within, away from the surface of my life" (EMF 28). Using a critique of her father's values as a tool to detach herself from his world, Fuller began in 1840–41 to turn within, toward the depths of her psyche.[16] The drama of her early career lies in her recovery of this hidden realm, submerged in the Underworld of her being. One route back into the depths of her self, she intuited, passed through her mother's garden—a secluded region where her thoughts and feelings could develop at their own tempo "in the nest" (32). Significantly, Fuller connects this imagined floral realm to what she terms "the enchanted gardens of Greek mythology." "This path," she affirms, "I followed, [and] have been following ever since" (30).

More precisely, in the exploration of her "inner life" (L 2:64), Fuller began to create her own unique amalgam of classical mythology, alchemy, Christian mysticism, and Germanic folklore. One of the challenges facing Fuller was to find a symbolic and mythic vocabulary that might capture the intensity of her changing moods. Early on, the image of the Titans assailing Olympus (an account found in Hesiod's *Theogeny*) had attracted her. "The Titans are the lower passions," she wrote to her friend Caroline Sturgis in 1838. "They dared to attempt to scale with ladders those serene heights where dwell the gods." But despite their defeat, the Titans embodied an energy (the "power to cause volcanoes") that Fuller admired (L 1:332). The following year, Fuller told Sturgis that the progress of life was an "undulating line" that included moments of "action and passion"—"the Titanic era" of "strife" (L 2:34). A little later, in a mythic "rhapsody," she confided to Sturgis that "I love the stern Titanic part, I love the crag, even the Drachenfels of life—I love its roaring sea that dashes against the crag—I love its sounding cataract, its lava rush, its whirlwind, its rivers generating the lotus and the crocodile . . ." (L 2:40). Passages like this probably motivated Channing's observation that "in temperament Margaret seemed a Bacchante, prompt for wild excitement, and fearless to tread by night the mountain forest, with song and dance of delirious mirth . . ." (M 2:92–93). But Fuller's reference to the Drachenfels in her letter to Sturgis gave her understanding of the self's energies a dangerous edge. In her private mythology, Fuller linked Titanic energy to the daemonic—a confrontation with powerful instinctive energies that she found in the Germanic legend of the Drachenfels (literally, "dragon crags" or "dragon rocks"), the site where maidens were exposed to deadly dragons.

While Emerson looked at "daemonology" and the "daemonic" with skeptical eyes, Fuller completely understood the significance of Goethe's concept of the unruly psychic "daemon" within that embodied turbulent and even dangerous feelings. Like Poe, she knew that the psyche contained an "imp of the perverse" that lay far beyond sunlight and abstract speculation. "As to the Daemoniacal," Fuller wrote in a letter that Emerson cites, "I know not that I can say to you anything more precise than you find in Goethe. There are no precise terms for such thoughts. The word *instinctive* indicates their existence. I intimated it in the little piece on the Drachenfels. It may be best understood, perhaps, by a symbol. As the sun shines from the serene heavens, dispelling noxious exhalations, and calling forth exquisite thoughts on the surface of earth in the shape of shrub or flower, so gnome-like works the fire within the hidden caverns and secret veins of earth ..." (M 1:225). "In genius, and in character," she continues, "it works, as you say, instinctively; it refuses to be analyzed by the understanding, and is most of all inaccessible to the person who possesses it" (M 1:225–26). Fuller's reference to "the little piece on Drachenfels" is a reference to her poem of that title, in which she evokes a sense of psychic expectation, "a high mysterious mood" that seems a "hieroglyphic spell" pointing toward hidden mystery. Elsewhere in her writing, Fuller refers to the Drachenfels in order to evoke a sense of psychological danger, in which she felt overwhelmed by anxiety and irrational impulse. "I am on the Drachenfels, and cannot get off;" she wrote Emerson in 1839, "it is one of my naughtiest moods" (L 2:104).

Fuller derived her image of the Drachenfels from one of the Rhine ballads that she reviewed for the *Dial*. For her, the image of a Rhine maiden exposed to the hungry dragon embodied a dark psychological truth: the recognition that on her lonely and dangerous pathway to illumination, no hero would happen along like St. George or Perseus to rescue her. Instead, Fuller had to face her inner demons alone. As Emerson notes, she chose the "sistrum" (or rattle) of Isis as her personal "emblem" (M 1:221). This is a particularly appropriate symbol, since the sistrum, shaken by the priests of Isis, was used to ward off dangerous powers such as Typhon, who—in the myth—had already dismembered the consort of Isis: Osiris. In a sense, Fuller's writing was the "sistrum" that she used to tame the dangerous psychological energies—such as loneliness, fear, and anxiety—that could overwhelm the self. It evoked the process of self-discipline and "purification" that Fuller needed to tame her unruly passions, the daemonic energies of the unconscious that blocked the pathway to inner illumination and self-reliance. "What demon," Fuller inquired of one of her friends, "resists our good angel, and seems at times to have the mastery?" (L 2:82).

In addition to expressing the turbulent energies of the self, Fuller turned to classical myth and Christian iconography to capture her sense of loss and pain. When Fuller learned in September 1839 that Samuel Gray Ward was leaving her for Anna Barker, she realized that he could no longer embody the "shrine at which I could rest upon my weary pilgrimage" (L 2:90). Instead, she felt like the Madonna, mourning at the tomb of her lost child (a theme that Fuller would expand five years later in her finest poem, "Raphael's Deposition from the Cross"). "But Oh," Fuller lamented, "it is waiting like the Mother beside the sepulchre for the resurrection, for all I loved in you is at present dead and buried . . ." (L 2:91). Over the next year, Fuller discovered a sense of resurrection not in the love of others, but in the depths of her self. Transposing her attention from secular to divine love, she wrote to Channing of her sense that the progress of the soul was "the one only true aim of our pilgrimage here" (L 2:110). By September 1840, she confided to Sturgis about "the mighty changes of my spiritual life" (L 2:158). "My life is now prayer;" she revealed to Emerson, "Through me sweetest harmonies are momently breathing" (L 2:160). This sense of spiritual ecstasy culminated in a remarkable letter that Fuller sent Caroline Sturgis on October 22, 1840. Written within a few weeks of the Ward-Barker wedding and near the five-year anniversary of her father's death, this letter captured the emotional and spiritual intensity of Fuller's season of crisis, at the same time that it raised it to a mythic level.

The focus of this letter is upon the receptive soul, nearing the end of its spiritual pilgrimage and awaiting the emergence of a new-born divinity (imagined as a divine "child") within the self. In a profound act of identification, Fuller takes Mary's transformation after the Annunciation as a model for the spiritual birth that she is seeking. "I cannot plunge into myself enough," Fuller ecstatically exclaims,

> I cannot dedicate myself sufficiently. The life that flows in upon me from so many quarters is too beautiful to be checked. I would not check a single pulsation. It all ought to be;—if caused by any apparition of the Divine in me I could bless myself like the holy Mother. But like her I long to be virgin. (L 2:167)

This passage justifies Kimberly VanEsveld Adams's observation that Fuller "found the Madonna a rich and empowering symbol for herself and other women."[17] Pairing the Madonna with the "Greco-Roman and Egyptian goddesses" in Fuller's pantheon, Adams interprets Mary as a figure who, after the Annunciation, mirrors the other "Virgin Goddesses."[18] This observation is validated by Fuller's presentation of the "idea of woman" three years later in "The Great Lawsuit," where Mary takes her own place alongside ancient goddesses such as Diana and Isis. The Madonna's role, Adams notes in passing, "touches that of Ceres [Demeter]."[19] Like Demeter searching for Persephone, Mary's life takes on meaning in relation to her divine child. Some commentators see Demeter and Persephone as two facets of the same being: the goddess who seeks and the divinity which embodies sacred power. This double identity became a crucial aspect of the way Fuller depicted her relationship to the great goddesses filling her writing. At some times, she longs to manifest their power; at others, she is a spiritual seeker hunting for a divine core of being that eludes her.

For example, in Fuller's letter of October 22, 1840, the figure of Mary functions both as a magnified symbol of the ideal self, and as an image of one's psychic being. Mary is a woman touched by divinity, but equally importantly she is a figure of spiritual longing. She represents spiritual pilgrimage and transfiguration, aspiration and ecstasy. Fuller found this double valence in the writing of the eighteenth-century French mystic Louis Claude de Saint-Martin, whom she cites near the beginning of *Woman in the Nineteenth Century* as exemplifying "a new hour in the day of man" (EMF 250). In *Le nouvel homme*, Saint-Martin depicted in detail the process of psychological transformation needed to make the new, spiritual man. Before "divinity penetrates us," he argued, "it must traverse us in our ignominy and in our grief."[20] After "nourishing within ourselves the . . . grief of spirit," we reach a moment of spiritual "virginity"; and, then, "the annunciation takes place in us, and not before long we perceive that the holy conception has taken place in us as well."[21] Finally, Saint-Martin affirmed, there appears in the soul the "infant annunciated in you by the angel."[22] This imagery of annunciation—spiritual pregnancy—and divine birth mirrors the language of Fuller's October 22, 1840 letter to Caroline Sturgis. In her psychological mythmaking, the psychic womb could gestate a divine child—a new self waiting to be born.

The complexity of Fuller's mythmaking becomes apparent in the rest of her letter. Speaking in exalted and prophetic tones, she announces a new revelation—a "Genesis" that she privately shares with her closest female friend. In this crucial letter, many of Fuller's most important symbols begin to appear, but they are not completely developed. At various points in her letter, Fuller presents three powerful symbols of transfiguration: she imagines herself (1) undergoing a spiritual pregnancy, (2) journeying into the depths of the self in quest for a glowing gem of illumination, and (3) experiencing a seasonal death and rebirth. In the opening of the letter, Fuller describes her sense of "nun like dedication" (L 2:168), which she links to an awareness of spiritual pregnancy. She senses that her "soul swells with the future" and that—within the depths of her self—a divine "child" of renewed selfhood has begun growing (167). For Fuller, this sense of inner growth was bound to an inescapable pain, which she characterizes as crucifixion, a "wound," and—most profoundly—as a purifying "fire" that "draws her to itself and consumes [her] mortal part." Such fiery purification leads to a second symbolic pattern, as Fuller imagines herself undertaking a subterranean quest into the depths of the psyche, "into the very heart of the untrodden mountain where the carbuncle has lit the way to veins of yet undreamed of diamond" (168). Entering the depths of an inner cavern, or what seems like a psychic "womb," Fuller imagines herself pursuing a glowing core of illumination that might manifest itself as a precious gem or a divine "child" waiting to be born. Finally, in a third symbol of personal transformation, Fuller imagines the changes taking place in her psyche in seasonal terms. She dramatizes the inner process that she is passing through as a psychic death and rebirth, as the "flower" of the inner self is converted "into dead-seeming seed," only to "bloom again" as a "Phenix" into "the tenderest spring" (169). But for the moment, Fuller laments, she is trapped in a state of "Northern winter," in which "the snowy shroud" of the soul's winter hides the spiritual changes that are secretly taking place within her.

As Fuller consolidated the insights gained through her spiritual crisis, she began constructing sustained mythical narratives of personal transformation. The two most striking are the mystical essays "The Magnolia of Lake Pontchartrain" and "Leila," which she published in the January and April 1841 issues of the *Dial*, respectively. In these two essays, we witness Fuller progressing from a personal testimony of spiritual aspiration to a sustained mythical narrative that dramatizes her emerging psychic energies through a syncretic goddess figure she names "Leila." Fuller attributed her mystical flower sketches ("Yuca Filamentosa" and "The Magnolia of Lake Pontchartrain") to an October 1840 conversation with a family friend, William Eustis. Visiting the Fuller household, Eustis recounted the imaginary histories of two plants—narratives that he presented "not like a botanist, but a lover" (L 2:165). Having heard Eustis's interpretation of one of the plants as "the type of pure feminine beauty in the moon's own flower," Fuller immediately saw its mythological potential. She wrote to her friend William Henry Channing that she perceived the lineaments of a "true poem" that "harmonizes with all legends of Isis,

Diana, &c.," as it revealed the presence of "a Divine Thought" (166). In "The Magnolia of Lake Pontchartrain," which Fuller published two months later in the *Dial*, she turned the Magnolia into a vivid narrative of spiritual aspiration. Her essay opens with a solitary male figure who finds his meditation on "nobleness" disrupted by a "fragrance beyond anything I had ever known" (EMF 44). Tracing this fragrance as one of "the monitions of [her] nature," the rider eventually finds a solitary mythic figure, which "he" identifies as "the Queen of the South." This "imperial vestal" (an avatar of the independent "virgin" goddesses that Fuller had been studying) manifests a self-reliant independence, since "there is no disturbance to prevent the full consciousness of power." Unlike female figures that have been "plucked from their home," she has escaped the fate of "princesses captive in the prison of a barbarous foe" (45). In Emerson's interpretation of this essay, he is the rider and Fuller is the "Queen of the South" luxuriating in a new spiritual independence that he identifies in a letter to Fuller as "a fervid Southern eloquence" (L 2:337).

But given Fuller's own appropriation and modification of Emersonian self-reliance, it is equally likely that both figures in her mystical narrative—the male rider and the Magnolia—are different versions of her self: the first a masculinized voice influenced by Emerson and Fuller's father and the second a new, female-centered mythic awareness that has disrupted her previous consciousness. As the Magnolia continues her narrative, she recounts how she changed from being a domesticated woman, "full clad in . . . golden fruit and bridal blossoms" (46), into a solitary figure who has been "driven back upon the centre of my being" (47). Discovering within hidden depths, the Magnolia found herself rejected by those who had earlier enjoyed her bounteous gifts. Unable to recognize her new self, they cast her out. But at the moment of rejection, the Magnolia recounts, "A mystic shudder of pale joy then separated me wholly from my former abode" (48). Suddenly, a mythological vista opened up for the Magnolia and she found herself "before the queen and guardian of the flowers. Of this being," she continues,

> I cannot speak to thee in any language now possible betwixt us. For this is a being of another order from thee, an order thou mayest feel, nay, approach step by step, but which cannot be known till thou art it, nor seen nor spoken of till thou hast passed through it. Suffice it to say, that it is not such a being as men love to paint, a fairy, like them, only lesser and more exquisite than they, a goddess, larger and of statelier proportions, an angel . . . only with an added power. . . . (48)

"Take a step inward, forget a voice, lose a power;" the queen of the flowers tells the Magnolia, "no longer a bounteous sovereign, become a vestal priestess and bide thy time in the Magnolia" (49). In this psychological allegory, Fuller recapitulated much of the imagery of her October 22nd letter to Sturgis. But in addition to announcing a new, mythic awareness, she constructed a dialogue between her emerging sense of divine being and an older persona anchored in masculinized patterns of thought that could not completely understand the significance of such goddess language.

Declaring her spiritual independence, the Magnolia proclaims that she will never again "detain a wanderer, luring him from afar, nor shall I again subject myself to be questioned by an alien spirit to tell the tale of my being in words that divide it from itself" (EMF 49). The fruition of this mythic dedication was Fuller's essay "Leila," which represents her most detailed account of the goddess symbolism that later structured "The Great Lawsuit" and *Woman in the Nineteenth Century*. Radically challenging the patriarchal spiritual models of the day, this essay presents the reader with an astounding alternative: the image of a female messiah/divinity who might become the object of spiritual aspiration and devotion. Following Emerson's belief that the self-reliant self must open pathways that connect self-awareness to an inner divine power, Fuller imagines that inner divinity in exclusively female terms: as a Goddess, rather than as Emerson's "god within." In the process, "Leila" presents a striking vision of the "divine feminine" as the center of being and the foundation for female self-reliance. Fuller imagines herself incarnating (or what she terms 'impersonating') the mythic mantle of Leila's divine energy, absorbing it into her self so that it might transfigure her awareness and being. Reading "Leila," one has the uncanny sense of reading Emerson transposed to an entirely different key—one that highlights the mythical dimensions of self-reliance in feminist terms. For Fuller stabilizes an imaginative structure that articulates self-reliance as a personal quest for an inner illumination figured as a female—not a male—power. But it is important to recognize that by 1841, Fuller had begun establishing her ideas upon a theological platform as profound as Emerson's. However, not everybody in her society was ready for a radically feminized redefinition of sacred myth. As Fuller asserts near the opening of her essay, "Most men, as they gazed on Leila were pained" (EMF 53).

In "Leila," Fuller supplements the patriarchal theology of her age by affirming a new goddess-language, a woman-centered vocabulary of spiritual awakening and exaltation. Characterizing Leila as "a bridge between [herself] and the infinite," she links her to goddesses such as Isis, Venus, Sophia, and Demeter. The narrator's relationship to Leila is one of ritual pursuit and meditation (recalling the rites of Demeter and Isis in Hellenistic mystery cults). Approaching Leila "in the singleness of prayer," she conjures Her from the "vasty deep" of a mystical "lake," until the Goddess "rises and walks on its depths" (54). But at other moments, Leila "passes" suddenly "into the back-ground of being," where the narrator must pursue her glowing energy in "the secret veins of earth" and hidden caverns. "I venerate her in all this," she reflects, "in awed silence." Seeking the hidden "abyss," she looks for "the star which glitters at the bottom." "O draw me, Star," she prays, "I fear not to follow. . . . Let me gaze myself into religion, then draw me down,—down." But in addition to summoning Leila from the depths of her psyche, Fuller's narrator also considers the revolutionary and utopian potential of unleashing mythic female powers on the earth. At times, Leila "bursts up again in . . . fire," unleashing volcanic energy on the earth. At other moments, she is the "Saint of Knowledge" or an "Angel" that "showers down on man balm and blessing." At the most ecstatic moments in Fuller's essay, Leila takes on the divine lineaments of the Great Mother as source of life and generative power. "The rivers of bliss flow forth at thy touch," Fuller writes, "and the shadow of sin falls separate from the form of light" (56). "At her touch," she continues, "all became fluid, and the prison walls grew into Edens," while "each serpent form soared into a Phenix" (57).

But in addition to its mythic intensity, an important quality in "Leila" is its evocation of emotional pain. Never far from the surface is the image of alchemical fire, melting and purifying the self. Fuller found the image of purifying fire in the myths of Demeter searching for her lost daughter Persephone, and of Isis hunting for her missing consort Osiris. In the Homeric "Hymn to Demeter," the Goddess interrupts her hunt to stop at Eleusis (the site of the Goddess's mystery cult), where she fosters the son of the local queen Metaineira. In order to make him immortal, Demeter placed the boy each night "like a brand in the fire, unknown to his dear parents."[23] In Plutarch's account of the myth of Isis, the Egyptian goddess performs the same action: nursing a royal child, "in the night she would burn away the mortal portions of his body."[24] Identifying with such mythic narratives of the divine mother purifying her foster child in fire, Fuller constructs a powerful account of her creative process. "Into my single life," she reflects, "I stooped and plucked from the burning my divine children." Only through the acceptance of suffering, "an elected pain," Fuller asserts, could she transform her self and finally achieve the "more beauteous forms" that are "Born from the suddenly darting flame" (57). In "Leila," Fuller terms this process "moral and mental alchymy," a purification of the self that might lead to the recovery of the divine and holy "child" waiting in the ashes of her soul's fire. In her October 22nd letter, Fuller had identified herself with the royal child purified in fire. "My Caroline," she exclaimed, "I am not yet purified. Let the lonely Vestal watch the fire till it draws her to itself and consumed this mortal part" (L 2:167). In "Leila," she plays both parts: the sorrowing mother goddess and the mortal being who is purified.

This double identification is even more visible when we consider the sexual politics of Fuller's quest for Leila. What is especially striking about her mythic narrative is the way in which an idealized female figure becomes the object of intense longing. We know that Fuller found one model of spiritual longing in Persian poetry. "When I first met with the name Leila," she observed, "I knew, from the very look and sound, it was mine; I knew that it meant night,—night, which brings out stars, as sorrow brings out truths" (M 1:293). The name Leila, which does mean 'night' in Persian, appears in the spiritual allegory *Layla and Majnun*. This is a story about lost love: a male figure (Majnun) pursues a beloved woman (Layla), who becomes the object of his spiritual aspiration. Fuller also encountered this pattern in the works of one of her favorite German writers, the poet Novalis. "I have never found any response to the psychological history of my childhood except in Novalis," she noted in one of her journals. "I do think I am not ignorant of his emblematic carbuncle."[25] In this journal, Fuller explicitly linked the symbol of the carbuncle to the "gleaming" image of Anna Barker. "I loved Anna," she reflected, "for a time with as much passion as I was then strong enough to feel—Her face was always gleaming before me, her voice was echoing in my ear, all poetic thoughts clustered round the dear image. This love was a key which unlocked for me many a treasure which I still possess, it was the carbuncle (emblematic gem) which cast light into many of the darkest caverns of human nature" (EMF 23). The symbol of the carbuncle allowed Fuller to treasure and simultaneously transform passion into permanent insight, as she sublimated her relationship with Anna Barker into an imagined relationship with a divine being, who radiates the gem-like fire that she associated with her lost friend. The erotic energy radiating from this glowing symbol recorded desire, at the same time that it provided a new center of imaginative orientation—one seemingly impervious to the vicissitudes of personal losses. Retreating at times "into the secret veins of earth," Fuller observes, there "glows through [Leila's] whole being the fire that so baffles men . . . the blood-red, heart's-blood-red of the carbuncle." This glowing energy provides Leila (and, one might read, Fuller herself) with "her own light"—a self-reliant illumination enabling her to aspire toward her "purest self" (EMF 55).

But Novalis did more than teach Fuller the symbolic language of the carbuncle as the goal of psychic and spiritual excavation. He also showed her how the pain of romantic loss could be transformed into an intense process of self-exploration. After the death of his beloved, Novalis underwent an intense spiritual transformation in which the pain of separation became transformed into a sense of illumination. "My love has become a flame that slowly consumes all that is earthly . . ." Novalis wrote to his friend Friedrich Schlegel. "Even now a new inner life is burgeoning within me."[26] In his *Hymns to the Night*, the Poet found his absent beloved in the depths of his soul's darkness. Following the glowing eyes of Anna Barker/ Leila into the soul's "Night," Fuller (like Novalis) learned how to transform the pain of loss into illumination. Reading her relationship with the lost Anna through the idealizing lens of Novalis, Fuller ended up in an analogous spiritual and psychological location. Like Novalis, she found both in the expanding depths of her self and in the recesses of nature that Novalis described as "the transfigured features of my beloved."[27] But there is one key difference. Novalis was a male romantic writer who used the figure of an absent female beloved to focus his spiritual aspiration. But writing as a *woman* expressing her emotional and spiritual longing for the absent *female* beloved, Fuller subtly changes the pattern. For she is able to play *both* parts, both the lovelorn poet as spiritual seeker and the exalted female figure the poet pursues. Pursuing an alter ego dramatized as Leila, Fuller projects a magnified image of *her own* hidden potential—a divine being imagined as her own spiritual center. Connecting with Leila and absorbing her energy, Fuller would learn how to become a self-reliant individual authorized by her relational ties to the god(dess) Leila within.

In "Leila," Fuller dramatizes her pursuit of exalted womanhood through a dual literary structure that oscillates between pilgrimage and epiphany, as it alternates between imagined scenes of pursuit and utopian moments of transfigured being. Constructing a dialectical interplay between two competing perspectives, she represents both the longing for fulfillment and a vision of transfigured being. On the one hand, we have the spiritual longing of the narrator as she pursues Leila; on the other, we encounter mythic dramatizations of a utopian "Leila-consciousness" that transfigures both awareness and reality. In this structure, the narrator pursues a personified ideal of transfigured consciousness and then periodically shifts into the very mythic awareness that she has been searching for. Put another way, "Leila" constructs an imaginary conversation between Fuller's own consciousness and an idealized self-image dramatizing the endpoint of her existential and spiritual aspiration. By the end of Fuller's essay, these two sides draw together, as Leila speaks to the narrator, accepting the narrator's desire to merge her aspiring awareness into the mythic power of the figure she has been pursuing. As she imagines *becoming* Leila and absorbing her divine powers, Fuller's narrator lifts her life up to a transcendent level equivalent—in many ways—to Emerson's vision of self-reliance. In *Nature*, for example, Emerson balanced an ascending rhetoric of spiritual aspiration against the utopian vision of a figure he describes near the end as an "Orphic poet." The ensuing double vision measures the longing for transcendence against a dramatization of the exalted being that Emerson defines as the endpoint of spiritual desire. But where Emerson describes the Orphic Poet as an acquaintance (perhaps Bronson Alcott), Fuller depicts Leila as an exalted version of *her self*—an avatar who possesses the illumination and power that she is seeking.

The next step in Fuller's mythmaking was her publication, in 1843, of her influential feminist essay: "The Great Lawsuit: Man *versus* Men. Woman *versus* Women." Building on her mythological explorations of the previous four years, she generalized her use of myth from being an instrument of personal exploration into functioning as a tool of cultural analysis. Placing a wide range of mythical personages alongside figures drawn from the Bible, literature, and history, Fuller offered myth as an equally valid part of the common idiom. In her usage, classical myths become models of psychological and social being. In the nineteenth century, references to Eve or Mary functioned as familiar cultural touchstones. In "The Great Lawsuit," Fuller added references to goddesses such as Isis, Ceres, Diana, and Minerva. Each of these beings, she explained, evoked different dimensions of "the idea" of woman (N 755–57). A primary goal of Fuller's essay was to define "new individualities" that might "be developed in the actual world" (777). But in the absence of stable role models exemplifying spiritual independence or fortitude, this process was impeded for women, who were trained to emulate flawed examples of submissiveness and passive domesticity. The prevailing ideal, Fuller knew all too well, was to create "model women of bride-like beauty and gentleness" (750) and not to promote the insight or strength of a goddess like Minerva (Athena). As a result, one half of human potential—the female side—remained underdeveloped. Part of the problem, Fuller realized, was that women lack "a standard" within themselves, an ideal of fulfilled being toward which they might aspire. There were passing hints of an enlarged ideal of womanhood, but these "gleams" and "dim fancies" were soon "obscured by the mists of sensuality, the dust of routine" (756). Only through a reorientation toward ideals of transfigured womanhood might it be possible to realize "crystallizations more pure and of more various beauty," a circulation of "divine energy" throughout the world that might lead to "a ravishing harmony" (752).

Projecting both a longing for cultural transformation and a utopian ideal of regenerated being, "The Great Lawsuit" thus generalizes and stabilizes the narrative structure that Fuller pioneered in "Leila." She alternates scenes of aspiration and fulfillment, balancing images of personal struggle against visions of transfigured being that function as a glowing beacon pulling the individual and society onward. Picking up the language that she had found in classical myths and had used in her letters, she characterizes men and women as undertaking a "pilgrimage" (N 766) toward the recognition of their divine destiny. Elsewhere, she depicts the end of this quest as contact with the divine core that transfigures the self and facilitates "self-reliance" (754). In a remarkable narrative moment, Fuller dramatizes her double role as pilgrim and transfigured hierophant by staging a dramatic encounter between two versions of her self: the essay's narrator and an alter ego named "Miranda" (753–54), who represents the self-reliant woman that the narrator and her readers might become. Conversing with an idealized version of herself, Fuller—at this moment—represents simultaneously both her struggle toward personal fulfillment and the ideal of perfected, self-sufficient being that oriented her life. The dialogue with Miranda subtly revises Emerson's rhetorical structure. Miranda functions like the "exemplary persona," the idealized model of self-fulfillment that Emerson presented as a role model in each of his essays.[28] But Fuller changes the rhetorical structure. In his essays, Emerson speaks to his aspiring readers from a position of intellectual and spiritual mastery, assuming the voice of an idealized persona that the reader is expected to emulate. But in "The Great Lawsuit," Fuller self-consciously plays the roles both of inspired speaker and aspiring reader. In the process, she opens up a dialogic space in her writing—a structure of double consciousness in which she can occupy both the position of spiritual pilgrim and of exalted being. She can be the searcher (Psyche, Demeter, or Isis), but also the triumphant goddess reunited with her lost other. Fuller expressed this doubleness of being in her 1841 Conversations, when she noted that Persephone and Ceres (Demeter) "were two phases of one thing."[29] In the (Eleusinian) mystery of personal transfiguration, both roles were necessary.

In "The Great Lawsuit," the lost child who is sought ultimately takes on the lineaments of Minerva (Athena)—the great warrior goddess of classical antiquity. "There are two aspects of woman's nature," she asserted, "expressed by the ancients as Muse and Minerva" (N 774). The Muse, Fuller knew, meshed easily with contemporary ideals of female beauty and influence. But the figure of Minerva evoked qualities that had been undervalued and dismissed by her society. In Fuller's hands, Minerva is not only the aggressive warrior who carries "the armor and the javelin," she is also the woman set apart, who "meditate[s] in virgin loneliness" (776). Independent, "self-centred" (777), and totally independent from the control of others, Fuller's Minerva represents "the soul which is poised upon itself" (774), an analogue of the Indian girl, "betrothed to the sun" (770), who "dedicate[d] herself to the ... Sun of Truth" (775). In Fuller's reading of history and classical mythology, there are many avatars of Minerva: the religious leaders St. Teresa, Joanna Southcote, and Mother Anne Lee, as well as mythical figures such as Electra and Cassandra (769–71). Each of these women—in Fuller's eyes—manifested an independence of being. But as she noted in later writings, some of them also experienced tragic destinies. Cassandra was a prophetess doomed to be misunderstood, and Iphigenia (who appears in Fuller's revision of "The Great Lawsuit" into *Woman in the Nineteenth Century*) was fated to be a human sacrifice to the gods of war.

The year following "The Great Lawsuit," 1844, was Fuller's *annus mirabilis*. In April, she completed *Summer on the Lakes*, a book-length narrative punctuated at key moments with mythological meditations. Over the summer, as she prepared for a momentous move from New England to New York City, Fuller explored her moods in a series of intensely mythic journal reflections and poems. Finally, at the end of the year, Fuller revised her mythological repertoire, as she expanded "The Great Lawsuit" into *Woman in the Nineteenth Century*. After 1844, mythological references largely disappeared from Fuller's writing. Her *New-York Tribune* essays tend to use the Bible as their primary point of orientation, until the final year of Fuller's life, when the cataclysmic events of the Roman Revolution motivated a return to some of her favorite mythological symbols.

In terms of Fuller's engagement with mythology, the two most significant moments in *Summer on the Lakes* are imaginary dialogues in which analogues of Fuller justify their interest in mythology, mysticism, and the occult. In the first a character named "M." addresses two traveling companions, modeled on James and Sarah Freeman Clarke. "My people work in the secret," M. tells them, "... they remain in the dark because only there such marvels could be bred." Echoing the language of the Gnomes in Goethe's *Faust*, Part Two, Fuller evokes the "daemonic" working of the unconscious—a process that she links to the work of "the alchymist" and which her companion J. identifies as an expression of "Bacchic energy" (EMF 78). The second dialogue builds on this subterranean imagery, when "Free Hope" tells her companions of her interest in "the hidden springs of life," a hidden site that contains "ore" which may be "unearthed" by "miners." After evoking the imagery of Fuller's mystical essay "Leila," Free Hope declares that: "All my days are touched by the supernatural, for I feel the pressure of hidden causes, and the presence, sometimes the communion, of unseen powers" (146). These passages reveal that the study of mythology, for Fuller, was not just an academic exercise but rather the exploration of a symbolic vocabulary that helped her navigate the spiritual and psychological dimensions of her life.

Fuller's 1844 poetry should be approached in that spirit, for successive verses show her struggling to achieve an expression of both spiritual aspiration and transfigured, mythic consciousness. For example, these poems are filled with mythic images of ritual death and rebirth. In "Boding raven of the breast," Fuller imagines her being planted in "a deep safe grave" from "Whence the soul may take its flight / Lark-like spiral seeking light" (EMF 228). While "Raphael's Deposition from the Cross" concludes with the image of the buried self, "transfused" with the "primal light" of Leila (who reemerges in Fuller's writing) until buried "life is risen to flower a God" (240). Finally, in "To the Face Seen in the Moon," Fuller imagines that the mythic conjunction of the male and female sides of her personality might allow her to "win the secrets of the tomb," and emerge "The worthy Angel of a better sphere" (241). In such texts, the psyche becomes the site of ritual transformation, as if it were an alchemical crucible or the temple of an ancient mystery religion. The goal of this mythic conjunction, in Fuller's poetic vocabulary, is an imaginary locale where "the perfect two embrace,/ Male & female, black & white" and "Soul is justified in space" ("Double triangle, Serpent and Rays," 233). Two of the 1844 poems return to the narrative of transformation found in Apuleius's *The Golden Ass*. "Sistrum" celebrates the sacred rattle of Isis, which Fuller interprets as the source of self-reliant power: "God-ordained, self-fed Energy" (235). "Leila in the Arabian zone" links Fuller's syncretic goddess to the great goddesses of antiquity: Io, Isis, Diana, Hecate, and Phebe ["Phoebe"?], at the same time that it recapitulates Lucius's famous vision of Isis with her "Blue black" robe "blazoned o'er with points of light." "The magic Sistrum arms her hand, /" Fuller continues, "And at her deep eye's command / Brutes are raised to thinking men / Soul growing to her soul filled ken" (233). Evoking the transfiguration of the self that fascinated Fuller throughout her career, these lines also anticipate one of the major concerns of *Woman in the Nineteenth Century*, which argues for the transformation of masculine sensibility from a predatory sensuality to a reverence for women and the feminine qualities that men also contain.

But of all Fuller's 1844 poems, the one that best captures her commitment to mythmaking is "Winged Sphynx," which opens with the lines:

> Through brute nature upward rising,
> Seed up-striving to the light,
> Revelations still surprising,
> My inwardness is grown insight.
> Still I slight not those first stages,
> Dark but God-directed Ages;
> In my nature leonine
> Labored & learned a Soul divine;
> Put forth an aspect Chaste, Serene,
> Of nature virgin mother queen;
> Assumes at last the destined wings,
> Earth & heaven together brings.... (EMF 234)

Here the two phases of Fuller's mythmaking are conjoined: the struggle of pilgrimage and the power of epiphany. The search for the divine power within is laborious and painstaking. But the fruition of spiritual aspiration into divine ascendancy rewards the struggle for self-reliant illumination. "I sit like Tantalus at the banquet;" Fuller recorded in an undated journal fragment, "I am not content to *see* the Gods. I would be one, else even nectar and ambrosia pall on the palate."[30]

But what Fuller found is that "nectar and ambrosia" do pall on the palate and that the longing for transfiguration is not always fulfilled. This was certainly the experience of the women whom she visited in Sing Sing Prison, as she was completing *Woman in the Nineteenth Century* in the fall of 1844. Instead of achieving divine epiphany, numerous women in the city found themselves in various states of suffering and captivity. As she completed her book, Fuller's use of mythology reflected her new awareness of the losses experienced by others. As embodiments of this political focus, a group of new figures appeared: "the Mater *Dolorosa*" (the grieving Madonna) (EMF 316), "the maiden, enlightened by her sufferings" (316), and the Scandinavian goddess Iduna returning from "the prison in which she sat mourning" (335). But perhaps the most significant of Fuller's additions is the figure of Iphigenia, Agamemnon's daughter.[31] A human sacrifice to male aggression and violence, Iphigenia became a fitting symbol for Fuller of the women who would be injured in the impending Mexican War. More generally, Iphigenia as sacrificial victim evoked the sexually exploited women of New York City, who had become "the sold and polluted slaves of men" (319–20). Fuller focuses primarily on Euripides' *Iphigenia in Aulis*, which was based on a variation of the myth in which Iphigenia, after her heroic decision to accept her sacrifice, is rescued from death by Artemis, who spirits her away to a deserted island. In *Woman in the Nineteenth Century*, Fuller highlights Iphigenia's loneliness and emotional suffering, as she "wander[s] alone at night in the vestal solitude of her imprisoning grave" (300).

In the final appendix of her book, Fuller clarified the appeal of Iphigenia's nobility and heroism. In a critical essay "borrowed from the papers of Miranda," she highlights the sacrificial nobility of classical tragic heroines. "A great occasion was given to each," Fuller writes, "whereby to test her character" (365). No one, "Miranda" rapturously asserts, knew Iphigenia better than she. Identifying with her heroine's tragic sorrow, Miranda recalls "the heavenly tears I have shed with [Iphigenia]," as well as her conviction that she "understood her wholly . . . better than she understood herself" (366). What captured Fuller's imagination was Iphigenia's heroic acceptance of her tragic destiny, manifested in the noble decision to give her self willingly to the sacrifice. Fuller found an analogous figure of noble suffering in Cassandra, the prophetess doomed by Apollo to be forever misunderstood. In Euripides' *The Trojan Women*, Fuller encountered the image of Cassandra as "the inspired child, the poet, the elected sufferer for the race" (375). In this passage, Fuller reveals her distance from earlier, ecstatic portraits of divine power which she hoped to absorb. If classical mythology taught her how to imagine the exaltation of the self, it also revealed the painful limits of human aspiration. It was one thing to imagine becoming a god; it was quite another to measure the departing footsteps of a divinity, who touched one's life but only imperfectly. The loneliness of Iphigenia and the frustration of Cassandra became fit emblems for a writer who dreamed of the self's expansion yet also recognized that—for many people—the "destined wings" that could seem so close were often furled.

Abbreviations in Notes

EMF *The Essential Margaret Fuller*, ed. Jeffrey Steele (New Brunswick, NJ: Rutgers University Press, 1992).
L   *The Letters of Margaret Fuller*, ed. Robert N. Hudspeth (Ithaca: Cornell University Press, 1983–94).
M   *The Memoirs of Margaret Fuller Ossoli*, ed. Ralph Waldo Emerson et al. (Boston: Phillips, Sampson and Co., 1852).
N   *The Norton Anthology of American Literature*, 8th ed., vol. B, ed. Nina Baym et al. (New York: W. W. Norton & Co., 2012).

Notes

1. Nancy Craig Simmons, "Margaret Fuller's Boston Conversations: The 1839–1840 Series," *Studies in the American Renaissance* (1994): 204. In the manuscript notes attributed to Elizabeth Palmer Peabody, only the second through sixth conversations deal directly with classical mythology. Starting in the seventh conversation, the focus shifted to the definition of beauty and—in later conversations—to a consideration of the social and psychological position of women.
2. Ibid., 205–8.
3. Ibid., 206.
4. Ibid., 207.
5. Apuleius, *The Metamorphosis, or Golden Ass*, trans. Thomas Taylor (London: J. Moyes, 1822), 88n.
6. Meg McGavran Murray, *Margaret Fuller: Wandering Pilgrim* (Athens, GA and London: University of Georgia Press, 2008), 5.
7. Caroline Healey Dall, *Margaret and Her Friends, or Ten Conversations with Margaret Fuller upon the Mythology of the Greeks and Its Expression in Art* (1895; rpt. New York: Arno Press, 1972), 161–62.

8. Dall, *Margaret and Her Friends*, 41.
9. Fuller papers, Houghton Library, Harvard, bMS 1086 (Box A), 1.
10. Luther H. Martin, *Hellenistic Religions: An Introduction* (New York and Oxford: Oxford University Press, 1987), 18, 25.
11. Martin, *Hellenistic Religions*, 59.
12. Arthur Versluis, *The Esoteric Origins of the American Renaissance* (Oxford: Oxford University Press, 2001) discusses this body of literature and its impact at length.
13. Robert D. Richardson, Jr., "Margaret Fuller and Myth," *Prospects: An Annual Journal of American Cultural Studies* (1979): 170–71.
14. *The Letters of Ralph Waldo Emerson*, ed. Ralph L. Rusk (New York: Columbia University Press, 1939), 2:336.
15. Sarah Way Sherman, *Sarah Orne Jewett: An American Persephone* (Hanover, NH and London: University Press of New England, 1989), 17.
16. Relocating the source of knowledge about being inward toward the self is common on the part of later women authors (e.g., Adrienne Rich, "Diving into the Wreck").
17. Kimberly VanEsveld Adams, "The Madonna and Margaret Fuller," *Women's Studies* 25 (1996): 385.
18. Ibid., 391.
19. Ibid., 391.
20. Louis Claude de Saint-Martin, *Le nouvel homme* (1792; rpt. New York: Verlag, 1986), 31.
21. Ibid., 46–47, 32.
22. Ibid., 89.
23. Hesiod, "To Demeter," in *The Homeric Hymns and Homerica*, trans. Hugh G. Evelyn-White (Cambridge, MA: Harvard University Press, Loeb Classical Library, 1967), 307.
24. Plutarch, *Morals*, V, "Isis and Osiris"; cited in Martin, *Hellenistic Religions*, 79. Such parallels, Martin argues, illustrate the way in which the "Mysteries of Isis . . . were apparently fashioned after the example of the Eleusinian Demeter, with whom the Greeks identified her" (78).
25. Journal fragment, Fuller papers, Massachusetts Historical Society.
26. Quoted by Donald Melcer, "Introduction" to Melcer, ed., *Novalis: Classics from the Journal for Anthroposophy* 80 (2009): 20.
27. Novalis, *Hymns to the Night* III, in *Novalis*, 130.
28. Lawrence Buell, *Literary Transcendentalism: Style and Vision in the American Renaissance* (Ithaca: Cornell University Press, 1973).
29. Dall, *Margaret and Her Friends*, 159.
30. Fuller papers, Houghton Library, Harvard, bMS 1086 (A)–2.
31. The classical playwright Euripides wrote two tragedies focusing on Iphigenia, a figure later revisited by Goethe in his verse drama *Iphigenie auf Tauris*.

Bibliography

Adams, Kimberly VanEsveld. "The Madonna and Margaret Fuller." *Women's Studies* 25 (1996): 385–405.

Apuleius. *The Metamorphosis, or Golden Ass*. Translated by Thomas Taylor. London: J. Moyes, 1822.

Buell, Lawrence. *Literary Transcendentalism*. Ithaca and London: Cornell University Press, 1973.

Dall, Caroline Healey. *Margaret and Her Friends, or Ten Conversations with Margaret Fuller upon the Mythology of the Greeks and Its Expression in Art*. 1895. Reprint, New York: Arno Press, 1972.

Emerson, Ralph Waldo. *The Letters of Ralph Waldo Emerson*. Edited by Ralph L. Rusk. New York: Columbia University Press, 1939.

Fuller, Margaret. *The Essential Margaret Fuller*. Edited by Jeffrey Steele. New Brunswick, NJ: Rutgers University Press, 1992.

———. Fuller papers, Houghton Library, Harvard, bMS 1086 (Box A).

———. Journal fragment, Fuller papers, Massachusetts Historical Society.

———. *The Letters of Margaret Fuller*. Edited by Robert N. Hudspeth. Ithaca: Cornell University Press, 1983–94.

———. *The Memoirs of Margaret Fuller Ossoli*. Edited by Ralph Waldo Emerson et al. Boston: Phillips, Sampson and Co., 1852.

Hesiod. *The Homeric Hymns and Homerica*. Translated by Hugh G. Evelyn-White. Cambridge, MA: Harvard University Press, Loeb Classical Library, 1967.

Martin, Luther H. *Hellenistic Religions: An Introduction*. New York and Oxford: Oxford University Press, 1987.

Melcer, Donald, ed. *Novalis: Classics from the Journal for Anthroposophy* 80 (2009).

Murray, Meg McGavran. *Margaret Fuller: Wandering Pilgrim*. Athens, GA and London: University of Georgia Press, 2008.

Richardson, Robert D., Jr. "Margaret Fuller and Myth." *Prospects: An Annual Journal of American Cultural Studies* (1979): 169–84.

Saint-Martin, Louis Claude de. *Le Nouvel homme*. 1792. Reprint, New York: Verlag, 1986.

Sherman, Sarah Way. *Sarah Orne Jewett: An American Persephone*. Hanover, NH and London: University Press of New England, 1989.

Simmons, Nancy Craig. "Margaret Fuller's Boston Conversations: The 1839–1840 Series." *Studies in the American Renaissance* (1994): 195–266.

Chapter 8

Remaking the Republic of Letters: James McCune Smith and the Classical Tradition
John Stauffer

James McCune Smith enjoyed exposing Americans' ignorance of classical languages and traditions. In 1859 he criticized the Supreme Court for misunderstanding the meaning of "citizenship" in the Roman Republic. Such ignorance had led the Court, in *Dred Scott v. Sandford* (1857), to conclude erroneously that neither slaves nor their descendants could be citizens; as Chief Justice Roger Taney wrote in his majority opinion, blacks "had no rights which the white man was bound to respect." In his supporting opinion, Justice Peter Daniel, a proslavery Virginian, quoted extensively from the Justinian code of Roman law, which had become an important source of American law concerning slavery. He too, made numerous errors in translation and interpretation, according to McCune Smith. Similarly, Theodore Woolsey, President of Yale College and arguably the nation's preeminent Greek scholar, also reviewed the classical quotations in Daniel's opinion and highlighted the justice's many "blunders" and "absurd" translations. McCune Smith praised Woolsey's review, but he also noted that on one point the professor was "hardly clear" and thus obfuscated the Roman law of slavery; so he corrected him:

> The term *ingenuus* not only meant "the child of freed persons," as the professor states; it was more especially applied to those who, having been free born, (*engenui*) and subsequently reduced to slavery by sale . . . were finally emancipated: an *ingenuus* therefore was a free-born emancipated slave, a *libertinus* a slave-born emancipated slave.[1]

McCune Smith's larger point was that free blacks' right to citizenship in the U.S., regardless whether they were born free or slave, was based upon the "firm foundation" of Roman law. This was because Roman law granted citizenship both to *engenui* and *libertini*, and since the U.S. Constitution lacked "any definition of the word" citizenship, "the word must bear the meaning which language itself attaches to it under like circumstances, to wit, when it expresses the relation of the individual to the general government, as in Roman polity." For McCune Smith, Roman law provided the precedent for blacks' right to citizenship in the U.S. "In order to impeach that right it will be necessary to blot out from history the annals of lofty Rome, to erase from language the word citizen, and to erase from human polity the relation which the individual bears to the State in a republic."[2]

What is remarkable about McCune Smith's critique of the Supreme Court and of Woolsey is that he himself had been born a slave. A *libertinus*, he was denied admittance to American colleges, which emphasized classical training, on account of his race. Yet his understanding of classical languages, literature, and law was superior to that of the Supreme Court justices; and his knowledge of Roman law and of the Latin language was such that he could correct Yale's president, a professor of classics.

As his reference to "lofty Rome" implies, McCune Smith adored the classics. Moreover, he believed that studying the history, literature, and languages of Greece and Rome pointed the way to reform and revolution in America. Greece and Rome had established republics, but ones fatally flawed by slavery. They thus illuminated the predicament in the United States, another slave republic that saw itself as a successor to these classical societies.[3] The histories of Greece and Rome presented cautionary tales for Americans. They served as warnings of what would happen if slavery persisted. For McCune Smith, the writings of the ancients emphasized the urgency of abolishing slavery in America and establishing a "pure Republic," in which all people enjoyed the right of citizenship.[4] For such a transformation to occur, however, he believed that Americans first needed to create a new "republic of letters," one inspired by the classical tradition, one that would yield a new social vision and the creation of a pure republic, a "glorious commonwealth, perpetually progressive, free from *caste*," and smiling upon "all her citizens."[5]

James McCune Smith was the foremost black intellectual in nineteenth-century America and the most educated before W. E. B. Du Bois. Born a slave in 1813 in New York City, the son of a white man and a self-emancipated bondwoman, he owed his liberty to the Emancipation Act of New York State, which freed the remaining slaves in New York on July 4, 1827.[6] He received his primary education at the Quaker-founded African Free School No. 2, which educated many of the nation's black leaders, including his mentor Peter Williams, Jr., the pastor of St. Philip's Episcopal Church, a center of black life in the city. McCune Smith graduated in 1828 and studied Latin and Greek with Williams to prepare for college, while also apprenticing to a blacksmith. The future essayist would always treat with dignity the "art" of manual labor.[7]

After being rejected from Columbia College and Geneva College (now Hobart and William Smith), he was admitted to the University of Glasgow, arguably more prestigious than any American college at the time. Black leaders raised enough money for him to attend, and he spent five years in Glasgow, obtaining his B.A. in 1835, his M.A. in 1836, and his M.D. in 1837, followed by a year-long residency in Paris. In each of his three degrees he graduated at or near the top of his class.[8]

Glasgow was indispensable to McCune Smith's development as a writer and scholar. He thrived at the same university that had educated Adam Smith and James Watt, and where Edmund Burke had held the ceremonial title of Rector. He absorbed the intellectual legacies of the Scottish Enlightenment. And he experienced a dearth of racism, enjoying a degree of freedom unknown to American blacks. He returned to New York City with as much training and confidence in his intellectual abilities as the most erudite white graduates, and he dedicated the rest of his life to educating and uplifting black and white Americans. He became a leading abolitionist, ran an interracial medical practice and pharmacy on fashionable West Broadway in New York City, and for twenty years served as chief physician at the New York City Colored Orphan Asylum, until racist anti-draft rioters burned it down during the Civil War.

As an abolitionist, educator, and physician, McCune Smith was an original essayist whose published work spanned multiple fields, from medicine, demography, and climate, to slavery and abolition, race, chess, poetry, and freemasonry. He broke the color barrier in medical scholarship by publishing two case studies in prestigious journals.[9] An accomplished statistician, he collaborated with the Harvard-educated physician and statistician Edward Jarvis to expose the errors of the 1840 U.S. Census, which erroneously suggested that slaves lived longer and healthier lives than free blacks. He was the first black to be elected to the American Geographical Society. He edited several New York City black papers and became the New York correspondent for

Frederick Douglass' Paper. Douglass thought so highly of him that he said: "No man in this country more thoroughly understands the whole struggle between freedom and slavery, than does Dr. Smith, and his heart is as broad as his understanding."[10]

McCune Smith loved languages: fluent in ancient Greek, Latin, and French, his writing also reveals varying degrees of proficiency in Spanish, German, Italian, and Hebrew. His reading was broad; among his favorites were Anacreon, Terence, Virgil, and Aristotle, along with British and American romantics. Much like Thoreau, he believed that languages and the humanities, along with the natural and social sciences, were necessary to "give an account of the nature of things." Only by treating all knowledge as "a systemic whole" could one ascertain one's world.[11] He was a central figure in what has sometimes been called the American and African American literary Renaissance, a time when writers and artists (mostly white) felt newly inspired by classicism.[12]

In his early essay, "The Destiny of the People of Color" (1843), McCune Smith established strategies for fighting slavery and racism that he would develop over the rest of his career. The classical tradition was central to these strategies, for, like other Americans, he saw the U.S. as following in the footsteps of Greece and Rome. All three countries only "pretended to be Republican in their form of government"; they were in fact "Polygarchies, or Tyrannies of many masters." He cited Demosthenes, who said that "a government built on a fictitious foundation must fail."[13] Such had been the fate of almost all Republics, he concluded. "The same epitaph is written over their graves—SLAVERY. . . . Slavery destroyed the Republics of Antiquity; shall it also destroy our Republic?"[14] The answer hung in the balance. Classical writers offered cautionary tales of destruction, but they also pointed the way to reform and the realization of a lasting Republic.

Aristotle provided one such cautionary tale. McCune Smith attributed to him the doctrine that "'Might makes Right': because men have the power, therefore, they have the right to keep other men enslaved."[15] He also noted that the ratio of slaves to masters in America was much lower than among the Ancients. American slaves could take advantage of Aristotle's doctrine. And so for both practical and moral reasons, McCune Smith revised the doctrine of "might makes right" (much as Lincoln later would); for McCune Smith, "right makes right."[16]

Terence the playwright offered inspiration, in the form of a "sublime truth" that "sprang from the bitterness of slavery."[17] As McCune Smith knew, Terence was a North African slave who was brought to the Roman Republic and then educated and freed by his master. He quotes Terence's sublime truth, from *Heauton Timorumenos* (*The Self-Tormentor*): "*Homo sum, humani nil a me alienum puto,*" which McCune Smith translates as "I am a man, and I deem nothing human alien from me." Terence's "glorious sentiment" functions as the foundation of McCune Smith's essay: "The common brotherhood of humanity is a doctrine inseparably linked with our fate. It is the necessary consequence of the equality of all the members of the human species," a fact that America's founding document had acknowledged. "We are destined to demonstrate that equality," McCune Smith declared.[18] Although he does not say it in his essay, he was himself demonstrating interracial equality as an erudite writer, educator, and physician. He urged his fellow blacks to remain in America, educate and uplift themselves, embrace the doctrine that "right makes right," and integrate with whites as equals in a common brotherhood of humanity.

The destiny of the people of color in America was, McCune Smith stated, "eminently conservative," for it borrowed classical doctrines and a classical form of government. "We [blacks] will save the [classical] *form* of government and convert it into a substance," he declared. Over the grave of slavery will grow a "pure Republic."[19]

Form was intimately linked to substance. For McCune Smith, the substance of a "pure republic" borrowed from and depended upon classical forms of representation. Symmetry, order, repetition, and experimentation reflected and shaped an egalitarian society, he believed; poetic meter needed to mimic what was sung or said. Significantly, McCune Smith argues that the origins of these classical forms were as much African as Greek or Roman. As he notes after quoting Terence, some of the "sublime truths" of classicism "sprang from the very bitterness of slavery" and "were indebted" to African slaves.[20]

McCune Smith develops the links between African and classical forms and the problems of slavery and racism in America in one of his most original essays, "The Critic at Chess," published in *Frederick Douglass' Paper* in January 1855. He portrays himself and his black friend Philip Bell (who wrote under the pseudonym "Fylbel") playing chess and discussing Tennyson's recently published poem on the battle of Balaclava in Crimea, "The Charge of the Light Brigade" (December 1854).[21] McCune Smith connects America to antiquity by setting the drawing room, where he and Fylbel play chess, in New York City, probably on Broadway. Through the plate glass window, McCune Smith sees "the giant spire of St. John's" church on West 30th Street, a block from Broadway; it "shot up into the dim invisible air a fitting conductor to our saintly thoughts."[22] But he also says that they "sat in the drawing room of the Sybarites," which refers to inhabitants of the lavish, ancient Greek city of Sybaris.[23]

As they sip coffee, McCune Smith thinks of friends who have "fallen in the way beneath our feet," and chants from Tennyson's poem:

> Half a league, half a league,
> Half a league onward.

"Isn't that fine?" Fylbel says, referring to the poem. McCune Smith agrees:

> Yes, it beats Virgil's "*quatit ungula campum*" [the hooves shook the plain]; for we have not only the sound of the horses' feet, as they begin with a canter, but the rush into the gallop; and the poet has not only mastered the difficulty of repeating the same phrase in the same words, but actually triumphs in the *cumulus* gained in the repetition, and bursting into the "*praeruptus aquae mons*" [the sheer mountain of water].[24]

McCune Smith compares Tennyson's poem to Virgil's *Aeneid* by describing how metrical form mimics the substance. In both poems, he suggests, the meter mimics the sound of horses' hooves, much as the Latin hexameter in *praeruptus aquae mons* evokes the sound of a mountain of water crashing against a boat.[25]

Additionally, McCune Smith argues that the meter and repetition of Tennyson's poem, and perhaps even of Virgil's *Aeneid*, owe a debt to a Congo chant that is "as old as Africa," which he had recently discovered in the French literary journal *Revue des Deux Mondes*.[26] He compares a stanza from the Congo chant with one from Tennyson's "Charge" and convinces Fylbel of Tennyson's formal "burglary":

> CONGO.
> Canga bafio te,
> Canga moune de le,
> Canga do ki la,
> Canga li.

TENNYSON.
Cannon to right of them,
Cannon to left of them,
Cannon in front of them
    Volleyed and thundered.[27]

"Hurrah for our mother-land," cries Fylbel. He becomes even more excited when McCune Smith tells him that the Congo chant had been used as a war cry by Saint Domingue slaves in their revolution of 1791, which led to the "pure republic" of Haiti that abolished slavery.[28]

In drawing attention to the formal similarities of Tennyson's "Charge," the Congo chant, and excerpts from Virgil's *Aeneid*, in a setting that conflates ancient Greece with America, McCune Smith connects Greece and Rome with the present; Europe and the United States with Africa; and whites with blacks. In so doing, he implies that the creation of a "pure republic" in the United States will require a co-mingling of ancient, African, and contemporary (romantic) influences, much as he has provided in "Critic at Chess." In fact, at the end of his essay he recasts Tennyson's "Charge of the Light Brigade" as a literary rather than a military attack. He quotes another stanza from "Light Brigade":

Flashed all their sabers bare,
Flashed all at once in air,
Sabring the gunners there,
Charging an army, while
    All the world wondered.

Fylbel asks: "what, connected with your light brigade, fits in with 'all the world wondered?'" The world "wondered to see a *light brigade of readable matter*" in the press, McCune Smith answers, by which he meant original work (like his essay) that spoke to pressing social problems, rather than stale excerpts "scissored" from other papers or "transcribed from Mother Goose's melodies [and] 'Sinbad the Sailor.'"[29]

Original work that highlighted the lines of influence and aesthetic borrowings between classical antiquity and the present, and between Africa, Europe, and the U.S., could be the engine of social change, McCune Smith believed. By asserting themselves as "co-workers in the kingdom of culture," he, Fylbel, and other blacks could create new cultural forms that would transform society. In this sense, McCune

Smith anticipates the cultural co-minglings of W. E. B. Du Bois, who had also been trained in the classics: "I sit with Shakespeare and he winces not," Du Bois would write. "I summon Aristotle and Aurelius and what soul I will, and they come all graciously with no scorn nor condescension."[30]

McCune Smith hoped to create a new Republic of Letters inspired by the classical tradition, one that would precipitate a "pure Republic" in America. "Heads of the Colored People," a series of ten biographical sketches published in *Frederick Douglass' Paper* from 1852 to 1854, are his most original and self-conscious attempt to remake the Republic of Letters and the American republic. In these sketches he portrays with dignity the lives and careers of New York City's working-class blacks, giving voice and personality to those who have been forgotten, excluded from the public sphere.[31] His subjects range from a legless news vender to a bootblack, washerwoman, sexton, steward and stewardess, editor, inventor, whitewasher, and schoolmaster. They are defined principally in terms of their work, which is the key to their character. Such work brings autonomy in this Republic of Letters, and thus the right to citizenship.

Throughout the sketches, McCune Smith responds to racist stereotypes. His title, "Heads of the Colored People," parodies the language of ethnology (the precursor of anthropology). While ethnologists argued that the crania of Africans contained smaller and thus inferior brains, the heads of McCune Smith's characters resemble those of whites.[32] His legless and illiterate news vender has "a fine long hooked nose," "hazel eyes," and a brow that resembles Thomas Jefferson's. Indeed his brow might "prove him the incontestable descendant of Thomas Jefferson and Black Sal [Sally Hemings]."[33] McCune Smith then stops himself from expounding on Jefferson's interracial family by quoting the Roman maxim, *"nil de mortuis nisi bonum"* ("nothing but good of the dead," or more commonly, "don't speak ill of the dead"). Although it was a popular Latin quotation in the nineteenth century, the copy-editor for *Frederick Douglass' Paper* misquoted McCune Smith by publishing it as *"nil de mortus nise."* Such errors were understandable (and not uncommon), since neither Douglass nor his copy-editors knew any Latin. (McCune Smith became so frustrated with printing errors of his Latin phrases—phrases that readers might therefore think came from a mere pretender to classical learning—that in his sketch, "The Editor," he accused black editors of sometimes being "ignorant of the alphabet.")[34]

Classical references and influences are everywhere in these sketches. Indeed, McCune Smith begins the series with an epigraph from one of the Odes of Anacreon, often called "The Portrait."[35] Since the printer of *Frederick Douglass' Paper* did not have Greek typeface, he transliterates two lines:

> Age Zographon ariste,
> Graphe Zographon ariste
> [αγε, ζωγραφων αριστε, / γραφε, ζωγραφων αριστε] [Come, best of painters! / Paint, best of painters][36]

He then includes two lines of his own, inspired by lines from "The Portrait":

> Best of Painters, come away,
> Paint me the *whitewash brush*, I pray.[37]

The imperative phrase "Paint me the *whitewash brush*" echoes the subtitle of his sketches: "Done With a Whitewash Brush." McCune Smith asks the painters in Anacreon's ode to paint him a whitewash brush in order to "do" the sketches. His sketches depend upon these painters. "Paint me the *whitewash brush*" refers to his efforts, aided by Anacreon's ode, to reconceive the Republic of Letters in America and in antiquity by *including* blacks in them. As he notes in his sketch on "The Whitewasher," both he and whitewashers are portraitists, who know the "secrets about lime [whites] and lamp black [blacks], and sizing and mixing colors."[38] Whitewashers mix "white and color," lime and lamp black. His point is that whites and blacks contain each other; they are of one blood.[39]

As for the subject of Anacreon's ode, a "lovely maid that's far away," whom the "best of painters come [to] portray," she seems almost as much African as Greek. She has "jetty [black] ringlets straying" and "tendrils playing"; and "where her tresses' curly flow / Darkles o'er the brow of snow." In antiquity as in America, there was a co-mingling and color-mixing of black and white.[40]

"Heads of the Colored People" represents McCune Smith's efforts to democratize American and classical letters. Immediately after his epigraph that begins the series, he writes:

> If Daniel Webster, in search of the presidency, quoted New Testament Greek, why may not [McCune Smith] draw upon old Anacreon in his endeavor to win the post of door keeper, not to the Senate (heaven save the mark!), but to the outermost enclosure leading to the Republic of

Letters? That glorious commonwealth, perpetually progressive [and] free from caste, . . . smiles upon all her citizens. . . . Dear old musical Anacreon! If any doubts the music, let them read the above motto ["Age Zographon ariste"], pronouncing the first word "agge" and the "o" as in "zone."[41]

Classicism can empower blacks and women as much as senators and presidential aspirants. McCune Smith hopes to transform his nation through the art of his portraits, inspired by the classical tradition. He draws attention to the beauty of Anacreon's ode and helps his readers appreciate its music. Such beauty should be accessible to all. And so he seeks a position not in the Senate, which needs saving, but as doorkeeper to the "outermost enclosure leading to the Republic of Letters." This will better enable him to open the floodgates and give voice to the voiceless, much as the portraitist, in a more limited way, does in Anacreon's ode. The poet ends his ode by saying of the maiden he portrays: "It glows, it lives, it soon will speak."[42] McCune Smith seeks the same thing for his subjects: to glow, live, and speak.

In his lifetime, McCune Smith's efforts to create a Republic of Letters, inspired by classicism, that would usher in a "glorious commonwealth" and smile upon "all her citizens," largely failed. His fear that slavery would destroy America, as it had ruined the republics of antiquity (in his estimation), was briefly realized with disunion and civil war. He died in November 1865, a month before the Thirteenth Amendment abolishing chattel slavery was ratified.[43] The postwar era witnessed a dramatic decline in classical training, and in the idea that a Republic of Letters could transform a nation. It also brought about the reforging of a white, "fictitious" Republic, as McCune Smith might have said, and the elision of the African American literary Renaissance.[44] After the war, his writings followed the Odes of Anacreon and fell into obscurity.[45]

Yet, he accurately predicted that African Americans would one day rise up through their art. As he noted in "The Destiny of the Colored People":

We are destined to write the literature of this republic, which is still, in letters, a mere province of Great Britain. We have already, even from the depths of slavery, furnished the only music which the country has yet produced. We are also destined to write the poetry of the nation. . . . We are destined to write the oratory of this Republic.[46]

In the twentieth century blacks were instrumental in remaking their Republic of Letters and their nation, but without the same degree of classical influence that McCune Smith had imagined would be part of this transformation.

In one sense McCune Smith predicted his own delayed influence, for he felt that his own work, like that of his beloved classical writers, was "not of today only but of centuries." In characterizing himself, this former slave, this *libertinus*, again found inspiration in the language and imagery of the ancients (here it is Ovid):

> In the series of metamorphoses I must have had a coral insect for a millio-millio-grandfather, loving to work beneath the tide in a superstructure that some day, when the labourer is long dead and forgotten, may rear itself above the waves, and afford rest and habitation for the creatures of his Good, Good Father and All.[47]

To the end of his life, James McCune Smith remained as much a classicist as an abolitionist or physician.

Notes

1. James McCune Smith, "Citizenship," *The Anglo-African Magazine*, vol. 1 (1859) (New York: Arno Press and The New York Times, rpt. 1968), 144–50, at 150; Theodore Woolsey, "Opinion of Judge Daniel, in the Case of Dred Scott," *The New Englander* 59 (August 1857): 345–65, at 348, 349; Paul Finkelman, ed., *Dred Scott v. Sandford: A Brief History with Documents* (Boston: Bedford Books, 1997), quotation from Roger Taney at 61. On Woolsey as the nation's preeminent Greek scholar, see *Proceedings of the American Academy of Arts and Sciences* 25 (May 1889–May 1990): 343–46, accessed April 27, 2017, https://www.jstor.org/stable/20020454?seq=1#page_scan_tab_contents.
2. McCune Smith, "Citizenship," 149.
3. On classicism in American intellectual life see Caroline Winterer, *The Culture of Classicism: Ancient Greece and Rome in American Intellectual Life, 1780–1910* (Baltimore: Johns Hopkins University Press, 2002); and Winterer, *The Mirror of Antiquity: American Women and the Classical Tradition, 1750–1900* (Ithaca: Cornell University Press, 2007), chap. 6, "The Greek Slave, 1830–1865"; and Eric Ashley Hairston, *The Ebony Column: Classics, Civilization, and the African American Reclamation of the West* (Knoxville: University of Tennessee Press, 2013).

4. McCune Smith, "The Destiny of the People of Color" (1843), reprinted in John Stauffer, ed., *The Works of James McCune Smith: Black Intellectual and Abolitionist* (New York: Oxford University Press, 2006), 48–60, at 55.
5. McCune Smith, "'Heads of the Colored People,' Done with a Whitewash Brush: The Black News-Vender," *Frederick Douglass' Paper*, March 25, 1852. On the significance of a "Republic of Letters," see Michael Warner, *The Letters of the Republic: Publication and the Public Sphere in Eighteenth-Century America* (Cambridge, MA: Harvard University Press, 1990); and Pascale Casanova, *The World Republic of Letters*, trans. M. B. DeBevoise (Cambridge, MA: Harvard University Press, 2004).
6. New York State began a process of gradual abolition in 1799 by freeing all children born to slave mothers after July 4 of that year, provided that they had served their masters until age twenty-eight (for women, age twenty-five). The Emancipation Act of 1827 freed the state's remaining slaves. See Arthur Zilversmit, *The First Emancipation: The Abolition of Slavery in the North* (Chicago: University of Chicago Press, 1967), 181–82, 208–15.
7. There is no biography of McCune Smith. For aspects of his life and work see John Stauffer, *The Black Hearts of Men: Radical Abolitionists and the Transformation of Race* (Cambridge, MA: Harvard University Press, 2002); Stauffer, *Works*; David W. Blight, "In Search of Learning, Liberty, and Self Definition: James McCune Smith and the Ordeal of the Antebellum Black Intellectual," *Afro-Americans in New York Life and History* 9.2 (July 1985): 7–26; Thomas M. Morgan, "The Education and Medical Practice of Dr. James McCune Smith," *Journal of the National Medical Association* 95.7 (July 2003): 603–14; Bruce Dain, *A Hideous Monster of the Mind: American Race Theory in the Early Republic* (Cambridge, MA: Harvard University Press, 2002), 237–63; Leslie Harris, *In the Shadow of Slavery: African Americans in New York City, 1626–1863* (Chicago: University of Chicago Press, 2003), 145–69, 274–78; Patrick Rael, *Black Identity and Black Protest in the Antebellum North* (Chapel Hill: University of North Carolina Press, 2002), 51–53, 60–61, 193–94, 243–44; Ronald K. Burke, ed., *American Public Discourse: A Multicultural Perspective* (Lanham, MD: University Press of America, 1992); and Carla L. Peterson, *Black Gotham: A Family History of African Americans in Nineteenth-Century New York City* (New Haven: Yale University Press, 2011).
8. Morgan, "Education and Medical Practice," 603–10; W. Innes Addison, ed., *The Matriculation Albums of the University of Glasgow, from 1728–1858* (Glasgow: James Maclehose and Sons, Publishers to the University, 1913); *Colored American*, September 23, September 30, and October 28, 1837.

9. James McCune Smith, "On the Influence of Opium Upon the Catamenial Functions," *New York Journal of Medicine* 2 (1844): 57–58; McCune Smith, "Lay Puffery in Homeopathy," *Annalist: A Record of Practical Medicine in the City of New York* 2.18 (June 15, 1848): 348–51; Morgan, "Education and Medical Practice," 608–10.
10. Frederick Douglass, "Dr. James McCune Smith," *Douglass' Monthly*, March 1859, reprinted in *Douglass' Monthly*, Vols. 1–3, 1859–61 (New York: Negro Universities Press, 1969), at 35; Edward Jarvis, "Insanity among the Coloured Population of the Free States," *American Journal of the Medical Sciences* 7.13 (January 1844): 71–83; McCune Smith, "From the N.Y. Tribune: Freedom and Slavery for Afric-Americans," *Liberator*, February 23, 1844; "A Colored Savant," *Provincial Freeman*, May 20, 1854; Morgan, "Education and Medical Practice," 610.
11. See Introduction to the present volume, [INSERT PAGE RANGE].
12. Winterer, *Culture of Classicism*, chap. 3; Gene Andrew Jarrett, ed., *A Companion to African American Literature* (New York: Wiley-Blackwell, 2010), chap. 7: "The 1850s: The First Renaissance of Black Letters."
13. McCune Smith, "Destiny of the People of Color," 54.
14. Ibid., 54. In a footnote, McCune Smith notes that "the little Republic of San Marino, where slavery has never existed, has endured thirteen centuries and manifests no sign of decay" (72n125).
15. In attributing the doctrine that "might makes right" to Aristotle, McCune Smith paraphrases *Politics* by quoting from James Beattie, the then well-known Scottish philosopher. In 1770 Beattie paraphrased Aristotle in his *Essay on the Nature and Immutability of Truth, in Opposition to Sophistry and Scepticism*: "Men of little genius and great bodily strength, are by nature destined to serve, and those of better capacity, to command, wherefore the nations of Greece and some other countries, being naturally superior in genius, have a natural right to empire; and the rest of mankind being naturally stupid, are destined to labor and slavery." Beattie's paraphrase stems from Aristotle's proslavery argument in *Politics*, Book 1, Chaps. 5–6: "That one should command and another obey is both necessary and expedient. Indeed some things are so divided right from birth, some to rule, some to be ruled. . . . [A]nything which conquers does so because it excels in some good. It seems therefore that force is not without virtue." Although he was familiar with Aristotle's *Politics*, McCune Smith in his footnote quotes Beattie's paraphrase of Aristotle. See McCune Smith, "Destiny of the People of Color," 71–72n118; James Beattie, *Essays on the Nature and Immutability of Truth* . . . (Edinburgh: William Creech, 1777), 309; Aristotle, *The Politics*, ed. and trans. T. A. Sinclair (New York: Penguin Books, 1992), 67, 72.

16. McCune Smith, "Destiny," in Stauffer, *Works*, 52; Lincoln, "Address at Cooper Institute," *Great Speeches* (New York: Dover, 1991), 51. In the 1850s, McCune Smith abandoned the nonviolent implications of the doctrine that "right makes right," much as Lincoln did fourteen months after ending his 1860 Cooper Union address with a similar doctrine: "LET US HAVE FAITH THAT RIGHT MAKES MIGHT." The belligerence and aggressiveness of proslavery Southerners convinced both men that armed resistance was the only way to preserve the Union and end slavery. Like most other black and many white abolitionists in the 1850s, McCune Smith realized that slavery itself constituted a state of civil war, and the only way to preserve the peace was to end the civil war. He became a friend and political colleague of John Brown and probable conspirator in Brown's interracial raid on Harpers Ferry in 1859, sparking the Civil War. See Stauffer, *Black Hearts of Men*, chaps. 5, 6, 8; and Stauffer, *Works*, ix, xxiii–xxviii.
17. McCune Smith, "Destiny," in Stauffer, *Works*, 53. On Terence see John Barsby, ed. and trans., *Terence, Volume 1: The Woman of Andros; The Self-Tormentor; The Eunuch*, Loeb Classical Library (Cambridge, MA: Harvard University Press, 2001).
18. McCune Smith, "Destiny," in Stauffer, *Works*, 53. McCune Smith's quotation from Terence appears in Act I of *The Self-Tormentor*. See Barsby, *Terence*, 186, 187. Barsby translates Terence's line as "I'm human, and I regard no human business as other people's" (187). Barsby gives Terence's Latin as *"nil,"* where other sources use *"nihil."*
19. McCune Smith, "Destiny," in Stauffer, *Works*, 53.
20. Ibid., 53.
21. McCune Smith's essay coincided with the birth of chess as a common recreation and the popularity of competitive chess, with public establishments setting aside rooms for chess playing. See Harry Golombek, *Chess: A History* (New York: Putnam, 1976); Richard G. Eales, *Chess: The History of a Game* (London: B. T. Batsford, 1985); and Harold J. R. Murray, *A History of Chess: The Original 1913 Edition* (New York: Skyhorse Publishers, 2012).
22. McCune Smith, "The Critic at Chess," in Stauffer, *Works*, 109. The location of the New York drawing room that McCune Smith describes is probably Donadi's on Broadway, where black and white men could play chess in luxury, and where one could see the large spire of St. John the Baptist Church, a block away on West 30th Street. His description of the interior of "the drawing room of the Sybarites" resembles the interior of Donadi's described in his 1859 essay, "Chess." See McCune Smith, "The Critic at Chess" and "Chess," in Stauffer, *Works*, 109 (quoted), 283–84.
23. McCune Smith, "Critic at Chess," 109.

24. Ibid., 109–10.
25. As McCune Smith no doubt knew, Virgil's line, *quadrupedante putrem sonitu quatit ungula campum* (resounding, the horses' hooves shook the crumbling plain), was often used in Latin textbooks to show how the meter (five feet of dactyls before a closing spondee) mimics the sound of horses' hooves. See McCune Smith, "Critic at Chess," 135n122. On the influence of classical literature on Tennyson, see A. A. Markley, "Tennyson," in *The Oxford History of Classical Reception in English Literature, Vol. 4 (1790–1880)*, ed. Norman Vance and Jennifer Wallace (Oxford: Oxford University Press, 2015), 539–57; Robert Pattison, *Tennyson and Tradition* (Cambridge, MA: Harvard University Press, 1979), 1–14, 128–52.
26. McCune Smith, "Critic at Chess," 110. The article that McCune Smith refers to is Gustave D'Alaux, "L'empereur Soulouque et son empire," *Revue des Deux Mondes* 10–12 (1850): 1041–65, with lines from the Congo chant as the epigraph at 1040; it was republished as "L'Illuminisme négre.—Les dévotions de madame Soulouque.—La chasse aux fétiches," in Gustave D'Alaux, *L'empereur Soulouque et son empire* (Paris: Michel Lévy, 1856), 63–78, with lines from the Congo chant at 63. D'Alaux also wrote on the Saint Domingue revolution. According to Mimi Sheller, D'Alaux was the penname of the French consul, General Maxime Reybaud. See Mimi Sheller, *Democracy after Slavery: Black Publics and Peasant Radicalism in Haiti and Jamaica* (Gainesville: University Press of Florida, 2000), 133.
27. McCune Smith, "Critic at Chess," 110.
28. Ibid.; D'Alaux, *L'empereur Soulouque et son empire*, 63–64.
29. McCune Smith, "Critic at Chess," 112 (emphasis added). McCune Smith often used both British and American spelling in the same essay, as in "saber" and "sabre" or "sabring"; "color" and "colour"; "labor" and "labour."
30. W. E. B. Du Bois, *The Souls of Black Folk* (1903; rpt. New York: Penguin Books, 1989), 90.
31. Stauffer, *Works*, 185–242.
32. George M. Fredrickson, *The Black Image in the White Mind: The Debate on Afro-American Character and Destiny, 1817–1914* (Middletown, CT: Wesleyan University Press, 1987), chap. 3; Stephen Jay Gould, *The Mismeasure of Man, Revised and Expanded* (New York: W.W. Norton, 1996), chaps. 2–3; Ann Fabian, *The Skull Collectors: Race, Science, and America's Unburied Dead* (Chicago: University of Chicago Press, 2010).
33. To support his contention that Jefferson sought "the dalliance of black women" and left "many descendants of mixed blood," he cites David Francis Bacon, *Wanderings on the Seas and Shores of Africa. Part I* (New York: Joseph W. Harrison, 1843), 111–12. McCune Smith, "The

Black News-Vender," in Stauffer, *Works*, 191, 236n13. On rumors in the antebellum era that Jefferson had fathered black children, see Annette Gordon-Reed, *Thomas Jefferson and Sally Hemings: An American Controversy* (Charlottesville: University Press of Virginia, 1997), Introduction, chap. 6.

34. McCune Smith, "Black News-Vender," 191. On the popularity of "*Nil de mortuis nisi bonum*," see William C. Smith, "The Note-Book of an Irish Barrister.—No. VI," *The Metropolitan Magazine* 22 (May to August, 1838) (London: Saunders and Otley, 1838), 3; "Nil De Mortuis Nisi Bonum. The Statement of Matthew Grime," *Chicago Tribune*, March 18, 1861; and "Nil de Mortuis Nisi Bonum," *Colby Stories, As Told By Colby Men of the Classes 1832 to 1902*, ed. Herbert Carlyle Libby (Concord, NH: The Rumford Press, 1900), 178–81. McCune Smith, "The Editor," in Stauffer, *Works*, 214–15.

35. On the spurious attribution of the Odes of Anacreon to Anacreon, and the relationship between Anacreon's poetry and the "Anacreon-tea," as the Odes came to be called, see David A. Campbell, ed. and trans., *Greek Lyric II: Anacreon, Anacreontea, Choral Lyric From Olympus to Alcman* (Cambridge, MA: Harvard University Press, 1988), 3–20; Tom Mason, "Abraham Cowley and the Wisdom of Anacreon," *The Cambridge Quarterly* 19, no. 2 (1990): 103–37; Bonnie MacLachlan, "Anacreon and Anacreontea," *The Classical Review* 54, no. 2 (October 2004): 297–99; Patricia A. Rosenmeyer, *The Poetics of Imitation: Anacreon and the Anacreontic Tradition* (Cambridge: Cambridge University Press, 1992); and John O'Brien, *Anacreon Redivivus: A Study of Anacreontic Translation in Mid-Sixteenth-Century France* (Ann Arbor: University of Michigan Press, 1995). The debate over the attribution of the Odes of Anacreon was apparently something McCune Smith was not aware of. As Mason notes, it was only beginning in the mid-nineteenth century that the association between the historical Anacreon and the Odes of Anacreon, first published by Henry Stephen in 1554, "began to collapse" among general readers (106). It was, however, clear to scholars by the early nineteenth century that the poems translated as the Odes of Anacreon "all dated from long after Anacreon's time." See "Anacreontea," *Oxford Classical Dictionary*, ed. Simon Hornblower and Antony Spawforth (New York: Oxford University Press, 1996), 80.

36. McCune Smith, "The Black News-Vender," 190. The translations are from Campbell, *Greek Lyric*, 182, 183.

37. McCune Smith, "The Black News-Vender," 190 (emphasis in the original).

38. Ibid., 190; McCune Smith, "The Whitewasher," in Stauffer, *Works*, 222.

39. McCune Smith, "The Whitewasher," 220, 222; Acts 17:26. My argument may seem counter-intuitive, since "whitewash" means to paint something white, or in the present day especially to conceal someone's faults, mistakes, or unseemly behavior. But it derives from McCune Smith's sketch of "The Whitewasher."
40. Thomas Moore, ed. and trans., *The Odes of Anacreon, with Fifty-Four Illustrative Designs by Girodet Roussy* (London: John Camden Hotten, Piccadilly, 1871), 118. My quotations are from ll. 3–4 of Moore's edition and translation: "Best of painters! come portray / The lovely maid that's far away." I have chosen Moore's translation because it is the one McCune Smith would have been most familiar with. Published in the U.S. as early as 1804, it was quite popular in America and Britain. In addition, Henry David Thoreau translated selections from the *Anacreontea*, which appeared in the *Dial* in 1843.

    On the image of blacks in antiquity, see especially Benjamin H. Isaac, *The Invention of Racism in Classical Antiquity* (Princeton: Princeton University Press, 2004); and David Bindman and Henry Louis Gates, Jr., ed., *The Image of the Black in Western Art: From the Pharaohs to the Fall of the Roman Empire* (1976; rpt. Cambridge, MA: Harvard University Press, 2010).
41. McCune Smith, "The Black News-Vender," 190–91.
42. Moore, *Odes of Anacreon*, 121. The ending of this ode in Campbell's edition is: "Soon, wax, you will be talking too." See Campbell, *Greek Lyric*, 185.
43. McCune Smith's writings contributed in a small way to the passage and ratification of the Reconstruction amendments, owing to his influence as a leading abolitionist and his friendships with Frederick Douglass and the abolitionist senator Charles Sumner. See Stauffer, *Black Hearts of Men*, chaps. 1–2, 5–8; Stauffer, *Works*, xiv, xvi; xxiv–xxviii; and James McCune Smith to Charles Sumner, December 15, 1863, The Papers of Charles Sumner, Houghton Library, Harvard University.
44. Winterer, *Culture of Classicism*, 5, chap. 5; Edward J. Blum, *Reforging the White Republic: Race, Religion, and American Nationalism, 1865–1898* (2007; rpt. Baton Rouge: Louisiana State University Press, 2015); Louis Menand, *The Metaphysical Club: A Story of Ideas in America* (New York: Farrar, Straus and Giroux, 2001), 369–75.
45. Mason, "Abraham Cowley and the Wisdom of Anacreon," 107. Mason notes that "for the last hundred years, classical students seem to have been quite sure that the three hundred years of European admiration for 'Anacreon' was merely an aberration. . . . Anacreon is not a poet who means much (if anything) to most twentieth-century Europeans. In effect Anacreon has become once again . . . an empty name."
46. McCune Smith, "Destiny of the People of Color," 59.

47. McCune Smith to Gerrit Smith, May 12, 1848, in Stauffer, *Works*, 308. Like McCune Smith, Ovid's *Metamorphoses* "calls attention to the boundaries between divine and human, animal and inanimate, raising fundamental questions about definition and hierarchy in the universe." See "Ovid," *Oxford Classical Dictionary*, 1085. Other classicists also invoked the metaphor of a "coral insect" [coral-polyp]: Oliver Wendell Holmes, "The Poet at the Breakfast Table. V," *Atlantic Monthly* 29.175 (May 1872): 618; Lydia Sigourney, "The Coral Insect," *Poems* (Philadelphia: T. K. Collins & Co., 1834), 167–68; Edward Rowland Sill, "Principles of Criticism," *Atlantic Monthly* 56.337 (November 1885): 674.

Bibliography

Addison, W. Innes, ed. *The Matriculation Albums of the University of Glasgow, from 1728–1858*. Glasgow: James Maclehose and Sons, Publishers to the University, 1913.

Aristotle. *The Politics* (1962). Edited and translated by T. A. Sinclair. New York: Penguin Books, 1992.

Bacon, David Francis. *Wanderings on the Seas and Shores of Africa. Part I*. New York: Joseph W. Harrison, 1843.

Barsby, John, ed. and trans. *Terence, Volume 1: The Woman of Andros; The Self-Tormentor; The Eunuch*. Cambridge, MA: Harvard University Press, 2001.

Beattie, James. *Essays on the Nature and Immutability of Truth in Opposition to Sophistry and Scepticism; On Poetry and Music, as they Affect the Mind; On Laughter, and Ludicrous Composition; On the Utility of Classical Learning*. Edinburgh: William Creech, 1777.

Bindman, David, and Henry Louis Gates, Jr., eds. *The Image of the Black in Western Art: From the Pharaohs to the Fall of the Roman Empire* (1976). Cambridge, MA: Harvard University Press, 2010.

Blight, David W. "In Search of Learning, Liberty, and Self Definition: James McCune Smith and the Ordeal of the Antebellum Black Intellectual." *Afro-Americans in New York Life and History* 9, no. 2 (July 1985): 7–26.

Blum, Edward J. *Reforging the White Republic: Race, Religion, and American Nationalism, 1865–1898*. 2007. Reprint, Baton Rouge: Louisiana State University Press, 2015.

Burke, Ronald K., ed. *American Public Discourse: A Multicultural Perspective*. Lanham, MD: University Press of America, 1992.

Campbell, David A., ed. and trans. *Greek Lyric II: Anacreon; Anacreontea; Choral Lyric From Olympus to Alcman*. Cambridge, MA: Harvard University Press, 1988.

Casanova, Pascale. *The World Republic of Letters.* Translated by M. B. DeBevoise. Cambridge, MA: Harvard University Press, 2004.

The Colored American (1837–41). Accessed April 27, 2017. http://www.accessible-archives.com/tag/the-colored-american/.

"A Colored Savant." *Provincial Freeman*, May 20, 1854.

D'Alaux, Gustave. *L'empereur Soulouque et son empire.* Paris: Michel Lévy, 1856.

Dain, Bruce. *A Hideous Monster of the Mind: American Race Theory in the Early Republic.* Cambridge, MA: Harvard University Press, 2002.

Du Bois, W. E. B. *The Souls of Black Folk* (1903). New York: Penguin Books, 1989.

Eales, Richard G. *Chess: The History of a Game.* London: B. T. Batsford, 1985.

Fabian, Ann. *The Skull Collectors: Race, Science, and America's Unburied Dead.* Chicago: University of Chicago Press, 2010.

Finkelman, Paul, ed. *Dred Scott v. Sandford: A Brief History with Documents.* Boston: Bedford Books, 1997.

Fredrickson, George M. *The Black Image in the White Mind: The Debate on Afro-American Character and Destiny, 1817–1914* (1971). Middletown, CT: Wesleyan University Press, 1987.

Golombek, Harry. *Chess: A History.* New York: Putnam, 1976.

Gordon-Reed, Annette. *Thomas Jefferson and Sally Hemings: An American Controversy.* Charlottesville: University Press of Virginia, 1997.

Gould, Stephen Jay. *The Mismeasure of Man, Revised and Expanded.* New York: W. W. Norton, 1996.

Hairston, Eric Ashley. *The Ebony Column: Classics, Civilization, and the African American Reclamation of the West.* Knoxville: University of Tennessee Press, 2013.

Harris, Leslie. *In the Shadow of Slavery: African Americans in New York City, 1626–1863.* Chicago: University of Chicago Press, 2003.

Holmes, Oliver Wendell. "The Poet at the Breakfast Table. V." *Atlantic Monthly* 29, no. 175 (May 1872): 608–18.

Hornblower, Simon, and Antony Spawforth, eds. *Oxford Classical Dictionary.* New York: Oxford University Press, 1996.

Isaac, Benjamin H. *The Invention of Racism in Classical Antiquity.* Princeton: Princeton University Press, 2004.

Jarrett, Gene Andrew, ed. *A Companion to African American Literature.* New York: Wiley-Blackwell, 2010.

Jarvis, Edward. "Insanity among the Coloured Population of the Free States." *American Journal of the Medical Sciences* 7, no. 13 (January 1844): 71–83.

Lincoln, Abraham. "Address at Cooper Institute" (1860). *Great Speeches.* New York: Dover, 1991.

MacLachlan, Bonnie. "Anacreon and Anacreontea." *The Classical Review* 54, no. 2 (October 2004): 297–99.

Markley, A. A. "Tennyson." In *The Oxford History of Classical Reception: Volume 4 (1790–1880)*, edited by Norman Vance and Jennifer Wallace, 539–57. Oxford: Oxford University Press, 2015.

Mason, Tom. "Abraham Cowley and the Wisdom of Anacreon." *The Cambridge Quarterly* 19, no. 2 (1990): 103–37.

Menand, Louis. *The Metaphysical Club: A Story of Ideas in America*. New York: Farrar, Straus and Giroux, 2001.

Moore, Thomas, ed. and trans. *The Odes of Anacreon, with Fifty-Four Illustrative Designs by Girodet Roussy*. London: John Camden Hotten, Piccadilly, 1871.

Morgan, Thomas M. "The Education and Medical Practice of Dr. James McCune Smith." *Journal of the National Medical Association* 95, no. 7 (July 2003): 603–14.

Murray, Harold J. R. *A History of Chess: The Original 1913 Edition*. New York: Skyhorse Publishers, 2012.

O'Brien, John. *Anacreon Redivivus: A Study of Anacreontic Translation in Mid-Sixteenth-Century France*. Ann Arbor: University of Michigan Press, 1995.

Pattison, Robert. *Tennyson and Tradition*. Cambridge, MA: Harvard University Press, 1979.

Peterson, Carla L. *Black Gotham: A Family History of African Americans in Nineteenth-Century New York City*. New Haven: Yale University Press, 2011.

Rael, Patrick. *Black Identity and Black Protest in the Antebellum North*. Chapel Hill: University of North Carolina Press, 2002.

Rosenmeyer, Patricia A. *The Poetics of Imitation: Anacreon and the Anacreontic Tradition*. Cambridge: Cambridge University Press, 1992.

Sheller, Mimi. *Democracy after Slavery: Black Publics and Peasant Radicalism in Haiti and Jamaica*. Gainesville: University Press of Florida, 2000.

Sigourney, Lydia. *Poems*. Philadelphia: T. K. Collins & Co., 1834.

Sill, Edward Rowland. "Principles of Criticism." *Atlantic Monthly* 56, no. 337 (November 1885): 665–76.

Smith, James McCune. "Citizenship." *The Anglo-African Magazine, Volume 1* (1859). New York: Arno Press and The New York Times, 1968, 144–50.

———. "From the N.Y. Tribune: Freedom and Slavery for Afric-Americans." *The Liberator*, February 23, 1844.

———. "Lay Puffery in Homeopathy." *Annalist: A Record of Practical Medicine in the City of New York* 2, no. 12 (June 15, 1848): 348–51.

———. "On the Influence of Opium Upon the Catamenial Functions." *New York Journal of Medicine* 2 (1844): 57–58.

Stauffer, John. *The Black Hearts of Men: Radical Abolitionists and the Transformation of Race*. Cambridge, MA: Harvard University Press, 2002.

———, ed. *The Works of James McCune Smith: Black Intellectual and Abolitionist*. New York: Oxford University Press, 2006.

Winterer, Caroline. *The Culture of Classicism: Ancient Greece and Rome in American Intellectual Life, 1780–1910*. Baltimore: Johns Hopkins University Press, 2002.

———. *The Mirror of Antiquity: American Women and the Classical Tradition, 1750–1900*. Ithaca: Cornell University Press, 2007.

Woolsey, Theodore. "Opinion of Judge Daniel, in the Case of Dred Scott." *The New Englander* 59 (August 1857): 345–65.

Zilversmit, Arthur. *The First Emancipation: The Abolition of Slavery in the North*. Chicago: University of Chicago Press, 1967.

Chapter 9

"In the face of the fire": Melville's Prometheus, Classical and Romantic Contexts

John P. McWilliams

As an example of how literary analogies create as well as define character, consider Melville's Captain Ahab. No dominant character has ever been more thoroughly fashioned from literary precedents. Ahab leads 'mad' black Pip by the hand with the tenderness of King Lear leading the Fool. Ahab exalts the possibilities of Man, but then undermines them, brooding upon his present inaction and planned destiny as if he were a New England Hamlet. Ahab withdraws into the defiant seclusion of his cabin like Manfred into his castle. Melville clearly intended the Parsee to serve as a Mephistopheles to Ahab's Faust. Ahab assaults God (or more often "the gods") from the vantage point of jealous and injured pride until, like Milton's Satan, he casts his "last cindered apple to the soil."[1] During the more admirable moments of declaring his monomania, Ahab even resembles Tennyson's Ulysses, sailing forth "to follow knowledge like a sinking star, / Beyond the utmost bound of human thought."[2]

Among these multiplying analogues, the significance of Prometheus has been comparatively neglected.[3] Although there are but two explicit references to Prometheus in *Moby-Dick*, their complexities deserve and reward detailed consideration. These complexities emerge from classical models of Promethean heroism, themselves contradictory. As studies of the changing characterization of Prometheus have shown, Prometheus has always served as a template for the age in which he is being reconsidered. In particular, the character of Ahab acquires resonance by being placed in the contexts of both Prometheus's classical origins and the so-called "Romantic Prometheus" first imagined by Goethe and then re-imagined by Byron, Mary Shelley, and Percy Shelley.[4] Through his references to Prometheus, Melville is not simply adding in another tired literary allusion; he is transforming a vital classical reference in ways dependent upon, but different from, his near contemporaries in the Romantic era. The cumulative Promethean legend becomes a clarifying lens through which Ahab sees himself, and Melville sees Ahab.

Two Passages: Contrarieties

After hours spent futilely trying to chart the location of Moby Dick, Ahab falls asleep with clenched hands, then awakens "with his own bloody nails in his palms," and rushes on deck as if "forks of flame" were issuing from the "hell in himself":

> For at such times, crazy Ahab, the scheming, unappeasedly steadfast hunter of the white whale; this Ahab that had gone to his hammock, was not the agent that so caused him to burst from it in horror again. The latter was the eternal, living principle or soul in him and in sleep, being for the time dissociated from the characterizing mind, which at other times employed it for its outer vehicle or agent, it spontaneously sought escape from the scorching contiguity of the frantic thing, of which, for the time, it was no longer an integral. But as the mind does not exist unless leagued with the soul, therefore it must have been that, in Ahab's case, yielding up all his thoughts and fancies to his one supreme purpose; that purpose, by its own sheer inveteracy of will, forced itself against gods and devils into a kind of self-assumed, independent being of its own. Nay, could grimly live and burn while the common vitality to which it was conjoined, fled horror-stricken from the unbidden and unfathered birth. Therefore, the tormented spirit that glared out of bodily eyes, when what seemed Ahab rushed from his room, was for the time but a vacated thing, a formless somnambulistic being, a ray of living light to be sure, but without an object to color, and therefore a blankness in itself. God help thee, old man, thy thoughts have created a creature in thee; and he whose intense thinking thus makes him a Prometheus; a vulture feeds upon that heart for ever; that vulture the very creature he creates. (202)

In Hesiod's *Theogony* and in Aeschylus's *Prometheus Bound*, Zeus sends an eagle with long wings to punish Prometheus for having stolen fire for the benefit of man. Melville, however, internalizes the agent of punishment; the "vulture" that torments Promethean Ahab is his own *self-created* mental state. Just as Melville follows

Marlowe's *Doctor Faustus* (1592) and Milton's *Paradise Lost* (1667) in redefining Hell as an interior mental condition, so he follows Byron's "Prometheus" (1816) in associating willed torture with a "vulture," not an "eagle."

The fire Prometheus brought to man becomes Melville's particular, almost obsessive concern. Throughout *Moby-Dick*, Melville ascribes consistently contradictory spiritual connotations to fire: inner burning (self-consumption as well as rage) but also cultural enlightenment (eradicating the evil of the old order) and prophetic insight (a clarifying of vision). Although the "independent being" controlling Ahab's "purpose" is declared to "burn" him, it is nonetheless identified as "a ray of living light," albeit without an "object to color." Ahab's hated whale therefore acquires characteristics, quite unlike Hesiod's or Aeschylus's Zeus, of a *deus absconditus*, especially with regard to his unforgettable "whiteness." The inner presence of the punishing agent does not, however, lessen Ahab's "grand, ungodly, god-like" qualities; his torment, true to the Aeschylean model, increases both his stature and his grandeur (79).

In his brooding intensity, Ahab so convincingly exemplifies what Melville called "this great power of blackness" that it is easy to overlook Ahab's insistence that his declared metaphysical purpose is to bring about enlightenment and a better world.[5] Responding to Starbuck's outcry that the pursuit of the white whale is outright blasphemy, "vengeance on a dumb brute," Ahab binds the crew to his purpose by exalting the force of free will in pursuit of now hidden, and perhaps forbidden knowledge:

> Hark ye yet again—the little lower layer. All visible objects, man, are but as pasteboard masks. But in each event—in the living act, the undoubted deed—there some unknown but still reasoning thing puts forth the mouldings of its features from behind the unreasoning mask. If man will strike, strike through the mask! How can the prisoner reach outside except by thrusting through the wall? To me, the white whale is that wall, shoved near to me. Sometimes I think there's naught beyond. But 'tis enough. He tasks me; he heaps me. I see in him outrageous strength, with an inscrutable malice sinewing it. That inscrutable thing is chiefly what I hate; and be the white whale agent, or be the white whale principal, I will wreak that hate upon him. Talk not to me of blasphemy, man; I'd strike the sun if it insulted me. (164)

Because Ahab meets his death, not in the jaws of Moby Dick but tangled in whaleboat lines symbolic of fate, the subtle specifics of Ahab's declaration of purpose can be easily overlooked. Beyond the unreasoning mask that hides truth are the yet undescried "features" of a power deemed to be a "reasoning thing." Ahab is not sure that the "reasoning thing" is an entity as specifically definable as the Greek God, the Calvinist God, or any other kind of deity or deities. His chief concern lies elsewhere. It is not the "strength" or the "malice" symbolized in the white whale he "chiefly hates." It is rather, the "wall" of inscrutability itself.

Ahab is fully aware that he cannot be certain that there is any power beyond the wall, nor does he know whether the whale is to be regarded as the "agent" or the "principal" of presumed evil; he is in essence defining deity as the term we ascribe to all those things we do not know. To *thrust* through the wall would be not only to kill the white whale but to burst the prison of blinded consciousness and thereby truly to *know*. Ahab would thereby rid the world of the hidden reasoning thing whose malice seems evident but not certain. To do so would raise human powers to the level of the sun's power to illuminate and/or to burn. To be sure, Melville leaves his reader free to regard Ahab's wording of his quest as a rationalization of personal injury, but the persuasive effect of Ahab's words upon the crew, including Ishmael, suggests that the redemptive purpose of Ahab's quest must be, at the least, seriously entertained.

As Ahab acquires Promethean qualities, he gains stature and grandeur at the expense of psychological integrity. Just as Ahab's body seeks escape from his cabin, so his mind is said to separate itself from his soul, his inner center bursting its protective shell in an effort to escape the "scorching contiguity" of the "frantic thing." However admirable Ahab's quest to confront malice and inscrutability may be, his self-creating quest becomes an "unbidden and unfathered birth," itself a kind of monstrosity, a focusing of light's energy upon vacancy. His quest is for white light with "no object to color." Just as the rhetoric through which Ishmael is rendering Ahab's psychic conflict risks impenetrability, so Ishmael's evaluation of Ahab's quest impels the reader toward contradictory responses. On the one hand, the daring of Ahab's purpose raises him to Promethean stature; on the other, Ishmael draws back from Ahab in fearful revulsion, culminating in the warning, "God help thee, old man; thy thoughts have created a creature in thee."

The second Promethean analogy occurs near the end of Ishmael's narrative, as Ahab orders Perth the blacksmith to fashion a special harpoon, the epic weapon with which Ahab will assault the white whale. Perth is a rapidly aging ex-alcoholic who, after losing his family and occupation ashore, has resigned himself to blacksmithing aboard a whaler. Ahab knows instinctively that Perth is one of those dogged laborers whose mind, working like an "unreasoning wheel," can easily be controlled by the cog of Ahab's purpose (468). While the carpenter and Perth are at work repairing Ahab's splintered leg, Ahab half-despairingly orders his own newly created self to be fashioned from the forge. He begins by referring ironically to Perth, not himself, as "Prometheus":

[Ahab]: "What's Prometheus about there:—the blacksmith, I mean—what's he about?"
[Carpenter]: "He must be forging the buckle-screw, sir, now."
[Ahab]: "Right. It's a partnership; he supplies the muscle part. He makes a fierce red flame there!"
[Carpenter]: "Aye, sir; he must have the white heat for this kind of fine work."
[Ahab]: "Um-m. So he must. I do deem it now a most meaning thing, that that old Greek, Prometheus, who made men, they say, should have been a blacksmith, and animated them with fire; for what's made in fire must properly belong to fire; and so hell's probable. How the soot flies! This must be the remainder the Greek made the Africans of. Carpenter, when he's through with that buckle, tell him to forge a pair of steel shoulder-blades; there's a pedlar board with a crushing pack."
[Carpenter]: "Sir?"
[Ahab]: "Hold; while Prometheus is about it, I'll order a complete man after a desirable pattern. Imprimis, fifty feet high, in his socks; then, chest modeled after the Thames Tunnel; then legs with roots to 'em, to stay in one place; then, arms three feet through the wrist; no heart at all, brass forehead, and about a quarter of an acre of fine brains—and let me see—shall I order eyes to see outwards? No, but put a sky-light on top of his head to illuminate inwards. There, take the order and away." (470)

The intricate intertextual cross-references of this passage are as perplexing as they are intriguing. Ahab would convince us that the modern Prometheus, to use Mary Shelley's term, is a melancholic blacksmith, a maker of hellish fire, his own ironic counterpart. Among the Greek and Roman deities, the god of the forge was, of course, Hephaistos (Vulcan), not Prometheus. In Aeschylus's *Prometheus Bound*, Hephaistos is compelled by Zeus to bind Prometheus to the rock, but Hephaistos does so with reluctance and admiring sympathy. Hephaistos expresses no resentment that Prometheus, by stealing fire, has co-opted his own special occupation for man's use.

Ahab is ordering the *Pequod*'s Prometheus to create a new man modeled upon himself. In Ahab's mind, blacksmithing, creation, Prometheus, and flaming fire are by now fully interconnected. The tradition that Prometheus, not Zeus, was the creator of mankind, modeling man from clay and water, originates not in Hesiod or Aeschylus, but independently; it is to be found in Aesop and Apollodorus, continued in Ovid, Catullus, and Horace, then restored and emphasized for Enlightenment purposes by Goethe and Percy Shelley. Coincidently, Ahab remarks at this point that he would also have Perth fashion for him "a pair of steel shoulder blades" as if he, Ahab, were Atlas (Prometheus's brother), condemned to be bearer of the world and its sufferings. This implied self-analogy, in turn, immediately gives way to yet another transformation of self, this time into John Bunyan's Christian, the pedlar-pilgrim knowingly carrying the "crushing pack" of Sin upon his shoulders.

The contemporary reference for Melville's second passage remains unmentioned. The very idea of having a man of commanding mind create a new and presumably better man almost certainly derives from Mary Shelley's *Frankenstein or The Modern Prometheus* (1818). The "desirable pattern" for man would be a Monster of a size and strength beyond the Monster Frankenstein created, but a Monster that, unlike Mary Shelley's prototype, has "no heart at all." His "quarter acre of fine brains" would not enable him to see outward; light could shine within upon his fine brain, but not outward from it. This fantastical new man is, of course, Ahab's ever-evolving self-image, his half-desired self emerging from his association of Prometheus with metaphysical overreaching.

But how is Melville's reader to assess such multifaceted attitudes? From Ahab's perspective, his words seem as jeeringly self-critical as they are self-aggrandizing. From Melville's perspective, is this characterization of the "Modern Prometheus" to be read as farce, as psychological insight, as ironic contrast to both Aeschylus and the Romantic Prometheus, or as a half-complimentary parody of Mary Shelley's novel? Elements of them all are here. One is tempted to avoid such questions by applying to this passage Ishmael's comment upon the very book he is writing, "I try all things; I achieve what I can" (345). But a return to Melville's sources, and to his other fictional references to Prometheus, provides clarification beyond simple surrender to the irresolvability of Melville's dazzling diversity of tone and seemingly improvisational contrarieties. Promethean

Ahab cannot be understood without knowledge of his classical and romantic origins.

References and Sources

In contrast to *Moby-Dick*, Melville's references to Prometheus in his other fictions are revealingly one-dimensional. They insist upon the futility of the quest for forbidden, presumably divine knowledge and they picture the inner torment of searching for it. Consider the following passage from *Mardi, and a Voyage Thither* (1849):

> For we are not gods and creators; and the controversialists have debated, whether indeed the All-Plastic Power itself can do more than mold. In all the universe is but one original; and the very suns must to their source for their fire; and we Prometheuses must to them for ours; which, when had, only perpetual vestal tending will keep alive.[6]

Melville's phrase "we Prometheuses" illustrates the truth in Albert Camus's observation: "We like to believe we live in Promethean times."[7] By 1849, many celebrators of mid-century American culture, confident of America's Manifest Destiny, technological sublime, and democratic progress, would have liked to believe that "we Prometheuses" were assaulting the heavens to repossess ultimate knowledge, technological and spiritual. Melville would remind the reader that there is in truth "but one original," a power of fire which is clearly beyond all observable suns. All "we" mortals can ever do is to search out fire in the suns we can see. The complex Promethean motivations of Ahab, an "original" character if ever there were one, are not yet within Melville's mythological compass.[8] His assumption is rather that every man is equal in facing the limitation placed upon Promethean purpose. Ahab, by contrast, was to acknowledge equality with no man and no god.

Young Wellingborough Redburn cannot forget the sight of an alcoholic sailor named Miguel Saveda, his "cadaverous face crawled over by a swarm of worm-like flames," dying of spontaneous combustion while his "whole face, now wound in curls of soft-blue flame, wore an aspect of grim defiance, and eternal death." In his very next sentence, Redburn finds an analogy for what he has just seen: "Prometheus, blasted by fire on the rock."[9] Miguel Saveda, like Prometheus, is being consumed from within, not by Zeus's eagle, but because he is somehow "blasted" by the very fire Prometheus had stolen. In this instance, Melville's Promethean metaphor has far overreached its referent. Saveda is mentioned in passing in one chapter only; his Promethean quest is never in any way explained.

In an equally self-destructive climactic moment, Pierre Glendinning proclaims himself "the fool of Truth, the fool of Virtue, the fool of Fate," rushes away from both Isabel and Lucy, searches out a brace of pistols, wonders "what wondrous tools Prometheus used," and then proclaims that his own pistols "in an instant, can unmake the topmost three-score-years-and-ten of all Prometheus' makings."[10] Promethean creativity is now applied to murderous as well as constructive purposes. In similar fashion, Bannadona, the arrogant architect of Melville's "The Bell Tower," is killed, like Frankenstein, by the mechanical servant he has secretly created. The narrator exposes the limitations of Bannadona's ambition: "With him, common sense was theurgy; machinery, miracle; Prometheus, the heroic name for machinist; man, the true God."[11] In none of these three characters is there the complicating Promethean quality of searching out the nature of malicious inscrutability in order to defy and possibly destroy it. Neither "grand" nor "godlike" is a word one could feasibly apply to any of the three characters, although Pierre might wish to claim such a stature for himself.

What can we ascertain about the source knowledge Melville brought to the multifaceted references to Prometheus in *Moby-Dick*? In all likelihood, Melville's first important exposure to Prometheus came not from literature but from painting. In May of 1847 Melville visited the New York Gallery of Fine Arts, where Thomas Cole was exhibiting his recently completed *Prometheus Bound*.[12] Cole placed the Titan bound to an immense crag thrusting high above a barren landscape into blue sky, with a long-winged bird, presumably an eagle, flying toward him from the lower left. Prometheus's body is placed very much in the manner of an early Italian Renaissance crucifixion, from a low vantage point, his nude pale body contorted, with his face resigned, facing the viewer. The first time Ishmael sees Ahab, he describes him not only as a man scorched by lightning and "cut away from the stake," but as one "stricken ... with a crucifixion in his face; in all the nameless regal overbearing dignity of some mighty woe" (123, 124). So begins the conflation—and divergence—of Ahab with Prometheus, Christ, Satan, and many other literary-mythological figures. Christ, we remember, brought saving knowledge of a redemptive God to man. Christ came to bruise the Serpent's heel; he also came, however, to bring not Peace, but a Sword.

"History," the lead essay in Emerson's *Essays: First Series* (1841), with which Melville became familiar in 1850, had also likened Prometheus to Christ:

> What a range of meanings and what perpetual pertinence has the story of Prometheus! Beside its primary value as the first chapter of the history of Europe, (the mythology thinly veiling authentic facts, the invention of the mechanic arts and the migration of colonies,) it gives the history of religion with some closeness to the faith of later ages. Prometheus is the Jesus of the old mythology.[13]

To Melville as to Emerson, Prometheus and Jesus belonged to history because both belonged to myth in the deepest sense of the term; they were integral to the "one mind common to all individual men," which the first line of Emerson's essay and book proclaims (3). Prometheus may be the champion of mankind because he invents "the mechanic arts," but the larger "story" of Prometheus belongs to the history of religion, to the search for the universals that would make the "faith of later ages" possible. For both authors, needless to say, the "faith of later ages" should be neither doctrinal nor dogmatic. Emerson therefore portrays Prometheus and Jesus as confident seekers of the still-unfolding sources of man's salvation.

Within the cumulative "matter" of Prometheus, which writings were known to Melville? Thanks to the research of Merton Sealts into Melville's reading and of Mary Berclaw into Melville's sources, we can be sure of the following. Melville had referred both to Byron and to Prometheus in the first number of "Fragments From a Writing Desk" (1837). In 1849, before his trip to England he purchased the thirty-seven-volume set of the Harper's Classical Library, which included the Robert Potter translation of Aeschylus's *Prometheus Bound* (1777), but not Hesiod. Among the books Melville brought back from London were Mary Shelley's *Frankenstein* (the 1831 revised edition with Mary Shelley's preface) and Goethe's *Autobiography, Aus Meinem Leben, Dichtung und Wahrheit* (1811–14), which contains Goethe's reflections on Prometheus, together with a reference to his poem "Prometheus" (c. 1773). Melville's sister Augusta had owned the *Complete Works of Byron* (1835) as early as 1842, and Elizabeth Melville's brother presented her with multiple volumes of Byron's writings in 1847.

Melville's familiarity with all of these texts can safely be assumed. As I hope to demonstrate, it is also hard to deny, though impossible to prove, that Melville had recently read or reread the poems titled

"Prometheus" by Goethe and Byron, as well as Shelley's *Prometheus Unbound* (1820). (Goethe's poem had been published in an English translation in 1831; in the late 1850s, Melville was to obtain editions of the poetry of Shelley and Byron, perhaps for purposes of studying versification). In all probability Melville had in September of 1850 also read Emerson's recently published essay on Goethe in *Representative Men* (1850) as well as parts of Emerson's *Essays: First Series* (1841). Given the references to Plato in Melville's writings and letters from 1847 to 1851, it seems at least possible that Melville knew Plato's *Protagoras*, in which Protagoras introduces Prometheus as the god who, by stealing fire and by his technical ingenuity, made it possible for Zeus to endow humankind with a civic and moral sense. The importance of these source details is twofold. They demonstrate the half-systematic, half-random way in which Melville internalized his readings, then assimilated them with seeming effortlessness into his fiction. But, more particularly for our purpose, they show that by 1850 Melville had acquired an understanding of both the Prometheus of classical tradition (itself quite varied) and the remarkably different Prometheus invoked by the generation of great poets that immediately preceded his own.

Transforming Tradition

Ovid and other Roman poets (Catullus, Horace, Propertius) conceived of Prometheus primarily as the potter-creator of mankind, mixing clay and water into human form, not as the fire-bringer.[14] This latter view, which would be crucial to the European romantic poets, is of little or no importance to Hesiod, earliest known source of the Greek myth. After picturing Zeus binding Prometheus to a pillar and sending an eagle to devour Prometheus's liver, Hesiod refers in passing to Prometheus's theft merely as "the ray, far-seeing, of unwearied fire."[15] Whatever metaphoric implications the word "fire" may have are far less important to Hesiod than Zeus's retaliatory creation of Woman (Pandora), source of all man's earthly trials, as punishment for Prometheus's recklessness. In *Theogony* and in *Works and Days*, three times as many lines are devoted to Pandora as to Prometheus's theft of fire. Whether Melville knew Hesiod's poems or not, Pandora's role in the Promethean legacy remained of minimal interest to him. Melville also disregards Hesiod's contrast between Prometheus ("Forethought") and his dull-witted brother Epimetheus ("Afterthought"), who had been gulled by Zeus's offering of Pandora. Ahab's confrontational directness has no place in Hesiod's *Theogony*; Hesiod's Prometheus is a would-be trickster god, the originator of animal sacrifice, who fully deserved punishment at the hands of all-mighty Zeus. The first five adjectives Hesiod applies to Prometheus in the *Theogeny* are, in order, "brilliant," "shifty," "clever," "audacious," and "sly" (39–41). The best Hesiod can muster on Prometheus's behalf is to close by informing his reader that, "kind" and "wise" though Prometheus may have been, "it is impossible to hoodwink Zeus" (43).[16]

For Melville, the significance of Prometheus originates in Aeschylus's *Prometheus Bound*.[17] As Kratos (Might) says in the opening words of the play, while dragging Prometheus to the rock, Prometheus is both the "champion of the human race" and "the rebel."[18] By these words, Prometheus's role is immediately exalted beyond Hesiod's imagining. The fire which Hesiod's Prometheus stole from heaven had primarily provided mankind with a means of cooking food and securing warmth; only secondarily was it a source of technology. To explain how "All human skill and science was Prometheus's gift," Aeschylus's Prometheus describes at length the benefits he has brought to humanity through the theft of fire: tools and skills, agriculture and navigation, medicines and metallurgy, all of them used to transform mankind's world thanks to Prometheus's skills at writing and mathematics, as well as his sense of historical time. Prometheus, in sum, gave humanity "mind and reason," enabling the human race to progress beyond the instinctive animality of the Titans to the arts of civilization (34). Prometheus's enumeration of his benefits to mankind ends by emphasizing a gift that was to be of special pertinence to Melville's Ahab as Ahab makes final preparations to confront Moby Dick. Prometheus has given mortals his own power of foresight, "various modes of prophecy:" "*signs from flames*, obscure before, I now made plain" (35, italics mine).

In post-Enlightenment cultural terms, Aeschylus's Prometheus sought to benefit the human race by bringing the gifts that would enable Greece to emerge from the Iron Age into the light of civilization. Ahab, by contrast, seeks to benefit humanity, not only by seeking forbidden knowledge, but by ridding the world of the agent or principal of inscrutable evil. However different the acts issuing from these motives, their shared determination to benefit humankind at any personal cost depends upon shared assumptions. Just as Ahab believes there is a power beyond the pasteboard mask and a power beyond the lightning, so Prometheus remains convinced there is a power beyond Zeus that is personified in the three Fates and the

Furies who "control Necessity" (35). Both heroes share an assumption that the god whom they challenge through their force of will is essentially malicious. Unlike Hesiod, Aeschylus claims that before Prometheus intervened to champion mankind, Zeus had wished to destroy humanity and create another race (27).

Prometheus denounces Zeus as a ruthless, immovable tyrant driven by "black ingratitude" and "merciless anger" (26, 27). Similarly, Ahab (convinced like Ishmael that the "invisible spheres were formed in fright") assumes that the viciousness of creatures beneath the mask of the sea's surface infers the malice of the godlike white whale (195). Nonetheless, despite their instinctive recognition of fatality, hope remains essential to them both. Although Hesiod's Pandora had released from her box (or, more accurately, from her urn) all human evils except Hope, Aeschylus's Prometheus explicitly endows humans with Hope as well as foresight, qualifying his gift by stating "I caused men no longer to foresee their death by planting blind hopefulness" (28).

The narrative structures of both *Prometheus Bound* and *Moby-Dick* rest upon a sequence of predictive warnings. First Hephaestus, then the Chorus, then Oceanus, then Io, and finally Hermes arrive on stage to comfort or taunt Prometheus, fixed immovably to the rocky mountain-top. All warn Prometheus against the consequences of his intransigence, his verbal fury, and his pride. Before the play ends in the thunderbolts and lightning that will bring on Zeus's punishing eagle, Hermes concludes that Prometheus's "thoughts and words . . . are what one may hear from lunatics" (51). Similarly, Starbuck, then Stubb and then the whale-ship captains met during the intermittent gams all try to dissuade the increasingly monomaniacal Ahab from his purpose. In both works the prophetic warnings become increasingly pointed as the rebellious hero becomes more belligerently intransigent. A significant difference, however, is that Ishmael, who serves as a kind of Chorus, refrains from ever directly confronting Ahab, whether from feelings of futility, fear or troubled admiration for the nobility of Ahab's purpose.

Goethe, Byron, Percy Shelley, Mary Shelley and Melville all refashion Prometheus for their own individual purposes, but they do so within a revolutionary, not yet democratic world riven with disorder. In the main, the rebellions of the Olympians and of Prometheus prefigure the rebellion of Enlightenment progressives and individualistic romantics against the tyrannies of the Old Order: monarchy, feudal hierarchy, canon law, and class privilege. The promise of Prometheus is now inseparable from his inner intellectual, spiritual, and aesthetic vision. His defiance of authority and his demand for man's freedom acquire greater importance than his technocratic benefits. Accordingly, fire is—for all these writers except Melville—replaced by light as the controlling metaphor for a future spiritual progress that should, and perhaps will, transform political and cultural institutions.

Early nineteenth-century romantic writers therefore imagine Prometheus less as a Titan than as the representative of mankind's fullest human potential. Romantic poets are drawn to invoke Prometheus in comparative isolation as a fully developed but alternative state of mind. Because there is no play-going audience to see Prometheus's bodily suffering, the physical freeing of Prometheus from his chains, even in a closet drama like Shelley's *Prometheus Unbound*, becomes cursory, almost incidental, sometimes even disregarded. Prometheus is to be seen as a cultural visionary whose creativity, determination, and suffering are forever inseparable from one another.

Intervening between the classical and romantic conceptions of Prometheus is the endlessly controversial figure of Milton's Satan. In passages that Melville surely read, both Goethe and Shelley weighed the appeal of Satan against that of Prometheus, and found Satan wanting. Goethe argued that "Milton's Satan, gallantly as he is portrayed, remains in a disadvantageously subaltern position as he attempts to destroy the splendid creation of a superior Being." Prometheus, by contrast, "has the advantage of being able to create and form in defiance of higher beings."[19] Shelley goes further, arguing that Satan is lessened by the "pernicious casuistry" with which he challenges God, whereas Prometheus, "a more poetical character than Satan," is "exempt from the taints of ambition, envy, revenge, and a desire for personal aggrandisement."[20] Like Melville's Ahab, Byron's Prometheus asserts his own dark, defiant will *in extremis*, but all three poets exalt the figure of Prometheus almost beyond fault. Neither Goethe nor Byron may have quite been prepared to argue, as Shelley did, that Prometheus is "the type of the highest perfection of moral and intellectual nature, impelled by the purest and the truest motives to the best and noblest ends" (205). For all three poets, however, Prometheus was to retain no trace of the petulance and sense of shame that had humanized him in Aeschylus's play, and had made Prometheus's eventual reconciliation with Zeus conceivable.[21] The romantic Prometheus therefore posed a conundrum; Prometheus the Titan was now to be a man, but a man who showed no smallness of character, none of the self-seeking human qualities that had compromised the Greek gods.

Important differences remain, as concisely summarized by Stuart Curran's formulation of three variations of the Romantic Prometheus: "the resolute humanism of Goethe's conception, or the defiant and universal refusal of Byron's, or the anarchist liberation inscribed in Shelley."[22] Goethe's Prometheus, not chained to any rock, but walking in a garden among his clay statues, is the godlike Man who, in Goethe's revision of Genesis 1:26–27, expresses rightful pride in essentially creating himself:

Hier sitz ich, forme Menschen	Here I sit, forming men
Nach meinem Bilde,	In my image,
Ein Geschlect, das mir gleich sei,	A race to resemble me:
Zu leiden, zu weinen,	To suffer, to weep,
Zu geniessen und zu freuen sich,	To enjoy, to be glad—
Und dein nicht zu achten.	And never to heed you,
Wie ich.	Like me! [23]

In his autobiography, Goethe had written "the myth of Prometheus came to life in me" when he realized that his literary creativity, a "natural gift," had become "the philosophical basis for my whole existence." His identification with Prometheus, Goethe contends, had encouraged him to become a committed artist, just as his poem "Prometheus" became "the tinder for an explosion" in German literature (469). Such an unfolding of Promethean creative ambition within the artist could certainly be applied to Herman Melville's sense of literary unfolding within himself, but it does not readily apply to Ahab's more Faustian kind of perceptual overreaching.[24]

In Byron's Prometheus, however, Melville could have found many qualities readily ascribable to Ahab. Bound to "the rock, the future and the chain," Byron's Prometheus suffers a "suffocating sense of woe" at the strife inflicted by "the inexorable Heaven / And the deaf tyranny of Fate."[25] Although Zeus is never named, Prometheus flings back the "Menace" and "Hate" of the "Thunderer" into the facelessness of whatever power(s) may control the world. The poem's closing lines credit Prometheus with a "firm will" that is "Triumphant where it dares defy," and thereby makes "Death a Victory." Unlike Goethe or Shelley, Byron refuses to grant Prometheus visions of a better future. An indescribable fatality and force always hover over him; he can only fleetingly foresee "His own funereal destiny / His wretchedness, and his resistance / And his sad unallied existence" (98). The formidable psychological and spiritual isolation of Byron's Prometheus, far more extreme than the Prometheus of Hesiod,

Aeschylus, Goethe, or Shelley, was to be recreated in Ahab, whether Ahab happens to be in his cabin or on deck. Byron has written an ode in which there is no other human presence save Prometheus himself, who remains wordless from beginning to end. Whatever murderous injustices Zeus, vulture, and whale may have inflicted, both Byron's Prometheus and Melville's Ahab are defined by their self-enclosed, self-tormented minds.

Shelley's *Prometheus Unbound* is quite another matter. Shelley replaces Pandora with Asia, thereby wedding Prometheus to the spirits of Love and Intellectual Beauty. Following Aeschylus's restoration of Hope as a Promethean gift, Shelley urges humankind, at poem's end, "to hope till Hope creates / From its own wreck the thing it contemplates" (268). The play's last two lines rhyme "free" with "victory." In political terms, Shelley prophesies a time when "Thrones, altars, judgment-seats, and prisons," themselves all attributes of Jupiter, will be but "the ghosts of a no-more-remembered fame" (253).

The controlling power in the world of Shelley's play is not Jupiter but the comparatively obscure Demogorgon, who speaks as Necessity and proclaims the utopian republic soon to come. Because Melville refers to Demogorgon in *Moby-Dick*, it seems likely that Melville had read Shelley's *Prometheus Unbound* with some care. If so, he would have known that Shelley's third act ends with the following prophecy by the Spirit of the Hour:

> The loathsome mask has fallen, the man remains
> Sceptreless, free, uncircumscribed, but man
> Equal, unclassed, tribeless, and nationless,
> Exempt from awe, worship, degree, the king
> Over himself. (253)

A great deal of often retrogressive European history, discouraging to romantic and Enlightenment hopes, was to intervene between 1820 and 1850. Melville's recognition that Ahab will never get behind the "pasteboard mask" is therefore as much the product of Melville's times, as Shelley's assurance that "the loathsome mask has fallen" had been of immediately post-Napoleonic Europe.

A still deeper reason for Melville's likely reservations about Shelley's poem stems from the basis of Shelley's poetics. Shelley's imagery, he insists, is "drawn from the operations of the human mind" (205). By evoking almost innumerable "Spirits" through sheer beauty of imagery and music of meter, but without providing context or connection between them, Shelley clearly believed he could bring such abstractions into being through incantatory words. From *Typee* (1846) to *Billy Budd* (1891, 1924), Melville wrote from very different aesthetic and epistemological assumptions. To be sure, words could be symbolic, even symbolic of personified spirits, but they must originate in what Emerson had called "natural facts."[26] Meaningful words are to begin in Aristotelian imitation (*mimesis*) of the world we know, however differently subsequent listeners or readers may understand them.

What drew Melville toward the implicit use he might make of Mary Shelley's *Frankenstein* as a portrayal of "The Modern Prometheus"? Surely it was not Mary Shelley's singling out the overreaching of modern scientific and material research into realms of forbidden knowledge and monstrous creation—twentieth-century eugenics, the Atom Bomb, cloning, recombinant DNA, and possibly the Human Genome Project.[27] Instead Melville emphasizes the consequence of pursuing forbidden knowledge until it leads to a self-created, self-punishing "monster," "daemon," "demon," "devil" or "thing," to use Mary Shelley's various terms. In his laboratory, Victor Frankenstein, driven by exalted Promethean purpose, creates a living man, but a man so repellent, so humanly inhuman, that the creature first pursues Frankenstein, and then is pursued by him, as a hideous psychological double. Similarly, Moby Dick can be viewed as the creation of Ahab's mind, a projection of the tyrannical, semi-divine power Ahab almost succeeds in wielding. Seemingly an enemy, but in fact a counterpart, the self-created monster of both authors must serve, ultimately, as the punishing eagle or vulture, be it the "agent" or "principal" of inscrutable evil.

Melville thus shares with Mary Shelley a desire to reveal that the end of the Promethean or Faustian quest cannot be the redemptive progress imagined for the individual artist by Goethe's "Prometheus" and for the entirety of human society by Shelley's *Prometheus Unbound*. Victor Frankenstein dies caught in the immense white ice floes of the Arctic; the Monster he created, who has lived for a time in the blindingly white ice caves on Mont Blanc, is last seen departing over the white Arctic ice toward his suicidal funeral pyre. Similarly, the body of Ahab is last seen bound by rope-lines of fate to the body of the "Albino" white whale, whose colorlessness "shadows forth the heartless voids and immensities of the universe" (263). Already engaged in pursuit of "the Ambiguities," Melville was not prepared to insist upon any judgment so one-dimensional as Victor Frankenstein's "Learn from me, if not by my precepts, at least by my example, how dangerous is the acquirement of knowledge, and how much happier that man is who believes his native town to be the world, than he who aspires to become greater than his nature will allow."[28] For both novelists, however, the end of the Promethean quest has to be death, not the salvation of humankind. The secret of life can no more be penetrated by a whale captain's harpoon than by a galvanic battery recharging human body parts. An implied warning against romantic idealism lingers in the reader's mind after the conclusion of both novels.

The spirit with which the two seekers meet their deaths could hardly be more different. Victor Frankenstein dies "fallen," "miserable," and "chained in an eternal hell," acknowledging to Walton, "from my infancy I was imbued with high hopes and a lofty ambition; but how am I sunk. Oh! my friend, if you had known me as I once was, you would not recognize me in this state of degradation" (152). Frankenstein accepts full responsibility for the Monster's killing of four innocent people, including Frankenstein's wife, brother, and intimate friend, yet the guilt Frankenstein feels does not preclude his rage to kill his second self.[29] Ahab feels neither guilt nor "degradation;" his quest has not yet killed anyone and he believes his monster enemy to be the agent or principal of evil. Ahab hurls his harpoon proclaiming that "my topmost greatness lies in my topmost grief," welcoming the "piled comber of my death," and spitting a last breath of hate at the "all destroying, but unconquering whale" (571). Ahab's defiant, supra-Byronic victory is to maintain his mad, noble purpose intact; he knows he can remain Ahab only by uniting himself with the whale.

Fire

For Melville, the deadly, self-consumptive force of fire was emerging as the dominant outcome of the Promethean legacy. Greek cultural practice, by contrast, had pursued celebratory fire ceremonies. To honor the gifts Prometheus brought to man, Periclean Athens conducted an annual torch race, the *Prometheia*. Runners, carrying a burning torch, raced from the altar of Prometheus at the Academy to the potters' quarter within the city.[30] Shelley, perhaps alone among contemporary poets, knew of this Athenian custom. In *Prometheus Unbound*, a torch-bearing "SPIRIT, in the likeness of a winged child" describes the altar and temple of Prometheus, then asserts that "the emulous youths / Bore to thy honour through the divine gloom / The lamp which was thine emblem; even as those / Who bear the untransmitted torch of hope / Into the grave, across the night of life" (249).

Throughout Shelley's poem, sun, fire and light remain as inseparable as flame, torch, and lightning. All are agents of the power of illumination that makes man free. Asia calls Prometheus "the sun of this rejoicing world" (234). The fire which Prometheus has "tamed," she says, is "most terrible, but lovely" (237). Earth later proclaims that, thanks to Prometheus, "The lightning is his [man's] slave; heaven's utmost deep / Gives up her stars" (264). Like François Guizot's characterization of Benjamin Franklin as the man who "brought down fire from heaven and a tyrant from his throne," Prometheus combines piercing intellect with an active will to liberate. A minor passage, spoken by the THIRD SPIRIT, conveys how these agents coalesce into a single force within the truthful, dreaming mind:

> I sate beside a sage's bed,
> And the lamp was burning red
> Near the book where he had fed,
> When a Dream with plumes of flame,
> To his pillow hovering came,
> And I knew it was the same
> Which had kindled long ago
> Pity, eloquence, and woe. (224)

Prometheus need not be specifically mentioned in such passages; he can be confidently evoked as the "long ago" source of prophetic knowledge for every succeeding sage. Light in all its benign connotations will presumably intensify and rise upward, even as it carries a measure of woe within it.

To Ahab and to Ishmael, however, fire and sun, flame and lamp, retain opposed qualities that portend a cataclysmic future symbolized by the fate of the *Pequod*. While gazing at whale blubber blazing into red flame within the try-works, Ishmael summons up a nightmarish revelation. "That darkness was licked up by the fierce flames, which at intervals forked forth from the sooty flues, and illuminated every lofty rope in the rigging, as with the famed Greek fire" (422). The phrase "famed Greek fire" probably contains an implied reference to Prometheus as well as to the suicidal fire ships used by the Greeks in their 1820s naval war for independence against the Turks. Although the flames transform the *Pequod* into the very picture of "red hell" (423), Ishmael envisions the fire as the emblem of his commander's singular psyche. Ishmael observes, "Like a plethoric burning martyr, or a self-consuming misanthrope once ignited, the whale supplies his own fuel and burns by his own body" (422). After gazing into the try-works, Ishmael identifies fire as the symbolic agent of Ahab's self-consumption: "The rushing *Pequod*, freighted with savages, and laden with fire, and burning a corpse, and plunging into that blackness of darkness, seemed the material counterpart of her monomaniac commander's soul" (423). At this moment, Promethean fire and hellish light converge to represent the forbidden, self-destructive knowledge Ahab seeks to discover behind the mask of the whale. For Melville, imagery of the visibility of fire-laden darkness stretches back from Goethe's *Faust* and Marlowe's *Doctor Faustus* to Dante, Virgil, and Homer. In that literary context, the light of Enlightenment Reason seems to be consuming itself.

The meanings Ishmael would draw from this nightmarish moment are, first, that his physical turn-about while manning the tiller, suddenly facing dangerously astern rather than ahead, is a symbol of the *Pequod*'s future; and second, that the "artificial fire" of the try-works must be shunned in order to experience the fire of the "natural sun ... the glorious, golden, glad sun, the only true lamp—all others but liars" (424). These two insights, so subversive of Shelley's certainties, support the climactic warning—phrased as a command—that Ishmael delivers both to himself and to the reader: "Look not too long in the face of the fire, O man!" (424). Ishmael knows he can never be certain exactly what "fire" signifies. Hellish though fire so obviously is, the fire has also furnished the source of the light by which Ishmael has seen the plight of his captain and his ship. Similarly, the "famed Greek fire" led contemporary Greeks toward freedom. Ishmael's warning does not require us to turn entirely aside from the search for the significance of fire; we must rather remain vigilant, weighing carefully the duration and intensity of the pursuit. Psychological cost (fiery self-consumption) must be balanced against spiritual and metaphysical discovery. Ishmael would leave to each of us the determination of how much time spent in fire-gazing will prove to be "too long."

Before Ahab summons the grand courage needed for his final assault on Moby Dick, his thinking narrows into a crazed example of Ishmael's prophetic warning. As Ahab destroys the quadrant, he curses the sun as the "high and mighty Pilot," that can tell him nothing of destiny, but has left him with "these old eyes even now scorched with thy light, O sun!" (501). The distinction Ahab had once accepted between the natural sun and the artificial fire has been forgotten; both now seem wholly destructive to him, just as they had seemed wholly constructive to Shelley's Prometheus. This shift prepares the reader for the fire imagery in the very next chapter, "The Candles." During a typhoon, the rods on the *Pequod*'s corpusants burn with St. Elmo's fire. Ahab stands erect before the "lofty, tri-pointed trinity of flames" and acknowledges that the fire he once worshipped, he now worships only through defiance (507). In addressing the lightning, Ahab knows that his spirit has become defined by the quest for fire, and that his defiance of fire can only prove self-destructive. Cursing a spirit he is not sure exists, he exclaims "Oh, thou clear spirit, of thy fire thou madest me, and like a true child of fire, I breathe it back to thee" (507). Milton's Satan hated the beams of the natural sun; Melville's Ahab must unite himself with hated forbidden fire, whether natural or artificial.

By novel's end, Ahab personifies an entire spectrum of madness, from crazed hyperbole, through monomania, to craziness, to prophetic inspiration, to the alternative possibility that "man's insanity is heaven's sense" (414). Wherever a reader may choose to situate Ahab along this spectrum, Ahab remains true, even in "The Candles," to his search for a hidden essence of meaning beneath and beyond the mask upon the surface. For him, this assumption has now become as applicable to fire, as it has long been to the whale:

> There is some unsuffusing thing beyond thee, thou clear spirit, to whom all thy eternity is but time, all thy creativeness mechanical. Through thee, thy flaming self, my scorched eyes do dimly see it. O thou foundling fire, thou hermit immemorial, thou too has thy incommunicable riddle, thy unparticipated grief. Here again, with haughty agony, I read my sire. (508)

If fire represents a knowledge beyond Prometheus's gifts to human civilization, what kind of divine being could possibly exist beyond the fire? Fire is the only Father ("sire") Ahab can ever know. Beyond is the incommunicable riddle, a grief one cannot voice, for which there are no words.

Ahab's search for forbidden knowledge, for the secret of inscrutability, thus suggests the possibility that there is, in fact, no meaning whatsoever. Not nihilism (a creed with a clear meaning), nor even the meaning of nothing, but no meaning at all. Neither Ahab nor Ishmael ever directly raises this possibility; it was not a prospect many readers or writers were in 1850 willing to entertain. Its closest approximation in Melville's novel is Ahab's unwelcome premonition about Moby Dick himself: "the dead blind wall butts all inquiring heads at last" (521). The near certainty of a dead blind wall, however, is insufficient reason for Ahab to abandon his search to know and to destroy the inscrutable. Melville will not allow his reader to forget that all but one of the *Pequod*'s shipmates pay the ultimate price for Ahab's Promethean venture to rid the world of evil. And yet, readers must uneasily admire Ahab despite the common moral and civic principles by which he can be readily condemned.

Notes

1. Herman Melville, *Moby-Dick or The Whale*, ed. Harrison Hayford, Hershel Parker, G. Thomas Tanselle et al. (Evanston and Chicago: Northwestern University Press and the Newberry Library, 1988), 545.
2. Alfred, Lord Tennyson, "Ulysses," in *Tennyson's Poetry*, ed. Robert W. Hill, Jr., 2nd ed. (New York and London: W. W. Norton & Co., 1999), 83. "Ulysses" was first published in 1842.
3. Two informative studies of the shifting characterization of Prometheus in literature, Carol Dougherty's *Prometheus* and Carl Kerenyi's *Prometheus: Archetypal Image of Human Existence*, do not mention Herman Melville or Captain Ahab. Recent, wide-ranging studies of the quest for forbidden knowledge by Roger Shattuck and Theodore Ziolkowski (see below, note 27), to both of which I am deeply indebted, consider *Billy Budd* but not *Moby-Dick*. More than a half century ago Richard Chase's *Herman Melville* claimed that there was a central opposition between "the true Prometheus" and "the false Prometheus" throughout Melville's works, but Chase's remarks on the subject have proven too schematic and too impressionistic to remain useful (3–4). Bruce Franklin's chapter on *Moby-Dick* in his *The Wake of the Gods: Melville's Mythology* is subtitled "An Egyptian Myth Incarnate" and deals with Vishnu and Osiris, not Prometheus. One chapter of Denis Donoghue's *Thieves of Fire*, his 1973 T. S. Eliot lectures at the University of Kent, compares *Moby-Dick* to Dostoevski's *The Possessed* in necessarily general terms. Since 1980, little scholarly attention seems to have been paid to the Promethean quest within Melville's works. Melville scholarship has clearly turned in other directions. One example: Clare Spark's massive study of the literary politics of the Melville revival, *Hunting Captain Ahab* (2001), posits, for the sake of writing a history of the culture wars, an image of Melville as "the Promethean artist following the facts wherever they led, who would then stand up to irrational authority, inspiring others to do the same" (7). Spark is not, however, primarily concerned with how the inner- or inter-textual meaning of Melville's references to Prometheus contribute to a cumulative, central myth of Western culture.

4. As *Clarel* and *Billy Budd* were to demonstrate, Melville's use of classical analogies to define inner character grew markedly in his later writings. The rich implications of the Prometheus passages in *Moby-Dick* thus comprise a crucial transition to his later practice.
5. Herman Melville, "Hawthorne and His Mosses," in *The Piazza Tales and Other Prose Pieces*, ed. Harrison Hayford, Hershel Parker, G. Thomas Tanselle et al. (Evanston and Chicago: Northwestern University Press and the Newberry Library, 1987), 243.
6. Herman Melville, *Mardi, and a Voyage Thither*, ed. Harrison Hayford, Hershel Parker, G. Thomas Tanselle et al. (Evanston and Chicago: Northwestern University Press and the Newberry Library, 1970), 229.
7. Albert Camus, *The Rebel: An Essay on Man in Revolt* (New York: Random House, 1991), 26.
8. I use the word "original" in the sense Melville applied it to Hamlet, Don Quixote and Satan in *The Confidence-Man*. An "original" character is like a revolving Drummond Light: "everything is lit by it, everything starts up to it" (*The Confidence-Man: His Masquerade*, ed. Harrison Hayford, Hershel Parker, G. Thomas Tanselle et al. [Evanston and London: Northwestern University Press and the Newberry Library, 1984], 239).
9. Herman Melville, *Redburn: His First Voyage*, ed. Harrison Hayford, Hershel Parker, G. Thomas Tanselle et al. (Evanston and London: Northwestern University Press and the Newberry Library, 1969), 244.
10. Herman Melville, *Pierre or the Ambiguities*, ed. Harrison Hayford, Hershel Parker et al. (Evanston and Chicago: Northwestern University Press and the Newberry Library, 1971), 358.
11. Herman Melville, "The Bell Tower," in *The Piazza Tales*, 184.
12. See Robert K. Wallace, *Melville and Turner: Spheres of Love and Fright* (Athens: University of Georgia Press, 1992), 117; William Truettner and Alan Wallach, *Thomas Cole: Landscape into History* (New Haven and Washington: Yale University Press and the National Museum of Art, 1994), 84.
13. Ralph Waldo Emerson, "History," in *Essays: First Series*, ed. Alfred R. Ferguson and Jean Ferguson Carr, *The Collected Works of Ralph Waldo Emerson* (Cambridge, MA: Belknap Press of Harvard University Press, 1987), 2:17.
14. See Carol Dougherty, *Prometheus* (London and New York: Routledge, 2006), 17.
15. Hesiod, *Theogony and Works and Days*, trans. Dorothea Wender (London and New York: Penguin, 1973), 41.
16. See D. J. Conacher, *Aeschylus' "Prometheus Bound:" A Literary Commentary* (Toronto: University of Toronto Press, 1980), 11–13.
17. Melville may have read *Prometheus Bound* in any of the following translations: Thomas Morrell (the first translation into English, 1773), Thomas Medwin (1832, 1837), Elizabeth Barrett Browning (1833),

Henry David Thoreau (1843), or Richard Potter (1777). The Potter translation was reprinted as part of the Harper's Classical Library, which Melville owned. The fact that so many English translations had appeared in so short a time shows the importance of Prometheus to Melville's era.
18. Aeschylus, *"Prometheus Bound" and Other Plays*, trans. Philip Vellacott (London and New York: Penguin, 1961), 20.
19. Johann Wolfgang von Goethe, *From My Life: Poetry and Truth*, Parts One to Three, trans. Robert R. Heitner (Princeton: Princeton University Press, 1984), 469–70.
20. Percy Bysshe Shelley, Preface to *Prometheus Unbound*, in *Poetical Works*, ed. Thomas Hutchinson and G. M. Matthews (Oxford and New York: Oxford University Press, 1970), 205.
21. From the eighteenth to the late twentieth century, it was confidently assumed that Aeschylus's *Prometheus Bound* was the first play in a trilogy, followed by plays titled *Prometheus Unbound* and *Prometheus the Fire-Bringer*, of which only fragments have survived. In *Prometheus Bound* Aeschylus implies that, after twenty-three generations, Herakles will free Prometheus with Zeus's approval. Based upon the assumption that this implication is true, scholars have asserted that Aeschylus intended to write a second trilogy, whose basic outlines might be plausibly reconstructed, expressing a progressive, even conciliatory sense of history similar to that found in the *Oresteia*.
22. Stuart Curran, "The Political Prometheus," *Studies in Romanticism* 25, no. 3 (1986), 431.
23. Johann Wolfgang von Goethe, *Selected Poems*, ed. Christopher Middleton (Princeton: Princeton University Press, 1983), 30: "Here I sit, forming men / In my image, A race to resemble me: / To suffer, to weep, / To enjoy, to be glad— / And never to heed you, / Like me!"
24. While writing *Moby-Dick*, Melville wrote to Hawthorne that "As with all great genius, there is an immense deal of flummery in Goethe, and in proportion to my own contact with him, a monstrous deal of it in me." However, the context of Melville's remark makes it clear that the "flummery" in Goethe was limited to Goethe's advocacy of the need to "*live in the all*" (i.e., participate in a life rooted in Emersonian pantheism), and not to Goethe's admiration of the artist's search for undiscovered truth. See Melville's letter to Hawthorne, June 1851, in *Correspondence of Herman Melville*, ed. Lynn Horth (Evanston and Chicago: Northwestern University Press and the Newberry Library, 1993), 193–94.
25. George Gordon, Lord Byron, *Poetical Works*, ed. Frederick Page (Oxford and New York: Oxford University Press, 1970), 98.
26. Ralph Waldo Emerson does so in the "Language" section of *Nature* (1836); see *"Nature," Addresses, and Lectures*, ed. Alfred R. Ferguson,

The Collected Works of Ralph Waldo Emerson (Cambridge, MA: Belknap Press of Harvard University Press, 1971), 1:17.
27. For speculations on the connection of these twentieth-century developments to the search for forbidden knowledge in general, and Prometheus in particular, see Roger Shattuck, *Forbidden Knowledge: From Prometheus to Pornography* (New York: St. Martin's Press, 1996); and Theodore Ziolkowski, *The Sin of Knowledge: Ancient Themes and Modern Variations* (Princeton: Princeton University Press, 2000). Hawthorne had memorably explored fire-gazing in "Ethan Brand" and scientific overreaching in both "Rappaccini's Daughter" and "The Birthmark." Nor is he the last to do so; e.g., Kai Bird and Martin Sherwin's recent 600-page biography of J. Robert Oppenheimer is titled *American Prometheus*. Roger Shattuck applies the Latin term *Libido Sciendi* and the Greek term *Pleonexia* ("insatiable greed for the unobtainable, ... refusing any limit, any horizon") to convey the timelessness of such quests (46, 105). As Shattuck points out, most Western writers beginning with Aeschylus have ignored the importance of Pandora's box of life's evil gifts to the beginnings of Promethean myth.
28. Mary Shelley, *Frankenstein; or the Modern Prometheus*, ed. J. Paul Hunter (New York: W. W. Norton, 2012), 32.
29. Mary Shelley's success in developing the motif of the döppelganger was to result in a telling misidentification. In the world of popular culture, the name Frankenstein has mistakenly been taken to refer to the Monster, not his creator. Mary Shelley conceived of Victor Frankenstein as a brilliant mind made up of contradictory cultural heritages: a would-be believer in alchemy, an Enlightenment rationalist, and a genteel Man of Feeling.
30. See Dougherty, *Prometheus*, 53–56, and Ziolkowski, *The Sin of Knowledge*, 27.

Bibliography

Aeschylus. *"Prometheus Bound" and Other Plays*. Translated by Philip Vellacott. London and New York: Penguin, 1961.
Aeschylus, and Percy Bysshe Shelley, *"Prometheus Bound" (The Medwin-Shelley Translation) and "Prometheus Unbound."* Edited and with a Foreword by John Lauritsen. Dorchester, MA: Pagan Press, 2011.
Bercaw, Mary K. *Melville's Sources*. Evanston: Northwestern University Press, 1987.
Bird, Kai, and Martin Sherwin. *American Prometheus: The Triumph and Tragedy of J. Robert Oppenheimer*. New York: Random House, 2006.
Byron, George Gordon, Lord. *Poetical Works*. Edited by Frederick Page and corrected by John Jump. Oxford and New York: Oxford University Press, 1970.

Camus, Albert. *The Rebel: An Essay on Man in Revolt*. New York: Random House, 1991.
Chase, Richard. *Herman Melville: A Critical Study*. New York: The Macmillan Company, 1949.
Conacher, D. J. *Aeschylus' "Prometheus Bound:" A Literary Commentary*. Toronto: University of Toronto Press, 1980.
Curran, Stuart. "The Political Prometheus." *Studies in Romanticism* 25, no. 3 (1986): 429–55.
Donoghue, Denis. *Thieves of Fire*. New York: Oxford University Press, 1974.
Dougherty, Carol. *Prometheus*. London and New York: Routledge, 2006.
Emerson, Ralph Waldo. *Essays: First Series*. Edited by Alfred R. Ferguson and Jean Ferguson Carr. Introduction and notes by Joseph Slater. *The Collected Works of Ralph Waldo Emerson*. Cambridge, MA: Belknap Press of Harvard University Press, 1987, vol. 2.
———. *"Nature," Addresses, and Lectures*. Edited by Alfred R. Ferguson. Introduction and notes by Robert E. Spiller. *The Collected Works of Ralph Waldo Emerson*. Cambridge, MA: Belknap Press of Harvard University Press, 1971, vol. 1.
Franklin, Bruce. *The Wake of the Gods: Melville's Mythology*. Stanford: Stanford University Press, 1963.
Goethe, Johann Wolfgang von. *From My Life: Poetry and Truth*, Parts One to Three. Translated by Robert R. Heitner. Princeton: Princeton University Press, 1984.
———. *Selected Poems*, Edited by Christopher Middleton. Princeton: Princeton University Press, 1983.
Hesiod. *Theogony and Works and Days*. Translated by Dorothea Wender. London and New York: Penguin, 1973.
Kerenyi, Carl. *Prometheus: Archetypal Image of Human Existence*. Translated by Ralph Mannheim. Princeton: Princeton University Press, 1963.
Melville, Herman. *The Confidence-Man: His Masquerade*. Edited by Harrison Hayford, Hershel Parker, G. Thomas Tanselle et al. Evanston and London: Northwestern University Press and the Newberry Library, 1984.
———. *Correspondence of Herman Melville*. Edited by Lynn Horth. Evanston and Chicago: Northwestern University Press and the Newberry Library, 1993.
———. *Mardi, and a Voyage Thither*. Edited by Harrison Hayford, Hershel Parker, G. Thomas Tanselle et al. Evanston and Chicago: Northwestern University Press and the Newberry Library, 1970.
———. *Moby-Dick or the Whale*. Edited by Luther S. Mansfield and Howard P. Vincent. New York: Hendricks House, 1962.
———. *Moby-Dick or The Whale*. Edited by Harrison Hayford, Hershel Parker, G. Thomas Tanselle et al. Evanston and Chicago: Northwestern University Press and the Newberry Library, 1988.

———. *The Piazza Tales and Other Prose Pieces*. Edited by Harrison Hayford, Hershel Parker, G. Thomas Tanselle et al. Evanston and Chicago: Northwestern University Press and the Newberry Library, 1987.

———. *Pierre or the Ambiguities*. Edited by Harrison Hayford, Hershel Parker et al. Evanston and Chicago: Northwestern University Press and the Newberry Library, 1971.

———. *Redburn: His First Voyage*. Edited by Harrison Hayford, Hershel Parker, G. Thomas Tanselle et al. Evanston and London: Northwestern University Press and the Newberry Library, 1969.

Plato, *Protagoras*. Translated by Adam Beresford. New York and London: Penguin, 2005.

Sealts, Merton M. *Melville's Reading: Revised and Enlarged Edition*. Columbia: University of South Carolina Press, 1988.

Shattuck, Roger. *Forbidden Knowledge: From Prometheus to Pornography*. New York: St. Martin's Press, 1996.

Shelley, Mary. *Frankenstein; or the Modern Prometheus*. Edited by J. Paul Hunter. New York: W. W. Norton & Co, 2012.

Shelley, Percy Bysshe. *Poetical Works*. Edited by Thomas Hutchinson and G. M. Matthews. Oxford and New York: Oxford University Press, 1970.

Spark, Clare L. *Hunting Captain Ahab: Psychological Warfare and the Melville Revival*. Kent, OH: Kent State University Press, 2001.

Tennyson, Alfred, Lord. *Tennyson's Poetry*. Edited by Robert W. Hill Jr. New York and London: W. W. Norton & Co. 1999.

Truettner, William, and Alan Wallach. *Thomas Cole: Landscape into History*. New Haven and Washington: Yale University Press and the National Museum of Art, 1994.

Wallace, Robert K. *Melville and Turner: Spheres of Love and Fright*. Athens: University of Georgia Press, 1992.

Wenke, John. "*Moby-Dick* and the Impress of Melville's Learning." In *Critical Essays on Melville's "Moby-Dick,"* edited by Brian Higgins and Hershel Parker, 507–22. New York: G. K. Hall, 1992.

Ziolkowski, Theodore. *The Sin of Knowledge: Ancient Themes and Modern Variations*. Princeton: Princeton University Press, 2000.

Chapter 10

Coleridge's Rome
Jonathan Sachs

In a remarkable series of essays written for the *Morning Post* in 1802, Samuel Taylor Coleridge suggested that the situation in Napoleonic France was not just parallel to that of Rome under the Caesars but a precise repetition of that earlier historical moment, with the only difference being "the degrees of rapidity with which the same processes have been accomplished." As Coleridge insists, "The reigns of the first three Caesars have been crowded into the three first years of the reign of Bonaparte."[1] Speed, then, is what distinguishes the present from the past. As Coleridge seeks to anticipate the outcome of Napoleon's rule, however, the legacy of imperial Rome, that earlier and slower historical moment, remains relevant as Coleridge uses the parallel between Napoleonic France and Rome under the Caesars to predict that Napoleon's decline will be as swift as his rise.

Coleridge's argument here echoes a common understanding of the modern world as the heir to the ancient, an issue of continuity that turned, through much of the eighteenth century, on whether Europe might repeat the ancient cycle of decline and fall under the conditions of modern debt-financed warfare. As Michael Sonensher suggests, in linking the classical past with the European present what came to matter in the eighteenth century was whether new mechanisms for financing warfare through national debt would produce a repetition of the ancient cycles of decline and fall. The threat to political stability and economic prosperity, in other words, "was not so much the inequality and luxury that, according to a long-standing tradition of political and historical analysis, had been responsible for earlier cycles of decline and fall, but the new financial instruments and fiscal resources that had accompanied the transformation of warfare during the seventeenth and eighteenth centuries."[2] Coleridge also links patterns of decline and fall in antiquity to his present moment, and he too moves away from an analysis of the link built around inequality and luxury, but for Coleridge the problem is not one of debt and credit. Rather, Coleridge adds to the issue of historical repetition and parallel the problem of historical speed or pace. Present events may repeat past events, but what distinguishes them is their "rapidity," the speed or pace at which they unfold. Coleridge, however, avoids the simple contrast between the slowness he associates with antiquity and the perceived speed of his present. What is most distinctive in Coleridge's thinking, as this chapter will show, is the dialectical merging of speed and slowness, antiquity and modernity, into an account where each is essential to understanding the other, and an account, moreover, in which attention to ancient Rome thus makes possible new ways of thinking about the relation between the past, present, and future.

In this reading, "Rome" functions as the sign for a series of events that form a complete set and whose outcome is known; it stands in contrast to the uncertain position in which Coleridge and his contemporaries find themselves in relation to their own present, but it can for them be used to shed light on that present and help imagine the potential futures that might flow from it. In this sense, Coleridge's use of Rome might be seen as an extension of exemplary history, or what Cicero calls *historia magistra vitae*, a type of argument that had long characterized European thinking in which perceived parallels between events or individuals in the past and the present were used to offer contemporary models of political and moral prudence. Reinhart Koselleck has suggested that while this topos varies greatly its very longevity indicates its elasticity and its usefulness. Whatever doctrines *historia magistra vitae* could be made to support, however, the topos works only as long as certain assumptions and conditions are upheld, namely the constancy of human nature and the constancy of circumstances that admitted the introduction of the initial parallel. Any social change that occurred would have to unfold "so slowly and at such a pace that the utility of past examples was maintained."[3] According to Koselleck, "The temporal structure of past history bounded a continuous space of potential experience."[4] He argues, however, that this tradition of understanding the relationship between past and future breaks apart at the end of the eighteenth century as a result of the French Revolution and a corresponding new sense of time, *Neuzeit*. This new time is predicated on a rupture between past and future as the experience of the past ceases to correspond with horizons of future expectation. Such a modern conception of time makes the future less and less knowable, less and less related to that which precedes it. It is precisely this sense of rupture that Coleridge pressures as he links France and Rome.

Coleridge, then, might be understood as an anomaly within the broad trajectory of Koselleck's account of *Neuzeit* and the changing significance of the past. For a start, Coleridge refuses to recognize a sundering of the present from the past, and he continues to assert that "As human nature is the same in all ages, similar events will of course take place under similar circumstances" (CW, 3:312). This is the very constancy of circumstances that Koselleck suggests is requisite for exemplary thinking, and we should therefore not be surprised when Coleridge's analysis of France under Napoleon uses Rome in an exemplary fashion. That analysis, however, also acknowledges the sense of temporal acceleration and the corresponding new time that Koselleck sees as formalized with the French Revolution and its aftermath. In Coleridge's account, analogies can be struck between Rome and contemporary European events, but those analogies must recognize one central distinction between the two, namely that the contemporary experience of time is different because things happen faster.

Coleridge, as we might expect, was not the only one to acknowledge the seemingly increased pace at which events unfolded. These kinds of claims for historical compression or intensification and a corresponding sense of temporal acceleration become commonplace by the end of the eighteenth century. William Eden, for example, when writing about the relationship between a particular point in time and a larger event that frames that moment, set out to characterize an "eventful period of history, in which a few years have given the experience of whole centuries."[5] Similarly, Byron's "Epistle to Augusta" suggests that he

> had the share
> Of life which might have filled a century
> Before its fourth in time had passed me by. (stanza 14, lines 110–12)

For Coleridge, Eden, Byron and others the present moment is an accelerated present. Time is speeding up and history produces more experiences in a shorter time than one might have at other times. Coleridge's account of this process is distinctive, however, because it seeks simultaneously to insist on the exemplary parallel between present and past while also recognizing the present as fundamentally distinct from the past, primarily on account of the rapidity at which events now unfold. Within this context, Rome stands for Coleridge as the standard of time against which the present is measured. If, as Coleridge suggests, events happen faster, they happen faster in comparison to the events of Roman history.

As this essay will argue, Rome was particularly important for Coleridge as he developed his ideas about the aftermath of the French Revolution, but it was also central to Coleridge's understanding of time and his historical situation in the broader sense. We can thus understand Coleridge's reflections on the links between Napoleonic France and imperial Rome as part of the effort to understand the initiation of "revolutionary time," that new sense of time thought by many circa 1800 to be a product of the French Revolution. In the context of revolutionary time, the possibility of change is both instantaneous and radically transformative because it produces a rupture between past and present. Coleridge, I will show, uses Roman history to clarify his present situation and to speculate about futurity, and in this way we might wonder about the perhaps paradoxical situation whereby ancient events were used to articulate a fundamentally modern conception of time, one grounded in the radical contingency and unknowability of a future divorced from a ready connection to past precedent, one seemingly cut free from the past. In this context antiquity, as we will see, serves as a stable anchor, a period of time that because it has finished can be known. More, for Coleridge Roman antiquity—and the transition from republic to empire most pointedly—comes to be associated with a particular pace and rate of change, and with slowness generally, a slowness that serves as a marked contrast to the apparent speed of his present moment. But the knowledge offered by the comparison of Roman antiquity with the European present comes at a cost, for by invoking the Roman parallel and using it to work out his prognostication of how events in France will turn out, Coleridge also undermines the potential applicability of an earlier historical trajectory (Roman antiquity) to the present because the two historical trajectories transpire at fundamentally different paces. What can be gained by comparison between two such temporally uneven durations of time? Is it even possible to link two series of events that are understood to unfold at different speeds? In developing his comparison between ancient Rome and revolutionary France, in other words, Coleridge understands his present moment as at once joined to the past and fundamentally sundered from it.

The argument of this essay, then, focuses on the reception of classical antiquity by one of the central figures of Anglo-American Romanticism, but it offers a way of thinking about reception that is different from the approach taken by many of the other essays in this volume. Specifically, it does not follow the influence or uses of particular classical authors, nor does it seek to answer questions about what specific invocations of particular classical texts do in the various contexts in which they are reused. The first approach generally looks at the transmission of a particular author or work, and can be associated with a range of methodologies from influence studies to the more theorized analysis of *Rezeptionsästhetik*. Among its best practitioners, it is a sophisticated and deliberately self-conscious technique to keep the meaning of texts open while continuously showing how meaning is created in the specific interpretations of classical texts by later readers.[6] This approach has been criticized as a "new aesthetics" by practitioners of a second approach to thinking about the uses of the classical past, one that deliberately aligns itself with cultural studies and seeks to move classical reception studies away from its focus on the tracing of literary influence through the textual reception of predominantly literary sources and to ask instead "what texts (images, music) do in society."[7]

While there is thus considerable disagreement about the proper scholarly method for articulating how the ancient world continues to shape our own and how the literature, politics and culture of classical antiquity have been transmitted, both approaches, I would argue, focus on the uses of classical texts and they tend to develop their arguments through an analysis of how specific texts from antiquity are re-appropriated in later contexts. My essay also generates its concerns from techniques of close reading, but its focus is not on particular classical texts, nor is it particularly concerned with models of influence and the transmission of the corpus of an author or authors. Instead, I am more invested in tracing how Roman history, and the transition from republic to empire specifically—more than a classical text, author, or set of authors—functions as a sign of the classical more generally, and on the subsequent uses to which that sign is put in an effort to comprehend an unfamiliar present and an uncertain future. "Rome" and "Roman history" in this context function less as part of a textual reception history and more as what Simon Goldhill has described as "a horizon of recognition, a more diffuse sense of antiquity, or a more general sign of the classical,"[8] one commonly overlooked by the specificity and particularity of other more text-based approaches to the reception of antiquity.

The French Revolution has commonly been understood to initiate a new, modern sense of time. With its self-conscious and deliberate attempts to destroy the symbols and traditions of the past and its reorganization and renaming of the months and weeks by which time is "kept" and understood, the Revolution sought to initiate a new chronology originating retroactively with the Year One.[9] As

Lynn Hunt argues, "A new relationship to time was the most significant change, and perhaps the defining development, of the French Revolution."[10] Most significantly for Hunt, the attempt of the Revolution to manage and control time signals a rupture, a break in secular time and a separation from the past. Like Hunt, Peter Fritzche also sees a break in the understanding of time around the French Revolution, which is similarly understood as a rupture between past and present. For Fritzche, "One of the distinguishing characteristics of the nineteenth-century sense of time ... is the dramatization of change as the restless iteration of the new, and also the insistence that the experience of this change is unique and foundational to the idea of modernity."[11] Modernity, then, comes into being in conjunction with novelty, specifically with the "restless iteration of the new." As the claims of Hunt and Fritzche indicate, what I have above called "revolutionary time," with its interpretation of change as sudden and transformative, is a concept whose meaning and implications scholars continue to try to reconstruct today.

Whether this "restless iteration of the new" is a product of the French Revolution, however, is an open question, and one that, as we will see, Coleridge's essays on France and the Caesars help to complicate. Either way, one effect of being freed from the contingencies of the past is that elements of the past can be invoked as part of the present selectively and without the burden of historical continuity. In Koselleck's terms, the topos of *historia magistra vitae* has ended and the future becomes a more open and unpredictable problem. The past, in turn, becomes available in a new way. It can be summoned no longer on the basis of a certain and secure parallel between a past and a present conceived as contiguous on the model of exemplarity, but rather more indiscriminately as a means to make an unfamiliar present seem familiar. This is something of what Marx was after when he described the French Revolution as being carried out through the precedents of the Roman republic. For Marx, the point here is that the invocation of Rome appears to be a summons to the past, but it is really a form of bringing a new future into being under the guise of repeating the past. As Marx explains:

> unheroic as bourgeois society is, it nevertheless took heroism, sacrifice, terror, civil war and battles of peoples to bring it into being. And in the classically austere traditions of the Roman republic its gladiators found the ideals and the art forms, the self-deceptions that they needed in order to conceal from themselves the bourgeois limitations of the content of their struggles and to keep their enthusiasm on the high plane of the great historical tragedy.[12]

The instantiation of Rome here functions as a kind of false consciousness: it uses the familiarity of past precedent and the glory of the Roman past to hide the limitations of a present struggle. But it is emphatically not a parody of the Roman past it invokes: "the awakening of the dead in those revolutions served the purpose of glorifying the new struggles, not of parodying the old; of magnifying the given task in imagination, not of fleeing from its solution in reality; of finding once more the spirit of revolution, not of making its ghost walk about again."[13] Invoking the past, for Marx, does not provide a model to constrain present possibilities; instead, it is the very invocation of the past that brings the future into being.

The particularity of the French use of Rome has now been amply documented by scholars,[14] but for my purposes here, the point is that Marx's interpretation of the French cult of antiquity insists on how the classical past can be used, intentionally or not, to forge new and previously unimaginable futures. But invoking the past to bring a new and previously unimagined future into being is, of course, not the only way of reading the French use of Rome or the particular processes of temporal acceleration and renewal in which they are enmeshed. In the context of a new sense of time marked by its seeming rupture from the past with all of the uncertainty about the future that this brings, Coleridge's voice stands out in the absolute confidence with which he nonetheless ventures a future prediction, and that confidence is based on a combination of difference and continuity and an assertion that time is not singular, that time is filled with the presence of the now that can explode out of the continuum of history.

We find this most clearly in the series of three essays by Coleridge written for the *Morning Post* in 1802 in which he compares the present state of France with that of Rome under the Caesars. Like Marx after him who insisted that "all facts and personages of great importance in world history occur, as it were, twice,"[15] Coleridge was obviously aware of those many French patriots, those Brutuses and Gracchis and Publicolas, who dressed the novelty of their revolutionary activities in the borrowed clothing and tongue of the Roman past. His implicit purpose in the essays was to deflect attention away from France's claim to be a "new Roman Republic" by suggesting instead that if France resembled any period of Roman history it was not the Republic, but the period "when Rome ceased to be a Republic" (CW, 3:314).

Having introduced the shift from republic to empire, Coleridge must work out the accuracy of the resemblance. Is it total, or only partial, he asks? Will it produce the same effects or have "the same duration" (CW, 3:314)? In response, Coleridge argues that the parallel is total, and over the course of his three essays he develops a sustained comparison between the conditions of the late Roman republic and Europe at the turn from the eighteenth to the nineteenth century. Enlightenment skepticism, in Coleridge's account, is akin to Epicurean metaphysics and ethics; the Roman agrarian laws are the equivalent of the nationalization of Church lands in France; the granting of universal suffrage matches the effects in Rome of extending full citizenship to the Italian states, and so on. The results of this general pattern are the same as their initial occurrence in Roman precedent: a weakening of what Coleridge calls the "natural aristocracy" through the internal dissolution of luxury and skepticism and a correspondent strengthening of the "mad tyranny of the multitude," all of which produce a power vacuum filled by the military and their generals.

In the case of Coleridge, the acknowledgement of the deep parallels between Napoleonic France and imperial Rome might be understood as problematic since, even if we associate the Roman Empire with precariousness and tyranny, it did last over four hundred years. This, however, is why intensification and acceleration are so central to Coleridge's claims. Rapidity is the quality that Coleridge most associates with the French Revolution. Bonaparte, for example, as Coleridge notes in "Affairs of France. II," should fear "the rapid spread of Royalism in France" (CW, 3:351). When France changes constitutions, it is a "rapid change of constitutions" that Coleridge describes in "On the Circumstances that Appear to Especially Favour the Return of the Bourbons at this Present Time" (CW, 3:360), and, in "Our Future Prospects," when the French armies triumph it is in a "chain of rapid successes" (CW, 3:421). Coleridge's invocation of historical parallel allows him to suggest that the future will unfold along predictable patterns gleaned from the classical past, but here and elsewhere, Coleridge's association of the French Revolution with rapidity means also that he can turn the increased speed at which events unfold in modernity to Britain's advantage in his prediction of the future. An emphasis on "degrees of rapidity" and related concepts like acceleration and intensification become the crucial distinctions around which Coleridge establishes the salient dissimilarity between imperial France and imperial Rome. According to Coleridge, the greater rapidity, the acceleration and intensification, with which the French empire has established itself under Bonaparte presages a shorter duration, "a duration as brief as its rise has been rapid" (CW, 3:324). This question of speed is central to Coleridge's analysis and it becomes the basis of the most significant differences he discerns between France and Rome.

Speed works in two ways in Coleridge's argument. First, he suggests that the establishment of the institutions of the Roman Empire was slow and deliberate. Augustus acted with "the utmost caution, slowness, and decency" (CW, 3:335). Popular liberties were not wiped out "at a blow" (CW, 3:336) and Augustan despotism, which maintained the forms of republican institutions, was "well concealed." Napoleon, in contrast, acted quickly and rashly in a manner that left his power like "an isthmus of Darien" by alienating both royalists and republicans. In the rapid establishment of his despotism, the French "are permitted to see what the Romans saw only after a lapse of forty-seven Augustan years" (CW, 3:336). Coleridge thus establishes the acceleration of contemporary historical processes through the prominent contrast between the speed of the present and the perceived slowness of the classical past. In characterizing the speed of events in France, Coleridge privileges the slowness of Augustus, which he associates with caution and decency. But it is the rapidity of Napoleon's rise that offers comfort and potential future security.

In this way, fast and slow can be understood to contain each other, and the process can be compared to a similar contrast in Wordsworth's Preface to the *Lyrical Ballads*, which was revised the same year that Coleridge's remarks were published. There, Wordsworth also expressed concern over the speed of contemporary life with his disdain for popular cravings after "extraordinary incident" that the "rapid communication of intelligence hourly gratifies."[16] For Wordsworth, such rapid communication and craving after incident produce a concomitant slowness, the "savage torpor" that blunts the discriminating powers of the mind. Coleridge privileges Augustan slowness but his perceived speeding up of contemporary time offers consolation because it augurs a more rapid end to the French regime; for Wordsworth the outlook is more ambivalent and, consistent with Fritzche's emphasis on the "restless iteration of the new" as the distinguishing feature of the nineteenth-century sense of time, the increased speed of modernity serves only to gratify a craving for novel incident or event. For both Wordsworth and Coleridge, however, acceleration and slowness exist in a complicated interrelation in which the perception of speed enables the recognition of slowness and vice versa. The difference here is that while both characterize speed through its interrelationship with slowness, for Coleridge slowness is explicitly associated with antiquity. Indeed, slowness functions for Coleridge as the sign of the classical, a point to which I will return.

The second aspect of speed in Coleridge's argument, one that might also be linked to Wordsworth's emphasis on "rapid communication," concerns Coleridge's awareness of how the very speed with which Napoleon established his dictatorship exposes him to a further kind of acceleration: specifically, the more rapid speed of communications technologies, especially the newspaper. Of course the hand press in 1800 was no faster than it was in 1500, but Coleridge perceives communication as quicker because of the late eighteenth-century proliferation of print wherein more presses produced more writing. The French government, Coleridge insists, is "insecure" because "The very newspaper, which our reader has now in his hand, and which, in a few hours hence, he may probably rumple up for 'vile uses,' is so powerful an agent as to constitute an essential difference between the probable duration of a despot's reign in the present age, and that which it often was in the time of Imperial Rome" (CW, 3:330). Coleridge describes the printing press as "the only 'infernal machine'" which is truly formidable to a modern despot. It is the means for acquiring and perpetuating freedom, and need only be feared by the enemies of freedom. Why is the press so formidable, why is it such a threat? Because of its speed, because "the rapid inter-communication of thoughts and discoveries, the amiable social vanity, that is the result of this free intellectual commerce..." (CW, 3:330). The point here is that like Wordsworth, Coleridge also associates acceleration with changes in communications technology, with what we would today describe as an explosion of print and with what has been called, in a much debated claim, a "reading revolution."[17] As more recent studies have made increasingly clear, romantic readers very much understood themselves to be living through a media as well as a political revolution, one that saw the creation of what Andrew Piper has described as "a new media reality" characterized by proliferation and excess, by the "imminent sense of too-muchness that surrounded the printed book."[18]

This raises an important question about Coleridge's analysis: is this modern sense of accelerated time, this increased rapidity of events, the result of the seeming eventfulness of the French Revolution, with its new calendar and its initiation of a corresponding new time, or is it rather a result of the seemingly increased speed of communications technologies and other processes of what we would today call mediation? The two explanations, of course, are not mutually exclusive. We have seen how Coleridge associates rapidity with the French Revolution, but, in addition to the analysis of the role of newspapers and media in Napoleonic France discussed above, a similar sense of rapidity also shapes Coleridge's understanding of communication generally. In his essay on Bonaparte from March 1800, Coleridge notes, "Yesterday we again received French Papers, and up to the 12th inst. The spring of the year approaching, in which nature begins to re-produce, and man re-commences the work of destruction, each successive communication, however undecisive the facts communicated may be, cannot but rise in interest. It is, therefore, a pleasing superstition, not wholly unworthy of momentary indulgence in a generous mind, to regard the late unwonted rapidity of intercourse as an happy omen."[19] Similarly, in an essay on peace from January 1800, Coleridge suggests that "No rapidity of mutual communication can be expected from different armies of different nations, equal to that which the armies of a single nation, acting under one plan, will easily realize."[20] In both instances, communication is evaluated on the basis of its speed.

And yet despite the fact that Coleridge associates rapidity with both the development of the French Revolution and with communications technologies, it is not events in France but rather, issues associated with an emergent print media apparatus, specifically the problem of what Coleridge calls "publicity," that provoke one of his most explicit assertions that there has been no rupture; that past and present are not discontinuous, and that the only way to see through the fog produced by the craving after incident and the novel "wonders of the day" is to look to the past and to recognize its relevance for the present. As he explains in *The Statesman's Manual*:

> If there be any antidote to that restless craving for the wonders of the day, which in conjunction with the appetite for publicity is spreading like an efflorescence on the surface of our national character; if there exist means for deriving resignation from general discontent, means of building up with the very materials of political gloom that stedfast frame of hope which affords the only certain shelter from the throng of self-realizing alarms, at the same time that it is the natural home and workshop of all the active virtues; that antidote and these means must be sought for in the collation of the present with the past, in the habit of thoughtfully assimilating the events of our own age to those of the time before us.[21]

With the term 'collation'—the action of comparing the sheets of a document or a printed book—Coleridge uses a bibliographical metaphor to understand historical parallelism. Such a move underscores Coleridge's shift in emphasis from the fear associated with dissemination and the rapid circulation of print, here associated with publicity, to a different kind of print, one associated with bibliography in which books are engines of slowness and the kind of media technology that allow for the "thoughtful" collation of present with past. Moreover, with its emphasis on the linking of present and past as a means to transcend the craving for novelty and its corresponding alarmism, the passage further underscores this process of collation as offering renewed grounds for hope in a context of "political gloom." In this way, it might serve as a blueprint for Coleridge's earlier comparison of Napoleon and the first three Caesars, which develops the analogy precisely as a means to broadcast hope through its ultimate prediction of Napoleon's rapid fall. In working out the particularities of his more general claim, Coleridge reinforces the connection between imperial Rome and the European present, but his analysis is surprising because he uses the classical past to ground his analysis of temporal acceleration, which he perceives to be a most contemporary phenomenon. Coleridge's reading of the increased speed and eventfulness of the present can be compared to related accounts of speed in more recent theorists of modernity,[22] but his argument is distinguished by its long reach back to the classical past and by its related account of speed and acceleration as enmeshed with patterns of slowness, especially the slowness that stands for Coleridge throughout the essays as a general sign of the classical.

Like Marx, Coleridge insists on the parallel between France and Rome. For Marx, the significance of that parallel hinges not around what Koselleck and others call exemplary thinking but rather, around a temporal rupture that enables the invocation of the past as the means to bring a new, bourgeois society into being. For Coleridge, in contrast, the link between France and Rome is genuinely backward looking, where the outcome of past events constrains future possibilities. But this constraint on future possibilities, in turn, makes the future more, not less, knowable, because the present situation in France is understood as being not just parallel to that of Rome under the Caesars, but a precise reduplication of that earlier series of events. History repeats itself.

We might even suggest that in Coleridge's account, past time gathers as water in a reservoir, to be reused and recycled as part of later present moments. In this way, Coleridge offers us an example of nonsynchronous time prior to that of Walter Benjamin in the twentieth century. Benjamin repeatedly distinguishes different senses of time as he introduces procedures of repetition and what he calls "the presence of the now" (*Jetztzeit*) in contrast to "the homogenous course of history." For Benjamin, significance is to be found not in "the concept of the historical progress of mankind" that stands inseparable from "the concept of its progression through a homogenous, empty time,"[23] but rather in those moments that manage to rupture the stasis associated with continuity. In testament to the potential violence of temporal change and the shift of temporal expectations, Benjamin continuously associates such interruptions of homogenous time with an explosive blasting: they "blast open the continuum of history" (262) or "blast a specific era out of the homogenous course of history—blasting a specific life out of the era or a specific work out of the lifework" (263). Such "blasting," which stands in marked contrast to Coleridge's gentler and less violent metaphor of collation, is especially marked in Benjamin's discussion of the French use of Rome, in which he introduces the concept of "now time": "History is the subject of a structure whose site is not homogenous, empty time, but time filled by the presence of the now [*Jetztzeit*]. Thus, to Robespierre ancient Rome was a past charged with the time of the now which he blasted out of the continuum of history" (261). In Benjamin's account, historical experience does not pass but instead accumulates; it can be recalled and reintroduced in new circumstances. Time is at once always moving and always stopped, always available, but the means through which what Benjamin calls *Jetztzeit*, or what I have been calling revolutionary time, can be claimed by the present is always violent.

For Coleridge also, we might venture, time is neither synchronous nor homogenous, though his understanding of temporal repetition and of historical lives and works shifting out of the continuum of time is less mystical, less messianic, and less violent than that of Benjamin. Repetition is possible, but it is understood in much less explosive terms than for Benjamin. If Napoleon appears to repeat almost verbatim the historical structure and outcomes of the first three Caesars, it is not because the Caesars have been "blasted" out of time to interrupt the continuity of history, but rather precisely because they have not broken that continuity, have not blasted through anything. Repetition provides not the enhanced awareness of the now and the uncertainty of a future ripe with new messianic possibilities, but the simple replay of the past. History repeats itself, the future is not open and unknown but rather, closed by the past. The future can be known, and this is why Coleridge can be so confident and so hopeful in his prediction of Napoleon's imminent decline.

Coleridge's understanding of historical repetition might also be likened to that of Giovanni Arrighi, the twentieth-century historian for whom later forms of capital accumulation are conceived as replicas or repetitions of earlier forms that recur within a structure of accelerated time and increased speed. Focusing on the shift of capitalist centers of production, Arrighi locates the origin of capitalist accumulation in a fifteenth-century Genoese-dominated model and traces its transition from the Italian states to seventeenth-century Amsterdam, nineteenth-century London, and twentieth-century New York. At each spatial shift, the later instantiation copies the forms of the earlier one. In Arrighi's account, however, the process is far more complex than simple imitation, because the growth and spread of capital (what Arrighi calls "systematic processes of accumulation") is accompanied by vast changes in the size, scale, and complexity of each successive regime. The process also develops more quickly at each successive stage in what Arrighi describes repeatedly as "the speed up in the pace of capitalist history" such that "as we move from the earlier to the later stages of capitalist development, it has taken less and less time for systemic regimes of accumulation to rise, develop fully, and be superseded."[24] For Arrighi, then, the growth of capitalism—like the parallel between France and imperial Rome in Coleridge's analysis—is a prolonged process of imitation and repetition, but under conditions of increasing speed and complexity. Though he does not describe it in these terms, the present that results from this process becomes, therefore, marked by a sense of time that is not singular but plural. Such non-singular time for Arrighi is uneven and driven by a theory of repetition in which each subsequent phase of capitalist accumulation repeats and intensifies that of the prior formation. The past, in other words, persists in the present and any one particular moment in the process functions as what Ian Baucom calls "an uncanny moment," a moment in which "present time finds stored and accumulated within itself a nonsynchronous array of past times."[25]

If Coleridge's understanding of the intensification and nonsynchronous character of historical change can thus be likened to both Benjamin and Arrighi, the salient distinction is that Coleridge rejects the language of violent rupture that Benjamin uses to characterize the re-emergence of the past in the present, with his language of blasting and exploding, in favor of a more bibliographically inspired language of interleaving and collation that produces a more predictable process of acceleration and intensification along the lines later modeled by Arrighi. The past is continuous with the present; it just unfolds at a more rapid pace. As Coleridge notes, France has been changed into an empire "by the same steps as the Roman Republic was, and under the same titles and phrases: only as before, differing in the degrees of rapidity with which the same processes have been accomplished. The reigns of the first three Caesars have been crowded into the three first years of the reign of Bonaparte" (CW, 3:316–17). For both Coleridge and Arrighi, the present moment is one whose "conditions of possibility have not waned but intensified, a present in which that 'past' survives not as a sedimented or attenuated residue but in which the emergent logics of this past find themselves enthroned as the dominant protocols of [a] 'nonsynchronous' contemporaneity."[26]

For Coleridge, the seemingly increased speed of the present is not a product of the French Revolution but is instead associated with a longer trajectory of print media and rapid communication. The French Revolution, in other words, does not set the inevitable conditions of Coleridge's modernity; rather it is modernity as a product of the increased speed of communications technology and the specific rapidity of print that constrains the French Revolution and shapes the conditions of possibility for its future outcomes. Within this context, Coleridge defines his media-saturated present through its processes of acceleration and intensification, but the meaning of these processes is brought into relief by their contrast with the slowness of imperial Rome. Rome and "the classical" more broadly then come to stand as a general sign for a slowness whose significance is elicited through its comparison with an accelerated present. Indeed, we might even venture to suggest that the reason that slowness is possible in Rome is because it provides an example of the full imperial cycle of rise, growth, decline, and fall in the absence of a network of mass media. In this sense, there are crowds and public opinion in imperial Rome, but what Rome lacks are the kind of media communications networks, increasingly associated with print and with newspapers in particular by the time of Coleridge's writing in the early nineteenth century, that turn public opinion into publicity and make the times, in Coleridge's description, "crowded," with news, with novelty and with "the wonders of the day."

The analysis can be compared to another more famous romantic touchstone in which the classical also serves as a mark of the slow. The speaker of Keats's "Ode on a Grecian Urn" begins his address to the urn by describing it as

> Thou still unravished bride of quietness,
> Thou foster-child of silence and slow time

Keats here associates the urn with the absence of sound, with quietness and silence. With his initial pun on the word 'still' the absence of movement is likened to undisturbed continuity through time, to a quality of being pure and "unravished." As the poem continues, it is this lack of movement and sound that most distinguish the scene depicted on the urn. It is a scene that is explicitly visual and not verbal, expressing its "flowery tale more sweetly than our rhyme," and while the speaker calls deliberate attention to the material and visual qualities of the urn, the longing of the "Ode" might also be understood as a longing to achieve a purity of representation akin to what Winckelmann described as the "edle Einfalt und stille Größe" (noble simplicity and grandeur) of classical material culture. In Keats's account, such purity of representation ultimately becomes so transcendent as to escape both the noise of mediation, those processes that come "in between" and transmit ideas through their materiality, and the noise of history, the realm in which things happen. It might even be argued that this quality of directness and purity associated with the lack of sound and the lack of movement come to stand in Keats's urn for a particular kind of classicism more generally, one whose origins extend back to Winckelmann's influence on eighteenth-century aesthetics. Neither the "Ode" nor the urn, of course, can achieve the unmediated qualities for which they long, and like the lovers who can "never, never" kiss, though "winning near the goal," the transparency to which they appear to aspire will never be reached. But like the lovers also, this failure has its compensations, in this case the reflections that the poem develops about the unavoidable quality of mediation and the rich potentialities of silence (those "unheard" melodies), stillness, and lack.

The contrasts through which these reflections are achieved and the manner in which the Ode constructs the classical are comparable to Coleridge's reflections on Rome. For Coleridge, as for Keats, the classical is marked by slowness, a slowness that acquires its full meaning through its contrast with the apparent speed of a newly mediated present, one driven by the "rapid inter-communication of thoughts and discoveries" made possible by the technologies of mediation like print. Print technology is understood to speed time; the classical, in contrast, stands as a space in which such technologies are absent, and in their absence a deliberate slowness emerges in Coleridge's account while for Keats, greater emphasis is placed on the stillness and silence that might nonetheless be associated with the slow. This is not to suggest that classical antiquity was any more slow or quiet than the present for Keats or Coleridge, but rather, that they use the perceived slowness and stillness that they associate with antiquity to mark the present as a time of increased speed and noise.

It is tempting to stop there, but there is something else in Keats's introduction of the urn. In addition to the urn's unspoiled quality, its stillness and quietness, and despite attempts to locate the scene on the "leaf-fringed legend" with a moment out of time, the poem cannot avoid acknowledging the movement of time, just as it cannot avoid acknowledging the inevitability of mediation. For the urn is a "foster-child" not only of "silence" but also of "slow time." It is a "sylvan historian" that keeps record of the deeds contained on its surface. Echoing the earlier description of the urn's "leaf-fringed legend" Keats's use of 'sylvan' here contains a pun that, like Coleridge's use of 'collation,' represents the slow time of antiquity through the bookish metaphor of the leaf. This characterization of the urn as a historian, and one explicitly associated with the book, works as a reminder of its time-keeping qualities, a reminder that the urn is a material remnant of the classical past. The time kept by the urn, though, is "slow time" and, just as in Coleridge's representation of imperial Rome, this works to further the association of the classical with slowness.

Slow time can also serve as a reminder, though, of a different kind of time, a time that we might today call "deep time" and that we would associate with geology, the earth sciences, and other emerging disciplines that, among other concerns, expanded estimates of the age of the earth and introduced the possibility of species adaptation and extinction. The temporal emphasis of this kind of thinking moves not toward the intensification described by Coleridge and others, but rather, toward the expansion of time found in the work of Buffon, Saussure, de Luc, Hutton, Blumenbach, Demarest, Lamarck, Cuvier, and others. What this means is that the perceived acceleration of modernity that marks Coleridge's account of Napoleonic France can be understood to develop in relationship to the longer timescales of natural or geological history. Perceptions of speed are inherently related to perceptions of slowness, and with the increasing awareness of the vastness of the timescale needed to grapple with the age of the earth and processes of species adaptation and extinction, the comparative eventfulness and speed of the present become clearer.

While Coleridge's reading of the seemingly increased speed and eventfulness of the present can, as this chapter has shown, be compared to related accounts of acceleration in Marx, Benjamin, Koselleck, Arrighi, and other more recent theorists of modernity, his argument differs from their diverse accounts. It is distinguished by the manner in which it uses its long reach back to the classical past and its invocation of a classical exemplar, imperial Rome, and a particular form of mediation, the arborially inspired book, to imagine a more complex temporal framework. In Coleridge's account, imperial Rome stands as a general sign of the classical, one that comes to mark forms of slowness more generally. But Coleridge does not simply contrast the slowness that he associates with antiquity with the speed and rapidity that he recognizes to be a fundamental, and fundamentally new, quality of the present. Instead, Coleridge understands speed and acceleration as enmeshed with patterns of slowness, especially the slowness that stands for Coleridge as a general sign of the classical. Coleridge's account, in other words, is motivated by a more dialectical incorporation of speed and slowness, antiquity and modernity, in which each quality is seen to contain the other. Coleridge thus represents time, and the complex layering of time that he understands as central to the interpellation of past and present, not as layers of different periods of time that can be sharply distinguished as "eras" or "ages" and understood as part of a movement in the direction of present and future progress, but rather as layers of different timeframes that can be analogized and understood in relation to one another despite the different speeds at which they unfold. Coleridge's Rome thus offers an opportunity to think about how "Rome" enabled new ways of thinking about both the future and the past, which simultaneously encouraged a sense of compression and expansion, disrupting progressivist historical assumptions and altering perceptions of the pace and scale of time.

Notes

1. Samuel Taylor Coleridge, *The Collected Works of Samuel Taylor Coleridge, Volume 3: Essays on His Times* in The Morning Post *and* The Courier, ed. David Erdman, 3 vols. (Princeton: Princeton University Press, 1978), 3:316–17. Further references to this edition will be provided parenthetically in the text with the initials CW.
2. Michael Sonensher, *Before the Deluge* (Princeton: Princeton University Press, 2007), 6.
3. Reinhart Koselleck, "*Historia Magistra Vitae*: The Dissolution of the Topos into the Perspective of a Modernized Historical Process," in *Futures Past: On the Semantics of Historical Time* (Cambridge, MA: MIT Press, 1985), 23.
4. Ibid.

5. William Eden, *Some Remarks on the Apparent Circumstances of the War in the Fourth Week of October 1795* (London, 1795), 38.
6. The seminal work for this hermeneutic approach is Charles Martindale, *Redeeming the Text: Latin Poetry and the Hermeneutics of Reception* (Cambridge: Cambridge University Press, 1993). For a more recent account of its claims, see Martindale, "Reception—A New Humanism? Receptivity, Pedagogy, the Transhistorical," *Classical Receptions Journal* 5, no. 2 (2013): 169–83.
7. Simon Goldhill, *Who Needs Greek?: Contests in the Cultural History of Hellenism* (Cambridge: Cambridge University Press, 2002), 10.
8. Simon Goldhill, *Victorian Culture and Classical Antiquity: Art, Opera, Fiction and the Proclamation of Modernity* (Princeton: Princeton University Press, 2011), 161.
9. For fascinating recent work on the calendar, see Sanja Perovic, *The Calendar in Revolutionary France: Perceptions of Time in Literature, Culture, Politics* (Cambridge: Cambridge University Press, 2012).
10. Lynn Hunt, *Measuring Time, Marking History* (Budapest and New York: Central European University Press, 2008), 68.
11. Peter Fritzche, *Stranded in the Present: Modern Time and the Melancholy of History* (Cambridge, MA: Harvard University Press, 2004), 53–54.
12. Karl Marx, *The Eighteenth Brumaire of Louis Bonaparte* (New York: International Publishers, 1963), 16–17.
13. Ibid., 17.
14. On the French appropriation of Rome, see Harold T. Parker, *The Cult of Antiquity and the French Revolutionaries* (Chicago: University of Chicago Press, 1937); Robert L. Herbert, *David, Voltaire, Brutus and the French Revolution: An Essay in Art and Politics* (New York: The Viking Press, 1972); Mona Ozouf, *Festivals and the French Revolution* (Cambridge, MA: Harvard University Press, 1988), 271–78; Norman Vance, *The Victorians and Ancient Rome* (Oxford: Blackwell, 1997), 24–26.
15. Marx, *Eighteenth Brumaire*, 15.
16. William Wordsworth and Samuel Taylor Coleridge, *Lyrical Ballads*, ed. R. L. Brett and A. R. Jones, 2nd ed. (London: Routledge, 1991), 239.
17. Rolf Engelsing, *Der Bürger als Leser: Lesergeschichte in Deutschland 1500–1800* (Stuttgart: Meltzler, 1974). Engelsing's argument, briefly, is that there was a revolutionary shift circa 1750 from intensive reading, where readers read repeatedly the few books that they owned, to extensive reading, where readers began to read as many books as they could.
18. Andrew Piper, *Dreaming in Books: The Bibliographic Imagination in the Romantic Age* (Chicago: University of Chicago Press, 2009), 4, 5. For additional arguments about Romanticism's "media revolution," see Celeste Langan and Maureen McLane, "The Medium of Romantic

Poetry," in *The Cambridge Companion to British Romantic Poetry*, ed. James Chandler and Maureen McLane (Cambridge: Cambridge University Press, 2008); and Maureen McLane, *Balladeering, Minstrelsy, and the Making of British Romantic Poetry* (Cambridge: Cambridge University Press, 2008), esp. 112–16.

19. From "Bonaparte. III: The Hope for Peace," CW, 3:214.
20. From "On Peace. II: Overtures," CW, 3:67.
21. Samuel Taylor Coleridge, *The Collected Works of Samuel Taylor Coleridge, Vol. 6: Lay Sermons*, ed. R. J. White (Princeton: Princeton University Press, 1972), 8–9.
22. In addition to Koselleck, as discussed above, and Giovanni Arrighi, discussed below, I have in mind here also Hartmut Rosa, Jürgen Habermas, and Paul Virilio. See Hartmut Rosa, "The Speed of Global Flows and the Pace of Democratic Politics," *New Political Science* 27, no. 4 (2005): 445–59, esp. 443; Hartmut Rosa, "Social Acceleration: Ethical and Political Consequences of a De- Synchronized High-Speed Society," with comments by William Scheuerman, Barbara Adam and Carmen Leccardi, *Constellations: An International Journal of Critical and Democratic Theory* 10, no. 1 (2003): 3–52; Jürgen Habermas, *The Philosophical Discourse of Modernity* (Cambridge, MA: MIT Press, 1987), especially "Modernity's Consciousness of Time and Its Need for Self-Reassurance," 1–22; and Paul Virilio, *The Virilio Reader*, ed. James Der Derian (London: Wiley Blackwell, 1998).
23. Walter Benjamin, "Theses on the Philosophy of History," in *Illuminations*, ed. Hannah Arendt (New York: Schocken Books, 1969), 261. Further page references to this edition are given parenthetically in the text.
24. Giovanni Arrighi, *The Long Twentieth Century: Money, Power, and the Origins of Our Time*, 2nd ed. (London and New York: Verso, 2010), 221–22.
25. Ian Baucom, *Specters of the Atlantic: Finance Capital, Slavery, and the Philosophy of History* (Durham, NC: Duke University Press, 2005), 29.
26. Ibid., 24.

Bibliography

Arrighi, Giovanni. *The Long Twentieth Century: Money, Power, and the Origins of Our Time*. 2nd ed. London and New York: Verso, 2010.

Baucom, Ian. *Specters of the Atlantic: Finance Capital, Slavery, and the Philosophy of History*. Durham: Duke University Press, 2005.

Benjamin, Walter. *Illuminations*. Edited by Hannah Arendt. New York: Schocken Books, 1969.

Coleridge, Samuel Taylor. *The Collected Works of Samuel Taylor Coleridge*. 16 vols. Princeton: Princeton University Press, 1969–2002.

Eden, William. *Some Remarks on the Apparent Circumstances of the War in the Fourth Week of October 1795.* London, 1795.
Engelsing, Rolf. *Der Bürger als Leser: Lesergeschichte in Deutschland 1500–1800.* Stuttgart: Meltzler, 1974.
Fritzche, Peter. *Stranded in the Present: Modern Time and the Melancholy of History.* Cambridge, MA: Harvard University Press, 2004.
Goldhill, Simon. *Victorian Culture and Classical Antiquity: Art, Opera, Fiction and the Proclamation of Modernity.* Princeton: Princeton University Press, 2011.
———. *Who Needs Greek?: Contests in the Cultural History of Hellenism.* Cambridge: Cambridge University Press, 2002.
Habermas, Jürgen. *The Philosophical Discourse of Modernity.* Cambridge, MA: MIT Press, 1987.
Herbert, Robert L. *David, Voltaire, Brutus and the French Revolution: An Essay in Art and Politics.* New York: The Viking Press, 1972.
Hunt, Lynn. *Measuring Time, Marking History.* Budapest and New York: Central European University Press, 2008.
Koselleck, Reinhart. *Futures Past: On the Semantics of Historical Time.* Cambridge, MA: MIT Press, 1985.
Langan, Celeste, and Maureen McLane. "The Medium of Romantic Poetry." In *The Cambridge Companion to British Romantic Poetry*, edited by James Chandler and Maureen McLane. Cambridge: Cambridge University Press, 2008.
Martindale, Charles. "Reception—A New Humanism? Receptivity, Pedagogy, the Transhistorical." *Classical Receptions Journal* 5, no. 2 (2013): 169–83.
———. *Redeeming the Text: Latin Poetry and the Hermeneutics of Reception.* Cambridge: Cambridge University Press, 1993.
Marx, Karl. *The Eighteenth Brumaire of Louis Bonaparte.* New York: International Publishers, 1963.
McLane, Maureen. *Balladeering, Minstrelsy, and the Making of British Romantic Poetry.* Cambridge: Cambridge University Press, 2008.
Ozouf, Mona. *Festivals and the French Revolution.* Cambridge, MA: Harvard University Press, 1988.
Parker, Harold T. *The Cult of Antiquity and the French Revolutionaries.* Chicago: University of Chicago Press, 1937.
Perovic, Sanja. *The Calendar in Revolutionary France: Perceptions of Time in Literature, Culture, Politics.* Cambridge: Cambridge University Press, 2012.
Piper, Andrew. *Dreaming in Books: The Bibliographic Imagination in the Romantic Age.* Chicago: University of Chicago Press, 2009.
Rosa, Hartmut. "Social Acceleration: Ethical and Political Consequences of a De-Synchronized High-Speed Society." With comments by William Scheuerman, Barbara Adam and Carmen Leccardi. *Constellations: An International Journal of Critical and Democratic Theory* 10, no. 1 (2003): 3–52.

———. "The Speed of Global Flows and the Pace of Democratic Politics." *New Political Science* 27, no. 4 (2005): 445–59.

Sonensher, Michael. *Before the Deluge*. Princeton: Princeton University Press, 2007.

Vance, Norman. *The Victorians and Ancient Rome*. Oxford: Blackwell, 1997.

Virilio, Paul. *The Virilio Reader*. Edited by James Der Derian. London: Wiley Blackwell, 1998.

Wordsworth, William, and Samuel Taylor Coleridge. *Lyrical Ballads*. Edited by R. L. Brett and A. R. Jones. 2nd ed. London: Routledge, 1991.

Chapter 11

The Classics and American Political Rhetoric in a Democratic and Romantic Age
Carl J. Richard

During the same period when new grammar schools, academies, and colleges were introducing the Greek and Roman classics to the western frontier of the United States, to a rising middle class, to girls and women, and to African Americans, states were expanding the voting population to include all free adult white males. While the spread of manhood suffrage led to a more democratic style of politics, the expansion of classical education ensured that American courtrooms, legislatures, newspapers, and private letters continued to bristle with classical allusions. Although some stump speeches lacked such references, most political leaders took advantage of every opportunity to showcase their classical learning, even to broader audiences they hoped might respect, if not fully comprehend, their allusions. Classically trained, most American politicians lived a double rhetorical life, attempting to assure common voters of their ability to empathize with their concerns while simultaneously demonstrating their learning, wisdom, and virtue to constituents of all classes through their knowledge of the classics.

Fifth-century BCE Athens, the first major democracy in history, provided a crucial bridge: American statesmen learned that they could not only make classical references but even ornament them in the aristocratic style of Cicero without seeming aristocratic, as long as their allusions concerned the glories of Athenian democracy. Despite their praise for the concise, plain, and rational speeches of the Athenians Pericles and Demosthenes, whose rhetorical style they claimed best suited a democratic age, their own speeches more often employed the copious, florid, and emotional style of Cicero.

This was because their education emphasized Latin over Greek and because the era in which they lived was as romantic in aesthetic sensibility as it was democratic in ideology. Furthermore, while southern politicians used classical precedents to support the institution of slavery, northern abolitionists used the classical theory of natural law to assault it.

The study of Latin dominated American education throughout the antebellum period (1820–61). While Homer and the Greek New Testament were also staples of classical training, the time allotted to Latin far outweighed that assigned to Greek. Nearly all colleges not only required a facility with the works of Cicero and Virgil for admission but devoted most of their curricula to expanding students' knowledge of Latin literature. At the secondary level, for instance, the Boston Latin School, aiming to help its students meet the Harvard admissions requirements, focused on Cicero, Caesar, Sallust, Tacitus, Virgil, and Horace. Even as the number of American colleges increased from 9 to 182 from the mid-eighteenth to the mid-nineteenth century, college entrance requirements and curricula remained largely unchanged, emphasizing Cicero, Virgil, Horace, and other Latin authors. New female academies and colleges offered similar training for girls and women. A few schools in large northern cities like Philadelphia also offered a classical education to African American students, female and male. Although the Greek quest for independence from the Ottoman Empire enthralled Americans, helping to produce a philhellenic strain that led to the inclusion of the Greek dramatists in college curricula for the first time, the educational system continued to emphasize Latin.[1]

Daniel Webster was typical of the politicians of his age. He loved the classics and peppered his addresses to august bodies, like Congress and the Supreme Court, with classical references, but also exhibited an occasional reticence about using them in speeches geared to less educated audiences. For instance, in arguing a famous case for Dartmouth College before the Supreme Court, Webster closed with a melodramatic, Ciceronian flourish: "Sir, I know not how others may feel (glancing at the opponents of the College before him), but, for myself, when I see my alma mater surrounded, like Caesar in the senate house, by those who are reiterating stab after stab, I would not, for this right hand, have her turn to me, and say, 'Et tu quoque mi fili!' 'And thou too, my son!'" Webster was not deterred by the irony involved in wrapping the words of Julius Caesar in a Ciceronian cloak, nor by the irony of the fact, later noted in his autobiography, that Dartmouth had given him only "a very scanty" classical training, a small store of knowledge that he himself had felt compelled to augment. Likewise, in 1851, the year before his death, while watching his beloved Union beginning to crumble before his eyes, Webster closed his last Fourth of July speech with a Latin line that meant: "I wish these things: one, that in dying I may leave a free people; nothing greater than this can be given me by the immortal gods; the second, that each man may prove worthy of the republic." Yet Webster avoided using Latin phrases in his appeals to juries and, in 1841, persuaded William Henry Harrison, an avid reader of Cicero and of Charles Rollin's *Ancient History*, to delete obscure classical references from his inaugural address. Webster joked that he had killed "seventeen Roman pro-consuls as dead as smelts." Unfortunately, Webster's failure to murder even more Roman references killed Harrison: delivered in the freezing rain, Harrison's inaugural address remains the longest in American history, leading to the president's death from pneumonia a month later and, thus, to the shortest presidential term in American history.[2]

It is true that, in the western states particularly, the "Age of Egalitarianism" opened political office to a number of men like Abraham Lincoln, Sam Houston, and Andrew Jackson who possessed little formal education. The son of nearly illiterate parents, Lincoln was raised in a rugged frontier environment in which study was regarded as laziness, an environment that, in Lincoln's own words, possessed "nothing to excite ambition for education." The backwoods schools Lincoln sporadically attended were conducted by teachers with meager qualifications. Lincoln joked, "If a straggler supposed to understand Latin happened to sojourn in the neighborhood, he was looked upon as a wizard." Though an avid reader who struggled tenaciously with words, passages, and ideas he did not understand, young Lincoln did not have access to a wide variety of books. His reading consisted of the Bible, *Aesop's Fables* (his sole classical reading as a child), *The Pilgrim's Progress*, *Robinson Crusoe*, and a few writings of Benjamin Franklin and George Washington. As a busy attorney, he read little more than newspapers and law books, the tools of his trade. Lincoln's law partner William Herndon remarked that Lincoln "read less and thought more than any man in his sphere in America."[3]

But the lack of a classical education did not necessarily make a man an enemy of the classics or prevent him from acquiring classical knowledge indirectly, through English translations or contemporary speeches and essays. Lincoln was proud of his command of Euclid's *Elements*, a level of mastery that awed Herndon and others. Herndon recalled that Lincoln often studied Euclid by candlelight until two in the morning, while the other attorneys riding circuit with him snored loudly. Lincoln frequently spoke of "the theorems and axioms of democracy," comparing them with Euclid's propositions.[4]

More important, as Garry Wills has demonstrated, the similarities between Lincoln's Gettysburg Address (1863) and Pericles's Funeral Oration (429 BCE) are so striking as to suggest at least some indirect influence on the part of the latter, especially since Pericles's famous speech, as recounted by Thucydides, was widely copied, praised, and cited in antebellum America. Just as the purpose of Pericles's oration had been to honor the Athenian dead of the Peloponnesian War, so Lincoln's intent was to memorialize the Union war dead. Yet both statesmen emphasized that the dead had won such honor through their own heroic sacrifice that mere words could hardly gain them any additional glory. Both stressed that the only way for the survivors to venerate the dead was to finish their crucial work of saving the democratic experiment from its enemies. Both appealed to revered ancestors—in Pericles's case the heroes of the Persian Wars, in Lincoln's the patriots of the Revolutionary War—thereby yoking the past to the present. Both employed such dichotomies as word versus deed, mortality versus immortality, the past versus the present, and democracy versus tyranny. Both speeches were extraordinarily concise, devoted to general principles rather than to particulars. Lincoln followed Edward Everett's two-hour Ciceronian oration, a speech filled with references to Periclean Athens, with a two-minute address stripped of all such allusions yet following Pericles's line of argument closely. In short, while Everett referred to Pericles, Lincoln embodied him. Nor was Roman influence completely absent from Lincoln's speech. He borrowed the phrase "a new birth of freedom" from the historian Livy, who had coined it in reference to the Roman law that ended enslavement for debt (*History of Rome* 8.28).[5]

Another Westerner who lacked formal training in the classics, Sam Houston, future congressman from and governor of Tennessee and future senator from and governor of Texas, memorized all five hundred pages of Alexander Pope's translation of the *Iliad* as a sixteen-year-old in 1809. When Houston demanded that his teacher at a local academy in eastern Tennessee teach the ancient languages and the teacher refused, Houston declared that he would never recite another lesson again and stormed out of the school. When Houston's brothers then found him living with the Cherokees, he told them that he "liked the wild liberty of Red men better than the tyranny of his own brothers, and if he could not study Latin in the Academy he could, at least, read a translation from the Greek in the woods, and read it in peace." The translation to which he referred was Pope's *Iliad*, which he recited to Cherokee girls from memory on long walks. Houston's biographer M. K. Wisehart attributes his flamboyance, heroic self-image, and oratorical and literary style to Pope's *Iliad*. While visiting Nashville in 1831, Houston commissioned a painting of himself as the Roman consul Marius. In a speech before Congress regarding the Compromise of 1850 Houston likened Henry Clay to Ajax in the thick of battle. On another occasion he compared his fallen comrades at the Alamo to the Spartans who died at Thermopylae.[6]

Even Andrew Jackson, who was once praised for his lack of classical learning, could still show his respect for the classics in symbolic ways. Andrew Stevenson of Virginia suggested that Jackson had benefited from his ignorance of Greek and Latin, writing: "Regular and classical education has been thought by some distinguished men to be unfavorable to great vigour and originality of the understanding; and that, like civilization, whilst it made society more interesting and agreeable, yet, at the same time, it leveled the distinctions of nature." Yet as president, Jackson appointed the famous neoclassical architect Robert Mills as the official architect of his administration. In fact, when Jackson's own estate, the Hermitage, burned in 1835, he appears to have sought Mills's advice in reconstructing it. The capitals of the new Corinthian columns that fronted the house were modeled on those of the Temple of the Winds in Athens. Jackson probably also sought Mills's advice concerning his domed tomb. For his home Jackson selected expensive wallpaper designed by the Frenchman Joseph Dufour, a panoramic series of panels that included Minerva tossing Telemachus off the cliffs of the island of Calypso in order to break the spell of the nymph Eucharis (a story told by François de Salignac de la Mothe-Fénelon in *Les Avantures de Télémaque* [1699]). Imitating Jackson in architecture as in other matters, Jackson's political ally and fellow Tennessean James K. Polk, who liked to converse with a former classmate in Greek, also built a home in the Greek Revival style in the early 1840s. On the grounds sat a Doric tomb, built to house Polk's remains soon after his death in 1849. As the historian Wendy Cooper has noted, "Just as Americans aped Europeans, so the fashions of the wealthy on this side of the Atlantic were copied by others aspiring to similar heights of refinement and fashion." This was true even of those who presented themselves as champions of the masses.[7]

It is true that some of the poorly educated new voters considered the classics useless vestiges of aristocracy, and that some politicians sought to capitalize on their anti-intellectualism by denigrating the classical languages. In 1859, for example, Senator John Hale of New Hampshire reflected the anticlassicism of some uneducated Americans when he remarked: "Whenever I hear a judge in court give an opinion in Latin, I generally conclude that he is about to announce some infernal doctrine that he is ashamed to speak in English."[8]

But most politicians acted differently when speaking to one another and, increasingly, when addressing any audience they thought might be even mildly learned or respectful of learning. In fact, when speaking to one another, they sometimes carried their classicism to absurd lengths. In 1841 John G. Palfrey complained that Virginia legislators were likely to flaunt their classical erudition "even on a question of renewing the upholstery of the Representatives' Chamber, or paying the Sergeant-at-Arms." When John Quincy Adams sneered at John Randolph's numerous quotations of Latin poets in Congress, calling them mere "scraps of Latin from the Dictionary of Quotations," the genuinely learned Randolph retorted that he had never met "a Yankee who knew anything about the classics." Both men understood the importance of maintaining their respective reputations for classical knowledge. Yet they at least avoided the extreme sensitivity of Judge John Rowan, who killed Dr. James Chambers in a duel over which man possessed the more thorough knowledge of Greek and Latin. Rowan went on to serve in the House of Representatives and the U.S. Senate, where he was presumably safe from any imputations against his classical prowess.[9]

Antebellum politicians learned quickly that one way to appear erudite and elegant without seeming aristocratic was to praise Athenian democracy in a Ciceronian speech. Whereas the founders had regarded the Roman republic, with its famous balance between the aristocratic Senate and the popular assemblies, as the greatest political model of antiquity and had feared the instability of democratic Athens, the antebellum generation embraced Athenian democracy. Yet, because of their Latin education and romantic sensibility and, perhaps more importantly, because their audiences possessed the same romantic aesthetic preferences, they often chose to praise Athens in a Ciceronian style rather than emulate the concise, plain, and rational addresses of the Athenian orators whom they themselves often claimed were the more appropriate models.

In his classic manual *The Orator* (55 BCE), Cicero opposed the "Attic style" made famous by Pericles's Funeral Oration and by the fourth-century BCE speeches of Demosthenes against the Macedonian king, Philip II. For instance, Cicero stressed the importance of emotion in addresses. Orators must touch the hearts of their audiences, he wrote, because, "Men decide far more problems by hate, or love, or lust, or rage, or sorrow, or joy, or hope, or fear, or illusion, or some other inward emotion, than by reality, or authority, or any legal standards, or judicial precedent, or statute." He cited the example of a virtuous Roman named Rutilius, who refused to allow his lawyers to play on the jury's emotions and was condemned to death as a result: "A man of such quality has been lost through his case being conducted as if the trial had been taking place in that ideal republic of Plato. None of his counselors groaned or shrieked, none was pained at anything, or made any complaint, or invoked the State, or humbled himself. In a word, not one of them stamped a foot during those proceedings, for fear, no doubt, of being reported to the Stoics." Attorneys must use emotion to counter the letter of the law when arguing for its spirit, just as politicians must use emotion to arouse a listless nation in some cases and to curb its impetuosity in others. The orator must comprehend the audience's biases in order to lead them where they were already willing to be led and must model the very emotion he wished to evoke. That emotion must be genuine, of course, and the orator must begin the speech calmly and rationally. But, as the oration progressed, he must gradually build emotion through rich, diversified language and an animated delivery. For this reason, Cicero also opposed the concision of the Attic style, which hindered the crucial ability to evoke emotion: "Concise or quiet speakers may inform an arbitrator but cannot excite him, on which excitement everything depends." As a result, Cicero drafted speeches that were copious and florid without being redundant. While varying his vocabulary, he avoided meaningless synonyms, selecting each word for its peculiar force.

By the early nineteenth century Cicero, aided by his central place in American education and by the increasing romanticism of the age, had clearly prevailed in the field of American political rhetoric, however much Americans might praise the Attic style in theory. While in retirement in the 1810s and 1820s, Thomas Jefferson, who possessed an uncommon command of the Greek language and a style that was profoundly Attic, watched the triumph of Ciceronian rhetoric with increasing dismay. Jefferson claimed that the three qualities most essential to republican oratory were simplicity, brevity, and rationality, the very qualities exemplified by the Attic style. Even as a youth, Jefferson had copied into his literary commonplace book this passage on the virtue of rhetorical simplicity from the fifth-century BCE dramatist Euripides: "The words of truth are simple, and justice needs no subtle interpretations, for it has a fitness in itself; but the words of injustice, being rotten in themselves, require clever treatment." Now Jefferson wrote: "Amplification is the vice of modern oratory. It is an insult to an assembly of reasonable men, disgusting and revolting instead of persuading. Speeches measured by the hour die by the hour. . . . In a republican nation whose citizens are to be led by reason and persuasion, and not by force, the art of reasoning becomes of the first importance." As a result of his Attic preferences, Jefferson not only detested the Ciceronian rhetoric then popular in the House of Representatives but also warned that it would undermine the Constitution by exciting such disgust in the people that they would transfer their allegiance from the legislative to the executive branch.[10]

In anticipating a revolt against Ciceronian oratory Jefferson failed to recognize the increasing romanticism of most Americans, who, in this age before radio, film, and television, considered long, florid speeches their principal form of entertainment. Thus, while many American speakers agreed with Jefferson in theory, most imitated Cicero in practice. John Quincy Adams declared approvingly regarding Demosthenes: "His eloquence is characteristic of democracy, as that of Cicero is of aristocracy. It is the Doric to the Corinthian pillar." Thomas Dew, president of the College of William and Mary, agreed, adding that while Cicero's flashiness might have won more applause from his audiences, Demosthenes's simplicity was more persuasive: "When Cicero spoke, the man was admired, the oration was praised. When Demosthenes had spoken, the crowd went away denouncing Philip." Dew added, "The history of ancient republics has most conclusively proven that no audience is so favorable to the production of close, concise, and powerful oratory as the popular assembly." Following the profusion of stump speeches delivered throughout the United States as part of the presidential campaign of 1840, the *Southern Literary Messenger* declared: "Our country seems fast approaching to that peculiar state which called forth the unrivalled efforts of Grecian oratory. We seem destined to enact Greece, if I may so say, on a gigantic scale. . . . All history has shown that genuine eloquence can only flourish under institutions of republican character. Under arbitrary governments . . . persuasion is of no avail. . . . The oratorical campaign of 1840 has, in truth, furnished the true key to the secret of Grecian eloquence; henceforth, the American student will find no difficulty in understanding the real character of Demosthenes." The author included the usual statement of preference for Demosthenes over Cicero, noting concerning the former's speeches: "They are always to the point; there are no digressions—no common-places—nothing for mere ornament . . . whereas Cicero often amplifies and deals in philosophical reflections, some of which are mere common-places."[11]

But this preference for Attic over Ciceronian rhetoric was, if the pun may be allowed, merely rhetorical. For every Periclean oration like Lincoln's Gettysburg Address, there were innumerable Ciceronian speeches, such as Edward Everett's oration preceding Lincoln's. Everett could get away with adopting the aristocratic style of Cicero partly because it better suited a romantic age and partly because he shrewdly employed it to glorify Periclean Athens. In his speech Everett directly connected Athens to American democracy in one of the longest sentences in human history:

> Shall I, fellow citizens, who, after an interval of twenty-three centuries, a youthful pilgrim from the world unknown to ancient Greece, have wandered over that illustrious plain, ready to put off shoes from my feet, as one that stands on holy ground—who have gazed with respectful emotion on the mound which still protects the dust of those who rolled back the tide of Persian invasion, and rescued the land of popular liberty, of letters, and of arts, from the ruthless foe—stand unmoved over the graves of dear brethren who so lately, on three of the all-important days which decide a nation's history—days on whose issue it depended whether this august republican Union, founded by some of the wisest statesmen that ever lived, cemented with the blood of some of the purest patriots that ever died, should perish or endure—rolled back the tide of invasion, not less unprovoked, not less ruthless, than that which came to plant the dark banner of Asiatic despotism and slavery on the free soil of Greece? Heaven forbid!

Everett concluded his speech: "'The whole earth,' said Pericles as he stood over the remains of his fellow citizens, who had fallen in the first year of the Peloponnesian War, 'the whole earth is the sepulchre of illustrious men.' All time, he might have added, is the millennium of their glory. . . . Wheresoever throughout the civilized world the accounts of this great warfare are read, and down to the latest period of recorded time, in the glorious annals of our common country, there will be no brighter page than that which relates to The Battles of Gettysburg."[12]

At any rate, classical speeches, whether of the simple Attic or of the more ornate Ciceronian variety, were highly valued in antebellum America. As the historian Daniel Walker Howe has written: "By stressing the arts of rhetoric, classical studies helped direct political argumentation toward the declamatory style of Webster and Calhoun. The political speeches of the time, like the lyceum lectures, sermons, ceremonial discourses, and lawyers' arguments, constituted a popular body of oral literature. Paradoxically, the written culture of the classics underwrote and legitimated this oral culture." Perhaps this was because classical culture had been an oral one too; since written manuscripts were rare and expensive in antiquity, nearly all classical authors intended their works to be read aloud and, therefore, focused considerable attention on perfecting their aural qualities.[13]

The growth of democracy in antebellum America was not the only reason the southern perception of Athens shifted from the founding generation's belief that the polis was too democratic and unstable. Another factor was Athens's usefulness in support of the southern argument that slavery was a positive good. Ironically, when Athens finally achieved the popularity it had been denied for over two millennia because of its political egalitarianism, that popularity, at least in the South, was based partly on its social inequalities.

Southern proslavery appeals to classical history took several forms. Some references merely alluded to the universality of slavery, implying that anything universal must be natural and, therefore, good. Others emphasized slavery's venerable antiquity, implying that anything old and lasting must be natural and, therefore, good. Others involved the claim that since the Greeks and Romans, whom most Americans considered to have been admirable peoples, owned slaves, slavery must be good. Finally, it was asserted that the dazzling cultural achievements of Greece and Rome and the liberty and political equality singularly associated with the classical republics constituted evidence of the positive good of slavery. This use of the classical republics conferred enormous psychological benefits on proslavery southerners. As the historian Joseph Berrigan put it: "By becoming another Athens the South came into a rich inheritance of political and cultural responsibility. She ennobled her experience and dignified her action[s]. . . . Her defense of her way of life now seemed the battle against barbarians or against those who did not respect the values of Athens-South."[14]

Southern advocates of slavery thus attributed to it the love of liberty, equality among citizens, stability, and intellectual and artistic achievements of the classical republics. Thomas Dew wrote: "It has been contended that slavery is unfavorable to a republican spirit; but the whole history of the world proves that this is far from being the case. In the ancient republics of Greece and Rome, where the spirit of liberty glowed with the most intensity, the slaves were more numerous than the freemen. Aristotle and the great men of antiquity believed slavery necessary to keep alive the spirit of freedom."[15]

Best of all, the peculiar institution produced intellectual genius and artistic achievement. George Fitzhugh claimed regarding slavery: "To it Greece and Rome, Egypt and Judea, and all the other distinguished States of antiquity, were indebted for their great prosperity and high civilization, a prosperity and a civilization which appears almost miraculous, when we look to their ignorance of the physical sciences. The lonely and time-defying relics of Roman and Grecian art, the Doric column and the Gothic spire, alike attest the taste, the genius and the energy of society where slavery existed. . . . Scipio and Aristides, Calhoun and Washington, are the noble results of domestic slavery."[16]

If Athens was the social model of most southern advocates of slavery, Aristotle was their favored spokesman. In the *Politics* (1.2) Aristotle had argued that some men were born to lead and others to follow: "The element which is able, by virtue of its intelligence, to exercise forethought is naturally a ruling and master element; the element which is able, by virtue of its bodily power, to do the physical work, is a ruled element, which is naturally in a state of slavery." Just as the mind should rule the body, so those with better minds should rule those with better bodies. Aristotle connected slavery with the universal rule of humans over animals, adults over children, and males over females, power relationships he considered equally natural (though he claimed that the rule of male over female should more closely resemble that of a statesman over fellow citizens than that of a monarch over subjects). Slavery was both natural and beneficial to the slave (1.5): "Those whose function is to use the body and from whom physical labor is the most that can be expected are by nature slaves, and it is best for them, as it is for all inferior things I have already mentioned, to be ruled." The master was distinguished from his slave not only by his greater intelligence (though Aristotle conceded that in actual practice the slave was sometimes more intelligent than his master) but also by his greater love of liberty. At one point Aristotle implied that anyone who would allow himself to be enslaved, rather than taking his own life, did not possess the passion for liberty requisite for a citizen in a republic: "For he is by nature a slave who is capable of belonging to another and therefore does belong to another." Aristotle sometimes seemed to suggest, as had Plato (*Republic* 5.469–70), that while it was wrong to enslave fellow Greeks, it was appropriate to enslave at least some barbarians—a doctrine useful to Aristotle's pupil Alexander the Great in his conquest of the Persian Empire. For centuries slaveholders throughout the Americas wielded Aristotle's defense of slavery as a powerful weapon.[17]

Antebellum southerners were no exception. In 1840 John C. Calhoun had advised a young man to study ancient history "and to read the best elementary treatises on Government, including Aristotle's, which I regard as among the best." George Fitzhugh called Aristotle "the wisest philosopher of ancient times." He concluded: "The Bible (independent of its authority) is (by far) man's best guide, even in this world. Next to it, we would place Aristotle."[18]

Aristotle's concept of the "natural slave" was ideally suited to southern advocates of slavery, who had only to racialize it to suit their purposes. In his *Disquisition on Government* John C. Calhoun sounded much like Aristotle: "It is a great and dangerous error to suppose that all people are equally entitled to liberty. It is a reward to be earned, not a blessing to be gratuitously lavished on all alike— a reward reserved for the intelligent, the patriotic, the virtuous, and deserving, and not a boon to be bestowed on a people too ignorant, degraded, and vicious to be capable either of appreciating or of enjoying it. . . . Every effort to elevate a people in the scale of liberty above the point to which they are entitled must ever prove abortive and end in disappointment. The progress of a people rising from a lower to a higher point in the scale of liberty is necessarily slow." Through this implicit denigration of the intellectual and moral capacities of African Americans, Calhoun converted them into Aristotle's "natural slaves," thereby denying them the same right of resistance to "majority tyranny" he recognized for southern whites.[19]

While the northern Transcendentalists embraced Plato, whose *Republic* had championed socialism and the removal of children from their parents (at least among the elite), antebellum southerners preferred Aristotle, who had considered the family unit coextensive with civilized humanity. Fitzhugh compared modern abolitionists to utopians like Plato, whom the realistic Aristotle had far surpassed in wisdom. In Fitzhugh's eyes, nature itself was under assault from modern Platonists in the form of the socialist, feminist, and abolitionist movements. While Plato had proposed "to throw husbands, wives and children into a sort of common public stock," Aristotle had considered the preservation of the family the first duty of the polis.[20]

Most abolitionists responded by arguing that slavery had been the greatest flaw of Athens and the other classical republics; instead, they invoked the classical theory of natural law, the theory from which modern republicans like the founders had derived the theory of natural rights. The historian David Brion Davis has written, "Assuming that cultural achievement could never depend on moral evil, most historians and classicists tended to ignore ancient slavery or to relegate it as a deplorable defect unrelated to the glories of Greece and Rome." The Frenchman Henri Wallon, who published the first comprehensive study of ancient slavery in 1847, wrote regarding the Greek and Roman civilizations, "The bad points were the direct results of slavery, the good ones of freedom." Frederick Douglass, who had learned to read by studying the neoclassical speeches of Edward Everett contained in the 1832 edition of *The Columbian Orator*, proudly called Boston "the Athens of America," though he also argued that slavery had been the downfall of the first Athens, as well as of ancient Egypt, Israel, and Rome. Prejudice had deprived these states of the full use of all their citizens.[21]

Douglass also used the Egyptian influence on Greece to disprove the theory that light-skinned people were intellectually superior to dark-skinned people. He claimed: "Greece and Rome—and through them Europe and America—have received their civilization from the ancient Egyptians. . . . The ancient Egyptians were not white people but were, undoubtedly, just about as dark in complexion as many in this country who are considered genuine negroes. . . . The Egyptians were once superior to the Greeks, and the Greeks to the Romans, and the Romans were superior to the Normans, and the Normans superior to the Saxons, and now the Anglo-Saxon is boasting his superiority to the negro and to the Irishman."[22]

The historian David S. Wiesen noted the power of the Christian and classical traditions over the abolitionists. Wiesen wrote: "The most ardent enemies of slavery always used as a touchstone to prove the natural gift of Negroes for civilization, first their readiness to be Christianized and then their association with the classical tradition, either in historical fact or in their ability to absorb the best classical education." Indeed, the abolitionist propensity to highlight the classical knowledge of some African Americans as proof of the intellectual capacity of the whole race tended to encourage such learning wherever possible. During the Reconstruction period, Booker T. Washington marveled at the "craze for Greek and Latin learning" among the new freedmen, a craze he attributed to the widespread belief "that a knowledge, however little, of the Greek and Latin languages would make one a very superior human being, something bordering almost on the supernatural."[23]

There was even a sustained effort by antebellum abolitionists to portray runaway slaves as classical heroes. In 1837 the *Anti-slavery Record* compared the act of escape by runaway slaves to the retreat of the Greeks under Xenophon from the heart of the Persian Empire in 401 BCE, explaining, "To escape from a powerful enemy often requires as much courage and generalship as to conquer." When a runaway slave named Margaret Garner, on the verge of being captured by a posse of armed men in 1856, killed her own children rather than see them re-enslaved, Ellen Wilkins Harper published a poem comparing her to Roman heroes. Harper added: "Even Rome had altars 'neath whose shade / Might crouch the wan and weary slave." This was a reference to the Roman practice of allowing abused slaves to seek refuge at sanctuaries. Other abolitionists compared Garner to Verginius, who had killed his daughter Virginia rather than see her enslaved.[24]

Even Senator Charles Sumner of Massachusetts, who was more critical of Greco-Roman civilization than most, could not help fixating on a few obscure critics of slavery among the ancients. Sumner asserted: "We learn from Aristotle himself that there were persons in his day—pestilent Abolitionists of ancient Athens—who did not hesitate to maintain that liberty was the great law of Nature, and to deny any difference between master and slave—declaring at the same time that slavery was founded upon violence, and not upon right, that the authority of the master was unnatural and unjust. 'God sent forth all persons free; Nature has made no man a slave' was the protest of one of these agitating Athenians against this great wrong." Sumner added that the antislavery statements of these Athenians were identical to those asserted at modern abolitionist meetings.[25]

Abolitionists also championed the classical theory of natural law, the belief in a universal code of ethics inherent in nature, but interpreted it in a different manner from the ancients themselves, to invalidate slavery. Whereas Plato, Aristotle, and other classical philosophers, as members of highly communal societies faced with the constant threat of war, had interpreted the theory narrowly to recognize few individual rights, modern republicans had placed a new emphasis on the natural rights to life, liberty, and property. This emphasis had culminated in the Glorious and American revolutions and in the English and U.S. bills of rights.[26]

Antebellum opponents of slavery often invoked the theory of natural law. In an 1851 speech to his fellow citizens of Concord concerning the Fugitive Slave Law of 1850, Ralph Waldo Emerson cited Cicero on the principle that "an immoral law could not be valid," a truth the Roman had considered "the foundation of States." Emerson then noted the doctrine of the Greek playwrights that divine justice inevitably overtook those who violated natural law. The same year, when the abolitionist journalist Horace Greeley visited Rome, he could not help but make an implicit comparison between the Roman violation of natural law in the case of gladiatorial combat and the Fugitive Slave Law's compulsion of northern citizens to aid in the return of runaway slaves.[27]

In an 1852 speech proposing the repeal of the Fugitive Slave Law, Charles Sumner cited Cicero on natural law. He related: "After assailing indignantly that completest folly which would find the rule of justice in human institutions and laws, and then asking if the laws of tyrants are just simply because [they are] laws, Cicero declares that, if edicts of popular assemblies, decrees of princes, and decisions of judges constitute right, then there may be a right to rob, a right to commit adultery, a right to set up forged wills; whereas he does not hesitate to say that pernicious and pestilent statutes can be no more entitled to the name of law than robber codes; and he concludes, in words as strong as those of St. Augustine, that an unjust law is null." (Sumner neglected to mention that Cicero, like nearly all aristocratic Romans, owned slaves.) It was no accident that Sophocles's *Antigone*, a play about a woman who violates the edict of a ruler on behalf of a higher law, became popular in the 1840s and 1850s, the very decades when the dispute over slavery reached its height.[28]

In 1860 Charles Sumner used natural law to combat what he considered the illegitimate use of another venerable Greek theory, the theory of popular sovereignty. This theory, which held that the people had the right to choose their own form of government, had proved as crucial to the American Revolution and to the U.S. Constitution as the theory of natural law. In 1854 the Kansas-Nebraska Act had nullified the prohibition of slavery in Kansas and Nebraska that had been instituted by the Missouri Compromise (1820), replacing it with the right of settlers in these territories to determine for themselves whether to permit slavery. Sumner declared at the Massachusetts Republican Convention: "The sacred name of Popular Sovereignty is prostituted to cover the claim of a master over his slave.... To protect this 'villainy,' as John Wesley would call it, the right of the people to govern themselves is invoked—forgetful that this divine right can give no authority to enslave others." William Seward made a similar appeal to the classical theory of natural law that year, declaring that there was a "higher law" than the U.S.

Constitution, which condoned slavery, a declaration that probably cost him the Republican nomination and the presidency.[29]

The abolitionists regarded slavery as the greatest flaw of the democratic civilization of Athens, just as it was now the greatest flaw of the democratic civilization of the United States. But they chose to regard slavery as an incidental element of classical civilization, not a core element, a choice that allowed them to continue revering their favorite classical heroes and imitating their political rhetoric. Since classical civilization had supplied the founders with the intellectual resources necessary to defend republicanism against monarchy, not even the staunchest abolitionist could feel entirely comfortable assaulting the fountainhead of republicanism for what he perceived to be its greatest impurity.

But slavery was an important element of classical civilization, not an aberration, a universally accepted practice, not a passing evil, and Greco-Roman slavery exerted a profound influence on the antebellum South. While the classics provided vital inspiration to the forces of republicanism and democracy in the United States during the American Revolution, the Constitutional Convention, and the age of Jacksonian democracy, they also provided equally essential support to the proslavery forces of the Old South. While they helped build the modern Athens, they also helped cleave it asunder.

As with so much else, the Civil War was the great turning point in the history of both the classics and political rhetoric in America. The war laid to rest the issue of slavery and produced new controversies, nearly all of them economic. The Industrial Revolution, which received much of its initial capital in the United States from the Union government's massive wartime spending, transformed American life, creating for the first time a large European-style proletariat. The agricultural lifestyle experienced a dramatic decline, not since reversed; put out of work by the global glut of grain that resulted from European peace and the farmer's own productivity, many farmers migrated to the cities to hold factory jobs. The classics could not address the prevailing political issues of the protective tariff, the gold standard, and the regulation of corporations. Neither could the classics offer much in the dispute over Charles Darwin's theory of natural selection, though the ancient philosopher Anaximander had been the first to allude to the possibility of evolution. Economics, engineering, and the sciences were viewed as the proper objects of study in an industrial age; indeed, the federal government subsidized the study of engineering and agriculture under the Morrill Act of 1862. Most of the leading industrialists, the era's greatest role models, were self-made men with little formal education who scoffed at the classics. Meanwhile, the growth of international trade placed a premium on the knowledge of modern languages, and science so captivated public adulation that even the study of humanity was reconceived under the rubric of "social science." The Civil War, a catastrophe that caused the death of one out of every fifty Americans, appeared to many a monumental refutation of the Aristotelian notion that humans were rational creatures capable of discerning and applying universal moral laws. Finally, the aristocratic intellectual class, the historic defenders of the classics, began abandoning their traditional post because the antebellum period had, by democratizing the classics, drastically reduced their utility as aristocratic markers. By the Gilded Age, the very time when the classics seemed to be losing their intellectual utility, the American elite had lost their age-old monopoly of knowledge about them, so that Latin and Greek no longer served as a reliable badge of social status. In short, a perfect storm of rising skepticism and moral relativism, materialism spawned by the Industrial Revolution, the increasing glorification of science, and the changing self-interest of the American elite finally granted the utilitarians the victory that had so often eluded them in the past.[30]

In 1886 Harvard eliminated its Greek entrance requirement. Other older universities like Yale, as well as new universities like Cornell, Johns Hopkins, and the University of Chicago, followed suit in the ensuing decade, as universities moved toward curricula that allowed greater specialization in business, science, and other "majors." There were thirty-nine different degrees by 1900, and graduate programs arose. By that time only one-third of Harvard students elected to take Latin, only one-sixth Greek. A 1912 study of 155 colleges found that two-thirds required neither Greek nor Latin. Like other college teachers, classics professors became specialized and insular, rarely writing for the general public. As the percentage of educated Americans studying the classics decreased, the role of classical knowledge in the political culture declined.[31]

Notes

1. Edward L. Pierce, ed., *Memoir and Letters of Charles Sumner* (London: Sampson Low, 1878), 1:37; George P. Schmidt, "Intellectual Crosscurrents in American Colleges, 1825–1855," *American Historical Review* 42, no. 3 (1936): 46, 62, 66; Edgar W. Knight, ed., *A Documentary History of Education in the South before 1860* (Chapel Hill: University of

North Carolina Press, 1949–53), 3:244, 297–98, 375; 4:308–9, 324, 331–33, 399, 441–42; 5:413–16, 421, 440; Walter R. Agard, "Classics on the Midwest Frontier," *Classical Journal* 51, no. 1 (1955): 106–10; Charles Coleman Sellers, *Dickinson College: A History* (Middletown, CT: Wesleyan University Press, 1973), 221; Meyer Reinhold, *Classica Americana: The Greek and Roman Heritage in the United States* (Detroit: Wayne State University Press, 1984), 333; Barbara Solomon, *In the Company of Educated Women: A History of Women and Higher Education in America* (New Haven: Yale University Press, 1985), 23; Christie Ann Farnham, *The Education of the Southern Belle: Higher Education and Student Socialization in the Antebellum South* (New York: New York University Press, 1994), 15, 17–18, 20, 22, 24–25, 27, 31–32; Wayne K. Durill, "The Power of Ancient Words: Classical Teaching and Social Change at South Carolina College," *Journal of Southern History* 65, no. 2 (1999): 483; Caroline Winterer, *The Mirror of Antiquity: American Women and the Classical Tradition, 1750–1900* (Ithaca: Cornell University Press, 2007), 146, 150, 181–82, 187.

2. "Daniel Webster Argues the Dartmouth Case, 1819," in Richard Hofstadter and Wilson Smith, eds., *American Higher Education: A Documentary History* (Chicago: University of Chicago Press, 1961), 1:212–13; "Autobiography, 1829," in Charles M. Wiltse, ed., *The Papers of Daniel Webster: Correspondence* (Hanover, NH: University Press of New England, 1974–), 1:13; Marcus Cunliffe, *George Washington: Man and Monument* (Boston: Little, Brown, 1958), 192; Edwin A. Miles, "The Young American Nation and the Classical World," *Journal of the History of Ideas* 35, no. 1 (1974): 267; Freeman Cleaves, *Old Tippecanoe: William Henry Harrison and His Time* (New York: Scribner's Sons, 1939), 6, 10.

3. Douglas L. Wilson, "What Jefferson and Lincoln Read," *Atlantic* 267, no. 1 (1991): 54–57, 60.

4. William Herndon, *Herndon's Life of Lincoln* (Cleveland: World Publishing Company, 1942; reprint, New York: Da Capo Press, 1983), 248; Garry Wills, *Lincoln at Gettysburg: The Words That Remade America* (New York: Simon and Schuster, 1992), 174.

5. Wills, *Lincoln at Gettysburg*, 41, 52–59, 249–54.

6. Susan Ford Wiltshire, "Sam Houston and the *Iliad*," *Tennessee Historical Quarterly* 32, no. 3 (1973): 249–54.

7. Miles, "Young American Nation and the Classical World," 265; Talbot Hamlin, *Greek Revival Architecture in America* (Oxford: Oxford University Press, 1944), 46, 238–39; Winterer, *Mirror of Antiquity*, 38; Elizabeth Fox-Genovese and Eugene D. Genovese, *The Mind of the Master Class: History and Faith in the Southern Slaveholders' Worldview* (Cambridge: Cambridge University Press, 2005), 254; Wendy A. Cooper, *Classical Taste in America, 1800–1840* (New York: Abbeville Press and Baltimore Museum of Art, 1993), 73.

8. Miles, "Young American Nation and the Classical World," 267n34.
9. Edwin A. Miles, "The Old South and the Classical World," *North Carolina Historical Review* 48, no. 1 (1971): 258; Richard Beale Davis, *Intellectual Life in Jefferson's Virginia* (Chapel Hill: University of North Carolina Press, 1973), 111, 380; Fox-Genovese and Genovese, *Mind of the Master Class*, 250.
10. Douglas L. Wilson, ed., *Jefferson's Literary Commonplace Book* (Princeton: Princeton University Press, 1989), 71; Albert Ellery Bergh and Andrew A. Lipscomb, eds., *The Writings of Thomas Jefferson* (Washington: Thomas Jefferson Memorial Association, 1903), Jefferson to John Wayles Eppes, January 17, 1810, 12:343; Jefferson to David Harding, April 20, 1824, 16:30.
11. Thomas R. Dew, *A Digest of the Laws, Customs, Manners, and Institutions of the Ancient and Modern Nations*, 2nd ed. (New York: D. Appleton, 1870), 153, 159; Charles Francis Adams, ed., *Memoirs of John Quincy Adams, Comprising Portions of His Diary from 1795 to 1848* (Philadelphia, 1874–77; reprint, New York: AMS Press, 1970), December 21, 1811, 2:331; "Ancient and Modern Eloquence," *Southern Literary Messenger* 8, no. 1 (1842): 169, 179–80, 185.
12. Wills, *Lincoln at Gettysburg*, 215, 247.
13. Daniel Walker Howe, "Classical Education and Political Culture in Nineteenth-Century America," *Intellectual History Newsletter* 5, no. 1 (1983): 12.
14. Joseph R. Berrigan, "The Impact of the Classics upon the South," *Classical Journal* 64, no. 4 (1968–69): 19.
15. Susan Ford Wiltshire, "Jefferson, Calhoun, and the Slavery Debate: The Classics and the Two Minds of the South," *Southern Humanities Review* 11, no. 1 (1977): 37.
16. George Fitzhugh, *Sociology for the South, or The Failure of Free Society* (Richmond: A. Morris, 1854; reprint, New York: Burt Franklin, 1965), 89–90, 147, 241–44.
17. Susan Ford Wiltshire, "Aristotle in America," *Humanities* 8, no. 1 (1987): 8–11.
18. Calhoun to A. D. Wallace, December 17, 1840, in Robert Meriwether et al., eds., *The Papers of John C. Calhoun* (Columbia: University of South Carolina Press, 1959–), 15:389; George Fitzhugh, *Cannibals All! or, Slaves without Masters* (Richmond: A. Morris, 1857; reprint, Cambridge, MA: Harvard University Press, 1960), xxxii–xxxiii, 12–13, 53; Fitzhugh, *Sociology for the South*, 253.
19. John C. Calhoun, *A Disquisition on Government and Selections from the Discourse*, ed. C. Gordon Post (New York: Macmillan, 1953), 42–44.
20. Fitzhugh, *Cannibals All!* 194, 207–8; Fitzhugh, *Sociology for the South*, 253; Jennifer Tolbert Roberts, *Athens on Trial: The Antidemocratic Tradition in Western Thought* (Princeton: Princeton University Press,

1994), 281; Harvey Wish, *George Fitzhugh: Propagandist of the Old South* (Baton Rouge: Louisiana State University Press, 1943), 230–31.
21. David Brion Davis, *Slavery and Human Progress* (Oxford: Oxford University Press, 1984), 24, 112; "To the Editor of the *Salem Gazette*," in Walter M. Merrill et al., eds., *The Letters of William Lloyd Garrison* (Cambridge, MA: Harvard University Press, 1971–81), 1:20; Garrison to Henry E. Benson, November 4, 1836, in ibid., 2:181; December 17, 1836, in ibid., 2:192n; Daniel Walker Howe, *Making the American Self: Jonathan Edwards to Abraham Lincoln* (Cambridge, MA: Harvard University Press, 1997), 150; "The Significance of Emancipation in the West Indies," August 3, 1857, in John W. Blassingame, ed., *The Frederick Douglass Papers* (New Haven: Yale University Press, 1979–), 3:193; "Fighting the Rebels with One Hand," in ibid., 3:470, 474; Waldo E. Martin, *The Mind of Frederick Douglass* (Chapel Hill: University of North Carolina Press, 1984), 168.
22. "We Are in the Midst of a Moral Revolution," May 10, 1854, in Blassingame, *Frederick Douglass Papers*, 2:488; "The Clans of the Negro Ethnologically Considered," July 12, 1854, in ibid., 2:508.
23. David S. Wiesen, "Herodotus and the Modern Debate over Race and Slavery," *Ancient World* 3, no. 1 (1980): 11; Elzbieta Foeller-Pituch, "Ambiguous Heritage: Classical Myths in the Works of Nineteenth-Century American Writers," *International Journal of the Classical Tradition* 1, no. 4 (1995): 101.
24. Winterer, *Mirror of Antiquity*, 185, 187.
25. "White Slavery in the Barbary States," February 17, 1847, in Charles Sumner, *The Works of Charles Sumner* (Boston: Lee and Shepard, 1874–1883), 1:396–98.
26. Paul A. Rahe, *Republics, Ancient and Modern: Classical Republicanism and the American Revolution* (Chapel Hill: University of North Carolina Press, 1992), 71, 115, 509; Paul K. Conkin, *Self-Evident Truths* (Bloomington: Indiana University Press, 1974), 92, 95, 100.
27. "The Fugitive Slave Law, May 3, 1851," in Ralph Waldo Emerson, *The Complete Works of Ralph Waldo Emerson* (Boston: Houghton Mifflin, 1903–4; reprint, New York: AMS Press, 1968), 11:226–27, 238–39; Lurton D. Ingersoll, *The Life of Horace Greeley* (New York: Beekman Publishers, 1974), 250–51.
28. Sumner, "Freedom National, Slavery Sectional, August 26, 1852," in *Works of Charles Sumner*, 3:192–93; Caroline Winterer, "Victorian Antigone: Classicism and Women's Education in America, 1840–1900," *American Quarterly* 53, no. 1 (2001): 75.
29. Sumner, "Presidential Candidates and the Issues, August 29, 1860," in *Works of Charles Sumner*, 5:252–53. For reference to the development of the Greek theory of popular sovereignty and its importance see Conkin, *Self-Evident Truths*, 30, 50–51, 54, 59.
30. Michael Meckler, "The Rise of Populism, the Decline of Classical Education, and the Seventeenth Amendment," in Michael Meckler,

ed., *Classical Antiquity and the Politics of America: From George Washington to George W. Bush* (Waco, TX: Baylor University Press, 2006), 69–71; A. R. Burn, *The Pelican History of Greece* (New York: Penguin, 1965), 130.
31. Caroline Winterer, *The Culture of Classicism: Ancient Greece and Rome in American Intellectual Life, 1780–1910* (Baltimore: Johns Hopkins University Press, 2002), 100–101, 107, 117–119, 142, 147–148; Robert A. McCoughey, "The Transformation of American Academic Life: Harvard University, 1821–1892," *Perspectives in American History* 8, no. 1 (1974): 242; Reinhold, *Classica Americana*, 333.

Bibliography

Adams, Charles Francis, ed. *Memoirs of John Quincy Adams, Comprising Portions of His Diary from 1795 to 1848*. Philadelphia, 1874–77. Reprint, New York: AMS, 1970.

Agard, Walter R. "Classics on the Midwest Frontier. *Classical Journal* 51, no. 1 (1955): 103–10.

Auer, Jeffrey, ed. *Antislavery and Disunion, 1858–1861: Studies in the Rhetoric of Compromise and Conflict*. New York: Harper and Row, 1963.

Berrigan, Joseph R. "The Impact of the Classics upon the South." *Classical Journal* 64, no. 4 (1968–69): 18–20.

Blassingame, John W., ed. *The Frederick Douglass Papers*. 6 vols. New Haven: Yale University Press, 1979- .

Botein, Stephen. "Cicero as Role Model for Early American Lawyers." *Classical Journal* 73, no. 1 (1978): 313–21.

Bruce, Dickson D., Jr. "The Conservative Use of History in Early National Virginia." *Southern Studies* 19, no. 2 (1980): 128–46.

Burn, A. R. *The Pelican History of Greece*. New York: Penguin, 1965.

Calhoun, John C. *A Disquisition on Government and Selections from the Discourse*. Edited by C. Gordon Post. New York: Macmillan, 1953.

Davis, David Brion. *Slavery and Human Progress*. Oxford: Oxford University Press, 1984.

Dew, Thomas R. *A Digest of the Laws, Customs, Manners, and Institutions of the Ancient and Modern Nations*. 2nd ed. New York: D. Appleton, 1870.

Durill, Wayne K. "The Power of Ancient Words: Classical Teaching and Social Change at South Carolina College." *Journal of Southern History* 65, no. 2 (1999): 469–98.

Faust, Drew Gilpin. *A Sacred Circle: The Dilemma of the Intellectual in the Old South, 1840–1860*. Baltimore: Johns Hopkins University Press, 1977.

Fitzhugh, George. *Cannibals All! or, Slaves Without Masters*. Cambridge, MA: Harvard University Press, 1960.

———. *Sociology for the South, or the Failure of Free Society*. New York: Burt Franklin, 1965.
Fox-Genovese, Elizabeth, and Eugene D. Genovese. *The Mind of the Master Class: History and Faith in the Southern Slaveholders' Worldview*. Cambridge: Cambridge University Press, 2005.
Frothingham, Paul Revere. *Edward Everett: Orator and Statesman*. Port Washington, NY: Kennekat, 1971.
Gillespie, Neal. *The Collapse of Orthodoxy: The Intellectual Ordeal of George Frederick Holmes*. Charlottesville: University Press of Virginia, 1972.
Harris, J. William. "Last of the Classical Republicans: An Interpretation of John C. Calhoun." *Civil War History* 30, no. 3 (1984): 255–67.
Hofstadter, Richard, and Wilson Smith, eds. *American Higher Education: A Documentary History*. 2 vols. Chicago: University of Chicago Press, 1961.
Howe, Daniel Walker. "Classical Education and Political Culture in Nineteenth-Century America." *Intellectual History Newsletter* 5, no. 1 (1983): 9–14.
Kelley, Mary. "Reading Women/Women Reading: The Making of Learned Women in Antebellum America." *Journal of American History* 83, no. 3 (1996): 401–24.
Knight, Edgar W., ed. *A Documentary History of Education in the South Before 1860*. 5 vols. Chapel Hill: University of North Carolina Press, 1949–53.
Martin, Waldo E., Jr. *The Mind of Frederick Douglass*. Chapel Hill: University of North Carolina Press, 1984.
McCoughey, Robert A. "The Transformation of American Academic Life: Harvard University, 1821–1892." *Perspectives in American History* 8, no. 1 (1974): 237–332.
Meckler, Michael, ed. *Classical Antiquity and the Politics of America: From George Washington to George W. Bush*. Waco, TX: Baylor University Press, 2006.
Meriwether, Robert et al., eds. *The Papers of John C. Calhoun*. Columbia: University of South Carolina Press, 1959–.
Merrill, Walter M. et al., eds. *The Letters of William Lloyd Garrison*. 6 vols. Cambridge, MA: Harvard University Press, 1971–81.
Miles, Edwin A. "The Old South and the Classical World." *North Carolina Historical Review* 48, no. 1 (1971): 258–75.
———. "The Whig Party and the Menace of Caesar." *Tennessee Historical Quarterly* 27, no. 4 (1968): 361–79.
———. "The Young American Nation and the Classical World." *Journal of the History of Ideas* 35, no. 1 (1974): 259–74.
Miller, William Lee. *Arguing about Slavery: The Great Battle in the United States Congress*. New York: Alfred A. Knopf, 1996.

Moltke-Hansen, David, and Michael O'Brien, eds. *Intellectual Life in Antebellum Charleston*. Knoxville: University of Tennessee Press, 1986.

Moroney, Siobhan. "Latin, Greek, and the American Schoolboy: Ancient Language and Classical Determinism in the Early Republic." *Classical Journal* 96, no. 1 (2001): 295–307.

Niven, John. *John C. Calhoun and the Price of Union: A Biography*. Baton Rouge: Louisiana State University Press, 1988.

O'Brien, Michael, ed. *All Clever Men, Who Make Their Way: Critical Discourse in the Old South*. Athens: University of Georgia Press, 1992.

———. *A Character of Hugh Legaré*. Knoxville: University of Tennessee Press, 1985.

———. *Conjectures of Order: Intellectual Life and the American South, 1810–1860*. Chapel Hill: University of North Carolina Press, 2004.

Paskoff, Paul F., and Daniel J. Wilson, eds. *The Cause of the South: Selections from De Bow's Review, 1846–1867*. Baton Rouge: Louisiana State University Press, 1982.

Pierce, Edward L., ed. *Memoir and Letters of Charles Sumner*. 2 vols. London: Sampson Low, 1878.

Reinhold, Meyer. *Classica Americana: The Greek and Roman Heritage in the United States*. Detroit: Wayne State University Press, 1984.

Roberts, Jennifer Tolbert. *Athens on Trial: The Antidemocratic Tradition in Western Thought*. Princeton: Princeton University Press, 1994.

Rudolph, Frederick. *Curriculum: A History of the American Undergraduate Course of Study Since 1636*. San Francisco: Josey-Bass, 1977.

Schmidt, George P. "Intellectual Crosscurrents in American Colleges, 1825–1855." *American Historical Review* 42, no. 3 (1936): 46–67.

Sellers, Charles Coleman. *Dickinson College: A History*. Middletown, CT: Wesleyan University Press, 1973.

Shalev, Eran. *Rome Reborn on Western Shores: Historical Imagination and the Creation of the American Republic*. Charlottesville: University Press of Virginia, 2009.

Shewmaker, Kenneth E., ed. *Daniel Webster: "The Completest Man."* Hanover, NH: University Press of New England, 1990.

Solomon, Barbara. *In the Company of Educated Women: A History of Women and Higher Education in America*. New Haven: Yale University Press, 1985.

Sumner, Charles. *The Works of Charles Sumner*. 15 vols. Boston: Lee and Shepard, 1874–83.

Tolley, Kim. "Science for Ladies, Classics for Gentlemen: A Comparative Analysis of Scientific Subjects in the Curricula of Boys' and Girls' Secondary Schools in the United States, 1794–1850." *History of Education Quarterly* 36, no. 2 (1996): 129–53.

Webster, Daniel. *The Great Speeches of Daniel Webster*. Boston: Little, Brown, 1919.

Wiesen, David S. "Herodotus and the Modern Debate over Race and Slavery." *The Ancient World* 3, no. 1 (1980): 3–16.
Wills, Garry. *Lincoln at Gettysburg: The Words That Remade America.* New York: Simon and Schuster, 1992.
Wiltse, Charles M. *John C. Calhoun.* 3 vols. Indianapolis: Bobbs-Merrill, 1944–51.
———, ed. *The Papers of Daniel Webster: Correspondence.* Hanover, NH: University Press of New England, 1974–77.
Wiltshire, Susan Ford. "Aristotle in America." *Humanities Review* 8, no. 1 (1987): 8–11.
———. "Jefferson, Calhoun, and the Slavery Debate: The Classics and the Two Minds of the South." *Southern Humanities Review* 11, no. 1 (1977): 33–40.
———. "Sam Houston and the *Iliad*." *Tennessee Historical Quarterly* 32, no. 3 (1973): 249–54.
Winterer, Caroline. *The Culture of Classicism: Ancient Greece and Rome in American Intellectual Life, 1780–1910.* Baltimore: Johns Hopkins University Press, 2002.
———. *The Mirror of Antiquity: American Women and the Classical Tradition, 1750–1900.* Ithaca: Cornell University Press, 2007.
———. "Victorian Antigone: Classicism and Women's Education in America, 1840–1890." *American Quarterly* 53, no. 1 (2001): 70–93.
Wish, Harvey. "Aristotle, Plato, and the Mason-Dixon Line." *Journal of the History of Ideas* 10, no. 1 (1949): 254–66.
———. *George Fitzhugh: Propagandist of the Old South.* Baton Rouge: Louisiana State University Press, 1943.
Wright, Louis B. *Culture on the Moving Frontier.* Bloomington: Indiana University Press, 1955.

Chapter 12

Gibbon, Virgil, and the Victorians: Appropriating the Matter of Rome and Renovating the Epic Career
Edward Adams

The Essence of My Argument: Gibbon to Ruskin to Proust and Beyond

> To fill the ditch, was the toil of the besiegers; to clear away the rubbish, was the safety of the besieged; and, after a long and bloody conflict, the web that had been woven in the day was still unraveled in the night.

Although Wordsworth, the strongest, to use Harold Bloom's term, English romantic poet, expended some of his strength translating Virgil's *Aeneid*, and although Tennyson, his successor as laureate and the definitive Victorian poet, remains the most Virgilian among the major English poets, still the established view holds true that Virgil's critical and cultural stock dropped sharply, especially in comparison to Homer's primitive originality, as urbane eighteenth-century neoclassical standards ceded to nineteenth-century romantic ones such as Schiller's notion of the naïve. Ironically, during just this period and development, Virgil's most abiding claim, his long dominance of the matter of Rome, was itself succumbing to a rival, one not less but more urbane, namely, the supremely elegant Edward Gibbon. His judicious and rationalized prose history, not the poet's learned and secondary epic, became, for numerous aspiring historians, poets, and novelists, the go-to source for productive encounters with Rome's cultural significance. What's more, Gibbon's pretensions exceeded supplanting Mantuan Virgil to challenging Carthaginian Augustine (and his Versailles epigone Bossuet, whose suave polemics had led to Gibbon's brief conversion to Roman Catholicism). Augustine immortalized his personal repudiation of Virgilian pathos in his *Confessions* and his historical rejection of Virgil's Rome in his *City of God* for Biblical models of individual suffering, salvation, and seeking for a more truly eternal city. Gibbon's monumental reworking of Virgil simultaneously and notoriously doubted, even satirized Augustinian hopes for personal salvation along with the claims of his Christianized Rome. This questioning was part of a larger eighteenth-century phenomenon, one surveyed delightfully by Carl Becker in his *Heavenly City of the Eighteenth-Century Philosophers*, but epitomized by Gibbon's life and work. Thus, to return to Wordsworth, this poet and translator of Virgil evinces Gibbon's remarkable, though unremarked upon achievement when he cites, in book one of his *Prelude* (1850), the story of Odin's Gothic revenge upon Roman tyranny as the most tempting among many possible epic themes: yet he found this imperial subject, not in *The Aeneid*, but in *The Decline and Fall of the Roman Empire* (1776–88). His eventual decision to devote himself to an autobiographical, not military or historical, epic also owes much to Gibbon, now his *Memoirs of My Life* (1796), the first major authorial autobiography in English, published just before *The Prelude*'s 1798 first drafts. Gibbon anticipates Wordsworth's anxious listing of epic themes by also dramatizing his vocational quest, one similarly replete with numerous false starts. Tennyson, too, for all his tearful Virgilian melancholy, long labored over a learnedly historiographical, not muse-inspired epic, a declinist history centered not on a rising ideal but, like Gibbon's Antonine Rome, on a complacent, decadent, Arthurian Camelot. This always-already ruined city defines his decades-long project and reflects Gibbon's self-consciously wrecked and fallen—not Virgil's confidently eternal and triumphant—Rome.

Major scholars long ago outlined, and more recently have detailed Gibbon's achievement in terms of his synthesis of several early modern historiographical traditions, in particular the sweeping generalizations of *philosophes* like Voltaire and the exacting accuracy of *erudits* like Tillemont.[1] His *Decline and Fall* looms, for this reason alone, as the principal monument of an age abounding in superlative works of art and scholarship. In addition to the cutting-edge historiography underpinning its narrative of ancient civilization from its peak in the Age of the Antonines to its death throes in Mahomet II's siege of Constantinople, it boasts groundbreaking chapters on religion and theology, ethnography, law, ethics, philosophy, and even archeology. (His original theme had been the ruination of Rome's buildings, a subject he bequeathed directly to Ferdinand Gregorovius and, in Venetian disguise, to his loud critic and secret admirer, John Ruskin). It also possesses witty and innovative footnotes where all the gold of the most up-to-date scholarship glitters.[2] Nonetheless this modern historiographical appreciation has tended to overlook another key feature of Gibbon's work, namely, how it repeatedly returns to self-consciously literary, often epic set-pieces centered upon heroic warrior-emperors such as Julian and Heraclius, long-suffering commanders like Belisarius and his rival Narses, or romantic medieval adventurers from Robert Guiscard to Godefroy of Bouillon. This last is the hero of the *Gerusalemme Liberata*, one of Gibbon's favorite poems, and an important model for his famous quest for an appropriately grand theme, since Tasso, after long deliberation, so masterfully combined history with poetry: "A splendid scene! Among the six subjects of epic which Tasso revolved in his mind, he hesitated between the conquests of Italy by Belisarius and by Narses."[3] Scholarly tradition, intent upon historiography, has largely ignored this poetic dimension of Gibbon's inheritance and legacy.[4]

Thus, his Tassonian, Homeric, and Thucydidean concluding siege of Constantinople combines much-admired historiography with much-neglected literary artistry, in a chapter studded both with learned footnotes and epic scenarios rendered in balanced, couplet-like sentences. Examples include the epigraph (with its awkward but recognizable invocation of Penelope's nightly labors) and summaries of poetic themes within the body of the text itself. All represent his conscious desire to write a historical prose epic in the heroic style.[5] Often both Gibbon's content and form spring from epic, the latter directly modeled after Dryden's and Pope's popular techniques for translating, sanitizing, and civilizing Virgil and Homer for a more elegant era.[6] His regular practice confirms this basic tension between the historiographical need to distill evidence from his sources and a literary desire to soften their graphic details: "I have selected some curious facts, without striving to emulate the bloody and obstinate eloquence."[7]

Nonetheless, Gibbon's historiographical calling and prosaic actuality resist any full claim to the title of poet. Indeed, it is a term with which he sometimes takes issue, as in his negative judgment upon Voltaire's shortcomings, which he attributes to his leading French rival being too much the poet and too little the scholar.[8] Poetically extravagant ambition divorced from solidly grounded knowledge similarly guides Gibbon's critique later in the same chapter (see its note 53) of his leading English intellectual and literary rival, Dr. Johnson. With similar vigilance, Gibbon eschews any Homeric echoes that ring too readily, as in note 63, where he dismisses one historian's assertion that "Constantinople was sacked by the Asiatics in revenge for the ancient calamities of Troy" along with the penchant of fifteenth-century grammarians "to melt down the uncouth appellation of Turks, into the more classical name of Teucri."[9] Northrop Frye delineated how the European veneration for the epic calling led poets such as Milton to aspire to universal knowledge in their works, but Gibbon, with due Enlightenment modesty, restricts himself to merely suggesting his poetic ambitions while eagerly highlighting his historiographical credentials.[10] Gibbon's rhetoric explains the lack of scholarly attention to his epic qualities that I am attempting to redress here, even as such self-presentation masks what seems, at times, a fundamentally literary project.

To a profound and underappreciated extent, Gibbon's widespread influence on a range of ambitious nineteenth- and twentieth-century historians arises precisely from his lurking poetic ambitions, above all from his reworking of the *Aeneid* in *The Decline and Fall* and his conscious recasting of the *cursus honorum* model of the poetic career in his *Memoirs*—for Virgil, not Tasso, guided Gibbon's life and epic ambitions. This transformation, however cautious and rationalized, proved brilliantly successful in appropriating what T. S. Eliot considered the West's central poem as the primary source for the greatest of all epic historical subjects, the matter of Rome. It also allowed Gibbon to supplant Virgil and to top his literary success, thereby achieving the supreme ambition of epic poets for almost 1,800 years. At the same time, the *Decline and Fall* turned mere hints and possibilities, doubts or worrisome trends in Virgil (and Livy) into a story dominated by decadence and decline, ruin and failure that came to haunt Gibbon himself, to plague his Victorian followers, and to obsess our Proustian age. For Proust, too, is one of Gibbon's heirs—as his moment of vocational discovery, tasting a cookie dipped in tea, indicates—the most famous of many successors to the historian-artist who intimated his literary immortality amidst the ruins of Virgil's Capitol on that fateful evening in 1764.[11]

The guiding logic and chief allure of Gibbon's formal mirroring, yet renovation and rationalization of Virgilian poetry into prose history is matched and intensified by his thematic retelling of civilization's renewal and rationalization through falling into the darkness of barbarism and religion, only to be blessed by a stronger return to reason and progress. Nonetheless, the inevitable curse of this happy story is that such an ironic and secular renewal holds little promise of recovering even Virgil's fond hopes for eternal fame and rule. Gibbon's formula made built-in obsolescence and decadence so central that they follow logically upon even the greatest triumph, whether literary or historical. This well-nigh mathematical result of "the translation of empire" most clearly manifests itself in perhaps Gibbon's greatest heir, Henry Adams, who saw his own even more ironic and rationalized form of epic history as a failure from the very moment of its publication; and his better version of Gibbon's Enlightened Europe, Jeffersonian America, as suffering an ironic unraveling of its ideal project during the very administration of the third president who had so earnestly set out to realize it.

Gibbon's Followers: The Willing and the Unwilling

From the time his completed, six-volume history's prestige was bolstered by the posthumous publication of his autobiography, Gibbon's monumental history and innovative life began to serve as models for subsequent grand historical narratives and for aspiring historians imagining their careers. This influence lingers, for example, in Shelby Foote's boast upon completing his massive *Civil War* (1958–74): "[T]he total [is] 1,500,000-plus words: a third of a million longer than Gibbon's Decline & Fall, which I took about the same length of time to write. Funny; I thought those old boys wrote a lot faster than we do, not being much concerned about mot juste and suchlike."[12] Foote's ignorance demotes Gibbon to a mere benchmark of epic largesse, but the Victorians, who carefully attended to his autobiography, were not so presumptuous as to assume he was not a meticulous artist. Charles Merivale recalls, in the context of a larger discussion of "genius" and "perseverance," that "Gibbon wrote his first chapter over three times."[13] Elsewhere even Foote acknowledges that equaling Gibbon involves more than being able to add: "they tell me he makes me out to be an American Gibbon."[14] Few now strive to be the "American Virgil," but many seek the title Foote claims cautiously with his indefinite article. He was wise to deploy it, since he and his history are not the first in line. Gibbon's cultural status derived from his studious reworking, rationalization, modernization, and, finally, subsuming of the *Aeneid*'s narrative ideology along with the Virgilian career's traditional allure. His history effectively recasts Virgil's ancient poetic epic for a more prosaic world, and his autobiography came to serve as a practical substitute for Virgil's legendary poetic *cursus honorum*. The latter dictated aspiring poets should ascend from minor to major forms, from pastoral to georgic to epic, ending in one supreme epic life work—the *Aeneid* or the *Decline and Fall*.

Gibbon's influence, though often resisted, was most pervasive during the nineteenth century. During his lifetime, Gibbon's success encouraged his friend William Mitford to embark upon his epic *History of Greece* (1784–1810). Figures of higher literary and historiographical significance who admired and imitated Gibbon's history and autobiography later ranged from François Guizot in Napoleonic and Jules Michelet in Republican France to Henry Adams in pre-Civil War America. Gibbon loomed as their primary historiographical, literary, and vocational model. While the self-consciously pious Victorians often tried to elude his satanic charms, they, too, regularly succumbed—and, like Thomas Carlyle, often lost their faith as a result of reading him. Thus in 1825 Thomas Bowdler followed up his notorious but popular blue-penciling of Shakespeare (dropping the bawdy bits) with a bowdlerized Gibbon (without the irreligion). Gibbon ranked next to Shakespeare—at least in his potent combination of literary appeal and cultural danger.

This influence persisted well into the late twentieth century, indeed intensifying in the early years of the twenty-first. For now a series of ageing British historians testifies to this upsurge. Among the more important is Norman Davies in his recent and much-admired *Vanished Kingdoms* (2011). It begins with a nod to the effect of Gibbon upon his epic history of declining and falling states and of Gibbon's autobiography upon his budding career:

> I followed the advice of my history master to spend the summer vacation reading Edward Gibbon's *Decline and Fall of the Roman Empire*, together with his *Autobiography*. Gibbon's subject was, in his own words, "the greatest perhaps and most awful scene in the history of mankind." I have never read anything to surpass it.[15]

There are novelists too. In 2012 Caleb Carr published an epic historical fantasy novel, *Broken*, whose premise is that yet another "vanished kingdom" of European history once flourished deep in the interior of late antique Germany and that lost records of its history were discovered by none other than Edward Gibbon. Carr's book alternates between a translation of this manuscript and pastiche-Gibbon footnotes upon it.

Michelet's admission that not only Gibbon, but the Gibbonian career, served as a touchstone for his own aspirations is perhaps the most telling evidence of all, partly because of the enormous range and brilliance of Michelet's achievement, and partly because of his overtly romantic, revolutionary, and French agenda, so different from Gibbon's neoclassical, conservative, and English prejudices:

> The dry, cold Gibbon, himself expresses a melancholy emotion upon the conclusion of his great work* [here Michelet footnotes Gibbon's *Memoirs*], and I, too, if I may so speak, anticipate, with as much fear as desire, the period when I shall have terminated the long crusade through the heart of centuries, which I am undertaking for my country.[16]

In short, Gibbon stands alone in vocational influence among not just Victorian and modern English, but French, German, and American historians. In particular, Gibbon's pull has altered the narratives of nineteenth-century historians of Rome, whether admirers or critics, including Guizot, Michelet, and Renan; Milman, Arnold, Merivale, and Bury; Niebuhr, Mommsen, Burckhardt, and Gregorovius. Merivale concludes his multi-volume *History of the Romans* (1850–62):

> I have now reached the point at which my great predecessor Gibbon commences, and much as I regret that the crisis should be unfolded to the English reader by one who, unhappy in his school and his masters, in his moral views and spiritual training approached it, with all his mighty powers, under a cloud of ignoble prejudices, I forbear myself from entering the lists in which he has long stalked alone and unchallenged.[17]

Merivale intended to proceed further and challenge his predecessor, but opted for discretion over such valor. Theodor Mommsen published his best-selling *History of Rome* in the 1850s and almost fifty years later won the Nobel Prize for Literature largely for that work. (The only other historian to win the literature Nobel, Winston Churchill, is a more straightforward admirer of Gibbon.[18]) Though he set out to cover the full arc of Roman history from rise to fall and though his self-confident mastery of the latest scholarship was unrivaled in his day and superior to Gibbon's eighteenth-century accomplishments, his narrative never made it past Julius Caesar. His history's comment on Gibbon, one echoed by several private admissions, suggests why: "From Caesar's time, as the sequel will show and Gibbon has shown long ago, the Roman system had only an external coherence and received only a mechanical extension, while internally it became even with him utterly withered and dead."[19]

What's particularly revealing here is that the translation's phrase, "as the sequel will show and Gibbon," one vetted by Mommsen, obscures the original's explicit promise of additional volumes (that never came): "wie die spateren Bucher dies darlegen werden und Gibbon."[20] This change, though subtle, still manages to suggest Mommsen's growing anxiety that, like Merivale, he too would not fulfill his earlier plans and promises. Whether historians resisted Gibbon's skeptical ideology or felt superior as scholars, they nonetheless left his monumental work unchallenged and organized their narratives around his abiding achievement.

Appropriating the Matter of Rome: Virgil and Gibbon (via Asimov)

J. W. Burrow in his fine introductory study on *Gibbon* (1985) provides the initial insight: "[Virgil's] *Aeneid* is the story of the fall of a city, Troy, and its rebirth as Rome. The scope of Gibbon's *Decline and Fall* is wider, but its shape is similar; it ends with the Renaissance."[21] The bestselling science fiction writer Isaac Asimov furnishes additional clues that bring us closer to a full understanding of how specifically important Virgil's imperial epic of fall and rise is to the structure of Gibbon's narrative—along with how Gibbon has largely replaced Virgil: "Why shouldn't I write of the fall of the Galactic Empire and the return of Feudalism, written from the viewpoint of someone in the secure days of the Second Galactic Empire? I thought I knew how to do it for I had read Edward Gibbon's *Decline and Fall of the Roman Empire* from first page to last at least twice, and I had only to make use of that."[22] Asimov is only the most forthright of numerous twentieth-century science fiction writers whose space operas spring from the matter of Rome, not as it was formulated by Livy or Virgil, but as reformulated by the *Decline and Fall*. In Gibbon's history of ancient Roman collapse and modern European ascent, Asimov finds the basis for both the narrative pattern and narrative vantage of his account of galactic decline, fall, and rise in *Foundation, Foundation and Empire, Second Foundation* (1951–53).

Asimov's deliberate imitation of Gibbon's emplotment of the progress of civilization from a fallen Rome to a risen Europe and of Gibbon's self-complacent dramatization of his privileged narratorial vantage and advantage helps to clarify that Gibbon appropriated these narrative and narratorial elements from Virgil, and that once Gibbon adapted them to historical narration, they quickly become the markers of a new Gibbonian epic historical tradition. Asimov is in one sense my best evidence, insofar as his apparently total ignorance of Virgil along with the popularity of his text shows that Gibbonian epic history emerged in the late eighteenth century as a highly productive reworking of the classical epic tradition. Mass culture in mid-twentieth-century America, which remained largely unaware that such a poem as the *Aeneid* even existed, has nonetheless produced scores of recognizably Virgilian narratives of the fall and rise of Roman-like empires. Yet Asimov's trilogy possesses its two core elements: its Galactic Empire and Second Galactic Empire repeat the Troy and New Troy or Rome and New Rome sequence of the *translatio imperii*; and its dramatization of a tradition of great "psychohistorians" extending from the founder Hari Seldon refashions the paradigm of the Virgilian epic poet or the *translatio studii*. (Asimov's Seldon derives his scientific pretensions most directly from such theoriticians of civilizations' rise and fall as Henry and Brooks Adams, H. G. Wells, Arnold Toynbee, and Oswald Spengler, but all these historians looked to Gibbon, not Virgil.)

Virgil, Gibbon, and Asimov each deals with essentially the same anxiety regarding the prospects of secular civilization within the disconcerting vistas of an endless timescape. And all share a trope in their representation of historical progress in terms of the journey or physical movement of a civilization or a people: Virgil and Gibbon after him use the westward course of empire model, while Asimov revels in the vaster spaces of outward stellar exploration. In all three cases, the movement from the old to the new, the story of the fall and the rise, is narrated by a poet/historian from the perspective of the fully achieved restoration: Augustan Rome, Enlightenment Europe, "the secure days of the Second Galactic Empire." In each instance the intervening period takes the form of a wandering and searching for the path to the right future accompanied by a fear of somehow going wrong and repeating the mistakes of the past. The metaphorical notion of historical progress in time has been literalized into an actual journey through space. The wanderers' task is to discover the difficult path to a glorious future. Their burden is to forge the right balance between preserving the best part of the old and barren, while successfully searching out and adopting new and kindling energies.

The *Aeneid* allegorizes this historical dilemma as follows: Virgil's Trojans must take the long, hard route to Rome, not the easy one of quickly nestling in some little imitation Troy or of readily accepting the invitation to join in the nearly completed Carthage—for Carthage also merely repeats the flawed pattern of Eastern, now Tyrian, civilization. The Trojan founders of Rome find the true path by merging with the hardy barbarians of Italy, whereas Dido's Tyrians fail to do the same with the natives of North Africa. Aeneas accepts his fate and weds the Italian princess Lavinia. Dido refuses the African king Iarbas along with all other such conjugal prospects that would symbolize the union between a civilized, but decadent East and a vigorous, but primitive West. Virgil's Carthage turns inward upon itself, back to the same Eastern failure; his Rome reaches outward to embrace (long before Frederick Jackson Turner articulated it; but then Turner, too, was schooled by Gibbon's Virgilian ideology) a Turnerian status as a self-revivifying western frontier culture.[23] Gibbon adapts Virgil's epic model of orientalism. His mapping of the rise of the modern West plots the necessary rigor of that progress against numerous decadent, Eastern traps of luxurious abandonment and idle resignation along the way.

Gibbon's Byzantium and its capital Constantinople figure as one ominous example of civilization taking the easy but mistaken path of simple repetition in the East. In Gibbon's plot, Byzantium represents an orientalist trap of luxury and ease that entices civilization away from its necessary and rigorous venture into the West. It is a parodic anti-Rome, a city and civilization that from its very birth under Constantine the Great was always and already decadent, dying, and deadly for the future of mankind:

> At the festival of the dedication, an edict, engraved on a column of marble, bestowed the title of SECOND or NEW ROME on the city of Constantine.... The manly pride of the Romans, content with substantial power, had left to the vanity of the East the forms and ceremonies of ostentatious greatness. But when they lost even the semblance of those virtues which were derived from their ancient freedom, the simplicity of the Roman manners was insensibly corrupted by the stately affectation of the courts of Asia.... By a philosophic observer the system of the Roman government might have been mistaken for a splendid theater, filled with the players of every character and degree, who repeated the language, and imitated the passions, of their original model.[24]

Constantinople, the "SECOND or NEW ROME," represents a crucial epoch in the orientalization and feminization of the masculine, once Western civilization of Rome. Gibbon follows Virgil in identifying the East with mere repetition ("repeated," "imitated"), even conscious fakery ("a splendid theater"). This process emerges as the most obvious mechanism driving the decline and fall of the classical world.

For Gibbon, the logic of repetition inevitably implies decadence and regression, not the energy and progress civilization should espouse. His chapter on the foundation of Constantinople subtly underscores the Virgilian origin of his thinking in its larger dynamics and smaller verbal nuances:

> *Ancient Troy, seated on an eminence* at the foot of Mount Ida, overlooked the mouth of the Hellespont, which *scarcely received an accession of waters from the tribute of those immortal rivulets* the Simois and Scamander.... Before Constantine gave a just preference to the situation of Byzantium, he had conceived the design of erecting the seat of his empire on *this celebrated spot, from whence the Romans derived their fabulous origin.*[25]

In addition to the Virgilian orientalism of this passage, it is possible to discern an allusion here to Milton as well. "Ancient Troy, seated on an eminence" in this context recalls the famous opening lines of book 2 of *Paradise Lost*: "High on a Throne of Royal State . . . Satan exalted sat, by merit rais'd / To that bad eminence." David Womersley has commented upon the clustering of Miltonic-Satanic references in Gibbon's ambiguously heroic portrait of Julian the Apostate.[26] But Gibbon's interest in Milton's Satan permeates his history: it reinforces his ruling Virgilian orientalist theme. Gibbon's critique of Constantine's tyranny and the false ambition inherent in the building of Constantinople, the gorgeous but mimic Rome, deploys the resources of English epic by alluding to Milton's Satan amidst the glories of his new capital Pandaemonium, a mimic of God's Heavenly Jerusalem above. Milton casts his hell as an oriental despotism. Gibbon artfully characterizes his eastern tyranny as a kind of Miltonic hell.[27]

The allusions to Virgil in this passage, however, more deeply inform its purposes. Gibbon echoes the *Aeneid* specifically in the mocking reference to the "immortal rivulets" which recalls Virgil's disdain for one of the Trojans' early attempts to refound Troy. In book 3:472ff Aeneas and his followers come across Helenus and Andromache. Their colony is nestled beside a mimic Simois ("falsi Simoentis ad undam"). Aeneas's account of this visit emphasizes his growing realization of the futility, even the danger, of such fond recreations. With mingled scorn and sadness he refers to the town as a "little Troy" ("parvam Troiam") with its "copy of Pergamus" ("simulata ... Pergama") beside a "dry stream named after Scamander" ("arentem Xanthi cognomine rivum"). Gibbon replays and exaggerates Virgil's rhetoric by turning it back upon Troy itself. Gibbon discovers the original Scamander not as the raging torrent of epic, but only a dry "rivulet" scarcely capable of adding to the waters of the Hellespont. Constantine's effort to revive the flagging Roman Empire by returning it to its mythic Trojan birthplace represents a fatally mistaken flight eastward into slavish repetition and permanent decline. Like the *Aeneid*, the *Decline and Fall* demands that civilization move westward into the regions of barbaric energy. This Virgilian narrative requirement, insofar as it strongly determined Gibbon's contempt for what many justifiably regard as a brilliant Byzantine civilization that spanned the next thousand years, thus underwrote one of Gibbon's most controversial historical judgments. Where Virgil derides mimic Troys and looks to a harder but finer future in Italy, Gibbon mocks mimic Romes and points the better way to a vigorous future in the lands of England, France, and Germany. Where Virgil composes amidst (and in order to praise as such) the glories of Augustan Rome, Gibbon self-consciously writes from amidst (and with the intent so to depict it) the vibrant European culture of London, Paris, and Lausanne.[28]

In the drama of the *Aeneid*, Carthage towers far more ominously over the attempt to found Rome than do these little Troys. Whereas Aeneas skeptically experiences the various mock Pergamums as pathetically comic renditions of the Trojan original, he first views Carthage with breathless delight and envy. Carthage stands as a more enticing example of orientalist repetition than the various Troylets: a stronger temptation which Aeneas and his followers encounter with more hazard, from which they escape with less assurance, and with which Rome continues to grapple as Carthage becomes its great world-historical enemy in a series of shattering wars. In this crucial role, Gibbon casts a different, more difficult danger than Byzantium. The major opponent and primary threat to the secular and progressive world Gibbon celebrates is Christianity, particularly Christianity in the form of a unifying Roman Catholic Christendom. The Christian papal state or Heavenly City on earth emerges as the prime enemy of Gibbon's progressive secular ideal.[29] The long dark night of the Middle Ages—a time of barbarism and superstition separating Antonine Rome from the European Enlightenment—corresponds in its narrative potency to the Carthaginian and Dido episode in the *Aeneid*. So, too, Virgil's Christian epic heirs in the form of Augustine's *Civitas Dei* and Bossuet's *Histoire Universelle* stand as the major historical rivals of the *Decline and Fall*—which, it will be remembered, strenuously maintains precisely the thesis Augustine set out to debunk, namely, that Rome's conversion to Christianity led to its fall.

As Gibbon tells his tale—one deliberately opposed to Augustine's and Bossuet's historical visions (thus his autobiography attributes Gibbon's descent into Catholicism to his reading of Bossuet; thus, too, Pascalian irony figures prominently in his rescue and subsequent revenge)—the emerging European commonwealth must free itself from the seductive dream of a centralized Papal state. That formulation figures as no true civilization, but only as a more ingeniously organized, ready-made Carthage-like repetition of the imperial, monopolistic, anti-Republican errors of the past—with cardinals as senators, a pope for an emperor, and a vast temporal church-state magisterium for the imperium. The extended European submission to papal rule and superstition functions as the central drama of false recovery and inauthentic renewal from which civilization must wake itself to realize its true destiny. As with Carthage, the power of Christianity does not quickly wither but persists in its battle against true civilization. Like Dido, this spurned, infamous thing angrily plunges a secularizing, Westernizing Europe into a long series of wracking wars.

In sum, Gibbon sees Christianity and Byzantium as parallel models of regressive civilization: "Nor shall I dismiss the present work till I have reviewed the state and revolutions of the ROMAN CITY, which acquiesced under the absolute dominion of the popes about the same time that Constantinople was enslaved by the Turkish arms."[30] The concurrence of these events—"absolute dominion" and "enslavement"—represents the closest Europe came to falling back into the disastrous, failed formulation of imperial Rome. Of these two main threats, barbarism and religion, however, Gibbon always remains more concerned with the latter. In a passage closely related to the one above, we can mark how subtly, even playfully, Gibbon sought to associate the power of the papacy with a parodic and negative repetition of the Roman paradigm: "Yet the same Aeneas, when he was raised to the papal throne under the name of Pius the Second, devoted his life to the prosecution of the Turkish war. In the council of Mantua he excited some sparks of a false or feeble enthusiasm."[31] The reappearance of "Aeneas" and "Pius" along with the birthplace of Virgil, "Mantua," insistently and curiously evokes the *Aeneid* and its hero famous for piety. Yet in this passage it is the "same Aeneas" and it is "Pius the Second" who feebly and unheroically prosecutes a vain war against his lesser eastern twin. Repetition proves catastrophic for the hopes of an energetic, progressive state. Gibbon's summary statement upon the papacy reiterates the main contrast:

> In Rome the voice of freedom and discord is no longer heard; and, instead of the foaming torrent, a smooth and stagnant lake reflects the image of idleness and servitude. A Christian, a philosopher, and a patriot, will be equally scandalised by the temporal kingdom of the clergy; and the local majesty of Rome, the remembrance of her consuls and triumphs, may seem to embitter the sense and aggravate the shame of her slavery.[32]

Again we have the positive symbolism of a torrent here set against not a dry "rivulet," as in the case of Byzantium, but a "stagnant lake." The pointed opposition of absolutist rule in Rome to a glorious past of consular and republican triumphs matches the initiating contrast of the opening Antonine chapters between the calm of the imperial city and the energy of an earlier republican state. The case of a Christendom ruled by popes is far worse than that of a Rome ruled by emperors, however, because the former represents the failure to learn from and move beyond the limitations of the latter, an ever worsening paradigm of deadening repetition and oppression.

In the *Aeneid* a fortunate fall narrative thus transpires against a backdrop of unfortunate fall. Troy is redeemed by its rebirth in the better Troy that is Rome: the Troy of the union of a seed of eastern civilization, the Trojans, with a larger mass of barbarian vigor, the Latins. Jupiter, in the conclusion of the epic, makes this settlement quite plain to a delighted Juno: "sermonum Ausonii patrium moresque tenebunt / utque est, nomen erit; commixti corpore tantum / subsident Teucri" (12:834–36). This is the solution proposed by the *Decline and Fall* for a Europe made up of fragments of the fallen, decadent, but still civilized classical world and the energetic, powerful, but still barbaric Germans.

> This diminutive stature of mankind, if we pursue the metaphor, was daily sinking below the old standard, and the Roman world was indeed peopled by a race of pygmies; when the fierce giants of the north broke in, and mended the puny breed. They restored a manly spirit of freedom; and after the revolution of ten centuries, freedom became the happy parent of taste and science.[33]

Gregorovius also makes this Germanic reinvigoration of an exhausted Mediterranean civilization the central ideological theme of the vast historical project he inherited from Gibbon: "The same sight three hundred years later inspired the English Gibbon with the idea of writing of Rome's ruin, an idea which he subsequently developed in his immortal work, *The Decline and Fall of the Roman Empire*. Though actuated by precisely similar feelings, it is needless to say that I do not for a moment desire to rival such men as these."[34] The historian here includes Claudian and Poggio as previous observers of the ruinous, though inspiring cityscape, but Gibbon arrives last and best as his closest and primary model, while Virgil (via Aeneas in book 8, where the hero also sees ancient ruins in the same spot that would in the poet's day boast architectural glories) has faded away. Ironic triumph now holds less appeal than ironic defeat. Once again, Gibbon has displaced Virgil for this matter of Rome, but now ironically, yet productively, Gibbon correlates historical ruin with the ultimately empty hope of literary immortality. He uses Virgil to make a cultural statement remarkably similar to the poet's own. Each wants to enforce a deeply held belief in his civilization's origins in a peerless but fallen pattern from the past: Virgil reiterates Roman claims to the mythological-historical exemplar of a fallen original, Troy, and Gibbon stages the same maneuver with the European historical ideal, Rome. Each, in turn, has severely criticized the eastern decadence of the flawed ideal and used orientalist discourse to explain why Troy (its dedication to Persian pleasures and a sensual effeminacy) or Rome (its descent into eastern, barbaric, and/or religious absolutism) fell. Each struggles to demonstrate how the heir to the fallen ideal has moved beyond eastern decadence, overcome the model's flaws, and achieved a reinvigorated perfection not subject to another decline and fall, though Gibbon is, as ever, duly skeptical.

Roman history was long the essence of history for Western civilization, and Virgil was its sourcebook. Gibbon effectively replaced him. Virgil's deployment of a fall and rise narrative pattern in conjunction with a *translatio imperii* or westward-course-of-empire paradigm served, for Gibbon, as the primary literary pretext for his own spatial mapping of a temporal model of historical progress. Moreover, to the extent that Virgil's story of the journey of a fallen people through geographical space to a new, better home became the foundation for Gibbon's fall and rise narrative of civilization's ultimately progressive journey through time, the *Aeneid* served as the paradigm of history for Gibbon and his Enlightenment epic, but one in need of a rationalization and modernization. Gibbon cemented his potent influence by becoming the new guide and new model, but one thus in need of further updating by ambitious historians who both followed him—and sought to leave his imperfectly enlightened civilization and his still too confident and too Virgilian narrative behind.

Renovating the Epic Historical Career: Ruskin, Wells, and Adams

> Monarchy may sometimes have taste, as in the France of Louis XIV and XV, but it concentrates everything at court . . . the English aristocracy had not one centre but hundreds, scattered all over the country in "gentlemen's seats" and provincial towns . . . Oxford University had done nothing for Gibbon, and royalty had nothing to say to him except, "Hey, what Mr. Gibbon, scribble, scribble, scribble!" But the reading public of the day was just of the size and quality to give proper recognition to his greatness the moment his first volume appeared (1776). (Trevelyan, 3:104)

Such claims of a Gibbonian tradition warrant a minimum of three case studies to demonstrate a meaningful straight line, but just here only one can figure prominently. John Ruskin's epic account of Venetian history in terms of that city's buildings, *The Stones of Venice* (1851–53), is a thoroughgoing, if deeply conflicted, example of a Gibbonian transformation of Virgilian history. In turn, Ruskin's *Praeterita* (1889) tells the story of its author in light of Gibbon's reworking of the Virgilian career.[35] In a less conflicted manner, H. G. Wells's *Outline of History* (1920) redoes Gibbon's redoing of Virgil before his *Experiment in Autobiography* (1933) redoes Gibbon's *Memoirs*. Between Ruskin and Gibbon, Henry Adams, who looked to the former for his own *Mont-Saint Michel and Chartres* (1904) and bestowed upon the latter the ambition to turn history into a science, figures prominently. His brilliant *History of the United States* (1891) and subsequent *Education of Henry Adams* (1918) must here do triple duty.

G. M. Trevelyan's enthusiastic praise, in the epigraph, has clearly sloughed off the ambivalent admiration exhibited by the early and high Victorians. Coming from no less a star of early twentieth-century British historiography than the great-nephew of Macaulay, it reflects the kind of uncritical devotion Burrow locates in Trevelyan's contemporaries, Strachey and Churchill—and which he seems to require of true followers.[36] But the emergence of such nostalgia, instead, presents both additional evidence and points toward an ironic corollary. Trevelyan's, Strachey's, and Churchill's bland longing for Gibbon's brand of eighteenth-century history and Gibbon's ideal of a liberal, aristocratic, decentralized civilization stands in marked contrast to my final example of his more enduring legacy. Henry Adams is a more innovative historian than Trevelyan or Churchill—certainly than Strachey. He does not suppress, but programmatically magnifies the earlier Victorian ambivalence. In so doing, he demonstrates the deeper logic of Gibbon's achievement. Adams carried forward the lesson of Gibbon's critical transformation of Virgil and did not seek stalely to repeat his enlightened historiographical and aristocratic ideology of progress. Instead, he followed Gibbon's lead by endeavoring to surpass and reinvent Gibbon's own formulae with a new, more enduring kind of history and with a new hardier civilization than that centered upon Britain's moribund great houses and their easy residents.[37] For Gibbon's *Decline and Fall* is shaped by its wary admiration for Virgil's Rome and epic, a probing, rationalizing admiration sketched in Gibbon's early critical essays on Virgil and epic conventions, then realized in his monumental historical narrative of Rome's fall and Europe's rise.

In turn, the odd logic of Adams's success seems to lie in his judicious incorporation of a healthy pessimism and an anxious sense of failure throughout all of his equally innovative attempts to reinvent his great model. His much-acclaimed autobiography, *The Education of Henry Adams*, though it recounts many of Adams's failures, circles around the grandest of them all, one it chooses to honor only in the breach. His epic historical answer to Gibbon's *Decline and Fall*, *The History of the United States*, figures in his autobiography in the gap between "Chapter XX—Failure (1871)" and "Chapter XXI—Twenty Years After (1892)." Those twenty years saw the planning, writing, and publication of his history, something Adams never discusses. In that autobiography, however, Adams repeatedly cites "his idol Gibbon" and, while admiring and casting him as his chief model, still proclaims Gibbon's ultimate, Adams-like failure:

> The problem became only the more fascinating. Probably, it was more vital in May, 1860, than it had been in October, 1764, when the idea of writing the *Decline and Fall* of the city first started to the mind of Gibbon, "in the close of the evening, as I sat musing in the Church of the Zoccolanti or Franciscan Friars, while they were singing Vespers in the Temple of Jupiter, on the ruins of the Capitol." *Murray's Handbook* had the grace to quote this passage from Gibbon's *Autobiography*, which led Adams more than once to sit at sunset on the steps of the Church of Santa Maria di Ara Coeli, curiously wondering that not an inch had

been gained by Gibbon,—or all historians since,—towards explaining the Fall. The mystery remained unsolved; the charm remained intact. Two great experiments of western civilization had left there the chief monuments of their failure, and nothing proved that the city might not still survive to express the failure of a third.[38]

That third is less Gibbon's Enlightenment Europe than its purer offspring, Adams's Jeffersonian America. The principal effort of his meticulous rendering of the administrations of Jefferson and Madison was to discover if his history could solve the riddle that had stumped Gibbon, and if America could transcend the patterns of imperial rise and fall that plagued Europe. His history's opening suggests his final answer:

> ... their Capitol threatened to crumble to pieces and crush the Senate and House under ruins, long before the building was complete.
>
> A government capable of sketching a magnificent plan, and willing to give only a half-hearted pledge for its fulfillment; a people eager to advertise a vast undertaking beyond their present powers, which when completed would become an object of jealousy and fear,—this was the impression made upon the traveller who visited Washington in 1800, and mused among the unraised columns on the destiny of the United States.[39]

This scene of a rising America clearly prefigures its classicizing limitations and its impending fall—along with the scene of inspiration for numerous future Gibbons musing in their turns amidst its ruins. Thus Adams entered upon his history already anticipating that it would be a failed reinvention of Gibbonian epic history. Nonetheless, it is crucial that Adams began by experimentally supposing he could refashion the practice of history, that he could do epic without warfare, that his civilized subject could free itself from that alluring heroic curse. In contrast to Gibbon's dashed hopes—for he had complacently completed his history in 1788, confident that his balanced Europe would escape Rome's centralized Caesarean fate—Adams's reworked version of epic history remained vigilantly skeptical of its subject, that is, the peaceful idealism of Jefferson's America. This paradigm spiraled into the same old routine: his history culminated in an account of America's slow and tortured entry into the War of 1812, itself part of a much larger world war fought so eagerly by the Europeans; Jefferson's optimistic innovation of the embargo and championing of a decentralized nation state succumbed to war's necessities; its centralizing imperialist logic recycled America, despite or because of its military victories, into the established pattern of rising and peaking, declining and falling.

In Adams's case, his history neatly, programmatically, and epically evokes the collapse of Gibbon's confidence that Europe would escape its Roman past in the reality of Virgilian-Napoleonic imperialism and Miltonic-Orientalist repetition that came about so soon after the pre-1789 issuing of Gibbon's history's final volumes and the post-Napoleonic publication of his posthumous autobiography.

> Most picturesque of all figures in modern history, Napoleon Bonaparte, like Milton's Satan on his throne of state, although surrounded by a group of figures little less striking than himself, sat unapproachable on his bad eminence; or, when he moved, the dusky air felt an unusual weight. His conduct was often mysterious, and sometimes so arbitrary as to seem insane; but later years have thrown on it a lurid illumination. . . . Ambition that ground its heel into every obstacle; restlessness that often defied common-sense; selfishness. . .; energy. . .; ignorance. . .; and a moral sense. . .;—such a combination of qualities as Europe had forgotten since the Middle Ages, and could realize only by reviving the Eccelinos and Alberics of the thirteenth century, had to be faced and overawed by the gentle optimism of President Jefferson and his Secretary of State.[40]

Adams's knowing history anticipates (in knowing contrast to his insufficiently skeptical model's ominously optimistic blindness) being dragged by Napoleon and the incorrigible Europeans back into the condition of narrating heroic and aristocratic warfare. Neither he nor his gentle hero Jefferson with his dreams of the embargo's efficacy (dreams America still seems to cherish) for confronting and dispelling war and imperialism through its more civilized, rational, and up-to-date political-economic modalities could elude the return of that repressed epic evil in the lurid form of the prototypically heroic Andrew Jackson and his traditionally decisive victory in the siege of New Orleans—the last great narrative flourish of Adams's history (much as the siege of Constantinople is Gibbon's) and the definitive sign that America would, in the end or even at the beginning, be no different than Europe or Rome or Troy. Adams's history proved little different from its Gibbonian model, except for this heightened self-consciousness and ironic realism. His subsequent speculations regarding the exciting possibilities for scientific history—and his full-blown experiment in aiding his brother Brooks's *Law of Civilization and Decay* (1895)—only confirmed this grander epic failure by giving absolutely no hope that any possible human future could escape the forces that had determined the human past—and would shape its various, but always bitterly tragicomic futures.

Adams's brilliantly staged failure, along with those of many another historian (Asimov's imaginary Hari Seldon being the successful exception who seems to confirm this cruel rule), hardly detracts from, indeed it magnifies, the rich cultural productivity of Gibbon and his history. After all, Gibbon's self-complacent failure clearly pointed the way forward to Adams's self-tortured dismay in that his confident theorization of Europe's avoidance of its Roman past proved so hollow so quickly: 1789 and Napoleon dashed his ivory dreams. Together his history and career have thus provided powerful formulae for ambitious historians questing for a great theme and for how to imagine vocational renewal within a living tradition. It was precisely through casting his history and his life as a rationalized prose updating of the central epic poem and poet of the West that Gibbon, like Virgil remaking Homer before him, became the founder of a new series of great epic narratives by coming second and by showing how the business of reworking a classic for a new and more anxious era was to be done. His legacy of complacent success and disappointed cynicism is with us still.

Notes

1. Arnaldo Momigliano, *Studies in Historiography* (New York: Harper and Row, 1966), 40–55, first succinctly theorized this important claim. J. G. A. Pocock, *Barbarism and Religion*, 6 vols. (Cambridge: Cambridge University Press, 1999–2015) massively documents this same historiographical achievement. Pocock not only provides the most authoritative account of Gibbon's achievement, but his historical writings and career constitute a contemporary example of the Virgilian-Gibbonian tradition of declinist history that is my literary subject here.
2. See Anthony Grafton, *The Footnote* (Cambridge, MA: Harvard University Press, 1997), 1–4 and 97–104, on Gibbon's footnotes. Ferdinand Gregorovius, *History of the City of Rome in the Middle Ages*, trans. Mrs. Gustavus W. Hamilton, 8 in 13 vols. (London: George Bell, 1900), 1:9–10, points to Gibbon as a key inspiration for his multivolume study.
3. Edward Gibbon, *The History of the Decline and Fall of the Roman Empire*, 3 vols. (London: Penguin, 1994), 2:751.

4. Edward Adams, *Liberal Epic: The Victorian Practice of History from Gibbon to Churchill* (Charlottesville: University of Virginia Press, 2011), 59–103.
5. "That nation was indeed pusillanimous and base; but the last Constantine deserves the name of an hero: his noble band of volunteers was inspired with Roman virtue; and the foreign auxiliaries supported the honour of Western chivalry." Gibbon, *Decline and Fall*, 3:950.
6. Gibbon admits his artistic relation to Thucydides, as a source of scene-painting, not facts: "I must confess that I have before my eyes the living picture which Thucydides . . . has drawn of the passions and gestures of the Athenians in a naval engagement in the great harbour of Syracuse." Ibid., 3:954.
7. Ibid., 3:951. Claude Rawson, *Satire and Sentiment* (New Haven: Yale University Press, 1994), 29–97, attends closely to the sanitizing and softening of graphic violence in eighteenth-century heroic literature. Rawson attributes to the dominance of mock epic what, in *Liberal Epic*, I ascribe to the rise of the modern law of war or *ius in bello*.
8. "A lively philosopher derides on this occasion the credulity of the Greeks. . . . Yet I dare not reject the positive and unanimous evidence of contemporary writers." The reader is here directed to a footnote: "See Voltaire. . . . He was ambitious of universal monarchy; and the poet frequently aspires to the name and style of an astronomer, a chymist, &c." Gibbon, *Decline and Fall*, 3:944.
9. Ibid., 3:963.
10. Northrop Frye, *Northrop Frye on Milton and Blake*, ed. Angela Esterhammer, vol. 16 of *Collected Works of Northrop Frye* (Toronto: University of Toronto Press, 2005), 36–42.
11. Pocock, *Barbarism and Religion*, 1:275–92, and David Womersley, *The Transformation of* The Decline and Fall of the Roman Empire (Cambridge: Cambridge University Press, 1988), 41–44, critically investigate Gibbon's famous moment of inspiration. They represent historians questioning what is essentially a poetic topos. Womersley waxes polemical in repudiating it, while Pocock exercises his usual caution, wise nuance, and exhaustive detail. Both are largely deaf to its obvious literary dimensions. One can only imagine what they would have made of Proust's bookend to his madeleine, when at the conclusion of *Remembrance of Things Past*, in *The Past Recaptured*, trans. Frederick Blossom, vol. 7 (New York: Random House, 1932), 990–1007, his text alternates inconsistently between a spoon, fork, and knife clanging on a plate. Would they therefore conclude it, too, didn't really happen? And if it didn't?
12. Jay Tolson, ed., *The Correspondence of Shelby Foote and Walker Percy* (New York: Norton, 1996), 188.
13. Charles Merivale, *The Autobiography of Dean Merivale* (London: E. Arnold, 1899), 189.

14. Tolson, *Correspondence*, 200.
15. Norman Davies, *Vanished Kingdoms: The Rise and Fall of States and Nations* (New York: Penguin, 2011), 2. See also Piers Brendon, *The Decline and Fall of the British Empire 1781–1997* (New York: Vintage, 2007), xv: "The title of this book, with its echo of *The History of the Decline and Fall of the Roman Empire*, needs an explanation—if not an apology. It was chosen not because I am setting up as a rival to Edward Gibbon but because his work has a profound and hitherto unexplored relevance to my subject. No historian in his senses would invite comparison with Gibbon. His masterpiece, sustained by a prodigious intellect and an incomparable style, has no competitors. It filled the imagination of readers for two centuries and it performed a unique function as a towering piece of literary architecture." My argument is, on the one hand, merely an elaboration upon this claim, and, on the other, an extension of it back to Virgil and forward to our own cultural fear of ruin.
16. Jules Michelet, *The History of France*, trans. Walter Keating Kelly, 2 vols. (London: Chapman and Hall, 1844), 1:401.
17. Charles Merivale, *History of the Romans Under the Empire*, 4th ed., 7 vols. (New York: Appleton, 1863–66), 7:496.
18. Adams, *Liberal Epic*, 256–81, presents a detailed account and Sir John Keegan, *Winston Churchill* (New York: Viking, 2002), 38, a brief one.
19. Theodor Mommsen, *The History of Rome*, trans. William Purdie Dickson, new ed., 5 vols. (London: Macmillan, 1913), 5:326.
20. Ibid., 3:462.
21. John Burrow, *Gibbon* (Oxford: Oxford University Press, 1985), 84.
22. Isaac Asimov, *In Memory Yet Green* (Garden City, NY: Doubleday, 1979), 311. Pocock's six-volume study presents the fullest analysis (and example) of Gibbon's influence and theme, but says little about his influence upon popular culture (thus far anyway). A broader attentiveness to Gibbon's influence upon declinist narratives generally (including mass cultural ones) is my focus here.
23. Frederick Jackson Turner, *Rereading Frederick Jackson Turner: "The Significance of the Frontier in American History" and Other Essays* (New York: Henry Holt, 1994), 31–60, presents the classic American version of the frontier thesis. Pocock's Volume 4 of *Barbarism and Religion* details the historiography, but, once again, misses the epic poetry informing Gibbon's ideological concern with barbarians and frontiers.
24. Gibbon, *Decline and Fall*, 1:520.
25. Ibid., 1:509–10, my emphases.
26. Womersley, *Transformation*, 81.
27. W. R. Johnson, *Darkness Visible: A Study of Vergil's* Aeneid (Berkeley: University of California Press, 1976), remains the definitive study of Virgil's Miltonic-Satanic dimension. Johnson's important study is also typical of a twentieth-century scholarly emphasis on seeing Virgil's epic

as being fundamentally self-divided, generally between its propagandistic and poetic purposes. Brooks Otis, *Virgil: A Study in Civilized Poetry* (Oxford: Oxford University Press, 1964), is another example of this trend, one both important for my reading of Gibbon's further "civilizing" efforts and less dark than Johnson's. Johnson, 1–48, presents a useful overview of the modern critical trends. Theodore Ziolkowski, *Virgil and the Moderns* (Princeton: Princeton University Press, 1993), provides a more detailed and authoritative account. My study's attention to the question of secular decline more generally and to Gibbon's appropriation of Virgil's themes moves away from the question of Virgil's and ancient Rome's relation to the development of Christianity or, rather, it casts that relation in a more skeptical light.

28. Jürgen Osterhammel, *The Transformation of the World*, trans. Patrick Camiller (Princeton: Princeton University Press, 2014) is regularly compared to Fernand Braudel, but in his massive account of the revolutionary changes of the global nineteenth century, he regularly cites Gibbon as an important model, always labels him "great" or "the greatest European historian of the age," and duly notes one elegant location of his composition: "the comfortable circumstances of a prosperous private scholar on the shores of Lake Geneva" (815).

29. Carl Becker, *The Heavenly City of the Eighteenth-Century Philosophers* (New Haven: Yale University Press, 1932), traces ironies besetting the eighteenth-century philosophical campaign against Roman Catholicism.

30. Gibbon, *Decline and Fall*, 3:786.

31. Ibid., 3:784.

32. Ibid., 3:857.

33. Ibid., 1:52.

34. Gregorovius, *History of the City of Rome in the Middle Ages*, 1: 9–10.

35. Ruskin's detailed annotations are in his personal copy of Gibbon's *Decline and Fall*, which his father presented him in the twelve-volume Henry Hart Milman edition to aid his son in crafting entries for Oxford's Newdigate Poetry Prize, one of which eventually earned this award. These marginal and end-paper annotations show signs of his careful reading and rereading and span the entirety of Ruskin's publishing career from the 1830s well into the 1880s. They confirm how important Gibbon first loomed and always remained for Ruskin's conception of the meaning of Roman history in particular and of decline in general. Nonetheless, Ruskin's published writings frequently testify to his deep ambivalence, to say the least, to Gibbon's secular imagination and periodic style. As just one example, the opening pages of his 1885 autobiography, *Praeterita*, point to his boyhood reading, now under the direction of his mother not his father, of the King James Bible as an early and strong protection against Gibbon's influence and appeal. John Ruskin, *Works of John*

Ruskin (Cambridge: Cambridge University Press, 1908), 35:13–14, thus dramatizes his early father-inspired love of Walter Scott's novels and Pope's translation of Homer's *Iliad* in contrast to his mother-directed daily study of the Bible. This grounding proved a firewall against his ever adopting Gibbon as an unquestioned model. James Engell's chapter for this volume, "The Other Classic: Hebrew Shapes British and American Literature and Culture" provides a valuable context for understanding the extent and depth of Ruskin's political, cultural, and literary resistance to Gibbon's Virgilian ideology and Latinate style.

36. John Burrow, *A History of Histories: Epics, Chronicles, Romances and Inquiries from Herodotus and Thucydides to the Twentieth Century* (New York: Knopf, 2008), 343–44, is simply mistaken in claiming that to locate any widespread influence of Gibbon upon Victorian historians one must also find simple veneration. Indeed the reverse seems to hold true: his most productive influence appears in historians who push back, like Adams and Ruskin, rather than those who tend to be more admiring, like Trevelyan, Churchill, and Strachey. Harold Bloom's scholarship remains the definitive account of how the most persuasive influences are usually combined with resistance, not straightforward admiration. Again, historians' inattention to Gibbon's literary dimension leads them astray.

37. Sir David Cannadine, *The Decline and Fall of the British Aristocracy* (New Haven: Yale University Press, 1990), supports this historical claim and exemplifies the influence of Gibbon upon ambitious narrative historians.

38. Henry Adams, *The Education of Henry Adams* (New York: Library of America, 1983), 803–4. Jeremy Popkin, *History, Historians, and Autobiography* (Chicago: University of Chicago Press, 2005), 116–19, argues that Adams's rhetoric subtly works to reverse his relation to Gibbon, ironically rendering his own apparent story of failure a record of deeper success, while Gibbon's story of triumph proves, in the end, one of failure. Such a reading, though befitting Adams's inveterate irony, nonetheless obscures the importance of Gibbon's own sense of inevitable failure, for both his civilization and himself, a double tragedy that Adams does not invert, but intensifies, in his paired autobiography, which Popkin analyzes, and his epic history, which Popkin does not. His subject is limited to the historians' autobiographies, while mine looks to the interrelation of such works and the historians' narrative histories.

39. Henry Adams, *History of the United States During the Administrations of Thomas Jefferson and James Madison* (New York: Library of America, 1986), 25.

40. Ibid., 227. This article is a simple epitome of a larger book-length study. I will here take the opportunity to thank Linda H. Peterson,

who generously guided it in its dissertation form. A house fire led me to shelve it for many years, while I pursued other projects. I have now returned to it (in greatly altered form), and such grateful recognition is too long overdue.

Bibliography

Adams, Edward. *Liberal Epic: The Victorian Practice of History from Gibbon to Churchill*. Charlottesville: University of Virginia Press, 2011.

Adams, Henry. *The Education of Henry Adams*. New York: Library of America, 1983.

———. *The History of the United States During the Administrations of Thomas Jefferson and James Madison*. New York: Library of America, 1986.

Asimov, Isaac. *In Memory Yet Green*. Garden City, NY: Doubleday, 1979.

Becker, Carl. *The Heavenly City of the Eighteenth-Century Philosophers*. New Haven: Yale University Press, 1932.

Brendon, Piers. *The Decline and Fall of the British Empire, 1781–1997*. New York: Vintage, 2007.

Burrow, John. *Gibbon*. Oxford: Oxford University Press, 1985.

———. *A History of Histories: Epics, Chronicles, Romances and Inquiries from Herodotus and Thucydides to the Twentieth Century*. New York: Knopf, 2008.

Cannadine, Sir David. *The Decline and Fall of the British Aristocracy*. New Haven: Yale University Press, 1990.

Davies, Norman. *Vanished Kingdoms: The Rise and Fall of States and Nations*. New York: Penguin, 2011.

Frye, Northrop. *Northrop Frye on Milton and Blake*. Edited by Angela Esterhammer. Vol. 16 of *Collected Works of Northrop Frye*. Toronto: University of Toronto Press, 2005.

Gibbon, Edward. *The History of the Decline and Fall of the Roman Empire*. 3 vols. London: Penguin, 1994.

Grafton, Anthony. *The Footnote*. Cambridge, MA: Harvard University Press, 1997.

Gregorovius, Ferdinand. *History of the City of Rome in the Middle Ages*. Translated by Mrs. Gustavus W. Hamilton. 8 in 13 vols. London: George Bell, 1900.

Johnson, W. R. *Darkness Visible: A Study of Vergil's* Aeneid. Berkeley: University of California Press, 1976.

Keegan, Sir John. *Winston Churchill*. New York: Viking, 2002.

Merivale, Charles. *The Autobiography of Dean Merivale*. London: E. Arnold, 1899.

———. *History of the Romans Under the Empire*. 4th ed. 7 vols. New York: Appleton, 1864–66.

Michelet, Jules. *The History of France*. Translated by Walter Keating Kelly. London: Chapman and Hall, 1844.
Momigliano, Arnaldo. *Studies in Historiography*. New York: Harper and Row, 1966.
Mommsen, Theodor. *The History of Rome*. Translated by William Purdie Dickson. New ed., 5 vols. London: Macmillan, 1913.
Otis, Brooks. *Virgil: A Study in Civilized Poetry*. Oxford: Oxford University Press, 1964.
Osterhammel, Jürgen. *The Transformation of the World*. Translated by Patrick Camiller. Princeton: Princeton University Press, 2014.
Pocock, J. G. A. *Barbarism and Religion*. 6 vols. Cambridge: Cambridge University Press, 1999–2015.
Popkin, Jeremy. *History, Historians, & Autobiography*. Chicago: University of Chicago Press, 2005.
Proust, Marcel. *The Past Recaptured*. Translated by Frederick Blossom. Vol. 7 of *The Remembrance of Things Past*. New York: Random House, 1932.
Rawson, Claude. *Satire and Sentiment*. New Haven: Yale University Press, 1994.
Ruskin, John. *The Works of John Ruskin*. 39 vols. Cambridge: Cambridge University Press, 1908.
Tolson, Jay, ed. *The Correspondence of Shelby Foote and Walker Percy*. New York: W. W. Norton, 1996.
Trevelyan, G. M. *Illustrated English Social History*. 3 vols. London: Longmans, 1949.
Turner, Frederick Jackson. *Rereading Frederick Jackson Turner: "The Significance of the Frontier in American History" and Other Essays*. New York: Henry Holt, 1994.
Womersley, David. *The Transformation of* The Decline and Fall of the Roman Empire. Cambridge: Cambridge University Press, 1988.
Ziolkowski, Theodore. *Virgil and the Moderns*. Princeton: Princeton University Press, 1993.

Coda

Chapter 13

The Other Classic: Hebrew Shapes British and American Literature and Culture
James Engell

In relation to the literary culture of the English language, no account of "the classics" can be complete without attention to Hebrew. From the mid-sixteenth through the mid-nineteenth century, learned individuals regarded Hebrew as one of the classical languages. Its literature shaped not only religious and biblical study but also lyric poetry, concepts of the sublime, the prophetic mode, innovations in poetic form, critical examination of allegory and symbol, and fundamental debates concerning government and political organization. During this time the study of Hebrew was often allied with the study of Greek and Latin.

Throughout the eighteenth and earlier nineteenth century, Greek and Latin enrich English poetry, drama, political and historical discourse, essays, rhetoric, philosophy, natural history, and the novel. Yet, it is Hebrew Scripture and literature that most strongly refresh older poetic forms and incite new ones. The most important developments in English and American poetry since 1700 emerge from a critical, fresh approach to ancient Hebrew poetry and its forms, from attention to its miraculous expression of everyday life yoked by imagery and parallelism to eternity and transcendent power. The study of Hebrew poetry prompts a reformed sense of poetry not as metrical composition but as impassioned expression, often in direct speech, frequently in parallel phrasing. Attention to Hebrew Scripture invigorates criticism and aesthetics. It reignites a sense of poetic prophecy. In some minds it also raises the old question: are Jerusalem and Athens, the Hebraic and Hellenic, compatible? After the Romantic era, the influence of Hebrew wanes into the twentieth century. Secularization clearly plays a hand, though so does a complex critical tendency (at times tinged with anti-Semitism) that minimizes the role of Hebrew in reshaping English verse and influencing English and American culture.

The most important figure in the earlier, upsurging transformation is Robert Lowth, the most influential text his *Lectures on the Sacred Poetry of the Hebrews*, delivered between 1741 and 1750 at Oxford. While an astute contribution to biblical studies, Lowth's criticism revolutionizes poetry and literary aesthetics.[1] Lowth knew Hebrew well. He delivers his lectures, as then required of the Professor of Poetry, in Latin. Published in that language in 1753, they appear in English in serialized extracts in 1753 and 1766–67, and in a full English rendering by George Gregory in 1787, the year that Lowth, then Bishop of London, dies. In 1783 Hugh Blair's popular *Lectures on Rhetoric and Belles Lettres* summarize Lowth's points. In 1839, when Lowth's reputation is passing its peak, *The Penny Cyclopaedia* claims that he "may be said to have opened an almost new subject, little attention having been previously paid to the laws of Hebrew poetry, or even to the fact that large portions of the Books of the Old Testament are poems in the strict and proper sense of the word."[2] Lowth, a superb scholar of Greek and Latin, drew some of his ideas concerning primitive poetry from Thomas Blackwell's *An Enquiry into the Life and Writings of Homer* (1735). Lowth's work on Hebrew poetry exhibits a tight nexus of biblical and classical scholarship turned to poetic and cultural ends.

As M. H. Abrams remarks in *The Mirror and the Lamp* (1953), Lowth alters "profoundly the standard doctrines of the nature of poetry."[3] Moreover, Hebrew Scripture, not the "exploded mythology" of Greeks and Romans, was seen to sustain a living faith. The phrase "exploded mythology" is Coleridge's (*Biographia Literaria*, chap. 18), but before him William Warburton employs it in his *Divine Legation of Moses* (1741, vol. 1, bk. 3, sect. 6). Warburton argues that Græco-Roman mythology came bankrupt at its birth. Yet, strangely regarding Hebrew as "the narrowest" and "the most barren of all languages," Warburton disputes with Lowth, who emerges triumphant.[4] By the twentieth century, though, Lowth is virtually forgotten. Newly established departments of English in universities pay scant attention to influences of Hebrew on British or American literature, a feature of their studies that alters only after World War II, and then but slowly. Whether claims concerning Hebrew as the other classic are solid or stretched, the reader may judge after examining this essay and its associated references.[5]

It is common to speak "of the two Classical languages."⁶ This usage, however, is relatively recent. For example, one nineteenth-century scholarly tradition studied ancient Greek and Latin, "the classical languages," to examine and analyze Hebrew. Holger Gzella comments, "Wilhelm Gesenius and, in a more radical fashion, his antipode Heinrich Ewald were among the first who . . . applied categories inspired by the classical languages to Hebrew and Arabic morphosyntax."⁷ Earlier, with study of Hebrew Scripture allied to knowledge of Greek and Latin and a desire to study all languages of the Christian Bible, Milton, Lowth, Johann David Michaelis, and Johann Eichhorn had followed a similar practice. This tradition extended back to the Humanism of the sixteenth century. Study of Greek and Latin allied itself with study of Hebrew, the latter gaining impetus and strength from advances in the former. The three languages often fused in the work of individuals, among them John Selden, Increase and Cotton Mather, Richard Bentley, Jonathan Edwards, Ezra Stiles, John Coleridge (the poet's father), and his son Samuel Taylor.⁸ Learned fusion of the three languages appeared later, too, for example, in Matthew Arnold. Whatever we call "the classical tradition" suffers insularity if cut off from awareness of the Judeo-Christian tradition that intersected with the Greece-Rome axis. The study of Hebrew, Greek, and Latin, taken together, was viewed as integral.

Thus, an older usage, common in the sixteenth through eighteenth centuries, before historical philology identified Greek and Latin as Indo-European and Hebrew as a Semitic language, identifies Hebrew equally, or even *primus inter pares*, as one of the classical languages. Alexander Broadie states, "The relations between the Reformation and the humanist movement . . . operate on many levels. One evident relation is the interest in the classical languages, Hebrew, Greek, and Latin."⁹ In the sixteenth century a desire for a critical edition of the Bible encouraged the study of Hebrew in France and England. It was linked with Greek and Latin, all three as languages of the Bible. "It was the revolutionary developments of the sixteenth century," states Stefan C. Reif, "which afforded Hebrew the opportunity of acquiring a more permanent place in the [Cambridge] university curriculum." In 1516, 1524, and 1530, statutes at St. John's, Cambridge, directed that students study Hebrew, listed "among the five classical languages in which conversations at Hall and disputations were exclusively to be conducted." Provisions were made for a lecturer in Hebrew.¹⁰ For the M.A. degree, some Cambridge colleges required Hebrew beginning in 1549. Since at least 1575 Oxford provided instruction in

Hebrew.[11] The teaching of Hebrew owed much to Humanism. M. L. Clarke notes, "Westminster boys in the seventeenth century were composing orations and verses in Hebrew, Arabic, and other oriental languages as well as in Latin and Greek." St. Paul's and Merchant Taylors' placed Hebrew in their curricula, as did all the London public schools, though Winchester and Eton did not. (At Harrow, James Townley instituted regular recitations in Hebrew only in the later eighteenth century. St. Paul's kept Hebrew until 1814, and Westminster through the mid-nineteenth century.) In effect, as Ian Green concludes, "more and more scholars" were switching "from a reliance on Latin . . . and having to acquire Hebrew and Greek for biblical study."[12]

The earliest plan of study at Harvard College included weekly instruction in Hebrew, Aramaic, and Syriac.[13] As Robert H. Pfeiffer notes, "Hebrew has been taught in American colleges from the beginning. The first colleges established in Colonial America, particularly in New England, gave special importance to the teaching of Hebrew. This is particularly clear in the early history of Harvard College. . . . In the first place, the founders of Harvard were following the example of their English ancestors." Roger Williams, the Puritan dissident who left the Massachusetts Bay Colony to found Providence, Rhode Island, had received Hebrew lessons from John Milton. In turn, Williams taught Milton Dutch.[14] Harvard College enrolled five Native American students in the colonial period, among them Benjamin Larnell. One of his Latin poems survives, probably written while at Boston Latin School. It seems that then and while at Harvard, "this young student from a native village near Taunton, Massachusetts, spent time writing verse not only in Latin, but in Greek and Hebrew as well."[15] (In the seventeenth century, some Christian Hebraists held that Native Americans were one or several of the lost tribes of Israel.)[16] At Dartmouth, itself with an interesting record of Hebrew instruction, Samson Occom of the Mohegan tribe "was a diligent student of Hebrew" and traveled to England, where he delivered several hundred sermons.[17]

Before the age of twenty-four, the classical scholar Richard Bentley, a graduate of St. John's, Cambridge, in 1680, having proceeded MA in 1683, "compiled his 'Hexapla' . . . a 300-leaf quarto book, whose parallel columns, written very small, index alphabetically every word in the Hebrew Bible, with its equivalents in different Latin and Greek translations, and also in Aramaic and Syriac texts."[18] In the eighteenth century such study continued. Cambridge University granted Benjamin Kennicott an annual stipend between

1760 and 1772 and permitted him to remove Hebrew manuscripts temporarily to Oxford so that he might pursue his project on the Hebrew Bible.[19] Raymond Hickey states that by 1700, largely due to religious and biblical study, "a triad of classical languages . . . were continually referred to," Hebrew, Latin, and Greek, with the added belief "that all languages can be traced to Hebrew,"[20] a view dating to Pico della Mirandola and the early European reception of Kabbalism. One Harvard thesis by a candidate for the AB in 1642 argued that "Hebrew is the mother of languages," a position again urged in a thesis of 1691.[21]

The fact that the study of Hebrew often accompanied that of Latin and Greek for so long suggests that a gap exists in our intellectual history. Indeed, Hebrew was generally considered the third classical tongue, one of what American colonists often called the "three learned languages." For almost three centuries no one was considered truly learned without some knowledge of it. As a survey of recent scholarship reveals, at various times Hebrew was securely included in "classical languages" or "the classical languages." Later, as a Semitic or Oriental language it is contrasted with "the European classical languages" (as Sanskrit commonly is), or with "the classical languages" if those are identified as Greek and Latin. For three centuries, from the mid-sixteenth through the mid-nineteenth, Hebrew was often a required part of mainstream learned culture in England and North America. In the English-speaking world, works in Hebrew exert formative influence and revolutionary effects on literature, government, and culture, especially from 1740 through 1880. Hebrew is the other classic.

Cromwell had permitted Jews to live in England from 1656, the year a group of Sephardic Jews was identified in London. The Hebraic spirit of the Puritans was proverbial, though it did not always produce tolerance, as Roger Williams discovered. In his dissident colony of Rhode Island, construction of a synagogue, later named Touro, was begun at Newport in 1759, where a Jewish population had arrived in 1658 from Barbados, declined, then revived in mid-eighteenth century by the arrival of Jews from Holland, England, Germany, and Portugal.[22] Congregationalist minister Ezra Stiles of Newport, grandson of the poet Edward Taylor and later president of Yale and its first professor of Semitics, attended the dedication of the Newport Synagogue during Chanukah celebrations in 1763. Stiles and Rabbi Hayyim Isaac Carigal established a friendship in 1773, and Carigal tutored Stiles in Hebrew. In 1778 Stiles delivered his inaugural address as president of Yale in Hebrew, and five years later called the new American republic "God's American Israel."[23] Timothy Dwight, president of Yale following Stiles, treated Lowth in his master's thesis and championed Hebrew poetry over Greek, a language he tried to displace from the center of Yale's curriculum.

Moses Mendes Seixas, soon president of the Newport Touro congregation, addressed George Washington on the president's visit to Newport in 1790. Washington would later echo Seixas's views on religious toleration. Touro is the oldest synagogue building in the United States.[24] One of the honorary pallbearers at the funeral of Benjamin Franklin was, by Franklin's wish, a rabbi. Gershom Mendes Seixas, brother of Moses and rabbi of Shearith Israel congregation in New York City (the oldest continually functioning Jewish congregation in the United States), attended George Washington's April 30, 1789, inauguration as one of fourteen official clergy. He was one of the first ministers to deliver a Thanksgiving Day sermon (November 26, 1789). In 1787 he became a trustee of Columbia College, also named as one of its incorporators, and remained a trustee until 1815, the only Jew to hold that position until the twentieth century.[25] (Samuel Johnson, founder of King's College, which became Columbia College, was himself a Christian Hebraist who "taught his two young sons to 'converse in Hebrew.'")[26] Gershom Mendes Seixas composed a Hebrew graduation oration for Sampson Simson, the first Jew to graduate from Columbia, and Simson delivered it on June 21, 1800.[27] The most common biblical subject of American poems (aside from hymns) printed between 1610 and 1820 is the Book of Job. Of particular interest is Chauncey Lee's *The Trial of Virtue* (1806).[28] Shalom Goldman points out that Jonathan Edwards applied his energy to Hebrew at Yale and later in life: "the importance of Hebrew studies to his work has yet to be fully explored." Stiles had praised the ability of Edwards in languages, "especially in Hebrew."[29]

The extent of Christian Hebraism should not, however, imply that Christian Hebraists were, as a group, welcoming to Jews or Judaism. Stiles is remarkable for his learning and his openness, but even he, especially early in life, lamented in his *Literary Diary* that Jews would not enter the Christian fold. The seal of Yale itself, with its Hebrew inscription "Urim Ve-Tumim," was designed to represent Christian truth.[30] Paradoxically, as Jacob Kabakoff notes, while "colonial American Jews" used Hebrew for "prayer and religious instruction" essential to their identities, they had, "with few exceptions . . . but a meagre knowledge of Hebrew."[31]

Milton's Shadow, the Sublime in Word and Music

Milton modeled *Samson Agonistes* on Greek tragedies and recommended it to readers with Greek, Latin, and Christian precedents. Nevertheless, the work derives its spiritual character from the Book of Judges. As Charles Martindale notes, while we have come to see the Hebraic and the Hellenic as opposed, even mutually exclusive, in *Samson Agonistes* "Milton can help us to see underlying similarities in two ancient societies far distant from his and our own."[32] Scholars have scrutinized Milton's involvement with Hebrew for decades, yet Erik Gray has recently explained how, in *Paradise Lost*, Milton employs—no fewer than five times—"one of the . . . chief motifs" of the Song of Songs, "the trope of *lech l'cha*," originally from Genesis 12:1, where it signals a shift in God's relation to Abraham and his descendants. Milton's use of this trope, whose origin he knew, is central to the relationship he depicts between Adam and Eve, and, in a different way, central to the relationship Satan establishes with them. Milton, says Gray, "clearly understands the Song literally, as a poem of erotic love, as well as allegorically."[33] The distinction Milton made between the "Judaic" and the "Hebraic" is complex, as are his attitudes to them.[34] The larger point is that to become immersed in Milton requires Christian Humanism but knowledge of Hebrew Scripture and sources, too. To be learned meant learning Hebrew. In *Religio Laici* (1682) Dryden remarks how the Hebraist Richard Simon's *A Critical History of the Old Testament in Three Books*, published that year, could help a country curate

> Save pains in various readings, and Translations;
> And without *Hebrew* make most learn'd quotations.
> (lines 242–43)

If the curate was without Hebrew he could use a crutch. Already, Dryden knew, corners were being cut. At Westminster and Trinity College, Cambridge, Dryden himself had likely studied Hebrew and was exposed to students and teachers who knew it well.

John Dennis in 1701 champions the poetry of David above that of Virgil and his translator Dryden. In one comparison concerning verse that describes storms and seas, Dennis states that when we "see how the Psalmist has treated the same subject in the eighteenth Psalm . . . we shall find, that the greatness of Virgil is littleness compared to his." Dennis makes this point about poets who relate the power of Zeus,

Jupiter, or Jehovah. The Hebrew poets win hands down: "The true divine poetry has the advantage of the Pagan poetry; that it satisfied the reason more, at the same time that it raises a stronger passion, and that it entertains the senses, and especially the eye, more delightfully."[35] Dennis rests his claim—and arguments about poetry—on "the true religion." However, when he compares Virgil, Dryden, and David, the last translated in the King James Bible, his preference for David seems decidedly aesthetic, too. In individual phrasing it exhibits a power and simplicity that disclose the "amazing effects" and "infinite wrath" of God. Concluding that the English version of the psalms, "a faint copy, nay, a prosaic copy" of David, is nevertheless superior to "*Virgil's* original," Dennis asks, "What force and what infinite spirit must there not have been in the original *Hebrew*?" He states, "I could produce a hundred passages more out of sacred writ, which are infinitely superior to any thing that can be brought upon the same subject from the *Grecian* and *Roman* poets."[36] Multiple passages from Dennis echo this conviction.[37]

Hebrew deeply informs the new valuation of the sublime, as well as a re-estimation of tragedy and the tragic. Earlier scholars note this,[38] though recent discussions of the sublime tend to skimp on its Hebrew sources. Longinus, a pagan author, cites Greek and Roman writers to illustrate the sublime. Yet, he cites the Hebrew Bible as a prime example of what, to him, is the deepest wellspring of sublimity. In the section of *Peri hypsous* related to "forming great conceptions" through "elevation of mind," a condition Longinus treats first because he claims that it is the most vital and holds "the foremost rank" among conditions that produce "elevated language," he turns to Moses: "The legislator of the Jews, no ordinary man, having formed and expressed a worthy conception of the might of the Godhead, writes at the very beginning of his Laws, 'God said,'—what? 'Let there be light, and there was light: let there be land, and there was land.'"[39] (Today, no one claims that Moses himself wrote the Torah.) Richard Steele in *Guardian* 86 (1713) claims that the Book of Job is superior to any Greek or Roman classic in raising the sublime: Job "would have given the great Wits of Antiquity new Laws for the Sublime, had they been acquainted with these Writings."[40] While sublimity exists in a classicizing aesthetics, at least if one accepts Longinus as part of that aesthetic, it is the presence of the other classic that gives sublimity as understood in English aesthetics of the eighteenth and early nineteenth century its greatest power.

To magnify what audiences regarded as the sublimity of Handel's *Messiah*, the number of performers would swell to scores, even thousands. (George Bernard Shaw later complained about this and insisted on a small number of instrumentalists and chorus members.)[41] In 1800 William Shields recounted the anecdote of Handel's servant witnessing the composer's "tears mixing with the ink, as he penned his divine notes; which are surely as much the pictures of a sublime mind as Milton's words." Handel's style commonly earned the praise "sublime and noble."[42] The prophet Isaiah rendered in the King James Version, as well as the Psalms as they appear in the Book of Common Prayer, supply large parts of the libretto for *Messiah*, which, however, is not always sympathetic to Jews. While Handel treated the Messiah and pagan subjects such as *Acis and Galatea*, *Hercules*, *Semele*, and *Xerxes*, his strongest line of success flowed from popular oratorios featuring Hebrew figures. Charles Jennens, his frequent librettist, knew Greek and Latin well yet edited English translations of Hebrew Scripture for maximum choral effect, just as Handel modified his musical style to highlight the parallel structures, repetitions, and antitheses of Hebrew poetry.[43]

Esther led to *Deborah* and many compositions with Hebraic figures, including *Samson* (Newburgh Hamilton based his libretto on Milton's *Samson Agonistes*) and *Jephthah*, Handel's last oratorio. Answering Filmer's invocation of Hebrew Scripture to support the divine right of kings, Locke, who was, according to Laud's statutes of 1636, required to display knowledge of Hebrew and Arabic for his MA at Christ Church, Oxford, had countered Filmer in his *Treatises of Government* with different interpretations of Hebrew Scripture and numerous times had invoked Jephthah, and other Hebrew figures. (According to H. R. Fox Bourne, Locke took Hebrew classes twice weekly during two or three of his years at Christ Church "and probably knew something of Hebrew before he left Westminster."[44]) Some admirers of Handel recommended that when attending his oratorios, "The Theatre . . . ought to be enter'd with more Solemnity than a Church." Two letters appearing in the *Daily Post* in April 1739 about *Israel in Egypt* stressed not only its sublime music but the sublimity of its words from Hebrew poetry.[45] Handel, a Christian, apparently did not know Hebrew and is reported to have said of his oratorio *Theodora*, uncharitably, "The Jews will not come to it because it is a Christian story; and the ladies will not come because it is a virtuous one." Yet, the overall point is the popularity, artistic appeal, and staying power of the Hebrew figures—conveyed by

Handel's music and by the libretti with predominant sources from Hebrew Scripture.

Hebrew subjects as the centerpiece of major works were of course not new. Matthew Prior's *Solomon on the Vanity of the World* (1718), a brief epic, is but one example. As an excellent student at Westminster and St. John's, Cambridge, Prior studied Hebrew. His second poetical work at Cambridge, after writing a parody of Dryden's *Hind and the Panther*, was an ode "on these Words, I AM THAT I AM," from Exodus 3:14. A modern biographer notes, "Apparently one of Prior's favorite serious pieces, he was to use the Exodus ode as the lead poem in both his collected editions of *Poems on Several Occasions*."[46] Although Samuel Johnson felt *Solomon* often lacked interest, he believed Prior had in places "heightened it to sublimity." Johnson remarks that *Solomon* is the work to which Prior "entrusted the protection of his name, and which he expected succeeding ages to regard with veneration."[47] The phrase "brief epic" attached to *Paradise Regained* comes from Milton's mention in the *Reason of Church Government* concerning "epic form whereof the two poems of Homer and those other two of Virgil and Tasso are a diffuse, and the Book of Job a brief model."[48]

Robert Lowth entitled his Lectures XXVII and XXVIII "The Sublime Style of the Hebrew Ode." In the second of these he cites Deuteronomy 32, the "prophetic ode of Moses," and advises, "Another specimen of the perfectly sublime ode will be found in the triumphal ode of Deborah."[49] In Lecture XIII, on personification, Lowth discusses Deborah but places greater stress on "Isaiah, whom I do not scruple to pronounce the sublimest of poets." Lowth freshly translates Isaiah in 1778. Among others, Coleridge and Matthew Arnold (see below) will consider Isaiah closely. Lowth dwells on Isaiah's description of the fall of the monarch of Babylon: "How forcible is this imagery, how diversified, how sublime!" For Lowth, this is not praise enough. Discussing Isaiah to conclude Lecture XIII, Lowth, a formidable classicist, takes a step further. Of the "perfect beauty and sublimity" of Isaiah he adds, "If, indeed, I may be indulged in the free declaration of my own sentiments on this occasion, I do not know a single instance in the whole compass of Greek and Roman poetry, which, in every excellence of composition, can be said to equal, or even to approach it."[50]

Lowth in his first lecture praises Latin and Greek poets but argues, akin to Dennis, that the highest poetry is allied with religion. For Lowth, this is "remarkably exemplified in the Hebrew poetry, than which the human mind can conceive nothing more elevated, more beautiful, or more elegant; in which the almost ineffable sublimity of the subject is fully equalled by the energy of the language, and the dignity of the style." He observes that Hebrew writings exceed in antiquity those of Greece, and "in sublimity they are superior to the most finished productions of that polished people." Hebrew poetry is for Lowth the origin "in which the only specimens of the primeval and genuine poetry are to be found." Lowth makes clear that he is not in this enterprise making theological points, but offering literary and aesthetic ones. By addressing the poetry of the Hebrews, he will "recommend to the notice of the youth who is addicted to the politer sciences, and studious of the elegancies of composition, some of the first specimens of poetic taste."[51]

In analyzing or teaching Burke's treatment of the sublime, it is common to cite his quotations from Milton. Yet, Hebrew Scripture is for Burke perhaps more important. Students of Burke's *Enquiry* will recall that he quotes Milton's descriptions of Death and Satan from *Paradise Lost* that epitomize "the force of a judicious obscurity," and it is natural to turn to them. However, after quoting these passages, Burke invokes Hebrew Scripture rendered from the King James Version—and he does so at length, quoting the Book of Job and the Psalms, remarking, "The Psalms and the prophetical books are crowded with instances of this kind," that is, "with every thing terrible in nature . . . called up to heighten the awe and solemnity of the Divine presence."[52]

When Burke introduces Job 4:13–17 before quoting those verses (save the last clause of verse 17), he identifies "this passage in the book of Job" as not only sublime but "amazingly sublime." He asks, "Is it not wrapt up in the shades of its own incomprehensible darkness?" To uphold his contention that "A clear idea is . . . another name for a little idea" and that the sublime appears when obscurity and uncertainty cloak power, he emphasizes these words from the Book of Job by putting them in roman type while the rest of the quotation from Job is in italics: "but I could not discern the form thereof," the form of the spirit that brings "*fear . . . and trembling, which made all my bones to shake.*" In sections 3–5 of Part II, Burke stresses, by using roman type within several otherwise italicized quotations, this single example from the Book of Job. This emphasis is his and not the compositor's; the words set in roman type explicitly refer to Burke's contention that an obscure form is more sublime, and that this passage is "amazingly sublime" for that reason. Two passages from Milton lead the examples in Part II, sections 3–5, of the *Enquiry*, but Burke includes, at greater length, five examples from the Book of Job and three from the Psalms, recommending the prophets and the songs of praise as "crowded with instances" that produce the sublime through obscurity and power. In length, detail, and perhaps in admiration, his analysis of Job and the Psalms exceeds his commentary on Milton and all other authors.[53]

I diverge from Howard Weinbrot's assertion that the "Anglo-Hebrew sublime" differs from Longinus's conception of the sublime and from Burke's as well. Burke cites both Job and the Psalms at length to exemplify the sublime, something Weinbrot does not note. True, Longinus does not cite Hebrew writers to the extent that Joseph Warton conjectured he might have done. Warton in 1753 projects Longinus as praising many Hebrew passages far above Greek and Roman ones. Yet, in the genuine work from antiquity and not in Warton's imagined rendering of it, Longinus quotes and praises the Book of Genesis, something Weinbrot and others do not register. I agree with Weinbrot that the presence of sublimity in ancient Hebrew, often based on simplicity, everyday experience, and divine power fused in powerful, direct phrasing, is more significant for conceptions of the sublime in England than habitually credited.[54] Warton's high claims concerning Hebrew and the sublime (using his faked manuscript of Longinus as a pretext), claims made in 1753, owe a debt to the lectures of Lowth, published that year in Latin and discussed from the time Lowth began delivering them in 1741. Warton, educated at Oxford where his father Thomas Warton the elder had been Professor of Poetry from 1718 to 1728, the office Lowth soon held, would have been remiss had he not known Lowth's lectures, which Lowth commenced at Oxford when Warton, studying at Oriel, was in his second year, admitted commoner in January 1740.[55] Perhaps the last word here should be given to Coleridge. As recorded in *Table Talk*, Coleridge at age fifty-nine asked, "Could you ever discover any thing sublime, in our sense of the term, in the classic Greek literature? I never could. Sublimity is Hebrew by birth." In Anne Gillman's Bible, Coleridge wrote, "What can Greece or Rome present, worthy to be compared with the 50th Psalm, either in sublimity of the Imagery or in moral elevation?"[56]

Foundational Myths

Several myths relate the founding of Britain. Among the oldest is that of Brutus, Brute of Troy, descendant of Aeneas. Geoffrey of Monmouth dwells on this Trojan line. Yet, the first appearance of this myth does not come from Geoffrey in the twelfth century. A Hebrew parallel introduced by Christian writers made its claim in a manner one could not hold either less factual or more fantastic. The *Historia Britonum*, a compiled text attributed to Nennius writing in the late eighth century, is the first to assert that Brutus founded Britain. It states that this happened when Eli was judge in Israel and the Philistines took the Ark of the Covenant. Diverging versions of the *Historia Britonum* claim that Brutus descended either from Japheth or Ham, Noah's sons, with Japheth, the older, more accepted.[57] Later founding myths of Britain are associated with Joseph of Arimathea. In some versions Joseph comes to Glastonbury with the Holy Grail and places his staff in the ground, where it flowers into a revered thorn bush. (Cut down and burned in the Civil Wars, the bush was replanted in 1951 from cuttings of the original; vandals damaged this "original" thorn in 2010.) Moreover, "Glastonbury and Somerset legends involve the boy Jesus together with his Great-Uncle, Joseph of Arimathea building Glastonbury's first wattle and daub church."[58] Blake's prefatory lyric to *Milton* alludes to this legend and associated ones: "And did those feet in ancient time." In 1773 and again in 1820, Blake engraved "Joseph of Arimathea among the Rocks of Albion." Glastonbury becomes a site for Arthur and Guinevere and the accepted place of their burial. Falstaff, that quintessential English quasi-hero, went to the bosom of—? Some texts of *Henry V* read Abraham, some read Arthur. "He's in Arthur's bosom"—is that the confusion of Hostess Quickly, of an actor or compositor, or has Shakespeare planted a deeper connection? These foundational myths link to Christian faith, in many cases back to the Hebrew. For example, Northrop Frye comments, "The relation of Arthur to Albion . . . is very similar to that of Joshua to Jesus in the Bible."[59] Yet, the Hebrew connection was often lost or dropped. At a time of rising prejudice against Jews, Geoffrey of Monmouth fails to state that connection, though he may well have known it, for he used at least one recension of the *Historia Britonum*.[60] In 1290 Edward I expelled most of the Jews from England.[61]

The Psalms and Lyric Expression

The Psalms were widely translated in verse and prose beginning in the early sixteenth century when the study of Hebrew began to flourish in England and France. One example is a translation into English from the Latin translation (*Psalmorum omnium*) of the

Hebrew by Jan van Campen, published in London in 1539. Jan van Campen held the chair of Hebrew at the University of Louvain, an early center of Hebrew study, as Cambridge was.[62] Another would be *David translated according to the veritie and truth of th'Ebrue, with annotacions moste profitable* (1557). Metrical translations in English appeared in print by the middle of the sixteenth century. Robert Crowley's *The Psalter of Dauid* (1549) puts the psalms into rough fourteeners. *The Bay Psalm Book*, properly *The Whole Book of Psalmes Faithfully Translated into English Metre*, published in Cambridge, Massachusetts, in 1640 by Stephen Day, is the first book printed in North America. Hezekiah Usher sold it at his shop in Cambridge. It is hard for an expert bibliographer to list the many editions and printings. Surprisingly, while printed in the Algonquin language in the mid-seventeenth century at Harvard, the Christian New Testament was not printed in the American colonies in English until after 1740. Daniel Fowle and Gamaliel Rogers issued it in Boston.

In the late seventeenth century, David's songs and other Hebrew texts, such as the Song of Deborah in the Book of Judges, altered English lyric practice significantly.[63] While the title page of Isaac Watts's *Horae Lyricae* (1706) sets epigraphs from Horace and [Pseudo-] Pythagoras, his Preface argues that the original of "Poesie ... is Divine." Explicitly, "The eldest song which history has brought down to our ears was a noble act of worship paid to the God of Israel, 'When his *right hand became glorious in power, when thy right hand, O Lord, dashed in pieces the enemy ... they sank as lead in the mighty waters*,['] Exod. 15." Watts invokes David, Solomon, and Isaiah. In the Preface he regrets that his own efforts present the "narrow numbers of our old Psalm-translators." His poems in this book show influence from Horace and Pindar, but the underlying message is that the source of highest verse comes from a faith they did not share, a language not theirs but that of the ancient Hebrews. Twenty-eight years later, in 1734, Watts publishes what he had written when younger: "Had *Horace* or *Pindar* written this ode [Psalm 137], it would have been the endless admiration of the critic, and the perpetual labor of rival translators."[64]

Lowth, faced with lecturing upon his appointment as Professor of Poetry in May 1741, "seems to have turned," says Stephen Prickett, "to his theme of the psalms almost by default."[65] Lowth emphasized oral culture, sound, musicality, imagery, rhythm, and apparent spontaneity as features of poetic expression more vital than rhyme and apparent meter. As a lyric revival spread in the 1740s, fostered by the Wartons and William Collins (who knew one another and were at Oxford when Lowth was lecturing), as well as by Gray and others, there arose new interest in the lyric and in songs of praise, voicing what was called a natural language of passion.

The work of Isaac Watts is well known. Another English verse translation of the Psalms later in the eighteenth century deserves mention. James Merrick knew Hebrew. Not a bad poet, he was accounted for almost a century a good one. One of his poems, "The Wish," Henry Mackenzie included in *The Man of Feeling*. Merrick had consulted Lowth when Lowth was Prebendary of Durham before becoming Bishop of London. Lowth read some of Merrick's translations, asked to see them all, offered criticism, and encouraged publication. Several editions earned success for four more decades, supplemented by annotations published separately. Oxford anthologies of religious verse soon included his poems. Merrick's *The Psalms, translated or paraphrased in English verse* appeared in 1765. He received his MA from Trinity College, Oxford, in 1742 and was a fellow in 1745, spanning the years when Lowth delivered his early lectures. It was this connection at Oxford—mentioned by Merrick regarding how Lowth had paid attention to the Psalms—that caused Merrick to turn to Lowth, who called Merrick one of the "most eminent of scholars."[66] Merrick acknowledged John Loveday's help in translating the Hebrew and tells the reader that his translations are not designed for public worship, as "his measures are all of the Lyric kind."[67] The list of subscribers to Merrick's *Psalms* includes members of the clergy and fellows of colleges at Oxford and Cambridge, Henry Thrale, Mrs. Thrale, Samuel Johnson (probably *the* Samuel Johnson, for Johnson had met the Thrales on January 9, 1765, early in the same year as publication of Merrick's *Psalms*), Benjamin Kennicott, Lowth, Joseph and Thomas Warton, the latter then Professor of Poetry at Oxford. Merrick employs both couplets and ballad stanzas. Following a line developed in Lowth's lectures that the original Hebrew lyrics are unsurpassed in any literature, Merrick stresses direct, passionate phrasing in the first person.

Lowth's Reach

The harp and the harpist became commonly associated with lyric, bardic, and romantic verse. For example, a harp adorns the statue of Fitz-Greene Halleck on Poets' Walk in Central Park, New York. Yet, the harp as a symbol of lyric is David's before it belongs to a northern bard. Christopher Smart had written in versions of *Jubilate Agno*, "For M is musick and Hebrew מ is the direct figure of God's harp" (B₂524). "For M is musick and therefore he is God" (C5).[68] At their asymptote, the harp and its music become the divine Logos. In *A Song to David* (1763), Smart writes of David: "God's harp thy symbol, and thy type." Geoffrey Hartman, referring to Smart's verses that participate in an "apotropaic iteration which limits an otherwise emancipated verse line," suggests that Smart's verses display parallel repetitions that would avert evil. Hartman connects this motive with the wager between God and the Accuser in the Book of Job.[69] Smart's verse technique and the antiphonal structure of *Jubilate Agno* would not, it seems, have developed without some knowledge of Hebrew.[70]

Lowth prompted Smart. William Force Stead, in Appendix IV, "On the Verse-form," of his 1939 edition of *Jubilate Agno*, remarks, "Smart was trying to introduce various characteristics of Hebrew poetry." Smart's ideas about that poetry derived in part from the King James Bible and Anglican liturgical practice. Yet, Stead provides evidence that those ideas also leaned on Lowth's published Latin lectures *De sacra poesi Hebraeorum*, which Smart admired. Smart praised Lowth's work in a written notice. William Bond identifies Lowth's "discussion of parallelism and antithesis" as vital for *Jubilate Agno*.[71] Lowth in Lecture XIX, "The Prophetic Poetry is Sententious," cites the composing and reciting of Hebrew poetry by alternate and antiphonal chanting of verses and by constant, correspondent or parallel additions that create apposition or opposition.[72] I Samuel 18:7 and Isaiah 6:3 describe such practice. Bond's analysis recognizes more than half of *Jubilate Agno* as a vast set of parallel verses written originally in a double folio. To determine which parts reflect Smart's knowledge of Hebrew, which parts Anglican liturgy (especially the Book of Common Prayer), and which parts Lowth's lectures, is hard. All contribute. Regarding verse in English, Bond states the major point that *Jubilate Agno* is "a conscious experiment in a form new to English poetry."[73]

Smart read Hebrew poetry in the King James Version (1611), "prepared by learned divines who were excellent Hebraists,"[74] and he relied on points and examples offered by Lowth. The question remains, did Smart really know Hebrew? In 1747 he had taken the MA at Cambridge. Hebrew was required and examined for that degree at some Cambridge colleges starting in 1549. An exhaustive study of Smart's career, as well as internal evidence from his poetry, indicate that he was a tolerable Hebraist and had probably entered Cambridge with some Hebrew. Charles Parish concludes: "there is no doubt about Smart's knowledge of Hebrew." It is hard to assess his exact grasp, "but there are some passages . . . that indicate a surprising ability in at least certain areas."[75]

Smart's *A Song to David* also reveals his immersion in Hebrew poetry. With political as well as poetic implications, Smart called David "the minister of praise at large."[76] He was fascinated with Hebrew sources, words, and letters. His parallel structures suggest that whether averting evil, praising God, or attempting to name the creations of God, all verses and all languages are radically imperfect—each verse must be supplemented, echoed, recast. As Howard Weinbrot puts it, "Repetition becomes an emblem of divine immanence."[77] *A Song to David*, composed after the fragments of *Jubilate Agno*, was Smart's first publication. His compositions feature "echoing repetition" in all forms—"assonance, alliteration, rhyme"—which contribute to parallelism in sound.[78] The echoing replays an endless or eternal act of creation. It foreshadows the emphasis of Coleridge and Schelling on divine creation as an ongoing energy and endless productivity, what Coleridge, defining the primary imagination, calls "an eternal act of creation in the infinite I AM."[79]

Looking at psalmists and figures such as Watts and Smart, Howard Weinbrot summarizes developments in lyric poetry to 1770: "David triumphs over Pindar." In addition, "British imitators and paraphrasts treat Hebrew poetry with the same liberty classical translators treat Greek and Latin."[80] At the same time, direct, formal imitation of Greek and Latin models declines. Samuel Johnson's *Vanity of Human Wishes* (1749) is the last major poem in English closely to follow a single Greek or Latin work. With the exception of one or two short odes by Horace, Johnson would not again practice such imitation.

Lowth and the publisher of George Gregory's English translation of Lowth's lectures, Joseph Johnson, belonged to a critical nexus that, aside from Lowth's influence on the Wartons, Smart, Merrick, and William Collins, embraced James Macpherson, Hugh Blair, Coleridge, Wordsworth, Blake, Whitman, and eventually Gerard Manley Hopkins. These writers produce a transatlantic and transgenerational renewal of poetry in English. Wordsworth and Whitman read Lowth through Blair's summary. Coleridge (and perhaps Wordsworth) studied Lowth directly. Macpherson associated himself with Hugh Blair, who, in his "Critical Dissertation on the Poems of Ossian, the Son of Fingal," cites Lowth in discussing Macpherson's work.[81] Macpherson drew on the Song of Songs in his *Fragments of Ancient Poetry, Collected in the Highlands of Scotland* (1760), especially "Shilric, Vinvela." By returning to Hebrew, Lowth rejuvenated English poetry and shaped its modern, post-classical forms. From his work and its impact grew experiments such as Whitman's and, eventually, free verse.[82]

As Lowth remained convinced that Hebrew poetry was metrical, though he could not unlock any metrical secret, Blake claimed for his prophetic books a metrical pattern, though that pattern varies from book to book. In addition, notes Northrop Frye, "Ossian played an important part in liberating Blake's meter." To develop his patterns and escape the confines of iambic pentameter, Blake called on several resources, including the "old fourteener," which he altered from seven feet to seven beats.[83] Another resource for Blake's style and versification is the King James Bible and its rendering of the Hebrew prophets.[84] The Wartons, Collins, Smart, Macpherson, Blake, Coleridge, Wordsworth, and Whitman: in all a debt to Hebrew Scripture—and to Lowth—shines through. This is especially true of Smart, Macpherson, Blake, and Whitman. They each employ types of parallelism that Lowth identified in Hebrew verse. As Howard Weinbrot remarks of Macpherson, "His roots, some thought, were as Hebraic as Celtic" (and some, such as Francis Wise, thought their languages related). In a wider claim, worthy of more attention, Weinbrot states, "the mid-century Celtic revival depends upon Hebrew language and genealogy.... Perhaps it makes as much, or as little, sense to call the eighteenth century the Hebraic as the Augustan Age."[85] Later, young Emerson read Lowth with care.[86] Almost certainly, so did Harriet Beecher Stowe, who helped redefine the Bible as literature in the nineteenth century and wrote *Woman in Sacred History: A Celebration of Women in the Bible* (1873). In 1829, seven years before their marriage, her future husband, Calvin Stowe, had edited the standard American edition of Lowth's *Lectures*.

Government

The political identification of the English, especially of Puritans in the Old or New World, with the nation of Israel is commonplace. Puritan voyages to Massachusetts would establish, in the words of John Winthrop, first governor of the Massachusetts Bay Colony, "a City upon a Hill" (from Matthew 5:14). William Bradford averred that Hebrew was the language of "the Law and the oracles of God," the language that "angels spake to the holy patriarks." He and William Brewster were Hebraists, and Bradford's manuscript *Of Plymouth Plantation* (1650) includes eight pages of Hebrew vocabulary notes, as well as a hymn to the study of Hebrew.[87] (In 1492, Columbus included on his voyage a man who knew Hebrew, in case any natives still spoke that language!)[88] Dryden presents an elaborate, semi-satirical scheme of Hebraic identification in *Absalom and Achitophel* (1681). Blake's political stance, traced by David Erdman in *Prophet Against Empire* (1954, 3rd ed. 1977), is indebted to the Hebrew prophets.[89] A prophetic critique of empire had grown, culminating in Blake yet with germs in Swift, also satirically with Sir Balaam in Pope's "Epistle to Bathurst" (1732), published one day before the king opened Parliament in 1732/33.[90]

Late in Burke's career, confronting the French Revolution and what he considered its ideologues, Burke followed the Hebrew prophets and echoed their admonitions. John Gunnell remarks of Burke, beset by events he judged tragic and misguided, "Although excluded from participation, he, like the Hebrew prophet, comes to see himself as the personification of the community. He feels the wounds of society more deeply partly because of this very exclusion and perceives more objectively, through his detachment, the condition of society." Extending Gunnell's observation, Frans De Bruyn notes of Burke: "Significantly, when he seeks for an example of the 'heroes and patriots of old' who came to their country's rescue, he passes over the obvious figures of Greek and Roman history in favour of the Jewish hero Judas Maccabaeus: 'Why should not a Maccabeus and his brethren arise to assert the honour of the ancient law, and to defend the temple of their forefathers, with as ardent a spirit, as can inspire any innovator to destroy the monuments of the piety and the glory of ancient ages?'"[91]

Until recent work by Bernard Levinson, Joshua Berman, Eric Nelson, Nathan Perl-Rosenthal, and Eran Shalev, many commentators assumed that English republican thought and the birth of the United States as a democratic republic were indebted almost solely to secular philosophers such as Locke, documents such as the English Declaration of Rights and the Dutch *Plakkaat van Verlatinge*, and the Roman republic. Yet, Locke (see above) wrote against the theories of Filmer, an absolute monarchist, and Filmer relied on the authority of Moses and Hebrew Scripture. Locke countered by analyzing scripture in his two *Treatises* (1689), especially the *First*.[92] Many in the seventeenth and eighteenth centuries who developed republican principles in the English-speaking world repeatedly quoted the Law and the Prophets.

In *The Hebrew Republic: Jewish Sources and the Transformation of European Political Thought* (2010), Eric Nelson examines the reforms in political theory of the sixteenth and especially the seventeenth century that resulted from conscious application of Hebrew Scripture, its injunctions against monarchy, and its statements favoring redistribution of land and the practice of toleration. As Nelson explains, "The Protestant summons to return to the Biblical text brought with it incessant appeals to God's constitutional preferences as embodied in Scripture." Specifically, "The Hebrew revival" introduced "the claim that monarchy is sin. It legitimized redistribution" and "rendered the practice of toleration not merely *politique* but also pious." Yet, by the later eighteenth century, the force of this revival of Hebrew thought had peaked.[93]

In the Third Part of *Leviathan* (1651), Thomas Hobbes employs prodigious biblical knowledge. Reading excerpts masks the length and detail of this learning and how much Hobbes values it. Some, of course, now appears faulty. No evidence exists that Hobbes knew Hebrew. He even seemed to believe that since English had come to Scripture and preaching, there was no longer great need of Greek, Latin, or Hebrew! Yet, Hobbes marshaled formidable biblical arguments. In his view, Hebrew Scripture contains the foundation for all later models of government and civil authority, as well as the basis "Of a Christian Commonwealth," his title for the Third Part. Chapter 40 holds up the covenant of God and Abraham as the archetype for a modern commonwealth. As Abraham bound his family and seed to God, so might a monarch or civil power representing God bind the people and their descendants. Hobbes argues how Moses assumed sovereignty, and in Chapter 41 how Jesus then assumes that sovereignty from the kings of Israel.

As Eric Nelson explains, for Hobbes, "The Christian commonwealth should model itself on the Hebrew republic, assigning complete jurisdiction over religious affairs to the civil magistrate." While Hobbes must overlook the irony that such a civil power might interpret Scripture in a manner other than he does, and therefore might negate his application of Scripture, his awareness of this pitfall causes him all the more diligently to argue for his own interpretation of Hebrew Scripture. Nelson concludes that the Third Part of Leviathan should be regarded "as Hobbes's own contribution to the *respublica Hebraeorum* genre." I agree with Nelson's stance that Hobbes does not steer his audience away from Scripture or cast doubt on it as a mediated, and therefore flawed, version of God's revelation, "the political constitution of a defunct republic."[94] Hobbes calls on Hebrew Scripture because he cares about its authority, not only its "prophetic" mode for the Jews, but also its "Kingdom of God by

Nature," in which "as many of mankind as acknowledge His providence" are governed (ch. 31). This parallels Increase Mather's idea of Israel regarded historically yet also spiritually (see below). If Hobbes were trying to dilute the influence of Hebrew Scripture over modern government, why would he select as an epigraph for his book, produced on the frontispiece, the verse from Job (41:24 in the Vulgate, 41:33 in the King James Version, 41:25 in the Masoretic text), "*Non est potestas Super Terram quae Comparetur ei Iob. 41.24*"? And why would he select as a title for his book the name of that animal described in Job 41 as the incomparable creature of God's irresistible power? "Upon earth there is not his like."

Nathan Perl-Rosenthal comments, "The argument [Thomas] Paine first made in 1776 grew out of a 'Hebraic' strand in English republicanism that first took shape in the seventeenth century. This tradition claimed, on the basis of the putative account of a 'Hebrew Republic' in the Bible, that God condemned monarchy ... and that only kingless governments enjoyed divine approval." Those who earlier advocated this position "were so successful that Hebraic republic arguments, though still present in those books, were effectively hidden in plain sight,"[95] a disappearance so complete that other sources for republics without kings—Rome's republic, Milton, Algernon Sidney, Locke, Montesquieu, Rousseau, and more—eventually crowded out the Hebraic heritage on which many of them, including Milton and Sidney, had relied.

Petrus Cunaeus (Pieter van der Cun, 1586–1638) had published *De republica Hebraeorum* in the early seventeenth century. The Dutch paid heed to it. Other scholars investigated the Hebrew republic for political purposes.[96] In the New as well as the Old World, as Robert Pfeiffer remarks, "The study of Hebrew was cultivated for purposes unrelated to religion." More than commonly recognized, many invoked the Old Testament for political reasons. "In England the Puritans ... compared their revolt to the Maccabean rebellion, the persecution under Laud to the proscription of Judaism by Antiochus Epiphanes." Puritans called Boston the "Jerusalem of this land," their people "Christian Israel," and the Atlantic Ocean "the Red Sea."[97] Maps of the United States record this identification—New Canaan, Promised Land, Zionsville, Mount Hermon, Shiloh—and gravestones record the plenitude of Hebrew given names.[98] Increase Mather studied the historical Israel, which he sometimes called "carnal" or "natural" Israel. He believed also in a spiritual Israel, for him a Christian nation, a Puritan settlement in the New World. He worried, though, that citizens of his modern version of the ancient state would stray from God as much as the prophets of old feared that their own people had done.⁹⁹ Much later, Herman Melville imagined in *White-Jacket* (1850) that "we Americans are the peculiar, chosen people—the Israel of our time; we bear the ark of the liberties of the world." Skeptics may wonder if "the political Messiah had come. But he has come in *us*, if we would but give utterance to his promptings."¹⁰⁰ Melville doubted, however, that America always gave faithful utterance to these promptings.

During the American Revolution and its aftermath, "New England ministers employed the Hebrew Republic into the 1780s as a model for the new republican governments then being formed."¹⁰¹ The precedent was not lost on all later scholars. Near the entrance of the United States into a war already raging, Robert Henry Pfeiffer inaugurated the academic year at Harvard Divinity School on September 23, 1941, with his address "The Patriotism of Israel's Prophets."¹⁰² However, why in the United States did the Hebrew Republic as an acknowledged model fade after 1790? Perhaps because it had succeeded—a republic relying on institutional forms of government had been embodied in a written Constitution with amendments. As Franklin and Washington reminded citizens, the republic relied on the virtue of the people, yet the republic also relied on a Hebrew idea that the forms and branches of government, their organization and balance, matter enormously. Not long after 1790, the Hebrew republic became hidden in plain sight.¹⁰³

To examples offered by Nelson, Perl-Rosenthal, and others, we add those of John Coleridge and his son Samuel Taylor. The Rev. Mr. John Coleridge was a good Hebraist, and his congregation, it was said, thought that when he spoke Hebrew it was the voice of the Holy Ghost. Such attitudes persisted in the countryside, where he preached. Some parishioners felt uneasy if their minister could not speak a language they did not understand. John Coleridge invoked Hebrew Scripture for political purposes, though not to argue for a kingless state. Later, his son's *Lay Sermons* (1816–17) did the same thing. However, the shift in cultural views from 1776 to 1816 meant that the attitude prevalent in the mid- and later eighteenth century regarding Hebrew sources of statecraft became increasingly obscured.

John Coleridge argued for political organization based on principles he found in the Hebrew prophets and, less so, in the Christian gospels. He was no republican, though. When faced in his *Miscellaneous Dissertations Arising from . . . the Book of Judges* (1768) with explaining the text, "In those days there was no king in Israel, but every man did that which was right in his own eyes," he would evade and revert to vague authority: "It has been also observed, that those words . . . are inserted to shew some irregular practices. The observation is reasonable." John Coleridge maintained this despite elsewhere referencing 1 Samuel, which many interpreted as God's rejection of monarchy.[104] Contending that all power and government derive from God, and repeatedly citing the Hebrew prophets as guides to understanding this providence,[105] John Coleridge foreshadowed what his son Samuel Taylor Coleridge later claims as the basis of his own *Statesman's Manual* (1816) and *Lay Sermon* (1817): "I persist in avowing my conviction, that the inspired poets, historians and sententiaries of the Jews, are the clearest teachers of political economy: in short, that their writings are the STATESMAN'S BEST MANUAL."[106] Yet, when Samuel Taylor Coleridge published this conviction, the American Revolution was four decades past, the French almost three. During those decades, the guidance of Hebrew Scripture was being written out of the story. Coleridge's enthusiasm for the words of "the inspired poets, historians and sententiaries of the Jews" as "the clearest teachers of political economy" seemed strange to Dorothy Wordsworth. "It is ten times more obscure," she wrote, "than the darkest parts of the Friend." Even the learned Robert Southey apparently agreed. When Southey's library was sold, his copies of the *Lay Sermons* remained uncut.[107]

Not only did the conviction of the political importance of Hebrew Scripture make sense to John Coleridge and George Washington's generation, many statesmen and divines regarded it as the *prevalent* way of treating religion and political affairs. In the seventeenth and eighteenth centuries, idolatry was a major political and religious subject. Monarchists and republicans invoked it. According to Bernard Levinson and Joshua Berman, the Pentateuch was accepted "as a divinely inspired guide for the ordering of contemporary human affairs." Even when eliminating sermons that make no reference to secular thinkers, in America "Deuteronomy was the most frequently cited book in popular writings on the Constitution . . . exceeding even Charles de Montesquieu's *The Spirit of the Laws*." After eight states ratified the Constitution and a ninth would assure adoption, Samuel Langdon, former president of Harvard, spoke to the General Court of New Hampshire in June 1788. He read aloud Deuteronomy, Chapter 4, to argue for the new form of government: "If I am not mistaken, instead of the twelve tribes of Israel, we may substitute the thirteen States of the American union."[108] Born in 1775, Lyman Beecher, Presbyterian minister and father of Harriet Beecher, later declared that the Constitution did not stem from "Greece or Rome" but "from the Bible," and he did not mean the New Testament.[109] While not advocating American independence, John Coleridge had reminded his audience of Genesis that, "the twelve sons of Ishmael were twelve princes." When John Coleridge claimed that "*He* shews the best patriotism, *who* reconciles the Love of God to *himself, as one branch of the nation*, by a sincere reformation of his life, and by a future obedience to the laws of God and his country,"[110] he was providing, forty-one years in advance, a summary of the closing exhortation that his son Samuel would write for his own *Lay Sermon*.[111] However, in the second decade of the nineteenth century, that exhortation found few adherents.

This secular, progressive shift away from the infusion of Hebrew in learned and political communities is reflected in the fact that the study of Hebrew at Harvard, required from the founding of the college and reinforced by John Harvard's 1638 bequest of "a number of Hebrew grammars—a reminder of the great interest of the Puritans in the Old Testament and in its original Hebrew language"—began to flag in the mid-eighteenth century. This waning occurred despite the appointment of Judah Monis as instructor in Hebrew from 1722 to 1760, and the establishment of an endowed chair for Hebrew in 1764.[112] (The Harvard Corporation had declined to appoint Monis, a Jewish convert who knew rabbinic, Kabbalistic, and biblical texts, as professor.) By the mid-1780s—the year given as 1785 or 1787—Hebrew was no longer required, though Stephen Sewall, the Hancock Professor of Hebrew from its inception until 1785, revitalized its study to some degree. One of Sewall's annual lectures treated theories of Hebrew poetry, and he approved of Lowth's ideas. Despite student complaints concerning Hebrew instruction as early as 1653, and despite declining interest in studying the language as early as 1740,[113] a Hebrew oration had always been delivered at commencement exercises. Then in 1817 Harvard College eliminated it,[114] the year Coleridge pled, apparently in vain, for the continued political relevance of ancient texts in that language.

Romantic Prophecy, Power, and Mythic Force

In the Romantic era, the desire for a new Bible or new scripture, personal or universal, a new mythology for belief not allusion—the avowed goal of Blake and Whitman, and akin to stated aims of Keats, Shelley, Novalis, Thoreau, and others—found sustenance in the archetypal power of Hebrew Scripture, in its imaginative linking and reconciling, through concrete images, of the daily and common with the eternal and transcendent, of meek with sublime, of material with spiritual. Moreover, Lowth's stress on Hebrew prophecy included aesthetic values that appealed to these writers. He believed that in attempting to express divinity "it is absolutely necessary to employ figurative language," and his views opened the Bible to wider interpretations and to a newer, flexible use of myth.[115]

Wordsworth was a great Virgilian, an aspect of his poetry not sufficiently appreciated,[116] but in diction and rhythm Wordsworth's *Michael* owes much to the King James translation of Hebrew Scripture. Readers will catch the allusion to the final lines of Milton's *Paradise Lost* near the beginning of *The Prelude* (1805, 1:15–19), yet the *first* touchstone in that long poem (1:6–7) is Exodus 13:3. In the genealogy Wordsworth creates, thinking of Milton, for "Those trumpet-tones of harmony that shake / Our shores in England," he cites two instances. One is Homer. The second is "the voice / Which roars along the bed of Jewish Song" (5:199–207). The Preface to *Lyrical Ballads* enjoys several texts in its pedigree. Stephen Prickett claims, "one of Wordsworth's main sources for his preface" is Lowth's *Lectures*.[117] In his note to "The Thorn" in the second edition of *Lyrical Ballads*, Wordsworth quotes the Song of Deborah to illustrate impassioned speech: "The mind luxuriates in the repetition of words which appear successfully to communicate its feelings. The truth of these remarks might be shown by innumerable passages from the Bible, and from the impassioned poetry of every nation. 'Awake, awake, Deborah!' &c. Judges, chap. v., verses 12th, 27th, and part of 28th. See also the whole of that tumultuous and wonderful Poem." Coleridge closes Chapter 17 of *Biographia Literaria*, the chapter that begins his critique of Wordsworth's poetry, by quoting Judges 5:27 as an example of passionate repetition. He attributes notice of it to Wordsworth.

However, either man may have found this exact example from Judges highlighted by Thomas Gibbons in *Rhetoric; Or a View of Its Principal Tropes and Figures* (1767), widely used in dissenting academies, which themselves emphasized the study of Hebrew. (The reformer William Frend, prompted in part by his study of Hebrew, left his ordained position in the Church of England, became a Unitarian, and undertook a new translation of Hebrew Scripture based on classical philological practice.) Discussing *epanaphora*, Gibbons invokes Deborah's "triumphal ode, where she describes the death of Sisera by Jael, *Judg.* v.27. 'At her feet he bowed, he fell, he lay down; at her feet he bowed, he fell: where he bowed, there he fell down dead.'"[118] These are the same words Coleridge uses to close his chapter, where he asserts, "Such repetitions I admit to be a beauty of the highest kind."[119] Lowth had originally discussed and analyzed the Song of Deborah, criticism that may have prompted Gibbons's remarks.

Coleridge was a fine classicist. Yet, we now add Coleridge to Isaac Watts, John Dennis, Joseph Warton, Lowth, and, in certain contexts, Burke, to those favoring Hebrew over Greek and Latin poetry. Coleridge's praise regards a quality of supreme importance, the imagination. In 1802 he writes to William Sotheby that in ancient Greece, "All natural Objects were *dead*,—mere hollow Statues—but there was a Godkin or Goddessling *included* in each. . . . At best, it is but Fancy, or the aggregating Faculty of the mind—not *Imagination*, or the *modifying* and *coadunating* Faculty. This the Hebrew Poets appear to me to have possessed beyond all others & next to them the English. In the Hebrew Poets each Thing has a Life of it's [sic] own, & yet they are all one life." This, Coleridge's first formulated distinction between fancy and imagination, is never quoted in its proper context, the Hebrew poets. It is here, too, with "coadunating," a word made from Latin words to signify "making into one," that Coleridge anticipates his later Greek coinage for an act paramount to the imagination: it is "esemplastic." Yet, the power of imagination and the power to shape "one life," which he associates with Wordsworth's gifts, derives first and foremost from "the Hebrew Poets."[120]

In the *Statesman's Manual* Coleridge devalues eighteenth-century allegories and offers his definition of symbol, yet in a context almost universally ignored—that of Hebrew Scripture and the history of Israel. Careful reading of this definition and his other comments on the concept of the symbol reveal close affinity with Lowth's definition of "mystical allegory," the highest kind in Hebrew poetry. Coleridge was familiar with Lowth. The emphasis is on something that exists and acts as itself but also is part of, and points to, something larger, effecting a union of material and spiritual, mundane and transcendent, temporal and eternal.[121] Coleridge and Hyman Hurwitz, a Jewish scholar who published a volume on the Hebrew language as well as the popular *Hebrew Tales* (1826), kept up a fruitful personal acquaintance. In the Preface to his *Tales*, Hurwitz notes that "the three moral Tales" are "admirably translated by my esteemed friend Mr. S. T. Coleridge" and "are, by his kind permission, inserted in this collection." Coleridge had included these tales in *The Friend*.[122] In 1828 Hurwitz became the first Jewish Professor of Hebrew Language and Literature at University College, London, his appointment actively supported by Coleridge, who helped Hurwitz prepare his *Introductory Lecture* there.[123] Writing about Hurwitz and Coleridge, Ewan James Jones concludes, "The philosophical and linguistic implications of Hebrew provided a central site" for Coleridge to engage his "philosophical thinking" with poetic form and expression. Jones examines several instances to support this claim, perhaps most notably Coleridge's treatment of the "*I am, that I am.*"[124] A decade before the collaboration of Hurwitz and Coleridge on *Hebrew Tales*, Byron's *Hebrew Melodies* (1815), a volume of verse with musical settings, sold more than 10,000 copies despite its high cost of a guinea.[125]

Waning Study

As decades pass in the late eighteenth and earlier nineteenth century, a growing tendency portrays Jews in history and national life. However, in a culture increasingly secular, drawing on Hebrew as a vital language and resource for literature and government becomes less common. Despite the earlier presence of Jewish scholars such as the Abendana brothers Isaac and Jacob in the later seventeenth century, by the mid-eighteenth century Hebraic studies were declining at Cambridge University.[126] We have noted a similar trend at Harvard. As Shalom Goldman notes, "The Hebraism of liberal Harvard and of more conservative Yale had waned by the first decade of the nineteenth century. Classicism thrived; Hebraism declined." In general, the Puritan tradition of biblical scholarship faded and the study of Greek and Latin tended to supplant it.[127] When John Smith, the uninspiring but learned linguist, died in 1809, leaving vacant the professorship of Hebrew at Dartmouth, that chair remained vacant until the 1980s—not a misprint, the *1980s*.[128] Thomas Grimké, a Yale graduate and scion of the prominent Charleston, South Carolina, family, called in 1829 for the Bible to replace "the heathen classics." In his proposed reforms he envisioned that, "Hebrew will become peculiarly, THE CLASSICAL LANGUAGE." Grimké died in 1834 at age thirty-eight, and while those supporting his movement succeeded at some institutions in reducing the sway of Greek and Latin, Hebrew failed to replace them.[129]

Henry Wadsworth Longfellow's poem "The Jewish Cemetery at Newport" appeared in the *Monthly Magazine* in 1854 and subsequently in the group of poems "Birds of Passage" included in *The Courtship of Miles Standish and Other Poems* (1858). (See above for the early history of the Newport synagogue. The cemetery, dedicated in 1677, precedes the synagogue building by more than eighty years). However sympathetic to Jewish life, Longfellow's poem envisions that in the New World, as well perhaps as the Old, a dominant culture will effectively eliminate the culture of Jews. Like the cultures of Native Americans, it will wither and become, with the gravestones in the cemetery, "like the tablets of the Law, thrown down / and broken." A sharp statement begins the final stanza: "But ah! what once has been shall be no more!" The last line concludes, "And the dead nations never rise again."[130] Longfellow had visited the cemetery on July 9, 1852, a time when, according to one scholar, no Jews remained living in Newport. There were, however, from 1853 to 1861 more than one hundred Jewish visitors, and irregular summer services were held.[131] In July 1867 Emma Lazarus, aged eighteen, later reported to have been jolted into a strong sense of Jewish identity by reading *Daniel Deronda*,[132] responded to Longfellow's poem with her own, "In the Jewish Synagogue at Newport," first published in *Admetus and Other Poems* (1871). The title of her volume, in which she often alludes to Greek mythology, is from the husband of Alcestis, saved by Apollo when Alcestis offers to die in his place.[133]

The point here is not to give a close reading of Longfellow's and Lazarus's poems (now linked in American studies) about the Newport cemetery and synagogue, but to highlight how Longfellow's attitude reflects one strand of American and British thought that caused the influence of Hebrew to decline: Jewish culture would fade or die as it weakened or was assimilated. Similarly, interest in Hebrew as one of "the classics" would also decline. In contrast, Lazarus vividly imagines a living Jewish past that may continue in the future. True, early in her poem the speaker visiting the synagogue reports, "No signs of life are here: the very prayers / Inscribed around are in a language dead; / The light of the 'perpetual lamp' is spent / That an undying radiance was to shed." Yet, even while the speaker concedes this erosion of time, she protests at the end, "Nathless [sic] the shrine is sacred yet." There is a "mystery of death" that suggests continuance—God remains at the shrine. The final lines, echoing yet altering Longfellow's "long, mysterious Exodus of Death," suggest survival beyond notions of personal or cultural death. The visitor is asked to act as if kneeling in presence "by the burning bush," afire but never consumed.[134] When Longfellow died, Lazarus wrote a notice for *The American Hebrew*: "Jewish hearers" of his poem about the cemetery, she says, "will not be so willing to accept the concluding stanzas of the poem," his sense of the Hebrews as dying off.[135] In *Songs of a Semite* (1882), struck by events in Europe and the United States, many anti-Semitic, Lazarus pursued Jewish themes. She dedicated the longest poem in that collection to the memory of George Eliot, "who did most among the artists of our day toward elevating and ennobling the spirit of Jewish nationality." The emphasis on "nationality" is crucial. Lazarus kept a picture of Eliot on her desk.[136]

The "perpetual lamp" at Touro was indeed revived, just as, after more than fifty years of quiescence, several scholars—Morris Uman Schappes, Albert Mordell, Heinrich Eduard Jacob, and Eve Merriam among them—revived the work of Emma Lazarus beginning in 1944. Yet only in the 1980s and 1990s did her poetry enter mainstream discussions of American Literature. Among earlier efforts to secure that place for Lazarus, in 1949 Max I. Baym presented a bound and inscribed gift copy of his *Emma Lazarus and Emerson*[137] to William A. Jackson, then director of the Houghton Library at Harvard. Emerson had called Lazarus "the great Hebrew Poetess," though had failed to include her in his anthology of verse.[138] Jackson, a man of eminent bibliographic skill, was less than favorably disposed to Jews. I have found no record of his response to the gift.

In American visual art, Thomas Cole's painting *The Oxbow* (1836) has attracted much attention in several fields, including environmental criticism. This picture, a complex visual puzzle, seems the equivalent almost of a modernist, Joyce-like play of signs, symbols, and self-reference; two figures of a question mark appear, one formed by birds wheeling in the sky, another by the view of the oxbow. Yet, the painting also represents a realistic landscape, the Connecticut River valley near Northampton, Massachusetts. On closer inspection, we see that Cole subtly supplies Hebrew letters on a hillside, formed by partial clearing of that hill. The letters seem to spell the name Noah, though seen upside down, some observers discern the name Shaddai or the Almightly. American Masonic lore identified the hills at this location with the mountains of Judea, and critics have made a link, too, with Solomon's Temple. Cole took the stance that Hebrew was the mother of all tongues and that its letters represented some object or animate being, a not uncommon view of the day also entertained by Emerson and Thoreau. There is not space here to elaborate, but it is clear, as David Bjelajac states, that Cole "drew on Puritan metaphors of the ancient Israelites' wilderness and pastoral economies to portray a rural American Zion untainted by the deleterious effects of commercial, industrial growth." Here is visual record of the deep entwining of the Hebrew, the modern, and the American desire for a new promised land.[139]

Hellenism and Hebraism: "Yet the days of Israel are innumerable"

In England, Thomas De Quincey maintained Lowth's high estimate of Hebrew over Greek:[140] "Speaking in the deep sincerities of the solitary and musing heart, which refuses to be duped by the whistling of names, we must say of the Greek that—*laudatur et alget*—he has brilliancies of earth, but on the deeper and more abiding nature of man he has no hold. [. . .] Whereas the Hebrew, by introducing himself to the secret places of the human heart, and sitting there as incubator over the awful germs of the spiritualities that connect man with the unseen worlds, has perpetuated himself as a power in the human system."[141] Daniel Roberts confirms that Lowth influenced De Quincey. While the Greek language, with "its greater intellectual resources," represents De Quincey's "literature of knowledge," Hebrew represents his "literature of power." Hebrew, for De Quincey the more profound language and sensibility, is, according to Roberts, "deeply spiritual" in expressing human relations with the divine.[142] Echoing this estimate of Hebrew, Carlyle spoke in 1840 of the Book of Job: "grand in its sincerity, in its simplicity; in its epic melody, and repose of reconcilement. . . . true eyesight and vision for all things; material things no less than spiritual. . . . There is nothing written, I think, in the Bible or out of it, of equal literary merit."[143]

De Quincey foreshadows Part IV of Matthew Arnold's *Culture and Anarchy* (1869), in later editions entitled "Hebraism and Hellenism," though Arnold never mentions De Quincey in his own book. As with other simple, seminal binaries—Joseph Addison's "natural" versus "learned" genius, for example (*Spectator* 160, September 3, 1711, where, incidentally, Addison states, "Homer has innumerable flights that Virgil was not able to reach, and in the Old Testament we find several passages more elevated and sublime than any in Homer")—Arnold's essay offers provocative generalizations. The pairing and sometimes proclaimed opposition of the Hellenic and the Hebraic had become common in German discourse by the mid-nineteenth century, and Arnold knew that discourse, some of which was colored by anti-Semitism. The brevity of Arnold's "Hebraism and Hellenism" leaves scant room for references or evidence. His pronouncements can spark quibbles, even ignite quarrels. He contends that the Hebraic or "Puritan" spirit has exerted such strength in Britain that his own day requires an antidote, a dose of Hellenism to elevate "knowing" and "thinking" above "doing." Hellenism embodies "the effort to see things as they really are" rather than "the effort to win peace by self-conquest," more "*spontaneity of consciousness*" above a "*strictness of conscience*," which, he says, characterizes Hebraism.[144] His comments are rightly interpreted by Miriam Leonard to reveal a nationalistic and racial basis, and, as Leonard states, "his ambivalence about English Semitism betrays his worries about the cultural force of Judaism," as contrasted with Hebraism, "in modern England."[145] Yet, Arnold was not only suspicious of theories claiming the superiority of the Anglo-Saxon race, he scorned them, for example, in his sarcastic attacks on Sir Charles Adderley and John Arthur Roebuck in "The Function of Criticism at the Present Time" (1864).

However, Arnold does identify the English as Indo-European, the Hebraic as Semitic, and calls for an increase in Hellenism. His use of Hebraism (and Hellenism) is, as Leonard notes, part real and part metaphorical.[146] One might say that he drains living Jewish experience out of the concept of Hebraism and leaves a cultural abstraction. However, when Arnold advises less Hebraism and more Hellenism he does so in the context of more recent English history, not as something always to be desired. Arnold reaffirms the Hebraic spirit not only of Great Britain but also of America. To be sure, he wrote *Culture and Anarchy* to further the work of the Society for Promoting Christian Knowledge, and Hebraism, he believes, has become, virtually unchanged, part of Christianity. So, he says, "Christianity changed nothing in this essential bent of Hebraism to set doing above knowledge." In achievement and ethical importance throughout history, he gives Hebraic and Hellenic equal weight; both seek to make us "'partakers of the divine nature.'"[147] It is a matter of balancing the two, an equipoise that, he claims, different periods of Western history have not honored. In short, if the Hellenic and its inheritor Rome form one classic of English-speaking culture, the Hebraic is the other classic.

It may rankle to hear Arnold argue that Hellenism should regain a balance that he claims is lost: "The nations of our modern world . . . inevitably stand to Hellenism in a relation which dwarfs it, and to Hebraism in a relation which magnifies it." Moreover, he asserts that "the human spirit is wider than the most priceless of the forces which bear it onward, and that to the whole development of man Hebraism itself is, like Hellenism, but a contribution." However, if Arnold laments that Hebraism in his own day has the upper hand, any assumption that he would place it in a permanently inferior category is dispelled by the Preface to *Culture and Anarchy*, a text as vital as the main body and often ignored. As if to answer Longfellow's lament that "dead nations never rise again," Arnold counters, "Yet *the days of Israel are innumerable*.... Now, and for us, it is a time to Hellenise.... But the habits and discipline received from Hebraism remain for our race an eternal possession; and, as far as humanity is constituted, one must never assign them the second rank to-day, without being prepared to restore them to the first rank to-morrow." (Here we also see the ambivalence that Leonard identifies: Arnold will in one sentence speak of "our race," by which he means the English and Europeans as Indo-European, not Semites, yet in the next he will invoke "humanity"—elsewhere he invokes "man" and "the human spirit"—as in need of the Hellenic and the Hebraic. Actual Jews and actual Greeks do not appear.) Special value, says Arnold, resides in "the discipline by which alone man is enabled to rescue his life from thraldom to the passing moment and to his bodily senses, to ennoble it, and to make it eternal. And this discipline has been nowhere so effectively taught as in the school of Hebraism."[148]

Arnold's main adversary, clear in his Preface, is not Judaism or Roman Catholicism. These he calls "cosmopolitan" and ranks them above the *"provinciality"* of Christian Nonconformists. Indeed, Arnold indicts Nonconformists and dissenting Protestants for their narrow-minded earnestness: "our puritans, ancient [from earlier English history] and modern, have not enough added to their care for walking staunchly by the best light they have ... they have developed one side of their humanity ... and have become incomplete and mutilated men in consequence." This contrasts with the spirit of Hebraism, which is "To walk staunchly by the best light one has, to be strict and sincere with oneself, not to be of the number of those who say and do not."[149]

Three years later Arnold arranges, edits, and publishes *The Great Prophecy of Israel's Restoration: Isaiah, chapters 40–66* (1872), directed to "young learners." Its alternate title is *A Bible-Reading for Schools*. In 1872 it enjoyed three printings, called by the publisher "editions." In 1889 a fifth printing or "edition" appeared. In 1875 Arnold had it set in larger typeface with a revised Introduction "because it has been found useful by many who are not school-children."[150] Arnold, a school inspector, aims to present young readers and others a "literary production of the highest order, which in our schools for the people can be ... apprehended as a connected whole.... Evidently the Old Testament offers more suitable matter for this purpose than the

New. Its documents exhibit Hebrew literature in its perfection, while the New Testament does not pretend to exhibit the Greek language and literature in their perfection." The Hebrew texts offer "poetry, rhythm, and eloquence" lacking in the New Testament. Arnold's substantial preface states that while the mass of people will not be reading Greek or Latin even in translation, many turn to the Bible regularly. When more advanced students do read Greek or Latin, he continues, "how little . . . do they get at its significance! how little do they *know* it! how little does it become a power . . . towards wide and complete knowledge!"[151]

Here Lowth again appears. Arnold, earlier Professor of Poetry at Oxford as Lowth had been, pays attention to his predecessor's translation of Isaiah and discusses Lowth's departures in vocabulary and verb tense from the Authorized (King James) version. In selective instances Arnold too changes verb tenses and word choice. He argues that these improve the 1611 rendering.[152] Arnold's Preface, a forerunner of the literary and educational stance that John Livingston Lowes will advocate in "The Noblest Monument of English Prose" (see below), states that it "would be possible that every child of twelve or thirteen years of age" might read and grasp "as a whole" the chapters from Isaiah that he presents.[153]

Hebraism in the American Renaissance

Elisa New contends, and I believe her correct, that "Melville is Hellenism's severest American critic, and that his greatest book," *Moby-Dick* (1851), is "a sustained defense of the Hebraic 'letter.'"[154] New argues that Ishmael is the orphan and preserver—and, one could add, he survives as Melville's strange reply to Longfellow even before Longfellow visits the cemetery at Newport in 1852. Longfellow called the deceased Jews who had come to the New World "These Ishmaels and Hagars of mankind." Less than a year before Longfellow's visit, *Moby-Dick* appeared, first in England as *The Whale*.

Multiple reincarnations of Hebrew figures populate *Moby-Dick*, each appearing in several, shifting guises: Job, Jonah, Ahab, and Rachel, as told by another, Ishmael, with the elusive presence of Leviathan, Moby Dick, the largest mammal that—perhaps one should say *whom*—the *Pequod* dares pursue. Yet, these figures do not simply repeat their biblical forebears. Melville makes them metaphoric extensions, telling new as well as old stories. His Hebraism is not lifted and transplanted statically. He does more than defend the Hebraic letter; he transposes and metamorphoses it, stretching its spirit. His creative power acts as an exponent of the Hebraic, honoring yet altering its original value, and combining it, too, with other traditions.[155] Melville's characters owe much to Hebrew stories, and so does his style. He employs a language that attempts to plumb depths in which the low and common sink and rise in a sea mysterious, inexplicable. With an almost ceaseless, varied repetition seeking to encompass the infinite yet pausing for the particular species, for the type of blubber or barnacle, his vocabulary and rhythm, his phrases, refrains, lists, and catalogues, these all contain, especially in *Moby-Dick*, more than traces of the parallelism and antiphonal soundings of Hebrew literature.[156] The stylistic fabric of the greatest American fiction exhibits a warp and woof of singular variety—Shakespeare, Rabelais, Cervantes, Hobbes, Carlyle, Coleridge, and more—yet its texture and quality frequently reveal the parallel motions of a textual shuttle whose guiding hand is Hebraic.

In Melville's long search for a sheet anchor of belief in a sea roiled by science, Darwinian evolution, and gale-force skepticism, his ungainly but striking poem *Clarel* (1876) stands out. Its genesis and place in Melville's corpus are not concerns here, nor its varied quality, ranging in 18,000 lines from the tired and verbose to the taut and vivid; rather, this: a key figure is the pilgrim Nathan, an American frontier Protestant of Puritan descent. Finding no faith satisfactory, he makes a pilgrimage to the Holy Land (Melville traveled there, as did many Americans after the Civil War), falls in love with Agar, a sympathetic and kind Jewish woman, converts to Judaism, marries her, and becomes a Zionist. Clarel, the main figure in the long poem, falls in love with the daughter of Agar and Nathan. All this does not mean that Melville had found the secure anchorage that he sought and just as constantly would suspect. Yet, he descried value and an ideal of conduct, if not of belief, in Hebraic culture. He worked ten years on *Clarel*. It achieved no commercial success. "Yet of all his works," Andrew Delbanco explains, "it is the one in which he best expressed the craving for belief that Hawthorne had detected in him ... talking of 'Providence and futurity and of everything that lies beyond human ken.'"[157] There are intriguing connections between Ishmael, *Moby-Dick*, and *Clarel*; it becomes impossible to separate the multiple Hebraic elements appearing in his novel and poem.[158]

Vincent Kenny in 1973 framed Melville's long poem as a variation on Hebraism and Hellenism: "In *Clarel* Melville wrote a Hebrew poem in a Greek mold."[159] This, as it turns out, was no chance coincidence with Arnold's terms. Melville wrote *Clarel* as he was immersing himself for more than a decade in the poetry and criticism of Arnold.[160] Melville in *Clarel* engaged Hebraism and Hellenism with Arnold in mind, though he did not repeat Arnold's conclusions.[161] Had Melville read Lowth? It's hard to say. At the Albany Academy, if he studied texts required for the English School, he had read Hugh Blair's *Lectures on Rhetoric and Belles Lettres*, which enthusiastically summarizes Lowth's work.[162]

In his late essay "Walking" (1862), Thoreau states gnomically, "It is too late to be studying Hebrew; it is more important to understand even the slang of today." His vantage here is looking westward to the future of the New World, not east to the past and the Old. Three paragraphs later he calls the West "but another name for the Wild," which sets up his famous statement, "In Wildness is the preservation of the World."[163] Thoreau sees a modern acceleration of knowledge and events, the rise of what Arnold would, somewhat differently, associate with a Hellenic spirit of science and curiosity. Thoreau himself promoted no organized religion. His Greek was the Greek of Homer, not of the Gospels, his Latin from Virgil, not the Vulgate. When he realized his life might soon end, he may have felt a twinge that not enough time remained to study Hebrew, a subject that at Harvard in the 1830s he declined to pursue, sharpening instead Latin, Greek, and several modern European languages.

However, to balance this seeming dismissal of Hebrew—Thoreau has a dialectical more than a polemical mind—the chapter "Reading" in *Walden* offers counterweight. There he advises, "The adventurous student will always study classics, in whatever language they may be written, and however ancient they may be." He regrets that this practice is uncommon. While "the college-bred" person may read "a Greek or Latin classic in the original," there will likely be no one with whom to discuss it. Yet, with even greater dismay, he asks that as far as reading "the sacred Scriptures, or Bibles of mankind, who in this town can tell me even their titles? Most men do not know that any nation but the Hebrews have had a scripture." Greek, Latin, all sacred scriptures, and the Hebrew nation have each produced "golden words" that merit perpetual study.[164] Emerson had commenced the final paragraph in his 1838 "Divinity School Address" this way: "I look for the hour when that supreme Beauty, which ravished the souls of those Eastern men, and chiefly of those Hebrews, and through their lips spoke oracles to all time, shall speak in the West also." Emerson inscribed a gift copy of his Address to "Henry D. Thoreau, With the regards of R. W. E."[165] In his own way, Thoreau had taken what Emerson in that last paragraph called the "immortal" but "fragmentary" sentences of "Hebrew and Greek Scriptures" and had tried to bring them, as Emerson had hoped a "new Teacher" would, "full circle;" then we "shall see their rounding complete grace; shall see the world to be the mirror of the soul."

"The worth of which exceeds all computation"

In his famous essay on the King James Bible, "The Noblest Monument of English Prose," first delivered as a lecture in 1923, John Livingston Lowes emphasizes "to what [a high] degree the Biblical vocabulary is compact of the primal stuff of our common humanity—of its universal emotional, sensory experiences." Moreover, "The Hebrew of the Old Testament"—though "to a less degree the Greek of the New"—is "supremely translatable, and it is so largely because of just these salient characteristics of its diction—its simplicity, its clarity, its directness, and its universal and immediate appeal." Lowes's father had urged him to learn Hebrew and Greek as well as Latin, and Lowes did. He pursued biblical studies before turning to modern literature.[166] As Arnold, Carlyle, De Quincey, Burke, Lowth, Dennis, and others had argued, Lowes believes that the language of Hebrew Scripture conveys elemental humanity, stylistic grandeur, and emotional intimacy.

Unlike Lowth, Burke, Dennis, and De Quincey, Lowes argues exclusively from the simplicity, the varied and majestic rhythms, the music, vivid images, and evocations of that language. He makes no plea whatever based on religious antecedence, belief, or credibility. He views English as highly fit for rendering biblical Hebrew—a point made as early as 1712 by Joseph Addison in *Spectator* 405—and hopes that such rendering might "be again a moulding force the worth of which exceeds all computation in the development of our literature and of our speech."[167] Lowes observes that much Hebrew Scripture dates "in large measure from that period of stress" when "the tragic problem of continued national existence merged—once more in the minds of prophets and poets and chroniclers alike—with the no less tragic spiritual problem of God's enigmatic dealings with his chosen race."[168] Here Lowes intertwines, as Coleridge earlier did, the fate of a nation, a political fate, with analysis and praise of the language of that nation. It is also interesting—and indicative of a growing amnesia that crept over the late nineteenth century and much of the twentieth—that Lowes never mentions Lowth, by 1923 a largely forgotten figure.

A Subject to Pursue

From the early-mid nineteenth to the mid- and even later twentieth century, what happened to the shaping presence that Hebrew and Hebrew Scripture had exerted so strongly over literature, criticism, and political theory written in English? Despite Arnold's stress on the Hebraic, the study of Hebrew in great universities had already become optional before 1800. Students, an increasing number no longer in religious study, began to ignore it. Even Arnold admitted that his own Hebrew was, for purposes of independent translation and correction, "totally inadequate." It allowed him, he said, only "in some degree to follow and weigh the reasons" of others.[169] Despite mention in a few editions of Longinus, Lowth's work languished. Charles D. Cleveland in 1872 called Lowth's *Lectures* "a work which unites a depth of learning to a discriminating criticism and a refined taste, in a very unusual degree; and while it is of inestimable value to the professed Biblical student, it affords equal pleasure and instruction to the general reader."[170] But this attitude was fading. In 1906 and 1926, Oxford published an edition of *On the Sublime* translated by A. O. Prickard with an appendix containing "Passages translated from Bishop Lowth's Oxford [Latin] lectures on Hebrew poetry." Several editions of Lowth's *Lectures* in English appeared in England and America between 1787 and 1847. This corresponds roughly with the period traditionally assigned to the Romantic era. Then, as far as I can ascertain, no edition or reprinting of Lowth's *Lectures* appeared between 1847 and 1969, when a German publisher reprinted the 1787 English translation.[171] In 1995, an English publisher reprinted Volume One of the 1787 English translation and the full 1775 Latin text published by Oxford.[172] In 2004 a reprint of an early English edition of the *Lectures* became available "on demand" or as an electronic book from a publisher of antiquated volumes.[173] Not until M. H. Abrams mentioned Lowth in *The Mirror and the Lamp* (1953) did the bishop resurface in English studies, and then briefly. More time would pass until Murray Roston in 1965, and then Stephen Prickett in 1984, gave substantive critical notice to Lowth.[174] The *MLA Bibliography* from 1926 to 1981 contains no article treating Lowth at any length. No part of Lowth's *Lectures* has ever appeared in *The Norton Anthology of English Literature*. More surprisingly, no excerpt from his *Lectures* appears in *The Norton Anthology of Theory and Criticism* or in any significant anthology of criticism. He is not mentioned in Gerald Chapman's splendid collection *Literary Criticism in England, 1660–1800* (1966), nor in any anthology of eighteenth-century or romantic writing that I know. Even the seventh edition of the *Oxford Companion to English Literature* (2009) offers no entry for Lowth.

Did the American and French Revolutions help to instigate the decline of the study of Hebrew? It is hard to say, but that close historical coincidence, while not proving cause and effect, is suggestive. In the eighteenth century it was common practice for Christians to appeal to their Old Testament to justify political ideas. This declined significantly by 1820. The influence of Lowth waned a few decades later. As university students not primarily in training for the ministry avoided Hebrew, and as the requirement to study it was dropped at institutions such as Harvard, Yale, Dartmouth, Cambridge, and others, Hebrew presented itself less forcefully in literary, historical, and political curricula, as well as in cultural consciousness. When the Faculty of Arts and Sciences at Harvard formed divisions and departments in 1890–91, it denominated "The Classics (Greek, Latin)" under the division of "The Ancient Languages." Another division, "The Semitic Languages and History," included Hebrew, though even then Hebrew was not named explicitly.[175] As Miriam Leonard remarks, nineteenth-century "developments in linguistics increasingly marginalized Hebrew in relation to other Eastern languages."[176] Hebrew became less valued, though Greek and Latin continued indispensable for decades.

Academic positions in English and American literature from the time departments were established until the mid-twentieth century, that is, from around 1880 to 1950 or a decade or two later, were not particularly open to Jews. Departments of English, some prone to anti-Semitism, could practice genteel bigotry or unconscious racism; many ignored Hebraic studies as contributing anything to English literature. (One refreshing exception to these attitudes was the interest that Edmund Wilson took in Judaic and Hebraic studies, as well as in American Jews.)[177] Scholars who expanded Hebraic studies in the nineteenth and twentieth centuries located themselves in departments of "Semitic" or "Oriental" languages. (At Harvard, the Hancock Professorship associated Hebrew with "Oriental languages" as early as 1765.) For all but specialists, the earlier, valued study of

Hebrew, recommended and even required from the sixteenth through the later eighteenth century, decayed. Secularization is certainly one large factor, but prejudice contributed. The study of modern Hebrew was not introduced into American colleges until 1934, first at New York University. The next twenty-five years saw expansion, especially after World War II.[178] Harvard College Library established its Judaica Division only in 1962. As noted above, Dartmouth revived the study of Hebrew in the 1980s after a hiatus of 175 years. Yet, the study of comparative literature that examines older Hebrew texts and the development of English literature—as opposed to biblical studies—was always full of potential. Scholars who explored this connection in the last two generations, M. H. Abrams, Murray Roston, Howard Weinbrot, Jason Rosenblatt, Robert Alter, and others, as well as those writing studies of the Hebrew republic and of writers such as Emma Lazarus, were Jewish. Since the time of Arnold and Lowes until recently, relatively few apart from those with a sense of Jewish history and heritage have ventured to examine the other classic with regard to literature in English.

More broadly, this suggests that the study of literature in English will always benefit from a diversity of backgrounds, ethnicities, beliefs, and convictions among the scholars, critics, and students who pursue it. Like the English language itself, literature in English from "Caedmon's Hymn" to the present is the result of wars, invasions, colonizations, expulsions, immigrations, rebellions, emigrations, identities assimilated and identities retained, as well as minorities and majorities ever shifting. And Ruth Wisse notes what has at times been forgotten concerning modern Jewish literary productions: "As with the Bible, the world will also value what the Jews find of value to themselves."[179]

Specialized articles and Howard Weinbrot's Part IV of *Britannia's Issue*, "Expanding the Borders. Jews and Jesus: This Israel, This England," which covers the late seventeenth century to about 1765, are invaluable.[180] And no one more than Robert Alter has brought to the reader fresh translations and guides to Hebrew Scripture and its literary resonances in English. Yet, there is, as far as I have been able to ascertain, no book-length study that systematically traces the formative power of Hebrew and Hebrew Scripture on literature in English during the eighteenth and earlier nineteenth centuries. Sheila Spector has, however, ushered forward two essay collections, *British Romanticism and the Jews: History, Culture, Literature*[181] and *The Jews and British Romanticism: Politics, Religion, Culture*.[182] These volumes chiefly engage historical, cultural, political, and intellectual issues. She has also written *Byron and the Jews* (2010), which examines the sense of religion, moral integrity, and alienation that Jews and Byron shared. In Hebrew and Yiddish translations of British romantic writers, Byron is most frequently cited.[183] A recent collection of essays, also edited by Spector, *Romanticism/Judaica: A Convergence of Cultures*,[184] covers various topics and offers reflections on earlier scholarship that engages Anglo-Jewish literature. Remarkably, in mid-2014 the online catalogue of the Library of Congress lists this as the *only* book under the subject heading "English literature—Hebrew influences." A parallel search for influences of Hebrew on American literature yields not one title at all, but rather, two books under a different subject, "Hebrew literature, Modern—American influences." In contrast, sixty-eight books fall under the heading "English literature—classical influences" (meaning Greek and Latin), and another ten under "American literature—classical influences" and closely related subjects. This essay, an admittedly imperfect conspectus, hopes to prompt further study and to secure continued attention for what every reader of literature in English should regard as the other classic.

Notes

1. For treatment of Lowth and references to commentary on his work, see James Engell, *The Committed Word: Literature and Public Values*, chap. 8, "Robert Lowth, Unacknowledged Legislator" (University Park: Penn State University Press, 1999), 119–40. Roston, Kugel, and Prickett produced earlier treatments of Lowth, and Balfour a subsequent one (see Bibliography).
2. *The Penny Cyclopaedia of the Society for the Diffusion of Useful Knowledge*, ed. George Long (London: Charles Knight, 1839), 14:179–80. The influential *English Cyclopaedia* of 1856 and *The English Encyclopedia* of 1867 reprint this statement.
3. M. H. Abrams, *The Mirror and the Lamp: Romantic Theory and the Critical Tradition* (Oxford: Oxford University Press, 1953), 78. Abrams notes that John Keble took up many themes of poetic expression explored by Lowth and earlier by Longinus.
4. See William R. McKelvy, *The English Cult of Literature: Devoted Readers 1774–1880* (Charlottesville: University of Virginia Press, 2007), 47–49.
5. Howard Weinbrot, *Britannia's Issue: The Rise of British Literature from Dryden to Ossian* (Cambridge: Cambridge University Press,

1993), Part IV, "Expanding the Borders, Jews and Jesus: This Israel, This England," 403–74, makes the best overall case for the presence and influence of Hebrew and Hebrew Scripture in British literature from 1660 to 1765. When I treat that time span, I draw on Weinbrot and supplement his work with further examples and claims.
6. E.g., Henry Stead, "Latin first and best," review of *Romans and Romantics, Times Literary Supplement* (June 28, 2013): 11.
7. Holger Gzella, "Expansion of the Linguistic Context of the Hebrew Bible," *Hebrew Bible / Old Testament: The History of Its Interpretation III/I: From Modernism to Post Modernism*, ed. Magne Sæbø (Göttingen: Vandenhoeck & Ruprecht, 2012), 134–67, at 143.
8. See Rudolf Pfeiffer, *History of Classical Scholarship 1300–1850* (Oxford: Clarendon Press, 1976).
9. Alexander Broadie, *The Tradition of Scottish Philosophy: A New Perspective on the Enlightenment* (Edinburgh: Polygon, 1990), 4.
10. Stefan C. Reif, *Hebrew Manuscripts at Cambridge University Library: A Description and Introduction*, University of Cambridge Oriental Publications 52 (Cambridge: Cambridge University Press, 1997), 3. This summarizes the study of Hebrew at Cambridge and includes political contexts ("Hebrew and Hebraists at Cambridge, An Historical Introduction," 1–35).
11. Robert H. Pfeiffer, "The Teaching of Hebrew in Colonial America," *The Jewish Quarterly Review* n.s. 45, no. 4 (April 1955): 363–73, at 363.
12. M. L. Clarke, *Classical Education in Britain, 1500–1900* (Cambridge: Cambridge University Press, 1959), 35; Ian Green, *Humanism and Protestantism in Early Modern English Education* (Farnham: Ashgate, 2009), 259–61, 19, with comments throughout on study of Hebrew (108, 119–21, 289–91, 299–300); Paul Elledge, *Lord Byron at Harrow School: Speaking Out, Talking Back, Acting Up, Bowing Out* (Baltimore: Johns Hopkins University Press, 2000), 8; James George Cotton Minchin, *Our Public Schools: Their Influence on English History* (London: Swan Sonnenschein, 1901), 245–46.
13. Reif, *Hebrew Manuscripts*, 6.
14. Pfeiffer, "Teaching of Hebrew," 363, 365.
15. Corydon Ireland, "Harvard's Indian College Poet," *Harvard Gazette* September 16, 2013, accessed April 27, 2017, http://news.harvard.edu/gazette/story/2013/09/harvards-indian-college-poet/.
16. See Richard H. Popkin, "The Rise and Fall of the Jewish Indian Theory," in Shalom Goldman, ed., *Hebrew and the Bible in America: The First Two Centuries* (Hanover, NH: University Press of New England for Brandeis University and Dartmouth College, 1993), 70–90; also Eran Shalev, *American Zion: The Old Testament as a Political Text from the Revolution to the Civil War* (New Haven: Yale University Press, 2013), 118–50.

17. Shalom Goldman, "Biblical Hebrew in Colonial America: The Case of Dartmouth," in Goldman, *Hebrew and the Bible in America*, 201–8, at 202–3.
18. Hugh de Quehen, "Bentley, Richard," *Oxford DNB Online*.
19. Reif, *Hebrew Manuscripts*, 17 and n65.
20. Raymond Hickey, "Attitudes and Concerns in Eighteenth-Century English," in *Eighteenth-Century English: Ideology and Change*, ed. Raymond Hickey, Studies in English Language (Cambridge: Cambridge University Press, 2010), 1–20, at 3.
21. Pfeiffer, "Teaching of Hebrew," 367–68.
22. For the history of Jews in Newport, also pertinent to a discussion of Longfellow and Lazarus (see in text below), see Morris A. Gutstein, *The Story of the Jews of Newport: Two and a Half Centuries of Judaism, 1658–1908* (New York: Bloch, 1936).
23. Shalom Goldman, *God's Sacred Tongue: Hebrew and the American Imagination* (Chapel Hill: University of North Carolina Press, 2004), 133. Goldman treats the relationship between Stiles and Rabbi Hayyim Carigal (63–66) and devotes chap. 3 to "Ambivalence and Erudition in New Haven: Ezra Stiles, Yale College, and the Jewish Tradition," 52–73. Arthur Hertzberg, "The New England Puritans and the Jews," in Goldman, *Hebrew and the Bible in America*, 105–21, paints a portrait of Stiles (113–15) as somewhat less sympathetic to Jews than Goldman himself does in *Sacred Tongue*. A third view is provided by Arthur A. Chiel, "Ezra Stiles and the Jews: A Study in Ambivalence," in Goldman, *Hebrew and the Bible in America*, 156–67. Tolerant by eighteenth-century standards, Stiles, as his career lengthened, became more open to the religion of the Jews and less concerned about conversion to Christianity. See also George Alexander Kohut, *Ezra Stiles and the Jews: Selected Passages from his Literary Diary Concerning Jews and Judaism* (New York: Philip Cowen, 1902) and Edmund S. Morgan, *The Gentle Puritan: A Life of Ezra Stiles, 1727–1795* (New Haven: Yale University Press, 1962), esp. chaps. 15 and 17.
24. Accessed April 27, 2017, http://www.tourosynagogue.org/index.php/history-learning/synagogue-history. For Rabbi Carigal, Stiles, and "How Hebrew Came to Yale," see also http://www.jewishvirtuallibrary.org/jsource/US-Israel/Yale.html, accessed April 27, 2017.
25. "Seixas," *The Jewish Encyclopedia*, ed. Cyrus Adler, Isidore Singer et al. (New York: Ktav, 1964 [1906]), accessed April 27, 2017, http://www.jewishencyclopedia.com/articles/13396-seixas ("unedited full-text of the 1906 *Jewish Encyclopedia*").
26. Goldman, *God's Sacred Tongue*, 129.
27. Jacob Kabakoff, "The Use of Hebrew by American Jews During the Colonial Period," in Goldman, *Hebrew and the Bible in America*, 191–97, at 194.

28. *A Bibliographical Description of Books and Pamphlets of American Verse Printed from 1610 Through 1820*, compiled by Roger E. Stoddard, ed. David R. Whitesell (University Park: Penn State University Press for the Bibliographical Society of America, 2012), 761 (entries 227, 493, 532, 820; entry 493 lists a revision of 227).
29. Goldman, *God's Sacred Tongue*, chap. 4, "All Knowledge is from the Hebrew: Jonathan Edwards as Biblical Exegete and Christian Hebraist," 74–88, at 78, 74. Goldman argues, "the references to Hebrew words, concepts, and texts in his writings reveal a growing familiarity with the Hebraic and Judaic traditions" (77).
30. Goldman, *God's Sacred Tongue*, 13–14.
31. Kabakoff, "The Use of Hebrew by American Jews During the Colonial Period," in Goldman, *Hebrew and the Bible in America*, 196.
32. Charles Martindale, "Milton's Classicism," in *The Oxford History of Classical Reception in English Literature, Vol. 3 (1660–1790)*, ed. David Hopkins and Charles Martindale (Oxford University Press, 2012), 63.
33. Erik Gray, "Come Be My Love: The Song of Songs, *Paradise Lost*, and the Tradition of the Invitation Poem," *PMLA* 128, no. 2 (March 2013): 370–85, at 381, 370–71, 375, 384, n11. The trope influenced medieval, courtly, and Renaissance love poetry, including Marlowe's "The Passionate Shepherd to His Love."
34. For example, see Samuel S. Stollman, "Milton's Dichotomy of 'Judaism' and 'Hebraism,'" *PMLA* 89, no. 1 (January 1974): 105–12. More recent, significant studies include Jason P. Rosenblatt, *Torah and Law in* Paradise Lost (Princeton: Princeton University Press, 1994), and Jeffrey S. Shoulson, *Milton and the Rabbis: Hebraism, Hellenism, and Christianity* (New York: Columbia University Press, 2001), which examines Milton's work in relation to midrash. Rosenblatt edited Milton's poetry and prose with an eye to biblical sources (W. W. Norton, 2011).
35. John Dennis, *The Advancement and Reformation of Modern Poetry: A Critical Discourse in Two Parts* (London: Rich. Parker, 1701), 178–91, at 183, 179. Spelling and capitalization are modernized.
36. Ibid., 178, 184, 186, 191.
37. For another view of Dennis and Hebrew, see Sarah B. Stein, "Translating the Bible to Raise the Fallen: John Dennis's Psalm 18," *Studies in Eighteenth-Century Culture* 43 (2014): 18–41. Stein's dissertation, "A Hebraic Modernity: Poetry, Prayer, and Translation in the Long Eighteenth Century" (Emory, 2012), challenges what it considers prevailing views of the Hebraic sublime and posits that the British, Christian use of Hebrew as a foil for Greek and Latin created "neohebraism," itself not authentically Hebrew. This in one sense must certainly be granted. British and American Christian Hebraists and authors interpreted Hebrew Scripture in specific ways, often adding Christian motives and

typology that would not meet the test of Jewish scholarship or exegesis then or now.

38. E.g., Samuel Holt Monk, *The Sublime: A Study of Critical Theories in Eighteenth-Century England* (Ann Arbor: University of Michigan Press, 1935), 77–83; Stephen Prickett, *Words and the Word: Language, Poetics, and Biblical Interpretation* (Cambridge: Cambridge University Press, 1986), 41; Robert H. Pfeiffer, "Hebrew and Greek Sense of Tragedy," *The Joshua Bloch Memorial Volume. Studies in Booklore and History*, ed. Abraham Berger, Lawrence Marwick, Isidore S. Meyer (New York: New York Public Library, 1960), 54–64.
39. *On the Sublime*, trans. W. Rhys Roberts (Cambridge: Cambridge University Press, 1899), 65.
40. Quoted by Weinbrot, *Britannia's Issue*, 425.
41. Sir Christopher Hogwood, *Handel* (London: Thames and Hudson, 1984), 267. In this section I am indebted to Hogwood and to Weinbrot, *Britannia's Issue*, 431–45. For further references, see Weinbrot, 432n33.
42. Hogwood, *Handel*, 142, 157.
43. Ibid., 154, 168–69.
44. H. R. Fox Bourne, *The Life of John Locke*, 2 vols. (New York: Harper & Brothers, 1876), 1:56.
45. Hogwood, *Handel*, 155, 157–58, 180–81.
46. *Poems on Several Occasions, by Matthew Prior, Esq.* Volume the second. The fourth edition. To which is prefixed, The Life of Mr Prior, by Samuel Humphreys, Esq. (London: C. Hitch, 1742), "Memoirs of the Life of Mr. Prior," xvi. Frances Mayhew Rippy, "Prior, Matthew," *Oxford DNB Online*.
47. Samuel Johnson, *The Lives of the Poets*, ed. John H. Middendorf, The Yale Edition of the Works of Samuel Johnson (New Haven: Yale University Press, 2010), 22:727, 726.
48. See Charles W. Jones, "Milton's 'Brief Epic,'" *Studies in Philology* 44, no. 2 (April 1947): 209–27, at 227. Jones argues that Milton, influenced by reading "Jerome's preface to his translation of the Book of Job," was convinced that Job contained both an external and internal form of epic that he might follow as a model (210–11). The argument relies in part on revealing that Milton, following Jerome and other sources, may have regarded Job as originally composed in hexameters.
49. Robert Lowth, *Lectures on the Sacred Poetry of the Hebrews*, trans. G[eorge]. Gregory, ed. Calvin Stowe (Boston: Crocker & Brewster, 1829), 232–33.
50. Lowth, *Lectures*, 108, 109, 110. Ian Balfour in his work on the sublime delivered a session in 2009 at the Harvard Humanities Center Reading Group on Dialectical Critical Thinking, "On the Judaic and the Sublime: Hegel Among Others."

51. Lowth, *Lectures*, 22, 29.
52. Edmund Burke, *A Philosophical Enquiry into the Origin of Our Ideas of the Sublime and Beautiful* (London: R. and J. Dodsley, 1759, 2nd ed.), 100, 121.
53. Ibid., 108–9, 108–22.
54. Weinbrot, *Britannia's Issue*, 425–28.
55. David Watson Rannie, *Oriel College*, University of Oxford, College Histories (London: F. E. Robinson, 1900), 144.
56. Samuel Taylor Coleridge, *Table Talk*, ed. Carl Woodring, 2 vols. (Princeton: Princeton University Press, 1990), 2:180; 1:312 and n26.
57. *Historia Britonum: The History of the Britons*, trans. Richard Rowley (Lampeter: Llanerch Press, 2005), 17, 21.
58. "Joseph of Arimathea," accessed April 27, 2017, http://www.glastonburyabbey.com/joseph_of_arimathea.php?sid=ddc4ffe380b2923c2a486b8f08723fb9. See also C. A. Ralegh Radford, *Glastonbury Abbey* (London: Pitkin, 1973), 11, 14. Abbot Beere promoted the cult of Joseph of Arimathea in the late fifteenth century.
59. Northrop Frye, *Fearful Symmetry: A Study of William Blake* (Princeton: Princeton University Press, 1947), 142.
60. Geoffrey of Monmouth, *The History of the Kings of Britain: An Edition and Translation of* De gestis Britonum (Historia regum Britanniae), ed. Michael D. Reeve, trans. Neil Wright (Woodbridge, UK and Rochester, NY: Boydell Press, 2007), lviii and nn61, 62.
61. Weinbrot discusses the various, deep identifications of England and Scotland with the Hebrew nation (*Britannia's Issue*, 408–23, 482–92).
62. Jan van Campen, *A Paraphrasis upon all the Psalmes of David, made by Johannes Campensis, reader of the Hebrue lecture in the universite of Louane [Louvain]* (London: Thomas Gybson, 1539).
63. See, for example, Prudence Steiner, "A Garden of Spices in New England: John Cotton's and Edward Taylor's Use of the Song of Songs," in *Allegory, Myth, and Symbol*, ed. Morton W. Bloomfield (Cambridge, MA: Harvard University Press, 1981), 227–43.
64. Isaac Watts, *Horae Lyricae, Poems, Chiefly of the Lyric kind, in Two Books* (London: Printed by S. and D. Bridge for John Lawrence, 1706), Preface; Watts, *Reliquiae Juveniles: Miscellaneous Thoughts in Prose and Verse . . . Written chiefly in Younger Years* (London: Richard Ford and Richard Hett, 1734), 75.
65. Stephen Prickett, "Biblical and Literary Criticism" in *The Bible and Literature: A Reader*, ed. David Jasper and Stephen Prickett (Oxford: Oxford University Press, 1999), 12–43, at 26.
66. J. R. Watson, "Merrick, James," *Oxford DNB Online*.
67. James Merrick, *The Psalms, translated or paraphrased in English verse* (Reading, 1765), Preface, iii–v, viii.

68. See William A. Kumbier, "Sound and Signification in Christopher Smart's *Jubilate Agno*," *Texas Studies in Literature and Language* 24, no. 3 (Fall 1982): 293–312, at 306.
69. Geoffrey H. Hartman, *The Fate of Reading* (Chicago: University of Chicago Press, 1975), "Christopher Smart's *Magnificat*: Toward a Theory of Representation," 88–96, at 89.
70. See Christopher Smart, *Jubilate Agno*, ed. W. H. Bond (Cambridge, MA: Harvard University Press, 1954), 16–25, and Bond, "Christopher Smart's *Jubilate Agno*," *Harvard Library Bulletin* 4, no.1 (Winter 1950): 34–52.
71. Bond, "Smart's *Jubilate Agno*," 44.
72. Ibid., 44–45.
73. Ibid., 52. Wide acceptance greeted the view that Lowth is vital for Smart's composition. However, Robert P. Fitzgerald, "The Form of Christopher Smart's *Jubilate Agno*," *Studies in English Literature, 1500–1900* 8, no. 3 (Summer 1968): 487–99, downplays this connection and argues that Smart may have begun "by creating a kind of prose original, in verses like those in the Psalter" (487).
74. Pfeiffer, "Teaching of Hebrew," 363.
75. Charles Parish, "Christopher Smart's Knowledge of Hebrew," *Studies in Philology* 58, no. 3 (July 1961): 516–32, 531–32 and n.
76. Quoted in Jasper and Prickett, *The Bible and Literature*, 150.
77. Weinbrot, *Britannia's Issue*, 470.
78. Kumbier, "Sound and Signification," 300.
79. Samuel Taylor Coleridge, *Biographia Literaria*, ed. James Engell and W. Jackson Bate, 2 vols. (Princeton: Princeton University Press, 1983), 1:304.
80. Weinbrot, *Britannia's Issue*, 459, 462.
81. *The Poems of Ossian*, translated by J. Macpherson, 2 vols. (London: A. Strahan and T. Cadell, 1796), 2:253–391, at 371n. In an earlier study of Lowth (see note 1 above), I stated that Macpherson attended some of Lowth's lectures, but this is almost certainly in error.
82. In contrast, for treatment of Lowth in the context of religious writing and the clerical hope for a more authentic Bible and English translation of it, see McKelvy, 39–55.
83. Frye, *Fearful Symmetry*, 184.
84. William A. Kumbier, "Blake's Epic Meter," *Studies in Romanticism* 17 (1978): 163–92, provides comprehensive discussion of the origins and development of Blake's epic meter. Kumbier notes (163–64 and n4) that George Saintsbury, John Hollander, and Alicia Ostriker cite the King James Bible, but he feels their analysis incomplete. Blake's metrical experiments are eclectic.
85. Weinbrot, *Britannia's Issue*, 474, 407.
86. Robert D. Richardson, Jr., *Emerson: The Mind on Fire* (Berkeley: University of California Press, 1995), 7, 11–13, 466.

87. Goldman, *God's Sacred Tongue*, 7.
88. Cyrus Gordon, "The Ten Lost Tribes" in Goldman, *Hebrew and the Bible in America*, 61–69, at 63.
89. Pfeiffer, "Teaching of Hebrew," 365. For Romantic prophecy, see also Murray Roston, *Prophet and Poet: The Bible and the Growth of Romanticism* (Evanston: Northwestern University Press, 1965) and Ian Balfour (who wrote previously on Northrop Frye), *The Rhetoric of Romantic Prophecy* (Stanford: Stanford University Press, 2002). For Blake, see David V. Erdman, *Prophet Against Empire: A Poet's Interpretation of the History of His Own Times* (Princeton: Princeton University Press, 3rd ed., 1977); also Sheila A. Spector, *Wonders Divine: The Development of Blake's Kabbalistic Myth* (Lewisburg, PA: Bucknell University Press, 2001); and Spector, *Glorious Incomprehensible: The Development of Blake's Kabbalistic Language* (Lewisburg, PA: Bucknell University Press, 2001), which treats Hebraic grammar and etymology in Blake's work. Chap. 1, "Contexts: The Languages of Eighteenth-Century England," 35–51, esp. 44–51, provides commentary regarding the study of Hebrew at that time.
90. For satire, the Bible, and prophecy, see Thomas Jemielity, *Satire and the Hebrew Prophets* (Louisville: Westminster/John Knox Press, 1992).
91. Frans De Bruyn, *The Literary Genres of Edmund Burke: The Political Uses of Literary Form* (Oxford: Clarendon Press, 1996), at 296, quotes from John G. Gunnell's *Political Theory: Tradition and Interpretation* (Cambridge, MA: Harvard University Press, 1979), 143. The observation concerning Burke on Judas Maccabaeus is at De Bruyn, 289–90.
92. For example, see *The Selected Political Writings of John Locke*, ed. Paul E. Sigmund (New York: W. W. Norton, 2005), xvi–xvii, 6–16, 21, 26–27, 39, 44, and 64–65 and 124, which appeal to Jepthah.
93. Eric Nelson, *The Hebrew Republic: Jewish Sources and the Transformation of European Political Thought* (Cambridge, MA: Harvard University Press, 2010), 2, 6, 138. I cannot here do justice to Nelson's detailed and convincing scholarship.
94. Nelson, *The Hebrew Republic*, 124, 123, 129; see also 21–26, 53–56, 123–30 and nn.
95. Nathan R. Perl-Rosenthal, "The 'divine right of republics': Hebraic Republicanism and the Debate over Kingless Government in Revolutionary America," *William & Mary Quarterly* Third Series 66, no. 3 (July 2009): 535–64, at 536. Perl-Rosenthal expresses indebtedness to scholars who published in specialized journals of Hebrew studies and history. He includes Eric Nelson, who published earlier on the subject in journal form (536n2 and 538n3).
96. Perl-Rosenthal, "The 'divine right,'" 537.
97. Peiffer, "Teaching of Hebrew," 364–65.
98. For a map giving a sample of biblical place names in the northeastern United States, see Goldman, *God's Sacred Tongue*, 8.

99. Robert Middlekauff, *The Mathers: Three Generations of Puritan Intellectuals, 1596–1728* (New York: Oxford University Press, 1971), 107–112.
100. Herman Melville, *White-Jacket, or, The World in a Man-of-War*, ed. A. R. Humphreys (London: Oxford University Press, 1966), 158.
101. Perl-Rosenthal, "The 'divine right,'" 537; see also 562–63.
102. *Harvard Divinity School Bulletin* 39, no. 14 (April 14, 1942): 45–54. A separate copy held in the Harvard University Archives gives its own pagination as 1–10.
103. For civic virtue and the specific form of government as distinct elements in sustaining a republic, see Perl-Rosenthal, 537, 542, 562–63 and nn.
104. John Coleridge, *Miscellaneous Dissertations Arising from the XVIIth and XVIIIth Chapters of the Book of Judges* (London: printed for the author, 1768), 113, 123. The volume contains an extensive list of subscribers.
105. John Coleridge, "Sermon preached at Ottery St. Mary, Devon, December 13th, 1776," 12, 5–11.
106. Samuel Taylor Coleridge, *Lay Sermons*, ed. R. J. White (Princeton: Princeton University Press, 1972), 128.
107. Coleridge, *Lay Sermons*, xxx and n.
108. Bernard M. Levinson and Joshua A. Berman, "The King James Bible at 400: Scripture, Statecraft, and the American Founding," 8, 10–11; Donald S. Lutz, *A Preface to American Political Theory* (Lawrence: University Press of Kansas, 1992), 12; see also Lutz, *The Origins of American Constitutionalism* (Baton Rouge: Louisiana State University Press, 1988), 140; Levinson, *"The Right Chorale": Studies in Biblical Law and Interpretation* (Tübingen: Mohr Siebeck, 2008), 1–6, 85–86; Levinson, "The First Constitution: Rethinking the Origins of the Rule of Law and Separation of Powers in Light of Deuteronomy," *Cardozo Law Review* 27:4 (February 2006): 1853–88.
109. Quoted by Shalev, *American Zion*, 82. In chap. 1, "'The Jewish Cincinnatus': Biblical Republicanism in the Age of the American Revolution," 15–49, Shalev discusses numerous examples of the Old Testament shaping the polity of the new republic. He later notes, "After the Civil War, the American Zion would become first and foremost a black Zion" (184).
110. John Coleridge, "Sermon," 7, 12.
111. Coleridge, *Lay Sermons*, 229–30; for Coleridge reaffirming in 1833 a view of the Bible, history, and national history as interrelated, see *Notebooks*, ed. Kathleen Coburn, 5 vols. (Princeton: Princeton University Press, 1957–2002), 5:6729.
112. Charles Berlin, *Harvard Judaica: A History and Description of the Judaica Collection in the Harvard College Library* (Cambridge, MA: Harvard College Library, 2004), 9. Berlin notes that the fire of 1764

destroyed the early Judaica collection, which, until the 1890s, then experienced "limited growth" (10).
113. For detailed treatment of Monis and Sewall, see Goldman, *God's Sacred Tongue*, chap. 2, "A Tale of Two Teachers: Hebrew at Harvard," 31–51; and Thomas J. Siegel, "Professor Stephen Sewall and the Transformation of Hebrew at Harvard," in Goldman, *Hebrew and the Bible in America*, 228–45. Siegel states, "Almost from the beginning . . . the tutors had difficulty convincing the students that the study of Hebrew was as important as that of Latin and Greek" (229); that the Corporation decided to hire Monis only as instructor (230); that Sewall, appointed in 1761 to teach Hebrew, was installed as Hancock Professor in 1765; and that Sewall treated Lowth in one of his lectures (234 and n28).
114. Pfeiffer, "Teaching of Hebrew," 366, 370.
115. Lowth, *Lectures*, 70. For Lowth and romantic prophecy, see Ian Balfour, *The Rhetoric of Romantic Prophecy* (Stanford: Stanford University Press, 2002), chap. 3, "Robert Lowth and the Temporality of Prophetic Rhetoric," 55–81, esp. 55, 67, 69, 77, 79. Lowth, according to Balfour, concentrated on the *mashal*, the figurative, the non-literal (69). David Stern, *Parables in Midrash: Narrative and Exegesis in Rabbinic Literature* (Cambridge, MA: Harvard University Press, 1991), notes that *mashal* "in the Bible," refers to language "used in a special way: to figures of speech, like metaphors or similes, to proverbs, and to allegories—though never . . . to the specific narrative forms that we call parables or fables" (9).
116. See James Engell, "Wordsworth, William" in *The Virgil Encyclopedia*, ed. Richard F. Thomas and Jan M. Ziolkowski, 3 vols. (John Wiley & Sons, 2014), 3:1397–99. That entry cites and is deeply indebted to the work of Bruce Graver.
117. Prickett, "Biblical and Literary Criticism," 27–28.
118. Thomas Gibbons, *Rhetoric; Or a View of Its Principal Tropes and Figures* (London: J. and W. Oliver, 1767), 207–8, 210.
119. Coleridge, *Biographia Literaria*, 2:57.
120. Samuel Taylor Coleridge, *Collected Letters*, ed. Earl Leslie Griggs, 6 vols. (Oxford: Clarendon Press, 1956–71), 2:865–66; see also *Biographia Literaria* 1:168–70, 295, 303.
121. For discussion and references, see Engell, *The Committed Word*, 138; also *Forming the Critical Mind: Dryden to Coleridge* (Cambridge, MA: Harvard University Press, 1989), 95–96.
122. Hyman Hurwitz, *Hebrew Tales Selected and Translated from the Writings of the Ancient Hebrew Sages* (New York: Spalding & Shepard, 1847), iv. The *Tales* first appeared in 1826 in London with Hurwitz's Preface complimenting Coleridge. See *The Friend*, ed. Barbara E. Rooke, 2 vols. (Princeton: Princeton University Press, 1969), 1:370n, and 370–73 for the three Moral Tales. Coleridge translated

two Hebrew dirges and hymns by Hurwitz, one for the funeral of Princess Charlotte (1817), a second for the funeral of George III (1820). T. Boosey & Sons published the second translation the year before that firm published the Faustus translation now attributed to Coleridge. Regarding Hurwitz's dirges, especially for Charlotte, see Karen Weisman, "Mourning, Translation, Pastoral: Hyman Hurwitz and Literary Authority" in *Romanticism/Judaica: A Convergence of Cultures*, ed. Sheila A. Spector (Burlington, VT: Ashgate, 2011), 45–55. Coleridge also translated Hurwitz's "Israel's Lament." For broad assessment, see Chris Rubinstein, "Coleridge and Jews," *The Coleridge Bulletin* n.s. 24 (Winter 2004): 91–96; also essays constituting Part IV, "Coda: Coleridge and Judaica," in *The Jews and British Romanticism: Politics, Religion, Culture*, ed. Sheila A. Spector (New York: Palgrave Macmillan, 2005), 233–97. For Hurwitz aiding Coleridge to strengthen his knowledge of Hebrew, see Ewan James Jones, *Coleridge and the Philosophy of Poetic Form* (Cambridge: Cambridge University Press, 2014), 161–66.
123. Coleridge, *Collected Letters*, 6:668, 709–10, 772, 775.
124. Ewan James Jones, "Coleridge, Hyman Hurwitz, and Hebrew Poetics," *The Coleridge Bulletin* n.s. 40 (Winter 2012): 59–68, at 68, 61–63.
125. See Sheila A. Spector, *Byron and the Jews* (Detroit: Wayne State University Press, 2010); also Gordon K. Thomas, "Finest Orientalism, Western Sentimentalism, Proto-Zionism: The Muses of Byron's *Hebrew Melodies*" in *Prism(s)* 1993 1:51–66; and Toby R. Benis, "Byron's *Hebrew Melodies* and the Musical Nation" in Spector, *Romanticism/Judaica*, 31–44.
126. Goldman, *God's Sacred Tongue*, 57, 10.
127. Ibid., 140, 201.
128. Goldman, "Biblical Hebrew in Colonial America," 205–6.
129. Goldman, *God's Sacred Tongue*, 165–66. Goldman quotes from Grimké's *Reflections on the Character and Objects of All Science and Literature* (1831).
130. Henry Wadsworth Longfellow, *The Courtship of Miles Standish and Other Poems* (Boston: Ticknor and Fields, 1864), 150–54.
131. For the absence of Jews when Longfellow visited Newport, see Lee Levinger, *A History of the Jews in the United States* (New York: Union of American Hebrew Congregations, 2007, 1st ed. Cincinnati, 1930), 74. The Touro Synagogue states on its official website, "Through the first half of the nineteenth century . . . the Jews of Newport dispersed. . . . The end of the nineteenth century ushered in new life for the Touro Synagogue with the arrival of eastern European Jews to the United States." Accessed April 27, 2017, http://www.tourosynagogue.org/index.php/history-learning/synagogue-history.

Touro Synagogue of Congregation Jeshuat Israel (Newport: The Society of Friends of the Touro Synagogue, 1948; rpt. and enlg., 1972), 12; Henry Wadsworth Longfellow Dana was one contributor to that collection of essays.

132. *Jewish American Poetry: Poems, Commentary, and Reflections*, ed. Jonathan N. Barron and Eric Murphy Selinger (Hanover, NH: Brandeis University Press, 2000), editors' Introduction, 6–7, where they say, "With Longfellow's representation of the Jews, the story of the Jewish presence in American poetry properly begins" (6).

133. For discussion of the paired Newport poems of Longfellow and Lazarus, see Max Cavitch, "Emma Lazarus and the Golem of Liberty" in *The Traffic in Poems: Nineteenth-Century Poetry and Transatlantic Exchange*, ed. Meredith L. McGill (New Brunswick: Rutgers University Press, 2008), 97–122, esp. 105–10; Barron and Selinger, *Jewish American Poetry*, 6–7; Christopher Benfy, *American Audacity: Literary Essays North and South* (Ann Arbor: University of Michigan Press, 2009), 61–66; Esther Schor, *Emma Lazarus* (New York: Schocken, 2006), 16–20; George Bornstein, *The Colors of Zion: Blacks, Jews, and Irish from 1845 to 1945* (Cambridge, MA: Harvard University Press, 2011), 82–83.

134. Emma Lazarus, *Admetus and Other Poems* (Cambridge, MA: Hurd and Houghton, Riverside Press, 1871), 160–62, at 162, 160 (ll. 5–8, 41, 43–44).

135. Quoted by Cavitch, "Emma Lazarus and the Golem of Liberty," 105, and Benfy, *American Audacity*, 61.

136. Quoted by Bornstein, *The Colors of Zion*, 84.

137. Reprinted from the *Publications of the American Jewish Historical Society* 38, no. 4 (June 1949): 261–87.

138. Barron and Selinger, *Jewish American Poetry*, 6.

139. David Bjelajac, "Thomas Cole's *Oxbow* and the American Zion Divided," *American Art* 20, no. 1 (Spring 2006): 60–83, at 74–75. Bjelajac's larger argument (69–81), on which I draw heavily (though first introduced to the painting and its Hebrew significance by Professors Samantha Harvey and Rochelle Johnson), considers Cole's painting as divided between dark and light, a struggle for a new Zion possibly encompassing race, industrialism, and swift changes in the landscape, with an allusion to John Bunyan's *The Holy War, made by Shaddai upon Diabolus* (1682). The railroad and industry were about to arrive—industry had already arrived—in the Connecticut valley.

140. See Daniel Sanjiv Roberts, "'Mix(ing) a Little with Alien Natures': Biblical Orientalism in De Quincey," in *Thomas De Quincey: New Theoretical and Critical Directions*, ed. Robert Morrison and Daniel S. Roberts (New York: Routledge, 2008), 19–44, esp. 33–35.

141. Quoted by Roberts, "'Mix(ing) a Little with Alien Natures,'" 34. The quotation is from De Quincey's manuscript "Greek and Hebrew" in the Berg Collection, New York Public Library. *The Works of Thomas De Quincey*, ed. Grevel Lindop et al., 21 vols. (London: Pickering & Chatto, 2000), vol. 20, ed. Barry Symonds et al., 20:350.
142. Roberts, "'Mix(ing) a Little with Alien Natures,'" 34.
143. Thomas Carlyle, *On Heroes, Hero-Worship, and the Heroic in History*, ed. Carl Niemeyer (Lincoln: University of Nebraska Press, 1966), 49. Interestingly, Carlyle introduces his praise by stating that because of its "noble universality, different from noble patriotism or sectarianism," as a result, "One feels, indeed, as if it were not Hebrew" (49).
144. Matthew Arnold, Part IV of *Culture and Anarchy: An Essay in Political and Social Criticism* (London: Smith, Elder, 1869), 142–64, at 142, 145, 147, 159.
145. Miriam Leonard, "Matthew Arnold in Zion: Hebrews, Hellenes, Aryans, and Semites," chap. 3 in *Socrates and the Jews: Hebraism and Hellenism from Moses Mendelssohn to Sigmund Freud* (Chicago: University of Chicago Press, 2012), 105–38, at 136. Her discussion is illuminating, though one conclusion seems strained: "For Arnold, Hebraism will always be not only a false start but a 'contravention' of nature" (129). She seems to overlook Arnold's remarks on Hebraism and Hellenism in the Preface to *Culture and Anarchy*.
146. Leonard, "Matthew Arnold in Zion," 136–37.
147. Arnold, *Culture and Anarchy*, 163, 147, 144.
148. Ibid., 157, 158, lviii–lx.
149. Ibid., xxi, xviii–xix, xvi, lix.
150. Thomas Burnett Smart, *The Bibliography of Matthew Arnold* (London: J. Davy & Sons, the Dryden Press, 1892), 37–38. A "fourth edition" of 1875 was printed at Cambridge by C. J. Clay. The large-type edition with a slightly different title, *Isaiah XL-LXVI with the Shorter Prophecies Allied to it*, with its own Introduction, was likewise issued in 1875 but printed at Oxford by E. Pickard Hall and J. H. Stacy. The publisher for both is listed as Macmillan (London). Arnold's remark about the book having "been found useful by many who are not school-children" is in his Introduction to the Oxford printing, 2.
151. Matthew Arnold, arr. and ed., *The Great Prophecy of Israel's Restoration: Isaiah, chapters 40–66* (London: Macmillan, 1872), xiii, vii.
152. Ibid., xxvi–xxvii.
153. Ibid., xxxiv.
154. Elisa New, "Bible Leaves! Bible Leaves! Hellenism and Hebraism in Melville's *Moby-Dick*," *Poetics Today* 19, no. 2 (Summer 1998): 281–303, 281. For detailed study of *Moby-Dick* and the Hebrew Bible, see Ilana Pardes, *Melville's Bibles* (Berkeley: University of California Press, 2008); also indispensable is Nathalia Wright, *Melville's*

Use of the Bible, with a New Appendix by the Author (New York: Octagon Books, 1980 [1st ed. Duke University Press,1949]).

155. Throughout *Melville's Bibles*, its chapters themselves structured by Job, Jonah, Ishmael, Ahab, and Rachel, Pardes stresses the shifting nature of Melville's Hebraic characters in *Moby-Dick*, their complexity and allusiveness.

156. Wright, *Melville's Use*, pays close attention to stylistic features throughout all of Melville's writing that ally it with Hebrew poetry and prose, 136–72, esp. 147–72.

157. I am indebted here to Andrew Delbanco, *Herman Melville: His World and Work* (New York: Alfred A. Knopf, 2005), 279–87, at 287.

158. Thomas L. Thompson, "Clarel, Jonah, and the Whale: A Question Concerning Rachel's Missing Children," *Leviathan: A Journal of Melville Studies* 12, no. 1 (March 2010): 53–65.

159. Vincent S. Kenny, *Herman Melville's* Clarel: *A Spiritual Autobiography* (Hamden, CT: Archon Books, 1973), 123.

160. Shirley M. Dettlaff, "Ionian Form and Esau's Waste: Melville's View of Art in *Clarel*," *American Literature* 54, no. 2 (May 1982): 212–28.

161. Peter Norberg, "Finding an Audience for *Clarel* in Matthew Arnold's *Essays in Criticism*," *Leviathan: A Journal of Melville Studies* 6, no. 1 (March 2004): 35–54; Shirley M. Dettlaff, "Counter Natures in Mankind: Hebraism and Hellenism in *Clarel*," in *Melville's Evermoving Dawn: Centennial Essays*, ed. John Bryant and Robert Milder (Kent, OH: Kent State University Press, 1997), 192–221.

162. *The Statutes of the Albany Academy, Passed December 5th, 1816, and Revised, September 14th, 1819* (Albany: Websters and Skinners, 1819), 12. Only the New Testament was assigned at the Academy (11). Melville attended the Academy in the early and mid-1830s on two different occasions and may have acquired some Latin there. Hebrew was not taught.

163. Henry D. Thoreau, *Excursions*, ed. Joseph J. Moldenhauer (Princeton: Princeton University Press, 2007), 201, 202.

164. Henry D. Thoreau, *Walden*, ed. J. Lyndon Shanley (Princeton: Princeton University Press, 1971), 106. I am indebted to Natasha Shabat for drawing attention to Thoreau's comments on Hebrew. She presented "Seeing the Divine in Nature: Discovering the Aleph Bet of Walden Pond" at the Thoreau Society Annual Gathering, July 11, 2013. Shabat connected Hebrew letters and names to the spirit of Thoreau as he found the divine in both words and natural phenomena, the two as closely related signs or presences.

165. Ralph Waldo Emerson, *An Address Delivered Before the Senior Class in Divinity College, Cambridge, Sunday Evening, 15 July, 1838* (Boston: James Munroe and Company, 1838), 31. The copy of this

edition inscribed to Thoreau is held in the Houghton Library Harry Elkins Widener Collection HEW 5.6.2, Harvard University.

166. John Livingston Lowes, "The Noblest Monument of English Prose," *Of Reading Books: Four Essays* (London: Constable, 1930), 53, 55. First delivered as a lecture February 19, 1923, and published in the *Harvard Alumni Bulletin* 25, no. 21 (February 22, 1923): 623–33. Larry Benson and W. Jackson Bate, "John Livingston Lowes," *American National Biography Online*, accessed April 27, 2017, http://www.anb.org/articles/16/16-01030.html (February 2000).

167. Cited from the last paragraph of Lowes's lecture (*Harvard Alumni Bulletin*, 633), which does not appear in the essay in book form seven years later. For Addison's view of Hebrew and English, see Weinbrot, *Britannia's Issue*, 429.

168. Lowes, in *Alumni Bulletin*, 631.

169. Matthew Arnold, *Isaiah XL–LXVI with the Shorter Prophecies Allied to It* (London: Macmillan, 1875), Introduction, 1.

170. Charles D. Cleveland, *A Compendium of English Literature, Chronologically Arranged, from Sir John Mandeville to William Cooper* (New York: A. S. Barnes, 1872), 674.

171. Hildesheim: Georg Olms, 1969, with an introduction by Vincent Freimarck.

172. London: Routledge/Thoemmes, 1995.

173. Kessinger Publishing, 2004.

174. Murray Roston, *Prophet and Poet: The Bible and the Growth of Romanticism* (Evanston: Northwestern University Press, 1965); Stephen Prickett, "Poetry and Prophecy: Bishop Lowth and the Hebrew Scriptures in Eighteenth-Century England," in *Images of Belief in Literature*, ed. David Jasper (New York: St. Martin's Press, 1984), 81–103; also Prickett, *Words and the Word*, with pages dispersed and numerous.

175. The President's Report from 1890–91 cites the creation of new "divisions," including "Semitic Languages and History" and "Ancient Languages" (see http://pds.lib.harvard.edu/pds/view/2574409?n=2325&s=4&printThumbnails=no, esp. 44 of the document. This description matches a vote taken by the Faculty of Arts and Sciences on May 5, 1891. My thanks to Susan Lively, current Secretary of the Faculty, for providing this research.

176. Leonard, "Matthew Arnold in Zion," 114.

177. See Goldman, *God's Sacred Tongue*, chap. 14, "A Long Affair: Edmund Wilson on Judaism, the Hebrew Language, and the American Jewish Community," 275–89.

178. Dwight MacDonald, "The Slave of Hebrew," *The New Yorker* (November 28, 1959): 57ff.

179. Ruth R. Wisse, *The Modern Jewish Canon: A Journey Through Language and Culture* (New York: The Free Press, 2000), 348.

180. Weinbrot, *Britannia's Issue*, 403–74.

181. Sheila A. Spector, ed., *British Romanticism and the Jews: History, Culture, Literature* (New York: Palgrave Macmillan, 2002). Spector's Introduction, 1–16, is helpful and laments the absence of the study of Jews and British Romanticism, a lack that her own volumes, authored and edited, have done much to redress.
182. Spector, *The Jews and British Romanticism* (see n122 above).
183. Spector, *Byron and the Jews*, 1. Spector provides excellent commentary on Byron's and the composer Isaac Nathan's *Hebrew Melodies*, 2, 19–22, 35–53.
184. Spector, *Romanticism/Judaica* (see n122 above).

Bibliography

Abrams, M. H. *The Mirror and the Lamp: Romantic Theory and the Critical Tradition*. Oxford: Oxford University Press, 1953.

Alter, Robert. *Pen of Iron: American Prose and the King James Bible*. Princeton: Princeton University Press, 2010.

Arnold, Matthew. *Culture and Anarchy: An Essay in Political and Social Criticism*. London: Smith, Elder, 1869.

———, arr. and ed. *The Great Prophecy of Israel's Restoration: Isaiah, chapters 40–66*. London: Macmillan, 1872.

Balfour, Ian. *The Rhetoric of Romantic Prophecy*. Stanford: Stanford University Press, 2002.

Barron, Jonathan N., and Eric Murphy Selinger, eds. *Jewish American Poetry: Poems, Commentary, and Reflections*. Hanover, NH: Brandeis University Press, 2000.

Baym, Max I. "Emma Lazarus and Emerson." *Publications of the American Jewish Historical Society* 38, no. 4 (June 1949): 261–87.

Bjelajac, David. "Thomas Cole's *Oxbow* and the American Zion Divided." *American Art* 20, no. 1 (Spring 2006): 60–83.

Benfy, Christopher. *American Audacity: Literary Essays North and South*. Ann Arbor: University of Michigan Press, 2009.

Benis, Toby R. "Byron's *Hebrew Melodies* and the Musical Nation." In *Romanticism/Judaica: A Convergence of Cultures*, edited by Shelia A. Spector, 31–44. Burlington, VT: Ashgate, 2011.

Berlin, Charles. *Harvard Judaica: A History and Description of the Judaica Collection in the Harvard College Library*. Cambridge, MA: Harvard College Library, 2004.

Bond, W. H. "Christopher Smart's *Jubilate Agno*." *Harvard Library Bulletin* 4, no. 1 (Winter 1950): 34–52.

Bornstein, George. *The Colors of Zion: Blacks, Jews, and Irish from 1845 to 1945*. Cambridge, MA: Harvard University Press, 2011.

Bourne, H. R. Fox. *The Life of John Locke*, 2 vols. New York: Harper & Brothers, 1876.

Broadie, Alexander. *The Tradition of Scottish Philosophy: A New Perspective on the Enlightenment.* Edinburgh: Polygon, 1990.

Burke, Edmund. *A Philosophical Enquiry into the Origin of Our Ideas of the Sublime and Beautiful*, 2nd ed. London: R. and J. Dodsley, 1759.

Carlyle, Thomas. *On Heroes, Hero-Worship, and the Heroic in History.* Edited by Carl Niemeyer. Lincoln: University of Nebraska Press, 1966.

Cavitch, Max. "Emma Lazarus and the Golem of Liberty." In *The Traffic in Poems: Nineteenth-Century Poetry and Transatlantic Exchange*, edited by Meredith L. McGill, 97–122. New Brunswick: Rutgers University Press, 2008.

Chiel, Arthur A. "Ezra Stiles and the Jews: A Study in Ambivalence." In *Hebrew and the Bible in America: The First Two Centuries*, edited by Shalom Goldman, 156–67. Hanover, NH: University Press of New England [for] Brandeis University Press and Dartmouth College, 1993.

Clarke, M. L. *Classical Education in Britain, 1500–1900.* Cambridge: Cambridge University Press, 1959.

Cleveland, Charles D. *A Compendium of English Literature, Chronologically Arranged, from Sir John Mandeville to William Cooper.* New York: A. S. Barnes, 1872.

Coleridge, John. *Miscellaneous Dissertations Arising from the XVIIth and XVIIIth Chapters of the Book of Judges.* London: Printed for the author, 1768.

———. "Sermon preached at Ottery St. Mary, Devon, December 13th, 1776." London: Printed for the Author, 1777.

Coleridge, Samuel Taylor. *Collected Letters.* Edited by Earl Leslie Griggs. 6 vols. Oxford: Clarendon Press, 1956–71.

———. *Biographia Literaria.* Edited by James Engell and W. Jackson Bate. 2 vols. Princeton: Princeton University Press, 1983.

———. *The Friend.* Edited by Barbara E. Rooke. 2 vols. Princeton: Princeton University Press, 1969.

———. *Lay Sermons.* Edited by R. J. White. Princeton: Princeton University Press, 1972.

———. *Notebooks.* Edited by Kathleen Coburn. 5 vols. Princeton: Princeton University Press, 1957–2002.

———. *Table Talk.* Edited by Carl Woodring. 2 vols. Princeton: Princeton University Press, 1990.

Coudert, Allison P., and Jeffrey S. Shoulson, eds. *Hebraica Veritas? Christian Hebraists and the Study of Judaism in Early Modern Europe.* Philadelphia: University of Pennsylvania Press, 2004.

De Bruyn, Frans. *The Literary Genres of Edmund Burke: The Political Uses of Literary Form.* Oxford: Clarendon Press, 1996.

Delbanco, Andrew. *Herman Melville: His World and Work.* New York: Alfred A. Knopf, 2005.

Dennis, John. *The Advancement and Reformation of Modern Poetry: A Critical Discourse in Two Parts.* London: Rich. Parker, 1701.

De Quincey, Thomas. *The Works of Thomas De Quincey*. Edited by Grevel Lindop et al. 21 vols. London: Pickering & Chatto, 2000.

Dettlaff, Shirley M. "Counter Natures in Mankind: Hebraism and Hellenism in *Clarel*." In *Melville's Evermoving Dawn: Centennial Essays*, edited by John Bryant and Robert Milder, 192–221. Kent, OH: Kent State University Press, 1997.

———. "Ionian Form and Esau's Waste: Melville's View of Art in *Clarel*." *American Literature* 54, no. 2 (May 1982): 212–28.

Elledge, Paul. *Lord Byron at Harrow School: Speaking Out, Talking Back, Acting Up, Bowing Out*. Baltimore: Johns Hopkins University Press, 2000.

Engell, James. *The Committed Word: Literature and Public Values*. University Park: Pennsylvania State University Press, 1999.

———. *Forming the Critical Mind: Dryden to Coleridge*. Cambridge, MA: Harvard University Press, 1989.

Emerson, Ralph Waldo. *An Address Delivered Before the Senior Class in Divinity College, Cambridge, Sunday Evening, 15 July, 1838*. Boston: James Munroe and Company, 1838.

Erdman, David V. *Prophet Against Empire: A Poet's Interpretation of the History of His Own Times*, 3rd ed. Princeton: Princeton University Press, 1977.

Fitzgerald, Robert P. "The Form of Christopher Smart's *Jubilate Agno*." *Studies in English Literature, 1500–1900* 8, no. 3 (Summer 1968): 487–99.

Frye, Northrop. *Fearful Symmetry: A Study of William Blake*. Princeton: Princeton University Press, 1947.

Geoffrey of Monmouth. *The History of the Kings of Britain: An Edition and Translation of* De gestis Britonum (Historia regum Britanniae). Edited by Michael D. Reeve. Translated by Neil Wright. Woodbridge, UK and Rochester, NY: Boydell Press, 2007.

Gibbons, Thomas. *Rhetoric; Or a View of Its Principal Tropes and Figures*. London: J. and W. Oliver, 1767.

Goldman, Shalom. "Biblical Hebrew in Colonial America: The Case of Dartmouth." In *Hebrew and the Bible in America: The First Two Centuries*, edited by Shalom Goldman, 201–8. Hanover, NH: University Press of New England [for] Brandeis University Press and Dartmouth College, 1993.

———. *God's Sacred Tongue: Hebrew and the American Imagination*. Chapel Hill: University of North Carolina Press, 2004.

———, ed. *Hebrew and the Bible in America: The First Two Centuries*. Hanover, NH: University Press of New England [for] Brandeis University Press and Dartmouth College, 1993.

Gordon, Cyrus. "The Ten Lost Tribes." In *Hebrew and the Bible in America: The First Two Centuries*, edited by Shalom Goldman, 61–69. Hanover, NH: University Press of New England [for] Brandeis University Press and Dartmouth College, 1993.

Gray, Erik. "Come Be My Love: The Song of Songs, *Paradise Lost*, and the Tradition of the Invitation Poem." *PMLA* 128, no. 2 (March 2013): 370–85.

Green, Ian. *Humanism and Protestantism in Early Modern English Education*. Farnham: Ashgate, 2009.

Gutstein, Morris A. *The Story of the Jews of Newport: Two and a Half Centuries of Judaism, 1658–1908*. New York: Bloch, 1936.

Gzella, Holger. "Expansion of the Linguistic Context of the Hebrew Bible." In *Hebrew Bible / Old Testament: The History of Its Interpretation III/I: From Modernism to Post Modernism*, edited by Magne Sæbø, 134–67. Göttingen: Vandenhoeck and Ruprecht, 2012.

Hartman, Geoffrey H. *The Fate of Reading*. Chicago: University of Chicago Press, 1975.

Hertzberg, Arthur. "The New England Puritans and the Jews." In *Hebrew and the Bible in America: The First Two Centuries*, edited by Shalom Goldman, 105–21. Hanover, NH: University Press of New England [for] Brandeis University Press and Dartmouth College, 1993.

Hickey, Raymond. "Attitudes and Concerns in Eighteenth-Century English." In *Eighteenth-Century English: Ideology and Change*, edited by Raymond Hickey, Studies in English Language, 1–20. Cambridge: Cambridge University Press, 2010.

Hogwood, Christopher. *Handel*. London: Thames and Hudson, 1984.

Ireland, Corydon. "Harvard's Indian College Poet." *Harvard Gazette*, September 16, 2013. Accessed April 27, 2017. http://news.harvard.edu/gazette/story/2013/09/harvards-indian-college-poet/.

Jemielity, Thomas. *Satire and the Hebrew Prophets*. Louisville: Westminster/John Knox Press, 1992.

Jewish Encyclopedia. Edited by Cyrus Adler, Isidore Singer et al. 1906. Reprint, New York: Ktav, 1964.

Jones, Charles W. "Milton's 'Brief Epic.'" *Studies in Philology* 44, no. 2 (April 1947): 209–27.

Jones, Ewan James. *Coleridge and the Philosophy of Poetic Form*. Cambridge: Cambridge University Press, 2014.

Kabakoff, Jacob. "The Use of Hebrew by American Jews During the Colonial Period." In *Hebrew and the Bible in America: The First Two Centuries*, edited by Shalom Goldman, 191–97. Hanover, NH: University Press of New England [for] Brandeis University Press and Dartmouth College, 1993.

Kenny, Vincent S. *Herman Melville's* Clarel: *A Spiritual Autobiography*. Hamden, CT: Archon Books, 1973.

Kohut, George Alexander. *Ezra Stiles and the Jews: Selected Passages from his Literary Diary Concerning Jews and Judaism*. New York: Philip Cowen, 1902.

Kugel, James L. *The Idea of Biblical Poetry: Parallelism and Its History*. New Haven: Yale University Press, 1981.

Kumbier, William A. "Blake's Epic Meter." *Studies in Romanticism* 17, no. 2 (1978): 163–92.

———. "Sound and Signification in Christopher Smart's *Jubilate Agno*." *Texas Studies in Literature and Language* 24, no. 3 (Fall 1982): 293–312.

Lazarus, Emma. *Admetus and Other Poems*. Cambridge, MA: Hurd and Houghton, Riverside Press, 1871.

Levinger, Lee. *A History of the Jews in the United States*. New York: Union of American Hebrew Congregations, 2007 [1st ed. Cincinnati, 1930].

Leonard, Miriam. *Socrates and the Jews: Hellenism and Hebraism from Moses Mendelssohn to Sigmund Freud*. Chicago: University of Chicago Press, 2012.

Levinson, Bernard M. "The First Constitution: Rethinking the Origins of the Rule of Law and Separation of Powers in Light of Deuteronomy." *Cardozo Law Review* 27, no. 4 (February 2006): 1853–88.

———. *"The Right Chorale": Studies in Biblical Law and Interpretation*. Tübingen: Mohr Siebeck, 2008.

Levinson, Bernard M., and Joshua A. Berman, "The King James Bible at 400: Scripture, Statecraft, and the American Founding." *The History Channel Magazine* (November 2010): 1–11.

Locke, John. *Selected Political Writings of John Locke*. Edited by Paul E. Sigmund. New York: W. W. Norton, 2005.

Long, George, ed. *The Penny Cyclopaedia of the Society for the Diffusion of Useful Knowledge*. London: Charles Knight, 1839.

Longfellow, Henry Wadsworth. *The Courtship of Miles Standish and Other Poems*. Boston: Ticknor and Fields, 1864.

Lowes, John Livingston. "The Noblest Monument of English Prose." In *Of Reading Books: Four Essays*, 45–77. London: Constable, 1930. Originally delivered as a lecture February 19, 1923, and published in the *Harvard Alumni Bulletin* 25, no. 21 (February 22, 1923): 623–33.

Lowth, Robert. *Lectures on the Sacred Poetry of the Hebrews*. Translated by G[eorge]. Gregory. Edited by Calvin Stowe. Boston: Crocker & Brewster, 1829.

Lutz, Donald S. *The Origins of American Constitutionalism*. Baton Rouge: Louisiana State University Press, 1988.

———. *A Preface to American Political Theory*. Lawrence: University Press of Kansas, 1992.

MacDonald, Dwight. "The Slave of Hebrew." *The New Yorker* (November 28, 1959): 57ff.

Macpherson, James. *Fragments of Ancient Poetry, Collected in the Highlands of Scotland*. Edinburgh: G. Hamilton and J. Balfour, 1760.

———, trans. *The Poems of Ossian*. 2 vols. London: A. Strahan and T. Cadell, 1796.

McKelvy, William R. *The English Cult of Literature: Devoted Readers 1774–1880*. Charlottesville: University of Virginia Press, 2006.

Martindale, Charles. "Milton's Classicism." In *The Oxford History of Classical Reception in English Literature, Volume 3: 1660–1790*, edited by David Hopkins and Charles Martindale, 53–90. Oxford: Oxford University Press, 2012.

Melville, Herman. *White-Jacket, or, The World in a Man-of-War*. Edited by A. R. Humphreys. London: Oxford University Press, 1966.

Merrick, James. *The Psalms, Translated or Paraphrased in English Verse*. Reading, 1765.

Middendorf, John H., ed. *The Lives of the Poets*. Vols. 21–23 of The Yale Edition of the Works of Samuel Johnson. New Haven: Yale University Press, 2010.

Middlekauff, Robert. *The Mathers: Three Generations of Puritan Intellectuals, 1596–1728*. New York: Oxford University Press, 1971.

Minchin, James George Cotton. *Our Public Schools: Their Influence on English History*. London: Swan Sonnenschein, 1901.

Monk, Samuel Holt. *The Sublime: A Study of Critical Theories in Eighteenth-Century England*. Ann Arbor: University of Michigan Press, 1935.

Morgan, Edmund S. *The Gentle Puritan, A Life of Ezra Stiles, 1727–1795*. New Haven: Yale University Press, 1962.

Nelson, Eric. *The Hebrew Republic: Jewish Sources and the Transformation of European Political Thought*. Cambridge, MA: Harvard University Press, 2010.

New, Elisa. "Bible Leaves! Bible Leaves! Hellenism and Hebraism in Melville's *Moby-Dick*." *Poetics Today* 19, no. 2 (Summer 1998): 281–303.

Norberg, Peter. "Finding an Audience for *Clarel* in Matthew Arnold's *Essays in Criticism*." *Leviathan: A Journal of Melville Studies* 6, no. 1 (March 2004): 35–54.

Pardes, Ilana. *Melville's Bibles*. Berkeley: University of California Press, 2008.

Parish, Charles. "Christopher Smart's Knowledge of Hebrew." *Studies in Philology* 58, no. 3 (July 1961): 516–32.

Perl-Rosenthal, Nathan R. "The 'divine right of republics': Hebraic Republicanism and the Debate over Kingless Government in Revolutionary America." *William and Mary Quarterly* 3rd ser., 66, no. 3 (July 2009): 535–64.

Pfeiffer, Robert H. "Hebrew and Greek Sense of Tragedy." In *The Joshua Bloch Memorial Volume. Studies in Booklore and History*, edited by Abraham Berger, Lawrence Marwick, and Isidore S. Meyer, 54–64. New York: New York Public Library, 1960.

———. "The Patriotism of Israel's Prophets." *Harvard Divinity School Bulletin* 39, no. 14 (April 14, 1942): 45–54.

———. "The Teaching of Hebrew in Colonial America." *The Jewish Quarterly Review* n.s. 45, no. 4 (April 1955): 363–73.

Pfeiffer, Rudolf. *History of Classical Scholarship 1300–1850*. Oxford: Clarendon Press, 1976.

Popkin, Richard H. "The Rise and Fall of the Jewish Indian Theory." In *Hebrew and the Bible in America: The First Two Centuries*, edited by Shalom Goldman, 70–90. Hanover, NH: University Press of New England [for] Brandeis University Press and Dartmouth College, 1993.
Prickett, Stephen. "Biblical and Literary Criticism." In *The Bible and Literature: A Reader*, edited by David Jasper and Stephen Prickett, 12–43. Oxford: Oxford University Press, 1999.
———. "Poetry and Prophecy: Bishop Lowth and the Hebrew Scriptures in Eighteenth-Century England." In *Images of Belief in Literature*, edited by David Jasper, 81–103. New York: St. Martin's Press, 1984.
———. *Words and the Word: Language, Poetics, and Biblical Interpretation*. Cambridge: Cambridge University Press, 1986.
Radford, C. A. Ralegh. *Glastonbury Abbey*. London: Pitkin, 1973.
Rannie, David Watson. *Oriel College*. University of Oxford College Histories. London: F. E. Robinson, 1900.
Reif, Stefan C. *Hebrew Manuscripts at Cambridge University Library: A Description and Introduction*. University of Cambridge Oriental Publications 52. Cambridge: Cambridge University Press, 1997.
Richardson, Robert D., Jr. *Emerson: The Mind on Fire*. Berkeley: University of California Press, 1995.
Roberts, Daniel Sanjiv. "'Mix(ing) a Little with Alien Natures': Biblical Orientalism in De Quincey." In *Thomas De Quincey: New Theoretical and Critical Directions*, edited by Robert Morrison and Daniel S. Roberts, 19–44. New York: Routledge, 2008.
Rosenblatt, Jason P. *Torah and Law in* Paradise Lost. Princeton: Princeton University Press, 1994.
Roston, Murray. *Prophet and Poet: The Bible and the Growth of Romanticism*. Evanston: Northwestern University Press, 1965.
Rowley, Richard, trans. *Historia Britonum: The History of the Britons*. Lampeter: Llanerch Press, 2005.
Rubinstein, Chris. "Coleridge and Jews." *The Coleridge Bulletin* n.s. 24 (Winter 2004): 91–96.
Schor, Esther. *Emma Lazarus*. New York: Schocken, 2006.
Shalev, Eran. *American Zion: the Old Testament as a Political Text from the Revolution to the Civil War*. New Haven: Yale University Press, 2013.
Shoulson, Jeffrey S. *Milton and the Rabbis: Hebraism, Hellenism, and Christianity*. New York: Columbia University Press, 2001.
Siegel, Thomas J. "Professor Stephen Sewall and the Transformation of Hebrew at Harvard." In *Hebrew and the Bible in America: The First Two Centuries*, edited by Shalom Goldman, 228–45. Hanover, NH: University Press of New England [for] Brandeis University Press and Dartmouth College, 1993.
Smart, Christopher. *Jubilate Agno*. Edited by W. H. Bond. Cambridge, MA: Harvard University Press, 1954.

Smart, Thomas Burnett. *The Bibliography of Matthew Arnold*. London: J. Davy & Sons, the Dryden Press, 1892.
Spector, Sheila A., ed. *British Romanticism and the Jews: History, Culture, Literature*. New York: Palgrave Macmillan, 2002.
———. *Byron and the Jews*. Detroit: Wayne State University Press, 2010.
———. *Glorious Incomprehensible: The Development of Blake's Kabbalistic Language*. Lewisburg: Bucknell University Press, 2001.
———, ed. *The Jews and British Romanticism: Politics, Religion, Culture*. New York: Palgrave Macmillan, 2005.
———, ed. *Romanticism/Judaica: A Convergence of Cultures*. Burlington, VT: Ashgate, 2011.
———. *Wonders Divine: The Development of Blake's Kabbalistic Myth*. Lewisburg: Bucknell University Press, 2001.
Stead, Henry. "Latin first and best," review of *Romans and Romantics*. *Times Literary Supplement* (June 28, 2013): 11.
Stein, Sarah B. "Translating the Bible to Raise the Fallen: John Dennis's Psalm 18." *Studies in Eighteenth-Century Culture* 43 (2014): 18–41.
Steiner, Prudence. "A Garden of Spices in New England: John Cotton's and Edward Taylor's Use of the Song of Songs." In *Allegory, Myth, and Symbol*, edited by Morton W. Bloomfield, 227–43. Cambridge, MA: Harvard University Press, 1981.
Stern, David. *Parables in Midrash: Narrative and Exegesis in Rabbinic Literature*. Cambridge, MA: Harvard University Press, 1991.
Stoddard, Roger E., comp., and David R. Whitesell, ed. *A Bibliographical Description of Books and Pamphlets of American Verse Printed from 1610 through 1820*. University Park: Pennsylvania State University Press for the Bibliographical Society of America, 2012.
Stollman, Samuel S. "Milton's Dichotomy of 'Judaism' and 'Hebraism.'" *PMLA* 89, no. 1 (January 1974): 105–12.
Thomas, Gordon K. "Finest Orientalism, Western Sentimentalism, Proto-Zionism: The Muses of Byron's *Hebrew Melodies*." *Prism(s)* (1993) 1:51–66.
Thompson, Thomas L. "Clarel, Jonah, and the Whale: A Question Concerning Rachel's Missing Children." *Leviathan: A Journal of Melville Studies* 12, no. 1 (March 2010): 53–65.
Thoreau, Henry D. *Excursions*. Edited by Joseph J. Moldenhauer. Princeton: Princeton University Press, 2007.
———. *Walden*. Edited by J. Lyndon Shanley. Princeton: Princeton University Press, 1971.
van Campen, Jan. *A Paraphrasis upon all the Psalmes of David, made by Johannes Campensis, reader of the Hebrue lecture in the universite of Louane [Louvain]*. London: Thomas Gybson, 1539.
Watson, J. R. "Merrick, James." *Oxford Dictionary of National Biography*.
Watts, Isaac. *Horae Lyricae, Poems, Chiefly of the Lyric kind, in Two Books*. London: Printed by S. and D. Bridge for John Lawrence, 1706.

———. *Reliquiae Juveniles: Miscellaneous Thoughts in Prose and Verse... Written chiefly in Younger Years*. London: Richard Ford and Richard Hett, 1734.

Weinbrot, Howard. *Britannia's Issue: The Rise of British Literature from Dryden to Ossian*. Cambridge: Cambridge University Press, 1993.

Weisman, Karen. "Mourning, Translation, Pastoral: Hyman Hurwitz and Literary Authority." In *Romanticism/Judaica: A Convergence of Cultures*, edited by Sheila A. Spector, 45–55. Burlington, VT: Ashgate, 2011.

Wisse, Ruth R. *The Modern Jewish Canon: A Journey Through Language and Culture*. New York: The Free Press, 2000.

Wright, Nathalia. *Melville's Use of the Bible, with a New Appendix by the Author*. New York: Octagon Books, 1980.

Contributor List

Edward Adams is Professor of English at Washington and Lee University. He is the author of *Liberal Epic: the Victorian Practice of History from Gibbon to Churchill* (University of Virginia Press), which won the Barbara and George Perkins Prize awarded by the International Society for the Study of Narrative (ISSN) to the most significant book published in the field in 2012. He is currently working on a study of Roman history, the decline and fall of the British aristocracy, and visions of national destiny from the early Victorian period through the 1930s, tentatively entitled *The School of Gibbon:* The Decline and Fall of the Roman Empire *and Anglo-American Historiography*.

Margaret Doody is John and Barbara Glynn Family Professor of Literature at the University of Notre Dame. She is the author of many articles on writers including Swift, Sterne, and Austen, and of *A Natural Passion: A Study of the Novels of Samuel Richardson* (Clarendon Press); *Frances Burney: The Life in the Works* (Rutgers University Press; rpt. Cambridge University Press); and *The Daring Muse: Augustan Poetry Reconsidered* (Cambridge University Press). Her interests have broadened in pursuit of the novel in its many developments as a form. She is best known internationally for *The True Story of the Novel* (Rutgers University Press); her most recent book, *Tropic of Venice* (University of Pennsylvania Press), treats that city as a text. She received an NEH fellowship in 2007 for a project tracing the roots of the Enlightenment in the Renaissance, dealing with thinkers such as Pico and Paracelsus on change, chaos, love, and progress. She is also the author of the "Aristotle, Detective" series.

James Engell is Gurney Professor of English and Professor of Comparative Literature, Harvard University. A former chair of the Department of English, of the Department of Comparative Literature, and of the Committee on Degrees in History and Literature at Harvard, he is the author of *The Creative Imagination: Enlightenment to Romanticism* (Harvard University Press), *Forming the Critical Mind: Dryden to Coleridge* (Harvard University Press), and *The Committed Word: Literature and Public Values* (Penn State University Press); coauthor with Anthony Dangerfield of the award-winning

Saving Higher Education in the Age of Money (University of Virginia Press); editor of *Johnson and His Age* (Harvard University Press), *Coleridge: The Early Family Letters* (Clarendon Press), and of *Samuel Taylor Coleridge: Poetry for Young People* (Sterling); coeditor with W. Jackson Bate of the *Biographia Literaria* (2 vols.) in *The Collected Works of Samuel Taylor Coleridge* (Princeton University Press / Routledge & Kegan Paul), with David Perkins of *Teaching Literature: What Is Needed Now* (Harvard University Press), and with Glenn Adelson, Brent Ranalli, and K. P. Van Anglen of *Environment: An Interdisciplinary Anthology* (Yale University Press). He contributed the entry for Wordsworth in *The Virgil Encyclopedia*. A member of the American Academy of Arts and Sciences, he recently served as a Senior Fellow at the National Humanities Center writing an intellectual and critical biography provisionally entitled *Coleridge: A Divided Self Reconciled*, as well as editing with Michael D. Raymond an illustrated and annotated edition of William Wordsworth's *The Prelude* (David R. Godine and Oxford University Press).

Christoph Irmscher is Provost Professor of English at Indiana University, Bloomington. He is the author of two books on Longfellow: *Public Poet, Private Man* (University of Massachusetts Press), and *Longfellow Redux* (University of Illinois Press). He has also written *The Poetics of Natural History: From John Bartram to William James* (Rutgers University Press), and *Masken der Moderne* (Königshausen und Neumann); he is coeditor with Alan Braddock of *A Keener Perception: Ecocritical Studies in American Art History* (University of Alabama Press). His biography *Louis Agassiz: Creator of American Science* was recently published by Houghton Mifflin Harcourt.

Mary Louise Kete, Associate Professor of English and Women's Studies at the University of Vermont, is the author of *Sentimental Collaborations: Mourning and Middle-class Identity in 19th Century America* (Duke University Press); and coeditor of the *McGraw-Hill Anthology of Women's Writing World Wide in English* (McGraw-Hill). She is currently coediting a special issue of the *C. L. R. James Journal* entitled "The Challenge of Lemuel Haynes"; and has finished a book manuscript entitled *American Ekphrasis: Slavery and the Problem of the Representative Self*.

John P. McWilliams, College Professor of the Humanities at Middlebury College, is the author of *Political Justice in a Republic: James Fenimore Cooper's America* (University of California Press), *Hawthorne, Melville and the American Character: A Looking-Glass Business* (Cambridge University Press), *The American Epic: Transforming A Genre* (Cambridge University Press), *The Last of the Mohicans: Civil Savagery and Savage Civility* (Twayne-Macmillan), and *New England's Crises and Cultural Memory* (Cambridge University Press); coauthor with Maxwell Bloomfield and Carl

Smith of *Law and American Literature* (Alfred A. Knopf); editor of James Fenimore Cooper's *The Last of the Mohicans* (Oxford University Press); and coeditor with George Dekker of *James Fenimore Cooper: the Critical Heritage* (Routledge & Kegan Paul).

Carl J. Richard is Professor of History in the University of Louisiana at Lafayette. He is the author of six books: *The Founders and the Classics: Greece, Rome, and the American Enlightenment* (Harvard University Press), *The Golden Age of the Classics in America: Greece, Rome, and the Antebellum United States* (Harvard University Press), *Why We're All Romans: The Roman Contribution to the Western World* (Rowman and Littlefield), *Greeks and Romans Bearing Gifts: How the Ancients Inspired the Founding Fathers* (Rowman and Littlefield), *The Battle for the American Mind: A Brief History of a Nation's Thought* (Rowman and Littlefield), and *Twelve Greeks and Romans Who Changed The World* (Rowman and Littlefield; rpt. Barnes and Noble).

Jonathan Sachs is Professor of English at Concordia University in Montreal. He is the author of *Romantic Antiquity: Rome in the British Imagination, 1789–1832* (Oxford University Press), and has published articles on topics including Percy Shelley's late poetry, the Jacobin novel, and Robert Wood and Homeric orality in the eighteenth century. Forthcoming articles include work on Adam Smith, decline and futurity, and Romanticism and the decline of literature. Sachs is coeditor (with Andrew Piper of McGill University) of a special issue on "Romanticism and the Cultures of Print" in *Romanticism and Victorianism on the Net*. With the aid of a Canadian Social Sciences and Humanities Research Council grant, he is currently completing *Decline and the Depths of Time: Historicity and the Forms of Ruin in British Romanticism*, which seeks to explain anxieties about decline in connection with new Enlightenment and post-Enlightenment ways of understanding time and historical experience.

John Stauffer is Professor of English and of African and African American Studies at Harvard University. He is the author or editor of fifteen books and over 100 essays, including forty peer-reviewed articles. *The Black Hearts of Men* (Harvard University Press) won the Frederick Douglass Book Prize and was runner-up for the Lincoln Prize. *GIANTS: The Parallel Lives of Frederick Douglass and Abraham Lincoln* (Twelve) was briefly a national bestseller and recipient of the Iowa Author award and a Boston Authors Club award. *The State of Jones* (Doubleday), coauthored with Sally Jenkins, is the basis of the 2016 feature film directed by Gary Ross and starring Matthew McConaughey. *The Battle Hymn of the Republic* (Oxford University Press), coauthored with Benjamin Soskis, was a Lincoln Prize finalist. His essays have appeared in *Time*, *The Wall Street Journal*, *New York Times*, *Washington Post*, and *Huffington Post*.

Jeffrey Steele is Professor of English at the University of Wisconsin, Madison. The author of a critical biography, *Transfiguring America: Myth, Ideology, and Mourning in Margaret Fuller's Writing* (University of Missouri Press), and of *The Representation of the Self in the American Renaissance* (University of North Carolina Press), he has also edited *The Essential Margaret Fuller* (Rutgers University Press). He served as president of the Margaret Fuller Society and is currently pursuing research on spatial paradigms and urban consciousness in antebellum New York writers; and on representations of race in late nineteenth-century American literature and advertising.

Steven Stryer is Associate Professor of English at the University of Dallas. A graduate of Harvard College with highest honors in the classics, he is currently revising his Oxford D. Phil. dissertation (supervised by Professor David Womersley) into a book entitled, "The Past/Present Topos in Eighteenth-Century English Literature: A Pattern of Historical Thought and its Stylistic Implications in Historiography, Poetry, and Polemic." His articles include "'A loftier tone': 'Laodamia,' *The Aeneid*, and Wordsworth's Virgilian Imagination" (in *Studies in Philology*); "Burke's Vehemence and the Rhetoric of Historical Exaggeration" (in *Rhetorica*); and "Allegiance, Sympathy, and History: The Catholic Loyalties of Alexander Pope" (in *Religion in the Age of Enlightenment*).

Herbert F. Tucker is John C. Coleman Professor of English at the University of Virginia. He is the author of *Epic: Britain's Heroic Muse, 1790–1910* (Oxford University Press), *A Companion to Victorian Literature and Culture* (Blackwell Publishers), *Under Criticism: Essays in Honor of William H. Pritchard* (Ohio University Press), *Tennyson and the Doom of Romanticism* (Harvard University Press), and *Browning's Beginnings: The Art of Disclosure* (University of Minnesota Press; coeditor (with Dorothy Mermin) of *Victorian Literature 1830–1900* (Harcourt College Publishers); and editor of *Critical Essays on Alfred Lord Tennyson* (G. K. Hall & Company).

K. P. Van Anglen is recently retired from Boston University, where he was Senior Lecturer on English. He is editor of the *Translations* volume in *The Writings of Henry D. Thoreau* (Princeton University Press), which (among other things) presents Thoreau's English versions of two plays by Aeschylus, and of selections from Pindar and the *Anacreontea*; he is also an editorial contributor to a dozen other Princeton Thoreau Edition volumes, including *Excursions*, the source of the text treated in his chapter for this volume. He has contributed articles on the classics and their reception by the Transcendentalists to numerous journals and reference works, most recently the *Virgil Encyclopedia*. He is author of *The New England Milton: Literary Reception and Cultural Authority in the Early Republic* (Penn State University Press); editor of *"Simplify, Simplify" and Other Quotations from Henry David Thoreau* (Columbia University Press), and coeditor with Glenn Adelson, James Engell, and Brent Ranalli of *Environment: An Interdisciplinary Anthology* (Yale University Press). He has served as a member of the Board of Directors of the Thoreau Society and as coeditor of the journal *Religion and the Arts*, as well as Keeper of the F. O. Matthiessen Room at Harvard. He is editor (with Kristen Case) of a volume of essays celebrating the bicentennial in 2017 of Thoreau's birth, *Thoreau at Two Hundred: Essays and Reassessments* (Cambridge University Press), and is writing a book entitled *Hawthorne's Milton: Aspects of American Aristocracy*. He received the Walter Harding Distinguished Service Award from the Thoreau Society in 2012.

Index

abolitionism, 2, 300–304; *see also* McCune Smith, James
Abrams, M. H., 379
　The Mirror and the Lamp: Romantic Theory and the Critical Tradition, 7, 342, 377, 380n
acceleration, historical, 23–24; *see also* revolutionary time
Adam and Eve, 347
Adams, Brooks, 321
　The Law of Civilization and Decay, 331–32
Adams, Edward, 24–25
Adams, Henry, 25, 317, 318, 321
　The Education of Henry Adams, 328, 329–30, 336n
　History of the United States During the Administrations of Thomas Jefferson and James Madison, 328, 329, 330–32
Adams, John Quincy, 294, 296
Adams, Kimberly VanEsveld, 203–4
Adams, Stephen, 156
Adams, Stephen, and Donald Ross, Jr., *Revising Mythologies: The Composition of Thoreau's Major Works*, 173
Adderley, Sir Charles, 371
Addison, Joseph, 370, 376
Aeneas, 47, 51n, 170, 322–25, 327, 352
Aeneid (Virgil), 28n, 160–61, 168, 178
　Dryden and, 50n
　Everett and, 105–6
　Gibbon and, 24, 316, 317–18, 323–24, 325–26, 327
　Gilpin and, 51n
　historical progress, 321–22
　Keats and, 8–9
　Longfellow and, 122n
　McCune Smith and, 225, 226, 234n
　Milton and, 170
　opening, 127
　Thoreau and, 165, 172
　Wordsworth and, 9, 313
Aeschylus, 10, 83, 165; *see also Prometheus Bound* (Aeschylus)
Aesop, 246

aesthetics, 1, 3–4, 271, 282
　Fuller and, 194
　Gilpin and, 44
　Hebrew and, 25, 341, 342, 348
　Wheatley and, 72n, 76n
African Americans, 388n
　education, 13, 290, 301
　literary Renaissance, 223, 229
　see also McCune Smith, James; Wheatley, Phillis
Agassiz, Louis, 116, 120, 187n
Age of Reason *see* Enlightenment
Ahab, Captain
　and Byron's Prometheus, 254–55
　conflation of mythical characters, 248
　and fire, 243, 245–46, 258–60
　and *Frankenstein*, 256–57
　intention to benefit humankind, 251–52
　literary analogies, 241
　mental vulture, 242–43
　monomania, 252
　Promethean analogies, 23, 244–45
　self-image, 246
　and the unknown, 243–44, 255, 260–61
Ajax, 293
alchemy
　Fuller and, 193, 198, 200, 201, 208, 214
　Victor Frankenstein and, 264n
Alcott, A. Bronson, 179, 195, 198, 211
Alpers, Paul, 163
Alter, Robert, 379
American Association for the Advancement of Science, 175–76, 187n
American Renaissance, 10, 223
American Revolution, 14, 130, 167, 292, 302
　Burke and, 27n
　classical inspiration for, 303, 304
　and Hebrew, 362, 378
Anacreon, 223, 228–29, 235n, 236n
Anaximander, 304
anti-Semitism, 342, 369, 370, 378
Anti-Slavery Record, 302
Apollo, 88, 139, 194–95
Apollodorus, 246

Apollonius Rhodius, *Argonautica*, 1, 144–45n
Apuleius, *The Metamorphosis, or Golden Ass*, 22, 195, 196, 198, 215
Arabic, study of, 343, 344, 349
Aramaic, study of, 344
Ariosto, Ludovico, 162, 183n
Aristotle, 5, 140
  McCune Smith and, 223, 232n
  Melville and, 256
  and natural law, 302
  and slavery, 299–300, 302
Arnold, Matthew
  and Hebrew, 25, 343, 392n
  Melville and, 375
  "The Function of Criticism at the Present Time," 371
  and Gibbon, 319
  The Great Prophecy of Israel's Restoration: Isaiah, chapters 40–66, 372–73
  "Hebraism and Hellenism" in *Culture and Anarchy*, 370–71, 372
Arrighi, Giovanni, 23, 280
art, representational, 45; *see also* Cole, Thomas; ekphrasis
Artemis, 216; *see also* Diana
Arthur, King, 353
Asimov, Isaac, 24, 320–21, 332
Athena, 198; *see also* Minerva
Athens
  American attitudes to, 289, 292–94, 297–302, 304
  and Jerusalem, 341
  Prometheia torch race, 257
Atherstone, Edwin, *The Fall of Nineveh: A Poem*, 146n
Atlas, 246
Attic vs. Ciceronian style, 294, 295–97
Augustine of Hippo, Saint, 314, 325
Augustus, Emperor *see* Octavian (Gaius Octavius, later Augustus)
Austen, Jane, 41
authority, writer's, 4
  Gilpin and, 11, 12, 35
  Landor and, 88
  role of the Muse, 127–28, 143–44, 145n, 147n
  Thoreau and, 177
  Wheatley and, 14–15, 54, 59, 62–63, 64–65, 68, 70
autobiography *see* Adams, Henry: *The Education of Henry Adams*; Coleridge, Samuel Taylor: *Biographia Literaria*; *Memoirs of My Life* (Gibbon); *Prelude, The* (Wordsworth); Ruskin, John: *Praeterita*; Thoreau, Henry David: *Journal* etc.
autonomy, personal *see* self-reliance

Bacchus, 36
Balfour, Ian, *The Rhetoric of Romantic Prophecy*, 389n

Barker, Anna, 197, 203, 209–10
Barlow, Joel, *The Columbiad: A Poem*, 10, 130
Barrett, Elizabeth *see* Browning, Elizabeth Barrett
Barsby, John, ed. and trans., *Terence, Volume 1*, 233n
Bate, W. Jackson, *From Classic to Romantic*, 7
Batstone, William, "Virgilian *Didaxis*: Value and Meaning in the *Georgics*," 176, 186n
Baym, Max I., *Emma Lazarus and Emerson*, 369
Beagon, Mary, 179
Beattie, James, *Essay on the Nature and Immutability of Truth. . .*, 232n
Becker, Carl, *Heavenly City of the Eighteenth-Century Philosophers*, 314
Beecher, Lyman, 363–64
Bell, Archibald, 55, 57, 58, 61
Bell, Philip ("Fylbel"), 224–27
Benjamin, Walter, 278–79, 280, 283
Bentley, Richard, 343, 344
Berclaw, Mary, 249
Berkeley, Bishop George, 160
Berlin, Sir Isaiah, 154
Berman, Joshua, 359, 363
Beulah, 137
Bible, languages of, 343; *see also* Hebrew: Scripture; King James Bible; New Testament; Old Testament
Bjelajac, David, "Thomas Cole's *Oxbow* and the American Zion Divided," 369, 391n
Blackwell, Thomas, *An Enquiry into the Life and Writings of Homer*, 342
Blair, Hugh
  "Critical Dissertation on the Poems of Ossian, the Son of Fingal," 357
  Lectures on Rhetoric and Belles Lettres, 342, 375
Blake, William, 5
  Fuller and, 22
  and Hebrew, 25, 359, 364
  and Lowth, 357
  metrical experiments, 358
  Jerusalem: The Emanation of the Giant Albion, 143–44
  see also Milton: A Poem
Blessington, Marguerite, Countess of, 83
Bloom, Harold, 313
Boehme, Jacob, 22, 198, 200
Böhme, Jakob *see* Boehme, Jacob
Bond, William, 356
Book of Common Prayer, 349, 356
Bossuet, Jacques-Bénigne, 314, 325
Boston
  Common, 120n
  Fuller's classes for women, 22, 193
  Latin School, 290

Longfellow's opposition to Charles River Marshes development, 19, 117–18
and slavery, 53, 54, 301
Wheatley and, 61, 75n
Bourne, H. R. Fox, 349
Bowdler, Thomas, 318
Bowles, William Lisle
  The Grave of the Last Saxon; or, The Legend of the Curfew: A Poem, 131
  The Spirit of Discovery; or, The Conquest of Ocean: A Poem, 135
Bradford, William, *Of Plymouth Plantation*, 358–59
Brendon, Piers, *The Decline and Fall of the British Empire 1781–1997*, 334n
Brewster, William, 358–59
Brisman, Leslie, *Romantic Origins*, 147n
Broadie, Alexander, 343
Brown, John, 233n
Brown, William Wells, *Clotel, or, The President's Daughter*, 16
Browning, Elizabeth Barrett, 83, 262n
  The Battle of Marathon, 141
Brutus (mythical founder of Britain), 352–53
Bryant, William Cullen, 103
bucolic, the *see* pastoral
Buell, Lawrence, 155–56
Bunyan, John
  The Holy War, made by Shaddai upon Diabolus, 391n
  The Pilgrim's Progress, 246
Burckhardt, (Carl) Jacob (Christoph), 319
Burke, Edmund, 8, 222
  Gilpin and, 35, 40, 47–48
  and Hebrew, 351, 359, 366
  A Philosophical Enquiry into the Origin of Our Ideas of the Sublime and Beautiful, 351
Burrow, J. W.
  Gibbon, 320
  A History of Histories: Epics, Chronicles, Romances and Inquiries . . ., 328, 336n
Burwick, Frederick, *Mimesis and its Romantic Reflections*, 60, 73n
Bury, J. B., 319
Buxton, John, 85
Byron, George Gordon, 6th Baron Byron of Rochdale
  classical background, 1, 5, 9
  and Hebrew, 380, 395n
  influence of, 146n
  Janus-faced stance, 184n
  "school" of poetry, 6, 7
  Don Juan, 128, 141
  "Epistle to Augusta," 269
  Hebrew Melodies, 367
  see also "Prometheus" (Byron)
Byzantium, 24, 322–23, 324, 325–26

Caesar, Gaius Julius, 46–47, 107, 290
Calhoun, Charles C., 116

Calhoun, John C., 298, 299
  A Disquisition on Government, 300
Calypso, 293
Cambridge University, 5
  and Hebrew, 343, 344–45, 350, 354, 356, 367, 378
Camden, William, *Britannia*, 39
Campen, Jan van, 354
Camus, Albert, 247
Cannadine, Sir David, *The Decline and Fall of the British Aristocracy*, 336n
capitalism, development of, 280
Carigal, Rabbi Hayyim Isaac, 345
Carlyle, Thomas, 318, 374
  On Heroes, Hero-Worship, and the Heroic in History, 370, 392n
Carr, Caleb, *Broken*, 318
Carretta, Vincent, *Phillis Wheatley: Biography of a Genius in Bondage*, 55, 56, 74n, 75n
Carthage, 24, 51n, 321–22, 324
Cassandra, 22, 213, 216–17
Catullus, Gaius Valerius, 83, 89, 99n, 246, 250
Ceres, 211; *see also* Demeter
Cervantes, Miguel de, 374
Chambers, Dr. James, 294
Channing, Edward Tyrell, 161, 162, 166, 203
Channing, William Henry, 195–96, 197, 201, 205
  Memoirs, 194
Chapman, Gerald, *Literary Criticism in England, 1660–1800*, 378
Chase, Richard, *Herman Melville*, 261n
Christ *see* Jesus
Christianity
  classical vs., 8, 94, 97, 196
  iconography, 203
  Milton and, 181n, 183n
  and mysticism, 198, 201
  secularization vs., 24
  and slavery, 56, 59, 74n, 301
  see also Protestantism; Puritan Hebraism; Roman Catholicism
Churchill, Winston, 319, 328, 336n
Cicero, Marcus Tullius
  historia magistra vitae, 268, 272
  and natural law, 302–3
  Stowe (estate) and, 36
  U.S. politicians and, 13, 289, 290–91, 294, 295–97
Civil War, American, 167, 222, 304, 305, 388n
  Gettysburg Address, 292, 297
  McCune Smith and, 229, 233n
Civil War, Roman, 19, 168
Clarke, M. L., 344
classical reception, 18, 26–27n, 270–71; *see also* Latin and Greek
Claudian (Claudius Claudianus), 186n, 327
Clausen, Wendell, 174

Cleveland, Charles D., 377
Cole, Thomas (painter), 182n
  The Oxbow, 369, 391n
  Prometheus Bound, 248
Coleridge, Henry Nelson, *Introductions to the study of the Greek classic poets . . .*, 162, 166
Coleridge, John, 343, 362–63, 364
Coleridge, Samuel Taylor
  classical background, 1, 9
  comparing Napoleonic France with imperial Rome, 267, 270, 273–75, 278, 279, 281
  and creation, 357
  and Hebrew, 25, 26, 343, 350, 352
  and Hurwitz, 366–67, 389–90n
  Janus-faced stance, 184n
  literary criticism, 8, 9
  and Lowth, 357
  Melville and, 374
  and *Neuzeit*, 268–69
  perceptions of time *see* collation; revolutionary time; slowness of antiquity
  Wordsworth and, 139
  Biographia Literaria; or Biographical Sketches of My Literary Life and Opinions, 6, 365, 366
  Lay Sermons, 362, 363
  "Ode to an Ass," 6
  The Statesman's Manual, 277, 363, 366
  Table Talk, 352
collation, 277–78, 279, 280–81
Collins, William, 6, 355, 357
Columbia College, 346
communications technology, 276–78, 281, 282, 285n
Concord, Thoreau and, 156–57
Congo chant, 225–26, 234n
Conington, John, *Publi Vergili Maronis Opera*, 122n
Constantine the Great, Emperor, 322, 323–24, 333n
Constantinople, 322–23
  siege of, 314, 315, 316, 325, 331
Constitutional Convention, U.S., 304
Cook, William, and James Tatum, *African American Writers and Classical Tradition*, 76n
Cooper, J. G., *Publii Virgilii Maronis Opera; or, The Works of Virgil . . .*, 110, 111, 122n
Cooper, James Fenimore, 10, 182n
Cooper, Wendy, 293
Copway, George (Kah-ge-ga-gah-bowh), 104
Cornell University, 305
cosmos, 21, 160
  and empiricism, 155, 156, 169, 175
  epos of, 177
  nature of, 170–71
Cottle, Joseph, 129

Cowley, Hannah, *The Siege of Acre: A Poem*, 133
Cramer, Jeffrey S., 186n
creation myths
  British, 131, 352–53
  Greek, 164, 246, 250, 253
  Hebrew, 357
  Roman, 324, 327
Cromwell, Oliver, 345
Crowley, Robert, *The Psalter of David*, 354
Cumberland, William and Richard Bland Burges, *The Exodiad: A Poem*, 140–41
Cumberland, William, *Calvary; or The Death of Christ: A Poem*, 130, 134, 148n
Cunaeus, Petrus (Pieter van der Cun), *De republica Hebraeorum*, 361
Cupid, 195, 196
Curran, Stuart
  Poetic Form and British Romanticism, 17, 18, 25, 29n, 167, 168
  "The Political Prometheus," 254
cursus honorum
  influence of, 3, 28n, 159, 160–61, 175, 185n
  Keats and, 8–9
  recast by Gibbon, 24, 316, 317–18, 328
  Thoreau and, 20–21, 155, 162–65, 169, 173–74, 178
  see also epic; georgic; pastoral

Dall, Caroline Healey, 196
Daniel, Justice Peter, 220
Dante Alighieri, 104, 108–9, 162, 163, 183n, 259
Dartmouth College, 290–91, 344, 367, 378, 379
Darwin, Charles, 153, 155, 157, 175, 177, 304
Darwin, Erasmus, 184n
David, King *see* Psalms of David
Davidson, Joseph, 108, 109, 110, 112, 114
Davies, Norman, *Vanished Kingdoms*, 318
Davis, David Brion, 301
Day, Stephen, *The Bay Psalm Book* (*The Whole Book of Psalmes Faithfully Translated into English Metre*), 354
De Bruyn, Frans, 359
De Quincey, Thomas, 25, 370
de Selincourt, Ernest, 84–85
Deborah, 350, 354, 365–66
decline and fall, cycles of, 267, 281; *see also History of the Decline and Fall of the Roman Empire, The* (Gibbon)
Delbanco, Andrew, 374
Demagorgon, 255
Demeter, 196, 197, 198, 204, 208, 213; *see also* Ceres
democracy, 2, 304
  American, 12–13, 247, 359
  American politicians and Athens, 289–90, 292, 294, 296–97, 298

Demosthenes, 223, 289, 294, 296–97
Dennis, John, 25, 347–48, 366
Derrida, Jacques, 64
Descartes, René, 48, 158
Dew, Thomas, 296, 298–99
Dial, 193, 202, 205, 236n
dialogue form, 36, 214
Diana, 22, 196, 198, 204, 206, 211, 215;
  see also Artemis
Dido, 51n, 322, 324, 325
Dilworth, Ernest, 91
Donoghue, Denis, *Thieves of Fire*, 261n
Doody, Margaret A., 10–11
Dougherty, Carol, *Prometheus*, 261n
Douglas, Gavin, 165
Douglass, Frederick, 236n, 301; *see also Frederick Douglass' Paper*
Drachenfels, 201, 202
Dryden, John, 347–48, 350, 359
  and Virgil, 46, 50n, 108, 109, 110, 112, 115, 315
Du Bois, W. E. B., 15, 221, 227
Dufour, Joseph, 293
Dutch (language), 344
Dwight, Timothy, 346

eclogue
  Thoreau and, 21
  Virgil and, 8–9, 18–19, 20
Eclogues (Virgil), 9, 28n, 104–5, 106–7, 168
  Eclogue 1, 107–8, 160, 174, 185n
  Eclogue 6, 164
  Eclogue 7, 164–65, 184n
  Thoreau and, 20, 164–65, 174, 184n
  Wordsworth and, 185n
  see also "Virgil's First Eclogue" (Longfellow)
Eden, William, 269
education, Latin and Greek
  in America, 12–13, 178–79, 290, 293–94
  in Britain, 8, 9, 12
  see also Hebrew: studied as classical language
Edward I, King, 353
Edwards, Jonathan, 343, 346
egalitarianism, 2, 13, 56, 224, 291, 298
Egypt, ancient
  goddesses, 203, 208
  Israel in Egypt (Handel), 349
  and slavery, 299, 301
Eichhorn, Johann, 343
ekphrasis, 72n, 73n, 77n
  Wheatley and, 14, 53–54, 60, 65–66, 67–68, 70, 71n, 76n
Electra, 213
elegy, 7, 21, 89, 94, 120, 175
Eleusinian Mysteries, 196, 213, 218n
Elgin Marbles, 82
Eliot, George, *Daniel Deronda*, 368, 369
Eliot, T. S., 4, 7, 316

Emancipation Act, New York State (1827), 221–22, 231n
Emerson, Ralph Waldo, 157
  classical background, 10
  Fuller and, 194, 197, 198–99, 201–2, 203, 206, 207
  and Hebrew, 369
  Melville and, 248, 250
  and Lowth, 358
  and natural law, 302–3
  "The American Scholar," 162
  "Divinity School Address," 375–76
  Memoirs of Margaret Fuller Ossoli, 199
  Nature, 211
Emmons, Richard, *The Fredoniad; or, Independence Preserved; An Epic Poem*, 10, 135–36, 146n
empire
  British, 57, 68
  critiques of, 168, 170, 359
  Ottoman, 290
  Persian, 300, 302
  Roman, 68, 172, 174, 178; *see also* Coleridge, Samuel Taylor: comparing Napoleonic France with imperial Rome; *History of the Decline and Fall of the Roman Empire, The* (Gibbon)
  see also translatio imperii
empiricism
  and cosmos, 155, 156
  Enlightenment, 154
  Thoreau and, 21, 156–58, 160, 166, 169, 171, 178, 180n
Empson, William, 123n, 170
Engell, James, 7, 25–26, 67, 76n
Engelsing, Rolf, *Der Bürger als Leser: Lesergeschichte in Deutschland 1500–1800*, 285n
Enlightenment, 19, 126, 154–55, 177
  equation with Augustan Rome, 321, 324
  Gibbon and, 316
  and Prometheus, 252–53, 259
  Scottish, 222
epic, 9, 10, 17–18, 24, 28n, 29n
  as adjective, 17, 167, 175
  Americans and, 167–68
  apocalyptic, 146n
  generic secession, 138
  Gibbon and, 315, 316
  history, 137–38
  "I sing" convention, 127, 129, 130, 142
  Milton and, 26, 350
  neoclassical theory, 126, 141–42
  pastoral and, 164
  prose as, 160
  similes, 169, 170
  Thoreau and, 21, 171
  see also invocation
epigram, 80, 85, 89, 99n
Epimetheus, 250–51
epiphany, 197, 210–11, 215, 216

epos, 24, 177
epyllion, 83
Erdman, David, *Prophet Against Empire*, 359
ethnology, 227
ethos
  artist's, 53, 58, 66
  of freedom, 69
  as patron, 65, 66–67
  poetic, 14, 54, 56, 63, 64–65
  reader's, 58, 68
  for slavery, 59, 62
  theorization of, 77n
Euclid, *Elements*, 291–92
Euripides, 216–17, 218n, 295–96
Eurydice, 197
Eustaphieve, Alexis, *Demetrius: The Hero of the Don*, 130
Eustis, William, 205
Everett, Edward, 292, 297, 301
Everett, William, 104, 105–7, 108, 112, 115, 121n
Ewald, Heinrich, 343
exceptionalism, 130–31
excursion *see* Gilpin, William; "Walk to Wachusett, A" (Thoreau)
exodus (Israelites from Egypt), 140–41; *see also* Old Testament: Exodus
experience *see* personal experience

Fairer, David, 1
Fates, 96, 97, 129, 251
Felton, C. C., 161–62
Fénelon, François de Salignac de la Mothe-, *Les avantures de Télémaque*, 138, 293
Ferry, David, 108, 109–10, 110–11, 113
Fields, James, 116, 120, 120n
Filmer, Robert, 349, 359
Fischer, Barbara K., *Mediations: Reframing Ekphrasis in Contemporary American Poetry*, 72n
Fitzgerald, Robert P., "The Form of Christopher Smart's *Jubilate Agno*," 386n
Fitzhugh, George, 299, 300
Foote, Shelby, *Civil War*, 317
Forde Abbey, 41–42
Forster, John, 81
Fortuna, 196
Fowle, Daniel, 354
Franklin, Benjamin, 291, 346
Franklin, Bruce, *The Wake of the Gods: Melville's Mythology*, 261n
Frederick Douglass' Paper, 223, 224, 227–28
Free Soil movement, 153
free verse, 358
French Revolution
  Burke and, 359
  Coleridge and, 23, 24, 270, 281
  Gibbon and, 330, 331
  and Hebrew, 378
  Henry Adams and, 332
  and Muse of Freedom, 130
  Roman republic as precedent, 272–73, 279
  see also revolutionary time
Frend, William, 365
Friend, The, 366
Fritzsche, Peter, 272, 275
Frye, Northrop, 316, 353, 358
Fugitive Slave Law (1850), 302–3
Fuller, Margaret, 10
  classical background, 21–22, 193
  combining myths, 197
  Conversations, 194–95, 198, 217n
  identification with Madonna, 203–4
  identification with myth, 195–96, 198–200, 200–202
  mythmaking, 193–94, 200, 211–12
  and mythology, 194–95, 198, 214, 216
  personal crisis, 197–99, 200, 203, 205
  transformational mythmaking, 204–6, 210–11
  "Autobiographical Romance," 200
  "Boding raven of the breast," 214
  "Double triangle, Serpent and Rays," 215
  "Drachenfels," 202
  "To the Face Seen in the Moon," 214
  "God-ordained, self-fed Energy," 215
  "The Great Lawsuit: Man *versus* Men. Woman *versus* Women," 204, 207, 211–13
  "Leila," 205, 207–11, 212, 214
  "Leila in the Arabian zone," 215
  "The Magnolia of Lake Pontchartrain," 205, 206–7
  "Raphael's Deposition from the Cross," 203, 214
  "Sistrum," 215
  Summer on the Lakes, 213, 214
  "Winged Sphynx," 215
  "Yuca Filamentosa," 205
  see also Woman in the Nineteenth Century (Fuller)
Fuller, Timothy, 200–201
future
  constrained, 278, 279, 281, 332
  divination, 97
  divorced from past, 270, 272
  progressive, 321, 375
  via invocation of past, 268, 271, 273, 274
Fylbel (Philip Bell), 224–27

Gale, Robert L., 121n
Garner, Margaret, 302
Genette, Gérard, *Seuils*, 127, 145n
Geoffrey of Monmouth, 352–53
georgic, 9, 21, 160, 161, 175
Georgics (Virgil), 28n, 168, 176, 178, 186n
  Thoreau and, 20, 159, 172, 186n
Germany, equated with Roman republic, 326–27
Gerusalemme Liberata (Tasso), 315

Gesenius, Wilhelm, 343
Gibbon, Edward, 8; see also History of the Decline and Fall of the Roman Empire, The (Gibbon); Memoirs of My Life (Gibbon)
Gibbons, Thomas, Rhetoric; Or a View of Its Principal Tropes and Figures, 365–66
Gibson, Bishop Edmund, 39
Gilbank, William, The Day of Pentecost, or Man Restored, 132
Giles, Paul, "American Literature and Classical Consciousness," 187n
Gill, Stephen, 1
Gilpin, William, 10–12
 architectural disapproval, 41–42, 43–44
 background, 35–36
 and Latin, 44
 and the Sublime, 47–48
 A Dialogue upon the Gardens of the Right Honourable the Lord Viscount Cobham, at Stow [sic] in Buckinghamshire, 36–38
 "Observations," 38–39
 Observations, Relative Chiefly to Picturesque Beauty . . ., 41
 Observations on the River Wye . . ., 40
 Observations on the Western Parts of England . . ., 45–49
Glasgow, University of, 222
Glorious Revolution (England), 140, 302, 359
Glover, Richard, The Athenaid, A Poem, 129
goddesses, 196, 198, 200, 207–8, 210, 211–12
Goethe, Johann Wolfgang von
 classical background, 9
 Fuller and, 22, 198, 200, 201–2, 214
 and Prometheus, 23, 241, 246, 249–50, 253, 254
 Thoreau and, 157, 158, 162, 166
 Die Italienische Reise, 166
 Faust, 259
 Iphigenie auf Tauris, 218n
Golden Ass, The see Apuleius, The Metamorphosis, or Golden Ass
Goldhill, Simon, 271
Goldman, Shalom, 25, 346
 God's Sacred Tongue, 383n, 389n
Gothic architecture, 11–12, 43, 44
Graeme, Elizabeth, "Invocation to Wisdom," 138
Graver, Bruce, 1, 27n, 389n
Gray, Erik, 347
Gray, Thomas, 6, 49, 51n, 355
Greece, ancient
 architectural influence, 293
 and slavery, 221, 223, 300, 302
 see also Athens
Greek see Latin and Greek
Greeley, Horace, 22, 193, 303

Green, Ian, 344
Greenwood, Emily, "The Politics of Classicism in the Poetry of Phillis Wheatley," 71–72n
Gregorovius, Ferdinand, 315, 319, 326–27
Gregory, George, 342, 357
Grimké, Thomas, 367
Guizot, François, 258, 318, 319
Gunnell, John, 359
Gzella, Holger, 343

Hale, Senator John, 294
Halmi, Nicholas, 1
Hamilton, Newburgh, 349
Handel, George Frideric, 25, 349–50
Hare, Archdeacon Julius, 81
harp, the, 131, 134, 135, 140, 142, 355–56
Harper, Ellen Wilkins, 302
Harper's Classical Library, 249, 263n
Harrison, William Henry, 291
Hartman, Geoffrey, 356
Harvard University
 admissions requirements, 290, 305
 Divinity School, 362
 Emerson and, 162
 and Hebrew, 344, 354, 363, 364, 367, 378, 394n
 libraries, 369, 379
 Longfellow and, 105, 107, 109, 115, 117–18
 Thoreau and, 20, 161–63, 166, 182n, 375
Harvey, Samantha, 391n
Hastings, Selina, Countess of Huntingdon, 53, 56, 57, 58, 65, 75n
Hawthorne, Nathaniel, 200, 263n, 264n
Hazlitt, William, 2, 9, 67, 184n
Hebraism see Puritan Hebraism
"Hebraism and Hellenism" in Culture and Anarchy (Arnold), 370–72
Hebrew
 Cole and, 369
 and decline of Greek and Latin models, 357
 Dryden and, 359
 English poetry and, 354–55, 356–58
 and foundational myths, 353
 literature in English and, 365–67, 379–80
 Lowes and, 376
 McCune Smith and, 223
 Melville and, 373–74
 modern, 379
 neohebraism, 383–84n
 poetry, 341–42, 350–51
 Scripture and myth, 364–65
 Scripture as political model, 359–61, 362–64, 378; see also Hebraism
 Smart and, 356–57
 studied as classical language, 1, 25–26, 341, 343–45, 347–48
 and the sublime, 348, 349
 Thoreau and, 25, 369, 375–76, 393n

Hebrew (cont.)
  waning popularity, 364, 367, 368, 377, 378–79
  and Western culture, 25–26
Hebrew Melodies (Byron), 367
Hebrew Tales Selected and Translated from the Writings of the Ancient Hebrew Sages (Hurwitz), 366–67, 389n
Hecate, 215
Helen (of Troy), 91, 94–95
Hellenism, 132, 162, 196, 208
  Hebraism and, 341, 370–72, 373, 375–76
Hephaestus, 245–46, 252
Hera, 198
Herakles, 263n
Heringman, Noah, 175
Hermes, 88, 252
Herndon, William, 291–92
Hesiod, 22–23, 163, 201, 242, 250–51
Hickey, Raymond, 345
Higginson, Thomas Wentworth, 200
Hiltner, Ken, 116, 123n
historia magistra vitae, 268, 272
historiography, 25, 314–15, 316, 318, 328, 329
history, 1, 3–4
  Arnold and, 371
  Coleridge and, 388n
  Fuller and, 211, 213
  Jewish, 366, 367, 379
  progressive, 321–22, 327, 329
  repeating itself, 278, 279–80
  Thoreau and, 155, 172, 173
  Whig, 12, 159–60
  see also slavery; time
History of the Decline and Fall of the Roman Empire, The (Gibbon)
  challenging St. Augustine, 314
  Christianity equated with Carthage, 324–26
  correlations with *Aeneid*, 327
  dangers of orientalization, 322–24
  epic heroes, 315
  Henry Adams and, 328, 330–32, 336n
  historiography, 25, 314–15
  influence on historians, 317, 318–20, 321, 326–27, 328–29, 332, 335n, 336n
  influence on science fiction, 320–21
  Ruskin and, 328, 335–36n
  and secularization, 24, 317, 321, 324, 325, 335n
  supplanting Virgil, 313–14, 320–21, 327–28
  Wells and, 328
  Wordsworth and, 314
  Zeitgeist, 316–17
History of the United States During the Administrations of Thomas Jefferson and James Madison (Henry Adams), 330–32
Hobbes, Thomas, *Leviathan*, 360–61, 374
Hogg, James, *Queen Hynde*, 140

Holford, Margaret
  Margaret of Anjou: A Poem, 133–34
  Wallace; or, The Fight of Falkirk: A Metrical Romance, 132, 134
holism, rational vs. empirical, 155, 157, 166, 169, 171, 187n
Homer
  American imitators, 10
  compared unfavorably with Old Testament, 370
  Emmons and, 136
  and epic, 18, 127
  Gibbon and, 315, 316
  Gilpin and, 46
  Keats and, 15, 70
  Landor and, 83, 96
  Melville and, 259
  rise in popularity, 313
  Ruskin and, 336n
  scholarship, 161–62
  Thoreau and, 21, 26n, 158–59, 163–64, 166, 169, 176–77
  in U.S. education, 290
  Virgil and, 332
  Wheatley and, 15, 63, 66–68, 69, 70
  Wordsworth and, 365
  see also Iliad (Homer)
Hopkins, Gerard Manley, 357
Horace (Quintus Horatius Flaccus), 76n
  Byron and, 9
  Johnson (literary figure) and, 357
  Gilpin and, 11, 12, 43–44
  Landor and, 80, 90
  and Prometheus, 246, 250
  in U.S. education, 290
  Watts and, 354
  see also Wheatley, Phillis: "To Maecenas"
Houston, Samuel "Sam," 291, 292–93
Howe, Daniel Walker, 297–98
Hoyle, Charles, *Exodus*, 130
Hulme, T. E., "Romanticism and Classicism," 7
Humanism, 158, 178, 254
  and Hebrew, 343, 344, 347
humanities, 21, 223
humanity (quality), 74n, 165, 300, 372, 376
Humboldt, (Friedrich Wilhelm Heinrich) Alexander von, 21, 153, 163, 175, 181n, 182n
  empirical holism, 155, 157, 166, 169, 187n
Hunn, Anthony, *Sin and Redemption: A Religious Poem*, 138–39
Hunt, Lynn, 272
Hurwitz, Hyman, 366–67, 389n

Iduna, 216
Iliad (Homer), 68, 72n, 145n, 161
  Pope's translation, 292, 293, 336n
  Thoreau and, 164, 165
individualism, 2, 16, 80, 84, 211, 252

industrialization, 19, 116–17, 175, 304–5, 369, 391n
interracialism, 222, 224, 233n; see also miscegenation
invocation
  agnostic, 146n
  Christian, 129–30, 132, 137
  of Freedom, 130, 140
  hedged, 138–39
  mistrusted, 144–45n
  musical, 131–32, 134, 135, 140
  paratextual temporality, 127, 145n
  of patriotism, 131
  rejection of, 129
  relation to narrative, 139–44, 147n
  see also Muse, the; Wheatley, Phillis: "To Maecenas"
Io, 215
Iphigenia, 22, 216, 217
Irmscher, Christoph, 18
Isaiah, 349, 350, 354, 372–73
Isis, 193, 196, 197
  Apuleius and, 198
  "The Great Lawsuit" and, 211, 213
  "Leila" and, 208
  sistrum, 202, 215
Israel
  Historia Britonum and, 353
  identification of Native Americans as lost tribes, 344
  John Coleridge and, 366
  political identification with, 346, 358–59, 360–63, 369
  and slavery, 301
Israel in Egypt (Handel), 349

Jackson, Andrew, 291, 293
Jackson, William A., 369
Jacob, Heinrich Eduard, 369
Janus-faced stance, 2–3, 17, 167, 184n
  Milton and, 181n, 183n
  and pastoral, 168
  Thoreau and, 20–21, 169, 177, 178
  Virgil and, 174, 186n
Japheth (son of Noah), 353
Jarvis, Edward, 222
Jefferson, Thomas, 56, 227, 234–35n, 295–96; see also History of the United States . . . (Henry Adams)
Jennens, Charles, 349
Jephthah, 349
Jesus, 248–49, 353, 360
Jetztzeit, 279
Jews, 345–46, 353, 367–69, 390n
  and academia, 378, 379
  Byron and, 380
Job, Book of, 346, 348, 351–52, 361, 370, 384n
Johns Hopkins University, 305
Johnson, Joseph, 357
Johnson, Rochelle, 391n
Johnson, Samuel (American educator), 346

Johnson, Samuel (British literary figure)
  Gibbon and, 316
  and Merrick's *Psalms*, 355
  on Prior, 350
  A Dictionary of the English Language, 167
  The History of Rasselas, Prince of Abissinia, 171
  The Vanity of Human Wishes, 357
Johnson, W. R., *Darkness Visible: A Study of Vergil's Aeneid*, 334–35n
Jones, Ewan James, 367
Jordan, June, "The Difficult Miracle of Black Poetry in America: Something like a Sonnet for Phillis Wheatley," 75n
Joseph of Arimathea, 353
Judas Maccabaeus, 359
Juno, 326
Jupiter, 194–95, 326

Kabakoff, Jacob, 346
Kabbalism, 345
Kansas-Nebraska Act (1854), 303
Keats, John, 1, 8–9, 67, 364
  The Fall of Hyperion, 8, 147n
  "On First Looking into Chapman's Homer," 15, 70
  Hyperion, 8, 139, 147n
  "Ode on a Grecian Urn," 281–82
  "Ode to a Nightingale," 8
  "Ode to May: Fragment," 139
  Sleep and Poetry, 8
Keble, John, 380n
Kelly, Andrea, 84
Kennicott, Benjamin, 344–45
Kenny, Vincent, 374–75
Kerenyi, Carl, *Prometheus: Archetypal Image of Human Existence*, 261n
Kermode, Sir (John) Frank, 4
Kestner, Joseph, 83
Kete, Mary Louise, 13–14
King James Bible, 348, 349
  Arnold and, 373
  Blake and, 358
  Burke and, 351
  Lowes and, 376–77
  Ruskin and, 335–36n
  Smart and, 356
  Wordsworth and, 365
Klevay, Robert, "The Reader and the Classics in Thoreau's *Walden*," 185n
Koselleck, Reinhart, 23, 268–69, 272, 278

Landor, Walter Savage
  appreciation of classical in the romantic, 16–17, 85–88, 100n
  classical background, 83
  and classical ideal, 81–83
  critical perspectives, 84–85, 87–88, 91, 92
  Ianthe poems, 89–97
  rebellious nature, 29n
  short lyric poems, 88–89

Landor, Walter Savage (*cont.*)
  works in Latin, 84
  "With An Album," 80
  "Apology for *Gebir*," 85–86
  "Apology for the *Hellenics*," 84
  "To the Author of *Festus*: on the Classick and Romantick," 86–87, 88
  "Child of a Day," 89
  "On the Classick and Romantick," 16
  Crysaor, 83
  Gebir, 83, 85–86, 99n, 129
  Hellenics, 83–84, 85
  Imaginary Conversations, 81
  Imaginary Conversations of Greeks and Romans, 83
  "The Loves who many years held all my mind," 92, 93
  "Memory," 95
  "Past ruin'd Ilion Helen lives!" 91
  Pericles and Aspasia, 83
  The Phocaeans, 83
  Poems from the Arabic and Persian, 85
  "To Shelley," 86
  "Written in Malvern," 92–93
Langdon, Samuel, 363
language
  classical reforming modern, 176
  of flowers, 200
  Longfellow and, 18–19, 103–4, 108–9, 119
  Thoreau's primitive, 176, 187n
Larnell, Benjamin, 344
Latin and Greek, 4–5
  African Americans and, 13, 221–22, 223, 301
  as credential, 44, 289–90
  decline in America, 304–5
  decline of formal imitation, 357
  Landor and, 83–84
  retaining popularity, 378
  Thoreau and, 21
  U.S. politicians and, 294
  see also education, Latin and Greek
Laud, Archbishop William, 349
Lavinia, 322
Layla and Majnun, 209
Lazarus, Emma, 25, 368–69, 379
Le Bossu, René, 126
Lee, Chauncey, *The Trial of Virtue*, 346
Lee, Mother Anne, 213
Leonard, Miriam, "Matthew Arnold in Zion: Hebrews, Hellenes, Aryans, and Semites," 371, 372, 378, 392n
Levinson, Bernard, 359, 363
Lewin, Jane E., 145n
Lincoln, Abraham, 7, 233n, 291–92
Lively, Susan, 394n
Livy (Titus Livius), 292
Locke, John, 48, 361
  Two Treatises of Government, 349, 359
Longfellow, Henry Wadsworth
  classical background, 10, 103–4
  environmentalism, 19, 116–19, 123n
  "foreignization" in translation, 18–19, 108–9, 119
  and Harvard, 105, 107, 109, 115, 117–18, 182n
  and Hebrew, 25
  later life, 115–16
  poetic style, 104
  translation of Dante's *Divina Commedia*, 104, 108–9
  translations of Michelangelo, 103
  "The Day is Done," 115
  Evangeline: A Tale of Arcadie, 104, 107
  "The Jewish Cemetery at Newport," 367–68, 390n
  Kéramos and Other Poems, 103, 108
  "From My Arm-Chair," 119
  Poems of Places, 120
  A Song of Hiawatha, 104
  "Three Friends," 120
  "The Village Blacksmith," 119
  Voices of the Night, 103
  see also "Virgil's First Eclogue" (Longfellow)
Longinus, *On the Sublime*, 28n, 348, 352, 377, 380n
Lorraine, Claude (painter), 45
Louvain, University of, 354
Lowell, James Russell, 115, 120n
Lowes, John Livingston, 25
  "The Noblest Monument of English Prose," 373, 376–77
Lowth, Bishop Robert, *Lectures on the Sacred Poetry of the Hebrews*, 25, 26, 342, 343, 354–55, 365
  Arnold and, 373
  Blair and, 375
  Coleridge and, 366
  De Quincey and, 370
  Dwight and, 346
  influence, 357–58, 380n
  Joseph Warton and, 352
  and *mashal*, 389n
  Smart and, 356, 386n
  and Song of Deborah, 366
  "The Sublime Style of the Hebrew Ode," 350–51
  waning popularity, 377–78
  Wordsworth and, 365
Lucian, 83
Lucius (character), 196, 215
Lucretius (Titus Lucretius Carus), 83

Macaulay, Thomas Babington, 1st Baron Macaulay, 24, 328
  Lays of Ancient Rome, 9–10
McCune Smith, James
  and Civil War, 233n
  classical background, 221–22
  irritated by ignorance, 220, 227
  overcoming color barrier, 222–23
  and Reconstruction, 236n

Republic of Letters, 15–16, 221, 227, 228–30
and right to citizenship, 220–21, 227
spelling variations, 234n
"The Critic at Chess," 224–27, 233n
"The Destiny of the People of Color," 223, 229, 232n
"'Heads of the Colored People' Done With a Whitewash Brush," 227–29
"The Whitewasher," 228, 236n
Mackenzie, Henry, *The Man of Feeling*, 355
McKeon, Michael, 168
Mackie, George, 108, 112, 114, 115
Macpherson, James, 10, 25, 386n
 Fragments of Ancient Poetry, Collected in the Highlands of Scotland, 357–58
McWilliams, John P., Jr., 22–23
 The American Epic: Transforming a Genre, 145n, 147n
Madison, James, 330
Madonna, the, 203–4, 216
Maecenas, historical, 65, 66
Magna Dea, 196, 199, 200
Manifest Destiny, 181n, 247
Marlowe, Christopher, *Doctor Faustus*, 243, 259
Martin, Luther H., *Hellenistic Religions: An Introduction*, 196, 218n
Martindale, Charles, 26n, 28n, 183n, 285n, 347, 383n
Marx, Karl, 272–73, 278
Mason, Tom, "Abraham Cowley and the Wisdom of Anacreon," 236n
Massachusetts Bay Colony, 358
Mather, Cotton, 343
Mather, Increase, 343, 361, 361–62
Mays, James, 1
Meares, Captain John, *Voyages Made in the years 1788 and 1789, from China to the West Coast of America*, 47–48, 50–51n
Medwin, Thomas, 262n
Melville, Herman
 classical analogies, 262n
 education, 393n
 and Goethe, 263n
 and Hebrew, 25
 and the novel, 10
 and Prometheus, 246–51; see also Ahab, Captain
 scholarly analysis, 261n
 and Shelley, 255–56
 "The Bell Tower," 248
 Billy Budd, 256, 261n
 Clarel, 374–75
 The Confidence-Man: His Masquerade, 262n
 Mardi, and a Voyage Thither, 247–48
 Typee, 256
 White-Jacket, 362
 see also *Moby-Dick*

Memoirs of My Life (Gibbon)
 Henry Adams and, 328, 329–30
 influence of, 318, 319
 recasting *cursus honorum*, 24, 316, 317–18
 Ruskin and, 328
 Wells and, 328
 Wordsworth and, 314
Mercury, 194
Merivale, Charles, 317, 319, 320
Merriam, Eve, 369
Merrick, James, *The Psalms, translated or paraphrased in English Verse*, 355, 357
Michaelis, Johann David, 343
Michelangelo Buonarroti (as poet), 103
Michelet, Jules, 24, 318, 319
Miller, James E., Jr., *The American Quest for a Supreme Fiction: Whitman's Legacy in the Personal Epic*, 147n
Mills, Robert, 293
Milman, Henry Hart, 319, 335n
 Samor, Lord of the Bright City: An Heroic Poem, 131
Milton, John
 and *cursus honorum*, 8
 and education, 179
 and epic, 10, 18, 127, 129
 Gibbon and, 323
 and Hebrew, 25, 26, 343, 344, 347
 Holford and, 134
 Landor and, 94
 republicanism, 129, 179, 361
 Thoreau and, 162–63, 165, 169–70
 and Virgil, 9, 28n
 Wordsworth and, 185n
 "L'Allegro" and "Il Penseroso," 162
 Lycidas, 94
 Paradise Regained, 350, 384n
 The Reason of Church-Government Urged against Prelaty, 350
 Samson Agonistes, 347, 349
 see also *Paradise Lost*
Milton: A Poem (Blake), 137–38, 141, 353
mimesis, 256; see also ekphrasis
Minerva, 22, 195, 211–12, 213, 293; see also Athena
miscegenation, 227, 228, 234–35n
Missouri Compromise (1820), 303
mist, 47–48, 51n, 115
Mitchell, W. J. T., *Picture Theory: Essays on Verbal and Visual Representation*, 14, 29n, 72n, 77n
Mitford, William, *The History of Greece*, 318
Mnemosyne, 139
Moby-Dick (Melville)
 Hebraism of, 373–74
 narrative structure, 252
 see also Ahab, Captain
modernism, 7, 369
Mommsen, (Christian Matthias) Theodor, *The History of Rome*, 319–20

Monis, Judah, 364, 389n
Montesquieu (Charles-Louis de Secondat, Baron de La Brède et de Montesquieu), 361, 363
Montgomery, James, *The World before the Flood*, 129
Moore, Thomas, ed. and trans. *The Odes of Anacreon . . .*, 236n
Mordell, Albert, 369
Morrill Act (1862), 304
Morning Post, 267
Morrell, Thomas, 262n
Moses, 348, 360
Most, Glenn W., 28n, 159, 169
Murphy, Henry, *The Conquest of Quebec: An Epic Poem*, 132–33, 146n
Murphy, Trevor, 177–78
Murray, Meg McGavran, 195
Muse, the
  as allegory for poetic genius, 126
  alternatives to *see* invocation
  and authority, 127–28, 143–44, 145n, 147n
  female poets and, 133–34, 138
  memory as, 139–40
  as poetic assistant, 129
  shapeshifting, 135–36, 146n
  topos, 19–20
Muses, 131
  Blake and, 137–38
  Landor and, 87, 95
  mother of, 139
  rejected, 132, 134, 181n
  Thoreau and, 173, 183n
  Wheatley and, 63, 66, 68–69
mysticism, European, 198, 201
mythology
  foundation *see* creation myths
  Hebrew Scripture and, 342, 364–65
  Landor and, 84, 87, 88, 91, 93–95, 96
  Lazarus and, 368
  Thoreau and, 164, 172
  truth of, 93, 163
  see also Fuller, Margaret; Muses; Prometheus

Napoleon Bonaparte, 267, 275, 277, 331, 332
Native Americans, 75, 103–4, 344, 354, 368
natural law, 290, 301, 302–4
natural sciences, 13, 154
  Thoreau and, 21, 153, 158–59, 177, 178
nature writing
  Gilpin's, 11, 38
  Thoreau's, 10, 153, 155, 166–67, 177, 179; *see also* "Walk to Wachusett, A" (Thoreau)
Naturphilosophie, 156
Nelson, Eric, 25
  The Hebrew Republic: Jewish Sources and the Transformation of European Political Thought, 359–60

Nennius (attrib.), *Historia Britonum*, 353
neoclassicism, 5, 18
  epic theory, 126, 141–42
Neuzeit, 268–69
New, Elisa, 373
New Testament, 354, 373
New York City
  McCune Smith and, 225, 227, 233n
  Shearith Israel congregation, 346
New York State Emancipation Act (1827), 221–22, 231n
New-York Tribune, 193, 213
New York University, 379
Newman, F. W., 26n
Newport, Rhode Island *see* Touro Synagogue, Newport
newspapers *see* communications technology
Newton, Isaac, 45, 48
Niebuhr, Barthold Georg, 319
Nitchie, Elizabeth, 88
Norton, Charles Eliot, 116, 117
Novalis (Georg Philipp Friedrich Freiherr von Hardenberg), 364
  Fuller and, 22, 198, 209, 210
Nuttall, A. D., *Openings: Narrative Beginnings from the Epic to the Novel*, 145n, 148n

Occom, Samson, 56, 344
Octavian (Gaius Octavius, later Augustus), 107, 108, 112–14, 168, 174
  Coleridge on, 275
odes, 87, 139
  Anacreon's (attrib.), 228, 229, 235n, 236n
  Hebrew, 350, 354, 365
  Horace's, 62, 70, 80, 90, 104
  Pindar's, 103
  see also Keats, John
Ogden, James, *The Revolution: An Epic Poem*, 138, 140
Old Testament, 347
  Arnold and, 372–73
  compared favorably with Homer, 370
  as poetry, 342, 347–48
  and politics, 361
  Deuteronomy, 363
  Exodus, 350, 365
  Genesis, 347, 352, 364
  Judges, 347, 354, 362–63, 365
  Song of Songs, 347, 357, 383n
  see also Isaiah; Job, Book of; Psalms of David
oratorio, 349
orientalism, 85, 322–24, 327, 331
Orpheus, 197
Osiris, 196, 197, 202, 261n
Ossian *see* Macpherson, James
Osterhammel, Jürgen, *The Transformation of the World*, trans. Patrick Camiller, 335n
Otis, Brooks, *A Study in Civilized Poetry*, 335n

Ovid (Publius Ovidius Naso)
  Fuller and, 22
  Landor and, 83, 89
  McCune Smith and, 230, 237n
  and Prometheus, 246, 250
  Stowe (estate) and, 36
Oxford History of Classical Reception in English Literature, The, 26–27n
Oxford University
  and Hebrew, 343–44, 349
  Landor and, 29n, 83
  and Latin and Greek, 5
  Lowth and, 342, 352, 355

Paine, Thomas, *Common Sense*, 20, 361
painting, 6, 45, 48, 72n, 293
  McCune Smith and, 228, 236n
  see also Cole, Thomas
Palfrey, John G., 294
Pandora, 250–51, 252
papacy, 24, 324–25, 325–26
Paradise Lost (Milton)
  Burke and, 351
  debt to Hebrew Scripture, 347
  Gibbon and, 323
  invocation, 162, 181n, 183n
  Melville and, 243
  Satan, 170, 185n, 253
  Thoreau and, 163, 169–70, 183n, 185n
  Wordsworth and, 185n, 365
Parish, Charles, 356–57
Parthenon marbles, 82
pastoral
  environmental significance, 116, 117, 123n
  in painting, 45, 369
  rebelled against, 5
  retained, 168
  Thoreau and, 21, 160, 166–67, 175, 179, 183–84n; *see also* "Walk to Wachusett, A" (Thoreau)
  Virgil and, 9, 134, 163; *see also Eclogues* (Virgil)
  Whitman and, 7
Patterson, Orlando, *Slavery and Social Death*, 75n
Paul, Sherman, 156
Paulding, James, *The Backwoodsman: A Poem*, 130
Peabody, Elizabeth Palmer, 195, 217n
Peacock, Thomas Love, *The Four Ages of Poetry*, 6
Pericles, 289
  Funeral Oration, 292, 294, 297
Perkins, David, 6
Perl-Rosenthal, Nathan, 359, 361
Persephone, 196, 197, 198, 204, 208, 213
personal experience
  Coleridge and, 24
  Fuller and, 22
  Gilpin and, 11, 41
  Landor and, 17, 84, 87, 89, 90, 91, 93–98
  Thoreau and, 21, 154, 155, 171–72, 172–73, 176
Pfeiffer, Robert H.
  "The Patriotism of Israel's Prophets," 362
  "Teaching of Hebrew," 344, 361
Phillips, Christopher N., 17–18, 167
Phoebe, 215
Pico della Mirandola, Giovanni, 345
picturesque, the *see* Gilpin, William
Pike, Sara Lee, "Introduction" to *Israel*, 138
pilgrimage
  Fuller and, 195–96, 197, 203–4, 210–11, 212–13, 215
  Melville and, 246, 374
  Thoreau and, 173
Pindar, 10, 83, 103, 354
Pinsky, Robert, 16, 85, 88
Piper, Andrew, 276
Pius II, Pope, 325–26
Plato
  Coleridge and, 9
  Emerson and, 10
  Fuller and, 198
  Melville and, 250
  and natural law, 302
  and Prometheus, 23
  Republic, 300
  and slavery, 299
Platonic ideal, 154
Plautus, Titus Maccius, 115–16
Pliny the Elder, *Historia Naturalis*, 9, 21, 177–79
Plotinus, 9, 10
Plutarch, 22, 208
Pocock, J. G. A., *Barbarism and Religion*, 181n, 333n, 334n
poet-prophets *see* vatic tradition
Poggio Bracciolini, 327
Polk, James K., 293
Pollok, Robert, *The Course of Time*, 130, 136–37
Pope, Alexander, 6, 12, 315
  and *cursus honorum*, 28n
  "Epistle to Bathurst," 359
  Gilpin and, 36
  translation of *Iliad*, 292–93, 336n
Popkin, Jeremy, *History, Historians, and Autobiography*, 336n
Porden, Eleanor, *Coeur de Lion*, 138
Potter, Richard, 263n
Potter, Robert, 249
Pound, Ezra, 16
Prelude or, Growth of a Poet's Mind; An Autobiographical Poem, The (Wordsworth), 51n, 139–40, 141, 147–48n
  influences, 314, 365
Preston, William, trans., *Argonautica* (Apollonius Rhodius), 1, 144–45n
Prickard, A. O., 377

Prickett, Stephen, 25, 377
primitive style
   Homer and, 162, 165, 313
   Lowth and, 342
   Ossian (Macpherson) and, 10
   Thoreau and, 176, 178, 187n
printing *see* communications technology
Prior, Matthew, *Solomon on the Vanity of the World*, 350
Prometheus
   as creator of mankind, 246, 250
   Enlightenment and, 252–53
   and forbidden knowledge, 264n
   Melville and, 22–23, 246–51; *see also* Ahab, Captain
   Romantics and, 241–42, 253–55
"Prometheus" (Byron), 23, 241, 243, 249–50, 252, 253, 254–55
"Prometheus" (Goethe), 256
Prometheus Bound (Aeschylus), 9, 242, 243, 245–46, 251–52, 253
   translations, 249, 262–63n
Prometheus Unbound (Shelley), 250, 253, 255–56, 256, 257–58
Propertius, Sextus, 89, 250
Protestantism, 39, 56, 360, 372
   Gilpin and, 11–12, 36, 38, 40, 43
   see also Puritan Hebraism
Proust, Marcel, 24, 28n, 316, 333n
Psalms of David
   Book of Common Prayer, 349
   compared favorably with Virgil, 347–48
   English poetry and, 355–58
   translations of, 351, 352, 353–55
Psyche (Cupid's lover), 138, 195, 196, 197, 213
psyche (inner self), 194, 197, 198, 201–2, 208, 258
psychology, transformational, 204, 205, 209, 210, 214–15
Puritan Hebraism, 25, 344, 358–59, 361–62
   Arnold and, 370, 372
   Cole and, 369
   waning, 364, 367
Putnam, Michael C. J., 164
Pye, Henry James, *Alfred: An Epic Poem*, 130
Pythagoras, 9, 354

Rabelais, François, 374
racial inferiority, perceived, 54, 57, 75n, 371; *see also* slavery: classical precedents for antebellum American
racism, 69, 222, 223, 224; *see also* anti-Semitism; ethnology; interracialism
Radcliffe, Ann, *The Mysteries of Udolpho*, 51n
Randolph, John, 294
Rawson, Claude, *Satire and Sentiment*, 333n
Reconstruction, 236n, 301; *see also* Thirteenth Amendment
Reif, Stefan C., 343
Renaissance, African American literary, 223, 229
Renan, (Joseph) Ernest, 319
republic, pure, 224, 226, 227
Republic of Letters, 15–16, 221, 227, 228–30
republicanism, 5, 359–60, 361, 362–63, 388n
   Milton and, 129, 179, 361
   and oratory, 295–96, 297
   tyranny vs., 223, 275
   see also natural law; slavery
revolutionary time, 20, 268–70, 271–72, 274–76, 279, 283–84
revolutionary traditionalism, 3, 4, 20, 160, 168, 181n
Reynolds, Sir Joshua, *Discourses*, 5
Rhea, 196
rhetoric, 4, 130, 161, 183n, 341
   Emerson's, 211, 212
   Gibbon's, 316, 324
   Hebrew, 365–66, 389n
   Henry Adams's, 336n
   Melville's, 244
   political, 13, 289–90, 295–96, 297–98, 304
   see also ekphrasis
Richard, Carl J., 12–13
Richardson, Robert D., 199
rights
   declarations of, 74n, 302, 359
   natural, 301, 302
   of slave owners, 65, 220
Risinger, Jacob, 1
Roberts, Adam, *Landor's Cleanness: A Study of Walter Savage Landor*, 100n
Roberts, Daniel Sanjiv, 370
Roberts, William, *Judah Restored*, 130
Robinson, David M., 155
Roebuck, John Arthur, 371
Rogers, Gamaliel, 354
Rollin, Charles, *Ancient History* (*Histoire Ancienne*), 291
Roman Catholicism
   Arnold and, 372
   Enlightenment and, 335n
   Gibbon and, 314, 324–26
   Gilpin's aversion to, 11–12, 39, 40–41, 43
Roman Revolution (1848), 213
Romantic period, narrowness of definition, 5–7, 38
Rome, ancient
   Coleridge and, 23–24, 267, 268, 269–70, 273–75
   Gibbon and *see History of the Decline and Fall of the Roman Empire, The* (Gibbon)
   model for later republicans, 359
   Republic and slavery, 220–21, 223, 224, 302

Republic as precedent for French Revolution, 272–73, 279
signifying the classical, 270
U.S. politicians and, 294
Rosa, Salvator (painter), 45
Rosenblatt, Jason, 379
Rosicrucianism, 198
Ross, Donal, Jr., 156
Roston, Murray, 377, 379
Rousseau, Jean-Jacques, 361
Rowan, Judge John, 294
Rugby School, 29n, 83
ruins
  Camden and, 39
  Gibbon and, 24, 314, 315, 316, 327, 329–30
  Gilpin and, 11, 12, 37–38, 40–43, 44, 49
  Stukely and, 45–46
Ruskin, John, 335–36n
  Praeterita, 328, 335n
  The Stones of Venice, 315, 328

Sachs, Jonathan, 23–24
Said, Edward, *Beginnings: Intention and Method*, 147–48n
Saint-Martin, Louis Claude de, *Le nouvel homme*, 22, 204
Saintsbury, George, 85, 92
Sallust (Gaius Sallustius Crispus), 290
Sappho, 83, 134
Sattelmeyer, Robert, 156
Schappes, Morris Uman, 369
Schelling, Friedrich Wilhelm Joseph, 357
Schlegel, Friedrich von, 162, 210
"schools" of English poetry, 6
science
  and belief, 374
  earth, 283
  fiction *see* Asimov, Isaac
  Hellenic, 375
  history as, 328, 331–32
  interdisciplinary approach, 175–76, 179, 184n, 186–87n, 326, 351
  overreaching, 256, 264n
  social, 223, 305
  study of, 304–5, 378, 394n
  see also natural sciences
Scott, Sir Walter, 6, 10, 87, 336n
  The Lady of the Lake, 131–32
Sealts, Merton, 249
secularization
  Gibbon and, 24, 317, 321, 324, 325, 335n
  and Hebrew, 342, 363, 364, 367
  and politics, 130, 359
Seixas, Gershom Mendes, 346
Seixas, Moses Mendes, 346
Selden, John, 343
self-reliance
  Emerson and, 211, 212–13

Fuller and, 194–95, 197–99, 206, 207, 210, 212–13, 215
Wheatley and, 14–15
Sewall, Stephen, 364, 389n
Seward, William, 303–4
Seybold, Ethel, 176–77
Shabat, Natasha, "Seeing the Divine in Nature: Discovering the Aleph Bet of Walden Pond," 393n
Shakespeare, William, 165, 166, 176, 227, 353, 374
  bowdlerization, 318
Shalev, Eran, 25, 359
  American Zion, 388n
Shattuck, Roger, *Forbidden Knowledge: From Prometheus to Pornography*, 261n, 264n
Shearith Israel congregation, NYC, 346
Shelley, Mary, *Frankenstein; or, The Modern Prometheus*, 23, 241, 246, 249, 256, 264n
Shelley, Percy Bysshe, 1, 9, 184n, 364
  and Prometheus, 23, 242, 246, 253, 255–56
  A Defence of Poetry, 6
Shields, John C., 14, 67, 77n
Shields, William, 349
Sidney, Algernon, 361
Sidney, Philip, 163, 179
Simon, Richard, *A Critical History of the Old Testament*, 347
Simson, Sampson, 346
Skene, George, *Donald Bane: An Heroic Poem*, 129
slavery, 13, 73–74n
  in ancient Greece, 221, 223
  classical precedents for antebellum American, 290, 298–99, 300, 304
  in Roman Republic, 220–21, 292
  see also abolitionism; Wheatley, Phillis
Smart, Christopher, 25, 356–57, 386n
Smith, Charles, *The Mosiad, or Israel Delivered: A Sacred Poem*, 130
Smith, James McCune *see* McCune Smith, James
Smith, John, 367
Solomon, 350, 354, 369
Sonensher, Michael, 267
Sophia, 208
Sophocles, 82, 83, 303
Sotheby, William, 141–42, 366
Southcote, Joanna, 213
Southern Literary Messenger, 296
Southey, Robert, 9, 87, 129, 363
  Joan of Arc, 130
Spark, Clare, *Hunting Captain Ahab*, 261n
Spector, Sheila, 25, 379–80, 395n
Spengler, Oswald, 321
Spenser, Edmund, 8, 89, 90, 134, 162, 163
Stauffer, John, 15
Stead, William Force, 356

Steele, Jeffrey, 22
Steele, Richard, 348
Stein, Sarah B., "A Hebraic Modernity: Poetry, Prayer, and Translation in the Long Eighteenth Century," 383n
Stern, David, *Parables in Midrash: Narrative and Exegesis in Rabbinic Literature*, 389n
Stevenson, Andrew, 293
Stiles, Ezra, 343, 345–46, 382n
Stoicism, 8, 9, 179, 295
Stonehenge, 45–47
Stowe, Calvin, 358
Stowe, Harriet Beecher, 363
  Uncle Tom's Cabin, or, Life Among the Lowly, 55, 74n
  Woman in Sacred History: A Celebration of Women in the Bible, 358
Stowe, landscape gardens, 35, 36–38
Strachey, Lytton, 328, 329, 336n
Stryer, Steven, 16–17
Stukeley, William, *Stonehenge. A Temple Restor'd to the Ancient Druids*, 45
Sturgis, Caroline, 197, 201, 203, 204, 209
sublime, the
  Handel and, 349
  Hebrew and, 341, 348, 350–52, 365, 370, 377, 383–84n
  the picturesque and, 35, 40, 47, 48
  Thoreau and, 163
  see also Longinus, *On the Sublime*
suffrage
  American white male, 12, 13, 289, 293–94
  post-revolutionary France, 274
Sumner, Charles, 120, 236n, 302, 303
Supreme Court, U.S., 220, 221, 290
Swedenborg, Emanuel, 22
Swift, Jane Sophia, 90
Swinburne, Algernon, "Song for the Centenary of Walter Savage Landor," 82–83
Sympson, Joseph, *Science Revived, or The Vision of Alfred*, 140
Syriac, study of, 344

Tacitus, Publius (or Gaius) Cornelius, 46, 290
Taney, Chief Justice Roger, 220
Tasso, Torquato, 145n, 315, 316, 350
Taylor, Thomas, 195
Telemachus, 293
Tennyson, Alfred, 1st Baron Tennyson, 9, 313, 314
  "The Charge of the Light Brigade," 224–27
  "Ulysses," 241
Terence (Publius Terentius Afer)
  McCune Smith and, 16, 223, 224, 233n
  Wheatley and, 15, 63, 68–69
Teresa, Saint, 213
Thelwall, John, *The Hope of Albion; or, Edwin of Northumbria: An Epic Poem*, 138
Theocritus
  Landor and, 83–84
  Thoreau and, 179, 183n
  Virgil and, 106, 119, 163, 164
Theodorakopoulos, Elena, 168, 174
Thirteenth Amendment to the U.S. Constitution, 229
Thomson, J. A. K., 87–88
Thoreau, Henry David, 364
  and Aeschylus, 263n
  classical background, 10, 103, 176–77, 183–84n, 187n
  and *cursus honorum*, 20–21, 155, 162–65, 169, 173–74, 178
  and Harvard, 20, 161–63, 166, 182n, 375
  and Hebrew, 25, 369, 375–76, 393n
  intellectual generalism, 153–54, 155, 175–77, 178–79, 187n
  Janus-faced stance, 20–21, 177, 178
  Princeton Edition, 180n
  Cape Cod, 21, 175
  "Dark Ages," 163
  "The Dispersion of Seeds," 177, 178
  Faith in a Seed, 158, 175
  "Homer, Ossian, Chaucer," 164, 166
  Journal, 153, 158, 164–65, 166, 175, 177
  The Maine Woods, 21, 175, 185n
  "Natural History of Massachusetts," 186n
  Walden, 21, 175, 176, 375, 376
  "Walking," 156, 375
  A Week on the Concord and Merrimack Rivers, 21, 156, 175
  "Winter Walk, A" (Thoreau), 156
  and Wordsworth, 170, 185n
  see also "Walk to Wachusett, A"
Thrale, Henry and Mrs., 355
Thucydides, 292, 315, 333n
Ticknor, George, 109, 182n
Tighe, Mary, *Psyche*, 138
Tillemont, Louis-Sébastien Le Nain de, 314
time
  acceleration of, 23–24, 280
  and collation, 277–78
  compression of, 269
  continuity through, 281–82
  geological, 283
  Gilpin and, 40–41
  non-synchronous, 278–79
  slowness of antiquity, 267, 268, 270, 275, 281–83
  see also revolutionary time
Tintern Abbey, 40
Titans, 201
topos *see* invocation; Muse, the
tourism, 11, 12, 35, 36, 38, 115

Touro Synagogue, Newport, 345, 346, 367–68, 369, 390n
Toynbee, Arnold, 321
traditionalism *see* revolutionary traditionalism
Transcendentalism, 6–7, 10, 300
    Fuller and, 193, 198–99
    Thoreau and, 155, 158
    W. H. Channing and, 194, 195–96
translatio imperii, 24, 160, 181–82n, 317, 321, 327
translatio studii, 160, 321
translations, 4
    biblical, 25, 344, 347, 350, 353–55, 379; *see also* King James Bible
    of Camden, 39
    Coleridge's, 389–90n
    Dryden's, 50n, 315, 347
    Keats's, 8
    Longfellow's own and read, 18–19, 115–16, 121n, 122n; *see also* "Virgil's First Eclogue" (Longfellow)
    of Lowth, 357, 373, 377
    McCune Smith's own and read, 220, 224, 236n
    making classics available, 12, 13, 291–92
    Pope's, 292–93, 315, 336n
    read by Fuller, 195
    read by Melville, 249–50, 262–63n
    Thoreau's own and read, 10, 26n, 165, 236n
    Wheatley's, 56
    Wordsworth's, 9, 313
Trapp, Joseph, 108, 109, 110, 112, 114, 115, 122n
travel literature *see* Gilpin, William; "Walk to Wachusett, A" (Thoreau)
Trevelyan, G. M., 24, 328, 336n
Tucker, Herbert F., 17, 19–20, 167
Tucker, Nathaniel, *America Delivered*, 130, 145n
Turner, Frederick Jackson, 322
Tuveson, Ernest Lee, *Redeemer Nation: The Idea of America's Millennial Role*, 181n
Typhon, 202

University of Chicago, 305
Usher, Hezekiah, 354
utilitarianism, 305

Van Anglen, K. P., 20
    "True Pulpit Power: 'Natural History of Massachusetts' and the Problem of Cultural Authority," 186–87n
vatic tradition, 160, 162, 163, 164, 169, 181n
Venus, 36, 51n, 195, 208
Very, Jones, 10
Virgil (Publius Vergilius Maro)
    American imitators, 10
    compared unfavorably with King David, 347–48
    critical perspectives, 4
    Dryden and, 9, 46, 50n
    and epic, 18, 134
    Fuller and, 22
    Gibbon and, 24
    Gilpin and, 12, 47, 49, 51n
    and Homer, 161
    Janus-faced stance, 174, 186n
    Longfellow and *see* "Virgil's First Eclogue" (Longfellow)
    McCune Smith and, 223
    and Maecenas, 65
    Melville and, 259
    Stowe (estate) and, 36
    Thoreau and, 21, 158–59, 163, 164–65
    in U.S. education, 290
    waning popularity, 313
    Wheatley and, 15, 69
    see also Aeneid (Virgil); *cursus honorum*; *Eclogues* (Virgil); *Georgics* (Virgil)
"Virgil's First Eclogue" (Longfellow), 18, 103, 104–5, 108–15, 119–20, 120n
Virgin Mary, 203–4, 216
Vishnu, 261n
Voltaire (François-Marie Arouet), 314, 315, 333n
    La Henriade de M. de Voltaire, 126

Walden Pond, 157
"Walk to Wachusett, A" (Thoreau), 20–21
    background, 155–56
    and epic, 170, 171, 173, 175
    influence of Homer and Virgil, 158–60, 163, 164–65
    influence of Humboldt, 157–59, 160
    Janus-faced stance, 169
    Naturphilosophie, 156–57
    Princeton Edition, 186n
    and sensation, 171–72, 172–73
Walker, Alice, "In Search of Our Mother's Gardens," 75n
Walker, William, *Gustavus Vasa*, 130, 140
Wallon, Henri, 301
Walls, Laura Dassow, 156–58, 181n, 182n, 187n
War of 1812, 135, 330–31
Warburton, William, *The Divine Legation of Moses . . .*, 342
Ward, Samuel Gray, 197, 203
Warton, Joseph, 6, 352, 355, 366
Warton, Thomas, 6, 352, 355
Washington, Booker T., 301
Washington, George, 291, 299, 346
Watts, Isaac, 25, 366
    Horae Lyricae, 354
Webster, Daniel, 290–91, 298

Weinbrot, Howard, 25, 352, 357, 358
    "Expanding the Borders. Jews and Jesus: This Israel, This England," 379, 380–81n
Wells, H. G., 25, 321, 328
Westminster School, 349, 350
Wharton, Richard, *Roncesvalles*, 146n
Wheatley, Phillis, 13–14, 60
    front matter to *Poems on Various Subjects, Religious and Moral*, 53, 55, 57–62, 67, 69–70
    position as slave, 53, 54–56, 57–59, 62, 68, 74n, 75n
    "Niobe in Distress," 138
    "On Imagination," 67
    "To Maecenas," 14–15, 53–54, 62–68, 69, 70, 138
Wheeler, Kathleen, 8
Wheeler, Stephen, 89
Whiggism, 12, 159–60
Whitefield, George, 56, 74n
Whitman, Walt
    and epic, 10
    and Hebrew, 25, 357, 358, 364
    "Inscriptions," 147n
    Leaves of Grass, 113
    "Out of the Cradle Endlessly Rocking," 138
    "Song of the Exposition," 147n
    "When Lilacs Last in the Dooryard Bloom'd," 7
Wiesen, David S., 301
Williams, Helen Maria, *Peru*, 129
Williams, Peter, Jr., 222
Williams, Roger, 344, 345
Wills, Garry, 292
Wilson, Edmund, 378
Wilson, Penelope, 28n
Winckelmann, Johann Joachim, 282
Winterer, Caroline, 230n, 232n, 236n, 240n, 306n, 309n
Winthrop, John, 358
Wise, Francis, 358
Wisehart, M. K., 293

Wisse, Ruth, 379
Wolf, Friedrich August, 161–62
Woman in the Nineteenth Century (Fuller), 194, 204, 207, 215, 216–17
    appendix, 198
    poem within, 197
    revision of "The Great Lawsuit," 213
Wood, Gordon S., *Revolutionary Characters: What Made the Founders Different*, 73n
Woods, George B. ed., *Poetry of the Victorian Period*, 7
Woolsey, Theodore, 220, 221
Wordsworth, Dorothy, 363
Wordsworth, William
    and Hebrew, 25, 365
    Landor and, 84, 87
    and Lowth, 357
    stoicism, 9
    Thoreau and, 170, 185n
    and Virgil, 9, 313
    vision of "cultivated man of action," 179
    The Excursion, 139
    Michael, 365
    Preface to *Lyrical Ballads*, 6, 275, 365
    Preface to *Poems*, 185n
    "Prospectus," 147n
    The Recluse, 139
    see also *Prelude or, Growth of a Poet's Mind; An Autobiographical Poem, The* (Wordsworth)
Womersley, David, *The Transformation of The Decline and Fall of the Roman Empire*, 333n
Wrangham, Francis, 108, 109, 110, 112

Yale University, 305, 345–46, 367, 378
Yiddish, 380

Zeus *see* Prometheus
Ziolkowski, Theodore
    The Sin of Knowledge: Ancient Themes and Modern Variations, 261n
    Virgil and the Moderns, 335n

EU representative:
Easy Access System Europe
Mustamäe tee 50, 10621 Tallinn, Estonia
Gpsr.requests@easproject.com

www.ingramcontent.com/pod-product-compliance
Lightning Source LLC
Chambersburg PA
CBHW052054300426
44117CB00013B/2116